The Treasury of Knowledge

Book Six, Part Three:

Frameworks of Buddhist Philosophy

A Systematic Presentation of
the Cause-Based Philosophical Vehicles

The publication of this work has been made possible through
the generous support of the Tsadra Foundation.

The Treasury of Knowledge

Book Six, Part Three:

Frameworks of Buddhist Philosophy

A Systematic Presentation of
the Cause-Based Philosophical Vehicles

Jamgön Kongtrul Lodrö Tayé

KALU RINPOCHÉ TRANSLATION GROUP
under the direction of Venerable Bokar Rinpoché

This volume
translated, introduced, and annotated by
Elizabeth M. Callahan

Snow Lion Publications
Ithaca, New York
Boulder, Colorado

Snow Lion Publications
P.O. Box 6483
Ithaca, New York 14851 USA
607-273-8519
www.snowlionpub.com

Printed in Canada on acid-free recycled paper.

ISBN 978-1-55939-277-8

Library of Congress Cataloging-in-Publication Data

Koṅ-sprul Blo-gros-mtha'-yas, 1813-1899.
[Śes bya mtha' yas pa'i rgya mtsho. English. Selections]
The treasury of knowledge : Book six, part three, frameworks of Buddhist philosophy, a systematic presentation of the cause-based philosophical vehicles / Jamgön Kongtrul Lodrö Tayé ; Kalu Rinpoché Translation Group under the direction of Bokar Rinpoché ; this volume translated, introduced, and annotated by Elizabeth M. Callahan.
p. cm.
Includes bibliographical references and index.
ISBN-13: 978-1-55939-277-8 (alk. paper)
ISBN-10: 1-55939-277-0 (alk. paper)
1. Buddhism—Doctrines. 2. Buddhist sects. 3. Buddhism—China—Tibet—Doctrines. I. Callahan, Elizabeth M. II. Title.

BQ4140 . K672513 2007
294.3'420423—dc22

2007010391

CONTENTS

FOREWORD

༄༅། །འཇམ་མགོན་བློ་གྲོས་མཐའ་ཡས་ཀྱིས་མཛད་པའི་ཤེས་བྱ་ཀུན་ཁྱབ་མཛོད་ལས། མཚན་ཉིད་ཐེག་པའི་རྣམ་པར་གཞག་པ་ལེགས་པར་ཤེས་ན། འཁོར་ལོ་དང་པོའི་ངེས་འབྱུང་དང་གང་ཟག་གི་བདག་མེད་ཀྱི་རྣམ་གཞག་ལེགས་པར་ཤེས་པར་འགྱུར་ཞིང་། འཁོར་ལོ་བར་པའི་སྟོང་ཉིད་སྤྲོས་པའི་མཐའ་ཐམས་ཅད་དང་བྲལ་བ་དང་། ཆོས་ཐམས་ཅད་ཀུན་རྫོབ་རྟེན་འབྲེལ་སྣང་ཙམ་དུ་ཤེས་པར་འགྱུར་ཞིང་། དེ་ལས་རྣམ་དག་གསུམ་དང་ཡོངས་དག་བཅུ་གཉིས་ལ་འཇུག་བདེ་བར་འགྱུར་ཞིང་། འཁོར་ལོ་གསུམ་པའི་དགོངས་པ། སེམས་ཀྱི་གནས་ལུགས་འོད་གསལ་བདེ་གཤེགས་སྙིང་པོ་ངོ་བོ་ལ་དྲི་མ་མེད་ཅིང་དྲི་མ་རང་ཤར་རང་གྲོལ་དུ་ཤེས་པར་འགྱུར་ཞིང་། དེ་ལ་བརྟེན་ནས་རྡོ་རྗེ་ཐེག་པའི་དུག་ལྔ་ཡེ་ཤེས་ལྔ་རུ་ཤར་ཚུལ་ཤེས་པར་འགྱུར་བའི་དེ་ཉིད་ཀྱི་ཕྱིར། འདི་ཤིན་ཏུ་གལ་ཆེ་བ་ཡིན་པས་བློ་གྲོས་མཆོག་དང་ལྡན་པ་རྣམས་ཀྱིས་ལེགས་པར་ཁོང་དུ་ཆུད་པར་མཛོད་ཅིག །

མཁན་མིང་ཚུལ་ཁྲིམས་པས་སྨྲས་སོ། །

If you thoroughly comprehend the philosophical vehicles presented in Jamgön Lodrö Tayé's *Treasury of Knowledge,* you will develop the firm resolve to emerge from saṃsāra and will understand the absence of the self of persons. These are the teachings of the first turning of the dharma wheel.

You will understand emptiness, which is freedom from all conceptually elaborated extremes, and will know that, on a conventional level, all phenomena are simply dependently originated appearances. Having understood these things, you will understand the threefold enumeration of utter purity and the twelvefold enumeration of complete purity[1] with ease. These are the teachings of the middle turning of the dharma wheel.

You will recognize that the abiding nature of mind, luminous sugatagarbha, is stainless in nature: stains are self-arising and self-liberated. This is the thought of the third turning of the dharma wheel.

On the basis of this, you will know the way in which the five poisons are the five wisdoms, as is taught in the Vajrayāna.

It is precisely for these reasons that this section of the *Treasury of Knowledge* is of the utmost importance. May those of great intelligence master this.

Spoken by Tsülgyam, who is only called "Khenpo"
(Khenpo Tsültrim Gyamtso Rinpoche)
5 November 2005

INTRODUCTION

For Buddhists, the study of philosophy has a single goal: awakening. Study (or, as it is traditionally undertaken, listening) is the first of the three means to knowledge, the other two being reflection and meditation. All Buddhist practitioners engage in some form of study, though for many of those whose main interest is meditation, the formal study of philosophy, with its branch areas of epistemology and logic, seems quite unnecessary. Yet, as Khenpo Tsültrim Gyamtso Rinpoche's foreword explicates, the systematic study of the topics contained in this volume will lead us from the foundational Buddhist teachings on the four truths to the Madhyamaka of Secret Mantra, and thence to awakening.

Khenpo Tsültrim teaches that there are four ways to approach the realization of mahāmudrā: through training progressively in the view, meditation, conduct, or the tantras. In the Karma Kagyu tradition, training in meditation starts with the four common preliminaries and four uncommon preliminaries,[2] and is followed by shamatha (calm abiding) and vipashyanā (superior insight) meditations according to either a Sūtrayāna or a Vajrayāna approach. When training in conduct, the first step is to do no harm, either to oneself or to others; subsequent training in altruistic behavior may be followed by instruction in other styles of conduct appropriate to one's level of practice.[3] To train according to the tantras is to practice the meditations of the four sets of tantra in sequence, starting with kriyā (action) tantras, charyā (conduct) tantras, yoga tantras, and finally anuttarayoga (highest yoga) tantras. Khenpo Tsültrim explains that while any of these three approaches will lead to the realization of mahāmudrā, training in the stages of the view, such as presented by Jamgön Kongtrul in this section of his *Treasury of Knowledge,* is the most profound way to proceed.[4]

Jamgön Kongtrul Lodrö Tayé and the Rimé Movement

Jamgön Kongtrul Lodrö Tayé[5] (1813–1900) was a Tibetan polymath: an erudite and eclectic scholar, teacher, meditation practitioner, and even a skilled political mediator when needed. Along with other luminaries of his time, such as Dza Paltrul,[6] Jamyang Khyentsé Wangpo,[7] Chokgyur Lingpa,[8] and later Ju Mipham,[9] Jamgön Kongtrul contributed to the revitalization and preservation of many lineages and traditions of Buddhist teachings in what is called the Rimé (*ris med*), or nonsectarian, movement. His outstanding quality as a synthesizer and harmonizer, both on a secular and a religious level, is just one of the reasons for his leading role as a nonsectarian. There are many good accounts of Jamgön Kongtrul's life and times, such as Gene Smith's (2001) "'Jam mgon Koṅg sprul and the Nonsectarian Movement," *The Autobiography of Jamgön Kongtrul* (Barron 2003), and Ringu Tulku's (2006) *The Ri-me Philosophy of Jamgön Kongtrul the Great.*[10] Here we will look at those aspects of his thought that are most relevant to this book.

The origins of the Rimé movement

The nineteenth-century Rimé movement was both a reaction to its times and a reflection of the views of its proponents. The religious climate in Tibet (which was intertwined with its politics) had become highly partisan, and the Rimé movement was a push towards a middle ground where the various views and styles of the different traditions were appreciated for their individual contributions rather than being refuted, marginalized, or banned. Jamgön Kongtrul and others brought to light many valuable teachings in both their own and others' traditions, some of which had been dangerously close to being lost, and to reduce the Rimé movement to the redressing of religious power or prestige would be to undervalue its fundamental ecumenical spirit. The Rimé masters' contribution is not simply one of balance: it enables us to experience the rich wisdom and means found in a variety of approaches.

It should be mentioned that a Rimé approach does not mix traditions. Each tradition of Buddhism in Tibet has its own meditation texts and commentaries, and its own approach to training practitioners. Jamgön Kongtrul and his contemporaries were concerned with preserving and promulgating these traditions, each in its own right; by doing so, they ensured their availability for subsequent generations of practitioners and scholars.

Jamgön Kongtrul's influences

Two aspects characteristic of the Rimé movement are seen in Jamgön Kongtrul's presentation of Buddhist doctrine in general and its philosophy in particular. The first is a return to emphasizing Indian sources—to fundamentals (though not to fundamentalism)—and the other is the revival of the Shentong system and the establishment of its place in the study of Madhyamaka philosophy. As we shall see, he drew upon the works of Indian masters, from Nāgārjuna, Asaṅga, and Vasubandhu to Chandrakīrti and Shāntarakṣhita. For his Shentong presentation, he relied primarily on the works of two more recent Shentong masters: the Sakya scholar Shākya Chokden[11] and the Jonang master Tāranātha.[12]

Tibetans rely more on the Indian exegetical works than sūtras: "original" sources often means the writings of Nāgārjuna, Asaṅga, and Vasubandhu, rather than the words of the Buddha found in the sūtras. One reason for this is that the great Indian masters systematized, and in that process clarified, the words and thought of the Buddha; and, of course, each generation usually finds recent works more accessible than the ancient texts, both conceptually and linguistically.

Jamgön Kongtrul states that what became known in Tibet as Shentong (Extrinsic Emptiness or Empty-of-Other)[13] was known in India as Yogāchāra-Madhyamaka. This stream of teachings began with the Buddha's third turning of the dharma wheel[14] and was later elucidated by Maitreya, Asaṅga, Vasubandhu, and Nāgārjuna in his Collection of Praises.[15] Dolpopa Sherab Gyaltsen[16] of Jonang monastery in Tibet is generally considered to be the first to use the terms Shentong and Rangtong (*Rang stong*; Intrinsic Emptiness or Empty-of-Self) in an extensive way. Jamgön Kongtrul says that many Kagyu and Nyingma masters[17] explain the key points of this system as the definitive meaning, specifically citing the third Karmapa, Rangjung Dorjé,[18] and the great Nyingma master Longchen Rabjam.[19] The Yogāchāra-Madhyamaka, or Shentong, view is also an intrinsic part of mahāmudrā teachings and of the Vajrayāna. The great yogi Milarepa sang many songs that express this view, as well as songs that express its counterpart, Rangtong.[20]

The Jonang school and Shentong teachings were banned in Central and

Western Tibet during the mid-seventeenth century owing, it seems, largely to a change in political power. Its texts were sealed and their printing was forbidden, and Jonang monastery was converted to a Geluk monastery.[21] Despite these restrictions, the Jonang Shentong teachings and practices continued even in Central Tibet, albeit in a reduced way, and in its fairly isolated affiliated monasteries in the eastern areas of Tibet (Amdo). During the eighteenth century, there was a revival and open reinstatement of the Shentong view within the Kagyu and Nyingma schools, which began with Kaḥ-tok Rikdzin Tsewang Norbu,[22] Situ Paṇchen Chökyi Jungné,[23] and Getsé Paṇḍita Gyurmé Tsewang Chokdrup.[24] Tsewang Norbu received the transmission of the Jonang teachings from Kunzang Wangpo,[25] a student of one of Tāranātha's disciples, Kunga Tayé.[26] Tsewang Norbu also strongly influenced the adoption of Shentong views by Situ Paṇchen Chökyi Jungné of the Karma Kagyu school, who regarded his Shentong views to be in accordance with those of the seventh Karmapa, Chödrak Gyamtso,[27] and Shākya Chokden.[28] Another important contributor to the Shentong revitalization was Shalu Ri-buk Tulku, Losel Ten-kyöng,[29] who enabled the reprinting of Tāranātha's banned works in 1874.[30] In this section of his *Treasury of Knowledge,* Jamgön Kongtrul carries on their work, clarifying and reaffirming the place of this system within the traditionally accepted hierarchy of four philosophical schools.

Jamgön Kongtrul's literary works

Jamgön Kongtrul's prodigious literary output (over ninety volumes) is contained in collections known as the Five Great Treasuries,[31] which comprise meditation practices, empowerments, and commentaries, as well as his own compositions. His own writings are found in *The Treasury of Extensive Teachings*[32] and *The Treasury of Knowledge,* also known as *The Encompassment of All Knowledge* (see below). His collections of texts are *The Mantra Treasury of the Kagyu School, The Treasury of Precious Terma Teachings,* and *The Treasury of Instructions.*[33]

The Treasury of Knowledge

The work translated in *Frameworks of Buddhist Philosophy: A Systematic Presentation of the Cause-Based Philosophical Vehicles*[34] is one section of *The Encompassment of All Knowledge* and its auto-commentary, *The Infinite*

Ocean of Knowledge.[35] Together these texts are often called (and hereafter will be referred to as) *The Treasury of Knowledge,*[36] the name given to them by Jamyang Khyentsé Wangpo.

Although Jamgön Kongtrul began compiling the texts for *The Mantra Treasury of the Kagyu School* first, *The Treasury of Knowledge* is generally regarded as his first work. He undertook it at the request of Ngédön Tenpa Rabgyé,[37] who had asked him to compose a treatise on the three vows: the Hīnayāna vows of individual liberation (*prātimokṣha, so sor thar pa'i sdom pa*), the Mahāyāna vows of a bodhisattva (*byang chub sems dpa'i sdom pa*), and the samayas, or commitments, of Secret Mantra (*gsang ba sngags kyi dam tshig 'am sdom pa*). Jamgön Kongtrul recounts the circumstances in his autobiography:[38]

> Prior to this, Lama Karma Ngédön had urged me to write a treatise on the three levels of ordination, saying that if I did so he would write a commentary. But my feeling was that there were already any number of treatises on this subject, and that if I were to write a treatise it should be more comprehensive in scope, something that would be of use to people who had not studied much. So in the periods between my meditation sessions I had been composing the source verses to my treatise *The Encompassing of the Knowable* [or *The Encompassment of All Knowledge*] a treatise dealing with the three higher trainings.[39] Later, I offered this to my lord guru for his inspection, and on that occasion he gave me great encouragement, saying, "This is definitely due to the blessings of your spiritual masters and the power that comes from having the *ḍākinīs* open up your subtle channels. We will call this *The Treasury of the Knowable* [or *Treasury of Knowledge*] the first of the five great Treasuries you will produce. Now you must write your own commentary to it."

Begun in 1863, the root text and its three-volume auto-commentary were probably completed by Jamgön Kongtrul in 1865. Certainly they were completed by mid-1867 when Jamgön Kongtrul recorded that he gave the oral transmission for the work to the Ngor master Ngawang Rinchen.[40] Although it was originally intended to discuss only the three vows, this work came to be a comprehensive treatise on Buddhism, covering all areas of knowledge and interest to the Buddhist population of Tibet. It is the last great Tibetan encyclopedia. Additionally—and not insignificantly—it provides us with a clear picture of Jamgön Kongtrul's nonsectarian approach to Buddhist practices and study.

The Treasury of Knowledge: Style and Contents

As befitting a compendium of this nature, *The Treasury of Knowledge* draws on and from the writings of both Indian and Tibetan masters. An important aspect of Buddhist scholarship is to ground one's presentation in the works of previous masters, a tradition stretching back to the time of the Buddha Shākyamuni. Readers should bear in mind that *The Treasury of Knowledge* is as much a compilation as it is an original work, and this should be understood from the traditional Buddhist context, where reliance on scripture is not only laudable but to varying degrees mandatory; where passages may be borrowed in their entirety without attribution; and where original writing—that is, something wholly self-created—is considered a fault.

Growing from the original section on the three vows, *The Treasury of Knowledge* is divided into ten sections (*gnas*)—called "books" in this translation series—each with four parts (*skabs*) of varying lengths. As we can see from the following overview, it begins with cosmology and history, moves on to survey vast and varied areas of knowledge, then discusses meditation practices, and concludes with sections on the path and the fruition of nirvāṇa. Each book has a theme that it discusses in its four parts from various perspectives: sometimes in terms of the Hīnayāna, Mahāyāna, and Vajrayāna approaches; at other times according to the different Tibetan traditions; in some cases, a section will be an in-depth look at one or more areas of the book's broad topic.

Book One: *Myriad Worlds: Buddhist Cosmology in Abhidharma, Kālacakra, and Dzog-chen* (1995)
- Part 1: The Cosmology of the Universal Way [Mahāyāna]
- Part 2: Our Universe according to the Individual and Universal Ways [Hīnayāna and Mahāyāna]
- Part 3: Space and Time in the Tantra of the Wheel of Time [Kālachakra]
- Part 4: The Causes of Cyclic Life [and the Primordial Purity of the Universe]

Book Two: The Advent of the Buddha[41]
- Part 1: Our Teacher's Path to Awakening
- Part 2: The Buddha's Enlightenment
- Part 3: The Buddha's Twelve Deeds
- Part 4: Enlightenment's Bodies and Realms

Book Three: The Buddha's Doctrine—The Sacred Teachings
- Part 1: What Are the Sacred Teachings?
- Part 2: Cycles of Scriptural Transmission
- Part 3: Compilations of the Buddha's Word
- Part 4: The Origins of the Original Translations' Ancient Tradition [Nyingma]

Book Four: Buddhism's Spread Throughout the World
- Part 1: Buddhism's Spread in India
- Part 2: How Buddhist Monastic Discipline and Philosophy Came to Tibet
- Part 3: Tibet's Eight Vehicles of Tantric Meditation Practice
- Part 4: The Origins of Buddhist Culture

Book Five: *Buddhist Ethics* [The Training in Higher Ethical Conduct] (1998)
- Part 1: The Qualities of the Spiritual Teacher and Student
- Part 2: The Vows of Personal Liberation
- Part 3: The Commitments of Awakening Mind [Bodhichitta]
- Part 4: The Vows and Pledges of Secret Mantra

Book Six: The Topics for Study
- Part 1: A Presentation of the Common Fields of Knowledge and Worldly Paths
- Part 2: The General Topics of Knowledge in the Hīnayāna and Mahāyāna
- Part 3: *Frameworks of Buddhist Philosophy: A Systematic Presentation of the Cause-Based Philosophical Vehicles*
- Part 4: *Systems of Buddhist Tantra: The Indestructible Way of Secret Mantra* (2005)

Book Seven: The Training in Higher Wisdom

Part 1: Gaining Certainty about the Keys to Understanding

Part 2: Gaining Certainty about the Provisional and Definitive Meanings in the Three Turnings of the Wheel of Dharma; the Two Truths; and Dependent Arising

Part 3: Gaining Certainty about the View

Part 4: Gaining Certainty about the Four Thoughts that Turn the Mind

Book Eight: The Training in Higher Meditative Absorption [Samādhi]

Part 1: Shamatha (Calm Abiding) and Vipashyanā (Profound Insight)

Part 2: The Stages of Meditation in the Cause-Based Approaches[42]

Part 3: *The Elements of Tantric Practice: A General Exposition of Secret Mantra Meditation Systems*[43]

Part 4: *Esoteric Instructions: A Detailed Presentation of the Process of Meditation in Vajrayāna*[44]

Book Nine: An Analysis of the Paths and Levels to Be Traversed[45]

Part 1: The Paths and Levels in the Cause-Based Dialectical Approach[46]

Part 2: The Levels and Paths in the Vajrayāna

Part 3: The Process of Enhancement

Part 4: The Paths and Levels in the Three Yogas

Book Ten: An Analysis of the Consummate Fruition State

Part 1: The Fruition in the Dialectical Approach

Part 2: The More Common Attainments in the Vajrayāna

Part 3: The Fruition in the Vajrayāna

Part 4: The Fruition State in the Nyingma School

Books One through Four cover Buddhist views on the world and Buddhist history. What follows, beginning with Book Five's presentation of the three vows, is the content of Buddhist doctrine. Book Six—the topics for study—sits between the training in ethical conduct (Book Five) and the trainings in wisdom and samādhi (Books Seven and Eight respectively). This organization suggests that the material in Book Six is designed to provide practitioners and scholars with the understanding that they will reflect upon (aided by Book Seven) and cultivate in their meditation (as set out in Book Eight).

Part One of Book Six is a presentation of what are called common fields of knowledge (*thun mong rig pa'i gnas*), which are areas of learning common to Buddhists and non-Buddhists. These subjects, which include a study of valid means of cognition (*pramāṇa, tshad ma*), cover the tools necessary for Buddhist philosophical studies. Part Two of Book Six, The General Topics of Knowledge in the Hīnayāna and Mahāyāna, begins with an overview of what distinguishes Buddhism from non-Buddhist systems and then surveys the ways Buddhist yānas (*theg pa*, vehicles) and philosophical tenet systems (*siddhānta, grub mtha'*) are categorized and enumerated. Jamgön Kongtrul concludes this opening with the most well-known framework: three yānas and four philosophical systems.[47] This is the framework that Part Three of Book Six, our present work, presents in some detail.

BOOK SIX, PART THREE: *Frameworks of Buddhist Philosophy*

In Part Three of Book Six, *A Systematic Presentation of the Cause-Based Philosophical Vehicles,* Jamgön Kongtrul presents an overview of the main aspects of the Hīnayāna and Mahāyāna systems (leaving out the Vajrayāna segment of the Mahāyāna),[48] and highlights the important points of their approaches. These are "cause-based yānas" (*rgyu'i theg pa*), in contrast to the "result-based yānas" (*'bras bu'i theg pa*), which is a common name for the Vajrayāna. As Jamgön Kongtrul says,[49] cause-based yānas employ "that by which we travel," a cryptic phrase meaning that these yānas use the causes of buddhahood as their path. Result-based paths use "where we are traveling to" as their means; that is, their method is the result itself: the wisdoms and pure appearances of buddhahood. (Result-based approaches are treated in Part Four of Book Six, *Systems of Buddhist Tantra.*) Speaking generally, from a Hīnayāna perspective, the causes are the renunciation of saṃsāra, the cultivation of ethical conduct, and the realization of the absence of a self of persons (*pudgalanairātmya, gang zag gi bdag med*). The Mahāyāna adds to that list the cultivation of the six pāramitās and the realization of the absence of a self-entity of phenomena (*dharmanairātmya, chos kyi bdag med*).

These yānas are also called "philosophical" (*lakṣhaṇa, mtshan nyid*). The term translated here as "philosophical" in other contexts is translated as "characteristics," "defining characteristics," or "dialectics." In Chapter Five of this book, Jamgön Kongtrul states that the Pāramitāyāna part of the

Mahāyāna "is called a philosophical [yāna] because it portrays (*mtshon par byed pa*) the path and its attributes that directly connect us to the unified state of Vajradhara, the final fruition." Thus the term refers to these yānas' descriptions of the characteristics that make up the path. They do this by means of categorizations and definitions, analysis and reason, rather than faith and devotion. Here, the application of the term is broad since it covers the early Buddhist schools through Madhyamaka, including the Madhyamaka character of Secret Mantra.

As is the case throughout *The Treasury of Knowledge,* many topics simply mentioned in this volume are explained in detail elsewhere.[50] In this book we find a general presentation of the Hīnayāna and Mahāyāna doctrines, paths, and results with an emphasis on the specifics of their philosophical tenet systems. In terms of Buddhist literature, we could say broadly that this section conforms to the genre of doxography or tenet systems (*siddhānta, grub mtha'*).[51] In fact, this section often serves as such for the Karma Kagyu tradition these days, which makes it important not just as a general document or a reflection of Jamgön Kongtrul's Rimé perspective, but as a textbook in a contemporary and vital tradition. Before we look at the structure and content of Jamgön Kongtrul's presentation, some background and context for this work may be helpful.

Doxography: An overview of shifting structures

Doxography is the systematization of views, the classification of fluid lines of thought into discrete, hierarchical categories that suggest uniformity where it may not exist. It should be kept in mind from the outset that these pedagogical frameworks, into which centuries of works are placed, are the creation of Buddhist thinkers: each one is an artifact (and sometimes an artifice). They do not necessarily describe or reflect historical facts—none of the Indian teachers they categorize thought of themselves as belonging to any such "schools" (or even necessarily holding the views that are ascribed to them). They evolved into their present forms mainly because they were so enthusiastically embraced by Tibetan scholars.

Nāgārjuna[52] (ca. second century CE) was the earliest Mahāyāna philosopher to provide a systematic exposition of emptiness. In his *Fundamental Treatise on the Middle Way,*[53] Nāgārjuna demonstrates through reasoning that phenomena have no nature and specifically refutes assertions held by the major abhidharma schools of his time, such as the Vaibhāṣhikas, or Sarvāstivādins.[54] In doing so, he is considered to have established the Middle Way, or Madhyamaka, system. Traditionally, three sets of texts are attributed to Nāgārjuna: Collection of Reasonings,[55] Collection of Praises, and Collection of Advice.[56] The works in his Collection of Reasonings and the texts of his student Āryadeva are considered models of Madhyamaka philosophy.[57]

During the fourth century, Asaṅga[58] and his brother Vasubandhu[59] wrote a large number of treatises, some of which comment on the Prajñāpāramitā sūtras, while others amplify teachings found in the third turning of the dharma wheel, such as the three characteristics,[60] *ālaya* consciousness, and buddha nature (*tathāgatagarbha*). Vasubandhu, having begun his scholastic career studying the Hīnayāna systems, wrote a major text on Vaibhāṣhika abhidharma (*Treasury of Abhidharma*),[61] while Asaṅga wrote the Mahāyāna equivalent, the *Compendium of Abhidharma.*[62] As a whole, their works can be seen as supplementing Nāgārjuna's Collection of Reasonings and providing a balance for any Buddhists who mistook his presentation of emptiness for a kind of nihilism. They also furnished Mahāyāna practitioners with detailed descriptions of the path and practices leading to awakening, both practical and vitally important topics (as attested by the fact that the basis for the Prajñāpāramitā studies in the Tibetan monastic colleges is one of the texts Asaṅga received from Maitreya, the *Ornament of Clear Realization*). Later, the works of Asaṅga and Vasubandhu were called Yogāchāra (and, in Tibet, either Chittamātra or Shentong).

Dignāga (ca. fourth/fifth century) developed a Buddhist system of logic and epistemology, which was furthered by the works of Dharmakīrti in the seventh century. Until the middle of the sixth century, there is no evidence that Mahāyāna followers perceived themselves as being divided into different schools or representing different points of view.[63]

The first compendium of Buddhist and non-Buddhist Indian philosophical systems was written by the great sixth-century philosopher and debater Bhāvaviveka[64] in his *Heart of the Middle Way*[65] and the auto-commentary, *Blaze of Reasoning.*[66] Bhāvaviveka is remembered for other firsts: he was the first to cast Madhyamaka arguments in the logical forms developed by Dignāga; perhaps the first to have used the terms Madhyamaka and Yogāchāra to refer to systems of thought; the first to criticize the views of those he calls Yogāchāras;[67] and the first to "divide" the ultimate into what he called "nominal ultimate" and "non-nominal ultimate."[68] Bhāvaviveka also took exception to the way Buddhapālita (early sixth century) presented the reasonings found in Nāgārjuna's *Fundamental Treatise on the Middle Way,* which later earned Bhāvaviveka the position as the founder of *Svātantrika-Madhyamaka.

Although one of the most famous Madhyamaka scholars for Tibetans and a brilliant scholar, Chandrakīrti (sixth century) was probably not widely influential in India. He is most well known for his *Entrance to the Middle Way,*[69] a commentary on the *Fundamental Treatise on the Middle Way,* in which he refutes the ideas of non-Buddhists and Buddhists. In *Lucid Words,*[70] Chandrakīrti defends Buddhapālita's approach and criticizes Bhāvaviveka's critique of the latter, for which Chandrakīrti is credited with being the founder of the *Prāsaṅgika branch of Madhyamaka. The crux of the disagreement between Bhāvaviveka and Chandrakīrti is whether Mādhyamikas should or can use the formal inferences, as developed by Dignāga and Dharmakīrti, when arguing for Madhyamaka emptiness, Chandrakīrti's position being that they should not.[71]

By the eighth century, the presentation of four tenet systems—Vaibhāṣhika, Sautrāntika, Yogāchāra, and Madhyamaka—appears in works such as Āryadeva's short *Compendium on the Heart of Primordial Wisdom*[72] and Shāntarakṣhita's *Compendium on Suchness*[73] and *Ornament of the Middle Way.*[74] This systematization continues to be found in the writings of eleventh-century Indian authors, such as Bodhibhadra,[75] Jetāri,[76] Maitrīpa,[77] Sahajavajra,[78] and Mokṣhākaragupta,[79] with some variation and individuality.

Tibetans received their first teachings on Madhyamaka philosophy from Shāntarakṣhita, who also set the tone for their approach to studying philosophical tenet systems. His *Ornament of the Middle Way*[80] demonstrates the flaws of the lower Buddhist tenet systems (Vaibhāṣhika through Yogāchāra), pointing out in each case their error of reification, but it concludes:[81]

> On the basis of the Mind Alone,
> We should know that outer things do not exist.
> On the basis of the method set forth here,
> We should know that mind is utterly devoid of self.
>
> Those who ride the chariot of the two approaches,
> Who grasp the reins of reasoned thought,
> Will thus be adepts of the Mahayana,
> According to the sense and meaning of the word.

As this demonstrates, Shāntarakṣhita's approach was to unite Yogāchāra and Madhyamaka, with the latter expressing the highest view. The importance of Madhyamaka studies was confirmed for Tibetans when, following the debate between Shāntarakṣhita's student Kamalashīla and the Chinese master Heshang Moheyan,[82] the Tibetan king Trisong De-tsen[83] (742–797) declared that Tibetans would henceforth follow the view of Nāgārjuna.[84] It was later decreed that among the eighteen Hīnayāna orders, only the texts belonging to the Mūlasarvāstivādin (which includes the Vaibhāṣhika and Sautrāntika tenet systems) would be translated,[85] which certainly accounts for the limited representation of non-Mahāyāna commentarial works in Tibetan. Attention would still be paid to the texts and doctrine of the so-called lower tenets, but often as supplemental studies. In keeping with Shāntarakṣhita's Yogāchāra-Madhyamaka synthesis, Yogāchāra texts continued to be translated and studied, along with the epistemological works by Dignāga and Dharmakīrti, and, of course, Madhyamaka texts.

By the eighth century, subdivisions had already been introduced into the presentations of four tenet systems. In the above-mentioned Indian texts of this period, Yogāchāra is typically split into Proponents of Images (*Sākāravādin, rNam pa dang bcas pa*) and Proponents of Nonexistent Images (*Nirākāravādin, rNam pa med pa*).[86] As Jamgön Kongtrul recounts in Chapter Seven, Madhyamaka was classified in a variety of ways by Indian masters.[87] Tibetans contributed to this by creating new subdivisions, starting with the first Tibetan doxographical works written by the ninth-century translators Shang Yeshé Dé[88] and Kawa Pal-tsek,[89] who introduced the terms Sautrāntika-Madhyamaka and Yogāchāra-Madhyamaka[90] and applied them to Bhāvaviveka and Shāntarakṣhita respectively. Since these neologisms reflect the different ways these masters explained conventional reality (*saṃvṛitisatya, kun rdzob bden pa*), they began to be incorporated into doxographical schemas during the later spreading of Madhyamaka, as evidenced by the eleventh-century Rongzom Paṇḍita Chökyi Zangpo's[91] works.

A significant contribution to Tibetan Madhyamaka studies occurred in the eleventh century when Pa-tsap Lotsāwa Nyima Drak[92] translated Chandrakīrti's *Lucid Words* and *Commentary on the "Entrance to the Middle Way,"*[93] and prepared a new translation of his *Entrance to the Middle Way*. Although Atīsha had introduced Tibetans to Prāsaṅgika and singled out Nāgārjuna and Chandrakīrti as the ones who had realized emptiness,[94] the works of Chandrakīrti had not been studied extensively prior to the time of Pa-tsap Lotsāwa. (As mentioned earlier, Chandrakīrti was not widely studied in India; and the only commentary on his works by an Indian master, that by Jayānanda, was composed in the eleventh century.[95]) Patsap Lotsāwa is credited with coining the now-famous terms Svātantrika and Prāsaṅgika[96] and setting in motion the propagation of Chandrakīrti's Prāsaṅgika view, which in time became accepted as the highest form of Madhyamaka view.[97] This did not happen immediately: the Svātantrika approach was favored and taught extensively by the eleventh- and twelfth-century masters such as Ngok Lotsāwa Loden Sherab[98] and Chapa Chökyi Seng-gé.[99] The terms Svātantrika and Prāsaṅgika became more or less universally adopted by the fourteenth and fifteen centuries,[100] for instance by the great Nyingma master Longchen Rabjam, who used them in his *Precious Treasury of Philosophical Systems*.[101]

A notable occurrence on the philosophical landscape of the fourteenth century, with far-reaching doxographical implications, was Dolpopa Sherab Gyaltsen's proclamation of Shentong as the highest interpretation of Madhyamaka view. Dolpopa's presentation of Shentong, or what he calls Great Madhyamaka, is a synthesis of the teachings found in the Prajñāpāramitā sūtras,[102] commentaries on the tantras (especially the Three Commentaries by Bodhisattvas),[103] and the works of Nāgārjuna, Asaṅga, Vasubandhu, and Maitreya. One of his main points is that the teachings of the second and third turnings of the dharma wheel[104] are fundamentally in agreement, and that they teach that wisdom is empty of what is extrinsic to it (*gzhan stong*), not empty of its own nature (that is, intrinsically empty, *rang stong*). Another noteworthy point, both generally and from a doxographical point of view, is that Dolpopa distinguished between a relative Chittamātra and an absolute Chittamātra, identifying the latter as Great Madhyamaka.[105] By promoting the terms Rangtong and Shentong in contradistinction and "clarifying" the Madhyamaka view, he introduced another wrinkle into the arrangement of doctrines. However, Dolpopa's views were regarded by many as radical and were vigorously refuted, particularly by Tsongkhapa and his followers, and, starting in the seventeenth century, were effectively banned; it is not until recently that we have access to his works (and not simply to accounts of what others claim he said, embedded in their refutations of him).[106] Dolpopa's presentations are of utmost importance for us, since, when it comes to subdividing the four tenet systems, Jamgön Kongtrul follows Dolpopa's main interpretation. In Chapter Seven,[107] Jamgön Kongtrul states that, generally speaking, there are two types of Mādhyamikas: Mādhyamika Proponents of the Absence of a Nature (*Niḥsvabhāvavādins*) and Yogāchāra-Mādhyamikas;

these became known in Tibet from the time of Dolpopa as Rangtong Proponents and Shentong Proponents .

Also living in the fourteenth century was Je Tsongkhapa,[108] founder of the Geluk tradition. In keeping with the continued interest in Chandrakīrti's works (set in motion by Pal-tsek and passed down to Tsongkhapa by the Sakya master Rendawa[109]), he emphasized Chandrakīrti's Prāsaṅgika as the pinnacle of views. Yet Tsongkhapa introduced what some regarded as new and unfounded interpretations, including a highly debated (and debatable) presentation of what constitutes Svātantrika and Prāsaṅgika and what distinguishes them.[110] In his *Essence of Eloquence,*[111] Tsongkhapa makes a modification to the tenet system classifications that changed the course of Tibetan doxographical literature: he designates Sautrāntika-Madhyamaka and Yogāchāra-Madhyamaka as subcategories of Svātantrika-Madhyamaka,[112] thus "lowering" the standing of Shāntarakṣhita and Bhāvaviveka.

As controversial as Dolpopa's views were for Tsongkhapa, some of Tsongkhapa's own views were regarded as equally controversial by his contemporaries. Refutations of Tsongkhapa's views are found in writings of the Sakya masters Tak-tsang Lotsāwa,[113] Gorampa Sonam Seng-gé,[114] and Paṇchen Shākya Chokden, as well as those of the eighth Karmapa, Mikyö Dorjé.[115] For Jamgön Kongtrul the most influential of these masters was Paṇchen Shākya Chokden, who gradually took a Shentong position in his writings, particularly once he met the seventh Karmapa, Chödrak Gyamtso. His Shentong views are not identical to Dolpopa's[116]—they could be said to be more moderate—but they are one of Jamgön Kongtrul's main sources. Eventually Shākya Chokden's works were banned in Central Tibet[117] (along with those of Dolpopa and Tāranātha).

The next major figure relevant to our present work is Tāranātha of the Jonang tradition, upholder of the teachings of Dolpopa. His works are Jamgön Kongtrul's other main source for the Shentong view. Tāranātha sets out his perspective on the four tenet systems in his *Essence of Shentong,*[118] where he divides Mādhyamikas into Ordinary Mādhyamikas (*dBu ma phal pa*) and Great Mādhyamikas (*dBu ma chen po*). He states that the ordinary Madhyamaka became known in Tibet as Rangtong and is the tradition of Buddhapālita, Bhāvaviveka, Vimuktisena, and Shāntarakṣhita (note the absence of Nāgārjuna and Chandrakīrti). Great Madhyamaka became known in Tibet as Shentong and is elucidated in the works of Maitreya, Asaṅga, Vasubandhu, and in Nāgārjuna's *Praise of the Dharmadhātu.*[119] Tāranātha was a brilliant and prolific writer, who did much to promote the Shentong teachings of Dolpopa. Unfortunately, his works were banned in the mid-seventeenth century.[120]

The establishment of the political rule of the fifth Dalai Lama in 1642 and the subsequent rise of the Geluk school to the stature of state religion in Central Tibet resulted in lean times for the Kagyu scholastic tradition. Some of its monastic seats were converted and its monastic colleges (*bshad grva*) were closed.[121] This, of course, interrupted its scholastic tradition, a situation which began to change only during the eighteenth century with Situ Chökyi Jungné and the subsequent flourishing of the Rimé movement in eastern Tibet.

As the Geluk school developed its strong monastic base and scholastic achievements, the genre of doxography rose to the level of an art form in Jamyang Shepa's mammoth *Great Exposition of Tenets.*[122] Written partly as a rebuttal of Tak-tsang Lotsāwa's criticism of Tsongkhapa, Jamyang Shepa's work in turn generated numerous supplemental texts, such as Chang-kya Rolpé Dorjé's *Beautiful Ornament of Philosophical Tenet Systems,*[123] Könchok Jigmé Wangpo's *Precious Garland,*[124] and Losang Könchok's *Clear Crystal Mirror.*[125]

By this point, the categories have been subdivided more extensively, so we no longer simply have a schema of four philosophical tenet systems. Only the first system, Vaibhāṣhika, remains the same (though Jamyang Shepa's explanation that they include all eighteen orders differs from Jamgön Kongtrul's presentation[126] and a Western academic perspective). The following outline shows the subdivisions for Sautrāntika, Chittamātra, and Madhyamaka, according to Jamyang Shepa.[127]

Vaibhāṣhika (Followers of the *Great Detailed Exposition, *Mahāvibhāṣha*)
Sautrāntika (Sūtra Followers)
- Followers of Scripture (*rLung gi rjes 'brangs*): followers of Vasubandhu's *Treasury of Abhidharma*
- Followers of Reasoning (*Rigs pa'i rjes 'brangs*): followers of Dignāga's and Dharmakīrti's texts on epistemology[128]

An alternative classification:
Sautrāntika
- Proponents of Perceptual Parity (*gZung 'dzin grangs mnyam*)
- Serial Pluralists (*sNa tshogs rim 'byung*)
- Non-Pluralists (*sNa tshogs gnyis med*)

Chittamātra (Mind Only)

- Followers of Scripture: followers of Asaṅga's Treatises on the Bhūmis[129]
  - Proponents of Real Images (True Aspectarians) (*rNam bden pa*)
    - Split-Eggists (*sGo nga phyed tshal pa*)
    - Proponents of Perceptual Parity
    - Non-Pluralists
  - Proponents of False Images (False Aspectarians) (*rNam rdzun pa*)
    - Proponents of Staining False Images (*rNam rdzun dri bcas*)
    - Proponents of Non-Staining False Images (*rNam rdzun dri med*)

- Followers of Reasoning: followers of Dignāga's and Dharmakīrti's texts on epistemology
  - Proponents of Real Images
    - Split-Eggists
    - Proponents of Perceptual Parity
    - Non-Pluralists
  - Proponents of False Images
    - Proponents of Staining False Images
    - Proponents of Non-Staining False Images

Madhyamaka

- Svātantrika ([Those Who Use] Independently [Verifiable Reasonings])
  - Sautrāntika-Svātantrika-Madhyamaka: Bhāvaviveka
  - Yogāchāra-Svātantrika-Madhyamaka
    - Proponents of Real Images: Shāntarakṣhita and Kamalashīla
    - Proponents of False Images: Haribhadra
      - Proponents of Staining False Images: Jetāri
      - Proponents of Non-Staining False Images: Kambala
- Prāsaṅgika (Consequence [System])
  - Proponents of the Model Texts (*phyi mo pa*): Nāgārjuna and Āryadeva
  - Partisan Prāsaṅgikas (*phyogs 'dzin pa*): Buddhapālita, Chandrakīrti, and Shāntideva
  - Non-Partisan Prāsaṅgikas: Nāgabodhi and Shākyamitra

What these categories may not reveal is that, as the centuries passed, the divisions between different schools of thought became more definitive and sharper; the non-Madhyamaka teachings became devalued, and even non-Prāsaṅgika thought was deprecated. The drawing of lines and the making of distinctions was not only a matter of doctrinal issue in Tibet. In a land with no separation of church and state, it certainly had political aspects. Thus, the doxographical literature became not just a means to sort out the complicated array of philosophical views, but also the forum for establishing the supremacy of one's interpretation. Nevertheless, it should be said that Tibetans were certainly commenting on and debating matters that were, and had been, of issue and contention throughout Buddhism's long history in both India and Tibet.

While this does not pretend to be a comprehensive overview of doxographical works or of the issues inspiring those divisions, it should provide a sense of how the literature (and classifications) evolved over the centuries, sometimes in response to, and as a reflection of, doctrinal conundrums. In India, the debates between Buddhists were largely between Abhidharma followers and Mādhyamikas, or Yogāchāras and Mādhyamikas. In Tibet, with the introduction of divisions of Madhyamaka, the debates became between different "forms" of Madhyamaka: Svātantrika versus Prāsaṅgika, Shentong versus Rangtong. One thing is certain: there were never four separate, monolithic philosophical tenet systems[130] with which people identified. Over the centuries, others applied the model backwards, sometimes categorizing someone's works as representing a particular tenet system but not categorizing that person as espousing that view (the most famous example being Vasubandhu and the Vaibhāṣhika system).[131] Nevertheless, despite the fluidity and imprecise nature of doxographical frameworks, they are useful as pedagogical tools.

The philosophers classified

Before looking at Jamgön Kongtrul's presentation, it may be helpful to see a chronological list of the Indian and Tibetan masters he uses as primary sources or mentions as proponents of a particular philosophical system (those mentioned in this introduction are included as well). The dates for many of the early Indian teachers are either uncertain or not agreed on, so rather than list the various positions and theories, a rough chronological order is given with only known or well-accepted dates provided. The philosophical school affiliations, when listed, are according to Jamgön Kongtrul.

First century CE
Buddhadeva (ca. first century CE): Vaibhāṣhika
Dharmatrāta (ca. first century CE): Vaibhāṣhika
Vasumitra (ca. first century CE): Vaibhāṣhika
Ghoṣhaka (ca. first century CE):[132] Vaibhāṣhika
Avitarka (ca. first century CE): Chittamātra

Second century
Nāgārjuna (second century): model Prāsaṅgika
Āryadeva (second to third century): model Prāsaṅgika
Āchārya Shūra (or Ashvaghoṣha) (second to third century)

Third century
Shrīlāta (330–410): Sautrāntika

Fourth century to fifth century
Asaṅga (late fourth to early fifth century)
Vasubandhu (late fourth to early fifth century)
Saṅghabhadra (late fourth to early fifth century): Vaibhāṣhika
Dignāga (late fifth to mid sixth century)

Sixth century
Saṅgharakṣhita (early sixth century): Sautrāntika
Buddhapālita (early sixth century)
Vimuktisena (early sixth century)
Sthiramati (ca. 470–550)
Bhāvaviveka (ca. 500–570): Sautrāntika-Svātantrika-Madhyamaka
Dharmapāla (ca. 530–561)

Seventh century
Dharmakīrti (ca. late sixth to early seventh century)
Chandrakīrti (sixth to seventh century): Prāsaṅgika-Madhyamaka
Shrīgupta (seventh century): Svātantrika-Madhyamaka

Eighth century
Shāntideva (early eighth century)
Jñānagarbha (700-760): Svātantrika-Madhyamaka

Āryadeva II
Shāntarakṣhita (725-783): Yogāchāra-Svātantrika-Madhyamaka
Kamalashīla (740–795): Yogāchāra-Svātantrika-Madhyamaka
Haribhadra (late eighth century): Svātantrika-Madhyamaka

Ninth to twelfth century

Yeshé Dé (early ninth century)
Kawa Paltsek Lotsāwa (early ninth century)
Thagana (ca. ninth century): Svātantrika-Madhyamaka
Jetāri (ca. eleventh century)
Bodhibhadra (ca. 1000)
Ratnākarashānti (early eleventh century)
Atīsha (982–1054): Svātantrika-Madhyamaka
Chandrakīrti the lesser (eleventh century)
Lakṣhmīkara (eleventh century)
Maitrīpa (1012–1097)
Sahajavajra (eleventh to twelfth century)
Rongzom Paṇḍita Chökyi Zangpo (eleventh century) (Nyingma)
Zu Gawé Dorjé (eleventh century): Shentong-Madhyamaka
Tsen Kawoché (b. 1021): Shentong-Madhyamaka
Yumo Mikyö Dorjé (b. 1027): Shentong-Madhyamaka
Milarepa (1040–1123)
Jayānanda (second half of the eleventh century)
Ngok Lotsāwa Loden Sherab (1059–1109)
Pa-tsap Lotsāwa Nyima Drak (b. 1055)
Abhayākaragupta (late eleventh to early twelfth century)
Mokṣhākaragupta (ca. eleventh to twelfth century)
Chapa Chökyi Seng-gé (1109–1169)

Thirteenth century on

Buddhajñānapāda (ca. thirteenth century): Svātantrika-Madhyamaka
Third Karmapa, Rangjung Dorjé (1284–1339): Shentong-Madhyamaka (Kagyu)
Dolpopa (1292–1361): Shentong-Madhyamaka (Jonang)
Longchen Rabjam (1308–1364): Shentong-Madhyamaka (Nyingma)
Rongtön Sherab Gyaltsen (1367–1449) (Sakya)
Tsongkhapa (1357–1419) (Geluk)

Tak-tsang Lotsāwa (b. 1405) (Sakya)
Gorampa Sonam Seng-gé (1429–1489) (Sakya)
Shākya Chokden (1428–1509): Shentong-Madhyamaka (Sakya)
Seventh Karmapa, Chödrak Gyatso (1454–1506) (Kagyu)
Karma Tinlé Choklé Namgyal (1456–1539) (Kagyu)
Eighth Karmapa, Mikyö Dorjé (1507–1554) (Kagyu)
Tāranātha (1575–1634): Shentong-Madhyamaka (Jonang)
Jamyang Shepa (1648–1721) (Geluk)
Kaḥ-tok Rikdzin Tsewang Norbu (1698–1755) (Nyingma: Shentong-Madhyamaka)
Situ Paṇchen Chökyi Jungné (1699–1774) (Kagyu: Shentong-Madhyamaka)
Chang-kya Rolpé Dorjé (1717–1786) (Geluk)
Könchok Jigmé Wangpo (1728–1791) (Geluk)
Losang Könchok (1742–1822) (Geluk)
Getsé Paṇḍita Gyurmé Tsewang Chokdrup (1761–1829) (Nyingma)
Dza Paltrul (1808–1887) (Rimé-Nyingma)
Jamgön Kongtrul (1813–1900) (Rimé-Kagyu-Nyingma)
Jamyang Khyentsé Wangpo (1820-1892) (Rimé-Nyingma-Sakya)
Chokgyur Lingpa (1829-1870) (Rimé-Nyingma)
Ju Mipham (1846–1912) (Rimé-Nyingma)

Jamgön Kongtrul's Presentation of Three Yānas and Four Tenet Systems

The text translated in *Frameworks of Buddhist Philosophy: A Systematic Presentation of the Cause-Based Philosophical Vehicles* is Jamgön Kongtrul's masterful survey of the broad themes and subtle philosophical points found in more than fifteen hundred years of Buddhist philosophical writings. In a clear, concise manner, he sets out the traditional framework of three yānas: Shrāvakayāna, Pratyekabuddhayāna, and Mahāyāna; and four philosophical tenet systems: Vaibhāṣhika, Sautrāntika, Chittamātra, and Madhyamaka. Of particular interest is his organization of the tenet systems and the texts on which he bases it, both of which reveal his own view as well as his sources of inspiration. Although he eschews a polemical approach, he does make statements on contested issues (often without identifying them as such), and refers to and comments upon others' positions. For those with some background in the subjects covered here, what Jamgön Kongtrul says and what he does not may be equally interesting.

Chapter One[133] begins with the statement that the three yānas were taught by the Buddha Shākyamuni, whereas the four philosophical tenet systems were demarcated by the Buddha's followers. The three yānas are characterized either in terms of the methods they employ or the intentions of their followers. Their methods are either cause-based or result-based. As mentioned above, "cause-based" means that the causes for awakening, for example, the six pāramitās for Mahāyāna practitioners, are practiced as the path. "Result-based" means that the results of awakening, the wisdoms and kāyas of buddhas, are meditated upon as the path.

The three yānas can also be distinguished from the perspective of their practitioners. The term "Hīnayāna" (Lesser Vehicle) is used to refer to the yānas practiced by those whose sole aim is their own liberation, and the "Mahāyāna" (Greater Vehicle) indicates that its practitioners strive to liberate others as well as themselves. Historically speaking, the terms Hīnayāna and Mahāyāna were only used by Mahāyāna followers—no one following the teachings designated by the term "Hīnayāna," or Lesser Vehicle, considered their approach "lesser."[134] There are, however, long-standing precedents in Buddhist history for redefining and refining terms, and these terms need not be regarded as historical relics, but may be considered from the perspective of a progressive path. Of course, some Buddhist practitioners prefer one mode of teachings to another, and continue with it throughout their lives, while others choose to train in the yānas in a graduated manner. In the latter approach, the Hīnayāna represents the foundational teachings and practices, and as such is an essential and integral part of the path for Mahāyāna practitioners. The Dzogchen Ponlop Rinpoche[135] presents this view:

> The Hīnayāna, which is associated with the first cycle of the Buddha's teaching, is translated as the "lower vehicle." However, this does not mean that the Hīnayāna is lower in quality. "Lower" refers to that which occurs at the beginning, the most fundamental part of our journey. The Hīnayāna is said to be lower than the other two vehicles[136] in the same way that the foundation of a house or building is lower than the upper floors . . . Many of the other factors that affect our journey are determined by how well we lay the foundation of the Hīnayāna path.

> If we attempt to leap right into Mahāmudrā or Dzogchen, then we are forgetting about Hīnayāna, which means we are forgetting about our foundation . . .
>
> The foundation that we are trying to develop consists of the Hīnayāna view of selflessness, the understanding of interdependent origination, and the path of revulsion and renunciation . . . When we develop a genuine understanding of suffering, renunciation, and the selfless nature of ego, we can properly enter the path of Mahāyāna.

It is with this view in mind that the term Hīnayāna is used in these pages.

The canonical sources Jamgön Kongtrul provides for the four philosophical tenet systems (*siddhānta, grub mtha'*) are both tantras: the *Hevajra Tantra* advises teaching the four systems sequentially, and the *Kālachakra Tantra* gives a symbolic account of their origins. Jamgön Kongtrul then explains that the four tenets systems[137] are the outcome (*grub don*) of the final view (*lta ba mthar thug*) that individuals reach through their own intellectual analysis, thus providing us with both an explanation of the origin of the tenets systems and the meaning of this term.

Within the three yāna structure, the first two yānas—the Shrāvakayāna and Pratyekabuddhayāna—are considered Hīnayāna. The Shrāvakayāna contains the first two of the four tenet systems: Vaibhāṣhika and Sautrāntika. The third yāna, Mahāyāna, contains the last two tenet systems: Chittamātra and Madhyamaka.

The four main sections of this book are the Shrāvakayāna, Pratyekabuddhayāna, Chittamātra tenet system, and Madhyamaka tenet system. Jamgön Kongtrul's systematic presentations of the Shrāvakayāna, Pratyekabuddhayāna, and Madhyamaka cover six topics: the meaning and etymology of their names; their entryways; their vows; their views; their results; and their classifications. (Madhyamaka has a seventh topic: a synopsis of its ground, path, and fruition.) For his presentation of Chittamātra, Jamgön Kongtrul chose a slightly different format that begins with the meaning and etymology of the name, and then incorporates seven topics from the *Compendium of the Mahāyāna*:[138] the source of knowable objects; the three characteristics; how to engage the import of those; the cause and result of that engagement; the unfolding; the three trainings; and the results of purification. The remainder of the Chittamātra chapter is devoted to its classifications. It is under the heading of the classifications in the Shrāvakayāna, Chittamātra, and Madhyamaka chapters (Chapters Two, and Six through Twelve) that we find the details of the four philosophical tenet systems.

Shrāvakayāna

Jamgön Kongtrul bases his discussion of the Shrāvakayāna (Chapter Two) on Vasubandhu's *Treasury of Abhidharma* and Asaṅga's *Compendium of Abhidharma*. Most of the chapter is an analysis of the four truths for noble ones (suffering, its origins, its cessation, and the path), which are the shrāvakas' entryway to their path and its results. Jamgön Kongtrul first treats these in general ways, discussing their essential qualities, defining characteristics, numbers, sequence, and etymologies, before turning to examine them individually. The truth of suffering is generalized as being of eight, six, three, or two kinds, with the threefold presentation probably being the most familiar: the suffering of suffering, the suffering of change, and the suffering of conditioned existence.

The origins of suffering are, as the *Compendium of Abhidharma* says, mental afflictions and defiled karma. Under the heading of the karmic origins of suffering, the ten unvirtuous actions (three of body, four of speech, and three of mind) are discussed in detail: each has a basis, intention, act, and completion that are needed to fulfill the karmic path of that action. Their divisions, worst instances, and three types of results (matured results, results that correspond to their causes, and dominant results) are also provided. Finally, six alternative classification schemes are given, making for a complete overview of the categories and topics related to karma.

Jamgön Kongtrul introduces the truth of cessation by saying that it is the attainment of separation from stains, and then describes its nature in terms of twelve aspects presented in the *Compendium of Abhidharma*. Cessation is the nirvāṇa attained through the Shrāvakayāna, and it is described in a number of short sections in Chapter Two, as well as in Chapter Three's explanations of the Vaibhāṣhika and Sautrāntika tenet systems and the classification of the result. The presentation of the truth of the path is simply a list of the five paths (accumulation, junction, seeing, meditation, and beyond training), as these paths are the main focus of Part One of Book Nine. This discussion of the four truths closes with a summary of their general characteristics.

The view for shrāvakas is primarily the realization of the absence of a self of persons (*pudgalanairātmya, gang zag gi bdag med*). As Jamgön Kongtrul recounts, some scriptures and Indian masters assert that shrāvakas (and pratyekabuddhas) also realize the absence of a self-entity of phenomena (*dharmanairātmya, chos kyi bdag med*); others do not. In Chapter Ten, Jamgön Kongtrul says one of the distinctive features of the Prāsaṅgikas' system is their assertion that shrāvakas and pratyekabuddhas realize both absences of self-entity. Chapter Two closes with a simple summary of the shrāvakas' result, nirvāṇa. It contains some technical differences in the positions ascribed to Vaibhāṣhikas and Sautrāntikas, but, simply put, their result is first nirvāṇa with the remainder of the aggregates and then, at death, nirvāṇa without remainder. (The details of the stages of the result are presented in the next chapter.)

Chapter Three is an account of three ways to classify the Shrāvakayāna: according to its tenet systems, its orders (*nikāya, sde pa*), and the attainment of results. Jamgön Kongtrul states that "the Shrāvakayāna contains numerous philosophical tenets with many subtle distinctions," but, to put this simply, it has two philosophical tenet systems: Vaibhāṣhika and Sautrāntika. This categorization, seemingly well-established by the eighth century in India, is probably derived from the fact that these were the two dominant abhidharma schools in northern India. Jamgön Kongtrul's observation that the Vaibhāṣhikas are a subdivision of the Mūlasarvāstivādins (one of the four main orders)[139] indicates that he does not regard the Vaibhāṣhikas as including or representing all eighteen orders, as other Tibetan doxographical works do.[140] It is also worth noting that Jamgön Kongtrul does not divide Sautrāntikas into Followers of Scripture and Followers of Reasoning, as is commonly done in the Geluk tenet system texts.

In Tibet, the primary source for the Vaibhāṣhika view is Vasubandhu's *Treasury of Abhidharma.* Its auto-commentary, the *Explanation of "The Treasury of Abhidharma,"* contains refutations of the Vaibhāṣhika positions and representations of Sautrāntika positions. Since the views of these tenet systems are complicated, digests like this are helpful places to start one's studies or simply to discover the main points. Jamgön Kongtrul begins with a succinct account of the points the Vaibhāṣhika and Sautrāntika positions have in common: they do not accept the Mahāyāna scriptures as the words of the Buddha Shākyamuni; they reject the notion of a permanent, single self; and they posit karma as the creator. This section also lists other topics they agree upon, from their classifications and definitions of phenomena (encompassing forms and mind) to their presentations of the paths and results.

Jamgön Kongtrul presents their views of the two truths as shared positions (whereas in Part Two of Book Seven he presents their positions on the two truths separately).[141] On the basis of a famous verse from the *Treasury of Abhidharma,* he explains that Vaibhāṣhikas and Sautrāntikas consider conventional reality to be anything that can be broken down, either physically or mentally, such that it is no longer understood to be that thing. If a table is broken apart, we no longer think "table" when we see the bits of wood. Thus, that "table" is only conventionally, or nominally, real. Ultimate reality is whatever is still cognized by a mind even when it is broken down into its individual parts.[142] It is the partless particles and irreducible moments of consciousness that serve as the building blocks of conditioned phenomena and mind.

Next, Jamgön Kongtrul looks at points of disagreement for Vaibhāṣhikas and Sautrāntikas. The first, and possibly seminal issue, is that Vaibhāṣhikas consider seven abhidharma texts to be the Buddha's words compiled by seven arhats, while Sautrāntikas consider them to have been composed by the seven arhats. Other points of difference are that Vaibhāṣhikas assert that, in most cases, sense consciousnesses and their objects arise simultaneously, whereas Sautrāntikas state that they arise sequentially, that is, that an object is the cause for its corresponding sense consciousness to arise. Vaibhāṣhikas consider the phenomena of the three times to be substantially existent, and Sautrāntikas consider them to be mentally imputed. Sautrāntikas state that external objects are hidden and that they cast an image (*ākāra, rnam pa*) that is apprehended by the sense consciousness. Sautrāntikas also assert reflexive awareness (*rang rig*). Vaibhāṣhikas do not accept either of these two positions. Vaibhāṣhika teachers include four masters whose views are cited in the *Treasury of Abhidharma*—Dharmatrāta, Vasumitra, Ghoṣhaka, and Buddhadeva—as well as Saṅghabhadra and Anantavarman.[143] Sautrāntikas are represented by Saṅgharakṣhita and Shrīlāta, and Vasubandhu's *Explanation of the "Treasury of Abhidharma."*

The second way to classify the Shrāvakayāna is according to its orders (*nikāya, sde pa*). Jamgön Kongtrul bases his presentation on Butön's *History of Buddhism*[144] and Pawo Tsuk-lak Trengwa's *Feast for Scholars: A History of the Dharma,*[145] both of which reflect descriptions of the orders found in the works of the Indian masters Vinītadeva, Shākyaprabha, Bhāvaviveka, and Padma.[146] The classification of the orders is looked at in three ways: as four main orders, as eighteen divisions, and as a twofold summation. Jamgön Kongtrul considers the four main orders, Mūlasarvāstivādins, Mahāsāṅghikas, Sthaviras, and Saṃmitīyas, in terms of such points as their names, lineages, and a few key tenets. The names of the eighteen orders are provided by a citation from Vinītadeva's *Compendium Showing the Different Orders.* These divisions developed for geographical and doctrinal reasons but, as a well-known sutra passage attests, each order contains a complete system of teachings that lead to liberation. Finally, the eighteen orders fall into two groups: those who propound the absence of a self of persons and those who assert an "inexplicable self [or person]." The latter, represented by the Vātsīputrīyas, "maintain that although the person cannot be described as being the same as or separate from the aggregates, or as permanent or impermanent, and so forth, it is substantially existent in the sense of being self-sufficient."[147] Needless to say, this view was repudiated by other Buddhists.

The third way to classify the Shrāvakayāna is in terms of its four results: stream enterers, once returners, nonreturners, and arhats. Jamgön Kongtrul treats these four in some detail; in fact, this is his most extensive coverage of these four levels in *The Treasury of Knowledge.* Again, the primary source for the complex architecture of approachers to and abiders in the results of stream enterers, once returners, nonreturners, and arhats, and their accompanying subdivisions, is the *Treasury of Abhidharma.* The *Compendium of Abhidharma* has similar categories, but its classifications and definitions are somewhat different.

Pratyekabuddhayāna

In Chapter Four, Jamgön Kongtrul turns to the second yāna, that of pratyekabuddhas. Pratyekabuddhas attain awakening in the periods when there are no buddhas or shrāvakas in the world. They are characterized as having a proud, independent nature, being intelligent, and possessing only a little compassion, although they do teach the dharma in nonverbal ways once they attain awakening. The systematic presentation of their yāna covers six topics: the meaning and etymology of their name; their entryway; their vows; their view; their results; and their classifications.

Pratyekabuddhas enter their path and attain nirvāṇa by contemplating the four truths and the twelve links of dependent origination. Observing the world, they see that all things arise from causes and conclude that if causes are interrupted, their results will not arise. Working their way back through the twelve links of dependent origination, they determine that if they uproot ignorance, the links following, through old age and death, will come to an end. All the traditional sources agree that pratyekabuddhas realize the absence of a self of persons. In addition, some texts, such as Maitreya's *Ornament of Clear Realization,*[148] say that they also realize that perceived objects have no self-entity. However, since they do not realize that the perceiving subject has no self-entity, pratyekabuddhas are said to realize only "half" of the absence of self-entity of phenomena (*dharmanairātmya, chos kyi bdag med*).

There are two types of pratyekabuddhas: the rhinoceros-like and the congregating practitioner. These categories are based on their dispositions and intelligence, with the rhinoceros-like being more inclined to solitude and of greater intelligence. All pratyekabuddhas attain the same results as the shrāvakas (stream-enterer through arhat). Jamgön Kongtrul concludes this chapter by remarking that although many Indian and Tibetan texts do not consider the philosophical tenet systems of shrāvakas and pratyekabuddhas separately, they do in fact have many differences. That, coupled with the prevalence of the phrase "three yānas" in the scriptures, warrants a separate presentation for pratyekabuddhas. Jamgön Kongtrul bases this section on the *Treasury of Abhidharma, Compendium of Abhidharma,* and Maitreya's *Ornament of Clear Realization.* This completes the Hīnayāna section.

Mahāyāna

Jamgön Kongtrul opens the Mahāyāna section (Chapter Five) by distinguishing it from the Hīnayāna in terms of its view (the realization of the twofold absence of self-entity); its trainings (the six pāramitās); its relinquishments (the afflictive and cognitive obscurations); its results (nirvāṇa that does not abide in the extreme of existence or peace); and its seven greatnesses, which are found in Maitreya's *Ornament of the Mahāyāna Sūtras.*[149] Jamgön Kongtrul begins his systematic presentation of the Mahāyāna by dividing it into the Pāramitāyāna and the Vajrayāna, of which the latter is the subject of Part Four of Book Six. In his overview of the Pāramitāyāna he states that the Pāramitāyāna is the cause-based part of the Mahāyāna path that leads to the primordial wisdom of buddhahood. In this he contradicts Tsongkhapa's position that final awakening can only be attained through the practice of the Vajrayāna. The remainder of Chapter Five is mainly devoted to an eleven-point discussion of the six pāramitās: their essential qualities; characteristics; etymologies; divisions and summaries; pure forms; most important types; distinctiveness; ways of training; results; numerical definitiveness; and order. The primary source for this is again Maitreya's *Ornament of the Mahāyāna Sūtras*.

The next major section on the Pāramitāyāna is a detailed presentation of its philosophical tenet systems, which will occupy the remaining seven chapters of the book (Chapters Six through Twelve). This may be the area of most interest to Buddhist practitioners and scholars, and it is where Jamgön Kongtrul's own views on the tenet systems are most clearly revealed.

Chittamātra

The Chittamātra system (Chapter Six) is treated in three parts: the meaning and etymology of its name, its seven bases, and its classifications (or subdivisions). The opening verse is a concise statement of one of the Chittamātras' main tenets: they assert consciousness to be truly existent. According to Jamgön Kongtrul, this assertion distinguishes this tenet system from Shentong-Madhyamaka. He states that Chittamātras are known as Proponents of Cognition (Vijñaptivādins) and Yogāchāras (Yoga Practitioners). It should be noted that Chittamātra is the more commonly used name for this system in Tibet, and that Jamgön Kongtrul also uses the latter two names for the Shentong tenet system (Chapter Eleven).[150]

Whether we call it Yogāchāra or Chittamātra, the teachings associated with this tenet system are based on the sūtras of the third turning of the dharma wheel and texts by Maitreya, Asaṅga, and Vasubandhu. They include a number of important topics: the eight modes of consciousness (rather than six) and the three characteristics or natures (*lakṣhaṇa, mtshan nyid*). Although Jamgön Kongtrul later indicates that he does not regard Asaṅga's teachings as Chittamātra, his summary of the seven bases, or topics, of the Chittamātra system is based on the ten topics (here condensed into seven) discussed in the ten chapters of Asaṅga's *Compendium of the Mahāyāna*. The first two topics are the source of knowable objects, which is the ālaya consciousness, and the three characteristics. The short presentation of the ālaya consciousness covers four points: the reasons for positing it; its characteristics; that its reversal is buddhahood; and that it is not a creator, single, a self, or permanent. The positing of the ālaya is integral to a Chittamātra presentation. The ālaya is the source of all we experience, which is characterized as threefold: dependent, imagined, and consummate.[151]

The dependent characteristic arises from the ālaya consciousness, and in its impure state it is called "the imagination of what is unreal." It is mere cognition appearing as the perceived images and the perceiving consciousness. It is called "dependent" because it manifests in dependence upon the force of habitual tendencies. The dependent characteristic is the basis for the designations of the imagined characteristics. Imagined characteristics are simply the names, labels, and notions that are applied to the dependent characteristic. These include the labels "big," "small," and notions of a self or true existence. The consummate characteristic is what exists ultimately: nonconceptual cognition empty of the duality of percepts and perceiver. Jamgön Kongtrul provides the subcategories of the three characteristics that are most well-known to Tibetans: imagined characteristics devoid of any characteristics and nominal imagined characteristics; impure and pure dependent characteristics; and the unchanging and the unerring consummate characteristics.

The classifications section of the Chittamātra system begins with another concise statement of its tenets: Chittamātras assert that external referents have no existence apart from being mere cognition (*vijñaptimātra, rnam rig tsam*). They consider external referents to be like the objects experienced in dreams for the following three reasons: First, referents (that is, all appearances) are only mental appearances, like the spots of light we see when we press on our closed eyelids. Secondly, if external appearances were to exist, they would exist for noble beings in meditative equipoise (which contradicts accepted Buddhist tenets). Thirdly, the same external appearances are experienced by different beings in quite different ways: for example, water is regarded as a home by fish, and something to drink by humans.

Given their assertion that appearances are simply mind and that mind (nondual cognition) is real, Chittamātras address the question of the status of these appearances, or what are called images (*ākāra, rnam pa*), in two ways. Some state that images are either "real" as mind, and others state that they are not; these account for the two main subdivisions of Chittamātra: Proponents of Real Images and Proponents of False Images.[152] Proponents of Real Images are subdivided based on how they posit the relationship between the cognizing mind and the images. The position of those called Split-Eggists is that the perceived objects and the perceiving mind are matching halves. Proponents of Perceptual Parity consider them to be in a one-to-one relationship: one consciousness for each image. Non-Pluralists say that there is only one consciousness, from which and to which many objects manifest. Jamgön Kongtrul's presentation of these subdivisions and their positions is based on Jetāri's *Explanation of "Differentiating the Sugata's Texts"*[153] and Shāntarakṣhita's *Ornament of the Middle Way*; both texts refute these positions.

Proponents of False Images say that images are not real; it is the force of ignorance and its attending habitual tendencies that cause the appearance of outer images. Those who subscribe to this view consider two issues: Is the mind tainted by images? Do buddhas experience dualistic appearances? The two responses to these issues yield two doxographical divisions: Proponents of Staining False Images and Proponents of Non-Staining False Images. The first are those who state that consciousness is tainted by images and that buddhas, while not being deluded themselves, do experience dualistic appearances. Those in the second category hold the positions that consciousness is not tainted by images and that buddhas do not experience dualistic appearances.

Jamgön Kongtrul then turns to the matter of whose works are considered Chittamātra. He states that although some Tibetans consider Vasubandhu's texts to be the scriptural source for the Chittamātra system, "This is simply the mistake of those who speak deviously by not distinguishing between Vasubandhu's assertion that primordial wisdom is truly existent and the Chittamātra system's statement that consciousness is truly existent." Under the heading, "The Masters Who Assert Chittamātra Positions," Jamgön Kongtrul first recounts the various views of Tibetans, and then introduces his first quotation from Dolpopa. After that, with characteristic brevity, Jamgön Kongtrul states what must be taken to be his own position regarding Chittamātra: "The great exalted one of Jonang and his followers maintain that Asaṅga and his brother were Madhyamaka masters and that their system of philosophical tenets is the Great Madhyamaka (*dBu ma chen po*)." If the texts by Asaṅga and Vasubandhu are not the source of the Chittamātra doctrine, we may wonder, who were the founding masters of the Chittamātra system? Drawing from texts by Tāranātha,[154] Jamgön Kongtrul says that the founders and promulgators of the Chittamātra system were "five hundred Mahāyāna masters, great exalted ones of earlier times, such as Avitarka, and others. 'Others' means some of their followers and some later Proponents of Mere Cognition (Vijñaptimātra)."

This chapter concludes with a brief account of why the Chittamātra system is refuted by Mādhyamikas. Chittamātras assert that reflexively aware, self-illuminating cognition, or consciousness, that is empty of the duality of percept and perceiver, exists ultimately. Since this constitutes a truly existing substratum, Mādhyamikas do not accept it. This, Jamgön Kongtrul says, is the primary difference between the Chittamātra and Madhyamaka systems.

Madhyamaka

The analysis of the Madhyamaka system (Chapters Seven through Twelve) has seven topics: the meaning and etymology of its names; its entryway; its vows; its view; its results; its classifications; and a synopsis in terms of ground, path, and fruition. Chapter Seven covers the first five topics and begins the subject of classification by surveying the various ways in which Madhyamaka is classified in India and Tibet. These classifications are derived from the way that Mādhyamikas explain the ultimate to be empty or the way they posit conventional reality. Jamgön Kongtrul's view is that there are two forms of Madhyamaka: Sūtra-Madhyamaka and Secret Mantra-Madhyamaka. The latter is the topic of the short but highly interesting Chapter Twelve. Sūtra-Madhyamaka is covered in Chapters Eight through Eleven. Its followers are divided into the Proponents of the Absence of a Nature (Niḥsvabhāvavādins) and the Yogāchāra-Mādhyamikas. Jamgön Kongtrul states that they became known in Tibet, from the time of Dolpopa onwards, as Rangtong Proponents and Shentong Proponents respectively.

Rangtong-Madhyamaka is the subject of Chapters Eight, Nine, and Ten. Chapter Eight begins with a brief introduction to the divisions of Rangtong, Svātantrika and Prāsaṅgika, which are derived from the differences between Bhāvaviveka and Chandrakīrti. Bhāvaviveka and his followers assert as part of their own system that phenomena are empty, and they primarily use independently verifiable reasonings in debate. Chandrakīrti and his followers accept that phenomena are empty only from the perspective of others, and since they do not accept that there are independently verifiable reasonings, they primarily use consequences in debate. Details of the differences between these two systems are found later in this chapter and in Chapter Nine. The majority of Chapter Eight is devoted to their shared approach to refuting the self of persons and the self-entity of phenomena through reasoning. Since reasoning is an important topic in the Rangtong system, it is treated at some length under four subheadings: the subject, object of negation, probandum, and reasons.

When Rangtong-Mādhyamikas engage in debate (without differentiating between whether they are Svātantrikas or Prāsaṅgikas), the subject is not something established by the valid cognitions of both the challenger and the opponent. The object of negation is only something imagined, not appearances. What is imagined is either something whose existence as a convention is negated (such as a self), or something whose ultimate existence is negated, but whose existence as a convention is not (e.g., pragmatic expressions). The probandum (what is to be proven) is a nonimplicative negation[155] that simply refutes the reality of the subject. Reasons are formulated either as negations or affirmations, but all five reasons used by Rangtong-Mādhyamikas are, in fact, negating reasons. The five are: (1) the vajra sliver reasoning, which refutes arising from the four extremes (self, other, both, or causelessly); (2) reasonings that refute the arising of a result that either exists at the time of its cause or does not exist then; (3) reasonings that refute arising from four possibilities;[156] (4) reasonings that refute that something is a single unit or a plurality; and (5) the reason of dependent origination, called the king of reasonings. These are also presented again in Chapter Ten, where some are delved into more extensively.

At the end of Chapter Eight Jamgön Kongtrul summarizes the Svātantrika and Prāsaṅgika positions. First and foremost, they do not disagree about ultimate reality. They only disagree about the way to posit conventional reality. There are three main areas of difference: (1) Svātantrikas either assert conventional reality according to a Sautrāntika position (that there are outer objects) or a Chittamātra position (that there are no outer objects, that objects are images of mind). Prāsaṅgikas make no assertions of their own regarding conventional reality: they simply comply with the everyday expressions that people ordinarily use. (2) Svātantrikas accept the pragmatic conventions of conventional reality as part of their own system; Prāsaṅgikas simply accept them for others, not as part of their own system. (3) In debate, Svātantrikas will establish their own position (emptiness or nonarising) and will use reasons that function by virtue of their relationship to real things, meaning reasons that are independently verifiable (*svatantra, rang rgyud*). Prāsaṅgikas state that they have no position. In debate, they primarily use consequences and do not accept the use of independently verifiable reasons.

In his Svātantrika presentation, here and in the following chapter, Jamgön Kongtrul synthesizes positions known to be held by those who are designated as Svātantrika masters, from Bhāvaviveka and Shāntarakṣhita to the early Tibetan masters Ngok Loden Sherab and Chapa Chökyi Sengé. Readers should be aware that all those designated as Svātantrikas do not necessarily hold all the positions attributed to this style of Madhyamaka. Although Jamgön Kongtrul's sources for this chapter are not certain, it seems that he has drawn much of the material in this chapter (and Chapters Nine and Ten) from Shākya Chokden's *Dharma Treasury.*[157]

Chapter Nine focuses on the Svātantrika system. Jamgön Kongtrul recounts again that the Svātantrika-Prāsaṅgika distinction began with Bhāvaviveka's criticism of Buddhapālita's way of commenting on Nāgārjuna's *Fundamental Treatise on the Middle Way* and Chandrakīrti's defense of Buddhapālita's approach. Bhāvaviveka advocated the use of formal inferences that have become known as "independently verifiable proof statements," and he later came to be considered the founder of the Svātantrika-Madhyamaka. As Jamgön Kongtrul's lengthy list of masters who embraced this system demonstrates, this approach was very popular in India from the sixth century onwards. Since its proponents differ in their assertions regarding the status of objects on a conventional level, they are categorized either as Sautrāntika-Svātantrika-Mādhyamikas, meaning they accept outer objects as mere conventions, or as Yogāchāra-Svātantrika-Mādhyamikas, meaning they assert that outer referents are simply consciousness. Bhāvaviveka is cited as the main proponent of the first division, and Shāntarakṣhita as the main proponent of the latter.

Mādhyamikas' entryway to their path and its results is the two truths. In the Svātantrika presentation, knowable objects are the basis for the classification of the two truths. Conventional reality is what exists from the perspective of a deluded mind; it is what cannot withstand rational analysis. A basis for the definition of conventional reality is a pot. Ultimate reality is that conventional phenomena, when analyzed, do not exist from the perspective of an undeluded mind; it is whatever can withstand rational analysis. A basis for the definition of ultimate reality is that a pot is empty of reality.

Jamgön Kongtrul lists the four possible relationships between the two truths: (1) they are synonyms; (2) they are discrete in their own natures, that is, completely separate from each other; (3) they are discrete simply in the sense that their sameness is negated; and (4) they are identical in nature but are discrete isolates.[158] Jamgön Kongtrul says that many Svātantrikas hold the fourth position. A distinguishing feature of the Svātantrika system is its divisions of the two truths: conventional reality is divided into correct conventionality and mistaken conventionality; and ultimate reality is divided into the nominal ultimate and the final ultimate. In this twofold explanation of the ultimate, the purpose of the nominal ultimate is to account for the role of inferential reasoning in relationship to the ultimate. Jamgön Kongtrul cites Jñānagarbha's *Differentiation of the Two Truths*[159] as the source of these classifications.

Chapter Ten discusses the Prāsaṅgika system under four headings: an account of Chandrakīrti's system; the Madhyamaka exposition according to the works of Nāgārjuna and Āryadeva, which are models for Madhyamaka; an explanation of ground, path, and result in Madhyamaka; and a synopsis of the main points of the Prāsaṅgika system. In his account of Chandrakīrti's system, Jamgön Kongtrul demonstrates the use of four types of reasonings unique to Prāsaṅgikas. These four are: (1) inferences based on what is commonly acknowledged by others; (2) consequences that expose the opponent's contradictions; (3) comparable applications of the opponent's reasons; and (4) demonstrations to the opponent of the irrelevance of proofs that are equivalent to the probandum. Following the procedure outlined by Shākya Chokden, Jamgön Kongtrul applies these four to the refutation of arising from the four extremes (self, other, both, and neither), the mode of reasoning called "the vajra sliver."

In Chandrakīrti's system, the two truths are presented as follows: Conventional reality is dependently originated phenomena appearing to the deluded mind because of the power of ignorance. It is defined as the object found by false seeing. The bases for this definition are, broadly, ignorance; specifically, the ignorance of taking things to be real; and, more particularly, the ignorance present in the mindstreams of ordinary beings. Ultimate reality is the expanse of the noble ones' primordial wisdom; what appears to an undeluded mind. It is defined as the object found by correct seeing. The basis for this definition is primordial wisdom, which directly realizes the absence of reality. Chandrakīrti's system does not divide the two truths and makes no distinction between correct and mistaken conventionalities. All conventional phenomena are equal in the same way that objects in dreams and the objects in waking states are equally "real" when we believe them to be so, yet equally not real in terms of their actual nature.

Under his second heading, "The Model Texts' Exposition of Madhyamaka," Jamgön Kongtrul cites the Sakya scholar Tak-tsang Lotsāwa as saying that the system of Nāgārjuna and Āryadeva explains emptiness in relationship to the three phases of analysis: no analysis, slight analysis, and superb (or thorough) analysis. This brief section makes two valuable points. First, if Buddhist scriptures are looked at from the perspective of these three levels of analysis, there are no internal contradictions. Teachings on the aggregates and constituents (skandhas and dhātus), the methods of the path, and the kāyas and wisdoms of buddhas are presented from the point of view of no analysis. Teachings that refute the existence of a self of persons and a self-entity of phenomena, and those that discuss emptiness and ultimate reality are presented from the perspective of a rational mind that analyzes slightly. The teachings that nothing exists in any way—not as something existent, nonexistent, permanent, impermanent, empty, not empty, or the like—reflect the perspective of thorough analysis. Secondly, these three levels of analysis provide a clear summary of the graduated approach to understanding emptiness. First, we turn away from the causes of suffering and take up what is positive, practices which require no analysis of the ultimate status of those objects. Next, by analyzing phenomena, we are able to counteract our belief in the true existence of our suffering, our emotions, and a self. Finally we must transcend all conceptual elaborations, even notions of emptiness.

In the third section on ground, path, and result, Jamgön Kongtrul says that the ground of the Madhyamaka system is the unity of the two truths, its path is the unity of method and wisdom, and its result is the unity of the two kāyas. Of these, only the first topic of the two truths is dealt with at length. Here, the two truths are described as method and what develops from method. Conventional reality, which consists of what is commonly accepted in the world, is the method for realizing the ultimate, and, in that sense, the ultimate is what develops from method. To bring about an understanding of the ultimate, Prāsaṅgikas use five types of reasons to prove the absence of a self-entity of phenomena, and employ a sevenfold reasoning to prove the absence of a self of persons. The five reasons are presented in detail here, and the sevenfold reasoning is treated briefly as it is discussed at greater length in Part Three of Book Seven.[160] The five reasonings (which are the same five discussed in Chapter Eight) are analyzed in terms of the formulations of the reason, the subject, subject property, and entailment. Here Jamgön Kongtrul says that the Prāsaṅgika position is that these five reasonings are commonly acknowledged by others, whereas the Svātantrika system regards them as independently verifiable reasonings. This discussion of the two truths closes with statements about the actual ultimate: The actual ultimate is beyond being an object of the intellect, and it transcends all conceptual elaborations. It is beyond the means used to cut through elaborations, and it is beyond being a position or thesis of any kind. It is simply to abide in peace, free from elaborations and reference points.

The fourth, and final, part of Chapter Ten is a synopsis of the main points of the Prāsaṅgika system. First, Jamgön Kongtrul presents what he considers to be the five distinctive positions of the Prāsaṅgika system: (1) All phenomena exist only nominally. (2) All conditioned phenomena are deceptive. (3) Taking things to be real is the afflictive obscuration (not the cognitive obscuration), which establishes that shrāvakas and pratyekabuddhas must realize the absence of a self-entity of phenomena. (4) The way dharmatā is seen is the same in all three yānas. (5) Buddhas' form kāyas and activities are simply appearances for others.

Jamgön Kongtrul closes with a list of what he calls "eight uncommon theses expounded by a later generation of Tibetans." These are Tsongkhapa's famous, yet highly controversial, "eight difficult points of the Prāsaṅgika-Madhyamaka." Jamgön Kongtrul cites Shākya Chokden's view of these: "[We can agree] only with the words of the statement 'Noble shrāvakas and pratyekabuddhas realize the absence of a self-entity of phenomena.' As for the other seven points, they are philosophical tenets that Prāsaṅgika-Mādhyamikas would not consider even in their dreams."

Shentong-Madhyamaka

Chapter Eleven is Jamgön Kongtrul's presentation of what he considers to be the highest expression of the Sūtra-Madhyamaka view: Shentong-Madhyamaka, known prior to the time of Dolpopa as Yogāchāra-Madhyamaka. For this chapter, it seems that Jamgön Kongtrul draws exclusively from the works of Tāranātha and Shākya Chokden, either as paraphrases or direct quotations (sometimes without attribution). The scriptural sources for Shentong-Madhyamaka are the five Dharma Treatises of Maitreya[161] and the commentaries on these by Asaṅga and Vasubandhu, which were transmitted in two streams. The general philosophical tenet system of the first three treatises—the *Ornament of Clear Realization, Ornament of the Mahāyāna Sūtras,* and *Differentiation of the Middle and the Extremes*—was transmitted by a lineage originating with Dignāga and Sthiramati. The uncommon philosophical tenet system of the last two treatises—the *Differentiation of Phenomena and Their Nature* and *Highest Continuum*—was transmitted orally in India, and passed to Tibet through the translators Zu Gawé Dorjé[162] and Tsen Kawoché.[163] The Tibetan mahāsiddha Yumo Mikyö Dorjé,[164] a forefather of the Jonang tradition, established this latter transmission as a system of standard texts. As mentioned before, Jamgön Kongtrul considers that the third Karmapa, Rangjung Dorjé, and the Nyingma master Longchen Rabjam explain the key points of the Shentong teachings as the definitive meaning. Dolpopa Sherab Gyaltsen "proclaimed the lion's roar of Shentong-Madhyamaka," setting out his views on Shentong in a clear and definitive manner. Significant contributions to the transmission of the Shentong teachings were made by Shākya Chokden and Tāranātha in the fifteenth and seventeenth centuries respectively. As has been the case with the other philosophical tenet systems, the teachers named as representatives of the Shentong system do not present all points in the same way.

Jamgön Kongtrul addresses one of these differences by presenting the views of both Shākya Chokden and Dolpopa on the categorization of the five Dharma Treatises of Maitreya, and in doing so he also establishes the rationale for why all five treatises are considered Madhyamaka. (Other Tibetan scholars classify these five treatises in various ways, from all being Chittamātra to some being Rangtong.)

The detailed explanation of the Shentong system covers three topics: the two truths; the way Shentong is not the same as Chittamātra; and the way Shentong and Rangtong differ. The presentation of the two truths is a long passage from Tāranātha's *Essence of Shentong* (though not so attributed), in which the two truths are discussed within the framework of the three characteristics. It begins with the first two verses of Maitreya's *Differentiation of the Middle and the Extremes.* In his explanation of these verses, Tāranātha demonstrates how conventional reality (the imagined and dependent characteristics) and ultimate reality (the consummate characteristic) transcend the extremes of nihilism and permanence.

Tāranātha describes the three characteristics: Imagined characteristics include nonentities (such as space), the objects that appear to our thoughts, and all the things that are conceptually imputed by the mind (big, small, good, bad, and so on). The dependent characteristic is mere consciousness that manifests as the entities of percept and perceiver. The consummate is reflexive awareness, self-illuminating and free from conceptual elaborations; it is known variously as dharmatā, thusness, and the ultimate. Imagined and dependent characteristics are equal in that they do not really exist, that they are delusive appearances, and that they are conventionalities and false. They are not, however, identical: imagined characteristics do not exist even on a conventional level, whereas the dependent do exist on a conventional level. The consummate characteristic does not exist conventionally and does exist ultimately; thus it really exists.

Tāranātha next turns to how each of the three characteristics exists, is empty, and is an inherent absence (*niḥsvabhāva, ngo bo nyid med pa).* These explanations are found in the *Sūtra Unraveling the Intention,*[165] Maitreya's *Ornament of the Mahāyāna Sūtras* and *Differentiation of the Middle and Extremes,* and Vasubandhu's *Thirty Verses.*[166] Imagined characteristics are imputedly existent; they are the emptiness of the nonexistent; and they are the inherent absence of characteristics. Dependent characteristics are substantially existent; they are the emptiness of the existent; and they are the inherent absence of arising. The consummate characteristic exists without conceptual elaborations; it is ultimate emptiness; and it is the ultimate inherent absence. Tāranātha then addresses questions that might arise regarding the consummate nature: If the consummate nature is truly existent, does it exist as something that comes or goes? Is it singular or is it a plurality? He replies that if it had any such characteristics, it would not really exist. The consummate nature is, in terms of its own nature, not something that arises or ceases—it is free from conceptual elaborations. It is permanent, partless, and omnipresent. Here, Jamgön Kongtrul adds that the Shentong presentation of the topics related to the ground (the two truths), the path (the pāramitās, five paths, and ten bhūmis), and the result (buddhahood with its kāyas and wisdoms) are for the most part in accord with the Chittamātra system.

The second topic in this chapter is the ways in which the Shentong system is free from the defects of the Chittamātra system, specifically that of the Chittamātra Proponents of False Images. (Some Tibetan scholars regard the Shentong system as being nothing more than that of the Chittamātra Proponents of False Images.) Jamgön Kongtrul provides a simple statement of their differences: Chittamātra Proponents of False Images assert that the ālaya consciousness truly exists, for which they are considered to be Realists. Shentong Proponents assert that primordial wisdom, which transcends consciousness and is free from elaborations, truly exists. Since primordial wisdom is not a conditioned phenomenon, they are free from the mistakes that characterize Realists.

The third topic is how Shentong differs from Rangtong and other points. First, Jamgön Kongtrul says that the Shentong and Rangtong systems do not differ in the way they determine all conventional phenomena to be empty, nor do they disagree that the extremes of conceptual elaborations cease during meditative equipoise. These two system only differ in the way they use conventional expressions in their exposition of their philosophical tenet systems. As a conventional position, Shentong Proponents say that the consummate characteristic, or dharmatā, exists, and Rangtong Proponents say that it does not exist. Shentong Proponents state that nondual primordial wisdom is truly established at the time of final analysis by means of reasonings that analyze for ultimacy, and Rangtong Proponents do not make such assertions. The Shentong position is that ultimate reality is not simply a nonimplicative negation—that is the way the imagined and dependent characteristics are empty. For them, the ultimate is primordial wisdom, which is empty of the duality of perceived and perceiver. Other points in this part include another lengthy quotation from Tāranātha's *Essence of Shentong*, answering critics of the Shentong position on sugatagarbha (buddha nature).

In the final section of this chapter Jamgön Kongtrul makes two recommendations. The first and most important is that we should understand that the system stemming from Nāgārjuna and the system originating with Maitreya and Asaṅga are both Madhyamaka, and that we should appreciate each for its specific contribution to the exposition of the Buddhist path. As Shākya Chokden says, the presentations of the ālaya and the three modes of emptiness (that is, the ways in which the three characteristics are empty), which are found in Asaṅga's texts, are necessary to explain topics found in the tantras, such as the bases for purification and the means of purification. The explanations of the way nondual primordial wisdom is empty of a nature, which are found in the Svātantrika and Prāsaṅgika texts, are needed to eliminate any reification of wisdom. The second point we should keep in mind is that Tāranātha and Shākya Chokden stress the need to distinguish between Chittamātra and Proponents of Cognition (Vijñaptivādins). For both these points, Jamgön Kongtrul quotes two passages from Shākya

Chokden's works, first his *Great Path of the Nectar of Emptiness,*[167] followed by his *Establishing the Unity of the Definitive Meaning.*[168]

Secret Mantra-Madhyamaka

Chapter Twelve is a pithy exposition of the Secret Mantra-Madhyamaka found in the tantras and their commentaries. Since the Madhyamaka found in Secret Mantra (Vajrayāna) emphasizes nondual primordial wisdom, it accords most with Shentong-Madhyamaka; nevertheless the Rangtong expression of Madhyamaka is relevant to, and necessary for, Vajrayāna practice. In this chapter, Jamgön Kongtrul shows how the Rangtong and Shentong modes relate to the two phases of Vajrayāna practice, the generation and completion stages.

Generation stage practice involves imagining deities and their maṇḍalas. The practice of the completion stage is to remain within primordial wisdom. Each stage has two aspects, for which either the Rangtong or the Shentong expression of Madhyamaka is more profound. The first aspect of generation stage practice is the ground for the arising of the deities. Shentong-Madhyamaka explanations clarify how the seed syllables and emblems (from which the deities manifest) arise within emptiness and are expressions of nondual primordial wisdom. The second aspect of generation stage practice is that these deities manifest without conceptual elaborations. Rangtong-Madhyamaka teachings are most useful for understanding this. In terms of the completion stage, first we must let go of any fixations on the generation stage by dissolving the visualization of the deities and maṇḍalas and resting without reference points. The Rangtong approach is most effective for this phase. However, simply resting without reference points is not the actual completion-stage wisdom. The second aspect of completion stage is the actual completion-stage wisdom: the primordial wisdom of connate great bliss. This is described in the Shentong-Madhyamaka teachings.

Jamgön Kongtrul concludes by saying that Sūtra-Madhyamaka and Mantra-Madhyamaka do not differ in terms of the object of their realization, which is freedom from elaborations. They are distinguished only from the perspective of the mind and its qualities of realization.

The book closes with a summary of all Madhyamaka systems in terms of the ground, path, and result and their transcendence of the two extremes. Ground Madhyamaka is the union of the two truths. The Madhyamaka view of the two truths is free from the extreme of nihilism because it accepts that, on a conventional level, appearances manifest due to interdependent causes and conditions. It is free from the extreme of permanence because its view of the ultimate does not involve any conceptually elaborated extremes. Path Madhyamaka is the union of wisdom and merit. In the cultivation of these, Madhyamaka practitioners avoid the extreme of nihilism by amassing merit out of their compassion for others, and they avoid the extreme of permanence by not reifying wisdom. Resultant Madhyamaka is the union of the two kāyas. It lies beyond the extreme of nihilism because of the manifestations of the form kāyas (nirmāṇakāya and sambhogakāya), and it is beyond the extreme of permanence because of the dharmakāya, which is beyond all conceptual elaborations.

The Four Tenet System Structure According to Jamgön Kongtrul

Hīnayāna
- **Vaibhāṣhika:** Dharmatrāta, Vasumitra, Ghoṣhaka, Buddhadeva, Saṅghabhadra, and Anantavarman
- **Sautrāntika:** Shrīlāta and Saṅgharakṣhita

Mahāyāna
- Pāramitāyāna
  - **Chittamātra**: five hundred Mahāyāna masters that include Avitarka
    - Proponents of Real Images
      - Split-Eggists
      - Proponents of Perceptual Parity
      - Non-Pluralists
    - Proponents of False Images
      - Proponents of Staining False Images
      - Proponents of Non-Staining False Images
  - **Madhyamaka**
    - Sūtra-Madhyamaka
      - Rangtong-Madhyamaka
        - Svātantrika: Bhāvaviveka, Shrīgupta, Jñānagarbha, Shāntarakṣhita, Kamalashīla, Vimuktisena, Haribhadra,

Buddhajñānapāda, Atīsha, Vitapāda, and Thagana
Sautrāntika-Svātantrika: Bhāvaviveka
Yogāchāra-Svātantrika: Shāntarakṣhita
Prāsaṅgika: Nāgārjuna, Āryadeva, and Chandrakīrti
Shentong-Madhyamaka: Maitreya, Asaṅga, Vasubandhu, Dignāga, Sthiramati, Zu Gawé Dorjé, Tsen Kawoché, Yumo Mikyö Dorjé, Rangjung Dorjé, Longchen Rabjam, Dolpopa, Shākya Chokden, and Tāranātha
Secret Mantra-Madhyamaka
Vajrayāna (the subject of Book Six, Part Four)

The Epilogue: Syncretism

In the course of fifteen hundred years of philosophical discourse Buddhists have been used to two broad approaches: the refutative and syncretic modes. The refutative method identifies and refutes flawed positions, while a more reconciliatory mode is syncretic in emphasizing the strengths of each philosophical system and incorporating them into a broad picture of philosophical endeavor. The syncretic approach is characteristic of many of the great Indian Buddhist teachers, from Asaṅga to Shāntarakṣhita, and the masters of the Kagyu tradition, such as Karmapa Rangjung Dorjé, Situ Chökyi Jungné, and Jamgön Kongtrul in the present volume. Refutation offers clarification of subtle and profound points, and is vital to the tradition at certain times (as was the case when Nāgārjuna wrote his *Fundamental Treatise on the Middle Way*). It is also more apt to appeal to scholars. The syncretic approach taken here by Jamgön Kongtrul is one well-suited for scholar-practitioners: those who seek awakening through the combination of analytical inquiry and meditation.

Having presented the progressive stages of view in this volume, in Book Eight, Part Two, Jamgön Kongtrul discusses the meditations of the cause-based philosophical yānas, concluding with a succinct summary of meditation as practiced in the two Rangtong-Madhyamaka systems and Shentong-Madhyamaka. The following verses from that section outline a progressive approach to meditating on emptiness, showing how the study of the view and the practice of meditation as found in the tenet systems result in the realization of mahāmudrā.

[Mahāyāna practitioners] primarily [meditate] upon the
meaning of madhyamaka.
For all, the preliminaries include analysis.
Svātantrikas rest in a spacelike nonimplicative negation.
For Prāsaṅgikas, dharmadhātu (the object of meditation)
and the mind (the meditator)
are inseparable, like water poured into water.
Shentong practitioners remain in great nonconceptual
luminosity.
All are in agreement concerning the vital point of simply [remaining] within a state free from conceptual elaborations.[169]

The Translation

Kyabjé Kalu Rinpoché's wish that Jamgön Kongtrul's *The Treasury of Knowledge* be translated into English has taken some time to fulfill. The complexity and concise nature of *The Treasury of Knowledge* requires that the translator either possesses a thorough knowledge of the topics, or that she (or he) receive explanations from living scholars of the traditions represented, and supplement those with textual research. This translation has been prepared by the latter method, for which I am indebted first to Khenpo Tsültrim Gyamtso Rinpoche, whose teachings on this book I heard over twenty years ago. Secondly, I have had the invaluable and tireless help of Āchārya Lama Tenpa Gyaltsen, a learned scholar of the Karma Kagyu tradition.

Following that, I have read, as much as time and resources permitted, the texts from which Jamgön Kongtrul either drew his presentations or directly quoted, as well as the related commentaries on quoted texts. This has proved to be illuminating, and revealed the vastness of the topics that are the subject of Jamgön Kongtrul's succinct exposition. These sources are named in the bibliography and the endnotes, which also include some discussion of difficult or controversial points. Since many of the subjects contained in this volume are found in the works of Western scholars, reference has been made to other works in English to which interested readers may turn for more details on a particular topic.

On the matter of translation style, there is, fortunately or unfortunately, no single approach for this series. Each volume has its own needs and each translator has her or his own response to that. In this volume, I have chosen to use the Sanskrit for some technical terms as well as the major yānas and school names, rather than introduce possibly new translations. Many technical terms are followed by the Sanskrit or the Tibetan to facilitate identification, and a trilingual glossary is provided. Given the highly technical nature of the subjects discussed here, accuracy and precision have been the foremost concern. Many of the notes should provide readers with the understanding and information that Jamgön Kongtrul presumed his audience to possess; however, exhaustive annotation is simply not possible (it would require an additional volume, at least). Numerous points or key terms simply mentioned in this volume are discussed or defined in other sections of *The Treasury of Knowledge*; some of these have been noted and cross-referenced, but a thorough cross-referencing must await the completion of this translation series.

The text translated in *Frameworks of Buddhist Philosophy* consists of root verses, an outline, and commentary. Following this introduction, the root verses are presented with the outline. Since root verses are often studied on their own and memorized, the outline is included to aid such an approach. The main body of this book (root verses, outline, and commentary) has been divided into chapters by the translator, and each chapter opens with its section of outline. Throughout this book any text found in brackets has been added by the translator, including bracketed subheads. The complete outline with page references may be found in the appendix.

Tibetan words are transliterated according to the Turrell Wylie system with the modification that the head letter is capitalized in proper nouns. For Sanskrit the following modifications are used: *ṛi, ch, sh,* and *ṣh* rather than *ṛ, c, ś,* and *ṣh* (although *cch* is used for *cch,* not *chchh*). Reconstructed Sanskrit is indicated on first instance and in the glossary with an asterisk.

ACKNOWLEDGMENTS

This translation is the result of the vision and generosity of many people. The first is Kyabjé Kalu Rinpoché, who initiated this project to translate *The Treasury of Knowledge* in 1988, whose simplicity and lucidity remain my model for all things. The second is Bokar Rinpoché, to whom I am grateful for the invitation to participate in fulfilling Kalu Rinpoché's plan for this project. The third is Khenpo Tsültrim Gyamtso Rinpoche, from whom I have had the great fortune of receiving teachings for the past twenty-two years. Khenpo Rinpoche's explanations of the key sections of this volume and related subjects have provided me with the foundation for undertaking this translation; his way of being demonstrates the joy that comes of combining study and meditation.

I am also grateful to the Dzogchen Ponlop Rinpoche for his teachings at Nitartha Institute, where I studied and translated with him some of the Hīnayāna sections of this text as well as Madhyamaka. Also in the context of Nitartha Institute, I owe much to the explanations of the Āchārya Sherab Gyaltsen and Āchārya Lama Tenpa Gyaltsen, and to the translations of Karl Brunnhölzl and Tyler Dewar. A fortunate chance meeting with Druppon Khenpo Lodrö Namgyal resulted in the clarification of a number of key points.

In particular, I am indebted to Āchārya Lama Tenpa Gyaltsen, who gave his time, energy, and knowledge unstintingly in Germany and again in Colorado; through our discussions and debate, my understanding of the topics in this book were sharpened. I owe many thanks to Karl Brunnhölzl, both for his direct help and for the benefit I derived from his translation of the Madhyamaka section of this book.

Numerous people generously provided me with the reference materials necessary for undertaking this project: Richard Barron, Ani Migme Chödrön, Eric Colombel, Ari Goldfield, Derek Kolleeny, Jules Levinson, Nancy Murphy, Linda Pritzker, Lodrö Sangpo, Peter Schaffranek, Mark Seibold, Gene Smith and the Tibetan Buddhist Resource Center, Tashi Wangmo, Scott Wellenbach, and Ngawang Zangpo. Pemo Lydia Brunet and Kunzang Olivier Brunet carefully researched the citations many years ago in Sonada, India.

This translation has been much benefited by the editorial expertise of Olive Colón, Richard Marshall, and Susan Kyser of Snow Lion Publications, all of whom bore the exigencies of translation (and the translator) with kindness and patience. Karl Brunnhölzl, Andy Karr, Ari Goldfield, George Marsden, Nancy Murphy, and Chryssoula Zerbini contributed useful suggestions for the introduction.

My thanks also to the other translators of this series, Richard Barron, Sarah Harding, Ingrid McLeod, and Ngawang Zangpo, all of whom helped this translation along; and to Sidney Piburn and Jeff Cox of Snow Lion Publications for their dedication to publishing this and other Buddhist works. I am forever grateful for the immutable friendships of Richard Marshall,

George Marsden, and Joan Baumbach, who, each in his or her own way, made the completion of this project possible and easier. Finally, many thanks to Eric Colombel and Lama Drupgyu of Tsadra Foundation for their vision, encouragement, and support.

May the study and contemplation of *Frameworks of Buddhist Philosophy* bring tolerance, joy, and wisdom to all beings.

THE ROOT TEXT
FRAMEWORKS OF BUDDHIST PHILOSOPHY
A Systematic Presentation of the Cause-Based Philosophical Vehicles

A General Statement [I]

The three yānas of Buddhism were expounded by the Victor.
The four philosophical tenet systems are the outcome
of the final view [reached] by individuals through their own intellectual processes.

The Specific Divisions [II]
A Systematic Presentation of the Hīnayāna [A]
An Overview [1]

The Hīnayāna consists of the Shrāvaka[yāna] and the Pratyekabuddha[yāna].

The Extensive Explanation [2]
The Shrāvakayāna [a]
The Meaning of the Term and Its Etymology [i]

Shrāvakas attend others and proclaim what they have heard.

The Explanation of Its Entryway [ii]

The Overview: An Enumeration [aa]

The entryway [for shrāvakas] is
the four truths of suffering, its origins, its cessation, and the path,
with their sixteen aspects of the acceptance of phenomena, knowledge of phenomena, subsequent acceptance, and subsequent knowledge.

The Extensive Explanation: The Defining Characteristics [of the Four Truths] [bb]

The Combined Explanation [1']

The Essence [of the Four Truths] [a']

In terms of their essence, [the four truths are] the continuity of the aggregates produced by previous karma and mental afflictions;
the karma and mental afflictions forming the causes for what will be appropriated in the future;
the relinquishment that has destroyed what is to be eliminated by means of the remedies;
and primordial wisdom, which has the power to relinquish and attain.

Their Defining Characteristics [b']

[The four truths] are characterized by being in agreement with [the Buddha's] teachings.

The Definitiveness of Their Numbers and Sequence [c']

Their numbers—in two sets of causes and results—and their sequence are definite.
They are what is to be understood, abandoned, attained, and relied upon.

Their Etymologies [d']

In terms of their essence, each is undeceiving; thus they are said to be truths.

The Individual Explanations of the Four Truths [2']
The Truth of Suffering, What Is to Be Understood [a']
Ascertaining Its Nature [i']

The nine levels within the three realms (which are the places where beings take birth)
and the beings who take birth there are of the nature of the truth of suffering.

The Categories [of Suffering] and Their Abridgement in Terms of Their Nature [ii']

In terms of their nature, [sufferings] can be condensed into eight, six, three, or two [categories].

The Truth of the Origins of Suffering, What Is to Be Relinquished [b']
An Overview [i']

The truth of the origins of suffering consists of the mental afflictions and defiled karma.

The Extensive Explanation [ii']
The Origins of Suffering in Terms of the Mental Afflictions [aa']
The Causes of the [Afflictive] Origins of Suffering [1"]

Subtle proliferators, observed objects, and incorrect mental engagement are the causes.

The Nature [of the Afflictive Origins of Suffering] [2"]

[The afflictive causes of suffering] are mental events characterized by a pronounced lack of tranquility.

The Classifications [of the Afflictive Origins of Suffering] [3"]

The motivating forces are the root mental afflictions,
the secondary ones, and the views.

The Origins of Suffering in Terms of Karma [bb']
The Nature [of the Karmic Origins of Suffering] [1"]

[They create] actions that are intentions and the physical and verbal actions produced by those.

The Classifications [of the Karmic Origins of Suffering] [2"]
The Classifications [of Karma] in Terms of Its Nature [a"]
The Root Text's Overview [i"]

[Karma is] unmeritorious, meritorious, or stable.

Alternative Classification Schemes [b"]

It is in terms of its impetus and completion; speed; performance and storage; strength;
mode of appearance; and being similar or not that [karma] causes [beings] to take rebirth in the three realms.

The Truth of Cessation, What Is to Be Attained [c']
An Overview of the General Points [i']

The attainment of separation brought about by the path is cessation, thusness.
Vaibhāṣhikas and Sautrāntikas [respectively] assert it to be a nonimplicative negation that is substantially established or that is not so established.

Ascertaining the Nature [of Cessation] [ii']

The nature [of cessation] is [described by its] twelve aspects: its characteristics, profundity, and so forth.

The Truth of the Path, What Is to Be Practiced [d']

The path is that which, once embarked upon, takes you to your goal.

It comprises the five paths: accumulation, junction, seeing, meditation, and beyond training.

The Presentation Summarizing the General Characteristics [of the Four Truths] [3']

Suffering [a']

[Suffering is] impermanent, suffering, empty, and without a self-entity.

Its Origins [b']

[The origins of suffering are] causes, origins, strong producers, and conditions.

Its Cessation [c']

[Cessation is] cessation, peace, goodness, and definitive release.

The Path [d']

[The path is] a path, suitable, effective, and what brings definite release.

The Vows to Be Guarded [iii]

The vows, that which are to be guarded, are the discipline of individual liberation, [motivated by the wish for] definitive release.

The View to Be Realized [iv]

The view is primarily the realization of the absence of a self of persons.

The Result to Be Attained [v]

Nirvāṇa is a nonarising, unconditioned phenomenon.

Vaibhāṣhikas assert that it is an implicative negation and
Sautrāntikas that it is a nonimplicative negation.
[Nirvāṇa] with remainder [is divided into] eighty-nine conditioned and unconditioned [results],
or into four results; [nirvāṇa] without remainder is the severing of continuity.

The Classifications [of the Shrāvakayāna] [vi]
The Classifications of Its Philosophical Tenet Systems [aa]
The Actual Classifications [1']

[The Shrāvakayana's] philosophical tenet systems are either Vaibhāṣhika or Sautrāntika.

A Description of Their Assertions [2']
Their Similar Assertions [a']

They agree in not accepting the teachings of the Mahāyāna scriptures.
They reject a permanent, single self and state that karma is the creator.

Observed objects either increase defilements or do not.
Thus conditioned phenomena are defiled phenomena; and the phenomena of the truth of the path and unconditioned phenomena are undefiled phenomena.
[Conventional reality] is whatever halts its perceiver
when it is destroyed or eliminated.

[Gross] entities and continuities are conventionally existent and ultimately do not perform functions.
Partless particles and instants of mind, which do not so halt,
are ultimately existent and perform functions.
They agree for the most part about the way conditioned phenomena arise and about the paths and results.

Their Dissimilar Assertions [b']
Vaibhāṣhikas' Assertions [i']

Points of dissimilarity are that the Vaibhāṣhikas assert that the seven [abhidharma] texts are [the Buddha's] words;
that there are partless, discrete particles with interstices between them;
that when of similar types, [such particles] perform the same activity, and that they are like [grasses in] a meadow;
that sense faculties see referents, and consciousnesses apprehend those [referents];
and that in most cases, percepts and perceivers, as causes and results, arise simultaneously.

[Vaibhāṣhikas] maintain that the five bases, [the phenomena of] the three times, and nirvāṇa exist substantially;
that unconditioned phenomena are permanent, and the truth of cessation is an entity;
that consciousnesses are aware of what is other; and other points.
The basis [of their system] was delineated by the four great ones and others in reliance upon scriptures.

Sautrāntikas' Assertions [ii']

Dārṣhṭāntikas mostly state the opposite of that.
Particles touch but do not join, like [the pages of] a book.
The sense faculties are matter; external referents are hidden phenomena.
The consciousnesses do not see these: they experience images as their referents.

Forms, mind, feelings, discriminations, and intentions exist substantially.
Everything else is imputedly existent; space and the others are nonimplicative negations.
They assert that [consciousness is both] a reflexive-awareness and an other-awareness; that [the phenomena of] the three times are imputed entities; and other points.
This is [the system] asserted by Saṅgharakṣhita, Shrīlāta, and others.

The Classifications of Its Orders [bb]
The Four Main Orders [1']

The main orders are the four: Sarvāstivādins,
Mahāsāṅghikas, Sthaviras, and Saṃmitīyas.

The Eighteen Divisions [2']

The divisions into five, seven, three, and three [result in] the eighteen [orders].

The Twofold Summation [3']
The Actual Twofold Summation [a']

They are grouped into propounders of a self and propounders of an absence of a self.

Ancillary Analysis [b']

[Shrāvakas] are flawed in their refutation of the Mahāyāna and in their assertion that [ultimate] reality is established.
On other [topics] they are not wrong; it is their own system.

The Classifications of Its Results [cc]
An Overview [1']

Having meditated on the sixteen aspects, one progresses through the five paths
by applying the factors for awakening, and attains the four types of results.

An Extensive Explanation [2']
A Detailed Explanation of the Gradual Type [a']
Stream Enterers [i']
Approachers to the Result of a Stream Enterer [aa']

Approachers to [the result of] a stream enterer may not have abandoned any of the desire realm afflictions,
or they may have abandoned the fourth or fifth, but to have abandoned the sixth is not possible.
They abide in one of the fifteen moments,
and are of two types: followers of faith and followers of the dharma.

Abiders in the Result of a Stream Enterer [bb']

Abiders in the result
have attained the realization of the sixteenth moment.
There are those of lower and higher acumen, those who will take seven rebirths, and those who will take two.

Once Returners [ii']
Approachers to the Result of a Once Returner [aa']

Through their meditation, they become approachers to a once returner.
They [will] abandon the sixth [affliction].

Abiders in the Result of a Once Returner [bb']

They have not abandoned the ninth [affliction] at all.
Abiders in the result who have one interruption will definitely return.

Nonreturners [iii']
Approachers to the Result of a Nonreturner [aa']

By exerting themselves continuously, they become approachers to a nonreturner.

Abiders in the Result of a Nonreturner [bb']

Those who abandon the ninth [affliction] abide in the result. They may go to the form realm,
where they pass beyond [misery] in the bardo, after birth, or [after] rising to a higher state;
they may go to the formless realm; they may [attain] peace in this lifetime; or they may physically actualize [nirvāṇa].

Arhats [iv']

Approachers to the Result of an Arhat [aa']

They approach the level of an arhat in order to abandon the ninth affliction of the [Pinnacle of] Existence.

Abiders in the Result of an Arhat [bb']

With the abandonment of that [ninth affliction], they are liberated from the bonds of the three realms and abide in the result.
[This result] is classified as those with twofold liberation and those liberated by wisdom;
those with the ornaments of the supercognitive abilities of magical powers and those without ornaments; and
those with a remainder of the appropriating aggregates and those without remainder.

An Explanation of the Skipping and Instantaneous Types as Supplementary Topics [b']

Of the four pairs of beings, or the eight types of individuals,
the first and last have the instantaneous type and the middle two have skippers.

The Pratyekabuddhayāna [b]

How Pratyekabuddhas Differ from Shrāvakas [i]

Swift pratyekabuddhas are released in three existences,

and the rhinoceros[-like take] one hundred aeons; they all give rise to [some qualities that] are strong, some that are weak, and others profound.

A Systematic Presentation of the Pratyekabuddhayāna [ii]
The Meaning of the Term and Its Etymology [aa]

The meaning of the term is that they awaken on their own without relying on others.

Its Entryway [bb]
An Overview of Its Entryway [1']

Their entryway is to take external causes and results as analogies
for the forward and reverse sequences of internal dependent origination.

A Detailed Explanation of Its Style of Meditation [2']

Saṃsāra and nirvāṇa both have two modes: forward and reverse.

The Vows to Be Guarded [cc]

Their vows are those of individual liberation.

The View to Be Realized [dd]

They realize the absence of a self of persons
and that perceived referents have no nature.

The Classifications [of Pratyekabuddhas] [ff]
The Rhinoceros-like [1']

Those of higher acumen
in their final phase of cyclic existence take rebirth on the basis of three aspirations.
They become fully ordained monastics and rely upon the special and final fourth [meditative concentration].

By meditating on the sixteen aspects [of the four truths],
on one seat,
they proceed from the heat of the path of junction to the attainment
of an arhat.

The Congregating Practitioners [2']

The lesser congregating practitioners are of lower acumen, the
greater congregating practitioners are of intermediate acumen.
They take two lifetimes, and bring [the doors of] liberation to mind.
They teach the dharma by means of silent physical communications.

A Systematic Presentation of the Mahāyāna [B]

A Description of the Differences between the Hīnayāna and Mahāyāna [1]

[Mahāyāna practitioners] realize both absences of self-entity; their
intention and practice accord with the pāramitās.
They abandon the two obscurations, and do not abide in the
extremes of existence or peace.
[The Mahāyāna] possesses seven greatnesses.

The Actual Systematic Presentation of the Mahāyāna [2]

The Pāramitāyāna: The Cause-Based Philosophical [Yāna] [a]

An Overview of Its Characteristics [i]

This is the Mahāyāna, [which leads practitioners to]
buddhahood
through its cause-based philosophical [path].

A Detailed Account of the Systematic Presentation [of the Pāramitāyāna] [ii]

General Statements about Undertaking the Training [aa]

The Person Who Trains [1']

People who make this journey
are highly intelligent; their acumen is at one of three levels.

The Application of the Training: The Six Pāramitās [2']

Following the generation of bodhichitta,
their undertaking is to train in the six pāramitās.
We should understand these in terms of their essential qualities; characteristics; etymologies;
divisions and summaries; pure forms; most important types; distinctiveness; ways of training;
results; numerical definitiveness; and order.

An Explanation of the Actual Practice: Shamatha and Vipashyanā [3']

The actual practice is first to cultivate shamatha, which is one-pointed concentration,
and then vipashyanā, which is the discernment of phenomena.

A Detailed Explanation of the Classifications of [the Pāramitāyāna's] Philosophical Tenet Systems [bb]

An Overview: Their Names [1']

[The Pāramitāyāna's] systems of philosophical tenets are either Chittamātra or Madhyamaka.

An Extensive Explanation of the Characteristics of [the Pāramitāyāna's Philosophical Tenet Systems] [2']

An Explanation of the Chittamātra System [a']

The Meaning of the Term and Its Etymology [i']

Chittamātras state that consciousness is truly existent.

A Summary of Its Seven Bases [ii']
An Overview [aa']

They condense the entire Mahāyāna path into seven bases.

An Extensive Explanation [bb']
The Source of Knowable Objects [1"]

The source of knowable objects is the ālaya consciousness.

The [Three] Characteristics of Those [Knowable Objects] [2"]
The Dependent [Characteristic], the Basis for Designations [a"]

As for the three characteristics: the dependent characteristic arises from that [ālaya consciousness].
It is the imagination of what is unreal, appearing through the force of habitual tendencies.
It does not remain for an instant and is governed by what precedes it.

The Imagined [Characteristic], What Is Designated [b"]

On top of that substantially existent basis for designations,
a self, "mine," and so forth are mistakenly imagined.

The Consummate [Characteristic], the Pervader [c"]

[The consummate is] the unconditioned, empty of the object of negation: imputed existence.
It is nonconceptual cognition, empty of duality, ultimately existent.

[How] to Engage the Import of Those [3"]

The practical engagement of those [three characteristics involves] three [determinations] free from discouragement; four abandonments;
devoted interest; knowing the absence of any reference;
abandoning imagination; and seeing correctly.

In this way, [bodhisattvas] enter the bhūmis of engagement
through belief, seeing, meditation, and completion.

The Cause and Result [of That Engagement] [4"]

The cause and result of that [engagement] are contained within the
conduct of the six pāramitās.

The Unfolding [5"]

The gradual progression is the unfolding of the modes of the ten
bhūmis.

The Three Trainings [6"]

The trainings are the three types of higher trainings.

The Results of Purification [7"]

The results are the excellences of relinquishment and primordial
wisdom.

The Explanation of the Classifications [of the Chittamātra System] [iii']

The General Explanation [aa']

The root of their assertions is that other than being mere
cognition,
external referents do not have even the slightest existence, like
dreams.

The Actual Classifications [of the Chittamātra System] [bb']

The Actual [Classifications] [1"]

Proponents of Real Images [a"]

The Assertions of the Proponents of Real Images [i"]

They hold [one of] two positions: [first,] Proponents of Real Images
assert that appearances are real in being the mind, which
is the perceived object.

A Description of Their Specific Classifications [ii"]

Split-Eggists [aa"]

> [Some state that both] cognition and [its] images are real in being reflexive parts.

Proponents of Perceptual Parity [bb"]

> [Others say that] the number of perceiving cognizers corresponds to the number of perceived images.

Non-Pluralists [cc"]

> [Some] say that even though there are various appearances, the entity [of cognition] is not a plurality.

Proponents of False Images [b"]

A General Explanation of Their Assertions [i"]

> Proponents of False Images assert that, like [the floaters seen] by the visually impaired,
> appearances are nonexistents vividly appearing, unreal and false;
> only cognition empty of duality is real.

Their Specific Classifications [ii"]

> Since [some] assert that appearances taint cognition and [some] do not,
> and [some] say that there are dualistic appearances on the bhūmi of buddhahood and [others] say there are not,
> there are the two divisions of Staining and Non-Staining.

Ancillary Points [2"]

The Masters Who Assert Those [Chittamātra Positions] [a"]

> This is the system of five hundred past masters and others.

The Way This [Chittamātra View] Is Refuted [b'']

All the flawed [assertions] of Realists are refuted by the texts of the noble [Nāgārjuna].

An Explanation of the Madhyamaka System [b']

The Meaning of the Term and Its Etymology [i']

Being free from extremes, Madhyamaka is the best philosophical tenet system.

Its Entryway [ii']

Its entryway is the two truths.
[Mādhyamikas engage] conventional reality knowing that from the perspective of no analysis, [things] appear and yet do not truly exist;
and they conduct themselves properly with regard to what is to be adopted and rejected.
They encounter ultimate [reality] by knowing that there is nothing to adopt or reject, block or encourage, in anything—
the very [moment] things simply appear, they are empty.
This [approach] integrates the two stores.

The Vows to Be Guarded [iii']

What are to be guarded are the bodhisattva vows.

The View to Be Realized [iv']

What is realized is that, on the conventional [level], phenomena appear while not existing, like the moon's reflection in water;
but, ultimately, all elaborations and characteristics subside.
They realize the two truths unerringly.

The Result to Be Attained [v']

The result is peace, the manifestation of the two kāyas.

The Classifications [of the Madhyamaka System] [vi']
An Overview [aa']

Although Madhyamaka is classified in many ways, its two main divisions are Sūtra-Madhyamaka and Mantra-Madhyamaka.

An Extensive Explanation [bb']
The Common Madhyamaka of the Sūtra System [1"]
An Overview: The Names [of Madhyamaka Schools] [a"]

The Sūtra system comprises [the teachings of] the Proponents of the Absence of a Nature and the Yogāchāras,
which correspond [respectively] to such terms as "ordinary" and "preeminent," or "broad" and "subtle."
In Tibet, they are known as Rangtong and Shentong.

An Extensive Explanation: The Characteristics [of Madhyamaka Schools] [b"]
Rangtong [i"]
A Brief Account of the Divisions [of Rangtong] [aa"]

The first has two [subschools:] the Svātantrika and Prāsaṅgika.

A Detailed Explanation of the Systematic Presentation [of Rangtong] [bb"]
The System Common to Prāsaṅgikas and Svātantrikas [(1)]
The Twofold Absence of Self-entity [(a)]

Their common [approach] is to use reasonings to refute
the two self-entities: of persons (the source of views) and of phenomena (the root of obscurations).

The Mode of Reasonings [(b)]

The object to be negated is something imputed to a subject.
Probanda are either facts or conventions.
Reasons analyze four points: cause, result, both of those, and nature.
These four forms of analysis eliminate the Realists' extreme of existence.

The reason of dependent origination, [used in] the analysis of mere appearances, eliminates both extremes.
Thus [Svātantrikas and Prāsaṅgikas] do not disagree about the ultimate.

The Explanation of Their Differences [(2)]

They differ over many issues: conventional [reality], statements in debate, and other points.

The Explanation of the Individual [Rangtong] Systems [(3)]
The Systematic Presentation of Svātantrika [(a)]
An Account of Its Specific Classifications [(i)]
Sautrāntika-[Svātantrika-] Mādhyamikas [(aa)]

Among those who commented on the thought of Nāgārjuna, Bhāvaviveka and his followers
accept positions of their own, such as emptiness,
and formulate reasons in which the three modes are established through the power of [their relationship to real] things.
They concur with Sautrāntikas about outer objects.

Yogāchāra-[Svātantrika-] Mādhyamikas [(bb)]

Shāntarakṣhita and others only assert mere consciousness,
not outer referents; in this presentation they are like Chittamātras.

A Concise Explanation of Its Systematic Presentation [(ii)]

Conventional [reality] is that, from the perspective of a deluded state of mind, phenomena exist.
Ultimate [reality] is that, from the perspective of an undeluded mind, there is no such existence.
The two truths are defined as either what can be negated by reasonings or what cannot be so negated.
They are one in essence but different isolates.
Conventional [reality] is presented as correct or mistaken according to
whether something is able to perform a function or not.

They prove a nonimplicative negation that is an exclusion: it [simply] refutes real entities.
The refutation of arising and so forth is the nominal ultimate.
The pacification of elaborations is the final ultimate.
They do not assert an ālaya, thus consciousness has six modes.
They say that fruition is the illusionlike appearances of primordial wisdom.

The Systematic Presentation of Prāsaṅgika-Madhyamaka [(b)]

A Brief Account of Chandrakīrti's Exegetical System [(i)]

For eradicating conceptually elaborated characteristics, Chandrakīrti's system
is exceptional and preeminent; it does not use independently [verifiable] reasons.
His own system is free from assertions except [for what is done] simply for others.
[This system uses] negations and affirmations that employ four valid means of cognition—
direct perception, inference, scriptural authority, and analogical proof, which are commonly acknowledged in the world;
and four types of reasons—inferences based on what is commonly acknowledged by others, consequences that expose contradictions,

comparable applications of [the opponent's] reasons, and [the
demonstration of] the irrelevance [of proofs that are equivalent
to the probandum].

A mind that discerns conventions is necessarily a mistaken cognition.
Correct and mistaken conventional [realities] are equal in their
performance and nonperformance of functions.
The presentation of the two truths is determined by the presence
of delusion and its absence.
In sum, this is the final exegesis of the Collection of Reasonings.

A General Description of the Model Texts' Exposition of Madhyamaka [(ii)]

A General Statement [(aa)]

Scholars say, "In the system of the noble father and son, which
serves as the model for all [Madhyamaka] texts,
the fundamental topic of profound emptiness
is explained in terms of the three phases."

The Specific Explanation [(bb)]

The ground, the sphere of conduct, and the result are presented
in accord with conventional expressions from a perspective of no
analysis.
The absence of self-entity and the ultimate are presented from the
perspective of slight analysis.
Superb analysis is the pacification of all conceptual elaborations.

The Specific Explanation of Ground, Path, and Result [in Madhyamaka] [(iii)]

Ground Madhyamaka: The Unity of the Two Truths [(aa)]

The Actual [Presentation of the Two Truths] [(1')]

It is taught that worldly conventional [reality] is the method
and ultimate reality is what develops from that method.

The Explanation of the Way [the Two Truths] Are Established [(2')]

For conventionality, [Prāsaṅgikas] cite what is commonly acknowledged by others in the world.
In terms of the ultimate, [Prāsaṅgikas] use five types of reasons to prove the absence of a self-entity of phenomena
and a sevenfold reasoning to prove the absence of a self of persons.

The actual ultimate is beyond the intellect; elaborations do not apply to it.
Cutting through elaborations, such as eliminating the eight extremes, is [itself] simply a convention.

A thesis is [the creation of] the intellect; the intellect is conventional.
Therefore, there are no independently [verifiable] theses or assertions.
Even nonarising and so forth are not a thesis,
because they [simply] banish fixation to never-existent entities.
It is taught that once [reification] is overturned, clinging to nonentities must be renounced.

The [Prāsaṅgika] philosophical system emphasizes abiding in unborn peace, free from elaborations;
this involves no mode of apprehension.

Path Madhyamaka: The Unity of Method and Wisdom [(bb)]

The unification of method and wisdom is gradually developed during the ten bhūmis
[when] primordial wisdom directly realizes [dharmatā].
[Primordial wisdom] is divided during subsequent attainment in that it is the support.

Resultant Madhyamaka: The Unity of the Two Kāyas [(cc)]

[The result] is asserted to be the unity of the two kāyas.

A Synopsis of the Main Points of the [Prāsaṅgika] Philosophical Tenet System [(iv)]

What is logically imputed is rejected: entities are simply names.
Conditioned phenomena are deceptive; nirvāṇa is not.
Taking things to be real and what that produces is the afflictive obscuration, the root of cyclic existence.
Because the three yānas' ways of seeing are similar, their paths of seeing are the same.

Since [from the perspective of buddhas] knowable objects have subsided, buddhas are simply appearances for others.
These are the main features of this philosophical tenet system.

The Explanation of the Shentong-Madhyamaka System [ii"]
An Overview of the [Shentong] System [aa"]

Maitreya's thought was explained by Asaṅga and his brother.
The two systems of Yogāchāra and Certainty about the Ultimate
do not differ in terms of the essence of their views.

However, in the system of the first Dharma Treatises there are three yānas [ultimately];
whereas the view of the *Highest Continuum* is that there is one yāna ultimately,
a bhūmi with the habitual tendencies of ignorance, and birth through undefiled karma.
These are ways for the common [disciples] to cut through conceptual elaborations and the uncommon [to become certain] about the ultimate.

A Detailed Explanation of [the Shentong] System [bb"]
The Way the Two Truths Are Ascertained [(1)]

First, imagination of what is unreal exists conventionally.
Percept and perceiver are simply imputed by mind and do not exist.

Primordial wisdom, free from conceptual elaborations, [exists] in the sense that it is the dharmatā of that [consciousness];
and within that [dharmatā], adventitious, removable stains exist.

Conventional [phenomena] are simply delusive appearances, empty of any nature.
Dharmatā is unchanging, not empty of a nature.
The imagined is nonexistent; the dependent exists conventionally.
The consummate does not exist conventionally but does exist ultimately.

These three [characteristics] are imputedly existent, substantially existent, and existent without conceptual elaborations.
They are the emptiness of the nonexistent, the emptiness of the existent, and the ultimate emptiness.
They are the inherent absence of characteristics, the inherent absence of arising, and the ultimate inherent absence.

Consequently, [Shentong Proponents] assert that all knowable objects are pervaded by emptiness.
They state that the consummate, in terms of its own nature, is not connected to conventional phenomena;
it precludes the triad of definition, definiendum, and illustration;
it is free from conceptual elaborations, permanent, partless, and omnipresent.
Their presentations of all other [topics] accord with the Chittamātra.

The Way [Shentong] Is Free from the Chittamātras' Defects [(2)]

The Proponents of False Images state that the entity of consciousness truly exists and
that it is an object of mind. This [Shentong system] asserts that primordial wisdom
truly exists; and yet, because it is not a conditioned phenomenon,
[their assertions about] the ultimate are free from the mistakes of the Realists.

An Explanation of the Ways that Rangtong and Shentong Differ and Other Points [(3)]

The Rangtong and Shentong [systems] do not differ over
the way that conventional [phenomena] are empty, nor do they disagree that the extremes of conceptual elaborations cease during meditative equipoise.
They differ over whether, as a convention, dharmatā exists during subsequent attainment or not,
and over whether primordial wisdom is truly established at the end of analysis or not.

[The Shentong system] asserts that [if] ultimate reality
were simply a nonimplicative negation, whereby its nature is not established,
it would be an inanimate emptiness.
[Shentong Proponents] present [ultimate reality] as being primordial wisdom empty of dualism, as being reflexive awareness.
This is asserted to be the profound view linking the Sūtra and Mantra [systems].

Additional Topics: Recommendations [cc"]

Most Tibetan teachers say, "This system is Chittamātra,"
and regard Maitreya's texts and Asaṅga and his brother as inferior.
The sun and moon that ornament the sky of the Sage's teachings
are the scriptural traditions of the two chariot[-systems].

The judicious thing is to give up fixed positions in which one repeatedly echoes the constellation[-like] minor texts,
and engage [these two systems] in an equal way.

The Profound Madhyamaka of Secret Mantra [2"]

The Madhyamaka of the profound Mantra [approach] is the basic state of all phenomena.
It is natural luminosity distinguished by great bliss;

it is primordial wisdom, the union of clarity and emptiness, bliss
and emptiness.
This is taught clearly in the *Five Stages,* Commentaries by Bodhisattvas, and other texts.

A Synopsis of What Is Taught in All Madhyamaka [Systems]: Its Ground, Path, and Fruition [vii']

As its ground, [Madhyamaka] does not denigrate conventionalities just as they appear,
and it is free from conceptually elaborated extremes regarding the abiding nature.
Its path is to relinquish the apprehension of characteristics through profound wisdom,
and to amass merit for the sake of others out of compassion.

Its result is the perfection of the dharmakāya, a state of peace,
and that the form kāyas nonconceptually benefit others.
These [three points] contain all that is taught in Madhyamaka.

1. THREE YĀNAS AND FOUR TENET SYSTEMS

I. A General Statement

The systematic presentation of the cause-based philosophical *yānas*, or vehicles, begins with two parts: a general statement; and the specific divisions.

A General Statement [I]

> **The three yānas of Buddhism were expounded by the Victor.**
> **The four philosophical tenet systems are the outcome**
> **of the final view [reached] by individuals through their own intellectual processes.**

Our Buddhist tradition[170] is renowned for its three yānas and four systems of philosophical tenets. Among these, the three yānas[171] are what the Victor [Buddha Shākyamuni] presented as his teachings; they are also what the victors who appeared earlier in this excellent aeon taught, and what the victors who will appear later will teach.

Generally, it is well known that a "yāna"[172] is [a form of transport] such as an elephant with its load; the term also carries the sense of that which is traveled on (*bgrod par bya ba*) while it bears its load. Accordingly, the means for traveling (*bgrod par byed pa*) to the supreme state while carrying the burden of benefiting ourselves and others is designated as a "yāna." Furthermore, [the yāna that employs] that by which we travel (*'dis bgrod pa*) [as its method] is referred to as a "cause-based path"; and [the yāna that uses] where we are traveling to (*'dir bgrod pa*) [as its method] is "a result-based yāna."[173] Also, the yāna that involves the greater burden of the welfare of both ourselves and others is designated as the Mahāyāna; the yāna that involves only the lesser burden of our own benefit is designated as the Hīnayāna.[174]

The four philosophical tenet systems are described in Secret Mantra[175] as follows. The *Glorious Two-Part* [*Hevajra Tantra*] states in its section on a gradual progression based on view:[176]

> Teach them the Vaibhāṣhika
> and Sautrāntika [systems].
> Explain Yogāchāra
> and, after that, Madhyamaka.

The Primordial Wisdom chapter of the *Kālachakra Tantra*[177] says that the four philosophical tenet systems arise from the four faces of the Bhagavat. Their names are mentioned simply for symbolic purposes; the tantra does not present them in terms of a threefold exposition of ground, path, and result, as it does for the three yānas. (The four Vedas[178] are also said to arise from the four faces of Kālachakra;[179] however, that does not mean that they were the Buddha's exposition.)

The four systems of philosophical tenets were set forth by individuals who appeared after the Teacher [Shākyamuni Buddha] and who were founders of particular chariot-systems. Therefore, the philosophical tenet systems are the outcome (*grub don*) of the final view (*lta ba mthar thug*) that individuals [reach] through their own intellectual analysis. For this reason, the omniscient Rongtön the Great[180] explains:

> As for the meaning of "philosophical tenet":[181] it is the outcome of thorough analysis, which individuals who are engaged in investigating what is to be accepted and what is to be rejected [arrive at] through their particular orientation (*'dod pa*).
>
> The meaning of the term signifies that what is established (*grub pa*) through the scriptures and reasonings of a particular system is not surpassed [for followers of that system].

SECTION I: HĪNAYĀNA

2. THE SHRĀVAKAYĀNA: AN OVERVIEW AND THE FOUR TRUTHS

II. The Specific Divisions
A. A Systematic Presentation of the Hīnayāna
1. An Overview
2. The Extensive Explanation
a. The Shrāvakayāna
i. The Meaning of the Term and Its Etymology
ii. The Explanation of Its Entryway
aa. An Overview: An Enumeration
bb. The Extensive Explanation: The Defining Characteristics [of the Four Truths]
1' The Combined Explanation
a' The Essence [of the Four Truths]
b' Their Defining Characteristics
c' The Definitiveness of Their Numbers and Sequence
d' Their Etymologies
2' The Individual Explanations of the Four Truths
a' The Truth of Suffering, What Is to Be Understood
i' Ascertaining Its Nature
ii' The Categories [of Suffering] and Their Abridgement in Terms of Their Nature
b' The Truth of the Origins of Suffering, What Is to Be Relinquished
i' An Overview
ii' The Extensive Explanation
aa' The Origins of Suffering in Terms of the Mental Afflictions
1" The Causes of the [Afflictive] Origins of Suffering

2" The Nature [of the Afflictive Origins of Suffering]
3" The Classifications [of the Afflictive Origins of Suffering]
bb' The Origins of Suffering in Terms of Karma
1" The Nature [of the Karmic Origins of Suffering]
2" The Classifications [of the Karmic Origins of Suffering]
a" The Classifications [of Karma] in Terms of Its Nature
i" The Root Text's Overview
ii" The Commentary's Addition: A Detailed Treatment
aa" Unmeritorious Karma
bb" Meritorious Karma
cc" Stable Karma
b" Alternative Classification Schemes
c' The Truth of Cessation, What Is to Be Attained
i' An Overview of the General Points
ii' Ascertaining the Nature [of Cessation]
d' The Truth of the Path, What Is to Be Practiced
3' The Presentation Summarizing the General Characteristics [of the Four Truths]
a' Suffering
b' Its Origins
c' Its Cessation
d' The Path
iii. The Vows to Be Guarded
iv. The View to Be Realized
v. The Result to Be Attained

[In this chapter, the main body of the volume begins with] the specific divisions, which has two main sections: a systematic presentation of the Hīnayāna; and a systematic presentation of the Mahāyāna.

A Systematic Presentation of the Hīnayāna [A]

This has two parts: an overview; and the extensive explanation.

An Overview [1]

> **The Hīnayāna consists of the Shrāvaka[yāna] and the Pratyekabuddha[yāna].**

The Extensive Explanation [2]

This has two divisions: the Shrāvakayāna; and the Pratyekabuddhayāna.

The Shrāvakayāna [a]

This presentation has six topics: the meaning of the term and its etymology;[182] its entryway; the vows to be guarded; the view to be realized; the result to be attained; and the classifications [of the Shrāvakayāna].

The Meaning of the Term and Its Etymology [i]

> **Shrāvakas attend others and proclaim what they have heard.**

The Sanskrit *shrāvaka*[183] is used to mean both "to listen" (*nyan pa*) and "to hear"[184] (*thos pa*). Therefore [it was translated into Tibetan as *nyan thos*, and as] "hearers" [in English]. This is similar to [the Tibetan translation of *buddha*]: since *buddha*[185] is used to mean both "to awaken" (*sangs pa*) and "to blossom" (*rgyas pa*), [it was translated into Tibetan as *sangs rgyas*,] meaning "awakened-blossomed one."[186] [*Shrāvaka* was translated into Tibetan] in another form: ["hearer-proclaimers" (*thos sgrog*),] since it is said that they attend others and proclaim what they have heard. Given that they attend their masters and proclaim what they have heard from them to others, they are called "those who proclaim what they hear," or "hearers."[187]

The Explanation of Its Entryway [ii]

This part begins with the overview: an enumeration; and is followed by the extensive explanation: the defining characteristics [of the four truths].

The Overview: An Enumeration [aa]

> **The entryway [for shrāvakas] is**
> **the four truths of suffering, its origins, its cessation, and the path,**
> **with their sixteen aspects of the acceptance of phenomena, knowledge of phenomena, subsequent acceptance, and subsequent knowledge.**

The entryway for shrāvakas is the sixteen moments of knowledge, which are comprised of the acceptance of phenomena, knowledge of phenomena, subsequent acceptance, and subsequent knowledge,[188] each occurring in relationship to one of the four truths of noble beings:[189] the truth of suffering, the truth of the origins of suffering, the truth of cessation, and the truth of the path.

The Extensive Explanation: The Defining Characteristics [of the Four Truths] [bb]

This is discussed in three sections: the combined explanation; the individual explanations of the four truths; and the presentation summarizing the general characteristics [of the four truths].

The Combined Explanation [1']

In this section, there are four parts: the essence [of the four truths]; their defining characteristics; [the definitiveness of] their numbers and sequence; and their etymologies.

The Essence [of the Four Truths] [a']

> **In terms of their essence, [the four truths are] the continuity of the aggregates produced by previous karma and mental afflictions;**
> **the karma and mental afflictions forming the causes for what will be appropriated in the future;**
> **the relinquishment that has destroyed what is to be eliminated by means of the remedies;**
> **and primordial wisdom, which has the power to relinquish and attain.**

- The essence of the truth of suffering is the continuity of the appropriated aggregates,[190] which are produced by the karma and mental afflictions of previous lives.
- The essence of the truth of the origins of suffering is karma and mental afflictions, which are the causes for future appropriated aggregates.
- The essence of the truth of cessation is the relinquishment that has destroyed the origins of suffering, which are the factors eliminated by means of the remedial path.
- The essence of the truth of the path is the primordial wisdom of noble ones, which has the power to relinquish the origins [of suffering] and to attain cessation.

The first two contain saṃsāra's causes and results, which are afflictive phenomena. The last two contain nirvāṇa's causes and results, which are purified phenomena.[191]

Their Defining Characteristics [b']

> **[The four truths] are characterized by being in agreement with [the Buddha's] teachings.**

This accords with the statement in the *Compendium*:[192]

> [The four truths] have the characteristic of not being in conflict with the doctrine.

- The defining characteristic of the truth of suffering is the defiled (*sāsrava, zag bcas*) aggregates, which are the results produced by the origins of suffering, just as [the Buddha] taught.
- The defining characteristic of the truth of the origins of suffering is whatever produces the aggregates, which appropriate suffering, as taught [by the Buddha].
- The defining characteristic of the truth of cessation is thusness (*tathātā, de bzhin nyid*) purified of adventitious stains, as [the Buddha] taught.
- The defining characteristic of the path is the passage that leads to liberation, as [the Buddha] taught.

The Definitiveness of Their Numbers and Sequence [c']

> **Their numbers—in two sets of causes and results—and their sequence are definite.**
> **They are what is to be understood, abandoned, attained, and relied upon.**

The truths are delineated as four, and two states are ascertained: saṃsāra and nirvāṇa. Since each state has its own set of causes and results, two sets of causes and results are ascertained as follows. In terms of saṃsāra, the truth of suffering is determined to be the result and the truth of its origins is the cause. In the context of nirvāṇa, the truth of cessation is the result, and the truth of the path is the cause. It is definite, therefore, that the number of truths is four. It is not, however, that the four truths include all knowable objects (*jñeya, shes bya*), because they do not include four types of phenomena: space, nonanalytical cessation, impure thusness, and completely pure worldly realms.

The sequence of the four truths, which are the objects, are presented according to the order in which they are comprehended by the perceiving mind. The *Treasury* [*of Abhidharma*] states:[193]

> The sequence [of the truths] accords with the process of comprehension.

[They are presented this way] because this is how our understanding develops. The first step is to identify the aggregates involving suffering in saṃsāra, as in identifying an illness. Next we recognize that the causes of those aggregates, that is, their origins—karma and mental afflictions—must be abandoned; this is like freeing ourselves from the causes of an illness. Then we know that cessation, the freedom from all suffering, is what is to be attained; this is like the comfort of being illness-free. Finally we conclude that meditation on the undefiled path, which is the method for [attaining] that [cessation], must be practiced, in the same way that we would take an efficacious medicine. This is stated in the *Highest Continuum*:[194]

> Just as an illness must be identified, its cause eliminated,
> well-being attained, and medicine taken,
> so must we identify suffering, abandon its causes,
> recognize cessation, and practice the path.

Their Etymologies [d']

> **In terms of their essence, each is undeceiving; thus they are said to be truths.**

The commonly [applicable explanation is that] in terms of their essence, each of the four aspects [of the four truths] is true and undeceiving (*mi bslu ba*). Therefore, when the natures of those [truths] are seen just as they are, an unmistaken state of mind (*phyin ci ma log pa'i blo*) occurs. This is why they are called "the truths of noble beings."[195] Their individual etymologies are given in the *Explanation of the "Treasury of Abhidharma"*:[196]

> Because it has the character of being distressful, it is suffering . . . Since it is the source, it is the origin . . . Because it is the disintegration of the aggregates, it is cessation . . . Since it refers to the journey, it is the path.

The Individual Explanations of the Four Truths [2']

In this section, there are four parts: the truth of suffering, what is to be understood; the truth of the origins of suffering, what is to be relinquished; the truth of cessation, what is to be attained; and the truth of the path, what is to be practiced.

The Truth of Suffering, What Is to Be Understood [a']

This has two divisions: ascertaining its nature; and the categories [of suffering] and their abridgement in terms of their nature.

Ascertaining Its Nature [i']

> **The nine levels within the three realms (which are the places where beings take birth)**
> **and the beings who take birth there are of the nature of the truth of suffering.**

The *Compendium of Abhidharma* says:[197]

> What is the truth of suffering? It is understood through the lives of sentient beings and the places where they are born.

The three realms divided in terms of their mental states, make nine levels (*bhūmi*, *sa*):

(1–4) four levels of the form realm, which are the four meditative concentrations (*bsam tan bzhi*);

(5–8) four levels of the formless realm, which are its four spheres;[198] and

(9) one level of the desire[199] realm, which is similar throughout.

These worlds (the inanimate environments) are the places where sentient beings take birth. They and the beings living there (who are the animate inhabitants) should be understood to be of the nature of the truth of suffering.

The Categories [of Suffering] and Their Abridgement in Terms of Their Nature [ii']

> **In terms of their nature, [sufferings] can be condensed into eight, six, three, or two [categories].**

Sufferings are classified in terms of their natures in the following ways.[200]

Eight [Sufferings]

The four types of suffering in relation to the internal [that is, your body] are birth, aging, sickness, and death. The three types of suffering in relation to external things are encountering unpleasant things, being separated from what is attractive, and not being able to obtain what you desire despite your efforts. The [*Compendium of*] *Abhidharma* states:[201]

> In brief, the five appropriated aggregates are suffering.

Accordingly, there is the one suffering of negative propensities,[202] which serves as the cause for all [the other kinds of suffering]. Those are the eight.

Six [Sufferings]

Those eight can be reduced to six. Since three—aging, sickness, and death—are related to changes in age, health, and vitality, they are counted as one: the suffering of change. When that is added to the remaining five, there are six.

Three [Sufferings]

Those can be further abbreviated into three.

(1) Of the eight kinds of suffering, the four of birth, aging, sickness, and death, plus the fifth of encountering what is unpleasant have the characteristic of being phenomena that are experienced as suffering. Thus, they are the suffering of suffering (*sdug bsngal gyi sdug bsngal*).

(2) Two—being separated from what is attractive and not being able to obtain what you desire despite your efforts—are characterized by being changeable phenomena that are initially experienced as pleasurable. Therefore, they are the suffering of change (*'gyur ba'i sdug bsngal*).

(3) The five appropriated aggregates, which involve negative propensities, are not liberated from pleasure or pain and are linked to what is impermanent. Since they exist that way and are not pleasurable, they are the suffering of conditioned existence (*'du byed kyi sdug bsngal*).

Two [Sufferings]

The eight kinds of suffering can be condensed into two. The first seven are so easy to understand that even worldly beings recognize them to be suffering. Because they are the objects of such [minds], those seven are suffering according to conventional truth.[203] The *Explanation of the "Treasury of Abhidharma"* says:[204]

> Immature beings are like the palm of the hand:
> they do not recognize the hair of the suffering of conditioned existence.
> Noble ones are like the eye:
> they are greatly disturbed by that hair.

The eighth type of suffering is difficult for worldly beings to understand, but those who have transcended the world know it to be suffering. Since it is the object for their minds, it is suffering according to ultimate truth.[205]

The Truth of the Origins of Suffering, What Is to Be Relinquished [b']

This has two divisions: an overview; and the extensive explanation.

An Overview [i']

> **The truth of the origins of suffering consists of the mental afflictions and defiled karma.**

The [*Compendium of*] *Abhidharma* states:[206]

> What is the truth of the origins of suffering? It is the mental afflictions and the karma that develops under the influence of the mental afflictions.

The mental afflictions (desire and the others) and defiled karma, which is driven by those mental afflictions, serve as the origin of suffering. Thus they are called "the truth of the origins [of suffering]."

The Extensive Explanation [ii']

This is discussed in two parts: the origins of suffering in terms of the mental afflictions; and the origins of suffering in terms of karma.

The Origins of Suffering in Terms of the Mental Afflictions [aa']

This has three topics: the causes of the [afflictive] origins of suffering; the nature [of the afflictive origins of suffering]; and the classifications [of the afflictive origins of suffering].

The Causes of the [Afflictive] Origins of Suffering [1"]

> **Subtle proliferators, observed objects, and incorrect mental engagement are the causes.**

The *Treasury of Abhidharma* says:[207]

> The causes of the mental afflictions are complete [when]
> the subtle proliferators have not been abandoned,
> their objects are present,
> and the mind engages incorrectly.

Mental afflictions arise based on the following three conditions:

(1) Their causal conditions (*rgyu'i rkyen*) are [present as long as] their seeds, "the subtle proliferators"[208]—which are that [mental afflictions] mature from subtle [propensities] in a way that is magnified—have not been eliminated.

(2) Their object conditions (*dmigs rkyen*) are the presence of things that are attractive, unattractive, and so forth.

(3) Their dominant conditions (*bdag rkyen*) are incorrect mental engagements, such as considering unpleasant objects to be attractive ones.

The Nature [of the Afflictive Origins of Suffering] [2"]

> **[The afflictive causes of suffering] are mental events characterized by a pronounced lack of tranquility.**

Whenever something arising within the mind involves distraction, mistakenness, agitation, torpor, recklessness, or a lack of restraint, it is characterized by a pronounced lack of tranquility. Because they arise from such [causes], the function, [or activity, of those mental events] is to make the mindstream very unpeaceful.

The Classifications [of the Afflictive Origins of Suffering] [3"]

> **The motivating forces are the root mental afflictions, the secondary ones, and the views.**

There are six root mental afflictions.[209] They are also counted as ten, since one, views, is divided into five types.[210] There are also twenty secondary mental afflictions,[211] which, although they do not create mental afflictions in the same way that the root ones do, are capable of creating mental afflictions that are subsidiary to those [root ones]. Their defining characteristics are as described earlier.[212]

Generally speaking, all mental afflictions are origins of suffering, which means they are causes that are the source of suffering. Nevertheless, ignorance is the fundamental, root cause of saṃsāra. Then what about the explanation in the [*Compendium of*] *Abhidharma* and other places that craving (*tṛiṣhṇā, sred pa*) is the origin of suffering?[213] Craving is described in that way because it is what immediately impels us into our next existence and is the principal cause that links us with our next birth. This accords with the *Commentary on Valid Cognition*:[214]

> Although lack of awareness is the cause of existence,
> that is not stated; it is craving that is named.
> It is the cause because it impels.
> Karma [is also not stated as the cause] because it is what
> comes next.

Thus it is that ignorance acts as the cause. Craving, being the linking factor, is the motivating force and the origin of karma.

The Origins of Suffering in Terms of Karma [bb']

This has two topics: the nature [of the karmic origins of suffering]; and the classifications [of the karmic origins of suffering].

The Nature [of the Karmic Origins of Suffering] [1"]

> **[They create] actions that are intentions and the physical and verbal actions produced by those.**

Karma[215] is of two types: actions that are intentions (*chetanākarma, sems pa'i las*) and actions that are the results of intentions (*chetayitvā karma, bsam pa'i las*).

(1) Intention is the motivating force (*kun slong*), the cause for performing a virtuous or unvirtuous action. It is always a mental act.
(2) The result of intentions (*bsam pa*) is the motivating force that occurs while the action generated by those intentions is performed. This may be physical, verbal, or mental.[216]

The Classifications [of the Karmic Origins of Suffering] [2"]

This has two parts: the classifications [of karma] in terms of its nature; and alternative classification schemes.

The Classifications [of Karma] in Terms of Its Nature [a"]

This has two sections: the root text's overview; and the commentary's addition: a detailed treatment.

The Root Text's Overview [i"]

> **[Karma is] unmeritorious, meritorious, or stable.**

All karmic paths[217] fall into these three categories:
(1) unmeritorious karma, which is negative actions;
(2) meritorious karma, which is virtuous actions; and
(3) stable karma, which is [the karma created by] degenerative samādhis.[218]

The Commentary's Addition: A Detailed Treatment [ii"]

This has three divisions: unmeritorious karma; meritorious karma; and stable karma.

Unmeritorious Karma [aa"]

The numerous types, or principal instances, of unvirtuous karmic paths are all included within ten categories: three of body, four of speech, and three of mind.[219]

The Three Types of Physical Karma

Killing

Killing involves five aspects: (1) The basis (*gzhi*) is a sentient being whose mindstream is different from one's own. (2) The intention (*bsam pa*) is being aware of that [other being] in an unmistaken way [with the intent to kill]. (3) The act (*sbyor ba*) is killing that being using poisons, weapons, magic spells,[220] and so forth, or to engage someone else to kill them. (4) The mental affliction is [any of] the three poisons generally; anger specifically completes the act (*rdzogs byed*). (5) The conclusion occurs when the victim dies before the killer.[221]

These five complete the karmic path of killing. When any one of these five aspects is not present, a wrongdoing occurs, but the karmic path is not complete. We should know that this applies in the case of all following negative actions.

Killing is categorized as three:

(1) killing out of desire, such as craving for meat;
(2) killing out of anger, such as vindictiveness; and
(3) killing out of bewilderment, such as offering a sacrifice.

The most evil form of killing is to kill your father if he is also an arhat.

Stealing

(1) The basis is things owned by others, objects dedicated to the three jewels, the wealth of nonhumans, and the like. (2) The intention is being motivated to take something through deceitful means, through force, or by stealth. (3) The act is stealing something yourself or asking someone else to do so. (4) The mental affliction is [any of] the three poisons in general; desire or avarice specifically completes the act. (5) The conclusion occurs when you have the thought that you have obtained such substances, regardless of whether they have been removed from their original location or not.

Stealing is of three types:

(1) stealing through the use of force, such as seizing things with no explanation;
(2) stealing by stealth, such as breaking into a building; and
(3) stealing by means of deceit, such as altering weights and measures.

The most evil kind of stealing is to steal what has been offered to the three jewels.

Sexual Misconduct

(1) The basis includes your own husband or wife; your relatives up to seven times removed even if they are not specifically committed to someone else; someone else's spouse; inappropriate sexual partners (such as bhikṣhus or bhikṣhuṇīs who are protected by their rules); anyone in unsuitable places (in the presence of representations of the three jewels and so forth); and anyone at an improper time (such as during daylight or when the other person [is observing] the lay precepts,[222] is pregnant, or is menstruating). (2) The intention is being motivated by the desire to have sexual intercourse with inappropriate sexual partners. (3) The act is undertaking that action. (4) The mental affliction is [any of] the three poisons; desire specifically completes the act. (5) The conclusion is to think with lust that you had an experience of pleasure arising from sexual intercourse.

Sexual misconduct is categorized as three:

(1) having sexual relations with those precluded by family ties (such as parents or siblings);
(2) having sexual relations with those precluded by their commitments (such as spouses); and
(3) having sexual relations with those excluded by their dharma vows (such as bhikṣhus or bhikṣhuṇīs).

In terms of improper desire, the greatest evil is sexual misconduct with your mother if she is also a female arhat.

The Four Types of Verbal Karma

Lying

(1) The basis is an object [i.e., a person] other than yourself. (2) The intention is being motivated by the desire to say something like "I saw that" about something you have not seen, with the objective of deceiving others. (3) The act is doing something cognizable[223] physically or verbally. (4) The mental affliction is any one of the three poisons, which will complete the act. (5) The conclusion occurs when someone else comprehends your meaning.

The application is not confined to a cognizable act of speech. One can create false impressions using symbolic gestures of the body, which constitute lying, such as remaining silent about having committed a downfall when questioned directly by the elders (*sthavira, gnas brtan*) during the purification-renewal ceremony.

There are three types of lies:

(1) defeating lies, such as lying about spiritual attainments;[224]
(2) major lies, which are ones that benefit yourself or harm others; and
(3) trivial lies, such as those that are neither beneficial nor harmful.

The worst type of lie is one that denigrates the tathāgatas or deceives your guru.

Divisiveness

(1) The basis is others who have a friendly relationship. (2) The intention is wishing to divide them. (3) The act is initiating the activity. (4) Among the three mental afflictions, aggression specifically completes the act. (5) The conclusion occurs when another person comprehends your meaning.

This includes any intention or action that subsequently alienates people after you have initiated harmonious relations.

There are three types of divisiveness:

(1) vehement divisiveness, such as directly separating close friends;
(2) indirect divisiveness, such as separating friends through oblique means; and
(3) covert divisiveness, such as secretly creating schisms.

The most evil kind of divisiveness is to cause a schism in the saṅgha.

Harsh speech

(1) The basis is anything that pertains to the mindstreams of sentient beings. (2) The intention is being motivated by the wish to speak in a displeasing way. (3) The act is saying something [harsh] that is verbally cognizable. (4) The mental affliction is [any of] the three poisons, and aggression completes the act. (5) The conclusion occurs when you are heard by someone and they comprehend your meaning.

Harsh speech is of three kinds:

(1) face-to-face harshness, such as disclosing someone's hidden flaws directly to them;
(2) indirect harshness, such as saying something mean to another mixed with jokes; and
(3) circuitous harshness, such as disclosing someone's hidden flaws to their close friends.

The most evil kind of harsh speech is to speak harshly to your parents or a noble being.

Idle talk

(1) The basis is as before. (2) The intention is being motivated by the desire to mindlessly chatter a lot. (3) The act is voicing something obsequious, to sing, or do something similar in a verbally cognizable way. (4) The mental affliction is [any of] the three poisons, and bewilderment specifically completes the act. (5) The conclusion occurs when you are heard by someone.

Idle talk is divided into three kinds:

(1) wrong idle talk, such as the recitations and talk of *tīrthikas*;[225]
(2) worldly idle talk, such as meaningless chatter; and
(3) truthful idle talk, such as teaching the dharma to those who are not suitable.

In terms of idle talk, the greatest evil is to distract those who desire the dharma.

The Three Kinds of Mental Karma

Covetousness

(1) The basis is another's external or internal possessions. (2) The intention is being motivated by a hope or aspiration for the wealth and possessions of others. (3) The act is thinking about that repeatedly. (4) The mental affliction is [any of] the three poisons, and desire completes the act. (5) The conclusion is to perform that repeatedly and not employ a remedy because you are neither ashamed nor embarrassed [about such actions].

Covetousness is of three types:

(1) covetousness towards what is yours, such as attachment to your family's status;
(2) covetousness towards what belongs to others, such as longing for others' wealth; and
(3) covetousness towards what belongs neither to yourself nor to others, such as wishing for the treasures beneath the ground.

The greatest evil in terms of covetousness is to covet the possessions of renunciates.

Malice

(1) The basis is the same as above. (2) The intention is being motivated by the wish to harm someone, such as by killing or beating them. (3) The act occurs when you contemplate that. (4) The mental affliction is [any of] the three poisons, and aggression completes the act. (5) The conclusion is to regard this [mental state] as a virtue and have no interest in remedying it.

Malice has three divisions:

(1) malice that arises from aggression, such as the intention to kill others during war;
(2) malice arising from jealousy, such as feeling ill will towards competitors; and
(3) malice arising from resentment, such as feeling hostile towards someone who has harmed you even though they have since apologized.

The most evil type of malice is to plan to commit one of the [five] acts of immediate consequence.[226]

Wrong views

(1) The basis is virtuous and unvirtuous phenomena. (2) The intention is being motivated by a belief that there are neither virtuous actions nor negative ones, by an incorrect view concerning causes and their results, and the like. (3) The act occurs when you contemplate that repeatedly. (4) Among the three mental afflictions, bewilderment is the one that completes the act. (5) The conclusion is to establish [such a view] and not remedy it.

There are three kinds of wrong views:

(1) wrong views about actions and their results, such as not accepting that virtuous actions are the causes of happiness and that negative actions are the causes of suffering;

(2) wrong views about the truth, such as not believing that you will attain the truth of cessation through your practice of the truth of the path; and

(3) wrong views about the three jewels, such as denigrating the three jewels.

The worst kind of wrong view is to hold a view to be supreme.

[The Results of Unvirtuous Actions]

Those [nonmeritorious actions produce] three kinds of results.

(1) Matured results (*rnam smin gyi 'bras bu*) refer to the fact that major results can mature from minor causes. In cases where the results do not match their causes in all regards [e.g., a result is experienced for a long time even though its cause was brief], the expression "matured karma" (*smin pa las*) is used. Furthermore, when an unvirtuous action is impelled by a strong motivation or done often, the result will be birth in the hells. When done with an intermediate motivation and frequency, it will result in birth as a hungry ghost. When done with a lesser degree of motivation and frequency, it will bring rebirth as an animal.

Secondly, there are results that correspond to their causes; and thirdly, there are dominant results that come to fruition even for beings in the higher realms.

(2) Results that correspond to their causes (*rgyu mthun gyi 'bras bu*) are of two kinds: (a) [resultant] actions that correspond to their causes and (b) [resultant] experiences that correspond to their causes. (2a) [Resultant

actions that correspond to their causes] are those actions which one naturally enjoys doing from the time of one's birth and which one is compelled to do because of one's previous actions. (2b) [Resultant experiences that correspond to their causes] are described in the *Precious Garland*:[227]

> Having killed, your life will be short.
> Having injured others, you will be greatly harmed.
> Having stolen, you will be materially impoverished.
> Having committed adultery, you will be [plagued by] enemies.
>
> Having lied, you will be disparaged.
> Having spoken divisively, you will be separated from your friends.
> Having used harsh language, you will hear unpleasant things.
> Having spoken meaninglessly, your words will not be honored.
>
> Covetousness will destroy your hopes.
> Malice will create fears.
> Wrong views [create] negative views.

(3) Dominant results (*bdag po'i 'bras bu*) mature environmentally. The same text says:[228]

> Externally, there will be little affluence and many dangers,
> swirling dust, smells, and [extreme] highs and lows [in the terrain],
> salt plains, and erratic [seasons];
> harvests will be minimal or nonexistent.

As for when those results will ripen, the *Explanation of the "Treasury of Abhidharma"* provides this quotation:[229]

> Whatever is heaviest in the cycle of karma
> will mature first.
> Next will be what is close, followed by what you are habituated to,
> and finally by what you did in previous [lives].

Engaging in those ten unvirtuous actions yourself is not the only way to complete a karmic path. When [a group of people have] a similar intention and activity—such as is the case with a group of soldiers—if one person commits the act of killing, the karmic path will be completed for all those in that gathering. The *Treasury* [*of Abhidharma*] states:[230]

> Because armies and the like have the same aim,
> all will have [the karma] of the one performing [the act].

This is certainly the case for the following as well. Bands of robbers, bandits, and others, who unite for the sake of stealing, [will experience] similar [results]. Anyone who causes someone else to commit one [of the ten unvirtuous actions] (with the exception of the three unvirtuous actions of mind) will complete the karmic path [of that action]. It is also taught that those who rejoice in [the negative actions] done by others will be tainted by a corresponding karma, and that those who rejoice in the virtue engaged in by others will obtain roots of virtue.

When those actions are considered in terms of the mental afflictions (i.e., whether they are committed with aggression, desire, or bewilderment), or in terms of their frequency (i.e., whether they are done innumerable times, many times, or just a few times), or in terms of their object (i.e., whether they are done in relation to supreme, middling, or inferior beings), they are said to cause rebirth as a hell being, hungry ghost, or animal. This is summarized in the *Precious Garland*:[231]

> Desire, aggression, stupidity,
> and the karma they generate are unvirtuous.
> From unvirtuous actions,
> suffering and all lower states arise.

The ten unvirtuous actions are committed in some form by the beings in the desire realms, with the exception of the beings in the hells and Unpleasant Sound.[232] In the higher realms [the form and formless realms], there are no unvirtuous actions. Also when a chakravartin[233] appears in the other continents of humans,[234] the ten unvirtuous actions are not evident owing to the force of his merit.

Meritorious Karma [bb"]

Meritorious karma is summarized in this quotation from the same text:[235]

Not killing, giving up stealing,
refraining from [sexual engagements] with others' spouses;
restraining oneself from speaking falsely, divisively,
harshly, or meaninglessly;

being without attachments or malice,
and renouncing views of nihilists
are the ten positive paths of action.

As is stated, the [ten] meritorious actions are the intention to renounce taking life through the intention to give up wrong views. Meritorious karma does not only involve [being free from] the mental afflictions, it must also include the four other aspects of basis, intention, act, and conclusion. These actions become distinguished when we go beyond, for example, simply not killing by committing ourselves to that with a vow, by protecting living beings, and by employing the means to extend the longevity of others. Such distinctions apply to the rest of the virtuous actions.

We should know that these actions bring about matured results, results that accord with their causes, and dominant results, and that they manifest correspondingly pleasurable [results], which are the direct opposites of the unpleasant results of the ten unvirtuous actions.

[The results of] these actions also differ according to whether their object is higher or lower and the frequency of their occurrence, as described above. This is summarized [in the *Precious Garland*]:[236]

The opposites of desire, aggression, stupidity,
and the karma they generate are virtuous.
From virtuous actions, happy states
and enjoyments in all lifetimes arise.

Stable Karma [cc"]

Stable [or unmoving] karma (*mi g.yo ba'i las*) is referred to as such because its maturation does not occur [or "move" to] anywhere but its originating states [which are the form and formless realms].[237] It is a state of equipoise and is not disturbed [or "moved"] by the faults of lower states. The same text states:[238]

> The concentrations, the immeasurables, and the formless [realm]
> bring the experience of the happiness of Brahmā and so forth.

[Stable karma] is described as the special mental state of the main absorptions (*snyoms 'jug dngos gzhi*) of the four meditative concentrations and four formless states, as is discussed in the earlier section on the paths to the elevated states (*mngon mtho'i lam*).[239]

Alternative Classification Schemes [b"]

> **It is in terms of its impetus and completion; speed; performance and storage; strength;**
> **mode of appearance; and being similar or not that [karma] causes [beings] to take rebirth in the three realms.**

Since [the Buddha's] teachings and the treatises treat the topic of karma and its results extensively, there are many ways it is categorized. The main ones are

(1) the classification of karma in terms of the four combinations of impetus and completion (*'phen rdzogs*);
(2) the classification of karma in terms of the speed of its maturation (*rnam smin myur bul*);
(3) the classification of karma in terms of whether it is performed and stored (*byas bsags*) or not;
(4) the classification of karma in terms of its strength (*stobs che chung*);
(5) the classification of karma in terms of its mode of appearance (*snang tshul*); and
(6) the classification of karma in terms of whether it is of a similar type (*rigs mthun*) or not.

It is on the basis of the causal karmic origins [of suffering] that there is the resultant suffering and [beings] take rebirth in the three realms.

To state this in a way that is easy to understand:

(1) [The classification of karma in terms of its impetus and completion] is fourfold.[240]
   (a) The driving impetus may be a positive action, but if the completing action is negative it will result, for example, in one becoming an impoverished human being.

(b) The action that is the driving impetus may be negative, but if the completing action is positive the result will be circumstances such as those of the wealthy nāgas.[241]

(c) If both the action that is the impetus and the completing action are negative, states such as the hells will be experienced.

(d) When both the action that is the impetus and the completing action are positive, the results include that of a chakravartin.

(2) [The classification of karma in terms of the speed of its maturation] is threefold:[242]

(a) "Karma experienced in this life": Karma propelled by a strong intention and activity, and done in relation to a supreme object, will ripen in the same lifetime. For example, the karma Devadatta[243] accrued by attempting to poison the Bhagavat with his fingernails produced the fires of hell at that very moment.

(b) "Karma experienced in the next life" is the experience of the maturation of an action in the life immediately after this lifetime. The five acts of immediate consequence[244] and the five secondary acts of immediate consequence[245] are examples of this type of karma.

(c) "Karma experienced in a succession of other lives" means that the experience of the maturation of an action can occur during three lifetimes [after the action was done] up to hundreds or thousands of lives later.

(3) [The classification of karma in terms of whether it is performed and stored or not]: Taking positive karma as an illustration, "performed and stored" would refer to making offerings to the three jewels with faith. "Not performed but stored" would be to rejoice in other's virtuous actions. "Performed but not stored" would be the recitations of a distracted mind. Actions neither performed nor stored are easy to understand. We should know that these distinctions apply in the case of negative actions as well.

(4) [The classification of karma in terms of its strength]: generally, if one does something that should be avoided, it will impel a result. The action of a remedy, however, is stronger because antidotes have the power to transform [karma].

(5) [The classification of karma in terms of its mode of appearance] is twofold:

(a) The karma related to shared appearances (*snang 'gyur thun mong ba'i las*) is that the appearances of the world, or environment, and all the beings living there manifest uniformly owing to the shared quality of [sentient beings'] accumulated karma.

(b) The karma related to unshared experiences (*myong 'gyur thun mong min pa'i las*) is that [beings have] unique pleasurable or painful experiences of different places, bodies,[246] and possessions. These are created by the karmic appearances of individual sentient beings.

(6) [The classification of karma in terms of whether it is of a similar type or not is threefold:]

(a) "Both are positive": in the case of offering to the guru with faith, since both the intention and the activity are a similar type—positive—the path of virtuous karma is completed.

(b) "Both are negative": in the case of taking life with the intent to kill, since both the intention and the activity are a similar type—negative—the path of unvirtuous karma is completed.

(c) "Mixed" can be a positive intention and a negative activity, as in the case of killing to protect many beings; or it can be a negative intention and a positive action, in the case of being generous for the sake of killing.

The Truth of Cessation, What Is to Be Attained [c']

This has two divisions: an overview of the general points; and ascertaining the nature [of cessation].

An Overview of the General Points [i']

The attainment of separation brought about by the path is cessation, thusness.
Vaibhāṣhikas and Sautrāntikas [respectively] assert it to be a nonimplicative negation that is substantially established or that is not so established.

The attainment[247] of separation from stains brought about by meditating on the path is referred to as "cessation" (*nirodha, 'gog pa*) or "thusness" (*tathātā, de bzhin nyid*). Vaibhāṣhikas assert that cessation is a nonimplicative negation[248] that is substantially established (*dravyasiddha, rdzas su grub pa*), and that it is a mere refutation equal in number to what is negated. Sautrāntikas assert that cessation is a nonimplicative negation that is not substantially established, in which, owing to antidotal meditation, the factors to be abandoned have become like a rainbow disappearing in the sky.

Ascertaining the Nature [of Cessation] [ii']

> **The nature [of cessation] is [described by its] twelve aspects: its characteristics, profundity, and so forth.**

The nature of cessation is described in the [*Compendium of*] *Abhidharma*:[249]

> What is the truth of cessation? The truth of cessation can be known through a description of its characteristics, profundity, conventional representation, ultimacy, incompleteness, completeness, absence of ornamentation, ornamentation, remainder, and absence of remainder, exalted state, and synonyms.

The nature of cessation is discussed extensively in terms of its twelve aspects, but here I will simply explain what is essential.

(1) How is cessation presented through its characteristics (*lakṣhaṇa, mtshan nyid*)? Its characteristics are as follows. Cessation is dharmatā, thusness. The undefiled path [leads to] cessation. It is the cessation, or nonarising, of the mental afflictions, the factors to be abandoned. Those are [respectively] the ground where cessation occurs, the methods by which cessation occurs, and the factors to be stopped, which are what cease. In brief, cessation is that, within the naturally pure dharmadhātu, by meditating on the path, adventitious stains cease.

(2) How is it profound (*gāmbhīrya, zab pa*)?

- Cessation cannot be said to be something that is other than the disintegration of all defiled formative forces (*'du byed zag bcas*), an implicative negation (*ma yin dgag*), and an entity (*dngos por 'gyur pa*), because if it were something other than those [that is, something separate from those], there would be no connection between a phenomenon and its dharmatā [its reality].[250]

- Cessation cannot be said to be something that is not other [than or separate from phenomena], because those [phenomena and dharmatā] do not have the same defining characteristics. If they did, cessation would be an afflictive phenomenon.
- Cessation cannot be said to be both [a phenomenon and its dharmatā], since both [the just-mentioned] faults would apply.
- It cannot be said to be neither of those: since [cessation] is what is intuitively cognized (*so so rang gis rig par bya ba*), it is not absolutely nonexistent.
- Why is it that cessation cannot be described in any of those ways? It is because the truth of cessation is the expanse (*dbyings*) in which all conceptual elaborations related to those four possibilities are absent.

(3) How is it conventionally represented (*saṃvṛiti, brda*)? A cessation in which the seeds of the factors to be abandoned have been restricted or suppressed by the paths of worldly beings is itself simply designated as a cessation, and is considered to belong to the category of cessation. Since [such cessations] are branches, or aspects, of complete cessation (*ma lus par 'gags pa*), they are taught to be nirvāṇa.

(4) What is ultimate cessation (*paramārtha, don dam*)? It is a cessation in which the seeds of the factors to be abandoned have been destroyed by the wisdom of noble beings (who have transcended the world), and in which those seeds will not re-arise.

(5) What is an incomplete cessation (*aparipūri, yongs su ma rdzogs pa*)? It is the cessation of noble beings in training, and refers to any of the following:

- the cessation of all factors to be abandoned by the path of seeing, which is the result of stream enterers;
- the cessation of the six factors to be abandoned during the path of meditation that pertain to the desire realm, which is the result of once returners; or
- the cessation of all the factors to be abandoned during the path of meditation that pertain to the desire realm, which is the result of nonreturners.

(6) What is a complete cessation (*paripūri, yongs su rdzogs pa*)? It is the cessation [attained by] noble beings beyond training when all factors to be abandoned are exhausted. This is the fruition of arhats.

(7) What is unornamented cessation (*niralaṃkāra, rgyan med*)? It is the cessation of arhats who, through their wisdom,[251] are liberated from only the afflictive obscurations (*nyon sgrib*) but are not adorned with supercognitive abilities or any similar qualities.

(8) What is ornamented cessation (*sālaṃkāra, rgyan dang bcas pa*)? It is the cessation of arhats who are liberated from both the afflictive obscurations and the obscurations to absorption (*snyoms 'jug gi sgrib pa*). Such arhats possess the six supercognitive abilities,[252] the three knowledges (knowledge of the process of death and rebirth, of previous and later lives, and of the exhaustion of defilements), and the eight excellent qualities.[253]

(9) What is cessation with remainder (*sheṣha, lhag bcas*)? It is a cessation in which there is the remainder of the five aggregates (which are the matured [result] of previous [karma]) in the case of beings of the desire or form realms and four aggregates in the case of beings of the formless realm. [These continue to be present] as long as [the arhats] remain in their [present] life, even though they have abandoned all their mental afflictions.

(10) What is cessation without remainder (*asheṣha, lhag med*)? It is a cessation in which aggregates [resulting from] matured [karma] do not remain because [the arhats] have passed from this life and have relinquished all their mental afflictions.

(11) What is its exalted state (*agra, khyad par du 'phags pa*)? It is the cessation that is the nirvāṇa that does not abide in either the extreme of existence or of peace. This is [attained] by buddhas and bodhisattvas through their wisdom and compassion, and [is exalted] because it is the source of ultimate benefit for all sentient beings and the source of their temporal happiness.

(12) What are its synonyms (*paryāya, rnam grangs*)? It has many synonyms: complete relinquishment, definite relinquishment, purification (*byang bar gyur pa*), exhaustion (*zad pa*), freedom from desire, cessation, complete peace, and disappearance (*nub pa*).

Thus it is said [in Asaṅga's *Compendium of Abhidharma*].[254]

The Truth of the Path, What Is to Be Practiced [d']

> **The path is that which, once embarked upon, takes you to your goal.**
> **It comprises the five paths: accumulation, junction, seeing, meditation, and beyond training.**

The nature of the path is that, once it is relied or embarked upon, it is the method that enables you to attain your goal of nirvāṇa. Although the path is classified in many ways in the Hīnayāna and Mahāyāna, we should know that all [the classifications] are contained in the five paths: the path of accumulation (*saṃbhāra mārga, tshogs lam*), path of junction (*prayoga mārga, sbyor lam*), path of seeing (*darshana mārga, mthong lam*), path of meditation (*bhāvanā mārga, sgom lam*), and path beyond training (*ashaikṣha mārga, mi slob pa'i lam*). A detailed exposition of these paths is found in the later section describing the path.[255]

The Presentation Summarizing the General Characteristics [of the Four Truths] [3']

This section is discussed in four parts: suffering; its origins; its cessation; and the path.

Suffering [a']

> **[Suffering is] impermanent, suffering, empty, and without a self-entity.**

The truth of suffering is summarized by four general characteristics. It is

(1) impermanent (*mi rtag*);
(2) suffering (*sdug bsngal*);
(3) empty (*stong pa*); and
(4) without self-entity (*bdag med pa*).[256]

It is said, "Everything conditioned (*saṃskṛita, 'dus byas*) has the characteristic of being impermanent. Everything impermanent is characterized by being suffering. All suffering has the characteristic of being empty. Whatever is empty has the characteristic of being without a self-entity."

Yogins and yoginīs should investigate [the truth of suffering] using these four points.

The etymologies or meanings of the terms for those four are found in the *Explanation of the "Treasury [of Abhidharma]"*:[257]

> Because [suffering] depends on conditions, it is impermanent. Because it has the character of being distressful, it is suffering. [Suffering] is empty since it is discordant with the view of "mine," and it has no self-entity since it is discordant with the view of a self-entity.

When these four aspects are fully comprehended, they are the remedies for the view [that suffering is] permanent, pleasurable, something that belongs to you, and something that has a self-entity.

Its Origins [b']

> **[The origins of suffering are] causes, origins, strong producers, and conditions.**

The general characteristics of the origins [of suffering] are that they are

(1) causes (*rgyu*);
(2) origins (*kun 'byung*);
(3) strong producers (*rab skye*); and
(4) conditions (*rkyen*).[258]

We should understand the following about these points:

(1) Karma and mental afflictions are characterized as being causes, because they are enabling causes[259] that plant the seeds of the habitual tendencies that will produce future lives in cyclic existence.
(2) They have the characteristic of being origins, because they are enabling causes that are the source of the six states of sentient beings, gods and the others. (All of these states have their respective manifestations and similar attributes, [which are caused by] their accumulated karmic tendencies.)
(3) They have the characteristic of being strong producers, because they are enabling causes that definitely give rise to specific, discrete mindstreams;[260] that give rise to different kinds of beings, types of

birth, and so forth; and that give rise to the Pinnacle of Existence,[261] the highest state of beings [in saṃsāra].

(4) [Karma and mental afflictions] have the characteristic of being conditions, since they are enabling causes for obtaining bodies [that is, rebirths] previously not attained and for leaving already obtained bodies.

The etymologies for those four are given in *Explanation of the "Treasury [of Abhidharma]"*:[262]

> [Origins] are causes in the sense of being phenomena that are seeds. They are origins in the sense of being phenomena that are sources. They are powerful producers in the sense of being connectors, and they are conditions in the sense of being creators of the actual [result]. These [work together] in the same way that a pot can be produced when a lump of clay, stick, wheel, rope, and water are assembled.

[Knowledge of] these remedy the wrong views [of thinking that suffering] has no cause, that it has only one cause, that it is a transformation of a causal [entity], and that it is a planned occurrence [i.e., something created by an all-powerful creator].

Its Cessation [c']

> **[Cessation is] cessation, peace, goodness, and definitive release.**

The general characteristics of cessation are that it is

(1) cessation (*'gog pa*);

(2) peace (*zhi ba*);

(3) perfection (*gya nom*); and

(4) definite release (*nges 'byung*).[263]

We should understand the following about these points:

(1) Cessation is the characteristic of being separated from all mental afflictions, which are the causes of suffering.

(2) Peace is characterized by the separation from suffering, that is, from the appropriated aggregates [and] formative forces (*saṃskāra, 'du*

byed), which create an unpeaceful state.

(3) Perfection has the characteristic of purity since it is free of the mental afflictions, and the characteristic of being happiness since it free from suffering.

(4) Definite release has the characteristic of being permanent since it will not revert, and the characteristic of being the foundation of benefit for others since, ultimately, it is what is virtuous.

The etymologies of those four are described in the *Explanation of the "Treasury [of Abhidharma]"*:[264]

> It is cessation because it is the disintegration of connections, since it is without any connections. It is peace because it is free from the three characteristics of conditioned phenomena.[265] It is perfection since it is virtuous. It is a definite release because it is a supreme state of confidence.

By meditating on these four, we will definitely emerge from the incorrect views of thinking, "There is no liberation"; "Suffering is liberation"; "The bliss of the meditative concentrations is perfection"; and "Liberation is not lasting."

The Path [d']

> **[The path is] a path, suitable, effective, and what brings definite release.**

The general characteristics of the path are that it is

(1) a path (*lam*);

(2) suitable (*rigs pa*);

(3) effective (*sgrub pa*); and

(4) what brings definite release [from saṃsāra] (*nges par 'byin pa*).[266]

We should understand the following about these points:

(1) [The meaning of] "path" is established by its linguistic root, as it is said:

> [Sanskrit] *mārga* means "to seek."[267]

Thus, the path is characterized as being the means for seeking and realizing the dharmadhātu.

(2) "Suitable" is its characteristic of being the antidote for mental afflictions, which are unsuitable.

(3) "Effective" is its characteristic of initiating the realization of suchness (*tattva, de kho na nyid*) and producing an unmistaken mind, having reversed mistaken [ideas], such as taking conditioned phenomena to be permanent.

(4) "Bringing definite release" is its characteristic of leading to the lasting state of nirvāṇa, which is unconditioned and permanent.

The etymologies of those four are presented in the *Explanation of the "Treasury [of Abhidharma]"*:[268]

> It is a path in the sense that it is what is traversed. It is suitable because it is appropriate. It is effective in the sense that it actually produces [the result of nirvāṇa]. It brings definite release because it brings true transcendence [of suffering].

Meditating on these four is the antidote for views involving mistaken analysis in which one thinks, "There is no path," "This path is bad," "Something else is the path," and "This path also can be reversed."

These descriptions of the four truths are topics of knowledge common to all yānas. Some of the categorization is derived from the *Compendium [of Abhidharma]*. In his *[Jeweled] Tree*,[269] Jetsün Drakpa Gyaltsen[270] discusses in detail that, overall, the *Compendium [of Abhidharma]* is to be considered a Sautrāntika text.

The Vows to Be Guarded [iii]

> **The vows, that which are to be guarded, are the discipline of individual liberation, [motivated by the wish for] definitive release.**

In the two Shrāvaka schools and the Pratyekabuddha[yāna], the vows to be guarded consist of the ethical conduct of individual liberation (*prātimokṣha, so so thar pa*). These vows are motivated by the wish for definite release [from saṃsāra] and involve the intention, and its congruent [mental events], to avoid harming others and the basis [of that harm]. This has already been explained in detail.[271] The explanations of the way the congruent [mental events] operate in the context of those [vows] differ in the higher and lower abhidharma [systems].[272]

The View to Be Realized [iv]

> **The view is primarily the realization of the absence of a self of persons.**

The view for shrāvakas is primarily the realization that a self of persons (*pudgalātman, gang zag gi bdag*) does not exist. The self of persons imputed by tīrthika practitioners to be permanent, single, clean, a creator, or independent does not exist. The mind that takes such a self of persons to exist is confused, because it is a mind [perceiving] something that is not there, like someone taking a striped rope to be a snake.

The aggregates are not the self of a person, because they are impermanent, multiple, and unclean. They are also not a creator because they are under the power of other things. There is also no self of a person apart from the aggregates, because "person" (*gang zag*) is [only] used to refer to the continuity of the aggregates, which are filled with (*gang*) and degenerated by (*zag pa*) causal karma and mental afflictions. This accords with the statement in the *Treasury* [*of Abhidharma*]:[273]

> No self exists—there are just aggregates.

[No self of persons exists apart from the aggregates,] because the mind that apprehends a self of persons comes into being when it observes the mere continuity of the aggregates.

In this root verse the term "primarily" is used for the following reason. Texts such as the *Sūtra on the Heavily Adorned Arrangement*[274] and the *Descent into Laṅkā Sūtra*[275] teach that shrāvakas and pratyekabuddhas do not realize the absence of a self-entity of phenomena (*dharmanairātmya, chos kyi bdag med*). Their view is that shrāvakas and pratyekabuddhas do not directly comprehend [the nonexistence of a self-entity of phenomena] through meditation. On the other hand, some [texts] explain that shrāvakas and pratyekabuddhas do realize both [absences of self-entity].

Their view is that the attentiveness [developed] during study, reflection, and familiarization assists shrāvakas and pratyekabuddhas in abandoning the mental afflictions experienced in the three realms.

Consequently, some Tibetan scholars say that the view of Nāgārjuna and his son [Āryadeva] is that shrāvakas and pratyekabuddhas realize the absence of a self-entity of phenomena, and the view of Asaṅga and his brother [Vasubandhu] is that shrāvakas and pratyekabuddhas do not realize this. These scholars maintain that they [i.e., Nāgārjuna and Āryadeva] assert that shrāvakas and pratyekabuddhas realize both absences of self-entity.[276]

The Result to Be Attained [v]

Nirvāṇa is a nonarising, unconditioned phenomenon.
Vaibhāṣhikas assert that it is an implicative negation and
Sautrāntikas that it is a nonimplicative negation.
[Nirvāṇa] with remainder [is divided into] eighty-nine
conditioned and unconditioned [results],
or into four results; [nirvāṇa] without remainder is the
severing of continuity.

In all three yānas the result to be attained is the same: nirvāṇa. Here, however, this is a nirvāṇa that is a cessation. The essence of nirvāṇa is described [by Chandrakīrti] in his *Commentary on the "Sixty Verses on Reasoning"* as follows:[277]

> Nirvāṇa is the nature of an entity [with] defining characteristics (i.e., the very essence of a form and so forth) that does not arise again owing to the absence of its causes and conditions, or karma and mental afflictions.

The shrāvakas' assertion [regarding nirvāṇa], as stated earlier,[278] is that, among conditioned and unconditioned [phenomena, nirvāṇa] is an unconditioned [phenomenon].

Kashmiri Vaibhāṣhikas say that there are three types of unconditioned phenomena,[279] and Magadha, or Central Indian, Vaibhāṣhikas assert that there are four types by adding thusness. Among those four, *Clarifying the Sage's Thought*[280] explains that Vaibhāṣhikas assert that [nirvāṇa] with remainder is an analytical cessation and [nirvāṇa] without remainder is a nonanalytical cessation, and Sautrāntikas assert that the absence of mental afflictions is an analytical cessation and the absence of the aggregates is a nonanalytical cessation. The *Explanation of the "Treasury [of Abhidharma]"* comments that although these schools agree that [nirvāṇa] is unconditioned, they differ in that Vaibhāṣhikas assert that it is an implicative negation and Sautrāntikas assert that it is a nonimplicative negation.[281] The meaning of their [positions] is that Vaibhāṣhikas say that [nirvāṇa] exists substantially (*dravya-sat, rdzas su yod pa*), thereby asserting that [nirvāṇa] is an existent entity (*dngos po yod pa*). Sautrāntikas say that it does not exist substantially, thereby asserting that [nirvāṇa] is not an existent entity.

In this presentation of [nirvāṇa] with remainder and without remainder, [nirvāṇa] with remainder means that all mental afflictions have been abandoned, but the continuity of the aggregates has not been severed. It [is divided into] eighty-nine conditioned [results] and eighty-nine unconditioned [results],[282] or the four results of shrāmaṇas.[283] [Nirvāṇa] without remainder is that when an arhat has relinquished all mental afflictions, the formative forces are cast aside and the continuity of the aggregates is severed. Thus, not even a trace of a remainder of suffering or aggregates is left, like a candle flame dying out. Both Shrāvaka schools assert that once arhats die, their awareness does not have any link with a subsequent life [i.e., does not take birth again].

3. THE SHRĀVAKAYĀNA: ITS TENET SYSTEMS, ORDERS, AND RESULTS

vi. The Classifications [of the Shrāvakayāna] [II.A.2.a.vi]
- aa. The Classifications of Its Philosophical Tenet Systems
  - 1' The Actual Classifications
  - 2' A Description of Their Assertions
    - a' Their Similar Assertions
    - b' Their Dissimilar Assertions
      - i' Vaibhāṣhikas' Assertions
      - ii' Sautrāntikas' Assertions
- bb. The Classifications of Its Orders
  - 1' The Four Main Orders
  - 2' The Eighteen Divisions
  - 3' The Twofold Summation
    - a' The Actual Twofold Summation
    - b' Ancillary Analysis
- cc. The Classifications of Its Results
  - 1' An Overview
  - 2' An Extensive Explanation
    - a' A Detailed Explanation of the Gradual Type
      - i' Stream Enterers
        - aa' Approachers to the Result of a Stream Enterer
        - bb' Abiders in the Result of a Stream Enterer
      - ii' Once Returners
        - aa' Approachers to the Result of a Once Returner
        - bb' Abiders in the Result of a Once Returner
      - iii' Nonreturners
        - aa' Approachers to the Result of a Nonreturner

bb' Abiders in the Result of a Nonreturner
iv' Arhats
aa' Approachers to the Result of an Arhat
bb' Abiders in the Result of an Arhat
b' An Explanation of the Skipping and Instantaneous Types as Supplementary Topics

....

[This chapter is a continuation of the discussion of the Shrāvakayāna by way of six topics.] Presented here is the sixth topic, the classifications of the Shrāvakayāna. This section has three main parts: the classifications of its philosophical tenet systems; the classifications of its orders; and the classifications of its results.

The Classifications of Its Philosophical Tenet Systems [aa]

This has two parts: the actual classifications; and a description of their assertions.

The Actual Classifications [1']

[The Shrāvakayana's] philosophical tenet systems are either Vaibhāṣhika or Sautrāntika.

The Shrāvakayāna contains numerous philosophical tenets with many subtle distinctions, having been formulated [on the basis of] the specific philosophical positions [taken by various] individuals. Nevertheless, for simplicity's sake, two divisions are made: Vaibhāṣhika and Sautrāntika.[284] [In his *Commentary on the "Compendium on the Heart of Primordial Wisdom,"*] the elder (*sthavira*) Bodhibhadra[285] says:

> Because they state that [the phenomena] of the three times exist as discrete particular substances (*rdzas kyi bye brag*),[286] they are referred to as such [that is, as Vaibhāṣhikas, Proponents of Particular (Substances)]. Alternatively, because they make statements in accord with the *Great Detailed Exposition*,[287] they are

> referred to by that [name: Vaibhāṣhikas, Proponents of the *Great Detailed Exposition*].

Among the orders (*nikāya, sde pa*), they are a subdivision of the Mūlasarvāstivādins.[288] From the same source:[289]

> Since they accept sūtras such as the *Six Doors* and *Excellent Conduct*[290] as literal and follow those sūtras, they are Sautrāntikas (Sūtra-followers). They are also known by the name of Dārṣhṭāntikas (Exemplifiers),[291] since they are skilled in teaching through examples.

A Description of Their Assertions [2']

This is discussed in two sections: their similar assertions; and their dissimilar assertions.

Their Similar Assertions [a']

> **They agree in not accepting the teachings of the Mahāyāna scriptures.**
> **They reject a permanent, single self and state that karma is the creator.**

Both Shrāvaka schools agree that the Mahāyāna scriptures, which comprise the middle and final teachings of the wheel of dharma, are not the words of the Victorious One, and thus they do not accept them. They say that the Mahāyāna scriptures contradict the four principles of the dharma[292] for the following four reasons: The Mahāyāna teaches (1) that the sambhogakāya is always present; (2) that bodhisattvas proceed to happiness; (3) that there is a supreme self, as in such statements as, "the supreme self, which is no-self, is attained"; and (4) that after shrāvakas and pratyekabuddhas have entered [nirvāṇa] without remainder, they must be roused [from that state] to then become buddhas.

Shrāvakas say that the Mahāyāna is not found within the eighteen orders of the Buddha's teachings and, therefore, is not a part of [the Buddha's teachings]. Also, the Mahāyāna teachings are not part of the three collections of scripture (*tripiṭaka, sde snod gsum*), because they do not appear in the common vinaya, do not fit within the sūtras, and contradict dharmatā [reality].

- Since the Shrāvaka schools do not consider the self-entity of phenomena or cognitive obscurations, they do not discuss the two types of absence of self-entity or the two obscurations.[293]
- Since they do not posit an *ālaya*[294] or an afflictive mind, they do not speak of eight modes of consciousness.
- Since they do not accept the extensive collection of the Mahāyāna sūtras, they do not assert the ten *bhūmis*,[295] which appear in the Mahāyāna sūtras.
- They believe that the bhūmi of a buddha has a remainder of karma and suffering and do not accept that all flaws are exhausted [in that state]; thus, they do not assert a transformation.[296]
- Since they do not accept that the sambhogakāya [forms of buddhas dwell] in Akaniṣhṭha, they do not assert or accept the three kāyas, four primordial wisdoms,[297] and so forth.

In the context of the bases (*mūla, gzhi*), neither school accepts, even on a conventional level, the self [of persons] imagined by non-Buddhists as being permanent, single, independent, and so forth, just as [they would not accept that] a striped rope is a snake. They assert that the environment and beings have no external creator, such as Cha or Īshvara;[298] they state that karma is the creator, as is said:[299]

> The myriad worlds arise from karma.

They concur in their presentations of the categories of the five aggregates, the eighteen constituents, the twelve sense spheres, the four modes of birth, the five kinds of beings, and the four kinds of food (coarse, of contact, mental, and of consciousness).[300]

[Phenomena and the Two Truths]

> **Observed objects either increase defilements or do not.**
> **Thus conditioned phenomena are defiled phenomena; and the phenomena of the truth of the path and unconditioned phenomena are undefiled phenomena.**
> **[Conventional reality] is whatever halts its perceiver when it is destroyed or eliminated.**

> **[Gross] entities and continuities are conventionally existent**
> **and ultimately do not perform functions.**
> **Partless particles and instants of mind, which do not so halt,**
> **are ultimately existent and perform functions.**

[The Shrāvaka schools] also agree on the main points regarding knowable objects, which are bases (*gzhi'i shes bya*): the way of positing defiled and undefiled phenomena[301] and the way of positing the two truths.

[Defiled phenomena] are what cause [mental] defilements (*āsrava, zag pa*), or mental afflictions, to increase and endure when a mind with desire cognizes and observes the nature of those phenomena. [Defiled phenomena cause mental defilements] by way of being observed objects (*dmigs pa*) or being [the mind and mental events, which] are congruent in five ways.[302] [Undefiled phenomena,] when observed, are what do not cause [mental defilements] to increase. Thus all conditioned phenomena, other than those included in the truth of the path, are illustrations (*mtshan gzhi*) of defiled phenomena; and the phenomena of the truth of the path and unconditioned phenomena are illustrations of undefiled phenomena.

The way of presenting the two truths[303] is given in the *Treasury* [*of Abhidharma*]:[304]

> Something that is no longer engaged by a mind
> when physically destroyed or mentally broken down
> exists conventionally, like vases or water.
> Everything else exists ultimately.

Conventional reality [is defined as] any phenomenon which is such that if it is physically destroyed or broken down into different parts by an eliminating mind (*sel byed kyi blo*), the mind perceiving it is halted.[305] Gross entities (such as the environment and its inhabitants) are false because they involve directional parts and because the mind can eliminate them [by separating them] into different parts. [Temporal] continuities (such as years, months, and days), which are imagined [to exist] in the three times, are not real since they can be divided into parts. All conventionally existent [phenomena] (*kun rdzob yod pa*) are ultimately unable to perform functions.

Ultimate reality is that which does not halt the mind perceiving it

[even] when it is broken down into parts.[306] It consists of (1) minute particles that truly exist (*bden par grub pa*) as the building blocks of things since they have no directional parts; and (2) the instants of the inner perceiving mind that exist as the building blocks of the temporal continuity [of mind]. All ultimately existent phenomena are capable of performing functions ultimately.[307]

The reason vases and so forth are conventionalities is that ultimately they are unable to perform functions. This is because, if one's position is that an object ultimately able to perform a function from its own side is a phenomenon, or referent, that intrinsically (*rang gi mtshan nyid la*) produces an unmistaken perceiver of itself, then those vases and so forth are conventionalities since the mind [perceiving them] relies upon inner contributory aspects, such as symbols, [to perceive them]. Thus it is said.

They agree for the most part about the way conditioned phenomena arise and about the paths and results.

Generally, [Vaibhāṣhikas and Sautrāntikas] agree that the definition of mind is that which apprehends simply the essential nature of an object, and mental events are what apprehend just the distinctive features [of an object]. They also are in agreement about the way conditioned phenomena arise, about which they state the following:

- The element-derivatives[308] of forms arise from the elements.
- The substances of cognitions (*shes rig gi rdzas*) arise in conjunction with the five congruent aspects.[309]
- The entities of [the formative forces] not associated [with forms or mind][310] arise from forms or minds, which are "that which bear a state"[311] (*gnas skabs can*).

In terms of the paths and their results, they agree

- on the main points of the illustrations and defining characteristics of the four truths, which are either objects to be adopted or to be rejected;[312]
- that, in terms of the subjective agent, there are five paths—accumulation, junction, seeing, meditation, and beyond training;
- on the enumeration of four pairs of beings, also called eight kinds of individuals;[313] and

- on most aspects of relinquishment and realization.

They are in agreement about the way [the Buddha] first developed bodhichitta, in the middle phase increased his stores [of merit and wisdom], and in the end became a buddha. They agree that in his last lifetime in cyclic existence when, as a prince, he was to accomplish his aim, he was an ordinary being on the path of accumulation and fully fettered (*'ching ba kun ldan*), even though he had perfected his stores of merit and wisdom during three incalculable [aeons].[314]

They do not assert that the Buddha awakened in Akaniṣhṭha, but rather that this occurred in front of the bodhi tree. At dusk, he tamed the thirty-seven million hordes of Māra. Then, on the same seat, at dawn he attained all the relinquishments and realizations—having progressed from the path of junction to the attainment of the knowledge of the exhaustion [of defilements] and their [subsequent] nonarising[315]—solely by means of the path of realizing the sixteen aspects of the four truths (impermanence and the others).

Prior to his awakening, the Buddha received key instructions on the worldly meditative concentrations from Arāḍha-kālāma and Udrakorāmaputra,[316] and through his practice of the absorptions of the sphere of Nothingness and the sphere of Neither Discrimination Nor Nondiscrimination, he became separated from passion. Thus the Buddha was free from passion prior to becoming a buddha.

They mostly agree on the presentation of the relinquishments and realizations for the twenty types of saṅgha[317] and on the way someone can regress from the attainment of relinquishments and realizations, with a few minor exceptions.[318] Their presentations of the excellent qualities of the four samādhis, the four formless states, and the four immeasurables are the same. They assert that the truth of suffering is [experienced] on the bhūmi of a buddha, meaning that the Buddha had matured aggregates that were impelled by previous karma and that he had a remainder of defiled karma.[319] They share the belief that the three types of nirvāṇa without remainder—which are [the fruitions attained by] shrāvakas, by pratyekabuddhas, and by buddhas—are the severing of the continuity of cognition (*rig pa rgyun chad pa*), just like [the extinction of] a fire when its wood is exhausted.

Their Dissimilar Assertions [b']

This has two parts: Vaibhāṣhikas' assertions; and Sautrāntikas' assertions.

Vaibhāṣhikas' Assertions [i']

> **Points of dissimilarity are that the Vaibhāṣhikas assert that the seven [abhidharma] texts are [the Buddha's] words;**
> **that there are partless, discrete particles with interstices between them;**
> **that when of similar types, [such particles] perform the same activity, and that they are like [grasses in] a meadow;**
> **that sense faculties see referents, and consciousnesses apprehend those [referents];**
> **and that in most cases, percepts and perceivers, as causes and results, arise simultaneously.**

Specific points of disagreements between the Vaibhāṣhikas' and Sautrāntikas' systems of philosophical tenets are found in abundance throughout the *Treasury* [*of Abhidharma*]. I will now summarize the Vaibhāṣhikas' positions in a general way.

Vaibhāṣhikas make the following assertions:

- The seven abhidharma texts[320] are compilations of teachings actually contained in sūtras that were extracted by individual arhats, just as was done with the *Collection of Meaningful Expressions*.[321] Thus, the seven abhidharma treatises are [the Buddha's] words (*vachana, bka'*).
- Since the collection of dharma—the scriptures and so forth—is a series of words, it is included within the category of non-associated formative forces.[322]
- Everything included with the category of forms is either an element or an element-derivative, or is composed of minute particles.
- When minute particles form gross phenomena, a middle particle is surrounded by particles of the six directions; and yet, partless discrete particles (*rdul phran cha med sil bu*) have interstices, or empty spaces, between them. Minute particles are substantially established (*dravya-siddha, rdzas su grub pa*). [When they are] of similar types, they perform the same activity. They are like [the hairs in] a yak's tail or [grasses in]

a meadow. Although discrete minute particles remain separate, they do not disintegrate because they are held together by karma or wind. Coarse phenomena are also drawn together in one direction by the wind that holds those [partless particles] together.[323]

- As for the way consciousnesses apprehend objects: sense consciousnesses apprehend their respective objects nakedly and immediately without an [intermediary] image,[324] like pliers [taking hold of] a lump of iron. Once a sense faculty sees the actual object (*don gyi rang mtshan*), a consciousness apprehends it. Vaibhāṣhikas assert that in most cases percepts and their perceivers, as causes and results, arise simultaneously, because a consciousness cannot be produced by something past or future.

[Vaibhāṣhikas] maintain that the five bases, [the phenomena of] the three times, and nirvāṇa exist substantially;
that unconditioned phenomena are permanent, and the truth of cessation is an entity;
that consciousnesses are aware of what is other; and other points.
The basis [of their system] was delineated by the four great ones and others in reliance upon scriptures.

- The five bases of objects of knowledge,[325] [the phenomena of] the three times, nirvāṇa, and, particularly, non-associated formative forces—which are referents (*don*) that are other than "that which bear a state" to which states are ascribed[326]—are substantially existent in the sense of being self-sufficient (*rang rkya thub pa'i rdzas yod*).[327]
- They assert the three kinds of unconditioned phenomena[328] to be permanent. Furthermore, since they are incapable of positing knowable objects that are not established by way of their essence (*ngo bos ma grub pa*), they assert that [unconditioned phenomena] are substances or entities that are [positive] determinations.[329] Although they consider unconditioned phenomena to be entities, they never assert them to be conditioned entities able to perform functions.[330] This is because they state that [unconditioned phenomena] have neither cause nor result, as is said [in the *Treasury of Abhidharma*]:[331]

> Unconditioned phenomena do not have those [that is, causes and results].

- They state that arhats can regress to the state of a once returner (*phyir 'ong*) and so forth.
- They say that the truth of cessation is something attained through the five faculties,[332] is the supreme of all phenomena, is the substance of separation (*bral ba'i rdzas*), and so forth; thus they consider the truth of cessation to be an entity.
- Citing the example of the way a sword cannot cut itself, they do not believe that consciousness (*shes pa*) can be a reflexive awareness [i.e., a consciousness aware of itself] (*rang rig*), or that it can experience itself. They state that every consciousness is an other-awareness [i.e., a consciousness aware of what is "other," meaning outer objects] (*gzhan rig*).

The phrase "and other points" in this root verse refers to other of their numerous unique positions, such as that they are not able to posit that the nonimplicative negation that is the simple negation of the self of persons is thusness.[333]

It is well known that the four great venerable ones,[334] the Kashmiri Saṅghabhadra,[335] the venerable Anantavarman,[336] and others, in reliance upon teachings found in scriptures [of the Buddha], clearly delineated the basis of this system of philosophical tenets.

Sautrāntikas' Assertions [ii']

> **Dārṣhṭāntikas mostly state the opposite of that.**
> **Particles touch but do not join, like [the pages of] a book.**
> **The sense faculties are matter; external referents are hidden phenomena.**
> **The consciousnesses do not see these: they experience images as their referents.**

Dārṣhṭāntikas (Exemplifiers), or Sautrāntikas,[337] mostly state the opposite of the Vaibhāṣhikas, meaning Sautrāntikas do not make the same assertions as the Vaibhāṣhikas on the topics just explained. It is said:

> *Jñānaprasthāna* (*Entering Primordial Wisdom*)[338] was composed by Kātāyanīputra;
> *Prakaraṇapāda* (*Correct Analysis*)[339] by Vasumitra;

Dharmaskandha (*Dharma Aggregate*)[340] by Shāriputra;
Prajñāptishāstra[341] (*Treatise on Designations*)[342] by Maudgalyāyana;
Vijñānakāya (*Collection of Consciousnesses*)[343] by Devasharman;[344]
Saṅgītiparyāya (*Enumerations of Persons*)[345] by Mahākauṣhṭhila; and
Dhātukāya (*Collection of Constituents*)[346] by Pūrṇa.

Sautrāntikas believe that these seven abhidharma texts[347] are treatises (*shāstras, bstan bcos*) [and not the words of the Buddha] because they were composed independently by those arhats.

- They assert that the collection of scriptural dharma—which has the characteristics of terms, and covers all that is contained in the scriptural tradition—is included within the aggregate of forms.
- As for forms, like [the Vaibhāṣhikas] above, they say that there are two types: minute particles, which are building blocks; and gross phenomena, which are constructed with those. Sautrāntikas, however, say that minute particles circle [each other] and do not join, but they also have no interstices between them. Hence, they are perceived as touching, like [the pages of] a bound book.[348]
- Sense faculties are matter (*bem po*) and, therefore, they are not what sees referents.
- External referents (*phyi don*) are considered to be hidden.[349] Because [external referents objects] are past [when a consciousness arises], they are not what a consciousness sees. Thus, [Sautrāntikas posit] what is called "an image,"[350] which is an appearance of consciousness that has been cast by the referent. Although the referent has ceased, the image that is consciousness set by that [referent] is experienced as the likeness of the referent. This is designated as the experience [of the referent]. A consciousness apprehending an object perceives by means of an image [acting] as an intermediary (*bar du chod pa*).
- Sautrāntikas state that percepts and their perceivers, as causes and results, arise sequentially, not simultaneously.

Given the Sautrāntikas' position that external referents are hidden [phenomena], they are similar to Chittamātra Proponents of Real Images in considering dualistic appearances to be cognition (*shes pa*). Nevertheless, these systems differ as to whether "what casts [images]" (*gtod byed*) is an external referent or not: [for Sautrāntikas, it is an external referent that casts the image; for Chittamātra Proponents of Real Images, it is not].

Forms, mind, feelings, discriminations, and intentions exist substantially.
Everything else is imputedly existent; space and the others are nonimplicative negations.
They assert that [consciousness is both] a reflexive-awareness and an other-awareness; that [the phenomena of] the three times are imputed entities; and other points.
This is [the system] asserted by Saṅgharakṣhita, Shrīlāta, and others.

- Among the five bases (which are knowable objects), forms, mind, and either two or three of the mental events—feelings, discriminations, and, [in some cases,] intentions—exist substantially.[351] Everything else is asserted to be imputedly existent entities—meaning that they are designated [as entities simply] in relation to [having some] aspects [of entities][352]—or to be imputedly existent nonentities (*dngos med*).
- They consider the three types of unconditioned phenomena (space and the others) to be permanent, but [simply] as nonimplicative negations that just refute their impermanence. In terms of what is determined,[353] this means that they assert [unconditioned phenomena] simply to be knowable objects that have no established essence, like the horns of a rabbit.
- Using the analogy that if something does not illuminate itself, it cannot illuminate something that is other than itself, they say that consciousness is twofold: it is reflexive awareness (*rang rig*), which is an inwards-facing experiencer, and it is other-awareness (*gzhan rig*), which is an outwards-facing experiencer. [The relationship between a consciousness and the objects it cognizes is like that of a crystal and the colors that appear within it:] colors appearing in a clear crystal are of the nature of that crystal. Thus, since a consciousness is that which is aware of referents that are of the same nature as itself, it is an authentic reflexive awareness (*rang rig mtshan nyid pa*) and a nominal referent-awareness (*don rig btags pa ba*).
- They maintain that [the phenomena of] the three times are not substantially established, that they are mentally imputed entities.

The phrase "and other points" in this root verse includes the following:

- Sautrāntikas assert that both nirvāṇa with remainder and without remainder are nonimplicative negations, which negate the factors that are to be abandoned by remedies; that is, they are a mere nothingness.
- They say that arhats regress just from the meditative concentration of resting at ease in the present life,[354] and these arhats are called "those who regress."[355] They do not accept, however, that arhats regress from their result.
- They assert that the truth of cessation is a nonentity for the following reasons: It cannot be observed by a valid cognizer[356] to be an entity, the way a form or feeling can be, or to be a potential (*nus pa*), the way the eyes can be. Also the sūtras refer to it as "separation," "exhaustion," "disappearance," and "cessation."
- Sautrāntikas are able to posit that the nonimplicative negation that is the mere negation of a self of persons is thusness.[357]

The basis of this system of philosophical tenets relies upon the sūtra section of the Victor's scriptures and is explained by the venerable Saṅgharakṣhita,[358] Shrīlāta,[359] and others. The details of the Sautrāntika philosophy can be understood from the *Treasury of Abhidharma's Auto-Commentary* [that is, the *Explanation of the "Treasury of Abhidharma"*].[360]

The Classifications of Its Orders [bb]

This has three parts: the four main orders; the eighteen divisions; and the twofold summation.

The Four Main Orders [1']

> **The main orders are the four: Sarvāstivādins,**
> **Mahāsāṅghikas, Sthaviras, and Saṃmitīyas.**

Although there are many descriptions by different masters of the way the Shrāvaka orders (*nikāya, sde pa*) are divided—such as that there was one [root order], two, three, and so on[361]—the presentation of four main orders is the most well-known.[362] The four are [Mūla]sarvāstivādins;[363] Mahāsāṅghikas; Sthaviras; and Saṃmitīyas.[364]

Mūlasarvāstivādins

Mūlasarvāstivādins (*gZhi thams cad yod par smra ba,* Proponents of the Existence of All Bases) are known by that name because they are the basis (*mūla, gzhi*) for all the orders; and because they state that the five bases (*mūla, gzhi*), which are knowable objects, exist (*asti, yod pa*) substantially.

- This order recited their scriptures in Sanskrit ("the well-formed language").
- Their lineage originated from Rāhula, a master of the warrior caste (*kṣhatriya*) who was devoted to the trainings (*bslab pa*).
- Their upper robe (*saṅghāṭī, snam sbyar*) had between nine and twenty-five patches (*snam phran*), and their symbol was a wheel and lotus.
- Their names ended with *shrī* (*dpal,* glorious), *bhadra* (*bzang po,* excellent), or *garbha* (or *sārā*) (*snying po,* heart).[365]
- Their philosophical tenets[366] included the positions that
  - [the phenomena of] the three times exist substantially;
  - all conditioned phenomena are momentary;
  - a self of persons does not exist; and
  - buddhahood is attained after three incalculable aeons.

Mahāsāṅghikas

Mahāsāṅghikas (*dGe 'dun phal chen pa,* Majority of the Community) are referred to as such because, at the time of the split, the majority of the saṅgha formed this group.

- This order [recited in] Prakṛit (the vernacular language).[367]
- Their [lineage originated from] Kāshyapa, a master of the Brahman caste who excelled in the ascetic practices.[368]
- Their [upper robe] had between seven and twenty-three patches, and their symbol was an endless knot (*shrivatsa*).
- Their names ended in *jñāna* (*ye shes,* primordial wisdom) or *gupta* (*sbas pa,* hidden).
- Their philosophical tenets included such assertions as
  - the self [of persons] and the aggregates are separate;
  - the [four] truths are seen all at once;[369]
  - it is possible to regress even from the level of supreme qualities;[370] and
  - the sense faculties do not apprehend objects.

Sthaviras

Sthaviras (*gNas brtan pa,* Elders or Firm Abiders) are called that because they state that they belong to the lineage of *sthavira* noble ones.

- This order [recited in] Pishācha (the flesh-eaters' language).[371]
- Their [lineage originated from] Kātyāyana, a master belonging to the caste of bamboo workers who was foremost in taming the people of the border lands.
- Their [upper robe] had between five and twenty-one patches, and their symbol was a conch.
- Their names ended in *ākara* (*'byung gnas,* source) or *varma* (or *sannāha*) (*go cha,* armor).
- Their philosophical tenets included assertions such as
  - the Buddha did not teach in Sanskrit;
  - mind is present during the absorption of cessation;[372]
  - mistaken consciousness (*log shes*) is not present [during absorption in cessation]; and
  - buddhahood is attained after ten incalculable [aeons] at the least and thirty at the most.

Saṃmitīyas

Saṃmitīyas (*Mang pos bkur ba,* Followers of Mahāsammata) are called that because they are holders of the lineage of the master Mahāsammata, [whose name means] he who was honored (*bkur ba*), or revered, by many (*mang ba*) beings.

- This order [recited in] Apabhraṃsha (the corrupted language).[373]
- Their [lineage originated from] Upāli, a master belonging to the caste of barbers who was supreme in upholding the vinaya.
- Their upper robe was similar to that of the Sthaviras.
- Their names ended in "commoner" (*'bangs*) or "class" (*sde*).
- Their philosophical tenets included assertions such as
  - the existence of an inexplicable self [or person];[374]
  - all knowable objects are considered to be both explicable and inexplicable;
  - conditioned phenomena with stable continuities are eliminated by destructive objects other than themselves; and
  - the path of seeing is [attained] after twelve moments.[375]

It is also explained that those orders had different ways of reciting the *Sūtra of Individual Liberation*[376] and formulating the proscriptions and downfalls (*bcas ltung*). There is also the explanation that the Mahāsāṅghikas were the basis of the [four] root [orders]. Name changes are [part of] the present-day [ordination ceremony], but were not part of the original ceremony.[377] The differentiation [of the orders in terms of their] robes, names, and so forth has been explained according to Atīsha's exegesis.

Since the *Hevajra Tantra*, in the fourth chapter of its second section, correlates the four orders to the four chakras,[378] and it is explained that the four faces of Kālachakra taught the four orders,[379] these are authoritative sources for the position that there were four root orders.

The Eighteen Divisions [2']

> **The divisions into five, seven, three, and three [result in] the eighteen [orders].**

The way the eighteen orders developed from the four main orders is stated in Vinītadeva's *Compendium on the Different Orders*:[380]

> Pūrvashailas,[381] Aparashailas,[382] Haimavatas,[383]
> Lokottaravādins,[384] and
> Prajñaptivādins[385]
> are the five orders of Mahāsāṅghikas.
>
> Sarvāstivādins,[386] Kāshyapīyas,[387]
> Mahīshāsakas,[388] Dharmaguptakas,[389]
> Bahushrutīyas,[390] Tāmrashāṭīyas,[391] and
> Vibhajvavādins[392]
> are the [seven] orders of Sarvāstivādins.
>
> Jetavanīyas,[393] Abhayagirikas,[394] and
> Mahāvihārins[395] are the [three] Sthaviras.
>
> Kurukullas,[396] Avantakas,[397]
> and Vatsīputrīyas[398] are
> the three Saṃmitīyas.

> These are the eighteen groups that formed because of
> their different geographical locations, points [of doctrine],
> and masters.

That is the explanation that the eighteen orders are the five Mahāsāṅghikas, the seven Sarvāstivādins, the three Sthaviras, and the three Saṃmitīyas. Their dissimilarities arose only because their followers lived in different areas, had different ways of asserting the points of their philosophical tenet systems, and had different founding masters; they do not differ in terms of being paths to liberation. The *Sūtra of a Teaching Given in a Dream*[399] to King Kṛikī states:

> Great king, you dreamt that you saw eighteen people divide a single piece of cloth and that each person received a piece without the original being diminished. This signifies that although the teachings of Shākyamuni will split into eighteen parts, the cloth of freedom will not be diminished.

We should know that the eighteen orders do not differ in terms of their qualities.

The Twofold Summation [3']

This has two divisions: the actual twofold summation; and ancillary analysis.

The Actual Twofold Summation [a']

> **They are grouped into propounders of a self and propounders of an absence of a self.**

If the eighteen orders are simplified, they fall into two groups: propounders of a self [of persons] and propounders of an absence of a self [of persons]. The five Saṃmitīyas (the Vātsīputrīyas and the others)[400] assert an inexplicable self [or person]. They maintain that although the person cannot be described as being the same as or separate from the aggregates, or as permanent or impermanent, and so forth, it is substantially existent in the sense of being self-sufficient. All the other Vaibhāṣhika orders, as well as the Sautrāntikas, state that there is no self [of persons]. The *Blaze of Reasoning* explains:[401]

> Among those orders, the eight Mahāsāṅghikas[402] (who were listed first) and (within the [ten Sthaviras] who were listed second) the Sthaviras, Sarvāstivādins, Mahīshāsakas, Dharmottaras,[403] and Kāshyapīyas are propounders of the nonexistence of a self [of persons]. They maintain that the self and "mine" imputed by the assertions of the tīrthikas are empty, and that all phenomena have no self-entity.
>
> The remaining five orders, Vātsīputrīyas and the others,[404] are propounders of a person. They state that while the person cannot be said to be identical with nor other than the aggregates, it is cognizable by the six consciousnesses and it is clearly what circles in saṃsāra.

Ancillary Analysis [b']

> **[Shrāvakas] are flawed in their refutation of the**
> **Mahāyāna and in their assertion that [ultimate] reality**
> **is established.**
> **On other [topics] they are not wrong; it is their own system.**

It is said that the Shrāvaka orders' refutation of the Mahāyāna is [a reflection of] their inability to comprehend the Mahāyāna's profundity and vastness, and that this is attributable to their inferior scholastic knowledge (*rtog ge nyid kyi shes rab*), beliefs, and weak merit. Their assertion that ultimate reality is substantially established reflects a similar flaw of not understanding the intention (*dgongs pa*) of [the Buddha's] teachings. It is for these reasons that the *Ornament of the Mahāyāna Sūtras*[405] and other texts discuss in detail how the Mahāyāna is in fact [the Buddha's] words.

The Vaibhāṣhikas' assertion of substantial existence is refuted by Sautrāntikas. The Sautrāntikas' position regarding imputed existence[406] is refuted by the Chittamātras by means of numerous scriptures and reasonings. In particular, since the belief in an inexplicable self [or person] is such an inferior view, it is thoroughly refuted in the *Root Commentary on the Kālachakra Tantra*,[407] *Entrance to the Middle Way*,[408] and other texts. Although [the Vaibhāṣhikas' and Sautrāntikas'] general presentations of ground, path, and result seem to conflict with those of the higher [philosophical tenet systems], they are not, however, wrong. They are the shrāvakas' own systems and, thus, they have merit.

The Classifications of Its Results [cc]

This has two parts: an overview; and an extensive explanation.

An Overview [1']

> **Having meditated on the sixteen aspects, one progresses through the five paths**
> **by applying the factors for awakening, and attains the four types of results.**

The Buddha appeared in the world and the doctrines he taught remain and are practiced. This makes it possible for one, first, to abide by the ethical conduct of one of the seven or eight sets of vows of individual liberation.[409] Then, with a qualified spiritual mentor, one studies, in keeping with the level of one's acumen, the nine scriptural categories[410] according to the shrāvakas, which are contained within the three collections of scripture. Study is followed by critical reflection. By meditating on the topics of reflection, which are the sixteen aspects of the four truths (impermanence and the others),[411] one will progress gradually through the five paths of the shrāvakas (accumulation, junction, and so forth) by applying the thirty-seven factors for awakening (*byang phyogs so bdun*). Finally one attains the four results: stream enterer (*srota-āpanna, rgyun zhugs pa*), once returner (*sakṛid-āgāmin, lan cig phyir 'ong ba*), nonreturner (*anāgāmin, phyir mi 'ong ba*), and arhat (*dgra bcom pa*).

An Extensive Explanation [2']

This is discussed in two sections: a detailed explanation of the gradual type; and an explanation of the skipping and instantaneous types as supplementary topics.

A Detailed Explanation of the Gradual Type [a']

In this section, there are four parts: stream enterers; once returners; non-returners; and arhats.

Stream Enterers [i']

This has two divisions: approachers to the result of a stream enterer; and abiders in the result of a stream enterer.

Approachers to the Result of a Stream Enterer [aa']

> **Approachers to [the result of] a stream enterer may not have abandoned any of the desire realm afflictions,**
> **or they may have abandoned the fourth or fifth, but to have abandoned the sixth is not possible.**
> **They abide in one of the fifteen moments,**
> **and are of two types: followers of faith and followers of the dharma.**

For those approaching the result of a shrāvaka stream enterer, the particular features of their relinquishment[412] are that it is possible that they have not relinquished any of the afflictions of the desire realm (*'dod nyon*), or that they may have abandoned the fourth or the fifth afflictions[413] of the desire realm. They will not have abandoned the sixth affliction at all for it is not possible that those approaching this result have abandoned the sixth.[414]

The particular features of their realization are that they abide in any one of the first fifteen of sixteen moments, which are the path of seeing.[415] The sixteen moments comprise the following:

- the acceptance of phenomena,[416] knowledge of phenomena,[417] subsequent acceptance, and subsequent knowledge[418] related to the truth of suffering (1–4);
- the acceptance of phenomena, knowledge of phenomena, subsequent acceptance, and subsequent knowledge related to the truth of the origins of suffering (5–8), related to the truth of cessation (9–12), and related to the truth of the path[419] (13–16).

Those approaching the result of a stream enterer fall into two categories: (1) followers of faith,[420] who are of lower acumen; and (2) followers of dharma,[421] who are of higher acumen.

Abiders in the Result of a Stream Enterer [bb']

> **Abiders in the result**
> **have attained the realization of the sixteenth moment.**
> **There are those of lower and higher acumen, those who will take seven rebirths, and those who will take two.**

The specifics of the relinquishments of those who abide in the result of a stream enterer are the same as those on the previous level. The distinctive feature of their realization is that they have attained the realization of the sixteenth moment, which is the subsequent knowledge of the truth of the path.[422]

There are four classifications[423] of abiders in the result of a stream enterer: (1) those of lower acumen, (2) those of higher acumen, and (3–4) [two] ways of taking birth.

First, there are two types in terms of acumen: (1) Those who were of lower acumen as approachers [to the result of a stream enterer now] become those who aspire through faith (*shraddhādhimukta, dad pas mos pa*). (2) Those who were of higher acumen become those who attain through seeing (*dṛiṣhṭiprāpta, mthong bas thob pa*).[424]

Second, in terms of the way they take rebirth, there are two types: (1) those who will take rebirth seven times in cyclic existence (*saptakṛitparamaḥ, lan bdun pa*); and (2) those who will take rebirth two times, who are called "those born into the same class" (*kulaṃkula, rigs nas rigs su skye ba*).

(1) For [those who take rebirth seven times,] the basic state is that of abiders in the result of a stream enterer [with the qualification that] they have not freed themselves at all from the afflictions of the desire realm. [Rebirth can manifest in the following two ways:] Those who attained that [result of a stream enterer] as a god will be reborn seven times as a god, then seven times as a human, and will [experience] two sets of seven states as a *bardo* being (*bar srid*), making twenty-eight [states] altogether. Those who attained [the result of a stream enterer] as a human will take rebirth as a human seven times, as a god seven times, and as a bardo being seven times during each [of those series of births], making twenty-eight.

Following those rebirths, they all become approachers to once returners. They are called "those who take rebirth in cyclic existence seven times" because the seven sets of lives have similar qualities. This is similar to the way that someone is called "wise in the seven things" [because they know topics grouped in sevens,] or a tree is called "seven-leafed" [because each branch has seven leaves].[425] There are, however, other ways that [taking seven rebirths] is explained.

(2) "Those born into the same class" have the same basic state of being an abider in the result of a stream enterer [with the qualification that] it is possible that they have abandoned either the third or the fourth affliction of the desire [realm, but] they will not have abandoned the fifth at all.[426] They will take two rebirths in the same class of being that they were when they attained [the result of a stream enterer], be it a god or human.[427]

Once Returners [ii']

This has two divisions: approachers to the result of a once returner; and abiders in the result of a once returner.

Approachers to the Result of a Once Returner [aa']

> **Through their meditation, they become approachers to**
> **a once returner.**
> **They [will] abandon the sixth [affliction].**

When those abiding in the result of a stream enterer exert themselves in the meditations of the path [of a once returner] with the aim of achieving the result of a once returner, they become approachers to a once returner. When they give up the sixth affliction [of the desire realm], they become abiders in the result of a once returner.

Abiders in the Result of a Once Returner [bb']

> **They have not abandoned the ninth [affliction] at all.**
> **Abiders in the result who have one interruption will**
> **definitely return.**

A subdivision of the abiders in the result of a once returner[428] is "those interrupted for one life."[429] As for their relinquishments and realizations: In terms of relinquishment, it is possible that they have abandoned the seventh and eighth afflictions of the desire realm, but they will not have abandoned the ninth affliction at all. Realization on this level is the same as before.

Even though "once returners" are the type who return once to the desire realm, if they exert themselves in the path of a nonreturner, they will proceed to that level. However, in the case of those belonging to the subdivision of "those having one interruption for one life," they will definitely return [to the desire realm for one more rebirth].

Nonreturners [iii']

This has two divisions: approachers to the result of a nonreturner; and abiders in the result of a nonreturner.

Approachers to the Result of a Nonreturner [aa']

> **By exerting themselves continuously, they become approachers to a nonreturner.**

To attain the result of a nonreturner, abiders in the result of a once returner exert themselves continuously on that path [of a nonreturner], through which they become approachers to the result of a nonreturner.

Abiders in the Result of a Nonreturner [bb']

> **Those who abandon the ninth [affliction] abide in the result.**
> **They may go to the form realm,**
> **where they pass beyond [misery] in the bardo, after birth, or [after] rising to a higher state;**
> **they may go to the formless realm; they may [attain] peace in this lifetime; or they may physically actualize [nirvāṇa].**

When approachers to a nonreturner have abandoned the ninth affliction of the desire realm,[430] they become abiders in its result. They fall into four main categories:

(1) those who go to the form realm (*gzugs su nyer 'gro*);
(2) those who go to the formless realm (*gzugs med nyer 'gro*);
(3) those who [attain] peace in this lifetime (*mthong chos la zhi*); and
(4) those who physically actualize [nirvāṇa] (*lus mngon byed*).

(1) Those who go to the form realm are of three types:
(a) those who pass beyond [misery] in the bardo (*bar dor 'da' ba*);
(b) those who pass beyond [misery] after birth (*skyes nas 'da' ba*); and
(c) those who rise to a higher state [and then attain nirvāṇa] (*gong du 'pho ba*).

(1a) [Those who pass beyond misery in the bardo:] The basic state is that of abiders in the result of a nonreturner. [Their specific characteristic is that] they are the type who pass beyond misery in the bardo that is a support for [i.e., is the state prior to or on the way to] any one of the sixteen levels of the form realm (with Great Brahmā being the one excluded).[431]

(1b) Those who pass beyond [misery] after birth are of three types:
(i) those who pass beyond [misery] after they are born (*skyes nas 'da' ba*);
(ii) those [who pass beyond misery] through application (*'du byed can*); and
(iii) those [who pass beyond misery] without application (*'du byed med pa*).[432]

(i) [Those who pass beyond misery after they are born] are the type who pass beyond misery as soon as they are born in any one of the sixteen levels of the form realm (with Great Brahmā again being the one excluded).
(ii) [Those who pass beyond misery through application] are the type who pass beyond [misery] by applying themselves with effort to the path after they have taken birth in [any one of] those states [of the form realm].
(iii) [Those who pass beyond misery without application] are the kind who pass beyond [misery] without any effort simply by engaging in the path after they have been born in [any one of] those [states of the form realm].

(1c) Those who rise to a higher state [and then pass beyond misery] are of two types:

(i) those who rise to Akaniṣhṭha[433] (*'og min du 'pho ba*); and

(ii) those who rise to the Pinnacle of Existence[434] (*srid rtser 'pho ba*).

(i) Those who rise to Akaniṣhṭha are of three kinds:

(aa) leapers (*'phar ba*);

(bb) half-leapers (*phyed 'phar ba*); and

(cc) those who rise through all [the levels] (*kun 'pho*).

(aa) [Leapers] are abiders in the result of a nonreturner who are born in their next life in Brahmā Type[435] and then leap to the state of Akaniṣhṭha, [thereby passing over fifteen levels of the form realm]. In Akaniṣhṭha they pass beyond misery.

(bb) [Half-leapers] are the kind who are born in Brahmā Type in their next life and then take birth in one of the four pure states.[436] Following that, they rise to the level of Akaniṣhṭha, where they pass beyond misery.

(cc) [Those who rise through all the levels] are the type who take birth in all sixteen levels of the form realm one after the other (with the exception of Great Brahmā). Following their [last] death, they pass beyond misery in the state of Akaniṣhṭha.

(ii) Those who rise to the Pinnacle of Existence are similar in that they are the kind who are born in Brahmā Type in their next life. Following that, they rise to the state of the Pinnacle of Existence, where they pass beyond misery.

(2) Those who go to the formless realm are the type who are born in their next life in one of the first three levels of the formless realm, after which they pass beyond misery in the state of the Pinnacle of Existence. It is said about this [type]:

> Wherever they die in the formless [realm], that is where [they pass beyond misery].[437]

[This category] does not have the type who pass beyond [misery] in the bardo.[438] It does, however, have three types who pass beyond misery after birth and three types of leapers, who are similar to the ones described above [for the form realm].[439]

(3) Those who [attain] peace in this lifetime are the type who pass beyond misery during the same state [i.e., life] in which they attained the level of abiding in the result of a nonreturner.

(4) Those who physically actualize [nirvāṇa] are the type who pass beyond misery having actualized the absorption of cessation.[440]

Arhats [iv']

This has two divisions: approachers to the result of an arhat; and abiders in the result of an arhat.

Approachers to the Result of an Arhat [aa']

They approach the level of an arhat in order to abandon the ninth affliction of the [Pinnacle of] Existence.

Abiders in the result of a nonreturner approaching [the result of an arhat] in order to abandon the ninth affliction of the [Pinnacle of] Existence (*srid nyon*) are called "approachers to an arhat."

Abiders in the Result of an Arhat [bb']

With the abandonment of that [ninth affliction], they are liberated from the bonds of the three realms and abide in the result.
[This result] is classified as those with twofold liberation and those liberated by wisdom;
those with the ornaments of the supercognitive abilities of magical powers and those without ornaments; and
those with a remainder of the appropriating aggregates and those without remainder.

With the abandonment of the ninth affliction of the [Pinnacle of] Existence, they are liberated from the bonds of the habitual conduct (*kun spyod*) of the three realms and become an abider in the result of an arhat.[441] This is classified in three ways:[442]

The twofold classification in terms of relinquishment:

(1) those with twofold liberation (*ubhayatobhāgavimukta, gnyis ka'i cha las rnam grol*), who are liberated from both the afflictive obscurations (*nyon sgrib*) and the obscurations to absorption (*snyoms 'jug gi sgrib pa*); and

(2) those liberated by means of wisdom (*prajñāvimukta, shes rab kyis rnam grol*), who are only liberated from the afflictive obscurations.

The twofold classification in terms of excellent qualities:

(1) those with the ornaments (*sālaṃkāra, rgyan can*) of the degenerative (*zag bcas*) supercognitive abilities (magical powers and the others)[443] that pertain to their respective level;[444] and

(2) those without ornaments (*niralaṃkāra, rgyan med*).[445]

The twofold classification in terms of liberation:

(1) those with the remainder (*sheṣha, lhag bcas*) of the aggregates, which appropriate suffering; and

(2) those called "arhats without remainder" (*asheṣha, lhag med*) because their [aggregates] have been exhausted[446] and their [state of an arhat] has been brought to completion (*mthar phyin pa*).

An Explanation of the Skipping and Instantaneous Types as Supplementary Topics [b']

Of the four pairs of beings, or the eight types of individuals, the first and last have the instantaneous type and the middle two have skippers.

Generally speaking, it is well known that the four results [are attained by] four pairs of beings. Specifically, since each level is subdivided into approachers and [abiders in] the result, these are the eight types of individuals. Among those [four], the first and last have the instantaneous type (*cig char ba*), whereas the middle two have the distinctions of the skipping type (*thod rgal ba*).[447] The instantaneous approach to [the relinquishment of] the factors to be abandoned is not [a topic] shared with the Shrāvaka[yāna]; it is taught, however, in the abhidharma that is unique to the Mahāyāna.[448]

4. THE PRATYEKABUDDHAYĀNA

b. The Pratyekabuddhayāna [II.A.2.b]
  i How Pratyekabuddhas Differ from Shrāvakas
  ii. A Systematic Presentation of the Pratyekabuddhayāna
    aa. The Meaning of the Term and Its Etymology
    bb. Its Entryway
      1' An Overview of Its Entryway
      2' A Detailed Explanation of Its Style of Meditation
    cc. The Vows to Be Guarded
    dd. The View to Be Realized
    ee. The Result to Be Attained
    ff. The Classifications [of Pratyekabuddhas]
      1' The Rhinoceros-like
      2' The Congregating Practitioners

[This chapter presents the second of the two divisions of the Hīnayāna, the Pratyekabuddhayāna.] It begins with a discussion of how pratyekabuddhas differ from shrāvakas, followed by a systematic presentation of the Pratyekabuddhayāna.

How Pratyekabuddhas Differ from Shrāvakas [i]

Swift pratyekabuddhas are released in three existences,
and the rhinoceros[-like take] one hundred aeons; they all
give rise to [some qualities that] are strong, some that
are weak, and others profound.

Shrāvakas and pratyekabuddhas are similar simply in terms of being [classified as] Hīnayāna; from the perspective of their causes and results, they are very different. From a causal perspective, the *Treasury* [*of Abhidharma*] says:[449]

> The swift are released in three existences.
> The rhinoceros [are released] through the causes [they cultivate] during one hundred aeons.

In terms of the result, the distinctive qualities of their type are as follows. Those of the pratyekabuddha[450] type have a strong sense of pride and, consequently, wish to manifest awakening on their own in a world devoid of buddhas and shrāvakas and without any teachers or rivals. They naturally have few mental afflictions, and thus they dislike distractions and seek solitude. Since their compassion is weak, they do not delight in benefiting others and the scope of their concern is limited. Given that their wisdom is more profound than that of the shrāvakas, they do not need to be taught by others and can manifest awakening using their own intelligence.

The distinctions of their path are as follows. In addition to understanding the sixteen aspects of the four truths (impermanence and the others),[451] pratyekabuddhas realize how the twelve links of dependent origination[452] are engaged and reversed (*'jug ldog*). On top of realizing the absence of a self of persons, they also realize that perceived objects have no nature. Thus it is taught that the pratyekabuddhas' realization is distinguished by their realization of one and a half absences of self-entity.[453]

A Systematic Presentation of the Pratyekabuddhayāna [ii]

This presentation has six topics: the meaning of the term and its etymology; its entryway; the vows to be guarded; the view to be realized; the result to be attained; and the classifications [of pratyekabuddhas].

The Meaning of the Term and Its Etymology [aa]

> **The meaning of the term is that they awaken on their own without relying on others.**

The meaning of the term *pratyekabuddha* (*rang sangs rgyas;* self[-realized] buddha) is as follows. Without relying on anyone else as their master, they manifest their own awakening through the power of their own wisdom and, therefore, are known as "self-awakened" (*rang byang chub*). Alternatively, in his *Commentary on the "Teachings Requested by Akṣhayamati,"*[454] [Vasubandhu] says that they are called "realizers by means of conditions" (*rkyen rtogs*)[455] because their primordial wisdom realizes dependent origination by means of the condition of an observed object.[456]

Its Entryway [bb]

This has two parts: an overview of its entryway; and a detailed explanation of its style of meditation.

An Overview of Its Entryway [1']

> **Their entryway is to take external causes and results as analogies**
> **for the forward and reverse sequences of internal dependent origination.**

The entryway for pratyekabuddhas is the twelve links of dependent origination, which has external and internal aspects. In terms of the first, the causal forms of external dependent origination include earth, water, fire, space, and time; and its resultant forms include roots, stalks, branches, leaves, flowers, and fruits. The forward sequence (*lugs 'byung*) is that when causes are present, their results will arise, and the reverse sequence (*lugs ldog*) is that when the causes are canceled, their results are canceled. Pratyekabuddhas take these as analogies for internal dependent origination. They examine a skeleton and understand that it comes from old age and death. Accordingly, they work through the steps to realizing that ignorance is the root of saṃsāra, thereby understanding the forward order of dependent origination. They also recognize that by reversing ignorance, the formative forces are canceled, and so on up through the reversal of old age and death; thus they realize the reverse sequence of dependent origination.

A Detailed Explanation of Its Style of Meditation [2']

> **Saṃsāra and nirvāṇa both have two modes: forward and reverse.**

Pratyekabuddhas' meditation on dependent origination involves two modes for both saṃsāra and nirvāṇa: a forward mode and a reverse mode.

First: Saṃsāra

The sequence of engaging saṃsāra through the power of afflictive phenomena (*saṃklesha, kun nyon*) is the process as it usually is. This is described in a sūtra:[457]

> The condition of ignorance produces the formative forces. The condition of the formative forces generates the consciousnesses . . . The condition of birth results in aging, death, misery, lamentation, suffering, unhappiness, and agitation. In this way, it is only a great mass of suffering that arises.

The reverse sequence is the reverse of that order, as is stated:

> Aging, death, and so forth follow birth. Birth comes from existence, and existence comes from grasping . . . Formative forces develop because of ignorance.

These sequences are distinguished from each other solely on the basis of their order; in fact, they are equivalent in terms of producing conviction about the causes and results of saṃsāra.

Second: Nirvāṇa

The sequence of engaging nirvāṇa through the power of purified phenomena (*vyavadāna, rnam par byang ba*) is stated as follows:

> From [the perspective of] the descending order, when ignorance is stopped, the formative forces are stopped. When the formative forces are halted, the consciousnesses are halted . . . When birth is stopped, aging, death, and so forth come to an end.

The reverse sequence is described as

> When birth is stopped, aging and death are stopped. When existence is halted, birth is halted . . . When ignorance is stopped, the formative forces come to an end.

These sequences are also simply different in terms of their order, but they are, in fact, identical ways to attain nirvāṇa. Therefore, because it is the case that when fundamental ignorance is stopped one is freed from all suffering, pratyekabuddhas set out to develop true wisdom in order to relinquish that ignorance.

The Vows to Be Guarded [cc]

> **Their vows are those of individual liberation.**

The vows of pratyekabuddhas are the ethical conduct of individual liberation, which are the same as for shrāvakas.

The View to Be Realized [dd]

> **They realize the absence of a self of persons**
> **and that perceived referents have no nature.**

The Treatises on the Bhūmis[458] explain that pratyekabuddhas, like shrāvakas, only realize the absence of a self of persons. On the other hand, the *Ornament of Clear Realization* says:[459]

> Know that the path of the rhinoceros-like is summarized accurately
> by [three things]:
> that they abandon the concept of perceived referents,
> that they do not relinquish [the notion] of a perceiver,
> and [the particular quality of] their support.

In addition to realizing the absence of a self of persons, pratyekabuddhas realize that perceived referents have no nature, which is one part of the self-entity of phenomena. This [interpretation] accords with the position of most [scholars].

The Result to Be Attained [ee]

Pratyekabuddhas attain the results of nirvāṇa with remainder and nirvāṇa without remainder. Since those are the same as the shrāvakas' results, I will not discuss their classifications here at all.[460]

The Classifications [of Pratyekabuddhas] [ff]

This has two divisions: the rhinoceros-like; and the congregating practitioners.

The Rhinoceros-like [1']

> **Those of higher acumen**
> **in their final phase of cyclic existence take rebirth on the basis of three aspirations.**
> **They become fully ordained monastics and rely upon the special and final fourth [meditative concentration].**
> **By meditating on the sixteen aspects [of the four truths], on one seat,**
> **they proceed from the heat of the path of junction to the attainment of an arhat.**

Rhinoceros-like (*khaḍgaviṣhāṇakalpa, bse ru lta bu*) pratyekabuddhas are of the highest acumen. Like the single horn of a rhinoceros,[461] they dwell alone out of their fear of busyness and distraction, and thus they are given that name.[462] For one hundred great aeons they please the buddhas who appear, thereby accruing stores [of merit and wisdom]. They also become proficient in the six topics of training: the aggregates, constituents, sense spheres, dependent origination, what is the case and what is not the case, and the truth.[463]

During their final phase of cyclic existence,[464] they make three aspirations: to be born in a world without buddhas and shrāvakas; to attain awakening on their own, not relying upon a master or anyone else; and to benefit others only by physical gestures that communicate the dharma, not by verbal communications. With these three aspirations they take their final birth in one of three castes[465] (and not the laborer, or *shūdra*, caste) in a world devoid of buddhas and shrāvakas. In that state [i.e., lifetime] through the force of their previous aspirations, they become fully ordained monastics without preceptors (*upādhyāya*) or masters (*āchārya*). They meditate on the sixteen aspects of the four truths (impermanence and the others), relying on the distinctive "final perfection," which is the fourth meditative concentration.[466] On one seat they proceed from the path of junction to the attainment of the primordial wisdom of an arhat, which is endowed with the knowledge of the exhaustion [of defilements] and the knowledge of their [subsequent] nonarising.[467] This explanation accords with the shrāvaka tradition.

The Mahāyāna's [*Compendium of*] *Abhidharma* explains that pratyekabuddhas require a series of lifetimes to proceed from the level of heat [on the path of junction] to the knowledge of the exhaustion [of defilements] and the knowledge of their [subsequent] nonarising.

The Congregating Practitioners [2']

> **The lesser congregating practitioners are of lower acumen,**
> **the greater congregating practitioners are of intermediate acumen.**
> **They take two lifetimes, and bring [the doors of] liberation to mind.**
> **They teach the dharma by means of silent physical communications.**

The pratyekabuddhas called "congregating practitioners" (*vargachārin, tshogs spyod*) are said to be like parrots, who fly in flocks. Thus, their basic quality is that they meditate with their companions. [There are two subtypes: the lesser congregating practitioners (*tshogs spyod chung ngu*) and the greater congregating practitioners (*tshogs spyod chen po*).]

The lesser congregating practitioners have accrued stores [of merit and wisdom] like the previous type [i.e., the rhinoceros-like pratyekabuddhas]. During their final phase of cyclic existence, they become learned in the six topics [of training] and develop through the middle level of patience [on the path of junction]. To progress through the rest of the paths, they again become proficient in the six topics. They take their last birth [propelled] by their three aspiration prayers and attain the result according to their type. This group is of lower acumen.

The greater congregating practitioners are similar to the previous type, except for the following differences. During their final phase of cyclic existence, they become learned in the six topics [of training], see the truth, and attain one of the first three results. Since they have been unable to attain the level of an arhat, they again become skilled in the six topics in order to attain that state. They take [their last birth] through [the force of] their three aspiration prayers and attain the result according to their type. This group is of intermediate acumen. Both [congregating types] take two lifetimes [to achieve their aims].

All three types of pratyekabuddhas bring to their minds profound dependent origination and the three doors to liberation.[468] To counteract others' lack of faith, they display whatever miraculous powers are appropriate. By being peaceful and restrained when they are out seeking alms, they teach the dharma that brings the realization of dependent origination through silent physical communications.

Generally, the Treatises on the Bhūmis explain shrāvakas and pratyekabuddhas in terms of higher and lower acumen and results, but since their expositions of the paths are mostly the same, they do not have separate collections of scriptures. In keeping with this approach, many Indian and Tibetan texts conflate the philosophical tenet systems of shrāvakas and pratyekabuddhas. On the other hand, the *Sūtra Dispelling the Remorse of [King] Ajātashatru*[469] and the *Kālachakra Tantra* state that pratyekabuddhas have their own collections of scriptures, and, following those, some texts make a distinction between their tenet systems. Here, I have made separate presentations of the philosophical tenet systems of shrāvakas and pratyekabuddhas because, despite the fact that their tenet systems are mostly the same, they do have many dissimilarities, and because the general expression "three yānas" is well known in the scriptures.[470]

SECTION II: MAHĀYĀNA

5. THE MAHĀYĀNA'S DISTINCTIONS AND TRAINING

B. A Systematic Presentation of the Mahāyāna [II.B]
- 1. A Description of the Differences between the Hīnayāna and Mahāyāna
- 2. The Actual Systematic Presentation of the Mahāyāna
  - a. The Pāramitāyāna: The Cause-Based Philosophical [Yāna]
    - i. An Overview of Its Characteristics
    - ii. A Detailed Account of the Systematic Presentation [of the Pāramitāyāna]
      - aa. General Statements about Undertaking the Training
        - 1' The Person Who Trains
        - 2' The Application of the Training: The Six Pāramitās
          - a' Their Essential Qualities
          - b' Their Characteristics
          - c' Their Etymologies
          - d' Their Divisions and Summaries
          - e' [Their Pure Forms]
          - f' Their Most Important Types
          - g' Their Distinctiveness
          - h' The Way to Train in the Pāramitās
          - i' Their Results
          - j' Their Numerical Definitiveness
          - k' Their Order
        - 3' An Explanation of the Actual Practice: Shamatha and Vipashyanā

bb. A Detailed Explanation of the Classifications of [the Pāramitāyāna's] Philosophical Tenet Systems
1' An Overview: Their Names

. . . .

[This chapter begins the second main section of this volume:] a systematic presentation of the Mahāyāna. It has two parts: a description of the differences between the Hīnayāna and Mahāyāna; and the actual systematic presentation of the Mahāyāna.

A Description of the Differences between the Hīnayāna and Mahāyāna [1]

[Mahāyāna practitioners] realize both absences of self-entity;
their intention and practice accord with the pāramitās.
They abandon the two obscurations, and do not abide in the extremes of existence or peace.
[The Mahāyāna] possesses seven greatnesses.

To begin a systematic presentation of the Mahāyāna, I will address the question of what the differences are between the Hīnayāna and Mahāyāna. Mikyö Dorjé[471] and his successors explain that they differ in terms of five points:

(1) their realizations of the view;
(2) the intentions and practices (*sbyor ba*) of their training;
(3) their relinquishments of the factors to be abandoned;
(4) the results they attain; and
(5) seven greatnesses.

First: [Realizations]

Those who, in addition to realizing the absence of a self of persons, clearly and completely realize the absence of a self-entity of phenomena, belong to the Mahāyāna; those without such realization belong to the Hīnayāna. This accords with [Nāgārjuna's] statement in his *Praises of the Transcendent One*:[472]

> You taught that those who do not realize
> that characteristics do not exist are not liberated.
> Therefore you presented this in its entirety
> in the Mahāyāna.

SECOND: [TRAININGS]

They differ [in terms of their training]: [Mahāyāna practitioners] are motivated by their intentions of love, compassion, and bodhichitta, and undertake to train in the six pāramitās; [Hīnayāna practitioners] have neither [such intentions nor such trainings]. This accords with the statement by Āchārya Shūra:[473]

> The rhinoceros-like
> have never heard even the words "six pāramitās."
> It is only the Bhagavat
> who abides in all six pāramitās.

THIRD: [RELINQUISHMENTS]

The Hīnayāna is able to remove the afflictive obscurations (*kleṣhāvaraṇa, nyon sgrib*) in their entirety, but cannot remove completely the cognitive obscurations (*jñeyāvaraṇa, shes bya'i sgrib pa*). The Mahāyāna is able to remove both obscurations along with all their habitual tendencies.

FOURTH: [RESULTS]

The Hīnayāna is inferior in terms of its method and wisdom, thus it is for those who aspire only for a nirvāṇa [that is] peace. The *Ornament of Clear Realization* states:[474]

> [Bodhisattvas] do not abide in existence owing to their wisdom,
> and they do not abide in peace owing to their compassion.

Accordingly, since the Mahāyāna teaches about profound wisdom and extensive methods, it is for those who aspire to and will achieve a nirvāṇa that does not consist of abiding in the extremes of existence or peace.

FIFTH: [SEVEN GREATNESSES]

The *Ornament of the Mahāyāna Sūtras* says:[475]

Because [the Mahāyāna] possesses [seven] greatnesses—
great focus;
the two accomplishments;
primordial wisdom; the cultivation of diligence;
skill in methods;

the greatness of true accomplishments;
and the great activity of the buddhas—
it is described definitively as "the Greater Vehicle."

To take those in order:

(1) [Greatness of focus means that Mahāyāna practitioners] focus on the great breadth of the Mahāyāna collection of scriptures (*piṭakas, sde snod*).
(2) [Its two accomplishments] are to be of benefit to oneself and others.
(3) [The Mahāyāna's primordial wisdom] is the realization of the twofold absence of self-entity.[476]
(4) [Bodhisattvas] cultivate the diligence of devoted application throughout three incalculable aeons[477] [on the Mahāyāna path].
(5) [The Mahāyāna's skillful methods mean that] since [bodhisattvas] have not forsaken [beings in] saṃsāra and have none of the afflictive phenomena (*saṃklesha, kun nyon*), they may, for example, do [any of] the seven physical or verbal unvirtuous actions.[478]
(6) [The true accomplishments of the Mahāyāna] are to perfectly achieve the strengths, fearlessnesses, and unique qualities of a buddha.[479]
(7) [Buddha activity] is spontaneous, uninterrupted activity.

The Mahāyāna possesses those [seven greatnesses]; the Hīnayāna does not.

The *Condensed* [*Perfection of Wisdom Sūtra*][480] says:

Because they have great generosity, great intellects, and great powers,
because they enter the supreme Mahāyāna of the victors,
wear great armor, and tame the magical displays of Māra,
they are called "mahābodhisattvas."

The *Compendium of the Mahāyāna* says:[481]

> The source of knowable objects; the characteristics; engaging those;
> its causes and results; its unfolding;
> its three trainings; and its results—the relinquishments
> and primordial wisdoms—are what make the [Mahā]yāna outstanding and distinguished.

Such quotations are representative of innumerable similar ones found in the teachings [of the Buddha] and the commentaries on their intention.

The Actual Systematic Presentation of the Mahāyāna [2]

This is discussed in two sections: the Pāramitāyāna: the cause-based philosophical [yāna]; and the Vajrayāna: the result-based [yāna] of Secret Mantra.[482]

The Pāramitāyāna: The Cause-Based Philosophical [Yāna] [a]

This has two parts: an overview of its characteristics; and a detailed account of the systematic presentation [of the Pāramitāyāna].[483]

An Overview of Its Characteristics [i]

> **This is the Mahāyāna, [which leads practitioners to] buddhahood**
> **through its cause-based philosophical [path].**

Entering this yāna provides us with the power to travel to buddhahood. It enables us to develop vast wisdom and a sphere of far-reaching activity, and to attain the joys of the elevated states[484] and the happiness of definitive excellence.[485] Thus it is termed "Mahāyāna" (Greater Vehicle). The *Condensed [Perfection of Wisdom Sūtra]* explains why:

> Why is it called the Mahāyāna of awakening?
> When traveled upon, it takes sentient beings beyond misery.
> This yāna is a palace of immeasurable proportions, like space.

It is the supreme of yānas: the means for truly attaining joy, pleasure, and happiness.

[The Pāramitāyāna] is called a philosophical[486] [yāna], because it portrays (*mtshon par byed pa*) the path and its attributes that directly connect us to the unified state of Vajradhara, the final fruition. In relationship to the primordial wisdom of unification (which is nonabiding nirvāṇa, the ultimate result), [the Pāramitāyāna] is referred to as the cause-based yāna since it takes as its practice the cause-based part [of the Mahāyāna path that leads] to that [primordial wisdom].[487]

A Detailed Account of the Systematic Presentation [of the Pāramitāyāna][488] [ii]

This has two topics: general statements about undertaking the training; and a detailed explanation of the classifications of [the Pāramitāyāna's] philosophical tenet systems.

General Statements about Undertaking the Training [aa]

This has three parts: the person who trains; the application of the training: the six pāramitās; and an explanation of the actual practice: shamatha and vipashyanā.

The Person Who Trains [1']

People who make this journey
are highly intelligent; their acumen is at one of three levels.

Generally speaking, people who journey on the Mahāyāna path possess great minds: their propensities (*rigs*) for the Mahāyāna have been awakened by circumstances, they have developed the intention of the two kinds of bodhichitta,[489] and they have the capacity to engage in the extensive conduct of awakening as their undertaking. With those [qualities] as a basis, there are three levels of acumen: lower, higher, and highest. Those of lower acumen have an interest in and forbearance for the pāramitā of wisdom, but when they engage in the first five pāramitās, such as generosity, they are unable to bring the pāramitā of wisdom to bear. Such people are known as beginning bodhisattvas. Those of higher acumen are able to apply the pāramitā of wisdom to their practice of generosity and the other pāramitās. Those who are of the highest acumen are able to bring a distinctive [aspect of] the pāramitā of wisdom to bear on their practice of generosity and the other pāramitās, meaning their intuitive reflexive awareness (*so so rang rig*) directly recognizes the natures [of the other five pāramitās].

The Application of the Training: The Six Pāramitās [2']

> **Following the generation of bodhichitta,**
> **their undertaking is to train in the six pāramitās.**
> **We should understand these in terms of their essential qualities; characteristics; etymologies;**
> **divisions and summaries; pure forms; most important types; distinctiveness; ways of training;**
> **results; numerical definitiveness;[490] and order.**

The training for all three levels of acumen is to engage in the conduct of awakening once bodhichitta has been aroused. This is mainly to train in the six pāramitās as one's undertaking. Although many of the topics concerned with these have already been discussed in the section on the vows of a bodhisattva,[491] I will give a brief account now [in terms of the following eleven points].

Their Essential Qualities [a']

The *Precious Garland* says:[492]

> Generosity means to give away your own wealth.
> Ethical conduct benefits others.
> Patience means to renounce anger.
> Diligence fully embraces virtue.
> Meditative concentration is one-pointed, free from mental afflictions.
> Wisdom ascertains the meaning of the truths.

Their Characteristics [b']

Each pāramitā has four characteristics: it diminishes its opposite quality (miserliness and so forth);[493] it is endowed with primordial wisdom, which does not conceive of the three spheres;[494] it fulfills the welfare of others through its practice; and it matures the mindstreams of beings. These accord with statements such as the one in the *Ornament* [*of the Mahāyāna Sūtras*]:[495]

> Generosity diminishes its discordant quality;
> it is endowed with nonconceptual primordial wisdom;
> it fulfills all wishes;
> and it matures all beings through the three means [or yānas].

Their Etymologies [c']

The same text states:[496]

> It is explained that they are
> what dispels poverty; what produces coolness; what
> prevents anger;
> what is the supreme application; what focuses the mind;
> and what knows the ultimate.

"What dispels poverty" is given as the etymology of *generosity*. The [Sanskrit] equivalent for generosity (*sbyin pa*) is *dāna*. *Dā* is from *dāridrya*,[497] meaning "poverty." *Na* is a negating word, [meaning] "eliminate." Since [*dāna*] means "to eliminate and dispel poverty," it is [the word] used for generosity. We should know that such explanations are given for all [the other pāramitās' names].[498]

Their Divisions and Summaries [d']

The Divisions

Each of the eighteen divisions of the root pāramitās, which were described in the section on the vows of a bodhisattva,[499] has the following six qualities, making one hundred and eight divisions of the pāramitās:

(1) it is done for the welfare of sentient beings;
(2) it is done in a way that does not harm sentient beings;
(3) it is done with forbearance for the sufferings involved with difficult deeds;
(4) it is done without being interrupted by other activities;
(5) it is done with an undistracted mind; and
(6) it is done with the understanding that everything is empty and illusionlike.

Alternatively, the *Ornament of Clear Realization* states:[500]

> Since each of them incorporates each of
> the six—generosity and the others—
> armor[like] accomplishment
> is described in terms of the six sets of six.

Since each of the six pāramitās incorporates the other six—such that there is the generosity of generosity, the ethics of generosity, and so forth—there are also thirty-six divisions of the pāramitās.

The Summaries

The *Ornament* [*of the Mahāyāna Sūtras*] says:[501]

> Generosity and ethical conduct
> contribute to the store of merit, and wisdom to [the store of] primordial wisdom.
> The other three belong to both.
> The [first] five can also belong to the store of primordial wisdom.

Thus it is said that [the six pāramitās encompass] the two stores. One alternative explanation is that when [the first five pāramitās] are embraced by wisdom, they become the store of primordial wisdom. Another is that since the first five [pāramitās] are method and the sixth is wisdom, [the pāramitās] are contained within method and primordial wisdom.

[Their Pure Forms] [e']

Our generosity is pure when we have no hopes for rewards or the maturation [of the act]. The *Ornament* [*of the Mahāyāna Sūtras*] states:[502]

> Generosity free from hopes;
> ethical conduct not concerned with [rewards] in future existences;
> patience in all ways;
> diligence that is the source of all excellent qualities;
>
> meditative concentration not [directed towards] the formless [realm];
> and wisdom endowed with methods
> are what those steadfast in the six pāramitās
> practice perfectly.

Their Most Important Types [f']

We should know that among all the types of generosity, generosity involving the dharma is the most important. The same text says:[503]

> Giving the dharma, maintaining pure ethical conduct,
> attaining patience with the unborn,
> cultivating diligence in the Mahāyāna [path],
> abiding in the final [equipoise] with compassion,[504]
> and wisdom are considered to be
> the most important pāramitās for the intelligent.

If we wish to incorporate those qualities associated with [the primary pāramitās], we must practice with the six genuine aspects (*dam pa drug*):[505]

(1) The genuine support (*rten dam pa*) is to possess bodhichitta.

(2) The genuine object (*dngos po dam pa*) is, for example, an object of generosity for which we have absolutely no partiality.

(3) The genuine goal (*ched du bya ba dam pa*) is to work for the welfare of others.

(4) The genuine method (*thabs dam pa*) is that [our practice of the pāramitās] is embraced by the wisdom that does not conceive of the three spheres.

(5) The genuine dedication (*bsngo ba dam pa*) is the sealing [of an act] by purely dedicating [the merit] to [the attainment of] awakening.
(6) The genuine purity (*dag pa dam pa*) is practicing [the six pāramitās] as the direct antidotes for the two obscurations.

Their Distinctiveness [g']

This has two aspects. [First,] there is the distinction between discordant qualities and their remedies. Those with the propensity for degeneration (*nyams pa'i skal ba can*) possess qualities discordant with generosity, such as attachment to pleasures. There are others with the propensity for distinction in that they possess the remedies [for discordant qualities], such as nonattachment. [The *Ornament of the Mahāyāna Sūtras*] says:[506]

> The causes of the degeneration of the steadfast ones' [pāramitās] are
> being attached to pleasures, being [morally] weak,
> being proud, having excessive desire [for comfort],
> indulging [in meditative concentration], and [holding on to
> reifying] concepts.
>
> Know that bodhisattvas who have
> the remedies for those
> have the qualities conducive to distinction,
> since they are able to overcome those [hindrances].

[Second,] there is the distinction between artificial [pāramitās] and true [pāramitās] as described in [The *Ornament of the Mahāyāna Sūtras*]:[507]

> It is taught that
> those who are false, are hypocritical,
> who make a show of being agreeable,
> apply themselves [only] intermittently,
>
> are [just] physically and verbally calm,
> or are [merely] eloquent,
> have divorced themselves from the practice of the [pāramitās].
> They are not true bodhisattvas.

> Those who practice the opposite of those
> are said to [posses] the true [pāramitās].

The Way to Train in the Pāramitās [h']

We should practice each [pāramitā] as incorporating all six pāramitās by being aware of their respective benefits and being aware of the faults of the qualities that are discordant with them. This can be illustrated by looking at generosity. When practicing the generosity of giving away our body, possessions, and roots of virtue, we should incorporate the other five pāramitās:

- by maintaining the ethical conduct of [observing] the vows and mental engagements of shrāvakas and pratyekabuddhas;
- by having patience for, and interest in, the qualities of omniscience;
- by having the diligence that will motivate us to increase those [pāramitās];
- by remaining in the meditative concentration of resting our minds one-pointedly without mixing in [things from] the Hīnayāna; and
- by sustaining the wisdom of recognizing that the object of generosity, the act of generosity, and the person who is generous are illusionlike.

Their Results [i']

The temporal [results] are described in the *Precious Garland*:[508]

> Generosity generates wealth; ethical conduct brings happiness.
> Patience [results in] radiance; diligence brings brilliance;
> meditative concentration [creates] peace; and intelligence liberates.

The final results are that the store of merit is the direct cause of a buddha's form kāyas;[509] the store of primordial wisdom is the direct cause of the dharmakāya; and diligence assists both, bringing about the attainment of these two kāyas [that is, the form kāyas and the dharmakāya].

Their Numerical Definitiveness [j']

That the pāramitās are definitely six is derived from the fact that when all the dharmas that the bodhisattvas practice are condensed, they are contained within the three trainings.[510] The *Ornament* [*of the Mahāyāna Sūtras*] explains:[511]

> The Victor perfectly elucidated the six pāramitās
> in the context of the three trainings.
> Three [pāramitās belong to] the first [training];
> the last two are the [other] two forms [of training];
> and one [pāramitā] accompanies all three [trainings].

Alternatively, the six pāramitās are described in relation to the elevated states and definitive excellence. Three pāramitās are performed for the sake of [results in] the elevated states: one is generous in order [to gain future] wealth; one maintains ethical conduct so that one will have a good physical body [in future lives]; and one is patient in order to [attract a favorable] entourage [in the future]. Three pāramitās are [performed for the sake of results] connected to definitive excellence: one practices meditative concentration in order to develop shamatha; one cultivates wisdom in order to develop vipashyanā; and one is diligent for the sake of increasing one's excellent qualities.

Their Order [k']

The same text says:[512]

> [The pāramitās] are presented in this order
> because the latter ones arise on the basis of the earlier ones;
> they [progress from] inferior to superior,
> and [grow] from coarse to subtle.

For those three reasons, the pāramitās (generosity and the others) are taught in this specific order.

An Explanation of the Actual Practice: Shamatha and Vipashyanā [3']

> **The actual practice is first to cultivate shamatha, which**
> **is one-pointed concentration,**
> **and then vipashyanā, which is the discernment**
> **of phenomena.**

The actual practice is described in the *Ornament of the Mahāyāna Sūtras*:[513]

> Shamatha and vipashyanā are that,
> on the basis of true abiding,
> mind rests within mind
> and phenomena are discerned.

As a beginning, one cultivates the one-pointed samādhi of shamatha first, and then one practices vipashyanā, which is the wisdom that discerns, or differentiates, phenomena. In the end, one meditates within the samādhi that fuses shamatha and vipashyanā, resting evenly in a natural way. Thus one is liberated from the bonds of cyclic existence and peace, and attains nonabiding nirvāṇa. The *Sūtra Unraveling the Intention* states:[514]

> A person who becomes familiar
> with vipashyanā and shamatha
> will be liberated from the bonds of taking on bad states
> and the fetters of characteristics.

An extensive systematic presentation of shamatha and vipashyanā will appear in the section on the stages of meditation.[515]

A Detailed Explanation of the Classifications of [the Pāramitāyāna's] Philosophical Tenet Systems [bb]

This is discussed in two parts: an overview of their names; and an extensive explanation of their characteristics.

An Overview: Their Names [1']

> **[The Pāramitāyāna's] systems of philosophical tenets are either Chittamātra or Madhyamaka.**

The cause-based philosophical yāna contains the philosophical tenets systems of the Chittamātras, who are the Proponents of Cognition,[516] and the Mādhyamikas, who are the Proponents of the Absence of a Nature.[517]

6. CHITTAMĀTRA

2' An Extensive Explanation of the Characteristics of [the Pāramitāyāna's Philosophical Tenet Systems] [II.B.2.a.ii.bb.2']

- a' An Explanation of the Chittamātra System
  - i' The Meaning of the Term and Its Etymology
  - ii' A Summary of Its Seven Bases
    - aa' An Overview
    - bb' An Extensive Explanation
      - 1" The Source of Knowable Objects
      - 2" The [Three] Characteristics of Those [Knowable Objects]
        - a" The Dependent [Characteristic], the Basis for Designations
        - b" The Imagined [Characteristic], What Is Designated
        - c" The Consummate [Characteristic], the Pervader
      - 3" [How] to Engage the Import of Those
      - 4" The Cause and Result [of That Engagement]
      - 5" The Unfolding
      - 6" The Three Trainings
      - 7" The Results of Purification
  - iii' The Explanation of the Classifications [of the Chittamātra System]
    - aa' The General Explanation
    - bb' The Actual Classifications [of the Chittamātra System]
      - 1" The Actual [Classifications]
        - a" Proponents of Real Images
          - i" The Assertions of the Proponents of Real Images
          - ii" A Description of Their Specific Classifications
            - aa" Split-Eggists
            - bb" Proponents of Perceptual Parity
            - cc" Non-Pluralists

b" Proponents of False Images
i" A General Explanation of Their Assertions
ii" Their Specific Classifications
2" Ancillary Points
a" The Masters Who Assert Those [Chittamātra Positions]
b" The Way This [Chittamātra View] Is Refuted

. . . .

[This chapter begins] the second part [of the detailed explanation of the classifications of the Pāramitāyāna's philosophical tenet systems:] an extensive explanation of their characteristics, which has two divisions: an explanation of the Chittamātra system; and an explanation of the Madhyamaka system.[518]

An Explanation of the Chittamātra System [a']

This presentation has three parts: the meaning of the term and its etymology; a summary of its seven bases; and the explanation of the classifications [of the Chittamātra system].

The Meaning of the Term and Its Etymology [i']

> **Chittamātras state that consciousness is truly existent.**

Those who assert that entities that are other than mind do not exist in any way, and that mind (that is, mere cognition) exists as a real entity (*bden pa'i dngos po*) are known as Chittamātras[519] or Proponents of Cognition (Vijñaptivādins).[520] The *Eight Thousand Stanza Perfection of Wisdom Sūtra* says:[521]

> O sons and daughters of the victors: all these three realms are simply mind (*sems tsam*).

Since they practice correctly bringing to mind the meaning of this quotation as it reflects [the actuality of] things (*dngos po dang mthun pa*), they are also known as Yogāchāras.[522]

A Summary of Its Seven Bases [ii']

This has two parts: an overview; and an extensive explanation.

An Overview [aa']

> **They condense the entire Mahāyāna path into seven bases.**

Chittamātras condense the whole Mahāyāna path into seven bases, following what is stated in the *Compendium of the Mahāyāna*:[523]

> The source of knowable objects; the characteristics; engaging those;
> its causes and results; its unfolding;
> its three trainings; and its results—the relinquishments
> and primordial wisdoms—are what make the [Mahā]yāna
> outstanding and distinguished.

An Extensive Explanation [bb']

This presentation has seven topics: the source of knowable objects; the [three] characteristics of those [knowable objects]; [how] to engage the import of those; the cause and result [of that engagement]; the unfolding; the three trainings; and the results of purification.

The Source of Knowable Objects [1"]

> **The source of knowable objects is the ālaya consciousness.**

It is taught that the source (*gnas*) of knowable objects is the ālaya consciousness (*ālayavijñāna, kun gzhi'i rnam shes*) so that we will become skilled in understanding the dependently originated causes of all phenomena.[524] There are four points involved in ascertaining this subject.

(1) The reasons that the ālaya exists are given in the *Sūtra Unraveling the Intention*:[525]

> The appropriating consciousness,[526] profound and subtle,
> flows with its seeds, like a river.
> It is wrong to regard it as a self;
> thus I do not teach it to the immature.

(2) The characteristics [of the ālaya] are as described in the *Abhidharma Sūtra*:[527]

> The expanse of beginningless time
> is the source of all phenomena.
> Since it exists, there are beings
> and the attainment of nirvāṇa.

Since [the ālaya consciousness], on the basis of the habitual tendencies for all afflictive phenomena,[528] holds the seeds [for such phenomena], it is the cause for the arising of all afflictive phenomena. Since it can become anything, it is also not obscured. It is indeterminate, because it is neither virtuous nor unvirtuous.

(3) As for when [the ālaya consciousness] is reversed (*ldog pa*): it engages (*'jug pa*) as long as beings are in saṃsāra, but it is reversed with the attainment of arhatship. This accords with the teaching:

> That which is like a flowing river
> is reversed with [the attainment] of arhatship.

When one becomes a buddha, it is reversed in the sense of being transformed, as is said:

> Whatever is of the ālaya consciousness
> becomes mirror[like] primordial wisdom.

(4) [The ālaya consciousness] is distinctly different from a creator, such as Īshvara. Īshvara and the like are considered to be the creator of all, single, a self, and permanent. The ālaya is notably superior since it is asserted that

it is present within each and every sentient being, and it is of the nature of the momentary dependent origination that is the differentiation of the nature [into phenomena].[529]

The [Three] Characteristics of Those [Knowable Objects] [2"]

This has three topics: the dependent characteristic, the basis for designations; the imagined characteristic, what is designated; and the consummate characteristic, the pervader.[530]

The Dependent [Characteristic], the Basis for Designations [a"]

> **As for the three characteristics: the dependent characteristic arises from that [ālaya consciousness].**
> **It is the imagination of what is unreal, appearing through the force of habitual tendencies.**
> **It does not remain for an instant and is governed by what precedes it.**

[Knowable objects] are categorized in terms of the three characteristics.[531] First, the dependent [characteristic] (*paratantra, gzhan dbang*) is what arises from that ālaya consciousness. It is referred to as "the imagination of what is unreal"[532] in that it is what appears as perceived aspects (*zung cha'i rnam pa*)—that is, what appears as the phenomena of the aggregates, constituents, and sense spheres—and it is what appears as the perceiving aspects (*'dzin cha'i rnam pa*)."

- Because [the dependent characteristic] arises through the force of its own habitual tendencies, which are previous seeds of similar types, it is [dependent] in terms of its *causes*.
- Because it is its nature not to remain for a second moment once it comes into existence, it is [dependent] in terms of its *nature*.
- Because it generates subsequent [moments of the dependent characteristic] as similar types, and because such later [moments] are governed by the previous ones, it is [dependent] in terms of its *results*.

In brief, [the dependent characteristic] is the basis for the designations of imagined [characteristics] and is part of the ālaya. It is the imagination of what is unreal, which is the mere cognition[533] (*vijñaptimātra, rnam rig tsam*) characteristic of [all beings in] the three realms.[534] Its nature is that it is substantially established.[535] From the perspective of delusion, it arises from causes and conditions.

The Imagined [Characteristic], What Is Designated [b"]

> **On top of that substantially existent basis for designations,**
> **a self, "mine," and so forth are mistakenly imagined.**

On top of that dependent [nature], which (as just stated) is the basis for designations and is substantially existent, the mental consciousness, that is, the imagination of what is unreal, mistakenly superimposes (*samāropa, sgro btags pa*) persons and phenomena, and imagines a self, "mine," names, reasons, and so forth.[536] [Imagined characteristics (*parikalpita, kun brtags*)] appear although ultimately they do not exist substantially in any way, just like floaters.[537] They are only the perceived objects of a deluded mind. To focus on these [imagined characteristics as existent] is contrary to liberation. The imagined aspect is utterly nonexistent, like the horns of a rabbit.[538]

The Consummate [Characteristic], the Pervader [c"]

> **[The consummate is] the unconditioned, empty of the object of negation: imputed existence.**
> **It is nonconceptual cognition, empty of duality, ultimately existent.**

The consummate[539] (*parinishpanna, yongs grub*) is what is unconditioned, and is empty of imagined [characteristics], which are the objects of negation and [only] imputedly existent. It is consummate in that it is nothing other than nonconceptual cognition (*shes pa*) empty of the duality of percept and perceiver, and it is the observed objects of [the path of] purification.

[An Overview of the Three Characteristics]

Imagined [characteristics] exist simply as imputations, because they do not exist as [functional] entities. Dependent [characteristics] exist substantially, because they are able to perform functions. The consummate [characteristic] exists ultimately, because it is the object of nonconceptual [cognition].

Consequently, in the sūtras, teachings that list nonexistents[540] are presentations of imagined [characteristics]. Teachings on illusions, dreams, mirages, and the like are about the dependent [characteristic]. The presentations of nonconceptuality and the unconditioned teach the consummate [characteristic].

Masters have given various accounts of the categorizations [of the three characteristics], of which the following are the most well-known for the majority of Tibetans.[541]

The imagined [characteristic] is twofold:

(1) Imagined [characteristics] devoid of any characteristics (*mtshan nyid chad pa'i kun brtags*) are what in fact do not exist, but are conceptually imputed, such as the belief in a self (*bdag lta*) or something being substantially established.

(2) Nominal imagined [characteristics] (*rnam grangs pa'i kun brtags*) are object-universals (*artha-sāmānya, don spyi*), which appear to thoughts, and the appearance of the dualism of perceived objects and perceiving subjects for the nonconceptual sense consciousnesses.[542]

The dependent [characteristic] has two aspects:[543]

(1) The impure dependent [characteristic] (*ma dag gzhan dbang*) is the mind and mental events of [beings in] the three realms, which, [though] not dual, are what appear as a duality because of their habitual tendencies.[544]

(2) The pure dependent [characteristic] (*dag pa gzhan dbang*) is the cognition [of noble beings during meditative equipoise,] which has no dualistic experience; and it is the cognition of noble beings during the subsequent state,[545] which does not fixate on appearances.

The consummate [characteristic] is also twofold:[546]

(1) The unchanging consummate [characteristic] (*nirvikārapariniṣhpanna, 'gyur med yongs grub*) is dharmatā, which is empty of both the dependent (the basis for delusion) and the imagined (the delusion). It is a nonimplicative negation, thusness, and what is unconditioned.

(2) The unerring consummate [characteristic] (*aviparyāsapariniṣhpanna,*

> *phyin ci ma log pa'i yongs grub*) is nondual cognition, which is what remains when [cognition] is empty of the duality of percept and perceiver. It is reflexive awareness, real (*satya, bden pa*), and substantially established. The path and its observed objects are considered part of this [unerring consummate] in the sense that they accompany it.[547]

In terms of conventions (*vyavahāra, tha snyad*), imagined [characteristics] are the actual conventions; dependent [characteristics] are the basis for conventions; and the consummate [characteristic] is without conventions.

In terms of the use of conventions, the imagined [characteristic] refers to the delusion of dualistic appearances. The dependent [characteristic] is used for the referent that is free from that [imagined nature]. The consummate [characteristic] refers to thusness.

It is clearly taught that a magical illusion serves as an analogy for these [three characteristics]. The mantras that create a phantom and the small piece of wood that serves as the basis for a phantom [equate, respectively, to] the fundamental mind and thusness. From those [manifests] the image (*ākāra, rnam pa*) that appears to be an elephant, which is the dependent [characteristic]. The elephant is the imagined [characteristic]. The nonexistence of that [elephant] in that [image of an elephant] is the consummate [characteristic].[548]

[How] to Engage the Import of Those [3"]

> **The practical engagement of those [three characteristics involves] three [determinations] free from discouragement; four abandonments;**
> **devoted interest; knowing the absence of any reference;**
> **abandoning imagination; and seeing correctly.**
> **In this way, [bodhisattvas] enter the bhūmis of engagement through belief, seeing, meditation, and completion.**

As for engaging those characteristics [of knowable objects], four [criteria must be present] in order for their import to be realized.[549]

(1) Who are the individuals that engage these? They are [bodhisattvas] who have amassed the two stores [of merit and wisdom] of the Mahāyāna.

(2) What causes this engagement?
- The strengths generated by roots of virtue.
- The three types of determination free from discouragement: having the determination that all sentient beings will achieve buddhahood; having the determination to engage in the pāramitās; and having the determination, "I will not be impeded by anything."
- The four abandonments: abandoning the mental engagements of shrāvakas and pratyekabuddhas; abandoning doubts about the Mahāyāna; giving up partiality with regard to dharma; and casting aside conceptuality.
- Engaging in shamatha and vipashyanā with devoted interest.

(3) How do we engage [these three characteristics as a path]? By means of the habitual tendencies of studying, we investigate the classifications of names, entities, natures, and specifics, and thereby come to understand that the three characteristics are not observable reference points. We do this in three stages: (1) by knowing that all those are merely imputedly existent; (2) by understanding them to be mere cognition; (3) and by reversing the idea that they are mere cognition.

In brief, we enter the path by recognizing delusion, which is the imagined [characteristic]; by abandoning the imagination, which is the dependent [nature]; and by directly seeing the consummate.

(4) What are the periods or phases of engagement? We engage gradually: first we [enter] the paths of accumulation and junction with engagement through belief; then we [proceed] on the paths of seeing, meditation, and completion.

The Cause and Result [of That Engagement] [4"]

> **The cause and result of that [engagement] are contained within the conduct of the six pāramitās.**

The graduated path of that engagement [proceeds] by means of the conduct of the six pāramitās: such conduct is the cause that initially gives rise to the path, and it is also the culminating result [of the path].

The Unfolding [5"]

> **The gradual progression is the unfolding of the modes of the ten bhūmis.**

The six pāramitās bring about the unfolding of the modes of the ten bhūmis (Very Joyful and the others) [according to] the ways of engaging cognition (*rnam par rig pa la 'jug pa'i tshul*). [The modes of the bhūmis] are included within [the discussions of] the way the bhūmis are traversed by means of the pāramitās, the way the bhūmis are attained, and the length of time it takes to progress through them.

The Three Trainings [6"]

> **The trainings are the three types of higher trainings.**

As stated above,[550] the six pāramitās are included within the three trainings, which are the foundations for bodhisattvas' trainings.

The training in higher ethical conduct is of three types: the ethical conduct of restraint and the others.[551] The term "higher" is used to indicate that these [trainings] are distinguished from those of the Hīnayāna by the arousing of bodhichitta and so forth.

The training in higher concentration[552] is to practice the bodhisattvas' heroic stride samādhi and the others[553] in order to meditate on the pāramitās, mature sentient beings, and achieve all the qualities of a buddha.

As for the training in higher wisdom:[554] once all concepts and characteristics have been relinquished, nonconceptuality is spontaneously present and the states subsequent [to meditative equipoise] are experienced as illusionlike. This is the pāramitā of wisdom.

In general, the trainings of bodhisattvas are immeasurable, but if they are abbreviated, they are contained within these [three trainings].

The Results of Purification [7"]

> **The results are the excellences of relinquishment and primordial wisdom.**

The results[555] that develop from those [trainings] are (1) the excellence of relinquishment, which is the conquering of the afflictive and cognitive obscurations; and (2) the excellence of primordial wisdom, which is the three kāyas—svabhāvakāya, sambhogakāya, and nirmāṇakāya—and their essence or characteristic—the dharmakāya. [The dharmakāya] is endowed with five attributes: it is a transformation; the basis for positive qualities; nondual; permanent; and inconceivable.[556] It is the source that radiates the immeasurable and inconceivable qualities of a buddha.

I will explain some topics related to the bhūmis, paths, and so forth later.[557] Those who wish to understand these in detail should refer to earlier Tibetan works, such as Jetsün Drakpa Gyaltsen's [*Jeweled*] *Tree*.

I have taken the assertions of earlier Tibetan [masters] as the basis for this presentation, and [followed] traditions that assert that Maitreya's Dharma Treatises[558] and the texts of Asaṅga[559] and his brother [Vasubandhu][560] are Chittamātra.[561]

The Explanation of the Classifications [of the Chittamātra System] [iii']

In this section, there are two parts: the general explanation; and the actual classifications [of the Chittamātra system].

The General Explanation [aa']

> **The root of their assertions is that other than being mere cognition, external referents do not have even the slightest existence, like dreams.**

The root of the Chittamātras' general assertion is that external referents (*bāhyārtha, phyi don*) do not have even the slightest existence other than being mere cognition, like appearances in dreams. Their reasons are as follows:

- Referents, such as forms, and everything such as the arising and ceasing of those [objects] are only mental appearances, like floaters or the appearance of two moons [when you press on your closed eyelids].
- If external referents were to exist in reality (*bden par yod*), it would follow that they would exist for the nonconceptual primordial wisdom of noble beings abiding in meditative equipoise; and yet they do not exist for [noble beings in that state].

- What appears to the six kinds of beings seems to be distinctly different even though [their perception] is not affected by superficial causes for [perceptual] error. To take one example: a river is seen as nectar by gods, as water by humans, as pus and blood by hungry ghosts, and as molten metal by beings in the hot hells, because of the positive or negative karma [of these beings].

Furthermore, the Chittamātras use many scriptural references and reasonings to refute external referents and prove that [all phenomena] are mere cognition.

The Actual Classifications [of the Chittamātra System] [bb']

This is discussed in two sections: the actual [classifications]; and ancillary points.

The Actual [Classifications] [1"]

This has two divisions: Proponents of Real Images; and Proponents of False Images.

Proponents of Real Images [a"]

This discussion has two parts: the assertions of the Proponents of Real Images; and a description of their specific classifications.

The Assertions of the Proponents of Real Images [i"]

> **They hold [one of] two positions: [first,] Proponents of Real Images**
> **assert that appearances are real in being the mind, which is the perceived object.**

As their principal philosophical tenets, Chittamātra Proponents hold [one of] two positions: that images are real (*satyākāra, rnam bden pa*) or that images are false (*alīkākāra, rnam rdzun pa*).[562]

As for the first, Proponents of Real Images assert that external referents do not exist as real entities and yet, owing to the habitual tendencies for conceiving [of appearances] as objects, cognition itself arises as the image of a referent, as in the analogy of a crystal with a color.[563] Thus, everything that appears as forms is simply the mind itself, which is the agent for appearances (*snang mkhan*) manifesting as distant cut-off objects (*rgyangs chad kyi don*) owing to the power of the deluded habitual tendencies. Moreover, [appearances,] in fact, are real in being the mind, which is the perceived object.[564] Therefore, the aggregates, constituents, sense spheres, and even true cessation (which is considered to be mind free from the factors to be abandoned), all of which are taught in the sūtras, are real in being mental phenomena, which is to say, they are [only] the mind itself. Owing to taking this position, they are known as Proponents of Real Images (*Satyākāravādin, rNam bden pa*).[565]

A Description of Their Specific Classifications [ii"]

This section has three parts: Split-Eggists; Proponents of Perceptual Parity; and Non-Pluralists.[566]

Split-Eggists [aa"]

> **[Some state that both] cognition and [its] images are real in being reflexive parts (*rang cha*).**

[Split-Eggists][567] are those who assert that perceived objects (which are cognitive images) and the perceiving cognition are [matching] halves, like an egg split [in half]. They also say that images are real in being the perceived parts, and cognition is real in being the perceiving part. The master Jetāri reports [their position]:[568]

> The consciousness appearing internally is other than this [external object], and what appears externally is also simply other than [the consciousness]. These two, however, are not a duality, because they are [both] simply reflexive awareness. Conceptuality, which arises through the force of those two, exaggeratedly considers them to be the two entities of percept and perceiver.

Proponents of Perceptual Parity [bb"]

> **[Others say that] the number of perceiving cognizers corresponds to the number of perceived images.**

[Proponents of Perceptual Parity][569] assert that the number of perceiving cognizers, which are discrete substances, equals the number of perceived images, which are discrete substances, such as white or red. In terms of appearances, many varieties of white or red manifest; in terms of what is real, those various[570] [appearances] are real in being individual substances. In the same way, the sense consciousnesses, which are the agents for appearances, are real in being multiple substantial entities. The *Auto-Commentary for the "[Ornament of] the Middle Way"* states:[571]

> Some say that like pleasure and so forth, images such as blue and so forth are only of an experiential character. Those cognitions are multiple, and they are always of similar types. They arise in the same way that multiple dissimilar-type cognitions arise simultaneously.[572]

Non-Pluralists [cc"]

> **[Some] say that even though there are various appearances,**
> **the entity [of cognition] is not a plurality.**

[Non-Pluralists][573] assert that it is just a single cognition that appears as white, red, and so forth. Therefore, even though the various appearances manifest as multiple, they are real in being the entities of [a single,] partless consciousness. Thus there is no plurality [of cognition]. This accords with the description [of their position] in the *Auto-Commentary for the "[Ornament of] the Middle Way"*:[574]

> They state that the entities of the varieties [of appearances] manifest from just a single consciousness, in the same way that [the various colors of] an onyx [appear].[575]

Proponents of False Images [b"]

This is discussed in two parts: a general explanation of their assertions; and their specific classifications.

A General Explanation of Their Assertions [i"]

> **Proponents of False Images assert that, like [the floaters seen] by the visually impaired,**
> **appearances are nonexistents vividly appearing, unreal and false;**
> **only cognition empty of duality is real.**

Chittamātra Proponents of False Images (*Alīkākāravādin, rNam rdzun pa*) state that all appearances of white, black, and so forth are nonexistents vividly appearing (*med pa gsal snang*), meaning that they appear while not existing, like the two moons seen when you press your eyes or the floaters seen by the visually impaired. In fact, they are not real but are false, like dreams and illusions; because, if [appearances] were real as cognition, objects (such as forms) would have to be cognizers (*rig pa*), which they are not. They assert that cognition empty of the duality of percept and perceiver is reflexively aware and self-illuminating (*rang rig rang gsal*), like a flawless crystal globe. It is not governed by referents and is not tainted by the stains of appearances. Only that [cognition empty of duality] is real.

To summarize [their view], they say that cognition is untainted by the stains of appearances; [it is pure,] like a pure crystal globe.[576] Appearances, like floaters, are false: even though they do not exist, they appear. Thus those who hold this position are known as Proponents of Nonexistent Images (*Nirākāravādin, rNam med pa*) or Proponents of False Images (*Alīkākāravādin, rNam rdzun pa*).[577]

Their Specific Classifications [ii"]

> **Since [some] assert that appearances taint cognition and [some] do not,**
> **and [some] say that there are dualistic appearances on the bhūmi of buddhahood and [others] say there are not,**
> **there are the two divisions of Staining and Non-Staining.**

Some say that although consciousnesses are, in fact, the perceiving aspect of pleasure, pain, and so forth, the force of ignorance causes them to appear as outer perceived images, and thus the entity of consciousness is tainted by those false images. Therefore, they are called Proponents of Staining

False Images (*Samala-alīkākāra, rNam rdzun dri bcas*).[578] Others state that ultimately the entity of consciousness is not tainted by outer images, that it is [pure,] like a pure crystal globe. Ordinary beings, however, do not realize this; it is realized only by buddhas. They are called Proponents of Non-Staining False Images (*Nirmala-alīkākāra, rNam rdzun dri med*).[579]

There is another explanation for the two divisions of Staining [False Images] and Non-Staining [False Images].

- [Proponents of Staining False Images] say that what appears as white or red is present at the bhūmi of buddhahood; nevertheless, [buddhas] are not deluded because they realize what is false to be false. Therefore, they say, "We do not state that referents and cognition are identical nor do we say that they are different." [Proponents of Staining False Images] assert that there are dualistic appearances at the bhūmi of buddhahood.
- [Proponents of Non-Staining False Images] say that if what appears as white or red were real in being the entity of cognition, it would appear also to buddhas, but it does not. They say, therefore, "Even though there is no connection between a cognition and a referent, [there are] appearances." [Proponents of Non-Staining False Images] assert that there are no dualistic appearances at the bhūmi of buddhahood.[580]

A Summary [of the Two Chittamātra Subschools]

Chittamātra Proponents of Real Images assert that everything that appears to the five sense consciousnesses as external referents is real in being the substance of the internal cognizer. Proponents of False Images say that everything that appears to the five sense consciousnesses as referents is not real in being the substance of the internal mind; rather, all is false and [only] imputedly existent. We should know that this accords with the explanations given by many scholars, such as Lakṣhmī.[581] Karma Tinlé[582] comments:

> Both Chittamātra [subschools] must be called Proponents of Cognition (Vijñaptivādins), or Chittamātras, because they assert each momentary, partless consciousness, which is free from percept and perceiver, to be ultimate reality. However, it is wrong to apply that [name Chittamātra] to those who only assert that appearing referents are mind, because that encompasses too much in that it applies to Sautrāntikas, and does not

encompass enough in that it does not apply to Proponents of False Images.

Both [Chittamātra subschools] assert that reflexively aware, self-illuminating cognition, which is without the duality of percept and perceiver, is ultimate. [In the ordinary state] it is covered by the obscurations of dualistic appearances; thus when the qualities of a noble being are attained, that [cognition] is simply free from dualistic appearances.

Some Tibetans cite the teachings of the master Vasubandhu as a scriptural [source] for these [Chittamātra views]. This is simply the mistake of those who speak deviously by not distinguishing between [Vasubandhu's] assertion that primordial wisdom is truly existent and [the Chittamātra system's] statement that consciousness is truly existent.

Ancillary Points [2"]

This has two sections: the masters who assert those [Chittamātra positions]; and the way this [Chittamātra view] is refuted.

The Masters Who Assert Those [Chittamātra Positions] [a"]

This is the system of five hundred past masters and others.

There are Tibetans who say unanimously that with the exception of the *Ornament of Clear Realization*, all the other Dharma Treatises of Maitreya[583] teach Chittamātra.[584] Some assert that the *Highest Continuum* keeps to the meaning of the Madhyamaka. Others assert that the final wheel of dharma presents only Chittamātra, not Madhyamaka. They say, "Asaṅga and his brother [Vasubandhu] were the co-founders of this chariot-system, and all their texts are Chittamātra. The Proponents of Real Images and of False Images and other [subdivisions] appeared among their followers. Dignāga[585] and his son [Dharmakīrti][586] asserted the positions of both the Proponents of Real Images and the Proponents of False Images."[587] Some say, "The noble Nāgārjuna[588] also asserted both those positions." And others state, "Although Asaṅga was a Mādhyamika master, that does not conflict with his having composed Chittamātra treatises, like Vasubandhu's composition[589] of the *Treasury of Abhidharma.*" There are many such statements expressing individual points of view.

The great omniscient dharma lord of Jonang [Dolpopa][590] states:

> The final wheel of dharma and the middle [texts][591] of Maitreya's Dharma Treatises do not present the Madhyamaka that Tibetans assert. These [texts] do, however, teach the Madhyamaka expounded by the Victor and his heirs. Tibetan assertions concerning the thought of the major texts of the noble [Nāgārjuna], such as his Collection of Reasonings,[592] and similar works, are quite limited and by no means final.

The great exalted one of Jonang and his followers maintain that Asaṅga and his brother were Madhyamaka masters and that their system of philosophical tenets is the Great Madhyamaka (*dBu ma chen po*).

You may wonder, in that case, who were the founding masters of the Chittamātra system? [The founders and promulgators of the Chittamātra system] were five hundred Mahāyāna masters, great exalted ones of earlier times, such as Avitarka, and others.[593] "Others" means some of their followers and some later Proponents of Mere Cognition (Vijñaptimātra).[594]

The Way This [Chittamātra View] Is Refuted [b"]

> **All the flawed [assertions] of Realists are refuted by the texts of the noble [Nāgārjuna].**

[Proponents of] False Images and [followers of the philosophical systems] below them assert that appearances are pervaded by delusion. Their positions concerning delusion and actions and agents are such that they cannot comprehend that there is no truly existing substratum.[595] They are, therefore, referred to as Realists.[596] Proponents of these lower [philosophical tenet systems] do—in relationship to a specific basis for negation [that they consider to be] truly existent—refute a specific object of negation that followers of a philosophical system lower than themselves imagine [to be truly existent]. Nevertheless, ultimately, all the flawed assertions in the Realists' philosophical tenets are thoroughly refuted by the noble [Nāgārjuna's] major texts, called the Collection of Reasonings,[597] and [the works of] of his followers. [Those texts] elucidate a special feature of Madhyamaka: knowing how to posit actions and agents despite the nonexistence of a substratum for delusion. Consequently, the *Synopsis of the View Asserted [by Mañjushrī]*[598] says:

> The main texts of the Vaibhāṣhikas, Sautrāntikas,
> and Yogāchāras
> contain a bit of truth as well as untruths.
> The Madhyamaka system is entirely true.

The Differences Between Chittamātra and Madhyamaka

Some say that there are major differences between the Chittamātra and Madhyamaka [systems] in terms of ground, path, and result and in other ways. However, the principal distinction between these two Mahāyāna schools is that [Chittamātras] assert that reflexively aware, self-illuminating cognition, empty of the duality of percept and perceiver, exists ultimately and Mādhyamikas do not. When explaining the Chittamātra philosophical tenet system, the *Compendium on the Heart of Primordial Wisdom*[599] and other texts say:[600]

> Consciousness free from percept and perceiver
> exists ultimately.

When explaining the Madhyamaka philosophical tenet system, these texts say:[601]

> The wise do not assert that
> consciousness exists ultimately.

7. AN OVERVIEW OF MADHYAMAKA

b' An Explanation of the Madhyamaka System [II.B.2.a.ii.bb.2'.b']
i' The Meaning of the Term and Its Etymology
ii' Its Entryway
iii' The Vows to Be Guarded
iv' The View to Be Realized
v' The Result to Be Attained
vi' The Classifications [of the Madhyamaka System]
aa' An Overview
bb' An Extensive Explanation
1" The Common Madhyamaka of the Sūtra System
a" An Overview: The Names [of Madhyamaka Schools]

[This chapter is a continuation of the detailed explanation of the classifications of the Pāramitāyāna's systems of philosophical tenets and its second part, an extensive explanation of their characteristics.] It is the second division: an explanation of the Madhyamaka system.[602] This presentation has seven topics: the meaning of the term and its etymology; its entryway; the vows to be guarded; the view to be realized; the result to be attained; the classifications [of the Madhyamaka system]; and a synopsis of what is taught in all Madhyamaka systems: its ground, path, and fruition.[603]

The Meaning of the Term and Its Etymology [i']

Being free from extremes, Madhyamaka is the best philosophical tenet system.

Those who propound a complete absence of reference points are free from [beliefs] in any extreme: existence or nonexistence, arising or ceasing, and so forth. Thus they are called "Mādhyamikas."[604] In the *Stacks of Jewels,* [the *Kāshyapa Chapter Sūtra*] says:[605]

> Do not think that phenomena are permanent. Do not think that they are impermanent. "Permanence" is one extreme and "impermanence" is a second extreme. The middle between two extremes cannot be analyzed and cannot be shown. It is not a support. It is devoid of appearance, devoid of cognition, and devoid of location. Kāshyapa: this is the middle way, the correct discernment of phenomena.

The shorter *Ornament of the Middle Way* states:[606]

> There is no existence nor nonexistence;
> neither both nor not both.
> Those who are free from the four extremes
> are referred to as "Mādhyamikas."

Its Entryway [ii']

Its entryway is the two truths.
[Mādhyamikas engage] conventional reality knowing that from the perspective of no analysis, [things] appear and yet do not truly exist;
and they conduct themselves properly with regard to what is to be adopted and rejected.
They encounter ultimate [reality] by knowing that there is nothing to adopt or reject, block or encourage, in anything—
the very [moment] things simply appear, they are empty.
This [approach] integrates the two stores.

The entryway for Mādhyamikas is the explication that, primarily from the perspective of their natures, all phenomena are included within the two truths.[607]

They engage conventional reality in the following manner. They know that unexamined and unanalyzed appearances, regardless of how they seem to be, do not truly exist as entities. Simply as interdependent connections [appearing] on the conventional level, [Mādhyamikas] undertake extensive virtuous actions (such as generosity) and avoid unvirtuous actions—all the while [maintaining] their motivation of bodhichitta and an awareness that things are illusionlike. In this way they train themselves in the scrupulous observance of what is to be adopted and what is to be rejected.

They encounter ultimate reality by knowing that actually there is nothing to adopt or reject, block or encourage, abandon or accept in any phenomenon. The very [moment] that things simply appear, they are empty of any nature.

Entering [the Madhyamaka path] through [understanding] the two truths is an approach that integrates the view and conduct, method and wisdom, and the two stores of merit and wisdom.

The Vows to Be Guarded [iii']

> **What are to be guarded are the bodhisattva vows.**

What is to be guarded is the ethical conduct of the bodhisattva vows. This is a practice that is empowered by great wisdom, which [knows] that, ultimately, [all phenomena] are free from conceptual elaborations and characteristics.

The View to Be Realized [iv']

> **What is realized is that, on the conventional [level], phenomena**
> **appear while not existing, like the moon's reflection in water;**
> **but, ultimately, all elaborations and characteristics subside.**
> **They realize the two truths unerringly.**

The view realized by Mādhyamikas is that, on the conventional [level], all phenomena appear while not existing, like the moon's reflection in water; and, ultimately, all conceptual elaborations and characteristics subside. In this way, they unerringly and fully realize the abiding nature of the two truths.

The Result to Be Attained [v']

The result is peace, the manifestation of the two kāyas.

The three yānas are similar in that nirvāṇa is the final result to be attained in each case. Mādhyamikas, however, do not assert that the mere cessation of the mental afflictions and the aggregates is nirvāṇa. They state that [nirvāṇa] is the unmistaken realization of the suchness (*tattva, de kho na nyid*) of all phenomena, both pure and impure, by means of the pacification of all conceptual elaborations. The *Fundamental Treatise on the Middle Way* says:[608]

What is without abandonment, without attainment,
without annihilation, without permanence,
without cessation, and without arising
is said to be nirvāṇa.

Praises of the Incomparable One says:[609]

You know that afflictive phenomena
and purified phenomena are of the same taste.
Thus, you are inseparable from the dharmadhātu,
and you are utterly and completely pure.

There are many such statements.

Nirvāṇa is presented as being twofold: with remainder and without remainder. A Mahāyāna explanation of this is found in the *Genuine Golden Light Sūtras*:[610]

The two kāyas are [nirvāṇa] with remainder;
the dharmakāya is [nirvāṇa] without remainder.

The noble Nāgārjuna also teaches these as the entryways to the three kāyas. He says that when one attains the nirvāṇa in which conceptual elaborations are pacified, by virtue of one's completion of the two stores of merit and wisdom, one manifests the dharmakāya for one's own sake and the two form kāyas [the sambhogakāya and nirmāṇakāya] for the sake of others. While remaining nonconceptual, like a precious gem, [the form kāyas] work for the welfare of the limitless beings to be tamed, both those with pure mindstreams and those with impure ones.

The Classifications [of the Madhyamaka System] [vi']

In this section, there are two parts: an overview; and an extensive explanation.

An Overview [aa']

Although Madhyamaka is classified in many ways, its two main divisions are Sūtra-Madhyamaka and Mantra-Madhyamaka.

Proponents of the Madhyamaka system of philosophical tenets were subdivided in several ways both in India and Tibet.[611] Some[612] say that there are three types: Sautrāntika-Mādhyamikas, Yogāchāra-Mādhyamikas, and Mādhyamikas Who Employ Worldly Consensus.[613]

(1) Sautrāntika-Mādhyamikas, such as Bhāvaviveka,[614] assert as conventions that external objects exist.

(2) Yogāchāra-Mādhyamikas, such as Shāntarakṣhita,[615] maintain that [even] as conventions external referents do not exist.

(3) Mādhyamikas Who Employ Worldly Consensus, such as Chandrakīrti,[616] speak about external objects [only] from the perspective of others, that is to say, only in terms of what is commonly acknowledged in the world.

Others say that two subdivisions can be made according to the way the ultimate is asserted: Those Who Logically Establish Illusion, and Proponents of Complete Nonabiding.[617]

(1) Those Who Logically Establish Illusion, such as Kamalashīla,[618] assert that ultimate reality is the combination of appearances' absence of reality and phenomena themselves (such as sprouts and other things).[619]

(2) Proponents of Complete Nonabiding, such as Buddhapālita,[620] assert that ultimate reality is what is determined (*pariccheda, yongs gcod*) as [a result of] excluding (*viccheda, rnam bcad*) all conceptual elaborations regarding appearances.

The master Ratnākarashānti[621] divides Mādhyamikas into two groups:[622]

(1) those who state that conventional [reality] is an image of cognition, and

(2) those who state that conventional [reality] is habitual tendencies.

The master Maitrīpa[623] makes two divisions:[624]

(1) Proponents of Illusionlike Nonduality, and

(2) Proponents of the Complete Nonabiding of All Phenomena.

The Kashmiri scholar Lakṣhmī[kara][625] provides a threefold classification:

(1) Sautrāntika-Madhyamaka;

(2) Yogāchāra-Madhyamaka; and

(3) Madhyamaka based on the Mother of the Victors.[626]

All such classifications of Madhyamaka are based on [the different explanations concerning] the way the ultimate is empty and, particularly, [the different] ways conventional [reality] is posited. Despite these many styles of classification, succinctly put, Madhyamaka is definitely of two types: Sūtra-Madhyamaka and Mantra-Madhyamaka.

An Extensive Explanation [bb']

This is discussed in two sections: the common Madhyamaka of the Sūtra system; and the profound Madhyamaka of Secret Mantra.

The Common Madhyamaka of the Sūtra System [1"]

This has two divisions: an overview: the names [of Madhyamaka schools]; and an extensive explanation: the characteristics [of Madhyamaka schools].

An Overview: The Names [of Madhyamaka Schools] [a"]

> **The Sūtra system comprises [the teachings of] the Proponents of the Absence of a Nature and the Yogāchāras,**
> **which correspond [respectively] to such terms as "ordinary" and "preeminent," or "broad" and "subtle."**
> **In Tibet, they are known as Rangtong and Shentong.**

Because of the slightly different systems, or styles, of commenting on the thought of the Mahāyāna sūtras, it is clear that there are two types [of Sūtra-Mādhyamikas]:

(1) Mādhyamika Proponents of the Absence of a Nature (Niḥsvabhāvavādins),[627] and
(2) Yogāchāra-Mādhyamikas.

Some use the terms "ordinary Madhyamaka" and "preeminent Madhyamaka" for these systems. The master Bhāvaviveka[628] and others use the phrase "broad, outer Madhyamaka" for the first and "subtle, inner Madhyamaka" for the second.[629] In Tibet, from the time of the great omniscient dharma lord of Jonang [Dolpopa] onwards, these have been known as the systems of Rangtong-Madhyamaka and Shentong-Madhyamaka.[630]

8. RANGTONG-MADHYAMAKA

b" An Extensive Explanation: The Characteristics [of Madhyamaka Schools] [II.B.2.a.ii.bb.2'.b'.vi'.bb'.1".b"]

- i" Rangtong
  - aa" A Brief Account of the Divisions [of Rangtong]
  - bb" A Detailed Explanation of the Systematic Presentation [of Rangtong]
    - (1) The System Common to Prāsaṅgikas and Svātantrikas
      - (a) The Twofold Absence of Self-Entity
      - (b) The Mode of Reasonings
    - (2) The Explanation of Their Differences

[This chapter, a continuation of the common Madhyamaka of the Sūtra system, presents] the second part, an extensive explanation of the characteristics [of Madhyamaka schools]. This has two divisions: Rangtong; and Shentong.

Rangtong [i"]

This has two parts: a brief account of the divisions [of Rangtong]; and a detailed explanation of the systematic presentation [of Rangtong].

A Brief Account of the Divisions [of Rangtong] [aa"]

The first has two [subschools:] the Svātantrika and Prāsaṅgika.

The first of the aforementioned [divisions of Sūtra-Madhyamaka], the Mādhyamika Proponents of the Absence of a Nature (Niḥsvabhāvavādin), are said to contain the two [subschools of Svātantrika and Prāsaṅgika][631] for the following [reasons].

The followers of Bhāvaviveka are called Svātantrikas because they assert, as a convention that is part of their own system, that all phenomena are without arising, are empty, and so forth. As proofs [of those assertions], they primarily use independently [verifiable] reasons[632] in which the three modes[633] are established through the power of [their relationship to real] things.[634]

The followers of Chandrakīrti are called Prāsaṅgikas, because they accept that [phenomena] are without arising, are empty, and so forth only from the perspective of others, which means that they commit to this only to refute others' mistaken ideas. [For Prāsaṅgikas] there are no independently [verifiable] reasons in which the three modes are established through the power of [their relationship to real] things. Therefore, they primarily just use consequences (*prasaṅga, thal 'gyur*) to demonstrate to Realists[635] their internal contradictions.[636]

A Detailed Explanation of the Systematic Presentation [of Rangtong] [bb"]

This is discussed in three sections: the system common to Prāsaṅgikas and Svātantrikas; the explanation of their differences; and the explanation of the individual [Rangtong] systems.

The System Common to Prāsaṅgikas and Svātantrikas [(1)]

This has two topics: the twofold absence of self-entity; and the mode of reasonings.

The Twofold Absence of Self-Entity [(a)]

Their common [approach] is to use reasonings to refute
the two self-entities: of persons (the source of views) and
of phenomena (the root of obscurations).

The common approach of both Svātantrika-Mādhyamikas and Prāsaṅgika-Mādhyamikas is to use many references to scriptures and a variety of reasonings (1) to refute a self of persons (*pudgalātman, gang zag gi bdag*), that is, the views concerning a self [of persons], as they are the source of all views and mental afflictions,[637] and (2) to refute a self-entity of phenomena (*dharmātman, chos kyi bdag*), that is, the taking of all outer and inner phenomena to be objectively real,[638] as that is the root of the two obscurations.[639] They then rest evenly in the absence of the two types of self-entity. These modes [of refutation and meditation] are discussed in some detail in the sections on reflection and meditation.[640]

The Mode of Reasonings [(b)]

The object to be negated is something imputed to a subject.
Probanda are either facts or conventions.
Reasons analyze four points: cause, result, both of those, and nature.
These four forms of analysis eliminate the Realists' extreme of existence.

The reason of dependent origination, [used in] the analysis of mere appearances, eliminates both extremes.
Thus [Svātantrikas and Prāsaṅgikas] do not disagree about the ultimate.

Subject

First, the subject (*dharmin, chos can*) is the basis for debate.[641] It is not something established by the valid cognitions[642] of both the challenger and the opponent, and it can be something coarse, such as an entity, or something small, such as a sprout. In these systems, the subject belongs to the set heterologous[643] to the probandum (*sādhya, bsgrub bya*), [and as such] is that which gives rise to reification.

Object of Negation

When a subject is analyzed, the object to be negated (*pratiṣhedhya, dgag bya*) is determined to be either an appearance or something imagined (*brtags pa*). It is not logical, [however,] to negate momentary appearances (*re zhig snang ba*), because reasonings cannot negate them. To take an example: for people with eye diseases, the appearances of floaters,[644] double moons, and the like do not stop as long as their eyesight is impaired. Similarly, as long as beings are not free from unafflicted ignorance,[645] illusionlike appearances [manifesting] to the six modes of consciousness do not stop.

It is not necessary to negate [appearances], because our mistakes[646] do not come from appearances: they arise from fixating on those [appearances]. This is the case because if we do not fixate on appearances, we are not bound—we are like a magician who, having conjured up a young woman, has no attachment towards her. [On the other hand, if,] like naïve beings attached to an illusory young woman, we fixate intensely [on appearances], our karma and mental afflictions will increase.

To intentionally negate appearances would be wrong because, if they were negated, emptiness would come to mean the [absolute] nonexistence of things. Another reason this would be a mistake is that yogins and yoginīs meditating on emptiness would fall into the extreme of nihilism since they would be applying their minds to a negation that [equals] the [absolute] nonexistence of everything.

Thus, [Mādhyamikas] set out to negate only what is imagined (*parikalpita, kun brtags pa*), because that is what can be negated. Like a rope [mistaken] for a snake, what is imagined does not conform to facts: it is simply the mind's fixations. [Dharmakīrti's] *Commentary on Valid Cognition* provides a further reason:[647]

> This [attachment] cannot be relinquished
> without the object's being invalidated.

The characteristic of things is that the perceiving mind cannot be negated unless its object is negated; therefore, we will not be able to negate the intense fixation of our perceiving mind unless its imagined object is negated. Without negating that intense fixation, we will not reverse afflictive phenomena,[648] because that [fixation] is their root.

Therefore, the object of negation for Mādhyamikas is only something imagined. It is of two types:

(1) objects whose existence even as a convention (*tha snyad tsam du grub pa*) is negated; and
(2) objects whose existence as ultimate (*don la grub pa*) is negated but whose existence as a convention is not.

The first type of object negated is a self either [of persons] or phenomena as imagined by proponents of our own [Buddhist] philosophical tenet systems or by proponents of other philosophical tenet systems. These do not exist even in terms of conventional reality (as was explained above).[649]

The second type of objects negated are the conventions of worldly consensus (*'jig rten grags pa'i tha snyad*), which are simply dependently originated according to their causes and conditions. These include things of immediate common consensus (such as [saying,] "I am going," "I am staying," or "I am eating"); and conventions that are suitable for common consensus, even though they may not be of things of immediate common consensus [now]. [The latter] are things about which there is common consensus in the [Buddhist] scriptures: causes and their results, the bhūmis and paths, factors to be abandoned and their remedies, and so forth.

Things commonly accepted as worldly conventions are not to be refuted as mere conventions. The reason this is not done is the same as what was said above about eliminating [or refuting] appearances.[650]

Probanda

There are two kinds of probanda (*sādhya, bsgrub bya*):
(1) proofs of facts (*don sgrub pa*); and
(2) proofs of conventions (*tha snyad sgrub pa*).[651]

Proofs of facts are of two types since debaters have different issues in question:
(a) nonimplicative negations[652] that [demonstrate that] the nature of a thing does not exist; and
(b) nonimplicative negations that [demonstrate that] the object of negation, just a nature, does not exist.[653]

In these systems, the probandum is a nonimplicative negation that is simply the refutation that a subject inherently exists, is real, and the like. It includes such nonimplicative negations as, "These appearances do not exist with a true nature," or "They do not exist in the way that they are imagined to be." [For Svātantrikas and Prāsaṅgikas, the probandum] is only an exclusion (*viccheda, rnam gcod*), merely the elimination of the object to be negated, and simply free from conceptual elaborations; they have no probandum that is something [positively] determined.[654]

Since they do not set forth any [affirmative probanda], there is also nothing that others could object to. In his *Rebuttal of Objections,* [Nāgārjuna] says:[655]

> If I were to have a proposition,
> I would have that fault.
> Since I have no proposition,
> I am without fault.
>
> If [I] were to observe something through
> direct perception or any other [means of valid cognition],
> [I] would either affirm it or deny it.
> Since there are no such things, I am beyond censure.

For these [systems,] the import of a nonimplicative negation is that it refers to nothing at all. It is said in the sūtras:

> Whoever understands that phenomena do not exist at all
> will not be attached to phenomena.

This shows that once the power of terms and concepts has been exhausted, [one's experience] will be like that of someone feeling rested after their hard work is over.

The point of negations and affirmations is summed up by the following [example]: When sound is proven to be impermanent by [the reason that] it is something produced, the actual object negated is the consciousness that ascribes (*sgro 'dogs pa*) permanence to sounds, and the actual object affirmed is the consciousness that ascribes impermanence to sound. This is the intention of Nāgārjuna's statement:[656]

> [Such statements] make us understand that no nature exists; they do not, however, eliminate arising.

Reasons

The means of proof are the reasons (*hetu, gtan tshigs*). In Madhyamaka reasonings, generally speaking, the evidence (*liṅga, rtags*) is presented in two ways:

(1) by setting up negations (*pratiṣheda, dgag pa*), or
(2) by setting up affirmations (*viddhi, sgrub pa*).

First: Negations

(1) Negation through the analysis of causes is called the "vajra sliver [reasoning]."[657]
(2) Negation by means of analyzing results refutes the arising of [a result] existent [at the time of its cause] and the arising of [a result that is] nonexistent [at the time of its cause].[658]
(3) Negation that employs the analysis of both causes and their results refutes arising from the four possibilities.[659]
(4) Negation that analyzes a nature [demonstrates that a phenomenon] is neither a single unit nor a plurality.[660]

The first type of negation is taught in the *Rice Seedling Sūtra*[661] and the last kind is presented in the *Descent into Laṅkā Sūtra*. The two middle ones appear in certain sūtras.[662] These four eliminate the Realists'[663] inflated ascription of inherent existence to things, thereby removing [their belief in] the extreme of existence.

Now we will look at these four in order.[664]

(1) The analysis of causes

When a sprout comes into being (*skye ba*), does it arise from itself? From something other than itself? From both? Or from no cause at all? This kind of analysis proves that, from a rational perspective, a sprout has no arising since it does not arise from anything at all.[665]

(2) The analysis of results

When a sprout arises, is this the arising of something that exists at the time of the seed? Or is this the arising of something that did not exist [at the time of its cause]?

If it were the arising of something that existed at the time of the seed, a sprout would not arise from the seed: its cause would serve no purpose, since the sprout already exists without depending on a cause. If it were the arising of something that did not exist [at the time of its cause], then it would be like the horns of a rabbit and its cause would have no potency (*nus pa*) at all.[666]

These reasonings refute [the possibility] that a combination of both is the case. It also is impossible [that a sprout arises] from neither being the case. [This analysis], therefore, proves that, in actuality, a sprout does not come into being.

(3) The analysis of both causes and results

From a mistaken perspective, it is not contradictory to make statements such as the following: "One sprout develops from one seed." "A single eye consciousness arises from the three conditions."[667] "One father produces many children." "A variety of crops grow from the combination of seeds, water, and manure." Nevertheless, from a rational perspective, the following four possibilities [for arising] are not feasible:

(a) that only one result manifests from just a single cause;
(b) that numerous results are produced by only one cause;
(c) that a single result comes from many causes; and
(d) that many results could arise from many causes.

Thus, from a rational perspective, a unity is untenable, and that also negates that a plurality could truly exist; thus it is proven that there is no arising.

(4) The analysis of a nature

Reasons stating that a sprout and other things are devoid of both real unity and real plurality prove that such things have no reality (*bden med*). This reasoning that something is neither a single unit nor a plurality is the root of all reasonings that negate true existence, which all four Buddhist philosophical systems [consider] to be the object of negation. It is taught that the *Fundamental Treatise on the Middle Way* is summarized by its refutation of eight points: arising and cessation, permanence and annihilation, going and coming, sameness and discreteness. The negations of the first six points depend upon the negation of sameness and discreteness (*gcig dang tha dad*), and the refutation of sameness and discreteness is simply [the argument] that no thing is a single unit or a plurality.[668]

[Second: Affirmations]

Affirmations are set up as evidence in the following way. The reasoning of dependent origination[669] is an analysis of mere appearances, and it is found in the *Questions of the Nāga King Anavatapta Sūtra.*[670] The reasoning that something is dependently originated proves that [the thing in question,] such as a sprout, has no reality. Its manner of presentation causes it to be categorized as an affirming reason; but, in fact, since it refutes reality, which is the object to be negated, it is a negating reason. This is the king of the reasonings used by Mādhyamikas to prove that things are empty of reality (*bden stong*), because it eliminates both the extreme of permanence and that of nihilism.

Since [phenomena] are dependently originated, they are not nonexistent as conventions; and thus the extreme of nihilism is avoided. [Phenomena also] are not objects that are permanent nor do they exist in terms of their own essence, because they depend on other causes and conditions. This establishes that [phenomena] have no nature and eliminates the extreme of permanence.

Questions of the Nāga King Anavatapta Sūtra says:

> The wise realize that all phenomena are dependently originated.
> They do not adhere to views involving extremes.

In the context of these [reasonings], it is impossible that a nature of things is a knowable object; and, therefore, there is no negative entailment,[671] since there is no link between what is to be pervaded and a pervader.[672] Nevertheless, in general, [Mādhyamikas may make statements] such as, "If a pot were to exist, it would follow that it must be either a unitary pot or a plurality." They also may use illusions, reflections, and so forth as concordant examples (*mthun dpe*). The object of comprehension (*prameya, gzhal bya*) for an inferential [cognition] based on such reasons is the probandum of these reasons [i.e., that all things have no nature].

Prāsaṅgikas and Svātantrikas do not disagree about these modes or the state of ultimate reality.

The Explanation of Their Differences [(2)]

> **They differ over many issues: conventional [reality], statements in debate, and other points.**

Both Prāsaṅgikas and Svātantrikas discuss the two truths. They do not disagree in the slightest way about ultimate reality (as was just mentioned), because if they were to, it would follow that one of them would not be Mādhyamikas, since the abiding nature of things is not multiple.

Differences Concerning Conventional Reality

They do disagree, however, about the presentation of conventional reality. Svātantrikas think that this should not be done according to the conventions of worldly people, because that would involve the possibility of error, as worldly people use conventions in a casual way without any rational analysis. Instead, they posit conventional [reality] in keeping with those who know how to apply reasonings, such as Proponents of Cognition (Vijñaptivādins) or Sautrāntikas. They maintain that even though Proponents of Cognition and the others have deviated from [a correct understanding of] ultimate reality, they have not done so with conventional reality.

Prāsaṅgikas say that someone who lacks the natural ability to climb trees and yet persists in doing so in a peculiar way—by letting go of a lower branch before grabbing hold of a higher one—will get nowhere, but will instead fall into the space between the branches. Similarly, Realists who, in their quest for suchness, put aside worldly conventions when they have not yet realized the true reality (*yang dag pa'i don*), will fall in between: into either the extreme of permanence or that of nihilism. Prāsaṅgikas state that Realists have deviated from [a correct understanding of] both truths, citing as their reason [Chandrakīrti's] statement in his *Entrance to the Middle Way*:[673]

> Those outside the path of the master Nāgārjuna
> lack the means for [achieving] peace.
> They have strayed from the conventional truth and that of suchness.
> Having strayed from those two truths, they will not attain liberation.

Prāsaṅgika masters, therefore, think that conventional reality should be posited according to the conventions of worldly people, not according to the proponents of other philosophical systems. This is because, in the same way that noble beings are the only valid authorities (*pramāṇa, tshad ma*) for ultimate reality, worldly people are the only valid authorities for the positing of conventional reality.

In sum, worldly people say, "A result comes from a cause," and understand it in just those [terms], without trying to analyze [whether the result arises] from itself, something other than itself, and so forth. Prāsaṅgikas' presentation of conventional [reality] accords with that [kind of general worldly understanding].

Differences Concerning the Acceptance of Conventions

Prāsaṅgikas and Svātantrikas differ regarding the acceptance of conventions (*vyavahāra, tha snyad*). Svātantrikas accept conventional reality as a [pragmatic] convention within their own system. Prāsaṅgikas, however, do not present anything as their own system either on the ultimate level or as a convention. Nevertheless, if it is called for, they will accept conventional reality—but only on the terms of worldly people. They do not accept it as part of their own system even as a mere [pragmatic] convention, citing the same text as their reason:[674]

> We do not accept conventional [reality]
> in the way you [Chittamātras] assert dependent entities.
> Nevertheless, we say, "Things exist," even though they do not,
> [deferring] to the world's perspective for the sake of the results.

Differences in Debate

When engaged in debate, Svātantrika masters assert that not presenting a system of one's own and only refuting others' systems is [sheer] sophistry[675] and, therefore, unacceptable. They say that if one does not establish one's own positions—emptiness, nonarising, and so forth—through valid forms of cognition,[676] one will be unable, simply by setting up consequences, to refute others' assertions that entities inherently arise. For these two reasons, they say that, as a convention, one should assert some points of one's own system that are established through valid forms of cognition; and such points would include the reasons and examples that prove one's own thesis (*pratijñā, dam bca'*) that there is no arising. This must be done because one cannot prove the thesis of one's own system using the reasons asserted by others.

Prāsaṅgikas say, "Those who have a thesis but do not posit it out of the fear that they will be subjected to others' criticism, and those who refute another's system with aggressive intentions using only [absurd] consequences are involved in a deceptive practice of sophistry. However, given that the Madhyamaka [system] does not have even the smallest position of its own to posit, what would be the point of troubling ourselves to search for a means to prove it? Actually, [the Madhyamaka approach] is not about refuting things. If we could observe a phenomenon to be negated, no matter how insignificant, it would be reasonable to refute it; but if we cannot observe a thing to be negated—not even the fragment left from splitting a hair's end a hundred times—how can we talk about negating it?" This accords with the opening statement in the *Entrance to the Wisdom* [*of the Middle Way*]:[677]

> It is only negation and affirmation that are negated.
> In fact, there is nothing to be negated or affirmed.

Prāsaṅgikas say that they present others' assertions in their treatises and analyze them rationally in numerous ways, not because they despise these other systems or take pleasure in debating, but for the sake of others: to overturn the reification of people trapped in conceptual nets. The *Entrance to the Middle Way* says:[678]

> The analyses in the *Treatise* are not presented out of fondness
> for debate.
> Suchness is taught for the sake of liberation.
> If others' scriptural systems collapse
> when suchness is presented, we are not to blame.

Each and every rational analysis found in the Madhyamaka treatises has the same objective: to overturn the concepts of superimposition or denial held by other parties.[679] But once their superimpositions and denials are eliminated, realization of the reality of the abiding nature will not arise through the force of analysis, because the abiding nature is not an object that can be analyzed by means of study or reflection. The same text states:[680]

Ordinary beings are bound by their concepts.
Yogins and yoginīs without concepts are liberated.
The wise, therefore, teach that the overturning of concepts
is the fruit of analysis.

Not only is there nothing for others to challenge in the Prāsaṅgika system, this system can invalidate everyone else's positions (*prakṣha, phyogs*), because, in their attempts to dispel their faults, all the answers they give to the Prāsaṅgika's reasonings are ineffective since [their answers are proofs that] are equivalent to their probandum.[681]

In brief, Prāsaṅgikas do not assert that there are independently verifiable reasons that function by virtue of [their relationship to real] things, because [for them] there are no forms of valid cognition that function by virtue of [their relationship to real] things that could prove such [reasons]. When, for the sake of others, they engage in negations and affirmations as one of two parties in debate, they employ four types of reasons and four valid means of cognition that are commonly acknowledged in the world.[682] Svātantrikas accept that there are reasons and forms of valid cognition that function by virtue of [their relationship to real] things, which [means that they are] independently verifiable.[683] Thus, the former [i.e., Prāsaṅgikas] have no probandum that is something [positively] determined;[684] they simply refute what others assert. Svātantrikas refute others' assertions by employing reasonings capable of cutting through conceptual elaborations, which are reasonings whose three modes are established by valid forms of cognition.

Further Differences

The phrase "other points" in this root verse refers to the numerous minor differences between these two systems.

- In the context of the ground, some points of difference are that Prāsaṅgikas do not assert that conventional [reality] is classified as either correct or mistaken, true or false, whereas Svātantrikas do.[685] Prāsaṅgikas assert that all objects are false and all states of minds (*blo*) are deluded, whereas Svātantrikas do not.
- In terms of the path, some of their minor differences include that during periods of study or reflection, Prāsaṅgikas do not prove a probandum that remains after an object of negation has been refuted, whereas

Svātantrikas do. Prāsaṅgikas do not state that they accept a view, Svātantrikas do.

- As for the result, some Svātantrikas believe that tathāgatas possess an illusionlike primordial wisdom that is a complete transformation (*gnas gyur pa*), and that conventional [reality] appears to them as illusionlike, but they are not deluded because they do not take [such appearances] to be real. Thus they say that impure karmic appearances exist for buddhas. Prāsaṅgikas assert that since appearances manifest from the habitual tendencies of unafflicted ignorance, they are delusive. Since tathāgatas have completely abandoned all delusions, all interactions with appearances have subsided; thus, no karmic appearances exist for buddhas.

9. SVĀTANTRIKA

(3) The Explanation of the Individual [Rangtong] Systems [II.B.2.a.ii.bb.2'.b'.vi'.bb'.1'.b".i".bb".(3)]

(a) The Systematic Presentation of Svātantrika

(i) An Account of Its Specific Classifications

(aa) Sautrāntika-[Svātantrika-]Mādhyamikas

(bb) Yogāchāra-[Svātantrika-]Mādhyamikas

(ii) A Concise Explanation of Its Systematic Presentation

[This chapter, a continuation of the detailed explanation of the systematic presentation of Rangtong, begins] the third part: the explanation of the individual [Rangtong] systems. This has two divisions: the systematic presentation of Svātantrika; and the systematic presentation of Prāsaṅgika.

The Systematic Presentation of Svātantrika [(a)]

This has two parts: an account of its specific classifications; and a concise explanation of its systematic presentation.

An Account of Its Specific Classifications [(i)]

This has two divisions: Sautrāntika-[Svātantrika-]Mādhyamikas; and Yogāchāra-[Svātantrika-]Mādhyamikas.

Sautrāntika-[Svātantrika-] Mādhyamikas [(aa)]

> **Among those who commented on the thought of Nāgārjuna,**
> **Bhāvaviveka and his followers**
> **accept positions of their own, such as emptiness,**
> **and formulate reasons in which the three modes are established through the power of [their relationship to real] things.**
> **They concur with Sautrāntikas about outer objects.**

[The Origin of the Svātantrika and Prāsaṇgika Division]

In general, the thought expressed in the noble Nāgārjuna's *Fundamental Treatise on the Middle Way, Called Wisdom,* was explained in many ways.[686] Nevertheless, these [commentarial modes] are mainly split in two ways: Prāsaṅgika and Svātantrika.[687] The *Fundamental Treatise* begins:[688]

> Entities do not arise
> at any time or any place:
> not from themselves nor from another,
> not from both, and not without cause.

The meaning of this verse has been discussed in a variety of ways. The master Buddhapālita[689] used the four theses (*pratijñā, dam bca'*) that arising does not occur from any of the four extremes to invalidate incorrect positions, but he did not put forth any means to prove an actual position (*prakṣha, phyogs*). Later, the master Bhāvaviveka criticized Buddhapālita's way of formulating his confutations. Bhāvaviveka set up the root statements[690] as independently [verifiable proof statements] and proved the subject property by independently [verifiable] means.[691]

After that, Chandrakīrti[692] demonstrated that Bhāvaviveka's criticisms of Buddhapālita were not applicable, and he explained that Bhāvaviveka's acceptance of independently [verifiable] reasons in the context of explaining the reasonings that analyze for ultimacy was flawed. Thus, Chandrakīrti is credited with being the one who delineated the system of Prāsaṅgika in a detailed manner.[693]

[The Divisions of Svātantrika]

The Svātantrika system was embraced by a great many masters, including Bhavya ([also known as] Bhāvaviveka),[694] Shrīgupta,[695] Jñānagarbha,[696] Shāntarakṣhita,[697] Kamalashīla,[698] Vimuktisena,[699] Haribhadra,[700] Buddhajñānapāda,[701] Dīpaṇkarabhadra ([also known as Atīsha]),[702] Vitapāda,[703] and Thagana.[704] If we group them according to [broad] types, there are two: Sautrāntika-[Svātantrika-]Mādhyamikas and Yogāchāra-[Svātantrika-]Mādhyamikas.[705] Bhāvaviveka[706] provides the reasons for such classifications by saying that, in terms of Nāgārjuna's text, there are two types of Mādhyamikas:

(1) the broad, outer Mādhyamikas, who accept outer objects merely as conventions for the sake of others; and
(2) the subtle, inner Mādhyamikas, who accept mere consciousness as a convention, but not outer objects.

Sautrāntika-[Svātantrika-]Mādhyamikas

Sautrāntika-[Svātantrika-]Mādhyamikas are the broad, outer Mādhyamikas. Prime examples are Bhāvaviveka and his followers. They maintain that their own positions, such as emptiness and nonarising, can be proven by valid cognition. Because of that, they formulate probative reasons (*sgrub byed kyi rtan tshig*) in which the three modes are established through the power of [their relationship to real] things.[707] They accept outer referents simply as conventions and discuss them in ways that concur with Sautrāntikas.

Yogāchāra-[Svātantrika-] Mādhyamikas [(bb)]

> **Shāntarakṣhita and others only assert mere consciousness,**
> **not outer referents; in this presentation they are like**
> **Chittamātras.**

Yogāchāra-[Svātantrika-]Mādhyamikas are, according to Bhāvaviveka's description, the subtle, inner Mādhyamikas. Prime examples are Shāntarakṣhita and others.

They do not differ from the previous ones [i.e., the Sautrāntika-Svātantrika-Mādhyamikas] in the way they put forth independently [verifiable] theses. As a convention, they accept mere consciousness but not, however, outer referents. In this regard, their presentation is like that of the Chittamātra-Yogāchāras.

A Concise Explanation of Its Systematic Presentation [(ii)]

Conventional [reality] is that, from the perspective of a deluded state of mind, phenomena exist.
Ultimate [reality] is that, from the perspective of an undeluded mind, there is no such existence.
The two truths are defined as either what can be negated by reasonings or what cannot be so negated.
They are one in essence but different isolates.
Conventional [reality] is presented as correct or mistaken according to
whether something is able to perform a function or not.

[The Two Truths]

Mādhyamikas subsume all phenomena, which are knowable objects, into the two truths. Knowable objects are the basis for the classification (*dbye gzhi*), and the two truths are the way they are classified. The Svātantrika system presents the two truths as follows.

- Conventional [reality] is what exists from the perspective of a deluded state of mind. A basis for the definition (*mtshan gzhi*) is a pot.
- Ultimate [reality] is that [conventional phenomena], when analyzed, do not exist from the perspective of an undeluded mind. A basis for the definition is that a pot is empty of reality.

[Here,] the meaning of something being real [or true] is that it is undeceiving (*mi bslu ba*) as the object of a particular mind, either a deluded one or an undeluded one. Phenomena are without any nature: they are empty of reality in terms of their own essence. This is the definition of mere reality (*bden pa tsam*).

[The Two Truths: Definitions and Positions]

- The definition of conventional reality is whatever cannot withstand rational analysis and, therefore, can be negated.
- The definition of ultimate reality is whatever can withstand rational analysis and, thus, is unable to be refuted.

In general, there are four positions regarding the two truths.[708]

(1) The two truths are synonyms (*ming gi rnam grang*), such that even the isolates[709] for their defining characteristics are not discrete.
(2) They are discrete in their own natures (*ngo bo tha dad pa*).
(3) They are discrete simply in the sense that their sameness is negated (*gcig pa bkag tsam gyi tha dad pa*): they cannot be described as different entities nor can it be said that they are identical.
(4) They are identical in nature but are discrete isolates (*ngo bo gcig la ldog pa tha dad pa*).

In this system there are many who hold the latter position.

[CONVENTIONALITIES]

Svātantrikas classify conventionalities as being either correct conventionalities (*yang dag kun rdzob*) or mistaken conventionalities (*log pa'i kun rdzob*):

(1) a correct conventionality is whatever is capable of performing a function[710] that is consistent with the way it appears [to its corresponding cognizer]; and
(2) a mistaken conventionality is whatever cannot perform a function consistent with its appearance.

(1) A correct conventionality is any phenomenon (such as a form) that has the following four characteristics:
  (a) it performs a function consistent with its appearance;
  (b) it has arisen from causes;
  (c) it is not something imagined; and
  (d) it appears [to its cognizing subject] in a way that is consistent with its respective class [of phenomena].[711]

Such phenomena exist as things capable of performing their respective functions.

(2) A mistaken conventionality is anything that appears but is unable to perform a function, such as the appearance of floaters [for the visually impaired][712] or the two moons [seen when you press your eyes]. Such appearances do not exist as things able to perform functions.

Svātantrikas consider that to be a thorough classification of conventionalities.

[The Ultimate and Other Points]

They prove a nonimplicative negation that is an exclusion:
it [simply] refutes real entities.
The refutation of arising and so forth is the nominal ultimate.
The pacification of elaborations is the final ultimate.
They do not assert an ālaya, thus consciousness has six modes.
They say that fruition is the illusionlike appearances of primordial wisdom.

Svātantrikas prove a nonimplicative negation that excludes [the possibility that the subject] does not possess [the quality of emptiness],[713] which negates any way of perceiving knowable objects as real entities. This is the ultimate, which they classify as being of two types:

(1) the nominal ultimate (*paryāyaparamārtha, rnam grangs pa'i don dam*) is the mere negation of actual arising and so forth, but it is not free from the conceptual elaboration of nonarising; and

(2) the final ultimate (*mthar thug gi don dam*) is the complete pacification of all elaborations, such as arising and nonarising.

These classifications are presented [by Jñānagarbha] in [his *Differentiation of*] *the Two Truths*.[714]

[Other Points]

Most masters of this school do not posit an ālaya; they state that consciousness consists of the six modes of consciousness. There are some Yogāchāra-Mādhyamikas, however, who take the position that there are eight modes of consciousness, which include the ālaya. [Svātantrikas, generally,] assert that fruition, which is the culmination of the path, is the independent (*rang rgyud pa*) appearances of the kāyas and primordial wisdoms, which exist in an illusionlike way.[715]

10. PRĀSAṄGIKA

(b) The Systematic Presentation of Prāsaṅgika-Madhyamaka [II.B.2.a.ii.bb.2'.b'.vi'.bb'.1".b".i".bb".(3).(b)]

(i) A Brief Account of Chandrakīrti's Exegetical System

(ii) A General Description of the Model Texts' Exposition of Madhyamaka

(aa) A General Statement

(bb) The Specific Explanation

(iii) The Specific Explanation of Ground, Path, and Result [in Madhyamaka]

(aa) Ground Madhyamaka: The Unity of the Two Truths

(1') The Actual [Presentation of the Two Truths]

(2') The Explanation of the Way [the Two Truths] Are Established

(bb) Path Madhyamaka: The Unity of Method and Wisdom

(cc) Resultant Madhyamaka: The Unity of the Two Kāyas

(iv) A Synopsis of the Main Points of the [Prāsaṅgika] Philosophical Tenet System

[This chapter, a continuation of the third part of the detailed explanation of the systematic presentation of Rangtong, the explanation of the individual [Rangtong] systems, presents] the second division: the systematic presentation of Prāsaṅgika-Madhyamaka. This section has four parts: a brief account of Chandrakīrti's exegetical system; a general description of the model texts' exposition of Madhyamaka; the specific explanation of ground, path, and result [in Madhyamaka];[716] and a synopsis of the main points of the [Prāsaṅgika] philosophical tenet system.

A Brief Account of Chandrakīrti's Exegetical System [(i)]

> **For eradicating conceptually elaborated characteristics, Chandrakīrti's system**
> **is exceptional and preeminent; it does not use independently [verifiable] reasons.**
> **His own system is free from assertions except [for what is done] simply for others.**

The master Chandrakīrti elucidates the way in which Buddhapālita comments on the intention of the noble Nāgārjuna's texts. Chandrakīrti's system is exceptional and preeminent for eradicating the conceptual elaborations associated with characteristics (*mtshan ma'i spros pa*), and he is a prime example of the Prāsaṅgika-Mādhyamika.

This system does not formulate independently [verifiable] probative reasons in which the three modes are established through the power of [their relationship to real] things. In order to refute the mistaken views of others, it accepts nonarising, emptiness, and so forth from the perspective of others, and it simply uses consequences to demonstrate to Realists their internal contradictions. Other than that, this system is free from any assertions, since there is nothing to be proven.

> **[This system uses] negations and affirmations that employ four valid means of cognition—**
> **direct perception, inference, scriptural authority, and analogical proof, which are commonly acknowledged in the world;**
> **and four types of reasons—inferences based on what is commonly acknowledged by others, consequences that expose contradictions,**
> **comparable applications of [the opponent's] reasons, and [the demonstration of] the irrelevance [of proofs that are equivalent to the probandum].**

In Chandrakīrti's own system, therefore, there is nothing to be negated nor affirmed through either nonimplicative negations or implicative negations. Nevertheless, for others, [his system] does employ negations and affirmations using the four valid means of cognition and four types of reasons.

The following are the four valid means of cognition, which, from the perspective of others, are commonly acknowledged in the world:

(1) direct perception (*pratyakṣha, mngon sum*);
(2) inference (*anumāṇa, rjes dpag*);
(3) scriptural authority (*āgama, lung*); and
(4) analogy (*upamāṇa, nye bar 'jal ba*).[717]

The four types of reasons (*liṅga, rtags*) used for others are:

(a) inferences based on what is commonly acknowledged by others (*gzhan la grags pa'i rjes dpag*);[718]
(b) consequences that expose the [opponent's] contradictions (*'gal ba brjod pa'i thal 'gyur*);
(c) comparable applications of the [opponent's] reasons (*rgyu mtshan mtshungs pa'i mgo snyoms*); and
(d) [demonstrations to the opponent of] the irrelevance of proofs that are equivalent to the probandum (*sgrub byed bsgrub bya dang mtshungs pa'i ma grub pa*).[719]

The dharma lord Gorampa[720] explains [the application of these reasons] as follows:

> Exposing contradictions (b) refutes that something arises from itself. Comparable applications of [the opponent's] reasons (c) refute arising from something other. [Demonstrations of the irrelevance of] proofs that are equivalent to the probandum (d) negate arising from both. Inferences based on what is commonly acknowledged by others (a) refute that things arise without any causes.

Serdokpa Dön-yö Pal[721] comments:

> [Gorampa,] although you are omniscient, what you say indicates that you still need to study Madhyamaka. These [four reasons should be used] as follows.
>
> Consequences that expose contradictions (b) create undesirable consequences for the reasons that the others accept. Comparable applications of the [opponents'] reasons (c) cause

> certainty about the entailment of these consequences to arise in your opponents' minds by using examples. [Demonstrations of the irrelevance of] proofs that are equivalent to the probandum (d) show [your opponents] that they cannot remove the difficulties that those consequences have created for them.
>
> Those three consequences (b-d) will prove the subject property and the entailment (which are commonly acknowledged by others) for your opponents' minds. Now you can use reasons based on what is commonly acknowledged by others (a) to generate an inferential valid cognition in your opponents' minds.

As we can see, it is explained that these four reasonings, which are unique to Prāsaṅgikas, are related to the negation of arising from each of the four extremes.[722] Since they are the main reasonings, I will discuss them now in some detail.

[The Vajra Sliver Argument and the Four Reasons]

[Refutation of arising from self]

First, we will look at the Sāṃkhyas'[723] belief that things arise from themselves. They assert that their statement, "Things arise from themselves," means that only things that exist at the time of their cause arise and that things that do not exist [at the time of their cause] do not arise. Sesame oil, they say, serves as an illustration: the reason sesame oil appears is that it already exists within sesame seeds, and the reason sesame oil does not appear from sand is that it does not already exist within sand. Prāsaṅgikas use the four reasonings to negate their position as follows.

- Prāsaṅgikas begin by saying, "It follows that for things, the subject, arising is pointless, because they already exist at the time of their causes." That is *a consequence that exposes [the opponents'] contradictions* (b).
- Sāṃkhyas then may say, "The entailment is not definite."[724] Prāsaṅgikas would reply, "It follows that things would arise endlessly, because even though something is already present, it can arise." That is *a comparable application of [the opponents'] reason* (c).
- Next, Sāṃkhyas may say, "Those two [cases] are not comparable for the following reason.[725] It is the pot that [is present] during the phase of the lump of clay that arises; [an already] manifestly perceptible pot does not arise [again]. These two are different: one is something manifestly perceptible and the other is not." Prāsaṅgikas would reply, "Referring to

the existence of 'the pot not manifestly perceptible during the clay-lump phase' is equivalent to your original probandum."[726] That is *[a demonstration to the opponents of] the irrelevance of proofs that are equivalent to the probandum* (d).

- Finally, Prāsaṅgikas say, "All outer and inner things, the subject, do not arise from themselves, because they [already] exist." That is *[the employment of] inferences based on what is commonly acknowledged by others* (a).[727]

[Refutation of arising from other]

In our [Buddhist] schools, there are Realists[728] who accept that phenomena arise from something other than themselves.[729]

- Prāsaṅgikas start with, "It follows that a seed and its sprout are not inherently different from each other, because a sprout arises from a seed." That is *a consequence that exposes [the opponents'] contradictions* (b).
- Realists may say, "The entailment is not definite."[730] Prāsaṅgikas would reply, "In that case, it follows that pitch-darkness could arise from flames, because even though something is inherently different from something else, it can arise [from that other thing]." That is *a comparable application of [the opponents'] reason* (c).
- Realists may counter with, "There is a difference between something that has the potential to produce [a result] and something that does not." Prāsaṅgikas would reply, "This is equivalent to your original probandum."[731] That is *[a demonstration to the opponents of] the irrelevance of proofs that are equivalent to the probandum* (d).
- Finally, Prāsaṅgikas say, "A sprout does not arise from a seed, because a seed and a sprout are inherently different from each other." That is *[the employment of] inferences based on what is commonly acknowledged by others* (a).

[Refutation of arising from both]

Nirgranthas [that is, Jains][732] assert that phenomena arise from both themselves and things other than themselves. They say that a clay pot's arising from the essential character of the clay is the sense in which it arises from itself. Its arising from the potter, a rope, water, and other factors is the sense in which it arises from something other than itself.

The reasonings refuting this position are the same ones used to refute arising from self and arising from other, as the *Entrance to the Middle Way* explains:[733]

> Arising from both is not reasonable,
> because the defects already explained apply.

[Refutation of arising without causes]

The Hedonists'[734] assertion that this world arises without causes is also negated in four steps.

- First Prāsaṅgikas say, "It follows that this world, the subject, is not perceived directly, because it is without causes." That is *a consequence that exposes [the opponents'] contradictions* (b).
- Hedonists then may say, "The entailment is not definite."[735] Prāsaṅgikas would reply, "It follows that the color and fragrance of a blue water lily [growing] in the sky[736] could be perceived, because even though something has no cause, it can be perceived." That is *a comparable application of [the opponents'] reason (c).*
- *Hedonists may reply*, "Those two [cases, this world and a flower growing in the sky,] are different: one has an existent nature and the other does not. Prāsaṅgikas reply, "This is equivalent to your original probandum." That is *[a demonstration to the opponents of] the irrelevance of proofs that are equivalent to the probandum* (d).
- Finally, Prāsaṅgikas say, "This world, the subject, does not arise without causes, because it arises sometimes."[737] That is *[the employment of] inferences based on what is commonly acknowledged by others* (a).

[The Two Truths]

> **A mind that discerns conventions is necessarily a mistaken cognition.**
> **Correct and mistaken conventional [realities] are equal in their performance and nonperformance of functions.**
> **The presentation of the two truths is determined by the presence of delusion and its absence.**
> **In sum, this is the final exegesis of the Collection of Reasonings.**

In this system, a mind that discerns conventions is necessarily a mistaken cognition. The *Commentary on Bodhichitta* says:[738]

> When we awaken from a dream [we see that
> dream objects and waking objects] do not differ in their
> performance of functions.

As is said, horses and elephants in dreams or illusions and actual horses and elephants, as well as cows in drawings and actual cows, are equivalent in the way that they perform functions from a mistaken perspective. They are also equivalent in not performing [functions] from a rational perspective. In terms of the things of worldly conventionality and yogic conventionality, [things are said] to be mistaken or correct; however, that is not [Chandrakīrti's] system.[739] His system asserts that there is nothing correct or mistaken in terms of yogic conventionality and, therefore, [yogic conventionality] is mere [conventionality].[740]

The criteria for positing the two truths is as follows.

- The essence of conventionality is the false appearances that [manifest] to a mind involved with delusion.
- The essence of the ultimate is what appears to an undeluded mind.

The first [conventional reality] is defined as the object found (*rnyed don*) by false seeing. The bases for this definition (*mtshan gzhi*) are, broadly, ignorance; specifically, taking [things] to be real; and, more particularly, the ignorance present in the mindstreams of ordinary beings.

The latter [ultimate reality] is defined as the object found by correct seeing. The basis for this definition is the opposite of ignorance: it is primordial wisdom, which directly realizes the absence of reality.

The *Entrance* [*to the Middle Way*] says:[741]

> All entities found bear two natures,
> owing to being seen correctly or falsely.
> It is taught that the object of correct seeing is suchness;
> [the object of] false seeing is conventional reality.

The same [text] says:[742]

> Those afflicted by eye diseases discern
> mistaken entities, such as floaters and so forth.

Perfect vision sees their nature.
This is the way to understand suchness here.

The meaning [of these verses] is as follows.

- Conventional reality is defined as what appears as the diversity of dependently originated [phenomena] through the power of ignorance.
- The ultimate is defined as the expanse of the noble ones' primordial wisdom, in which such appearances are not seen.

These are illustrated as follows: the appearance of floaters is an analogy for conventionality; that beings without eye diseases do not see those [floaters] in any way is an analogy for the ultimate.

To sum this up, most Tibetan scholars assert that this system is the final exegesis of the thought expressed in the Collection of Madhyamaka Reasonings.[743]

A General Description of the Model Texts' Exposition of Madhyamaka [(ii)]

This is discussed in two parts: a general statement; and the specific explanation.

A General Statement [(aa)]

Scholars say, "In the system of the noble father and son,
which serves as the model for all [Madhyamaka] texts,
the fundamental topic of profound emptiness
is explained in terms of the three phases."

Tak-tsang Lotsāwa[744] and most scholars after him agree in saying, "The heart of the tathāgatas' dharma is the unerring fundamental topic of profound emptiness. When this is explained in the system of the noble father and son [Nāgārjuna and Āryadeva], which serves as the model (*phyi mo*) for the Madhyamaka textual tradition, it is related to three phases:

(1) the phase of no examination or analysis;
(2) the phase when rational minds[745] analyze slightly; and
(3) the phase of superb analysis, which goes beyond verbal expression.

Since this makes the explanation and practice [of emptiness] quite easy, it is a genuine key instruction."

The Specific Explanation [(bb)]

> **The ground, the sphere of conduct, and the result are presented in accord with conventional expressions from a perspective of no analysis.**
> **The absence of self-entity and the ultimate are presented from the perspective of slight analysis.**
> **Superb analysis is the pacification of all conceptual elaborations.**

[Three perspectives can be distinguished] in the teachings of the middle wheel of dharma generally and in the texts of the father Nāgārjuna and his son specifically.

[First: No Analysis]

The ground (the aggregates, constituents, and sense spheres), the path (the sphere of conduct and methods), and the result (the kāyas, awakened activities, and so forth) are presented according to the expressions of worldly conventionality, that is, in terms of what is commonly understood from a perspective of no examination or analysis. Most of these topics accord with worldly conventionalities, either as things that are part of worldly consensus or as things that are suitable to become so.[746] Some topics, however, [only] accord with yogic conventionalities, such as the way things appear during meditative equipoise and the subsequent state of attainment.[747]

[Second: Slight Analysis]

The sections of teachings that refute the two self-entities (the objects to be negated) and then expound nonarising, emptiness, and ultimate reality are presented from the perspective of a rational mind that analyzes slightly.

[Third: Superb Analysis]

Many teachings, such as the majority of explicit statements in the Mother [Sūtras],[748] say that nothing exists in any way: not as something existent, nonexistent, permanent, impermanent, empty, not empty, or the like. They also say that nothing is suitable to be apprehended as anything at all. [This perspective is also expressed] in the first three lines of the following quotation from the *Fundamental Treatise* [*on the Middle Way, Called*] *Wisdom*:[749]

> Do not say "it is empty";
> do not state "it is not empty."
> Also do not say that it is both nor neither.
> [Such terms] should [only] be used as [conventional]
> designations.

By explaining these and the many similar passages in relationship to the phase of superb analysis, [the teachings] do not contradict each other in any way. The *Entrance to the Wisdom of the Middle Way* says:[750]

> In the primordial, unborn state,
> there is nothing to be negated and nothing to be affirmed.
>
> Transcending misery (nirvāṇa) and not
> are undifferentiated in the unborn state.
> Even nonarising itself is not so,
> because arising things do not exist.
>
> Conventionality does not exist, nor does the ultimate.
> Buddhas do not exist, nor do sentient beings.
> There is no view and no meditation;
> no conduct and no result.
>
> The import of that is what is to be meditated upon.
> Let the nonconceptual mind remain in its own peace.
> Without identifying anything or being distracted,
> meditate with clarity, free from characteristics.

[That expresses] the phase of thorough analysis, which is the final position of Prāsaṅgika-Mādhyamikas.

It is necessary to relate [the teachings on emptiness] to three phases for the following reasons. To begin with, we counteract nonmeritorious acts and proceed on the path to the higher states by taking up what is virtuous and turning away from what is negative. This does not require examination or analysis. In the middle, we reverse our belief in the two types of self-entity and progress on the path to liberation through practice that involves slight analysis. Finally, we eliminate all conceptual elaborations associated with a view and reach the end of the path to omniscience through the practice of superb analysis. Thus it is explained.

The Specific Explanation of Ground, Path, and Result [in Madhyamaka] [(iii)]

This is discussed in three sections: ground Madhyamaka: the unity of the two truths; path Madhyamaka: the unity of method and wisdom; and resultant Madhyamaka: the unity of the two kāyas.

Ground Madhyamaka: The Unity of the Two Truths [(aa)]

In this section, there are two parts: the actual [presentation of the two truths]; and the explanation of the way [the two truths] are established.

The Actual [Presentation of the Two Truths] [(1')]

> **It is taught that worldly conventional [reality] is the method and ultimate reality is what develops from that method.**

It is taught that conventional reality—which is whatever is commonly accepted as a convention in the world and talked about during the phase of no analysis using conceptual designations—is the method for realizing the ultimate. Ultimate reality is what develops from that method.[751] For Mādhyamikas, [the two truths] are the ground for [understanding] knowable objects. The way of unifying [an understanding of] the two truths is described in the words of the early Tibetan [masters]:

> Since there are appearances, we do not disregard the
> path of karma.
> Since they are empty, fixations do not arise.
> The unification of the two truths is the middle path.
> Heed this unerring, supreme [approach].

The Explanation of the Way [the Two Truths] Are Established [(2')]

> **For conventionality, [Prāsaṅgikas] cite what is commonly acknowledged by others in the world.**

As a general presentation of conventional [reality], which is the phenomena ascertained [in the world], [Prāsaṅgikas] simply cite that which is commonly accepted by others, such as valid and invalid means of cognition, or what is true and false in terms of correct and mistaken [conventionalities], all of which are part of worldly consensus. [Prāsaṅgikas] do not cite flawed philosophical tenet systems, such as those that assert permanence, nihilism, partless particles, or a truly existent cognition empty of duality.

> **In terms of the ultimate, [Prāsaṅgikas] use five types of reasons to prove the absence of a self-entity of phenomena**
> **and a sevenfold reasoning to prove the absence of a self of persons.**

The first type of valid cognizer to ascertain ultimate reality is an inferential [valid cognizer], which is a rational mind that is a special outcome of reflection. [Inferential valid cognition] is based on reasons,[752] of which there are many divisions. If we summarize these, [in this context,] they are, in fact, definitely only negating reasons: refutations of reality, which is the object to be negated. It is not possible that [Prāsaṅgikas] use affirming reasons as they are used in the field of logic (*rtog ge*). Even when they say, "[Phenomena] are illusionlike because they are dependently originated," [it is a negating reason]. The manner of presentation may make it seem that that is an affirming reason, but [if it were used in that way,] it would not result in the ascertainment of the ultimate. What [this reason] proves, in actuality, is the emptiness of reality (*bden stong nyid*), [and, therefore, it is a negating reason].

Negating Reasons

There are two types of negating reasons (*dgag rtags*):

(1) reasons of the imperception of something connected [to the predicate of the negandum],[753] and

(2) reasons of the perception of something contradictory [to the predicate of the negandum].[754]

The reason of dependent origination is the second kind of reason, and the other [four reasons] are the first type. The five great reasons are common to both the Prāsaṅgika and Svātantrika systems.[755] Here [in the Prāsaṅgika system], only these five (which include the reason that a phenomenon is neither a single unit nor plurality by analyzing its nature) are used to prove the nonexistence of a self-entity of phenomena. There is one reason that proves the absence of a self of persons and brings ascertainment of the ultimate: the sevenfold reasoning that uses the analogy of a chariot. This is the king of reasonings that prove the nonexistence of a self of persons.

The Five Great Reasons

First we will look at the five reasons in detail.

(1) The analysis of a nature: the reason of being neither a unity nor a plurality

The analysis of a phenomenon's nature, which proves that it is neither a single unit nor a plurality, demonstrates emptiness as [one of three] doors to liberation.[756]

[First:] The formulation of the reason

All phenomena (such as sprouts), the subject, do not really exist, because they are devoid of real unity or plurality. An example of this is a reflection in a mirror.

[Second: The modes of the proof]

- The *subject* of this reason is a mere appearance that is neither examined nor analyzed.
- The *subject property* that applies to this [subject]: [a mere appearance] is not a real unity because it has parts. It is not a real plurality because there are no real single units that are the building blocks [of a plurality].
- The *entailment*: if something were real, it would necessarily be either a single unit or a plurality. This [entailment] is established because those two [possibilities] are mutually exclusive, something that is accepted by [all Realists].[757]

(2) The analysis of causes: the vajra sliver reasoning

The analysis of a phenomenon's cause [employs] the vajra-sliver-like reason,[758] which shatters the Realists' rocky mountain of wrong views. It demonstrates the absence of characteristics (*animitta, mtshan ma med pa*) as a door to liberation.

First: The formulation of the reason

A sprout, the subject, does not really arise, because it does not arise from itself, from something other than itself, from both, or from neither. An example of this is a reflection.

Second: The modes of the proof

The *entailment* will always pertain to one of the four extremes [for arising, regardless of whether the assertion being refuted states that a thing] arises owing to the power of [real] things (*dngos stobs*), arises from the side of the object, or arises from the perspective of analysis.[759] Since [Nāgārjuna] considered this easy to understand, [he] did not discuss it in great detail in his [*Fundamental*] *Treatise* [*on the Middle Way*].[760]

The proof of the *subject property* has four parts:

(a) Establishing the reason that things do not arise from themselves

Sāṃkhyas assert that a sprout is simply a manifestation of the principal substance (*pradhāna, gtso bo*), and that the principal substance is the primal matter (*prakṛiti, rang bzhin*).[761] Therefore, a sprout arises from its own primal matter, an already existing permanent entity. [Prāsaṅgikas refute this, saying that] if that were the case a seed would arise endlessly, since it would not be feasible that the force of a sprout's arising should cause a seed to cease. If [Sāṃkhyas] were to assert that a seed (the cause) does not cease, its result, that is, a sprout's arising and its own colors and shapes, could never materialize. If something were to arise from itself, agents and their effects would be the same.

(b) Establishing the reason that phenomena do not arise from something other than themselves

Realist scholars say, "The way the Sāṃkhya's assertion that things arise from themselves is refuted is fine, but it is established by valid forms of cognition that phenomena arise from things other than themselves. This is because object-consistent consciousnesses arise from the four conditions,[762] and because most [other] entities arise from their causal and dominant conditions.[763] Causes and their results are not simply conceptual designations, they exist from their own sides. [Results are seen] to arise [from causes even] when they are thoroughly examined and analyzed."

Although there are many reasonings that negate this position, they come down to the following two points:

(i) It is impossible for things to arise from something other than themselves.

(ii) Otherness is impossible in [the framework of] arising.[764]

(i) [It is impossible for things to arise from something other than themselves]

[If phenomena were to arise from something other than themselves, it would follow that] from all things that are not causes of something, phenomena that are not their results would arise, because, [for example,] a barley seed and a rice seed are equivalent in being other than a rice sprout, [and this otherness] is established through their own natures (*rang gi ngo bo nas grub pa*).[765] [The reason] entails [the consequence,] because for things to be other, they [must] be present concurrently without depending upon each other, like [an animal's] left and right horns; and if such things were in a cause and result [relationship]—even while being [different from each other] in that way—there would be no reason why a rice seed, which is a substantial [cause],[766] should not produce a barley sprout.

(ii) Otherness is impossible in the framework of arising

Those who assert that a sprout arises from a seed cannot possibly also assert that those two are different, discrete substances, for the following [reasons]. The otherness of substances is established from the objects' own side, which is not possible when [two things] are not simultaneous; and the simultaneity of a cause and its result is logically refuted. The cessation of a cause and the arising of its result cannot possibly occur simultaneously, like the rising and falling of a scale's beam.[767] Furthermore, the simultaneity of a cause and its result is refuted by examining whether the result produced is existent [at the time of its cause] or not existent [at that time].[768]

(c) Establishing the reason that phenomena do not arise from both [themselves and things other than themselves]

Since the refutation [of arising from both self and other] is implicit in the [previous] two refutations, [the texts generally] do not present this in detail.

(d) The refutation of causeless [arising]

[The assertion that phenomena] arise without causes elicits the absurd consequences that entities would arise all the time, or that they would never arise. Like [other causeless phenomena, such as] lotuses [growing] in the sky, [which do not appear, all phenomena] would not be suitable to appear—but that contradicts our perception of causes and their effects as being clearly evident. Certain flawed philosophical systems maintain that the nonexistence of past and future lives has been proven, and thus they regard [both] body and mind to be of the nature of the elements. It is taught extensively that [such notions] are [merely] the product of mistaken direct perception that apprehends the elements.

(3) The analysis of results: the negation of the arising of an existent or a nonexistent

The analysis of results (which is an extension of the refutation of arising from something other) refutes the arising of [a result that is] existent [at the time of its cause] and the arising of [a result that is] nonexistent [at the time of its cause]. It demonstrates the absence of expectancy (*apraṇihita, smon pa med pa*) as a door to liberation.

Some may ask, "What is the result that arises: is it something that exists at the time of its cause or something that does not exist at such time?" Although Svātantrikas purportedly accept the latter [position] as a convention, [the refutations of these positions] are well established for the following reasons. If a result were to exist at the time of its cause, since it already exists in dependence on something else, what would its cause do? If [a result] were something completely nonexistent, again its cause would do nothing, as in the case of the horns of a rabbit. A combination of both [possibilities] is also not tenable.

(4) The analysis of both causes and results: the negation of arising from the four possibilities

The analysis of both a cause and its result refutes arising from the four possibilities.[769] As was stated above,[770] from a mistaken perspective, it is not contradictory to make statements such as, "One sprout develops from one seed." However, from a rational perspective, arising from any of the four possibilities—such as only one result manifesting from just a single cause—is untenable, since, in rational terms, a unity is not feasible, and that negates that a plurality could truly exist.

(5) The king of reasonings: the reason of dependent origination

The great reason of dependent origination is the king of reasonings used by Mādhyamikas to prove the absence of any reality. The *Fundamental Treatise* [*on the Middle Way*] says:[771]

> Whatever arises dependently
> is in its very nature a state of peace.

[An example of such reasoning is] the statement, "A sprout, the subject, does not truly exist, because it arises dependently." This [reasoning is applied] in two ways: (1) to eliminate the extreme of permanence, and (2) to eliminate the extreme of nihilism.

(1) Outer and inner entities, the subject, do not exist ultimately, because they are dependently originated.
(2) Those [entities], the subject, are not nonexistent conventionally, because they are dependently originated.

Prāsaṅgikas assert that these five reasonings are commonly acknowledged by others, whereas Svātantrikas state that they are independently [verifiable] reasonings.

To state this briefly: in the [Prāsaṅgika] system, arising from any of the four ways (self, other, and so forth) does not exist in the slightest, but since it is commonly understood in the world that arising exists, [Prāsaṅgikas] explain it accordingly. The *Entrance* [*to the Middle Way*] says:[772]

> Having simply sown a seed,
> worldly beings say, "I produced this boy,"

or think, "I planted a tree."
Therefore, even in the world, arising from something
other does not exist.

The Reasoning that Proves the Absence of a Self of Persons

The sevenfold reasoning [that uses the analogy of] a chariot proves the absence of a self of persons.[773] The *Entrance* [*to the Middle Way*] states:[774]

A chariot is not considered to be other than its parts.
It is not identical [with them,] nor does it possess them.
It is not in its parts, nor are the parts within it.
It is not the mere assembly nor the overall shape.

In addition to the fivefold [analysis[775] that begins with seeing that] a chariot is not something other than its parts (such as the nails), [Chandrakīrti] examines the collection [of parts] and the overall shape [of the chariot]. If we investigate [a chariot] using this sevenfold analysis, we will not find that it is the parts themselves nor will we find that it is something other than those [parts]. Similarly, if we look for a self using this sevenfold analysis, we will not find that it is something other than the aggregates nor will we find that it is the aggregates themselves. In this [analysis of the chariot], the overall shape and the collection are refuted implicitly, since they cannot be found apart from that which has the shape (*dbyibs can*) or that which is the collection (*tshogs pa can*).

[The Actual Ultimate]

The actual ultimate is beyond the intellect; elaborations do not apply to it.
Cutting through elaborations, such as eliminating the eight extremes, is [itself] simply a convention.

What is proven by these reasons is not, for example, an affirmation of the ultimate through the process of other-exclusion[776] on a conventional level. This is because mental elaborations do not apply to the actual ultimate (*don dam pa dngos nyid*), since it is far beyond being an object of the intellect (*blo*), or an object of terms and concepts. Therefore, techniques[777] such as eliminating the elaborations of the eight extremes—arising and cessation, permanence and annihilation, going and coming, sameness and discreteness—are [themselves] elaborations. In order to cut through the elaborations of conventionality, they are used simply as conventional expressions in keeping with what is commonly acknowledged by others.

A thesis is [the creation of] the intellect; the intellect is conventional.
Therefore, there are no independently [verifiable] theses or assertions.
Even nonarising and so forth are not a thesis,
because they [simply] banish fixation to never-existent entities.
It is taught that once [reification] is overturned, clinging to nonentities must be renounced.

A thesis, whatever it may be, is the creation of the intellect, and the intellect is a conventional, mistaken cognition. Therefore, for Prāsaṅgikas, there are no independently [verifiable] theses or assertions. Even nonarising, freedom from elaborations, and so forth are not put forth as independently [verifiable] theses for the following [two] reasons. (1) Although phenomena, persons, and so forth (which are verbally stated) have never existed, non-Buddhist and Buddhist Realists fixate upon them as [real] entities, because they have fallen into the extremes of superimposition or denial.[778] [Reasonings that demonstrate nonarising and so forth are stated only] to banish such [unwarranted] reification. (2) Once that reification is overturned, the intellect that clings to nonentities also must be renounced; and thus it is taught that [the ultimate] is beyond the intellect and without any clinging. This corresponds to Shāntideva's statement [in his *Entrance to the Bodhisattva's Way of Life*]:[779]

Once neither entities nor nonentities
are present for the intellect,
there are no other possibilities.
This is complete peace, free from referents.

The [Prāsaṅgika] philosophical system emphasizes abiding in unborn peace, free from elaborations;
this involves no mode of apprehension.

All [who follow] the noble father [Nāgārjuna] and his son [Āryadeva] emphasize that the rationally analyzed philosophical system of this tradition teaches that [the actual ultimate] is to abide in peace, which is unborn and free from all elaborations, and that this involves no mode of perceiving reference points.

Path Madhyamaka: The Unity of Method and Wisdom [(bb)]

> **The unification of method and wisdom is gradually developed during the ten bhūmis**
> **[when] primordial wisdom directly realizes [dharmatā].**
> **[Primordial wisdom] is divided during subsequent attainment in that it is the support.**

The master Chandrakīrti explains [the path] by bringing together the method (*upāya, thabs*) taught in the *Sūtra on the Ten Bhūmis*[780] and the wisdom (*prajñā, shes rab*) presented in the *Fundamental Treatise on the Middle Way*. He describes the way [method and wisdom] are unified through the gradual cultivation of the ten pāramitās during the ten bhūmis.[781] The essence of the ultimate is primordial wisdom that directly realizes dharmatā, which is free from all elaborations. As for the way in which dharmatā is realized: the primordial wisdom of noble beings does not see an essence of phenomena in any way. This is referred to with the conventional expression "realizing dharmatā." As [Atīsha] says [in his *Entrance to the Two Truths*]:[782]

> The most profound sūtras say
> it is the seeing of the unseen.

In the context of the subsequent states of attainment, primordial wisdom is divided slightly in that it is the support for the virtues of generosity and so forth.[783] The essence of primordial wisdom itself, however, has no divisions, because primordial wisdom and dharmatā are inseparable and the essence of dharmatā has no divisions.

Resultant Madhyamaka: The Unity of the Two Kāyas [(cc)]

> **[The result] is asserted to be the unity of the two kāyas.**

I will discuss the dharmakāya and the form kāyas without differentiating them in terms of their actual and nominal types.[784] As for the identification of the first, the dharmakāya is the space-like expanse free from the two obscurations and their habitual tendencies. This accords with the statement in the *Entrance to the Middle Way*:[785]

> When the dry wood of knowable objects is fully consumed,
> there is peace: the dharmakāya of the victorious ones.
> At that point, there is neither arising nor cessation.
> With the cessation of mind, the [sambhoga]kāya makes this
> [the dharmakāya] manifest.[786]

Given that, does primordial wisdom, in this system, exist at the bhūmi of a buddha or not? Jetsün Drakpa Gyaltsen[787] commented on this, saying:

> The assertion that, in the tradition of the master Chandrakīrti, primordial wisdom does not exist on a buddha's bhūmi denigrates both the master and the buddhas.

The dharma lord Sakya Paṇḍita[788] states:

> If you assert that, ultimately, on the bhūmi of a buddha, primordial wisdom is beyond existence and nonexistence and, conventionally, it is mind and mental events, then on the bhūmi of a buddha [primordial wisdom] does not exist, because a buddha has exhausted delusion.

The exalted Mikyö Dorjé, Silung Paṇchen [Shākya Chokden],[789] and others assert that, ultimately, on the bhūmi of a buddha, primordial wisdom is beyond existence or nonexistence, and, conventionally, primordial wisdom exists, because [the *Entrance to the Middle Way*] says:[790]

> With your excellent omniscience, you comprehend all knowable
> objects in a single moment.

In that case, if buddha[hood] is identified as being space-like dharmatā, does it mean that buddhas do not benefit others? [No, it does not, because] the power of the buddhas' previous aspirations and the merit of the beings to be trained cause [the buddhas' activities] to appear uninterruptedly with their two form kāyas, [which manifest] for the sake of others. This is like the way wish-fulfilling gems and wish-granting trees[791] can fulfill the needs and desires of those who pray to them even though they do not have the idea of doing so. The *Entrance [to the Middle Way]* says:[792]

> The kāya of peace is evident, like wish-granting trees,
> and, like wish-fulfilling gems, it is nonconceptual.
> Until all beings are liberated, it remains constant for the
> sake of enriching the world.
> It appears to those free from conceptual elaborations.

A Synopsis of the Main Points of the [Prāsaṅgika] Philosophical Tenet System [(iv)]

> **What is logically imputed is rejected: entities are simply names.**
> **Conditioned phenomena are deceptive; nirvāṇa is not.**
> **Taking things to be real and what that produces is the afflictive obscuration, the root of cyclic existence.**
> **Because the three yānas' ways of seeing are similar, their paths of seeing are the same.**
>
> **Since [from the perspective of buddhas] knowable objects have subsided, buddhas are simply appearances for others.**
> **These are the main features of this philosophical tenet system.**

This philosophical tenet system has many distinctive features, but the following five are the main ones.

First: [Phenomena Exist Only Nominally]

[Prāsaṅgikas] reject all discussions of valid forms of cognition and invalid forms of cognition, which are the logical imputations (*rtog ges btags pa*) of [the other philosophical systems] up through the Svātantrika system. [Prāsaṅgikas] reject these for their own Madhyamaka system and as worldly systems, even as mere conventional expressions, without even considering that such things [could be established] from a rational perspective. All phenomena (inner and outer, as well as causes and their results) are what is imagined (*blos brtags*), which [means that], from their own side as objects, they do not exist even as conventions: they are simply names and are [only] imputedly existent (*ming rkyang btags yod*). [Prāsaṅgikas] state that horses and elephants in dreams and the waking state are equivalent in terms of being real or false.[793]

Second: [Conditioned Phenomena Are Deceptive]

Whatever is conditioned is necessarily a false and deceptive phenomenon, since it does not remain for a second instant beyond its single instant of existence, and no agent and its object exist in that single instant. Not only are [conditioned phenomena] not able to withstand rational analysis, there is not even a trace of something that is established from a rational perspective. [Prāsaṅgikas,] therefore, maintain that there is no common locus (*gzhi mthun*) between conditioned phenomena and something established through valid forms of cognition. Although it is the case that when properly analyzed, nirvāṇa and any [hypothetically] superior phenomenon do not exist from their own side, [Prāsaṅgikas] assert that, from the perspective of slight analysis, the only thing that is undeceiving is nirvāṇa. This is stated in [the *Sixty Verses on Reasoning*]:[794]

> The victors teach that
> nirvāṇa alone is true.

Third: [The Afflictive Obscuration Is Taking Things to Be Real]

The root of cyclic existence is taking things to be real (*satyagrāha, bden 'dzin*). That [notion] and what it produces—the mental afflictions (such as attachment) and all their associated factors—are simply the afflictive obscuration (*kleṣhāvaraṇa, nyon sgrib*). Whereas [the cognitive obscuration (*jñeyāvaraṇa, shes bya'i sgrib pa*) is as the *Highest Continuum* says]:[795]

> All concepts of the three spheres[796]
> are asserted to be the cognitive obscuration.

It is also said:

> The cognitive obscuration is the one hundred [and eight] concepts concerned with percepts and perceivers.[797]

[Prāsaṅgikas] do not assert that there is a common locus between taking things to be real and the cognitive obscuration. Their assertion accords with statements such as [Nāgārjuna's in his *Precious Garland*]:[798]

> As long as one clings to the aggregates,
> [one will cling to a self.]

And:

> It is definite that the root of saṃsāra is taking things to be real.

This also establishes that it is impossible that shrāvakas and pratyekabuddhas do not realize the absence of a self-entity of phenomena.[799]

FOURTH: [THE REALIZATION OF DHARMATĀ IS THE SAME IN THE THREE YĀNAS]

The three yānas' paths of seeing do not consist of many moments, such as sixteen, fifteen, twelve, or four. The *Entrance* [*to the Middle Way*] says:[800]

> The intelligence that perceives suchness as its object is also
> not differentiated.

[Prāsaṅgikas] assert that the way dharmatā is seen is the same in all three yānas.

FIFTH: [BUDDHAS' MANIFESTATIONS ARE SIMPLY APPEARANCES FOR OTHERS]

The buddhas' unfathomable and indescribable form kāyas and activities are nonconceptual, just as are the achievements of wish-fulfilling gems and garuda stūpas.[801] Moreover, they are displays of appearances for others (*gzhan snang*) that do not require even the arousing of bodhichitta. Instead, their [manifestation] is attributable to the power of [the buddhas'] previous aspirations and the positive karma of those to be trained. Āryadeva describes the perspective of a buddha:[802]

When one wakens from the deluded sleep of ignorance,
these [states of] saṃsāra are not observed.

[Prāsaṅgikas] say that since, [from the perspective of a buddha,] all appearances of consciousness and knowable objects have subsided, buddhas are simply appearances for others.

[The Eight Uncommon Theses]

A later generation of Tibetans explains that this system has eight great, uncommon theses: four theses associated with refutation and four theses associated with affirmation.[803]

[The four associated with refutation]

(A1) The existence of things by way of their own specific characteristics (*svalakṣhaṇasiddha, rang mtshan kyis grub pa*) is not accepted even as a convention.

(A2) Independently [verifiable] reasons are not accepted even as conventions.

(A3) Reflexive awareness is not accepted even as a convention.

(A4) An ālaya is not accepted even as a convention.

[The four associated with affirmation]

(B1) External objects (*bāhyārtha, phyi don*) are accepted.

(B2) Taking things to be real is necessarily the afflictive obscuration.

(B3) Disintegration (*zhig pa*) is asserted to be a [functioning] thing (*dngos po*).

(B4) Noble shrāvakas and pratyekabuddhas realize the absence of a self-entity of phenomena.[804]

Regarding these [eight points], Serdok Paṇchen [Shākya Chokden] and his sons say, "[We can agree] only with the words of the statement 'Noble shrāvakas and pratyekabuddhas realize the absence of a self-entity of phenomena.' As for the other seven points, they are philosophical tenets that Prāsaṅgika-Mādhyamikas would not consider even in their dreams." The assertions of the eighth lord [Karmapa Mikyö Dorjé] are for the most part similar to that.[805]

11. SHENTONG-MADHYAMAKA

ii" The Explanation of the Shentong-Madhyamaka System [II.B.2.a.ii.bb.2'.b'.vi'.bb'.1".b"ii"]
aa" An Overview of the [Shentong] System
bb" A Detailed Explanation of [the Shentong] System
(1) The Way the Two Truths Are Ascertained
(2) The Way [Shentong] Is Free from the Chittamātras' Defects
(3) An Explanation of the Ways that Rangtong and Shentong Differ and Other Points
cc" Additional Topics: Recommendations

[This chapter, a continuation of the extensive explanation of the characteristics of the Madhyamaka schools, presents] the second division: the explanation of the Shentong-Madhyamaka system. This is discussed in three parts: an overview of the [Shentong] system;[806] a detailed explanation of [the Shentong] system; and additional topics: recommendations.

An Overview of the [Shentong] System [aa"]

> **Maitreya's thought was explained by Asaṅga and his brother.**
> **The two systems of Yogāchāra and Certainty about the Ultimate**
> **do not differ in terms of the essence of their views.**
>
> **However, in the system of the first Dharma Treatises there are three yānas [ultimately];**

whereas the view of the *Highest Continuum* is that there is one yāna ultimately,
a bhūmi with the habitual tendencies of ignorance, and birth through undefiled karma.
These are ways for the common [disciples] to cut through conceptual elaborations and the uncommon [to become certain] about the ultimate.

The Dharma Treatises of the exalted Maitreya[807] were explained by Asaṅga and his brother [Vasubandhu].[808] The general philosophical tenet system of these [texts] was taught in detail by many excellent disciple lineages, such as [those originating with] Dignāga and Sthiramati.[809] The uncommon philosophical tenet system [of Maitreya's texts] remained with supreme disciples, who transmitted it orally. In Tibet, this [uncommon explanation] was transmitted by the lotsāwas Zu Gawé Dorjé[810] and Tsen Kawoché[811] and was first established as a system of standard texts (*yig cha'i srol*) by the mahāsiddha Yumo [Mikyö Dorjé][812] and others. The uncommon key points of this view were elucidated in the teachings of the lord of victors Rangjung Dorjé,[813] the omniscient [Longchen] Drimé Özer,[814] and others, who also clearly maintained that this [view] was the final definitive meaning. In particular, the omniscient dharma lord Dolpopa the Great[815] proclaimed the lion's roar of "Shentong-Madhyamaka." Later, Serdok Paṇchen [Shākya Chokden],[816] the exalted Tāranātha,[817] and others clarified the uncommon key points of this system of philosophical tenets. [These are the masters who] appeared as the founders and promulgators of this great chariot-system.

The exegetical systems associated with those [treatises] differ in such a variety of ways that they could be [categorized] into subtler and broader subschools. Silung Paṇchen [Shākya Chokden]'s explanation is that principally there are two exegetical styles found in [Maitreya's Treatises]:[818]

(1) the exegetical style of the first three Dharma Treatises of Maitreya, which may be referred to as that of the Yogāchāra-Mādhyamikas, or

(2) the exegetical style of the *Highest Continuum*, which belongs to the Mādhyamikas with Certainty about the Ultimate (*don dam rnam par nges pa'i dbu ma pa*).

These two systems do not differ greatly in terms of the essence of their views, however, they do differ in the following specific ways:

(1) The system of the first Dharma Treatises of Maitreya explains that ultimately there are three yānas, and it does not make some points that are part of the presentation[819] found in the *Highest Continuum*.

(2) The thought of the *Highest Continuum* is expressed in the explanations that ultimately there is one yāna, that there is a bhūmi on which the habitual tendency of ignorance is present, and that birth can take place through undefiled karma.[820]

We should understand that these [two systems] are exegetical styles that are respectively (1) the means for common disciples to cut through conceptual elaborations by means of study and reflection;[821] and (2) the way for uncommon disciples to become definitively certain about the ultimate by means of meditation.

The majority of Tibetans say that [the first Dharma Treatises of Maitreya] are not Madhyamaka texts because they teach that ultimately there are three yānas. However, the masters who hold the positions [of the first Dharma Treatises] say that the explanation that shrāvakas and pratyekabuddhas do not enter the Mahāyāna path after having attained nirvāṇa without remainder is itself not enough justification to say that [these texts] are not to be considered Madhyamaka: being considered Madhyamaka is [determined] on the basis of the view. Their point is that [the first Dharma Treatises of Maitreya are Madhyamaka] because [they teach] the following special features of the Madhyamaka, as specified by the lord of scholars Kamalashīla and others:

(1) all knowable objects are of one taste, emptiness;

(2) all sentient beings are pervaded by the element of *sugatagarbha*;[822] and

(3) all beings are capable of the awakening [of a buddha].

The great omniscient one of Jonang [Dolpopa] states:[823]

> The five Dharma Treatises of Maitreya do not contain different views. The *Ornament of Clear Realization* does not explain the Rangtong view. None of these [texts] explain that ultimately there are three yānas and a cut-off potential.

Thus he does not subdivide Shentong-Madhyamaka into higher and lower [schools].

There are Tibetans who say that the Madhyamaka system of three of the Treatises of Maitreya is [in fact] the False Image system of the Chittamātra.[824] However, in general Tibetans make free use of the conventions "Real Images" and "False Images,"[825] which [they always consider] to belong to the Chittamātra [system]. [They make their categorization] simply [because] there are two types [of statements] that appear in these treatises: the images appearing as objects for cognition (which is [itself] appearing as referents) are real or they are false; [however, neither statement constitutes grounds for these texts to be considered as belonging to either Chittamātra subschool].

The following passage from [Serdok] Paṇchen Shākya Chokden is of particular relevance:[826]

> Those who assert that the view of the *Highest Continuum* is the Chittamātra view have no scriptures or reasonings to prove that, for the following reasons: In [the *Highest Continuum*'s] own system there are no scriptural quotations or reasonings that validate [such a categorization]. If they [instead] draw on scriptures and reasonings from other systems to prove [their point] and confute [other positions], they will never find a Mādhyamika who maintains the flawless Madhyamaka view.
>
> If [the fact that] the exalted Maitreya and Asaṅga have explained that [the *Highest Continuum*] is Madhyamaka is not enough proof [for them], they will never find a valid authority for these teachings.
>
> Bhāvaviveka and Kamalashīla prove that Nāgārjuna's scriptural tradition is Madhyamaka by using the argument that he was a noble being and was prophesied by the Sugata. Such [arguments] apply in this [case since both Maitreya and Asaṅga were noble beings and were prophesied by the Buddha].
>
> If [the *Highest Continuum*] is not considered Madhyamaka because it explains that the consummate [nature] is ultimate reality, how could the many earlier and later Tibetans[827] who assert that ultimate reality is emptiness in its aspect of a nonimplicative negation be considered Mādhyamikas?

Thus, Maitreya's and Asaṅga's own system does not explain that there are teachings [of the Buddha] or treatises that reveal a Madhyamaka view that is not found in the Madhyamaka taught in the last Dharma Treatise of Maitreya [the *Highest Continuum*]. This can be understood by reading not only the root texts of Maitreya but also the four Synopses[828] and the two Compendia,[829] because this system states:

> It is explained clearly that sūtras teaching that all phenomena have no inherent nature (*niḥsvabhāva, ngo bo nyid med pa*) are not to be taken literally. Anyone who accepts such [statements] as literal is a propounder of nihilism.

A Detailed Explanation of [the Shentong] System [bb"]

This discussion has three parts: the way the two truths are ascertained;[830] the way [Shentong] is free from the Chittamātras' defects; and an explanation of the ways that Rangtong and Shentong differ and other points.

The Way the Two Truths Are Ascertained [(1)]

> **First, imagination of what is unreal exists conventionally.**
> **Percept and perceiver are simply imputed by mind and do not exist.**
> **Primordial wisdom, free from conceptual elaborations, [exists] in the sense that it is the dharmatā of that [consciousness];**
> **and within that [dharmatā], adventitious, removable stains exist.**

The *Differentiation of the Middle and the Extremes* states:[831]

> Imagination of what is unreal exists;
> within it, duality does not exist.
> Emptiness exists within it,
> and it exists within that [emptiness].
>
> Thus all is explained
> as not empty and not non-empty.

Since [imagination] exists, [duality] does not exist, and
[imagination of what is unreal] exists [within emptiness, and emptiness within it],
this is the middle path.[832]

First, [the following is presented] from the perspective of cutting through conceptual elaborations concerning conventional [reality].[833] The mere imagination of what is unreal—cognition, which manifests as the variety of appearances—exists on a conventional [level]. The percepts and perceivers appearing to that [cognition] do not exist even conventionally, because they are simply imputed by the mind. Thus, conventional reality is free from the two extremes:

- It is free from the extreme of nonexistence, or nihilism, because the mere existence of imagination is accepted on the conventional level.
- It is free from the extreme of permanence, or existence, because it transcends superimposed, mutually dependent phenomena, such as percepts and perceivers.[834]

Primordial wisdom, emptiness free from conceptual elaborations, really exists (*bden par yod*) within that consciousness—i.e., within the imagination of what is unreal—in the sense that it is its dharmatā [its reality]. In the phase with stains, consciousness, "that which bears reality,"[835] exists within dharmatā as adventitious, removable stains; it is stains, [or] factors to be abandoned, which are of an unreal nature. Thus, ultimate reality is free from the two extremes:

- It transcends the extreme of nonexistence, or nihilism, because emptiness truly exists (*bden grub*).
- It transcends the extreme of existence, or permanence, because all phenomena comprising the duality of percept and perceiver (such as imagination) do not truly exist (*bden med*).

Conventional [phenomena] are simply delusive appearances, empty of any nature.
Dharmatā is unchanging, not empty of a nature.

That being the case, the conventional [phenomena of] percepts and perceivers are simply the manifestations of delusive appearances—they are not things that exist by way of their own natures. Thus, they are empty of any nature of their own. [Looking at this in the context of] a dichotomy between self and other, it is also not possible that a knowable object exists with a nature that is other [than its own]. Thus, since [conventional phenomena] are empty in all regards, they are not non-empty.

Primordial wisdom, which is dharmatā, exists originally by way of its own nature and never changes; therefore, it is *not* empty of a nature of its own, and it always exists.

[The Three Characteristics]

The imagined is nonexistent; the dependent exists conventionally.
The consummate does not exist conventionally but does exist ultimately.

You might wonder, did the sūtras not teach that even the dharmadhātu is empty? Generally speaking, it is empty, or emptiness, but that does not necessitate that it is empty of its own nature. Primordial wisdom [the dharmadhātu] is called "emptiness" because it is empty of all characteristics that are other than itself, that is, it is empty of all conceptual elaborations of percepts and perceivers.

Now [I will discuss] the three characteristics (*trilakṣhaṇa, mtshan nyid gsum*): the imagined (*parikalpita, kun brtags*), dependent (*paratantra, gzhan dbang*), and consummate (*pariniṣhpanna, yongs grub*).

Imagined [characteristics] are

- all non-entities (such as space);
- what appears as an object, such as a form manifesting to thought;
- the linking of names and their referents, where a name is taken to be its referent or a referent is mistakenly taken to be its name; and
- all perceived objects that are superimposed conceptually: outer and inner; end and middle; large and small; good and bad; directions; time; and so forth.

The dependent [characteristic] is mere consciousness that manifests as the entities of percept and perceiver, because it is an appearance that is governed by something other than itself, i.e., the habitual tendencies of ignorance.

The consummate [characteristic] is reflexive awareness, self-illuminating and free from conceptual elaborations. Synonyms for it are dharmatā, dharmadhātu, thusness, and the ultimate.

The dependent and imagined [characteristics] are equal in that they do not really exist (*bden par med*); equal in being delusive appearances; and equal in being conventionalities and false. It is necessary, however, to distinguish them in terms of their respective characteristics: imagined [characteristics] do not exist even on a conventional [level], whereas the dependent do exist conventionally. The consummate [characteristic] does not exist conventionally and does exist ultimately (*don dam du yod pa*), thus it really exists.

> **These three [characteristics] are imputedly existent, substantially existent, and existent without conceptual elaborations.**
> **They are the emptiness of the nonexistent, the emptiness of the existent, and the ultimate emptiness.**
> **They are the inherent absence of characteristics, the inherent absence of arising, and the ultimate inherent absence.**

The three characteristics [are discussed in the following three ways].

[Three Modes of Existence]

Imagined [characteristics] are imputedly existent (*btags pas yod pa*). Dependent [characteristics] are substantially existent (*rdzas su yod pa*). The consummate [characteristic] does not exist in [either of] those two [ways]—it exists without conceptual elaborations (*spros med du yod pa*).

[Three Modes of Emptiness]

Imagined [characteristics] are "the emptiness of the nonexistent" (*med pa'i stong nyid*). Dependent [characteristics] are "the emptiness of the existent" (*yod pa'i stong nyid*). The consummate [characteristic] is "ultimate emptiness" (*don dam stong nyid*).[836] The exalted [Maitreya in the *Ornament of the Mahāyāna Sūtras*] says:[837]

> Those who know the emptiness of the nonexistent,
> the emptiness of the existent,
> and natural emptiness
> are said to "know emptiness."

[Three Modes of Inherent Absence]

Imagined [characteristics] are the inherent absence of characteristics (*mtshan nyid ngo bo nyid med pa*).[838] Dependent [characteristics] are the inherent absence of arising (*skye ba ngo bo nyid med pa*).[839] The consummate [nature] is the ultimate inherent absence (*don dam ngo bo nyid med pa*).[840] [Vasubandhu's *Thirty Verses*] says:[841]

> Thinking of the three types of inherent absence
> of the three kinds of natures,
> it is taught that all phenomena have no nature.

[The Consummate Nature]

> **Consequently, [Shentong Proponents] assert that all knowable objects are pervaded by emptiness.**
> **They state that the consummate, in terms of its own nature, is not connected to conventional phenomena;**
> **it precludes the triad of definition, definiendum, and illustration;**
> **it is free from conceptual elaborations, permanent, partless, and omnipresent.**
> **Their presentations of all other [topics] accord with the Chittamātra.**

Consequently, this system asserts that all knowable objects are pervaded by emptiness and inherent absence. You may ask, "If the consummate [nature] is truly existent, does it exist as something that arises, abides, and ceases? Does it come or go? Change or disappear? Does it have spatial or temporal dimensions? Is it singular or is it a plurality?" It is none of those. If something were to have those [characteristics], it would follow that it does not really exist. This [consummate nature] has no connection to any such conventional phenomena: it is not something that arises, abides, and ceases, comes or goes. It is not singular nor is it a plurality; it is neither a cause nor a result. In terms of its own nature, it precludes the triad of definition, definiendum, and illustration. Since it is free from all conceptual elaborations, such as being something with spatial or temporal dimensions, [the consummate nature] is inherently permanent. Because it cannot be divided into discrete pieces, it is partless. Since it is the dharmatā of all phenomena, it is said to be omnipresent and all-pervading.[842]

[Shentong Proponents'] presentations of other [topics related to] ground, path, and result[843] are said for the most part to be in accord with the Chittamātra [system].

The Way [Shentong] Is Free from the Chittamātras' Defects [(2)]

The Proponents of False Images state that the entity of consciousness truly exists and
that it is an object of mind. This [Shentong system] asserts that primordial wisdom
truly exists; and yet, because it is not a conditioned phenomenon,
[their assertions about] the ultimate are free from the mistakes of the Realists.

The system known in Tibet as False Image Chittamātra states that the entity of the ālaya consciousness is truly existent; and consciousness, therefore, is an object of the intellect. Thus, they are [considered by others to be] Realists. This [Shentong] system asserts that the entity of primordial wisdom—which transcends consciousness and is free from all conceptual elaborations—truly exists. However, because this primordial wisdom beyond conceptual elaborations is not a conditioned phenomenon, they say that [their assertions about] ultimate reality are free from all the mistakes of the Realists.

An Explanation of the Ways that Rangtong and Shentong Differ and Other Points [(3)]

The Rangtong and Shentong [systems] do not differ over
the way that conventional [phenomena] are empty, nor do they disagree that the extremes of conceptual elaborations cease during meditative equipoise.
They differ over whether, as a convention, dharmatā exists during subsequent attainment or not,
and over whether primordial wisdom is truly established at the end of analysis or not.

[The Shentong system] asserts that [if] ultimate reality
were simply a nonimplicative negation, whereby its nature
is not established,
it would be an inanimate emptiness.
[Shentong Proponents] present [ultimate reality] as being
primordial wisdom empty of dualism, as being reflexive
awareness.
This is asserted to be the profound view linking the Sūtra
and Mantra [systems].

The two Madhyamaka [systems] renowned as Shentong and Rangtong do not differ in the way they determine all conventional phenomena to be empty, nor do they disagree that the extremes of conceptual elaborations cease during meditative equipoise. Nevertheless, they do differ in terms of the way they use conventional cognitive and verbal expressions during the subsequent state of attainment,[844] which is when philosophical tenet systems are distinguished. Simply as a conventional position, [Shentong Proponents] say that dharmatā or thusness exists, and [Rangtong Proponents] say that it does not exist. They also differ in their views of whether nondual primordial wisdom is truly established or not at the time of final analysis by means of reasonings that analyze for ultimacy.

Shentong Proponents, therefore, assert that imagined and dependent [characteristics] are conventionalities, and the consummate [characteristic] is ultimate reality. They also maintain that to view [ultimate reality] as being simply a nonimplicative negation, whereby its reality is not established, is [to regard ultimate reality as] an inanimate emptiness.[845] That is the way conventionalities are empty, but it is not the abiding nature of ultimate emptiness. Concisely put, that [ultimate] is primordial wisdom empty of the duality of percept and perceiver; it is intuitive reflexive awareness (*so so rang rig pa*). They state that since this way of presenting [the ultimate] is in complete harmony with the thought of the great tantras, it is the profound view linking the Sūtra and Mantra [systems], the pinnacle of Madhyamaka systems.

Now [we will look at] the summary of the essential points in the elimination of the extremes imputed by others [to the Shentong system] as presented by the exalted Tāranātha [in his *Essence of Shentong*]:[846]

There are those who quote the following passage from the *Descent into Laṅkā Sūtra*:[847]

> [Mahāmati] asked, "If sugatagarbha were to exist with its major and minor marks, would it not be similar to the self of [non-Buddhist] tīrthikas?"[848] [The Buddha] replied, "It is not similar because it is emptiness."

They say, "Sugatagarbha, therefore, does not really exist. If it had the major and minor marks and the like, this would be a tīrthika's system. The space-like complete absence of any existence is called sugatagarbha."

Such claims [limit] emptiness to mean the absence of reality and identify it as just the complete and utter absence of any existence. [Such ideas] belong to a flawed intellect that is attached to its inferior philosophical tenets. The sūtra states, as the reason why [sugatagarbha] is not similar to the tīrthikas' [self], that [sugatagarbha] is emptiness, but it does not say that [the reason it is not similar to the tīrthikas' self] is that it lacks the major and minor marks. Those who claim that sugatagarbha with its clearly evident and perfect major and minor marks is explained to be the provisional meaning are simply deceiving the world with their lies.

The statement that the assertion of [sugata]garbha as permanent belongs to the tīrthikas' systems again amounts to nothing more than a refutation of the sūtras on [sugata]garbha. It is not feasible to assert that the meaning of permanence [here] is the permanence of being continuous, because saṃsāra and all percepts and perceivers are the mere permanence of being continuous. Also, if the mere permanence of being continuous were sufficient [to qualify as] permanence, all conditioned phenomena would be permanent.

Some think, "[Sugatagarbha] is impermanent since first it has stains and later it becomes stainless." From the perspective of the dharmadhātu, it does not have stains at first, nor does it later become stainless. Nevertheless, the mode of having stains and becoming stainless is [simply something that appears] in relationship to the mindstreams of individuals. Thus, it is not the case that changes in the state of a sentient being result in changes to the state of dharmatā.

Others think, "It is not logical that the primordial wisdom of buddha[hood] exists within the mindstreams of sentient beings." This, however, contradicts the explicit statement [in the *Highest Continuum*]:[849]

> Because the primordial wisdom of buddha[hood] is present in all sentient beings . . .

Some say, "It is not feasible that the excellent qualities of buddha[hood] exist within the mindstreams of sentient beings. For example, if the strength of knowing what is the case and what is not the case[850] were to exist within the mindstreams of sentient beings, it would follow [absurdly] that sentient beings know what is the case and what is not the case." This statement is incorrect, because we do not say "Whatever is part of the mindstreams of sentient beings is buddha[hood]." If that were the consequence of saying that buddha[hood] and its excellent qualities reside in the mindstreams of sentient beings, would it also follow that when a buddha resides on a throne, the throne cognizes all knowable objects? Therefore, how could the mindstreams of sentient beings—that is, the eight modes of consciousness—be buddha[hood]? The buddha[hood] that resides [in the mindstreams of sentient beings] does not do so in the manner of a conventional support and something supported, [where buddhahood would be what is supported by a sentient being's mindstream]. It abides in the manner of being ultimate dharmatā.

Additional Topics: Recommendations [cc"]

Most Tibetan teachers say, "This system is Chittamātra,"
and regard Maitreya's texts and Asaṅga and his brother as inferior.
The sun and moon that ornament the sky of the Sage's teachings
are the scriptural traditions of the two chariot[-systems].

The judicious thing is to give up fixed positions in which one
repeatedly echoes the constellation[-like] minor texts,
and engage [these two systems] in an equal way.

Most earlier and later Tibetan teachers and some ordinary Indian paṇḍitas say, "This system is the Chittamātra philosophical tenet system," and thus they exclude it from the ranks of Madhyamaka. Many of them go further by conceitedly claiming to have fathomed the thought of the scholars [of this system], when [in fact] all they are doing is [simply] repeating [their own] exegetical system. By stating, "The exalted Maitreya's scriptural tradition and the noble Asaṅga and his brother are Chittamātra," they take them to be greatly inferior and the noble Nāgārjuna and others to be greatly superior. On the basis of that, they amass an infinite amount of the [bad] karma of rejecting the dharma.

What equal the sun and moon—which alone ornament the sky of the Sage's teachings—are none other than the scriptural traditions of the two great chariot[-systems].[851] Therefore, if we align ourselves with those, we will avoid repeatedly echoing the constellation-like minor texts of ordinary paṇḍitas, which involves devoting ourselves to the elaborations of refutations and proofs that rely on many spurious scriptures and reasonings. We will also avoid fixating on biased positions and providing limited explanations, the results of which will only bring ourselves and others into a pit of numerous faults. The supreme traditions of these two chariots do not contradict each other: one emphasizes outer principles, the other inner principles.[852] Therefore, the judicious thing to do is equally engage their points for study, reflection, and meditation.

The mahāpaṇḍita Shākya Chokden states:[853]

> Without the dharma system of the ālaya and the presentation
> of the three emptinesses
> found in the texts of Asaṅga's positions,
> how would we explain the bases for purification and the means
> of purifications,
> and the presentations of outer, inner, and other found in the
> texts of the great approach [i.e., the tantras]?
>
> Without [the explanations of] the way nondual primordial
> wisdom is empty of a nature

that are delineated by Prāsaṅgika and Svātantrika texts,
how would we give up taking profound and clear
primordial wisdom to be real
and our conceptual clinging to the sublime deities?

He also says:[854]

In this doctrine, there are two types of Madhyamaka:

(1) the ultimate essence of the definitive meaning of the texts of the exalted Maitreya; and

(2) the ultimate essence of the definitive meaning of the texts of the venerable Nāgārjuna.

(1) [The ultimate definitive meaning in Maitreya's teachings] is primordial wisdom, which is devoid of the duality of percepts and perceivers. The sources for this are [Maitreya's five Treatises:] the two *Ornaments*, two *Differentiations*, and *Highest Continuum Shāstra*. The *Differentiation of the Middle and the Extremes Shāstra* establishes this view as the Madhyamaka path, and the *Differentiation of Phenomena and Their Nature Shāstra* presents the stages by which the mind engages that [view and path].

(2) [The ultimate definitive meaning in Nāgārjuna's teachings] is a mere nonimplicative negation, which refutes all conceptually elaborated extremes. The sources for this are [Nāgārjuna's] Collection of Reasonings.[855] What is found in his Collection of Praises[856] is in keeping with Maitreya's Dharma Treatises.

Who were the establishing founders of these [systems]? The two: the venerable Nāgārjuna and the venerable Asaṅga. In what way were these established? As twofold: as the Rangtong system, which determines that both [conventional and ultimate] reality are empty of an essence; and as the Shentong system, which determines that only the nature of conventional [phenomena] is intrinsically empty (*rang stong*), and thereby eliminates conceptual elaborations concerning the ultimate.

Further, there are two [other systems]:

(1) the system of Āryavimuktisena[857] and Haribhadra,[858] which explains the thought of the *Ornament of Clear Realization* according to the Rangtong [perspective]; and

(2) the system of Abhayākaragupta[859] and Dharmapāla,[860] which explains the thought of [Nāgārjuna's] Collection of Reasonings according to the Shentong.

In sum, all four of these pioneering systems are equal in being Madhyamaka paths, because they are clearly stated to be Madhyamaka systems in the authentic scriptural traditions.

The Rangtong mode is explained to be the Madhyamaka path by masters who are Prāsaṅgika or Svātantrika proponents, because they explain emptiness in terms of the Rangtong-Madhyamaka, [following Nāgārjuna's] statement:[861]

Whatever is dependently arisen
is explained to be empty.
It is a dependent designation
and is itself the middle way.

The Shentong mode is asserted to be the Madhyamaka path by Asaṅga and his brother [Vasubandhu], because they assert emptiness in the Shentong style, [following the *Differentiation of the Middle and the Extremes*]:[862]

Since [imagination] exists, [duality] does not exist, and [imagination of what is unreal] exists [within emptiness, and emptiness within it],
this is the middle path.

In this regard, some in the Land of Snows [i.e., Tibet] think, "Madhyamaka, which is one of the four philosophical tenet systems, generally [consists of] the Prāsaṅgika and Svātantrika systems. [A system] superior to those could only be a path that is classified as Prāsaṅgika, since [the *Entrance to the Middle Way*] says:[863]

This profound and frightening suchness will definitely be realized by those who have previously familiarized themselves with it;

but others, even with their vast learning, will not be able to comprehend it.

[I will answer] that [by showing] the comparable application of [the opponent's reason] (*mgo mtshungs*) and the actual state of things (*rnal ma*).

First, [the comparable application of the opponent's reason]:

In that case, it would be [equally] reasonable to explain that the supreme type of Madhyamaka is only found in the Shentong mode, because the venerable Asaṅga explained it in that [way], and because he explained that the view of the Rangtong mode is a view of denial (*skur ba 'debs pa*) and a view for those of lesser acumen.[864] In this context of identifying the definitive meaning,[865] the venerable Asaṅga's scriptures are equally capable of negating or proving the same points that Chandrakīrti's scriptures are capable of negating or proving, because [the Buddha] prophesied that [Asaṅga] would be the master who would distinguish the provisional and definitive meanings in the sūtras. In brief, it is a matter of dispute who represents the Madhyamaka that is the pinnacle of the four systems of philosophical tenets propounded in the noble land [of India], because the Mahāyāna master Chandrakīrti did not explain the Shentong mode as Madhyamaka, and the noble Asaṅga—whose [stature] as a Mahāyāna master of the [Buddhist] doctrine is undisputed and unrivaled—explained that the Rangtong mode is not the scriptural tradition of the Madhyamaka.

Second, [the actual state of things]:

For explaining the thought of Nāgārjuna, the Rangtong exegetical system is superior; and for elucidating the thought of the exalted Maitreya, the Shentong mode is most profound. The scriptures and reasonings of one, therefore, are not able to negate the other.

If we do not look at it that way, we have [to regard] the venerable Asaṅga's scriptures and reasonings as predominant (*dbang btsan pa*), because he was prophesied as one who would attain the

> level of a noble being and delineate the definitive meaning, and he was [one of] the first founders of a system of the Mahāyāna. Chandrakīrti did explain that the venerable Asaṅga's exegetical style was not [in keeping with] the thought of Nāgārjuna, but he did not explain that the venerable Asaṅga had not internalized the meaning of Madhyamaka.

These masters [that is, Tāranātha and Shākya Chokden] make a distinction between Chittamātras and Proponents of Cognition (Vijñaptivādins), as is discussed in [*Distinguishing the*] *Two Modes* [and] *Establishing the Unity* [*of the Definitive Meaning*].[866] [The latter] states this in detail:

> The explanation that Proponents of Cognition (Vijñaptivādins) and Chittamātras are the same is derived from:
>
> (1) the confusion of the many Tibetans who accept that all [forms of] awareness and primordial wisdom are necessarily mind and mental events;
>
> (2) their mistake of not distinguishing primordial wisdom from consciousness; and
>
> (3) their failure to train properly in dharma terminology of the final teachings [of the Buddha, that is, the teachings of the third dharma wheel].
>
> You who assert that Proponents of Cognition (Vijñaptivādins) and Chittamātras are the same can understand that your position is not logical by simply reflecting on the meaning of passages that you chant, such as the following:
>
> From scriptures, [such as the *Differentiation of the Middle and the Extremes*]:[867]
>
> No phenomenon exists
> apart from the dharmadhātu.
>
> From sūtras, [such as the *Abhidharma Sūtra*]:[868]
>
> The expanse of beginningless time
> is the source of all phenomena.

From tantras, [the *Hevajra Tantra*]:[869]

> I pervade all these.
> [I] do not see another nature in beings.

Also from tantras:[870]

> Outside of the precious mind
> there are no buddhas or sentient beings.

> [When you reflect on] these sources, the expressions "dharmadhātu" and so on found in such scriptures must be explained as nondual primordial wisdom and the natural dharmakāya, because the scriptural traditions [of those texts] clearly state that.

This system of philosophical tenets is also called by the name "Madhyamaka" in the sūtras. The *Sūtra on Ultimate Emptiness* says:[871]

> The absence of one thing in something else is [that latter thing's] emptiness of that [first thing]. What remains there [i.e., emptiness] exists there. This is the middle path, the correct, unerring view about emptiness.

There are many such statements [in the sūtras]. The *Ornament of the Middle Way* states:[872]

> Therefore, forms and so forth are the mind itself;
> they are not asserted to be something external.
>
> On the basis of [knowing that appearances are] merely mind,
> know that external entities do not exist.
> On the basis of the mode [of reasoning explained] here,
> know that even that [mind] is utterly devoid of self-entity.

Nāgāmitra's *Entrance to the Three Kāyas* says:[873]

> The "middle path"
> is mere cognition.

If we analyze logically,
nothing else is feasible.

Ratnākarashānti's [*Instructions that*] *Ornament the Middle Way* begins:[874]

Here I will discuss the two truths
by means of the logic (*pramāṇa*) and scriptures
taught by Maitreya and Asaṅga
and presented by Nāgārjuna.

12. SECRET MANTRA-MADHYAMAKA

2" The Profound Madhyamaka of Secret Mantra [II.B.2.a.ii.bb.2'.b'.vi'.bb'.2"]

vii' A Synopsis of What Is Taught in All Madhyamaka [Systems]: Its Ground, Path, and Fruition [II.B.2.a.ii.bb.2'.b'.vii']

[This chapter presents] the second section [of the extensive explanation of the Madhyamaka system]: the profound Madhyamaka of Secret Mantra. [It concludes with the seventh topic of the explanation of the Madhyamaka system: a synopsis of what is taught in all Madhyamaka systems: its ground, path, and fruition.]

The Profound Madhyamaka of Secret Mantra [2"]

The Madhyamaka of the profound Mantra [approach] is the basic state of all phenomena.
It is natural luminosity distinguished by great bliss;
it is primordial wisdom, the union of clarity and emptiness, bliss and emptiness.
This is taught clearly in the *Five Stages,* Commentaries by Bodhisattvas, and other texts.

Since the Madhyamaka found in the approach of the profound Secret Mantra places a strong emphasis on nondual primordial wisdom, it is very much in harmony with Yogāchāra-Madhyamaka. This is because [Secret

Mantra] primarily ascertains and takes as its practice the nature of mind as it is taught extensively in the final wheel [of dharma], which is as follows: The nature of mind is natural luminosity, empty of all conceptual elaborations and characteristics. Its essence is that it is dharmatā-awareness, with the quality of being reflexive awareness. From the start, it is spontaneously present as the basic state of all phenomena.

This natural luminosity is distinguished by great bliss. It is emptiness (the letter E) and great compassion (the letter VAṂ).[875] It is primordial wisdom, which is the unification of clarity and emptiness, bliss and emptiness, and so forth. Since this subject is explained clearly and extensively in the *Five Stages*,[876] the Three Commentaries by Bodhisattvas,[877] and other texts, those texts should be consulted.

Here I will summarize [the key points of] a shared style of explanation. There are two points: Madhyamaka as it relates to the generation stage and Madhyamaka as it relates to the completion stage.[878]

Madhyamaka as It Relates to the Generation Stage

This has two modes:

(1) the mode [relating to] the ground for the creation of the deities; and

(2) the mode for the created deity to arise without conceptual elaborations.

(1) The Shentong mode of explanation [applies to how the deities] are created within nondual primordial wisdom, because [it clarifies how] the seed syllables and emblems that arise within emptiness are not beyond the primordial wisdom of the dharmadhātu.

(2) The way those created deities arise without conceptual elaborations is first ascertained by [being aware of the deities'] clarity and emptiness. Their clarity is the vivid appearance of the characteristics and attributes of the maṇḍalas of deities (the support and supported).[879] Their emptiness is that we do not cling to them in any way nor do we conceptualize them as anything, because if we fixate on the characteristics of those vivid appearances we will not transcend saṃsāra.

The mere cessation of concepts may be considered nirvāṇa, but it is not the transcendence of all flaws, because one has not reached the state of unification.[880] Therefore, we practice by unifying [clarity and emptiness]:

while the appearances of the deities are vivid, they are empty; while they are empty, they appear clearly. This is the unification of clarity and emptiness. In the key instructions, it is called "the inseparability of saṃsāra and nirvāṇa." In this context, objects manifest as the unification of appearances and emptiness, and cognition as the unification of clarity and emptiness. During the subsequent state of attainment,[881] which occurs when we arise from that [samādhi], we maintain the pride of being the deity and, therefore, we are engaged in a yoga with characteristics.

Madhyamaka as It Relates to the Completion Stage

This has two aspects:

(1) abandoning all fixations to the generation stage; and
(2) the actual completion-stage primordial wisdom.

(1) [The first aspect of the completion stage is] to gather [i.e., dissolve] the entire maṇḍala, both support and supported, using either a process of "grasping the whole" or "successive destruction,"[882] and then rest in a state without any reference points. [During] this [phase], the Rangtong mode[883] is the best for stopping the elaborations of thoughts. However, because it is not taught that [resting without reference points] is what is experienced by reflexively aware primordial wisdom, [simply resting without reference points] is not [the practice of] the actual completion-stage primordial wisdom.

(2) The actual primordial wisdom of the completion stage [is discussed] in terms of what is to be experienced in practice, the methods that bring about that experience, and the process by which [primordial wisdom] becomes fully manifest.

- What is to be experienced is the primordial wisdom of connate great bliss, which is reflexive awareness.[884]
- The means of experience are the stages of self-blessing[885] and reflexively aware primordial wisdom.
- [The actual completion-stage primordial wisdom] is nonconceptual, unmistaken primordial wisdom, and thus it is the view free from flaws. Nevertheless, at first when [primordial wisdom] simply manifests, one has not arrived at the bhūmis of noble beings, because [wisdom at this point] is simply illustrative primordial wisdom, which points [to the actual wisdom]. This is also called the "primordial wisdom of unified

bliss and emptiness" and the "connate primordial wisdom of melting bliss."[886]

I have presented this topic from the perspective of the shared abridged tantras (*laghu-tantra, bsdus rgyud*). For the distinctive and profound key points that correlate to the unique view of the *Kālachakra Tantra,* one must look elsewhere.

It is taught that the distinction between Sūtra-Madhyamaka and Mantra-Madhyamaka is based on their differences with regard to the subjective agent, that is, the qualities of their realizations; they do not differ in terms of the object [of their realization]: freedom from conceptual elaborations.[887]

A Synopsis of What Is Taught in All Madhyamaka [Systems]: Its Ground, Path, and Fruition[888] [vii']

As its ground, [Madhyamaka] does not denigrate
conventionalities just as they appear,
and it is free from conceptually elaborated extremes
regarding the abiding nature.
Its path is to relinquish the apprehension of characteristics
through profound wisdom,
and to amass merit for the sake of others out of compassion.

Its result is the perfection of the dharmakāya, a state
of peace,
and that the form kāyas nonconceptually benefit others.
These [three points] contain all that is taught in
Madhyamaka.

Everything that is taught in all the Madhyamaka systems is summarized by the following: Since [all Madhyamaka systems] do not denigrate conventionalities (*saṃvṛiti, kun rdzob*) just as they appear, they are free from the extreme of nihilism. Since they are free from any conceptually elaborated extremes regarding the ultimate abiding nature (*don dam pa'i gnas lugs*), they are liberated from the extreme of permanence. This is ground Madhyamaka: the union of the two truths.

[Mādhyamikas] are free from the extreme of permanence because, owing to their wisdom, they do not apprehend phenomena in terms of characteristics [that is, they do not reify phenomena in any way]. They are free from the extreme of nihilism because, out of compassion, they amass vast stores [of merit, which enable] them to benefit others. This is path Madhyamaka: the union of the two stores [i.e., primordial wisdom and merit].

[Mādhyamikas] are free from the extreme of permanence because they attain the dharmakāya, the state in which all conceptually elaborated characteristics have been pacified. They are free from the extreme of nihilism because their two form kāyas [that is, the sambhogakāya and nirmāṇakāya] benefit all those to be trained, both high and low, until saṃsāra is emptied. This is resultant Madhyamaka: the union of the two kāyas.

The point of all that is taught in the Madhyamaka is contained within these three [ground, path, and fruition].

This completes the explanation of the third part [of Book Six]: A Systematic Presentation of the Cause-Based Philosophical Vehicles.

APPENDIX: OUTLINE OF THE TEXT

GLOSSARY

English (or Sanskrit)	Sanskrit	Tibetan
abandonment, relinquishment	prahāṇa, prahīṇatva	spangs pa
abider in the result of a nonreturner		phyir mi 'ong 'bras gnas
abider in the result of a once returner		lan cig phyir 'ong 'bras gnas
abider in the result of a stream enterer		rgyun gzhugs 'bras gnas
abider in the result of an arhat		dgra bcom 'bras gnas
absence of a self of persons	pudgalanairātmya	gang zag gi bdag med
absence of a self-entity of phenomena	dharmanairātmya	chos kyi bdag med
absence of characteristics	animitta	mtshan ma med pa
absence of expectancy	apraṇihita	smon pa med pa
absence of nature		rang bzhin med pa
absence of reality, not really existing, not truly existing		bden med
absorption of cessation	nirodhasamāpatti	'gog snyoms
acceptance of phenomena	dharmakṣhānti	chos bzod
action	karma	las
actions that are intentions	chetanākarma	sems pa'i las
actions that are the results of intentions	chetayitvā karma	bsam pa'i las

ENGLISH (OR SANSKRIT)	SANSKRIT	TIBETAN
adventitious		glo bur
affirmation	viddhi	sgrub pa
afflictive mind	klishṭamana	nyon yid
afflictive obscuration	kleshāvaraṇa	nyon mongs pa'i sgrib pa
afflictive origins [of suffering]		nyon mongs kun 'byung
afflictive phenomena	saṃklesha	kun nas nyon mongs pa
aggregate	skandha	'phung po
Akanishṭha (Highest or Below None)	akanishṭha	'og min
ālaya consciousness	ālayavijñāna	kun gzhi'i rnam shes
analytical cessations	pratisaṃkhyānirodha	so sor brtags pas 'gog pa
appearance for others		gzhan snang
approacher to the result of a nonreturner		phyir mi 'ong zhugs pa
approacher to the result of a once returner		lan cig phyir 'ong zhugs pa
approacher to the result of a stream enterer		rgyun zhugs zhugs pa
approacher to the result of an arhat		dgra bcom zhugs pa
appropriated aggregates	upādānaskandha	nyer len gyi phung po
appropriating consciousness	ādānavijñāna	len pa'i rnam shes
arhat	arhat	dgra bcom pa
ascetic practices	dhūta guṇāḥ	sbyangs pa'i yon tan
aspect, image	ākāra	rnam pa
attainment	prāpti	thob pa
basis	mūla	gzhi
basis for the classification		dbye gzhi
basis for the definition, illustration		mtshan gzhi
bhūmi (level or ground)	bhūmi	sa
Brahmā Type	brahmakāyika	tshangs ris

English (or Sanskrit)	Sanskrit	Tibetan
buddha nature	tathāgatagarbha	de bzhin gshegs pa'i snying po
[Buddha's] words	vachana	bka'
capable of performing a function	arthakriyāsamartham	don byed nus pa
causal condition	hetupratyaya	rgyu'i rkyen
cause	hetu, kāraṇa	rgyu
cause-based yāna		rgyu'i theg pa
cessation	nirodha	'gog pa
Cha		chva
chakravartin (wheel-wielding monarch)	chakravartin	'khor lo sgyur ba
characteristic, definition, defining characteristic	lakṣhaṇa	mtshan nyid
Chittamātra (Mere Mind, Mind-Only, or Mere Mentalism)	*chittamātra	sems tsam pa
cognition		shes pa, rnam rig, shes rig
cognitive obscuration	jñeyāvaraṇa	shes bya'i sgrib pa
collection of scriptures	piṭaka	sde snod
common consensus, what is commonly acknowledged, worldly consensus	lokaprasiddha	'jig rten grags pa
common locus	samānādhikaraṇa	gzhi mthun
comparable application of the [opponent's] reason	*tulyahetu	rgyu mtshan mtshungs pa'i mgo snyoms
conceptual elaboration	prapañcha	spros pa
concordant example		mthun dpe
condition	pratyaya	rkyen
conditioned [phenomena]	saṃskṛita	'dus byas
congregating practitioner	vargachārin	tshogs spyod, tshogs shing spyod pa
congruent aspect		mtshungs ldan

English (or Sanskrit)	Sanskrit	Tibetan
consciousness	vijñāna	rnam shes
consequence	prasaṅga	thal 'gyur
consequence that exposes the [opponent's] contradictions	*virodhachodanā prasaṅga	'gal ba brjod pa'i thal 'gyur
constituent	dhātu	khams
consummate characteristic	parinişhpannalakşhaṇa	yongs su grub pa'i mtshan nyid, yongs grub
convention, conventional expression, [pragmatic] convention	vyavahāra	tha snyad
conventional reality	saṃvṛitisatya	kun rdzob bden pa
conventionality	saṃvṛiti	kun rdzob
conventions that are suitable for common consensus		grags rung gi tha snyad
correct conventionality		yang dag kun rdzob
defiled, degenerative	sāsrava	zag bcas
definite release	niryāṇam, niryā	nges 'byung
definition, defining characteristic, characteristic	lakşhaṇa	mtshan nyid
definitive excellence	niḥshreyasa	nges legs
definitive meaning	nītārtha	nges don
[demonstration to the opponent of] the irrelevance of proofs that are equivalent to the probandum	*sādhyasādhana-samāsiddha	sgrub byed bsgrub bya dang mtshungs pa'i ma grub pa
denial	apavāda	skur 'debs
dependent characteristic	paratantralakşhaṇa	gzhan gyi dbang gi mtshan nyid, gzhan dbang
dependent origination	pratītyasamutpāda	rten cing 'brel bar 'byung ba
determination, what is determined, [positive] determination	pariccheda	yongs gcod

English (or Sanskrit)	Sanskrit	Tibetan
Dharma Treatises of Maitreya		byams pa'i chos sde
dharmadhātu	dharmadhātu	chos dbyings
dharmakāya	dharmakāya	chos kyi sku
dharmatā (reality)	dharmatā	chos nyid
direct perception	pratyakṣha	mngon sum
direct perceptual valid cognition	pratyakṣhapramāṇa	mngon sum tshad ma
discrete, separate		tha dad pa
disintegration		zhig pa
dominant condition	adhipatipratyaya	bdag rkyen
dominant result	adhipatiphala	bdag po'i 'bras bu
dualistic appearance		gnyis snang
eight great, uncommon theses		thun mong ma yin pa'i dam bca' chen po brgyad
elder	sthavira	gnas brtan
element-derivative	bhautika	'byung 'gyur
elevated state	abhyudaya	mngon mtho
emptiness	shūnyatā	stong pa nyid
emptiness of the existent		yod pa'i stong nyid
emptiness of the nonexistent		med pa'i stong nyid
empty of reality		bden stong
enabling cause	karaṇahetu	byed rgyu
engagement through belief	adhimukticharyā	mos pas spyod pa
entailment	vyāpti	khyab pa
entity	bhāva, vastu	dngos po
essence, inherent nature, nature	svabhāva	ngo bo
established through the power of [a relationship to real] things	*vastubalapravṛitta	dngos stobs kyis grub pa, dngos po stobs zhugs kyis grub pa
ethical conduct	shīla	tshul khrims
etymology	nirukti	nges tshig

English (or Sanskrit)	**Sanskrit**	**Tibetan**
evidence, reason	liṅga	rtags
excellent quality, virtue	guṇa	yon tan
exclusion	viccheda	rnam bcad
exist in reality		bden par yod
exist ultimately		don dam du yod pa
existence of things by way of their own specific characteristics	lakṣhaṇasiddha	rang mtshan kyis grub pa
external referent	bāhyārtha	phyi don
extreme of nihilism	ucchedānta	chad mtha'
extreme of permanence	shāshvatānta	rtag mtha'
extrinsically empty, empty of what is extrinsic		gzhan stong
faculty	indriya	dbang po
final phase of cyclic existence	charamabhavika	srid pa tha ma pa
final ultimate		mthar thug gi don dam
five acts of immediate consequence	pañchānām ānantaryāṇām	mtshams med lnga
five secondary acts of immediate consequence		nye ba'i mtshams med pa lnga
floaters (*muscae volitantes*)	kesha, keshoṇḍuka	skra shad ['dzag pa]
form kāya	rūpakāya	gzugs sku
form, matter, visible form	rūpa	gzugs
formative force	saṃskāra	'du byed
formative force not associated [with forms or mind], non-associated formative force	viprayuktasaṃskāra	ldan min 'du byed
four possibilities	chatuṣhkoṭi	mu bzhi
four spheres of the form-less realms		gzugs med skye mched mu bzhi
four truths of noble beings	chaturāryasatya	'phags pa'i bden pa bzhi

English (or Sanskrit)	Sanskrit	Tibetan
free from conceptual elaborations	niṣhprapañcha	spros bral
fundamental mind		rtsa ba'i sems
Great Madhyamaka		dbu ma chen po
habitual tendency	vāsanā	bag chags
Hedonists (Materialists)	lokāyata	['jig rten] rgyang 'phen pa
heterologous set	vipakṣha	mi mthun phyogs
homologous set	sapakṣha	mthun phyogs
ignorance	avidyā	ma rig pa
illusion	māyā	sgyu ma
illustration		mtshan gzhi
image, aspect	ākāra	rnam pa
imagination of what is unreal	abhūtaparikalpa	yang dag min rtog, yang dag pa ma yin pa'i kun tu rtog pa
imagined [characteristic] devoid of any characteristics		mtshan nyid chad pa'i kun brtags
imagined characteristic	parikalpitalakṣhaṇa	kun tu brtags pa'i mtshan nyid, kun brtags
impetus and completion		'phen rdzogs
implicative negation	paryudāsapratiṣhedha	ma yin dgag
impure dependent [characteristic]		ma dag gzhan dbang
imputedly existent	prajñāptisat	btags pas yod pa, btags yod
incalculable aeon	asaṃkhyeya-kalpa	bskal pa grangs med pa
independently [verifiable]	svatantra	rang rgyud, rang dbang
individual liberation	prātimokṣha	so so thar pa
inexplicable self [or person]	*avaktavya pudgala	brjod du med pa'i bdag, brjod med kyi bdag
inference based on what is commonly acknowledged by others	*paraprasiddhānumāṇa	gzhan la grags pa'i rjes dpag

ENGLISH (OR SANSKRIT)	SANSKRIT	TIBETAN
inferential valid cognition	anumāṇapramāṇa	rjes dpag tshad ma
inherent absence	niḥsvabhāva	ngo bo nyid med pa
inherent absence of arising		skye ba ngo bo nyid med pa
inherent absence of characteristics		mtshan nyid ngo bo nyid med pa
inherent nature	svabhāva	ngo bo nyid
intellect, mind	buddhi	blo
intention, thought		bsam pa, dgongs pa
intrinsically empty, empty of self		rang stong
intuitive reflexive awareness	pratyātmavedanīya	so so rang rig
Īshvara	īshvara	dbang phyug
isolate	vyatireka	ldog pa
karma, action	karma	las
karma related to shared appearances		snang 'gyur thun mong ba'i las
karma related to unshared experiences		myong 'gyur thun mong min pa'i las
karmic origins [of suffering]		las kyi kun 'byung
karmic path	karmapatha	las kyi lam
knowable object	jñeya	shes bya
knowledge of phenomena	dharmajñāna	chos shes
knowledge of the exhaustion [of defilements] and the knowledge of their [subsequent] nonarising	kṣhayānutpattijñāna	zad (dang) mi skye shes pa
liberation	vimukti, mokṣha	rnam grol, thar pa
Mādhyamika Proponent of the Absence of a Nature	niḥsvabhāvavādin mādhyamika	ngo bo nyid med par smra ba'i dbu ma pa
Mādhyamika Who Employs Worldly Consensus	lokaprasiddhi mādhyamika	'jig rten grags sde spyod pa'i dbu ma pa

English (or Sanskrit)	Sanskrit	Tibetan
Mādhyamika with Certainty about the Ultimate		don dam rnam par nges pa'i dbu ma pa
Mādhyamikas (Those of the Middle or Centrists)	mādhyamika	dbu ma pa
Mahāsāṅghika (Majority of the Community)	mahāsāṅghika	dge 'dun phal chen pa
matter		bem po
matured result	vipākaphala	rnam smin gyi 'bras bu
meditative concentration	dhyāna	bsam gtan
mental affliction	klesha	nyon mongs
mental event	chaitta	sems byung
mere cognition	vijñaptimātra	rnam rig tsam
mere conventionality	saṃvṛitimātra	kun rdzob tsam
method	upāya	thabs
mind	chitta	sems
minute particle	paramāṇu	rdul phra rab
mistaken conventionality		log pa'i kun rdzob
moment	kṣhaṇa	skad cig
Mother of the Victors		rgyal ba'i yum
Mūlasarvāstivādin (Proponent of the Existence of All Bases)	mūlasarvāstivādin	gzhi thams cad yod par smra ba
nāga (water-dwelling animal or spirit)	nāga	klu
nature	svabhāva	rang bzhin, ngo bo
negating reason		dgag rtags
negative entailment	vyatirekavyāpti	ldog khyab
negative propensity	dauṣhṭhulya	gnas ngan len pa
Nirgranthas (Those Freed from Bondage)	nirgrantha	gcer bu pa ("naked ones")
nirmāṇakāya	nirmāṇakāya	sprul pa'i sku
nominal imagined [characteristics]		rnam grangs pa'i kun brtags
nominal ultimate	paryāyaparamārtha	rnam grangs pa'i don dam

English (or Sanskrit)	Sanskrit	Tibetan
nonabiding nirvāṇa	apratiṣhṭitanirvāṇa	mi gnas pa'i mya ngan las 'das pa
nonanalytical cessation	apratisaṃkhyānirodha	so sor brtags pa ma yin pa'i 'gog pa
nondual primordial wisdom	advayajñāna	gnyis med ye shes
nonentity	abhāva, avastu	dngos med
nonexistents vividly appearing		med pa gsal snang
nonimplicative negation	prasajyapratiṣhedha	med dgag
nonimplicative negation that excludes [the possibility that the subject] does not possess [the quality of emptiness]		mi ldan rnam gcod kyi med dgag
non-nominal ultimate	aparyāyaparamārtha	rnam grang ma yin pa'i don dam
Non-Pluralist		sna tshogs gnyis med pa
nonreturner	anāgāmin	phyir mi 'ong ba
not really existing, not truly existing, absence of reality		bden med
object condition	ālambanapratyaya	dmigs rkyen
object of comprehension	prameya, meya	gzhal bya
object to be negated	pratiṣhedhya	dgag bya
object-consistent consciousnesses		shes rig don mthun
object-universal	arthasāmānya	don spyi
observed object	ālambana	dmigs pa
once returner	sakṛid-āgāmin	lan cig phyir 'ong ba
order	nikāya	sde pa
other-awareness, awareness of something other	*anyavedana	gzhan rig
other-exclusion	anyāpoha	gzhan sel
pāramitā (perfection)	pāramitā	pha rol tu phyin pa
particle	aṇu, paramāṇu	rdul phran
partless particle		rdul phran cha med
path	mārga	lam

English (or Sanskrit)	**Sanskrit**	**Tibetan**
path beyond training	ashaikṣhamārga	mi slob pa'i lam
path of accumulation	saṃbhāramārga	tshogs lam
path of junction	prayogamārga	sbyor lam
path of meditation	bhāvanāmārga	sgom lam
path of seeing	darshanamārga	mthong lam
peace	shānta	zhi ba
perceived image, perceived aspect	grāhyākāra	zung cha'i rnam pa
perceiver	graha(na)	'dzin pa
perceiving aspect	grāhakākāra	'dzin cha'i rnam pa
percept, perceived object	grāhya	gzung ba
person	pudgala	gang zag
phenomenon	dharma	chos
philosophical tenet system, philosophy, doxography	siddhānta	grub mtha'
Pinnacle of Existence	bhavāgra	srid pa'i rtse mo
Pishācha	pishācha	sha za'i skad
position	prakṣha	phyogs
positive entailment	anvayavyāpti	rjes khyab
potency, potential		nus pa
power of [real] things		dngos stobs
Prakṛit	prakṛit, prakṛita	rang bzhin gyi skad
Prāsaṅgika (Consequentialist or Apagogist)	*prāsaṅgika	thal 'gyur pa
pratyekabuddha (self [-realized] buddha)	pratyekabuddha	rang sangs rgyas
primal matter	prakṛiti	rang bzhin
primordial wisdom	jñāna	ye shes
principal substance	pradhāna	gtso bo
probandum	sādhya	bsgrub bya
probative reason		sgrub byed kyi rtan tshig
profound	gāmbhīrya	zab pa
proof of a convention		tha snyad sgrub pa
proof of a fact		don sgrub pa

English (or Sanskrit)	Sanskrit	Tibetan
Proponent of Cognition	vijñaptivādin, vijñaptika	rnam rig smra ba
Proponent of Complete Nonabiding		rab tu mi gnas par smra ba
Proponent of Consciousness	vijñānavādin	rnam shes smra ba
Proponent of False Images	alīkākāravādin	rnam rdzun pa
Proponent of Illusionlike Nonduality	māyopamādvayavādin	sgyu ma ltar gnyis med du smra ba
Proponent of Images	sākāravādin	rnam pa dang bcas pa
Proponent of Nonexistent Images	nirākāravādin	rnam med pa
Proponent of Non-Staining False Images	nirmala-alīkākāra	rnam rdzun dri med pa
Proponent of Perceptual Parity		gzung 'dzin grangs mnyam pa
Proponent of Real Images	satyākāravādin	rnam bden pa
Proponent of Staining False Images	samala-alīkākāra	rnam rdzun dri bcas pa
Proponent of the Absence of a Nature	niḥsvabhāvavādin	ngo bo nyid med par smra ba
Proponent of the Complete Nonabiding of All Phenomena	sarvadharmāpratiṣhṭhāna-vādin	chos thams cad rab tu mi gnas par smra ba
proposition, thesis	pratijñā	dam bca'
provisional meaning	neyārtha	drang don
proximate condition	samanantarapratyaya	de ma thag rkyen
pure dependent [characteristic]		dag pa gzhan dbang
purified phenomena	vyavadāna	rnam par byang ba
Rangtong (Intrinsic Emptiness, or Empty-of-Self)		rang stong
rational mind		rigs shes
real entity		bden pa'i dngos po
Realist	vastusatpadārthavādin	dngos por smra ba, dngos po yod par smra ba

English (or Sanskrit)	Sanskrit	Tibetan
reality, real, true existence	satya	bden pa
really exist, truly exist		bden par yod
reason	hetu, nimitta	rgyu mtshan
reason of the imperception of something connected [to the predicate of the negandum]	saṃbhandhānupalabdhi-hetu	'brel zla ma dmigs pa'i gtan tshigs
reason of the perception of something contradictory [to the predicate of the negandum]	viruddhopalabdhihetu	'gal zla dmigs pa'i gtan tshigs
reason, evidence	liṅga	rtags
reason, reasoning	hetu	gtan tshigs
reasoning	nyāya, yukti	rigs pa
reasoning of dependent origination	pratītyasamutpādanyāya	rten 'brel gyi rigs pa
reasoning that [demonstrates that a phenomenon] is neither a single unit nor a plurality	ekānekaviyogahetu	gcig du bral gyi gtan tshigs
reasoning that negates arising from the four extremes		mtha' bzhi skye 'gog gi gtan tshig
reasoning that negates the arising of [a result] existent [at the time of its cause] and the arising of [a result that is] nonexistent [at the time of its cause]	*satasatutpādapratiṣhe-dhahetu	yod med skye 'gog gi gtan tshigs
reasoning that refutes arising from the four possibilities	chatuṣhkoṭyutpāda-pratiṣhedhahetu	mu bzhi skye 'gog gi gtan tshigs
referent, object	artha	don
reflexive awareness	svasaṃvedana, svasaṃvitti	rang rig
reification		dngos por zhen pa
relinquishment, abandonment	prahāṇa, prahīṇatva	spangs pa

English (or Sanskrit)	Sanskrit	Tibetan
result that corresponds to its cause	niṣhyandaphala	rgyu mthun gyi 'bras bu
result-based yāna		'bras bu'i theg pa
rhinoceros-like	khaḍgaviṣhāṇakalpa	bse ru lta bu
samādhi in which [appearances are seen to be] illusion-like		sgyu ma lta bu'i ting nge 'dzin
sambhogakāya	sambhogakāya	longs spyod rdzogs pa'i sku
sameness and discreteness		gcig dang tha dad
Sāṃkhya (Calculator or Enumerator)	sāṃkhya	grangs can pa
Saṃmitīya (Follower of Mahāsammata)	saṃmitīya	mang pos bkur ba
Sautrāntika (Sūtra-follower)	sautrāntika	mdo sde pa
Sautrāntika-[Svātantrika] Mādhyamika (Middle Way Proponent [of Independently Verifiable Reasons] Who [Accords with] Followers of the Sūtras)	*sautrāntika-[svātantrika-] mādhyamika	mdo sde spyod pa'i dbu ma [rang rgyud] pa
Sautrāntika-Mādhyamika (Middle Way Proponent Who [Accords with] Followers of the Sūtras)	*sautrāntika-mādhyamika	mdo sde spyod pa'i dbu ma
Secret Mantra		gsang sngags
self of persons	pudgalātman	gang zag gi bdag
self, self-entity	ātman	bdag
self-entity of phenomena	dharmātman	chos kyi bdag
self-illuminating		rang gsal
sense sphere	āyatana	skye mched
separate, discrete		tha dad pa
sevenfold reasoning [using the analogy of] a chariot		shing rta rnam bdun gyi rigs pa

ENGLISH (OR SANSKRIT)	SANSKRIT	TIBETAN
Shentong (Extrinsic Emptiness or Empty-of-Other)		gzhan stong
shrāvaka (hearer)	shrāvaka	nyan thos
simply a name and [only] imputedly existent		ming rkyang btags yod
skipping type		thod rgal ba
something cognizable	vijñapti	rnam pa(r) rig byed
space	ākāsha	nam mkha'
Split-Eggist		sgo nga phyed tshal pa
stable karma		mi g.yo ba'i las
Sthavira (Elder or Firm Abider)	sthavira	gnas brtan pa
stores of merit and wisdom		bsod nams dang ye shes kyi tshogs
stream enterer	srota-āpanna	rgyun zhugs pa
subject (of debate), that which bears reality, something possessing a quality	dharmin	chos can
subject property	pakṣhadharmatā/-tva	phyogs chos
subsequent acceptance	anvayakṣhānti	rjes bzod
subsequent knowledge	anvayajñāna	rjes shes
subsequent state of attainment	pṛiṣhṭhalabdha	rjes thob
substance of cognition		shes rig gi rdzas
substance of separation	visaṃyogadravya	bral ba'i rdzas
substantial cause	upādānakāraṇa	nyer len gyi rgyu
substantially established	dravyasiddha	rdzas su grub pa
substantially existent	dravyasat	rdzas su yod pa
substantially existent in the sense of being self-sufficient		rang rkya thub pa'i rdzas yod
subtle proliferator	anushaya	phra rgyas
suchness	tattva	de kho na nyid

English (or Sanskrit)	Sanskrit	Tibetan
suffering of change	vipariṇāmaduḥkhatā	'gyur ba'i sdug bsngal
suffering of conditioned existence	saṃskāraduḥkhatā	'du byed kyi sdug bsngal
suffering of suffering	duḥkhaduḥkhatā	sdug bsngal gyi sdug bsngal
sugatagarbha (heart of those gone to bliss)	sugatagarbha	bde bar gshegs pa'i snying po
supercognitive ability	abhijñatva	mngon par shes pa
superimposition	samāropa	sgro 'dogs
Svātantrikas (Those [Who Use] Independently [Verifiable Reasons] or Autonomists)	*svātantrika	rang rgyud pa
tathāgata (thus-gone-one)	tathāgata	de bzhin gshegs pa
that which bears a state		gnas skabs can
that which bears reality, something possessing a quality, subject (of debate)	dharmin	chos can
that which has the shape		dbyibs can
that which is the collection		tshogs pa can
thesis, proposition	pratijñā	dam bca'
thought, intention		bsam pa, dgongs pa
three characteristics	trilakṣhaṇa	mtshan nyid gsum
three collections of scripture	tripiṭaka	sde snod gsum
three doors to liberation	vimokṣhamukhatraya	rnam thar sgo gsum
three modes or criteria	trairūpya, trirūpa	tshul gsum
three natures	trisvabhāva	rang bzhin gsum
three spheres	trimaṇḍala	'khor gsum
thusness	tathātā	de bzhin nyid
tīrthika ("forder")	tīrthika	mu stegs pa
to arise, to come into being		skye ba
to take things to be real	*satyagrahaṇa	bden 'dzin

English (or Sanskrit)	**Sanskrit**	**Tibetan**
training in ethical conduct	shilashikṣhā	tshul khrims kyi bslab pa
training in higher concentration	adhichittaṃshikṣhā	lhag pa'i sems kyi bslab pa
training in samādhi	samādhishikṣhā	ting nge 'dzin gyi bslab pa
training in wisdom	prajñāshikṣhā	shes rab kyi bslab pa
transformation, complete transformation	āshrayaparivṛitti	gnas gyur, gnas yongs su gyur pa
treatise	shāstra	bstan bcos
true existence, reality, real	satya	bden pa
truly exist, really exist		bden par grub pa
truth of cessation	nirodhasatya	'gog pa'i bden pa
truth of origins	samudayasatya	kun 'byung gi bden pa
truth of suffering	duḥkhasatya	sdug bsngal gyi bden pa
truth of the path	mārgasatya	lam gyi bden pa
ultimate abiding nature		don dam pa'i gnas lugs
ultimate emptiness		don dam stong nyid
ultimate reality	paramārthasatya	don dam bden pa
unafflicted ignorance	akliṣhṭāvidyā	nyon mongs pa can ma yin pa'i ma rig pa
unchanging consummate [characteristic]	nirvikārapariniṣhpanna	'gyur med yongs grub
unconditioned phenomena	asaṃskṛita	'dus ma byas
undeceiving	avisaṃvādi	mi bslu ba
undefiled phenomena	anāsravadharma	zag pa med pa'i chos
unerring consummate [characteristic]	aviparyāsapariniṣhpanna	phyin ci ma log pa'i yongs grub
unique qualities of a buddha		sangs rgyas kyi chos ma 'dres pa
Unpleasant Sound	kuru	sgra mi snyan
upper robe	saṅghāṭī	snam sbyar
Vaibhāṣhika (Proponent of the [*Great*] *Exposition*)	vaibhāṣhika	bye brag smra ba

English (or Sanskrit)	Sanskrit	Tibetan
vajra sliver reasoning	vajrakaṇahetu	rdo rje gzegs ma'i gtan tshigs
valid cognition, valid form of cognition, valid authority	pramāṇa	tshad ma
valid form of cognition that functions by virtue of [its relationship to real] things	vastubalapravṛittān-umāna	dngos po stobs zhugs kyi tshad ma
vehicle	yāna	theg pa
view	dṛiṣhṭi	lta ba
vows of individual liberation	prātimokṣha	so sor thar pa'i sdom pa
what completes the act		rdzogs byed
what is determined, a determination, [positive] determination	pariccheda	yongs gcod
wisdom	prajñā	shes rab
with remainder	sheṣha	lhag bcas
without remainder	asheṣha	lhag med
worldly conventionality		'jig rten kun rdzob
yāna (vehicle or approach)	yāna	theg pa
Yogāchāra (Yoga Practitioner, Yoga Practice)	yogāchāra	rnal 'byor spyod pa
Yogāchāra-[Svātantrika] Mādhyamika (Middle Way Proponent [of Independently Verifiable Reasons] Who [Accords with] Yoga Practitioners)	*yogāchāra-[svātantrika] mādhyamika	rnal 'byor spyod pa'i dbu ma [rang rgyud] pa
Yogāchāra-Mādhyamika	*yogāchāra-mādhyamika	rnal 'byor spyod pa'i dbu ma pa
yogic conventionality		rnal 'byor kun rdzob

ENDNOTES

ABBREVIATIONS

ACIP	Electronic files of the Asian Classics Input Project (www.acip.org)
ALTG	Āchārya Lama Tenpa Gyaltsen (oral communications to the translator, 2003–2006).
ALTG notes	Notes on the Rangtong-Madhyamaka section compiled by Āchārya Lama Tenpa Gyaltsen for private tutoring, 2005.
Dg.K.	sDe-dge Black bKa'-'gyur: a reprint of a print from the Sde dge blocks originally edited by Si-tu Chos-kyi-'byung-gnas. Chengdu, China, 1999-.
Dg.T. Beijing	The collated sDe dge edition of the bsTan 'gyur. Beijing: Krung go'i bod kyi shes rig dpe skrun khang, 1995–2005.
Dharma	*Nyingma Edition of the sDe-dge bKa'-'gyur and bsTan-'gyur: Research Catalogue and Bibliography*. 8 vols. Oakland, CA: Dharma Press, 1980.
GTCD	Zhang, Yisun et al., ed. *Great Tibetan-Chinese Dictionary* (*Bod rgya tshig mdzod chen mo*). 3 vols. Beijing: Mi rigs dpe skrun khang, 1985.
KTGR	Khenpo Tsültrim Gyamtso Rinpoche (recorded oral teachings, n.d. and 1993).
MVP	*Mahāvyutpatti*. Ed. Sakaki. 2 vols. Kyoto, 1916–25 and 1928.

P.	*A Comparative Analytical Catalogue of the Kanjur Division of the Tibetan Tripitaka: Edited in Peking during the K'ang-hsi Era, and At Present Kept in the Library of the Otani Daigaku Kyoto*, 3 vols., The Otani Daigaku Library, Kyoto, 1930-1932. Otani University Shin-Buddhist Comprehensive Research Institute: Tibetan Works Research Project, 2005. http://web.otani.ac.jp/cri/twrp/tibdate/Peking_online_search.html
PKTC	Padma Karpo Translation Committee edition of *The Treasury of Knowledge*, 2000 (input of Zhechen Publications edition, a photographic reproduction of the original 4 vol. Palpung woodblock-print, 1844).
rTog Palace	*Tog Palace Manuscript of the Tibetan Kanjur.* Leh, Ladakh: Smanrtsis Shesrig Dpemdzod, 1975-(1980).
TN	Thubten Nyima. *Outline of the "Encompassment of All Knowledge"* (*Shes bya kun khyab kyi sa bcad*). Sichuan, China: Si khron mi rigs dpe skrun khang, 1990.
TOK	Jamgön Kongtrul Lodrö Tayé. *The Treasury of Knowledge* (*Shes bya mdzod/ Shes bya mtha' yas pa'i rgya mtsho*). 3 vols. Beijing: Mi rigs dpe skrun khang, 1982.
Toh.	*A Complete Catalogue of the Tibetan Buddhist Canons*. Ed. Ui, Suzuki, Kanakura, and Tada. Sendai, Japan: Tohoku University, 1934.

Notes

1 The threefold enumeration of utter purity (*rnam dag gsum*) and the twelvefold enumeration of complete purity (*yongs dag bcu gnyis*) refer to verses found in the *Prajñāpāramitā Sūtra in One Hundred Thousand Verses* that point out the intrinsic purity of all phenomena of saṃsāra and nirvāṇa. The threefold enumeration of utter purity links the three primary mental afflictions (desire, aggression, and bewilderment) to 108 phenomena, which encompass all phenomena in saṃsāra and nirvāṇa. The twelvefold enumeration of complete purity links the complete purity of the twelve synonyms for the self to a similar list of 108 phenomena. In recent years Khenpo Tsültrim Gyamtso Rinpoche has presented these topics as a succinct means to gain understanding of the profound view of both the Sūtrayāna and the Vajrayāna. He explains that the terms "utter purity" and "complete purity" are synonyms, but if one wants to differentiate them, utter purity indicates that the essence of a phenomenon is pure, and complete purity conveys that the phenomenon, as well as everything connected to it, is pure.

2 The four common preliminaries (*thun mong sngon 'gro*) are the contemplations on the precious human existence, death and impermanence, karmic causes and results, and the faults of saṃsāra. The four uncommon preliminaries (*thun mong ma yin pa'i sngon 'gro*) are refuge and bodhichitta, Vajrasattva meditation, maṇḍala offering, and guru yoga. See *Mahāmudrā: The Ocean of the Definitive Meaning* (*Phyag chen nges don rgya mtsho*) by the ninth Karmapa, Wangchuk Dorjé (Callahan 2001, 9–82).

3 *Mahāmudrā: The Ocean of the Definitive Meaning* lists five types of conduct: always-excellent conduct (*kun bzang gi spyod pa*); secret conduct (*gsang spyod*); the [yogic] discipline of awareness (*rig pa brtul zhugs kyi spyod pa*); conduct in a crowd (*tshogs spyod*); and conduct that is victorious-in-all-directions (*phyogs las rnam rgyal gyi spyod pa*). (See Callahan 2001, 267–8.) These types of conduct are discussed in Book Nine, Part Three, in the section on the conduct taught in the anuttara tantras (*The Treasury of Knowledge*, hereafter cited as *TOK*, III:533–66).

4 Many teachers combine these four approaches in various ways; they need not be practiced in isolation from each other.

5 Jamgön (The Protector Mañjushrī) (*'Jam mgon*) is a title indicating great learning and wisdom. Kongtrul (*Kong sprul*) is an abbreviation of his tulku name, "KONGpo Bamteng TRULku, the 'incarnation from Bamteng in Kongpo province' (in the south of Tibet)." (See Barron 2003, 306n184 and 23–4.) Lodrö Tayé (*Blo gros mtha' yas*) is his bodhisattva name.

6 Dza Paltrul (*rDza dpal sprul*) (1808–1887).

7 Jamyang Khyentsé Wangpo (*'Jam dbyangs mkhyen rtse'i dbang po*) (1820-1892).

8 Chokgyur Lingpa (*mChog gyur gling pa*) (1829-1870).

9 Ju Mipham (*'Ju mi pham*) (1846–1912).

10 In addition to these sources, for discussions related to the Rimé movement in Eastern Tibet during the nineteenth century, see Dreyfus 1997, 33–41; Kapstein 2000a, 106–19, 2000b and 2001, Chapter 12; Pettit 1999; Phuntsho 2005, 47–54; and Smith 2001, 24–5 and 227–33.

11 Paṇchen Shākya Chokden (*Paṇ chen shākya mchog ldan*) (1428–1509). See n. 721. See also Dreyfus 1997, 27–9.

12 Tāranātha (*sGrol ba'i mgon po*) (1575–1634). See n. 817.

13 For a history of the Shentong (*gZhan stong*) tradition, see Ringu Tulku 2006; and Hookham 1991. An excellent overview is found in Stearns 1999, as well as in a forthcoming section of *The Treasury of Knowledge* (Part Two of Book Four).

14 This includes such sūtras as the *Descent into Laṅkā Sūtra* (*Laṅkāvatārasūtra, Lang kar gshegs pa'i mdo*), *Sūtra Unraveling the Intention* (*Saṃdhinirmochanasūtra, dGongs pa nges par 'grel pa*), *Genuine Golden Light Sūtras* (*Suvarṇaprabhāsottamasūtra, gSer 'od dam pa'i mdo*). Note that the designations of texts as belonging to one of three turnings of the dharma wheel is thematic rather than based on historical chronology.

15 Collection of Praises (*bsTod pa'i tshogs*): see n. 856.

16 Dolpopa Sherab Gyaltsen (*Dol po pa shes rab rgyal mtshan*) (1292–1361): see Chapter 11, nn. 815 and 812; and Stearns 1999.

17 In Book Four, Part Two (*TOK*, I:461), Jamgön Kongtrul says that in addition to Dolpopa, Rangjung Dorjé, and Longchenpa, the Shentong teachings were spread by

the scholar Tsang Nakpa (*gTsang nag pa*) (?–1171); Minling Terchen Gyurmé Dorjé (*sMin gling gter chen 'gyur med rdo rje*) (1646–1714) and his brother, Minling Lochen Dharma Shrī (*sMin gling lo chen dharma shri*) (1654–1718); and the eighth Situpa, Paṇchen Chökyi Jungné (also known as Jé Tenpé Nyin-jé, *rJe bstan pa'i nyin byed*) (1699–1774) and his followers. See also Ringu Tulku 2006, 73.

18 Rangjung Dorjé (*Rang byung rdo rje*) (1284–1339): see n. 813.

19 Longchen Rabjam (*kLong chen rab 'byams*) (1308–1364): see n. 814.

20 Milarepa's *An Authentic Portrait of the Middle Way* (*dBu ma yang dag par brjod pa*) is an example of a song that contains statements reflecting both Rangtong and Shentong perspectives. See Khenpo Tsültrim Gyamtso 2003, 205–6.

21 For more on Shentong, the Jonang school, its banning and subsequent revival, see Stearns 1999, 62–77; and Kapstein 2001, 306–7.

22 Kaḥ-tok Rikdzin Tsewang Norbu (*Kaḥ thog rig 'dzin Tshe dbang nor bu*) (1698–1755).

23 Situ Paṇchen Chökyi Jungné (*Chos kyi 'byung gnas*) (1699–1774). For an account of Situ Paṇchen, see Smith 2001, 87–96.

24 Getsé Paṇḍita Gyurmé Tsewang Chokdrup (*dGe rtse paṇḍita 'gyur med tshe dbang mchog sgrub*) (1761–1829). It is interesting to note that Kapstein (2001, 307) says that "the account of the 'Great Madhyamaka' found in Dudjom Rinpoche's *Fundamentals,* part 3, is in most respects derived from the work of this master [Getsé Paṇḍita]." In a similar way Jamgön Kongtrul drew upon the writings of Tāranātha and Shākya Chokden for his presentation of Shentong in this book. See Chapter 11 in this volume.

25 Kunzang Wangpo (*Kun bzang dbang po*) (b. seventeenth century).

26 Kunga Tayé (*Kun dga' mtha' yas*) (b. seventeenth century).

27 Chödrak Gyamtso (*Chos grags rgya mtsho*) (1454–1506) is well known for his *Ocean of Texts on Reasoning* (*Tshad ma legs par bshad pa thams cad kyi chu bo yongs su 'du ba rigs pa'i gzhung lugs kyi rgya mtsho*).

28 See Stearns 1999, 74–6.

29 Shalu Ri-buk Tulku, Losel Ten-kyöng (*Zhwa lu ri sbug sprul sku, Blo gsal bstan skyong*) (b. 1804).

30 See Smith 2001, 250.

31 Five Great Treasuries (*mDzod chen lnga*).

32 *rGya chen bka' mdzod.* This is also known as *The Uncommon Treasury* (*Thung mong ma yin pa'i mdzod*).

33 *The Mantra Treasury of the Kagyu School* (*bKa' brgyud sngags mdzod*); *The Treasury of Precious Terma Teachings* (*Rin chen gter mdzod*); and *The Treasury of Instructions* (*gDams ngag mdzod*). *The Treasury of Instructions* also contains some of Jamgön Kongtrul's own writings.

For an overview of these, see Smith 2001, 262–6. For their tables of contents, see Barron 2003, 515–31.

34 *rGyu mtshan nyid theg pa rnam par gzhag pa'i skabs. "Frameworks of Buddhist Philosophy"* is the translator's addition. Jamgön Kongtrul's title appears as the subtitle.

35 *The Encompassment of All Knowledge* (*Shes bya kun khyab*); and *The Infinite Ocean of Knowledge* (*Shes bya mtha' yas pa'i rgya mtsho*).

36 *Shes bya mdzod.*

37 Ngédön Tenpa Rabgyé (*Nges don bstan pa rab rgyas*) (1808–1864 or 1867) was the first Dabzang Tulku (*Zla bzang sprul sku*), who founded Til-yag monastery in Nang chen, Eastern Tibet.

38 Barron 2003, 131.

39 The three trainings (*shikṣhā, bslab pa*) are the training in ethical conduct (*shilashikṣhā, tshul khrims kyi bslab pa*), the training in samādhi (*samādhishikṣhā, ting nge 'dzin gyi bslab pa*), and the training in wisdom (*prajñāshikṣhā, shes rab kyi bslab pa*).

40 See Barron 2003, 131, 137, and 138.

41 Forthcoming translation of Books Two, Three, and Four by Ngawang Zangpo.

42 Forthcoming translation of Book Eight, Parts One and Two, by Richard Barron.

43 Forthcoming translation by Elio Guarisco and Ingrid McLeod.

44 Forthcoming (2007) translation by Sarah Harding.

45 Forthcoming translation of Books Nine and Ten, *Journey and Goal*, by Richard Barron.

46 Note that the term "Dialectical Approach" is translated in this volume as "Philosophical Vehicles" (*mTshan nyid theg pa*).

47 See *TOK*, II:361–3.

48 The exception being its section on Secret Mantra-Madhyamaka in Chapter 12.

49 See Chapter 1, p. 83.

50 Specifically, readers should refer to Book Four, Parts One and Two, for relevant history; to Book Seven, Parts Two and Three, for related presentations of the definitive and provisional meanings, the two truths, and points on view; to Book Eight, Part Two, for discussion of the meditations; to Book Nine, Part One, for the path; and to Book Ten, Part One, for the fruition.

51 It should be noted that whereas most tenet system texts cover non-Buddhist Indian systems as well as Buddhist systems, this section of *The Treasury of Knowledge* only presents Buddhist systems.

For an overview of this genre, see Hopkins 1996. For relevant observations, see Cabezón 1990 and 2003, particularly 289–92.

52 See n. 588.

53 *Prajñā-nāma-mūlamadhyamakakārikā, dBu ma rtsa ba'i tshig le'ur byas pa shes rab ces bya ba.*

54 For a discussion of which schools and tenets Nāgārjuna refuted, see Walser 2005, 224–61.

55 Collection of Reasonings (*Rigs tshogs*): see n. 592.

56 Collection of Advice (*gTam tshogs*). This includes the *Precious Garland* (*Ratnāvalī, Rin chen phreng ba*) and *Friendly Letter* (*Suhṛlleka, Shes springs yig*).

57 The texts in Nāgārjuna's Collection of Reasonings and Āryadeva's works are considered models specifically for Rangtong Mādhyamikas, who were known in India as the Proponents of the Absence of a Nature (*Niḥsvabhāvavādin, Ngo bo nyid med par smra ba'i dbu ma pa*).

58 See n. 559.

59 See n. 560.

60 The three characteristics (*trilakṣhaṇa, mtshan nyid gsum*)—also known as "three natures" (*trisvabhāva, rang bzhin gsum*)—are imagined characteristics (*parikalpita, kun brtags*), dependent characteristics (*paratantra, gzhan dbang*), and the consummate characteristic (*pariniṣhpanna, yongs grub*). See Chapter 6, pp. 179–82, and Chapter 11, pp. 255–58.

61 *Abhidharmakoshakārikā, Chos mngon pa'i mdzod kyi tshig le'ur byas pa.*

62 *Abhidharmasamuchchaya, Chos mngon pa kun las btus pa.*

63 Tāranātha says in his *History of Buddhism in India* (Chimpa and Chattopadhyaya 1970, 187) that before the appearance of Buddhapālita and Bhāvaviveka, Mahāyāna followers shared the same dharma. "But these two *ācārya*-s [thought], 'The doctrines of *ārya* Nāgārjuna and of *ārya* Asaṅga are fundamentally different. The doctrine of Asaṅga is not indicative of the path of the Mādhyamika. It is merely the doctrine of *vijñāna* {consciousness}. What we uphold is the real view of *ārya* Nāgārjuna.' Saying this, they refuted the position of the others. As a result after the passing away of Bhavya, the Mahāyānī-s *{sic}* were split into two groups and started having controversies among themselves." (Brackets are in the original; my glosses are in braces.)

64 See n. 694.

65 *Madhyamakahṛidayakārikā, dBu ma'i snying po tshig le'ur byas pa.*

66 *Tarkajvālā, rTog ge 'bar ba.* See also nn. 614, 628, and 694.

67 Bhāvaviveka criticizes the view of the three natures in Chapter 25 of his *Lamp of Wisdom* (*Prajñāpradīpa, Shes rab sgron ma*), and replies to the Yogāchāra (as represented by Guṇamati and Dharmapāla) in Chapters 5 of his *Heart of the Middle Way* and *Blaze of Reasoning*. See Eckel 1985; and Brunnhölzl 2004, 492–3.

68 Bhāvaviveka uses "nominal ultimate" (*paryāyaparamārtha, rnam grangs pa'i don dam*) and "non-nominal ultimate" (*aparyāyaparamārtha, rnam grangs ma yin pa'i don dam*) in the third chapter of his *Blaze of Reasoning*.

69 *Madhyamakāvatāra, dBu ma la 'jug pa.*

70 *Mūlamadhyamakavṛittiprasannapadā, dBu ma'i rtsa ba'i 'grel pa tshig gsal ba.*

71 For more on the issues related to the use of formal inferences (what are also called "independently verifiable proof statements"), see n. 691.

72 *Jñānasāra-samuchchaya, Ye shes snying po kun las btus pa.* On the authorship of this text, see Mimaki 1987. For a translation, see Mimaki 2000.

73 *Tattvasaṃgraha, De kho na nyid bsdus pa'i tshig le'ur byas pa.* See Blumenthal 2004, 28.

74 *Mādhyamakālaṃkāra, dBu ma rgyan.* See Blumenthal 2004; Ichigō 1989; and Padmakara Translation Group 2005.

75 Bodhibhadra wrote a *Commentary on the "Compendium on the Heart of Primordial Wisdom"* (*Jñānasārasamuchchaya-nāma-nibandhana, Ye shes snying po kun las btus pa zhes bya ba'i bshad sbyar*).

76 Jetāri's eight-verse *Differentiating the Sugata's Texts* (*Sugatamatavibhaṅgabhāṣhya, bDe bar gshegs pa'i gzhung rnam par 'byed pa'i bshad pa*) is almost identical to verses 21–28 of Āryadeva's *Compendium on the Heart of Primordial Wisdom.*

77 Maitrīpa's *Precious Garland of Suchness* (*Tattvaratnāvalī, De kho na nyid kyi rin chen phreng ba*) is a discussion of three yānas: Shrāvakayāna, Pratyekabuddhayāna, and Mahāyāna; and four positions (*sthiti, gnas pa*): Vaibhāṣhika, Sautrāntika, Yogāchāra, and Madhyamaka (note that he classifies Sautrāntika as Mahāyāna).

78 Sahajavajra, a student of Maitrīpa, wrote a *Compendium of Positions* (*Sthiti-samuchchaya, gNas pa bsdus pa*), which presents the positions of the Vaibhāṣhika, Sautrāntika, Yogāchāra, Madhyamaka, and Mantra. He divides Yogāchāras into those who take the position of nonexistent images (*Nirākāravādin, rNam pa med pa'i gnas*) and those who take the position of images (*Sākāravādin, rNam pa dang bcas pa'i gnas*).

79 At the end of his *Discourse on Logic* (*Tarkabhāṣhā, rTog ge'i skad*), Mokṣhākaragupta discusses the views of the four tenet systems. See Kajiyama 1998.

80 *Mādhyamakālaṃkāra-kārikā, dBu ma rgyan gyi tshig le'ur byas pa.*

81 Verses 92 and 93 as translated by the Padmakara Translation Group (2005, 66).

82 *Hā shang Mahāyāna.*

83 Trisong De-tsen (*Khri srong sde btsan*).

84 See Wangdu and Diemberger 2000, 88; and Butön's *History of Buddhism* (Obermiller 1932, 198).

85 See Butön's *History of Buddhism* (Obermiller 1932, 198–9); Scherrer-Schaub 2002, 280; and Wangdu and Diemberger 2000, 23 and 24n6.

86 See nn. 562 and 565.

87 See Chapter 7, pp. 199–200.

88 Shang Yeshé Dé (*Zhang ye shes sde*) wrote *Distinctions of the View* (*lTa ba'i khyad par*).

89 Kawa Pal-tsek (*Ka ba dPal brtsegs*) wrote *Key Instructions on the Stages of the View* (*lTa ba'i rim pa'i man ngag*).

90 *Sautrāntika-Madhyamaka (*mDo sde spyod pa'i dbu ma*) and *Yogāchāra-Madhyamaka (*rNal 'byor spyod pa'i dbu ma*). (Note that the asterisk indicates reconstructed Sanskrit.)

91 Rongzom Paṇḍita Chökyi Zangpo (*Rong zom paṇḍita chos kyi bzang po*). These divisions are presented in three works: *Aide-Mémoire for the View* (*lTa ba'i brjed byang*), *Aide-Mémoire for the Tenet Systems* (*Grub mtha'i brjed byang*), and *Commentary on the "Garland of the View of the Key Instructions"* (*Man ngag lta ba'i phreng ba zhes bya ba'i 'grel pa*). See also Ruegg 1981, 55–72.

92 Pa-tsap Lotsāwa Nyima Drak (*Pa tshab lo tsā ba nyi ma grags*) (b. 1055).

93 *Madhyamakāvatāra-bhāṣhya, dBu ma la 'jug pa'i bshad pa.*

94 See Atīsha's *Entrance to the Two Truths* (*Satyadvayāvatāra, bDen pa gnyis la 'jug pa*), verse 14; Sherburne 2000, 355.

95 Jayānanda wrote a *Sub-Commentary on the "Entrance to the Middle Way"* (*Madhyamakāvatāraṭīkā, dBu ma la 'jug pa'i 'grel bshad*).

96 *Svātantrika (*Rang rgyud pa,* Those [Who Use] Independently [Verifiable Reasons]) and *Prāsaṅgika (*Thal 'gyur pa,* Consequentialists or Apagogists): see n. 631. Note that the Sanskrit "Svātantrika" and "Prāsaṅgika" are Sanskrit reconstructions of the Tibetan terms by modern scholars.

97 For a study of the issues dividing Svātantrika and Prāsaṅgika in the eleventh and twelfth centuries (here greatly simplified), see Vose 2005.

98 Ngok Lotsāwa Loden Sherab (*rNgog lo tsā ba blo ldan shes rab*) (1059–1109).

99 Chapa Chökyi Seng-gé (*Phyva pa chos kyi seng ge*) (1109–1169).

100 For an overview of Madhyamaka classification schemas in the intervening centuries in Tibet, see Brunnhölzl 2004, 336–40.

101 *Theg pa'i mchog rin po che'i mdzod.* See forthcoming translation by Richard Barron. In his *Precious Treasury of the Supreme Yāna,* Longchenpa divides Svātantrika into lower Svātantrika (*rang rgyud 'og ma*) and higher Svātantrika (*rang rgyud gong ma*), which Mipham follows in his *Compendium of Philosophical Tenet Systems* (*Yid bzhin mdzod kyi grub mtha' bsdus pa*) (see Phuntsho 2005, 238n38).

102 Specifically the *Bṛihaṭṭīkā* (*Yum gsum gnod 'joms*). See Stearns 1999, 89–98.

103 The Three Commentaries by Bodhisattvas (*Sems 'grel skor gsum* or *Byang chub sems dpa'i 'grel ba*): see n. 877.

104 Generally speaking, the scriptures of the second turning of the dharma wheel present emptiness, and the scriptures of the third turning present buddha nature (*tathāgatagarbha*) and the three characteristics (*trilakṣhaṇa, mtshan nyid gsum*).

105 See Stearns 1999, 91.

106 For translations of Dolpopa's works, see Stearns 1999; and Hopkins 2006. For refutations of Dolpopa and the views attributed to him, see, e.g., Hopkins 2002, 273–391.

107 See Chapter 7, p. 201.

108 Je Tsongkhapa Lo-zang Drakpa (*rJe Tsong kha pa blo bzang grags pa*) (1357–1419).

109 Rendawa (*Red mda' ba gzhon nu blo gros*) (1349–1412).

110 See Cabezón 2003; Eckel 2003; Ruegg 2000, 233–304; Yoshimizu 2003; and Yotsuya 1999.

111 *Legs bshad snying po.* See Thurman 1984, 266–77. It is said that Tsongkhapa wrote this in reaction to presentations such as those of Longchenpa and Dolpopa (see Hopkins 2003, 4).

112 Thus yielding the very awkward compounds: Sautrāntika-Svātantrika-Madhyamaka (*mDo sde spyod pa'i dbu ma rang rgyud pa*), Middle Way Proponents of Independently [Verifiable Reasons] Who [Accord with] Followers of the Sūtras; and Yogāchāra-Svātantrika-Madhyamaka (*rNal 'byor spyod pa'i dbu ma rang rgyud pa*), Middle Way

Proponents of Independently [Verifiable Reasons] Who [Accord with] Yoga Practitioners. See n. 705.

113 Tak-tsang Lotsāwa (*sTag tshangs lo tsā ba*) (b. 1405). Tak-tsang Lotsāwa's refutation of Tsongkhapa in his *Ocean of Excellent Explanations: An Explanation of "Freedom from Extremes through Understanding All Tenet Systems"* (*Grub mtha' kun shes nas mtha' bral grub pa zhes bya ba'i bstan bcos rnam par bshad pa legs bshad kyi rgya mtsho*) is found in Jamyang Shepa's *Great Exposition of Tenets* (*Grub mtha' chen mo*); see Hopkins 2003, 527–694.

114 Gorampa Sonam Seng-gé (*Go rams pa bsod nams seng ge*) (1429–1489).

115 Mikyö Dorjé (*Mi skyo rdo rje*) (1507-1603). For a comparison of Mikyö Dorjé's and Tsongkhapa's views, see Brunnhölzl 2004, 553–97.

116 See Tāranātha's *Twenty-one [Differences Regarding] the Profound Meaning* (*Zab don khyad par nyer gcig pa*), Mathes 2004; and Hopkins 2007, 117–36.

117 Although Shākya Chokden's works were banned in Tibet, they were preserved in Bhutan, where they were printed by Shākya Rinchen (1710–1759), the ninth Je Khenpo of Bhutan (also considered the reincarnation of Shākya Chokden).

118 *gZhan stong snying po*. See Hopkins 2007, 55–63. See Chapter 7, p. 201 for Jamgön Kongtrul's portrayal of this perspective. See also n. 630.

119 *Dharmadhātustava, Chos dbyings bstod pa.*

120 See Kapstein 2001, 306–7; Smith 2001, 95; and Phuntsho 2005, 48–9.

121 The Karma Kagyu monastic college was not reinstated until the 1980s at Rumtek monastery in Sikkim, India.

122 *Grub mtha' chen mo*. See Hopkins 2003.

123 Chang-kya Rolpé Dorjé (*lCang skya rol pa'i rdo rje*) (1717–1786). *Grub mtha' mdzes rgyan.* See Hopkins 1983; Klein 1991, 121–196; Lopez 1987; and Powell 1998.

124 Könchok Jigmé Wangpo (*dKon mchog 'jigs med dbang po*). *Grub pa'i mtha'i rnam par bzhag pa rin po che'i phreng ba.* See Hopkins and Sopa 1976/1989.

125 Losang Könchok (*Blo bzang dkon mchog*). The full title is the *Clear Crystal Mirror: A Word-Commentary on the Root Text on Tenets* (*Grub mtha' rtsa ba'i tshig tik shel dkar me long*). See Cozort and Preston 2003.

126 See Chapter 3, p. 125, where Jamgön Kongtrul says that Vaibhāṣhikas are a subschool of the Mūlasarvāstivāda. See also nn. 284 and 288.

127 See Hopkins 2003.

128 Specifically, Dignāga's *Compendium on Valid Cognition* (*Pramāṇasamuchchaya, Tshad ma kun btus*) and Dharmakīrti's Seven Treatises on Valid Cognition (see n. 586).

129 Tib. *Sa sde lnga.* This is a set of five texts: *Bhūmis of Yogic Practice* (*Yogāchārabhūmi, rNal 'byor spyod pa'i sa*); *Synopsis of Ascertainment* (*Nirṇayasaṃgraha, gTan la dbab pa bsdu ba*); *Synopsis of Bases* (*Vastusaṃgraha, gZhi bsdu ba*); *Synopsis of Enumerations* (*Paryāyasaṃgraha, rNam grangs bsdu ba*); and *Synopsis of Explanations* (*Vivaraṇasaṃgraha, rNam par bshad pa bsdu ba*).

130 The only "canonical sources" (that is, attributable to the Buddha) for four philosophical tenet systems that Jamgön Kongtrul provides are tantras (*Hevajra* and

Kālachakra). He follows this by saying that the four philosophical tenet systems were set out by those who appeared after the Buddha. See Chapter 1, p. 84.

131 It is well accepted that Vasubandhu wrote his *Treasury of Abhidharma* as an exposition of the Vaibhāṣhika abhidharma system, which he did not agree with as is clear from his criticism of some of their tenets in his *Explanation of the "Treasury of Abhidharma."*

132 Although there were several people called Vasumitra, Ghoṣhaka, and Dharmatrāta, the ones Jamgön Kongtrul refers to are presumably those cited in Vasubandhu's *Treasury of Abhidharma* and listed by Tāranātha (Chimpa and Chattopadhyaya 1970, 103) as Vaibhāṣhika teachers. The dating of them as ca. first century CE is based on Tāranātha's work, but it is conjectural. More accurately, it is probably best said that they lived some time between the second and fourth centuries.

133 All chapters are divisions introduced by the translator and are not part of Jamgön Kongtrul's outline (*sa bcad*).

134 Hirakawa observes (1990, 256): "The original meaning of the element *hīna* in the term 'Hīnayāna' is 'discarded'; it also denotes 'inferior' or 'base.' The appellation 'Hīnayāna' thus was a deprecatory term used by Mahāyāna practitioners to refer to Nikāya (Sectarian) Buddhism . . . It is unclear whether Mahāyānists referred to the whole of Nikāya Buddhism as Hīnayāna or only to a specific group."

135 Dzogchen Ponlop 2003, 11–13.

136 In this presentation, the second and third yānas are the Mahāyāna and Vajrayāna.

137 Philosophical tenet or tenet system (*siddhānta, grub mtha'*): literally, "established conclusion" or "limit of the established."

138 *Mahāyāna-saṃgraha, Theg pa chen po bsdus pa.*

139 It seems that, in fact, both Vaibhāṣhikas and Sautrāntikas were branches or factions within the followers of Sarvāstivāda abhidharma. See n. 284.

140 Jamyang Shepa says (Hopkins 2003, 219): "They [i.e., the eighteen schools] are not any tenet system except the Great Exposition School [Vaibhāṣhika]."

141 See n. 303.

142 See n. 305.

143 On the speculative identification of Anantavarman, see n. 336.

144 *Chos 'byung*, trans. Obermiller 1932.

145 *Chos 'byung mkhas pa'i dga' ston.*

146 Discussions of the orders are found in Vinītadeva's *Compendium Showing the Different Orders* (*Samayabhedoparachanachakre nikāyabhedopadeshanasaṃgraha, gZhung tha dad pa rim par bklag pa'i 'khor lo las sde pa tha dad pa bstan pa bsdus pa*); Shākyaprabha's *Luminous* (*Prabhāvatī, 'Od ldan*); Bhāvaviveka's *Blaze of Reasoning* (*Madhyamakahṛidayavṛittitarkajvālā, dBu ma'i snying po'i 'grel pa rtog ge 'bar ba*); and Padma's *Varṣhāgra-pṛicchā* (*dGe tshul gyi dang po'i lo dri ba* and *dGe slong gi dang po'i lo dri ba*).

147 Chapter 3, p. 139.

148 *Abhisamayālaṃkāra, mNgon rtogs rgyan.*

149 *Mahāyānasūtrālaṃkāra, Theg pa chen po mdo sde rgyan.*

150 In Chapter 11, Jamgön Kongtrul says that both Tāranātha and Shākya Chokden make a distinction between Chittamātra and Proponents of Cognition (Vijñaptivādins), with the latter name being reserved for Shentong-Madhyamaka (see p. 266). He also says that Yogāchāra-Madhyamaka is Shentong-Madhyamaka.

151 Khenpo Tsültrim Gyamtso Rinpoche often uses the example of a dream to illustrate the three characteristics. Our dreaming mind—which is mere cognition that is simply clear and aware—and the mere images in the dream are dependent characteristics (*paratantra, gzhan dbang*). Our ideas about what we experience in our dreams, such as thinking that those "lions and tigers and bears" are enjoyable, or that they are frightening, or that they are real external objects, are the imagined characteristics (*parikalpita, kun brtags*). The actual nature of our dreaming mind—cognition empty of the duality of perceived object and perceiving mind—is the consummate characteristic (*pariniṣhpanna, yongs grub*).

152 Proponents of Real Images (or True Aspectarians) (*Satyākāravādin, rNam bden pa*), and Proponents of False Images (or False Aspectarians) (*Alīkākāravādin, rNam rdzun pa*).

153 *Sugatamatavibhaṅgabhāṣhya, bDe bar gshegs pa'i gzhung rnam par 'byed pa'i bshad pa.*

154 Tāranātha's *Presentation of the Scriptures for the "Ornament of the Shentong-Madhyamaka"* (*gZhan stong dbu ma'i rgyan gyi lung sbyor ba*) and *History of Buddhism in India* (Chimpa and Chattopadhyaya 1970). See n. 593.

155 A nonimplicative negation (*prasajyapratiṣhedha, med dgag*) is one that does not indicate or imply anything in place of its object of negation.

156 The four possibilities (*chatuṣhkoṭi, mu bzhi*) are (1) that only one result manifests from just a single cause; (2) that numerous results are produced by only one cause; (3) that a single result comes from many causes; and (4) that many results could arise from many causes.

157 *The Dharma Treasury of an Ocean of Scriptures and Reasonings Ascertaining the Middle Way* (*dBu ma rnam par nges pa'i chos kyi bang mdzod lung dang rigs pa'i rgya mtsho*).

158 For a brief explanation of isolates (*vyatireka, ldog pa*), see n. 709.

159 *Satyadvaya-vibhaṇga, bDen gnyis rnam 'byed.* See n. 714.

160 See *TOK,* III:69–77.

161 For the five Dharma Treatises of Maitreya (*Byams pa'i chos sde*) see n. 807.

162 Zu Gawé Dorjé (*gZus dga' ba'i rdo rje*) (eleventh century).

163 Tsen Kawoché (*bTsan kha bo che*) (b. 1021).

164 Yumo Mikyö Dorjé (*Yu mo ba mi bskyod rdo rje*) (b. 1027).

165 *Saṃdhinirmochanasūtra, dGongs pa nges par 'grel pa.*

166 *Triṃshikākārikā, Sum bcu pa.*

167 *sTong nyid bdud rtsi'i lam po che.*

168 *Nges don gcig tu bsgrub pa.*

169 See *TOK,* III:156.14–18.

170 The Buddhist tradition refers to itself as "the insiders" (*nang pa*). This can be understood as meaning (1) those who are part of, or inside, the Buddhist teachings, i.e., anyone who has taken refuge in the Buddha, dharma (his teachings), and saṅgha (the community of practitioners); and (2) that followers of the Buddha are primarily concerned with what is inner, that is, the mind.

171 The three yānas (vehicles or approaches) (*theg pa*) are Shrāvakayāna, Pratyekabuddhayāna, and Mahāyāna. The first two are included in the Hīnayāna. Readers should note that although Vajrayāna is sometimes listed as the third yāna (the first two being the Hīnayāna and Mahāyāna), Jamgön Kongtrul is following the presentation in which Vajrayāna is one of two divisions of the Mahāyāna, the other being the Pāramitāyāna (see p. 165). See p. 158 for Jamgön Kongtrul's remarks on his reasons for presenting the Pratyekabuddhayāna as the second of three yānas.

172 Katz remarks (1983, 111–2), "Etymologically, the term [yāna] derives from the Sanskrit root *yā-,* 'to go,' and gives the sense of going or proceeding, as well as the means of carriage or vehicle, and is very close in many connotations to *mārga*, the path . . . Thus the term, derived from 'to go,' carries a range of meanings from a spiritual career, to a path or way, to a conveyance or vehicle."

173 This is a distinction that is applied, for example, to the two forms of Mahāyāna: Pāramitāyāna and Vajrayāna. In the cause-based yāna, we practice what takes us to the result, whereas in the result-based yāna, the result is practiced as the path. See also n. 487. The Dzogchen Ponlop Rinpoche explains (2003, 9–10) these two as follows:

> Yāna . . . means "the vehicle that brings us to our destination." Our destination here is enlightenment, liberation from saṃsāra . . . According to Shākyamuni Buddha, we can understand yāna in two different ways. We can understand the term to mean "the yāna that brings us to our destination" or "the yāna that brought us here"—in other words, to where we are right now.
>
> The first meaning of yāna, "the yāna that brings us to our destination," orients us to the future. The yāna, or vehicle, is the cause that brings us to our result: we are brought to the fruition stage, which is our destination. When we define yāna in this way, it is known as the causal yāna.
>
> The second meaning of yāna, "the yāna that brought us here," refers to the result or fruition. It is called the resultant yāna, or fruition yāna, because we have already been conveyed to our destination. We are already there.

174 As Jamgön Kongtrul states clearly, the distinction between the Hīnayāna, "Lesser Vehicle," and the Mahāyāna, "Greater Vehicle," is based on the scope of the intention of the individual practitioners. For more discussion of three yānas and the terms *Hīnayāna* and *Mahāyāna*, see the Introduction, p. 30.

175 Secret Mantra (*gSang sngags*) is another name for the Vajrayāna (*rDo rje theg pa*). This is the subject of Book Six, Part Four (Kongtrul 2005).

176 *dPal brtag pa gnyis pa.* The full title is *The King of Tantras, Called the Glorious Hevajra* (*Hevajra-tantra-rāja-nāma, Kye'i rdo rje zhes bya ba rgyud kyi rgyal po*) (Toh. 417 and 418). Part II, Chapter 8, verses 9cd–10ab.

Dg.K., vol. Nga, f. 53 and rTog Palace f. 288 read: *mdo sde pa yang de bzhin* ***no/ de nas*** *rnal 'byor spyod pa* ***nyid****/ de* ***yi*** *rjes* ***su*** *dbu ma bstan.* (Note that Dg.K. seems to be *de* ***mi*** *rjes la,* but that is not correct.) *TOK,* II:443.7 has *mdo sde pa yang de bzhin* ***te/*** *rnal 'byor spyod pa* ***de las phyis/*** *de* ***rjes dbu ma bstan par bya.*** These spelling differences do not change the meaning.

177 *Dus 'khor.* The full title of this work by Mañjushrī Yashas, the eighth king of Shambhala, is the *Glorious Kālachakra, the King of Tantras: Issued from the Supreme, Original Buddha* (*Paramādibuddhoddhṛita-shrīkālachakra-nāma-tantrarāja, mChog gi dang po'i sangs rgyas las phyung ba rgyud kyi rgyal po dpal dus kyi 'khor lo zhes bya ba*) (Toh. 362). The Primordial Wisdom chapter is the fifth chapter. This is a reference to verse 48cd, which says:

> From his eastern [face, he teaches] Yogāchāra, from his western, definitely all the Madhyamaka.
> He speaks the Sautrāntika from his right face, and the true Vaibhāṣhika from his white face.
>
> *shar nas rnal 'byor spyod pa nyid de slar yang nub kyi zhal nas nges par dbu ma mtha' dag go/ mdo sde pa ni g.yas kyi zhal nas gsungs te dkar po'i zhal nas dag pa'i bye brag smra ba'o.* Dg.T. Beijing 6:199–200.

178 The four Vedas are the major texts or sciences of ancient India that formed the basis of the Brahman tradition. Originally, there were three: Sacrifices or Offerings (*Yajur-Veda, mChod sbyin gyi rig byed*), Aphorisms (*Ṛig-Veda, Nges brjod kyi rig byed*), and Poetics (*Sāma-Veda, sNyan tshig gi rig byed*). Later, a fourth, Administration or Politics (*Atharva-Veda, Srid srung rig byed*), was added.

179 Verse 49ab says:

> The Lord of Victors teaches the *Ṛig-Veda* from his western face, and the *Yajur*[-*veda*] from his left face. From his right face, [he teaches] *Sāma*[-*veda*], and from the family of the supreme combustibles [i.e., the face of the fire god], which is his eastern face, [he teaches] the *Atharva*[-*veda*].
>
> *nub kyi zhal nas nges brjod rig byed dang ni rgyal ba'i dbang pos g.yon gyi zhal nas mchod sbyin gsungs/ g.yas kyi zhal nas snyan tshig rig byed mchog gi bsreg bya'i rigs la srid srung shar gyi zhal nas so.* Dg.T. Beijing 6:200.

180 Rongtön the Great (*Rong ston chen* po), also known as All-Knowing Rongtön (*Rong ston shes bya kun rig*) or Rongtön Sherab Gyaltsen (*Rong ston shes rab rgyal mtshan*) (1367–1449), was a great Sakya scholar, famous for his commentaries on the Prajñāpāramitā (perfection of wisdom) sūtras. He founded a monastery at Penpo Nalendra (*Phan po na lendra*) and his main students were Shākya Chokden (*Shākya mchog ldan*) and Gorampa (*Go ram pa*).

181 Philosophical tenet or tenet system (*siddhānta, grub mtha'*): literally, "established conclusion" or "limit of the established." For a presentation of a traditional etymology of *siddhānta* and *grub mtha',* see Hopkins 2003, 65–67.

182 The term *etymology* (*nirukti, nges tshig*) is used in a narrow or specific sense. It means that the word in question is analyzed in terms of its component parts in order to come to a precise understanding of the term. Such etymologies are not what is generally understood by this word in the West, i.e., the tracing of the phonetic, graphic, and semantic development of a word, identifying its cognates in other languages, and the like.

183 *TOK,* II:444.7: *shra ba ka* should be *shra' ba ka.*

184 This is generally glossed as "to cause [others] to hear" (*thos par byed pa*). See n. 187.

185 *TOK,* II:444.8: ***bu ddha*** should be ***buddha*** (Nyima 1990, hereafter cited as TN).

186 Tibetan translators expressed two "senses" of the Sanskrit *buddha* in their translation of the word as *sangs rgyas,* "awakened-blossomed one." These are derived from *pra-buddha* "to awaken" and *vi-buddha* "to blossom," and are presented by Yashomitra in his *Sub-Commentary on the "Treasury of Abhidharma"* (Dg.T. Beijing 80:6):

> As for [the meaning of the word] "*buddha*": Because his intelligence has blossomed, *buddha* means "to blossom" (*vi-buddha, rgyas pa*), as with a lotus flower that has blossomed. Another sense is that because he is free from the duality that is the sleep of ignorance, *buddha* means "to awaken" (*pra-buddha, sad pa*), as with a person who has awakened from sleep.
>
> *sang rgyas zhes bya ba ni blo rgyas pa'i phyir sangs rgyas te dper na padma kha bye ba zhes bya ltar rnam par rgyas zhes bya ba'i tha tshig go/ rnam pa gcig tu na ma rig pa'i gnyid gnyis dang bral ba'i phyir sangs rgyas te/ dper na skyes bu gnyis sad pa zhes bya ba ltar rab tu sad pa zhes bya ba'i tha tshig go.*

Subsequently, the Tibetan *sangs rgyas* (pronounced *sang-jay*) is explained as meaning "one who has awakened from the darkness of the two obscurations and who has fully developed (or 'blossomed' with) the brilliance of twofold knowledge" (*sgrib gnyis kyi mun pa sangs shing/ mkhyen gnyis kyi snang ba rgyas pa*) (*Great Tibetan-Chinese Dictionary,* hereafter cited as *GTCD*). See also the *Nighaṇṭu* (*sGra sbyor bam po gnyis pa*) (Toh. 4347; Dg.T. Beijing 115:316).

187 Hopkins discusses (1983, 840n495) the topic of two etymologies for *shrāvaka*:

> *Shrāvaka* (*Nyan thos*) is translated as 'Hearers' because they *hear* (*nyan*) the doctrine, practice it, and then *cause others to hear* (*thos par byed pa*) that they have actualized their goal (see Hopkins' *Compassion in Tibetan Buddhism* [London: Hutchinson, 1980], pp. 102–3). This etymology is built around active and causative uses of the verbal root for hearing, *shru*; one hears and then causes others to hear, in this case not what one has heard but what one has achieved after putting into practice the doctrines one has heard . . . [840] However, though there are two etymologies of *shrāvaka,* they are built not around different verbal roots but around the single root *shru* treated in active and passive modes with different interpretations of both what is heard . . . and what is proclaimed . . . [844]

188 These are discussed in the section Approachers to the Result of a Stream Enterer, p. 142.

189 Four truths of noble beings (*chaturāryasatya, 'phags pa'i bden pa bzhi*): Since the Sanskrit term *satya* (Tib. *bden pa*) means what is experienced as true or real, here "truth" (*satya, bden pa*) is used in the sense of an empirical truth or actual truth, not in the sense of a formal truth or logical truth. "Truth" is used throughout this translation for the familiar categories of "the four truths" or "two truths," and "reality" in most other cases. For more on the expression "four truths of noble beings," see n. 195.

190 According to the *GTCD,* the term "appropriated aggregates" (*upādāna-skandha, nyer len gyi phung po*) means that the defiled aggregates arose because of the appropriating action [or substantial cause] of previous karma and mental afflictions, and that

[these aggregates] create the appropriating action [or are the substantial cause] for future karma and mental afflictions (*nyer len gyi phung po/ las nyon snga ma'i nyer len las skyes pa dang/ las nyon phyi ma'i nyer len du 'gro ba'i zag bcas kyi phung po*). For a list of the five aggregates, see n. 300.

191 Phenomena are divided into two classes: the fifty-three afflictive phenomena (*saṃklesha, kun nas nyon mongs pa*) and the fifty-five purified phenomena (*vyavadāna, rnam par byang ba*). These two groups make up the 108 phenomena that are the bases for the explanations of emptiness and the path to its realization presented in the Prajñāpāramitā sūtras. For a complete list of these 108 phenomena, see Hopkins 1983, 201–12.

192 *bsDu ba.* I have not been able to identify this citation. It may be from Asaṅga's *Compendium of Ascertainments* (*Nirṇayasaṃgraha, gTan la dbab pa bsdu ba*); Toh. 4038.

193 *Abhidharmakoshakārikā, Chos mngon pa'i mdzod,* by Vasubandhu. Chapter 6, verse 2d. Toh. 4089, f. 18b5–6. Dg.T. Beijing 79:42. Note the following differences: Dg.T. Beijing 79:42: ***de dag ji*** *ltar mngon rtogs rim; TOK,* II:446.6: ***bden pa*** *ji ltar mngon rtogs rim.* See Pruden 1989, 896–7.

194 *Mahāyānottaratantrashāstra, Theg pa chen po rgyud bla ma'i bstan bcos,* by Maitreya. Chapter 4, seventh vajra point, verse 331. Toh. 4024, f. 69b7. See Fuchs 2000, 263.

195 Although the translation "four noble truths" (*chaturāryasatya, 'phags pa bden pa bzhi*) has become commonplace (it is found in *Webster's Third New International Dictionary Unabridged,* for example), it is nevertheless inaccurate. As even this brief explanation reveals, the term means "truths (or realities) for noble beings." Readers should be aware that these "truths" themselves are not noble as is evident from the following citations.

Vasubandhu discusses the term in his *Explanation of the "Treasury of Abhidharma,"* Chapter 6, commentary for verse 2cd (Dg. T. Beijing 79:683–4):

> The [phrase] "truths for noble ones" occurs in the sūtras. What does it mean? Because they are what is true for noble ones, the sūtras refer to them only as "truths for noble ones."
>
> Does that mean that they are false for those who are not noble ones? [No.] Because they [i.e., the truths] are not incorrect, they are true for everyone. However, noble ones see them just as they are, whereas others do not. Therefore, they are called "the truths of noble ones," and they are not [truths] for those who are not noble ones, because [such beings] see incorrectly . . .
>
> There are others who say that two are truths [only] for noble ones and two are truths for [both] those who are not noble ones and for noble ones.
>
> *mdo las 'phags pa'i bden pa rnams zhes 'byung ba de'i don ci zhe na/ 'di dag ni 'phags pa rnams la bden pas/ de lta bas na mdo kho na las/ 'phags pa'i bden pa rnams zhes bshad do/ ci 'di dag gzhan rnams la brdzun nam zhe na/ 'di dag ni phyin ci ma log pa'i phyir thams cad la bden na 'phags pa rnams kyis ni 'di dag ji lta ba de kho na bzhin du gzigs kyi gzhan dag gis ni ma yin pas de'i phyir 'di dag ni 'phags pa rnams kyi bden pa zhes bya ba'i phyin ci log tu mthong ba'i phyir 'phags pa ma yin pa rnams kyi ni ma yin te/ . . . gzhan dag na re gnyis ni 'phags pa rnams kyi bden pa yin la/ gnyis ni 'phags pa yang* [reading ***ma*** instead of ***yang***] *yin 'phags pa rnams kyi bden pa yang yin no zhes zer ro.*

As indicated in the Tibetan, I am reading *'phags pa* **yang** *yin* in the last sentence as *'phags pa* **ma** *yin*, following Pruden's translation of La Vallée Poussin, who notes that "others" are "according to P'u-kuang (TD 41, p. 333c2), the Sautrāntikas and the Sthaviras." See also Pruden 1989, 898. La Vallée Poussin adds the following (Pruden 1989, 1042n12):

> *Vibhāṣha*, TD 27, p. 401c27. What is the meaning of the term *āryasatya* ["noble truth"]? Are the truths so called because they are good, because they are pure (*anāsrava*), or because the Āryans [noble ones] are endowed with them? What are the defects of these explanations? All three are bad: 1. one can say that the last two truths are good; but the first two are of three types, good, bad, and neutral; 2. the last two are pure, but not the first two; 3. the non-Āryans are endowed with the truths, thus it is said, "Who is endowed with the truths of *duḥkha* [suffering] and of *samudaya* [the origin of suffering]? All beings. Who is endowed with the Truth of *nirodha* [cessation]? Those who are not bound by all the bonds (*sakalabandhana*, see *Kośa*, ii. 36c, English trans. p. 207)." Answer: One must say that, because the Āryans are endowed with them, these Truths are Āryasatyas . . .

196 *mDzod 'grel.* This refers to Vasubandhu's *Explanation of the "Treasury of Abhidharma"* (*Abhidharmakosha-bhāṣhya, Chos mngon pa'i mdzod kyi bshad pa*) (Toh. 4090), not Yashomitra's *Sub-Commentary on the "Treasury of Abhidharma"* (*Abhidharmakōṣhaṭīkā, Chos mngon pa'i mdzod 'grel bshad*) (Toh. 4092). This quotation is found in its entirety in the *Explanation of the "Treasury of Abhidharma,"* Chapter 7, in the discussion of verse 13a (Dg.T. Beijing 79:796), but only partially in the *Sub-Commentary on the "Treasury of Abhidharma"* (Dg.T. Beijing 80:1448–9). See Pruden 1990, 1110–11.

197 *Abhidharmasamuchchaya, Chos mngon pa kun las btus pa*, by Asaṅga. Chapter 2 (following the fivefold division of the Sanskrit text and Tibetan translation as noted by Griffiths 1999, 435). Toh. 4024, f. 73b2; Dg.T. Beijing 76:186. See Boin-Webb 2001, 81.

198 The four spheres of the formless realms (*gzugs med skye mched mu bzhi*): (1) the sphere of Limitless Space (*nam mkha' mtha' yas skye mched*); (2) the sphere of Limitless Consciousness (*rnam shes mtha' yas skye mched*); (3) the sphere of Nothingness (*ci yang med pa'i mtha' yas skye mched*); and (4) the sphere of Neither Discrimination nor Nondiscrimination (*'du shes med min gyi skye mched*).

199 *TOK*, II:447.8: ***gdod*** *khams* should be ***'dod*** *khams*. (TN)

200 See the *Compendium of Abhidharma*, Chapter 2. Dg.T. Beijing 76:189–90; and Boin-Webb 2001, 84–5.

201 Chapter 2. Toh. 4049, f. 74b4; Dg.T. Beijing 76:189. See Boin-Webb 2001, 84.

202 "Negative propensities" (*dauṣhṭhulya, gnas ngan len pa*) is a term that refers to both the presence of the seeds, or causes, of the mental afflictions and the habitual tendencies they create. It is similar to the term "appropriated aggregates." See n. 190.

203 Conventional truth (or conventional reality; relative truth) (*saṃvṛiti-satya, kun rdzob bden pa*). The point here is that whatever is an object for the mind of a worldly person is considered to be conventional reality.

204 This quotation is found in Chapter 6 (it is not a verse of the *Treasury of Abhidharma*). Toh. 4090; Dg.T. Beijing 79:685. See Pruden 1989, 900.

205 Since the eighth type of suffering—the suffering of negative propensities, or the suffering of conditioned existence—is an object for the mind of a noble being, it is considered to be ultimate reality. This is because whatever is seen by a noble being's wisdom is considered to be ultimate reality. It does not mean that this type of suffering is ultimately real. The suffering of conditioned existence appears (*snang ba*) to, or is seen (*gzigs pa*) by, a noble being's wisdom, but it is not felt (*tshor ba*) by that being's wisdom. (ALTG)

206 Chapter 2. Toh. 4049, f. 78b1; Dg.T. Beijing 76:198. See Boin-Webb 2001, 94.

207 Chapter 5, verse 34. Toh. 4089, f. 17a4–5; Dg.T. Beijing 79:39. Note minor differences: Dg.T. Beijing: *phra rgyas spangs par ma* ***yin*** *dang/ yul ni nyer bar* ***gnas*** *pa dang; TOK,* II:448.23: *phra rgyas spangs par ma* ***gyur*** *dang/ yul ni nyer bar* ***gyur*** *pa dang.*

208 Subtle proliferators (*anushaya, phra rgyas*) are the subject of Chapter 5 in the *Treasury of Abhidharma.* Vasubandhu explains in his *Explanation of the "Treasury of Abhidharma"* that latent mental afflictions are called "subtle proliferators" (*nyon mongs pa nyal ba la ni phra rgyas zhes bya*) (Dg.T. Beijing 79:558). See Pruden 1989, where the term is translated as "latent defilements," particularly 767, 770, 828–35, and 884n140.

209 The six root mental afflictions (*klesha, nyon mongs*) are (1) desire (*rāga, 'dod chags*); (2) anger (*pratigha, khong khro*); (3) pride (*māna, nga rgyal*); (4) ignorance (*avidyā, ma rig pa*); (5) doubt (*vichikitsā, the tshom*); and (6) views (*dṛiṣhṭi, lta ba*). See *TOK,* II:378–9; and Hopkins 1983, 255–8.

210 The five views (*dṛiṣhṭi, lta ba*) are (1) the view, or belief, in the perishing collection [i.e., the aggregates, as being a self] (*satkāyadṛiṣhṭi, 'jig tshogs la lta ba*); (2) wrong views (*mithyādṛiṣhṭi, log lta*); (3) a view holding to an extreme (*antagrahādṛiṣhṭi, mthar 'dzin gyi lta ba*); (4) holding a view to be supreme (*dṛiṣhṭiparāmarsha, lta ba mchog 'dzin*); and (5) holding an ethical conduct or a discipline to be supreme (*shīlavrataparāmarsha, tshul khrims brtul zhugs mchog 'dzin bcas*). See *TOK,* II:379; and Hopkins 1983, 258–61.

211 The twenty secondary mental afflictions (*nyer ba nyon mongs pa*) are wrath (*krodha, khro ba*); resentment (*upanāha, 'khon 'dzin*); concealment (*mrakṣha, 'chab pa*); spite (*pradāsha, 'tshig pa*); envy (*irṣhyā, phrag dog*); avarice (*mātsarya, ser sna*); hypocrisy (*māyā, sgyu*); deceit (*shāṭhya, g.yo*); self-satisfaction (*mada, rgyags pa*); violence (*vihiṃsā, rnam pa 'tshe ba*); non-shame (*āhrīkya, ngo tsha med pa*); non-embarrassment (*anapatrāpya, khrel med pa*); lethargy (*styāna, rmugs pa*); agitation (*auddhatya, rgod pa*); non-faith (*āshraddhya, ma dad pa*); laziness (*kausīdya, le lo*); non-conscientiousness (*pramāda, bag med pa*); forgetfulness (*mushitasmṛtitā, brjed nges pa*); distraction (*vikṣhepa, rnam par g.yeng ba*); and non-introspection (*asaṃprajanya, shes bzhin ma yin pa*). See *TOK,* II:381–2; and Hopkins 1983, 261–6.

212 See Book Six, Part Two (*TOK,* II:378–82).

213 See the *Compendium of Abhidharma,* Chapter 2. Dg.T. Beijing 76:198; and Boin-Webb 2001, 94.

214 *Pramāṇavārttika, Tshad ma rnam 'grel,* by Dharmakīrti. Chapter 2. This is Dharmakīrti's commentary on Dignāga's *Compendium on Valid Cognition* (*Pramāṇasamuchchaya, Tshad ma kun las btus pa*), and is one of Dharmakīrti's seven Treatises on Valid Cognition (see n. 586). Toh. 4210, f. 144b6; Dg.T. Beijing 97:517.

The translation follows the sNar edition of the text (as cited in Dg.T. Beijing 97:517) because it seems to be the edition that Jamgön Kongtrul used, with one exception (or spelling mistake). sNar edition: *mi shes **srid** pa'i rgyu yin kyang/ ma brjod **sred** pa nyid bshad pa/ **rgyu** ni 'phen **par** byed phyir dang/ de ma thag phyir las kyang yin.*

Compare with *TOK*, II:449.21: *mi shes **sred** pa'i rgyu yin kyang/ ma brjod **sred** pa nyid bshad pa/ **rgyu** ni 'phen **par** byed phyir dang/ de ma thag phyir las kyang yin;* and Dg.T. Beijing 97:517: *mi shes **srid** pa'i rgyu yin kyang/ ma brjod **srid** pa nyid bshad pa/ **rgyun** ni 'phen **pa** byed phyir dang/ de ma thag phyir las kyang yin.* The Dergé redaction: Although lack of awareness is the cause of existence, that is not stated; it is craving that is named because it impels the continuum. Karma [is also not stated as the cause] because it is what comes next.

215 "Karma" (*las*) means action, but the term can be used to mean the process of causes leading to their corresponding results. Readers should bear in mind that whenever "karma" is used, both meanings may be applicable.

216 This is the explanation found in the *Compendium of Abhidharma*, Chapter 2. See Dg.T. Beijing 76:215; and Boin-Webb 2001, 112. It may be compared to the *Explanation of the "Treasury of Abhidharma,"* Chapter 4, commentary for verse 1, which states that intended karma is either a physical action or verbal one (and not mental). See Dg.T. Beijing 79:409; and Pruden 1988, 551–2.

217 Karmic paths (*karma-mārga, las kyi lam*): Saṃsāra has three paths: the mental afflictions, karma, and suffering. On the basis of the mental afflictions, karma is created. On the basis of karma, suffering occurs. On the basis of suffering, mental afflictions arise again. These three constitute an uninterrupted cycle: the path, or modality, of saṃsāra (*'khor ba'i lam gsum/ nyon mongs pa'i lam dang/ las kyi lam/ sdug bsngal gyi lam gsum ste nyon mongs par brten nas las byed pa dang/ las byas par brten nas sdug bsngal 'byung ba/ sdug bsngal la brten nas nyon mongs pa skye zhing rgyun mi 'chad par 'khor ba'i rim pa'o*) (*GTCD*). See also *Treasury of Abhidharma*, Chapter 4, verse 78cd. Dg.T. Beijing 79:509; and Pruden 1988, 509.

218 Degenerative samādhis (*zag bcas kyi ting nge 'dzin*): The term "degenerative" (*sāsrava, zag bcas*) denotes that these states of meditation are tainted by ignorance, and thus cannot bring about liberation.

219 See also the *Treasury of Abhidharma*, Chapter 4, verses 68d–78; *Compendium of Abhidharma* (Chapter 2); and Gampopa's *Ornament of Liberation* (*Thar pa rin po che'i rgyan*).

220 Magic spells (or awareness-mantras) (*vidyāmantra, rig sngags*): In Buddhist practices, awareness-mantras are used only in positive ways, but in other traditions these powerful mantras are used to harm others, hence the translation "magic spells" in such contexts.

221 The *Treasury of Abhidharma* (Chapter 4, verse 72ab) says, "If one dies before or at the same time, the actual [karmic path of killing] has not occurred, because [the killer] has been reborn in another body" (*snga dang mnyam du shi ba la/ dngos med lus gzhan skyes phyir ro*). Dg.T. Beijing 79:30.

222 Lay precepts (*poṣhadha, gso sbyong*) (lit. "purification-renewal") are eight vows, which include celibacy, taken for one day. See Kongtrul 1998, 100–1. In other contexts *poṣhadha* is the monastic confession ceremony. See Kongtrul 1998, 131–3.

223 Something cognizable (*vijñapti, rnam pa rig byed*) is a technical term found in Sarvāstivādin (or Vaibhāṣhika) abhidharma's discussions on karma. It means an act that causes someone to know something, an act that is manifest to another

consciousness; it is contrasted with incognizable, or incommunicable, acts (*avijñapti-karma*). See the *Treasury of Abhidharma,* Chapter 4, verses 2–3.

224 Lying about spiritual attainments (*mi chos bla ma'i rdzun*) (lit. "a lie in which [one claims to have achieved] a state or qualities higher [than those of] human beings"): This type of lie constitutes a "defeat" (*pham pa*) in that it defeats or destroys one, and it specifically defeats or destroys a monastic's vow not to lie. See Kongtrul 1998, pp. 107–8; and *TOK,* II:53.

225 For a definition of *tīrthikas* ("forders") (*mu stegs pa*), see n. 848.

226 Five acts of immediate consequence (*mtshams med lnga*): (1) to commit patricide (*pha gsod pa*); (2) to commit matricide (*ma gsod pa*); (3) to kill an arhat (*dgra bcom gsod pa*); (4) to cause dissension among the saṅgha (*dge 'dun gyi dbyen byed pa*); and (5) to draw the blood of the Tathāgata with malicious intent (*de bzhin gshegs pa'i sku la ngan sems kyis khrag 'byin pa*). (*GTCD*)

227 *Ratnāvalī, Rin chen 'phreng ba,* by Nāgārjuna. Chapter 1, verses 14–16c. Toh. 4158, f. 107b2–3; Dg.T. Beijing 96:289. For verse 14d, the translation follows Dg.T. Beijing: *byi bo byed pas dgra* ***dang*** *bcas; TOK,* II:454.23: *byi bo byed pas dgra* ***zlar*** *bcas.* For verse 15c, the translation follows Dg.T. Beijing: ***tshig rtsub*** *nyid kyis mi snyan thos; TOK,* II:455.1: ***rtsub mo*** *nyid kyis mi snyan thos.*

228 This verse does not appear in the *Precious Garland* and it has not been located elsewhere.

229 Chapter 9. Toh. 4090; Dg.T. Beijing 79:908. See Pruden 1990, 1353. In the first line, the translation follows Dg.T. Beijing: *las* ***kyi*** *'khor* ***ba*** *lci gang dang; TOK,* II:455.8: *las* ***ni*** *'khor* ***bar*** *lci gang dang.*

230 Chapter 4, verse 72cd. Toh. 4089, f. 13b4; Dg.T. Beijing 79:30. See Pruden 1988, 649.

231 Chapter 1, verse 20ab and verse 21ab. Toh. 4158, f. 107b5; Dg.T. Beijing 96:290.

232 Unpleasant Sound (*Kuru, sGra mi snyan*) is the northern of the four continents described in abhidharma cosmology. See Kongtrul 1995, 110 and 113.

233 Chakravartin (wheel-wielding monarchs) (*'khor lo sgyur ba*): see Kongtrul 1995, 134–8.

234 This presumably means the three other continents—Majestic Body (*Videha, Lus 'phags po*), Bountiful Cow (*Godāniya, Ba lang spyod*), and Unpleasant Sound (*Kuru, sGra mi snyan*)—excluding our own "continent," which is called Jambu Continent (*Jambudvīpa, 'Dzam bu gling*).

235 *Precious Garland,* Chapter 1, verses 8–9c. Toh. 4158, f. 107a6; Dg.T. Beijing 96:289.

236 Chapter 1, verse 20cd and verse 21cd. Toh. 4158; Dg.T. Beijing 96:290.

237 See the *Explanation of the "Treasury of Abhidharma,"* Chapter 4, verse 46cd and its commentary. Dg.T. Beijing 79:473; and Pruden 1988, 622.

238 *Precious Garland,* Chapter 1, verse 24. Toh. 4158, f. 107b7; Dg.T. Beijing 96:290.

239 These are discussed in Book Six, Part One (*TOK,* II:348).

240 See the *Compendium of Abhidharma,* Chapter 2. Dg.T. Beijing 76:223; and Boin-Webb 2001, 126.

241 Nāgas (*klu*) are a non-human class of beings associated with water. Usually described as snakes with large hoods, they are considered to be very wealthy and dangerous to humans if disturbed.

242 See the *Compendium of Abhidharma*, Chapter 2 (Dg.T. Beijing 76:222–3; and Boin-Webb 2001, 125–6), and the *Explanation of the "Treasury of Abhidharma,"* Chapter 4, verse 50bc and its commentary (Dg.T. Beijing 79:476–7; and Pruden 1989, 625).

243 Devadatta was the Buddha Shākyamuni's jealous cousin, who tried to kill the Buddha on three occasions.

244 See n. 226.

245 Five secondary acts of immediate consequence (*nye ba'i mtshams med pa lnga*): (1) to have sexual intercourse with a female arhat (*dgra bcom ma la 'dod log spyod pa*); (2) to kill a bodhisattva dwelling in assurance (*byang sems nges gnas gsod pa*); (3) to kill a saṅgha member who is in training (*slob pa'i dge 'dun gsod pa*); (4) to misappropriate the saṅgha's property (*dge 'dun gyi 'du sgo 'phrog pa*); and (5) to destroy a stūpa (*mchod rten bshig pa*). (*GTCD*)

246 The translation follows PKTC reading *lus; TOK*, II:458.13 has *lugs*.

247 For discussions of Vaibhāṣhika and Sautrāntika theories of attainment (*prāpti, thob pa*), see Cox 1992 and 1995.

248 A nonimplicative negation (*prasajyapratiṣhedha, med dgag*) is one that does not indicate or imply anything in place of its object of negation. The other main type of negation used in Indo-Tibetan debate is an implicative negation (*paryudāsapratiṣhedha, ma yin dgag*), which implies or affirms something in place of the object of negation.

249 Chapter 2. Toh. 4049; Dg.T. Beijing 76:228. See Boin-Webb 2001, 133.

250 *Phenomenon* (*dharmin, chos can*) here is more literally "something possessing a quality." The addition of *can* indicates that the phenomenon (*chos*) possesses or is imbued with (*can*) the quality (*chos*) of dharmatā (*chos nyid*), its reality or ultimate nature.

251 The translation follows PKTC reading *shes rab* ***kyis*** *nyon sgrib; TOK*, II:460.19 has *shes rab* ***kyi*** *nyon sgrib*. PKTC accords with the *Compendium of Abhidharma* (Dg.T. Beijing 76:229): *shes rab kyis rnam par grol ba'i dgra bcom pa.*

252 Six supercognitive abilities (*mngon par shes pa*): (1) magical powers (*rdzu 'phrul*); (2) divine eye (*lha'i mig*); (3) divine ear (*lha'i rna*); (4) recollection of previous lives (*sngon gnas rjes dran*); (5) knowledge of others' minds (*gzhan sems shes pa*); and (6) knowledge of the exhaustion of defilements (*zag zad mkhyen pa*). The sixth is a quality that only buddhas possess (*GTCD*). These are discussed quite extensively in the *Treasury of Abhidharma,* Chapter 7, verses 42–56. See Pruden 1990, 1157–80.

253 The eight excellent qualities (*yon tan brgyad*) are not mentioned in the *Compendium of Abhidharma* (although the six supercognitive abilities and the three knowledges are). These may be the ones described in the *Unassailable Lion's Roar* (*Mi ldog pa seng ge'i nga ro*), which is Jamgön Kongtrul's commentary on the *Highest Continuum* (*Uttaratantra; rGyud bla ma*) (ALTG). Under the third vajra point, verse 14, the eight excellent qualities of the saṅgha are

- three excellent qualities of awareness (primordial wisdom that sees the true mode, primordial wisdom that sees all phenomena in their varieties, and the vision of inner primordial wisdom);

- three excellent qualities of liberation (the purification of the latent obscurations and the hindering obscurations, and possession of unsurpassable virtues); and
- the two [qualities], awareness and liberation, that are the basis for the classifications.

See Fuchs 2000, 109–110.

254 Jamgön Kongtrul has paraphrased Asaṅga's *Compendium of Abhidharma.* See Dg.T. Beijing 76:228–30; and Boin-Webb 2001, 133–37.

255 See Book Nine, Part One (*TOK*, III:464–508).

256 See the *Compendium of Abhidharma,* Chapter 2 (Dg.T. Beijing 76:190–5; and Boin-Webb 2001, 85–90), and the *Explanation of the "Treasury of Abhidharma,"* Chapter 7, commentary for verse 13a (Dg.T. Beijing 79:795–6; and Pruden 1990, 1110).

257 Chapter 7, commentary for verse 13a. Toh. 4090; Dg.T. Beijing 79:795–6. See Pruden 1990, 1110.

258 See the *Compendium of Abhidharma,* Chapter 2 (Dg.T. Beijing 76:227–8; and Boin-Webb 2001, 132–3), and the *Explanation of the "Treasury of Abhidharma,"* Chapter 7, commentary for verse 13a (Dg.T. Beijing 79:796; and Pruden 1990, 1110).

259 Enabling causes (*karaṇahetu, byed rgyu*) are one of six causes listed in the *Treasury of Abhidharma* (Chapter 2, verses 49-50). Wangchuk Dorjé in his *Youthful Play: An Explanation of the "Treasury of Abhidharma"* (*mNgon par mdzod kyi rnam bshad gzhon nu rnam rol,* hereafter cited as *Youthful Play*) (113) defines them as "all phenomena that are other than the [particular] conditioned phenomenon itself are causes that enable [the arising of] something conditioned" (*'dus byas rang las don gzhan pa'i chos thams cad 'dus byas kyi byed rgyu'i rgyu yin*). Jamgön Kongtrul (*TOK*, I:241) uses this definition with only minor word substitutions. See Kongtrul 1995, 182–3, where the term is translated as "productive causes."

260 The translation follows PKTC reading *so so rang rang gi* ***rgyud*** *tha dad; TOK,* II:462.19 has *so so rang rang gi* ***rgyu*** *tha dad.*

261 Pinnacle of Existence (*Bhavāgra, Srid pa'i rtse mo*) is the highest state attainable in the three realms of saṃsāra and is another name for the fourth level of the formless realm, the sphere of Neither Discrimination nor Nondiscrimination (*'du shes med min gyi skye mched*).

262 Chapter 7, commentary for verse 13a. Toh. 4090; Dg.T. Beijing 79:796. See Pruden 1990, 1110. Note the following wording and spelling variances: Dg.T. Beijing 79:796: *'byung ba'i* ***chos kyi*** *tshul gyis kun 'byung ba'o . . . mngon par sgrub pa'i con gyis* ***ni*** *rkyen te/ dper na* ***'jim pa'i*** *gong bu dang thal zhar dang 'khor lo dang* ***thag*** *gu dang . . . ; TOK,* II:463.2–4: *'byung ba'i tshul gyis kun 'byung ba'o . . . mngon par sgrub pa'i con gyis* ***na*** *rkyen te/ dper na* ***'ji ba'i*** *gong bu dang thal zhar dang 'khor lo dang* ***the*** *gu dang . . .*

263 See the *Compendium of Abhidharma,* Chapter 2 (Dg.T. Beijing 76:232; and Boin-Webb 2001, 140), and the *Explanation of the "Treasury of Abhidharma,"* Chapter 7, commentary for verse 13a (Dg.T. Beijing 79:796; and Pruden 1990, 1111).

264 Chapter 7, commentary for verse 13a. Toh. 4090; Dg.T. Beijing 79:796. See Pruden 1990, 1112.

265 The three characteristics of conditioned phenomena (*'dus byas kyi mtshan nyid gsum*) are arising (*skye ba*), impermanence (*mi rtag pa*), and aging (*rga ba*). These are discussed in Chapter 2 of the *Explanation of the "Treasury of Abhidharma,"* commentary for verse 45cd. See Dg.T. Beijing 79:199–200; and Pruden 1988, 238–9.

266 See the *Compendium of Abhidharma,* Chapter 2 (Dg.T. Beijing 76:252; and Boin-Webb 2001, 176), and the *Explanation of the "Treasury of Abhidharma,"* Chapter 7, commentary for verse 13a (Dg.T. Beijing 79:796; and Pruden 1990, 1111).

267 The word *mārga,* typically meaning "path," also has the meaning "to seek" (*'tshol ba*) from the root √*mārg,* "to look for" (Monier-Williams). This is often referred to in discussions of the meaning of the path. In his *Explanation of the "Treasury of Abhidharma,"* Vasubandhu says, "Why is the term *path* used? It is the path to nirvāṇa because it is what goes from here to there, and because it is [the means] through which nirvāṇa is sought" (*ci'i phyir lam zhes bya zhe na/ de nas der 'gro ba'i phyir ram/ 'dis mya ngan las 'das pa tshol ba'i phyir 'di ni mya ngan las 'das pa'i lam yin no*). Chapter 6, commentary for verse 65bd; Dg.T. Beijing 79:769.

268 Chapter 7, commentary for verse 13a. Toh. 4090; Dg.T. Beijing 79:796. See Pruden 1990, 1111.

269 *lJon shing/ rGyud kyi mngon par rtogs pa rin po che'i ljon shing.*

270 Jetsün Drakpa Gyaltsen (*rJe btsun Grags pa rgyal mtshan*) (1147–1216) was the third of the five patriarchs of the Sakya school.

271 See Kongtrul 1998, Chapter 2: The Vows of Personal Liberation, p. 85, The Definition [of the Vows of Personal Liberation] (*TOK,* II:35).

272 Higher abhidharma (*mngon pa gong ma*) refers to abhidharma teachings based on Asaṅga's *Compendium of Abhidharma.* Lower abhidharma (*mngon pa 'og ma*) means the abhidharma teachings based on Vasubandhu's *Treasury of Abhidharma.*

273 Chapter 3, verse 18a. Toh. 4089, f. 7b3; Dg.T. Beijing 79:16. See Pruden 1988, 399.

274 *Ārya-ghanavyūha-nāma-mahāyāna-sūtra, 'Phags pa rgyan stug po bkod pa zhes bya ba theg pa chen po'i mdo.* Toh. 110.

275 *Laṅkāvatārasūtra, Lang kar gshegs pa'i mdo.* Toh. 107; ACIP KL0107.

276 See Chapter 10, p. 246, where Jamgön Kongtrul states that, from a Prāsaṅgika standpoint, "it is impossible that shrāvakas and pratyekabuddhas do not realize the absence of a self-entity of phenomena." For discussion of this point, see Brunnhölzl 2004, 421–38; Padmakara Translation Group 2002, 310–14; and Lopez 1988a.

277 *Yuktiṣhaṣhṭikā-vṛitti, Rigs pa drug cu pa'i 'grel pa,* by Chandrakīrti. Toh. 3864; Dg.T. Beijing 60:951. This is commentary on verse 8 of Nāgārjuna's *Sixty Verses on Reasoning* (*Yuktiṣhaṣhṭikākārikā, Rigs pa drug cu pa'i tshig le'ur byas pa*) (Toh. 3825; Dg.T. Beijing 57:52).

The translation follows Dg.T. Beijing: *gzugs la sogs pa'i rang gi ngo'i mtshan nyid dngos po'i rang bzhin rgyu rkyen las dang nyon mongs pa dang mi ldan pas phyis mi skye ba gang yin pa de mya ngan las 'das pa.*

Compare with *TOK,* 2:466.5–6: *'on kyang rgyu dang rkyen las dang nyon mongs pa ma tshang ba las gzugs la sogs pa'i mtshan nyid dngos po'i rang gi ngo bo slar mi skye ba gang yin pa de mya ngan las 'das pa'o,* "Nevertheless, nirvāṇa is the very essence of an entity [with] defining characteristics, such as a form, that does not arise again owing to the incompleteness of its causes and conditions, or karma and mental afflictions."

278 See The Truth of Cessation section, p. 111.

279 The three types of unconditioned phenomena (*asaṃskṛita, 'dus ma byas*) are space (*ākāsha, nam mkha'*), analytical cessations (*pratisaṃkhyānirodha, so sor brtags pas 'gog pa*), and nonanalytical cessations (*apratisaṃkhyānirodha, so sor brtags pa ma yin pa'i 'gog pa*). Analytical cessations, or cessations resulting from knowledge, are the state of freedom from defiled phenomena, that is, mental afflictions. This cessation is attained through the power of the analysis of, or the wisdom (*prajñā, shes rab*) engaging, the four truths of noble ones. Nonanalytical cessations, or cessations not resulting from knowledge, are temporary absences of mental afflictions owing to the incompleteness of the necessary conditions. For example, when one concentrates intently on a specific task, one does not feel tired, but feelings of tiredness will return. See Pruden 1988, 59; and Hopkins 1983, 218.

280 *Thub pa dgongs gsal.* This may be *Thub pa dgongs pa rab gsal* by Sakya Paṇḍita, Kunga Gyaltsen (*Kun dga' rgyal mtshan*) (1182–1251); however, I was unable to locate this comment in that text.

281 I have not been able to locate this comment in the *Explanation of the "Treasury of Abhidharma."*

282 The eighty-nine conditioned results and the eighty-nine unconditioned results (*'dus byas brgyad cu rtsa dgu dang 'dus ma byas brgyad cu rtsa dgu*): There are eighty-nine paths of release (*rnam grol gyi lam*) with eighty-nine mental afflictions to be abandoned: paths 1–8 correspond to the path of seeing, where eight afflictions are abandoned; and paths 9–89 to the path of meditation, where on each of the nine bhūmis nine mental afflictions are abandoned. The paths of release are the conditioned results, and the abandonment of eighty-nine types of mental afflictions are the unconditioned results. This is discussed in Chapter 6, verse 51 of the *Treasury of Abhidharma;* see Pruden 1988, 992–3.

283 The four results of shrāmaṇas (*dge sbyong gi 'bras bu bzhi*) are stream enterer (*srota-āpanna, rgyun zhugs pa*), once returner (*sakṛid-āgāmin, lan cig phyir 'ong ba*), non-returner (*anāgāmin, phyir mi 'ong ba*), and arhat (*dgra bcom pa*). See A Detailed Explanation of the Gradual Type, pp. 142–149.

284 In Tibetan scholarship there are different views on the relationship between the Vaibhāṣhika and Sautrāntika philosophical tenet systems and the eighteen orders (*nikāya, sde pa*). The following is based on the excellent overview by Willemen and Dessein (Willemen et al. 1998, xi–xiii, 47, and 123–5). It seems that Sarvāstivādins developed from the Sthaviras (who with the Mahāsāṅghikas form the first division in the Shrāvakayāna followers) and mainly lived in Kashmir, Bactria, and Gandhāra. During the second century CE, Kashmiri Sarvāstivāda abhidharma scholars organized their literature into seven texts and wrote a compendium called the *Great Exposition* (**Mahāvibhāṣha*). Owing to doctrinal differences, they became known as Vaibhāṣhikas, "Proponents of the *Exposition.*" During this period, the old Sarvāstivādins in Bactria and Gandhāra were called Sautrāntikas, meaning simply that they were non-Vaibhāṣhika Sarvāstivādins and, as such, distinguished themselves, but they were not themselves a homogenous group. Kumāralāta (second century CE) is considered an important opponent of the Kashmiri Vaibhāṣhikas and a root teacher of the Sautrāntikas.

During the seventh century, the Kashmiri Vaibhāṣhikas declined in power (attributable to the loss of patronage), and the original Sarvāstivādins became the dominant Sarvāstivāda group through the ninth century. By the end of that century, some of them were calling themselves Mūlasarvāstivādins, reflecting their view that they represented the original Sarvāstivāda perspective. Willemen states (1998, xiii) that as they "are basically the continuation of old non-Vaibhāṣhika Sarvāstivādins, their views can be found in many older Chinese texts, and in many Indian Sarvāstivāda manuscripts." He concludes (ibid., xiii), "Actually, in the history of the Sarvāstivāda school, the Vaibhāṣhika 'orthodoxy' was a phenomenon limited in time and space. The mainstream [i.e., the non-Vaibhāṣhika Sarvāstivādins, also known as Sautrāntikas] temporarily lost ground, but after a few centuries regained it as Mūlasarvāstivāda."

285 Bodhibhadra (*Byang chub bzang po*) (ca. 1000) was a master at Nālandā and one of Atīsha's teachers. His *Commentary on the "Compendium on the Heart of Wisdom"* (*Jñānasārasamuchchaya-nāma-nibandhana, Ye shes snying po kun las btus pa zhes bya ba'i bshad sbyar*) (Toh. 3852; Dg.T. Beijing 57:891) is an explanation of Āryadeva's *Compendium on the Heart of Wisdom* (*Jñānasārasamuchchaya, Ye shes snying po kun las btus pa*) (Toh. 3851; Dg.T. Beijing 57:851).

286 Vasubandhu discusses the Vaibhāṣhikas' assertion that phenomena exist in the three times in his *Treasury of Abhidharma*, Chapter 5, verses 25–26 (see Dg.T. Beijing 79:586–97; and Pruden 1998, 806–20). They are said to hold this view on the basis of the Buddha's teachings and reasoning. Willemen summarizes (1998, 20) this as follows:

> (1) The past and future exist because the Bhagavat said that the knowledgeable, holy *Śrāvaka* does not take past matter (*rūpa*) into consideration and does not delight in future matter.
>
> (2) The Buddha also said that: "Consciousness arises because of two things: 1. the faculty of sight (*cakṣurindriya*) and the visible (*rūpa*), 2. the mind (*manas*) and factors (*dharma*)." As mental consciousness immediately follows visual perception, it is so that if the visible, perceived *before* by the organ of sight and therefore *past,* were no longer to exist, mental consciousness could not arise because of it.
>
> (3) If the object perceived, in the past, by the organ of sight were no longer to exist at the moment of consciousness, the latter would not arise, since there is no consciousness without an object.
>
> (4) If the past does not exist, how can a good or a bad action, in the future, yield its fruition? In fact, at the moment when the fruition is produced, the cause of maturation (*vipākahetu*)—i.e. the action—is past.

287 *Great Detailed Exposition* (*Mahāvibhāṣha, Bye brag tu bshad pa chen mo,* or *Bye brag bshad mdzod* [or *mtsho*] *chen mo*) (or *Treasury/Ocean of Great Detailed Exposition*), was translated into Tibetan from the Chinese by Fa Zun (*bLo bzang chos 'phags*) in 1949 but is yet unpublished. According to Buswell and Jaini (1996, 79 and 100), the *Mahāvibhāṣha* (*Great Exposition*) was written (or compiled) during the third council held in Kashmir (first century CE), when the Sarvāstivādin canon was codified. For a summary of the *Mahāvibhāṣha,* see Ichimura et al. 1996, 511–68; and Cox 1998, 229–39. (Note that the term *Mahāvibhāṣha* is not attested in Sanskrit; see Kritzer 2005, xxi.)

288 If the use of the name Mūlasarvāstivādin dates from the seventh century (as stated by Willemen in Willemen et al. 1998, xiii), this remark would be better as "[Vaibhāṣhikas] are a particular instance of the Sarvāstivādins." It could also apply to Sautrāntikas, who are also considered by some to be a subdivision of the Sarvāstivādins. See above n. 284; and Willemen et al. 1998, xii-xiii.

289 Toh. 3852; Dg.T. Beijing 57:892.

290 *Six Doors* (*Ṣhaṇmukha, sGo drug pa*) and *Excellent Conduct* (*Bhadracharyā-sūtra, 'Phags pa bzang po spyod pa*): I have been unable to identify these texts with any certainty.

291 Kritzer (2003a, 202) says:

> Closely associated with Sautrāntika is Dārṣṭāntika. This name is derived from the word *dṛṣṭānta* ("example"), and it appears to refer to the group's propensity for using examples or similes from the ordinary world to justify its doctrinal positions. It is not clear whether the terms Sautrāntika and Dārṣṭāntika are, respectively, positive and negative designations for the same group, different names for the same group at different periods, or terms for two different groups. However, . . . the commentators on the *Abhidharmakośabhāṣya* [*Explanation of the "Treasury of Abhidharma"*] tend to view Sautrāntika and Dārṣṭāntika as essentially synonymous (Cox *Disputed Dharmas* 37–41).

See also Cox 1988, 70n4; and Cox 1998, 106–10.

292 The four principles of the dharma (*chos kyi sdom bzhi*) are as follows. (1) All conditioned things are impermanent (*'dus byas thams cad mi rtag pa*). (2) Everything defiled involves suffering (*zag bcas thams cad sdug bsngal ba*). (3) All phenomena are empty and devoid of self-entity (*chos thams cad stong zhing bdag med pa*). (4) Nirvāṇa is a state of peace (*mya ngan las 'das pa zhi ba*). These are also known as the four seals of the Buddha's teachings (*lta bkar btags kyi phyag rgya bzhi*).

293 The two types of absence of self-entity are the absence of a self of persons (*pudgalanairātmya, gang zag gi bdag med*) and the absence of a self-entity of phenomena (*dharmanairātmya, chos kyi bdag med*). The two obscurations (*sgrib gnyis*) are the afflictive obscurations (*kleṣhāvaraṇa, nyon sgrib*) and the cognitive obscurations (*jñeyāvaraṇa, shes bya'i sgrib pa*).

294 *Ālaya* (*kun gzhi*) is translated in many ways, some of which are "all-basis," "universal ground," "all-ground," "basis-of-all," and "storehouse." For in-depth studies of ālayavijñāna, see Schmithausen 1987; and Waldron 2003.

295 Ten bhūmis (*sa bcu*; ten levels or grounds): (1) Very Joyful (*rab tu dga' ba*); (2) Stainless (*dri ma med pa*); (3) Illuminating (*'od byed pa*); (4) Radiant (*'od 'phro ba*); (5) Difficult to Overcome (*sbyang dka' ba*); (6) Manifest (*mngon du gyur pa*); (7) Gone Afar (*ring du song ba*); (8) Immovable (*mi g.yo ba*); (9) Excellent Intelligence (*legs pa'i blo gros*); and (10) Cloud of Dharma (*chos kyi sprin*). These are discussed in Book Nine, Part One (*TOK*, III:492–5).

296 This point is related to the statement on p. 129: "They assert that the truth of suffering is [experienced] on the bhūmi of a buddha, meaning that the Buddha had matured aggregates that were impelled by previous karma and that he had a remainder of defiled karma."

Although Jamgön Kongtrul says that Vaibhāṣhikas and Sautrāntikas agree about not asserting a transformation (*gnas gyur*), it is one of the issues Vasubandhu presents as a point of disagreement between Vaibhāṣhikas and Sautrāntikas in his *Explanation of the "Treasury of Abhidharma"* (Chapter 2, commentary for verse 36) (Dg.T. Beijing 79:177; see Pruden 1988, 209). It has been noted by Davidson (1985, 168) and King (1998) that Sautrāntikas do assert a "transformation of a basis" (*āshraya-parāvṛitta, rten 'gyur ba*). King states (1998):

In the critique of 'possession' (*prapti*) . . . Vasubandhu qua Sautrantika seems to utilise a notion which becomes of crucial importance in the subsequent Yogacara elaboration of the path to liberation, viz. *asraya-paravrtti*, the conversion of the basis. He states that verily, the physical basis of the Noble One has undergone transformation by virtue of the path of vision and the path of cultivation such that those defilements that are allayed no longer have the ability to shoot forth. As rice seeds that are in a non-germinal (or impotent) state, just so one is called a 'destroyer of the defilements' with reference to the defilements of the physical basis (*bhutasaraydh*).

297 The four primordial wisdoms (*jñāna, ye shes*) are mirrorlike wisdom (*me long lta bu'i ye shes*), discriminating wisdom (*sor rtogs ye shes*), the wisdom of equality (*mnyam nyid ye shes*), and the wisdom that accomplishes activities (*bya grub ye shes*). When five wisdoms are listed, the fifth is the wisdom of the dharmadhatu (*chos dbyings ye shes*).

298 Cha (*Chva*): the creator god of Bön, the pre-Buddhist religion of Tibet. Īshvara (*dBang phyug*): another name for the Hindu god Shiva.

299 *Treasury of Abhidharma*, Chapter 4, verse 1a. Toh. 4089; Dg.T. Beijing 79:24. See Pruden 1988, 551. Note that the word order is reversed: Dg.T. Beijing 79:24: ***las las*** *'jig rten sna tshogs skyes*; *TOK*, II:468.14: *'jig rten sna tshogs* ***las las*** *skyes.*

300 The five aggregates (*skandhas, phung po lnga*) are forms, feelings, discriminations, formative forces, and consciousnesses. The eighteen constituents (*dhātus, khams bco brgyad*) are the six objects of perception (visual forms, sounds, smells, tastes, tangible objects, and phenomena), the six sense faculties, and six consciousnesses. The twelve sense spheres (*āyatanas, skye mched bcu gnyis*) are the six objects of the sense consciousnesses and the six sense faculties. The four modes of birth (*skye gnas bzhi*) are birth from a womb, birth from an egg, birth from heat and moisture, and spontaneous birth. The five kinds of beings (*'gro ba lnga*) are hell-beings, hungry ghosts, animals, humans, and gods (demigods are included with gods).

GTCD: Among the four kinds of food (*zas bzhi*), coarse food (or "morsels") is for the growth of the sense faculties of this body; food of contact nourishes the consciousnesses; mental food is what propels one towards future existences; and food of consciousness is what finalizes the next existence (*zas bzhi/ kham gyi zas dang/ reg pa'i zas dang/ sems pa'i zas dang/ rnam shes kyi zas te bzhi ste/ tshe 'di la gnas dbang po rgyas pa'i don du kham zas dang/ brten pa rnam shes rgyas pa'i don du reg pa'i zas te gnyis dang/ phyi mar srid pa gzhan 'phen pa'i don du sems pa'i zas dang/ srid pa gzhan 'grub pa'i don du rnam shes kyi zas dang gnyis te bsdoms na bzhi'o*). (Note that *TOK*, II:468.17 has ***khams***, but according to the *GTCD* it should be **kham**.)

Ngawang Palden's (*Ngag dbang dpal ldan*) *Annotations* (Hopkins 2003, 224) says, "It is explained that morsels [that is, usual sorts of food] are only in the desire realm; the other three foods exist in all three realms—desire, form, and formless."

301 Defiled phenomena (*sāsrava, zag bcas chos*) and undefiled phenomena (*anāsrava, zag med chos*). For further discussions of these terms, see Pruden 1989, 834; and Norman 1990, 28–30, and 34n50.

302 Khenpo Tsültrim Gyamtso Rinpoche's *The Presentation of the Classifications of Mental States* (Khenpo Tsültrim Gyamtso 1996b/2000) states that mind (*chitta, sems*) and mental events (*chaitta, sems byung*) have five congruent aspects (*mtshungs ldan lnga*): (1) their support (*rten*): they depend on the same sense faculty; (2) their observed object (*dmigs pa*): they observe the same object; (3) their aspect (*rnam pa*): they have

the same objective aspect during their mode of apprehension; (4) their time (*dus*): they occur at the same time; and (5) their substance (*rdzas*): they share an equal number of moments of a similar type.

The same list is found in the *Treasury of Abhidharma,* Chapter 2, verse 34bd; see Pruden 1988, 205–6.

303 In this book Jamgön Kongtrul presents the Vaibhāṣhikas' and Sautrāntikas' positions on the two truths as a shared assertion. In Book Seven, Part Two, he presents the Vaibhāṣhika and Sautrāntika views on the two truths separately and as different. One thing this reflects is the different Tibetan views regarding which teachers represent the Sautrāntika system. In this section, Jamgön Kongtrul says that Sautrāntika teachers include Saṅgharakṣhita and Shrīlāta, and he makes no mention of Dignāga or Dharmakīrti in the Sautrāntika presentation. However, in Book Seven, Part Two (*TOK,* III:35), he quotes Dharmakīrti's *Commentary on Valid Cognition* (*Pramāṇavārttikakārikā, Tshad ma rnam 'grel*) as the source of the Sautrāntika definition of the two truths.

304 Chapter 6, verse 4. Toh. 4089; Dg.T. Beijing 79:43. See Pruden 1989, 910.

305 "To halt the perceiving mind" (*blo 'dor ba*) means that the mind no longer identifies the object. For example, when a table is broken up, the mind no longer thinks "table" when looking at the broken bits.

306 In his *Explanation of the "Treasury of Abhidharma"* (Chapter 6, commentary for verse 4), Vasubandhu explains ultimate reality as follows:

> Ultimate reality is that which, even when broken up, is engaged by the mind; and it is that which, even [if] the mind eliminates other qualities from it, is [still] engaged by the mind. An example is form. It is possible to reduce that to minute particles, and it is even possible for the mind to eliminate its qualities of taste, [but] there will [still] be the mind that engages the nature of form. The same is the case with feelings and so forth.
>
> *gang la bcom yang de'i blo 'jug pa kho na yin la/ blos chos gzhan bsal yang de'i blo 'jug pa de ni don dam par yod pa yin te/ dper na gzugs lta bu'o/ de la rdul phra bar tu bcom yang rung/ blos ro la sogs pa'i chos bsal kyang rung gzugs kyi rang bzhin gyi blo 'jug pa nyid de/ tshor ba la sogs pa yang de bzhin du blta bar bya'o.* Dg.T. Beijing 79:695–6.

Buescher demonstrates (2005, 74) that Shrīlāta (a Sautrāntika) provides a similar definition:

> Saṃghabhadra, in the *Samaya-pradīpika*, quoted the Sthavira sectarian Śrīlāta's definition of the two truths, which also relied upon the idea of substance:
>
>> That which exists in many substances is conventional; that which exists in a single substance is ultimate. Moreover, if, when one divides it, the thing (*dharma*) in question loses its original name, it is conventional; if it does not lose it, it is ultimate.

Cox explains (1995, 138) the position of Saṅghabhadra (a Vaibhāṣhika) as follows:

> Saṅghabhadra . . . distinguishes two types of existence: existence as a real entity (*dravyasat*), which is equated with absolute existence (*paramārthasat*), and existence as a provisional entity (*prajñāptisat*), equated with conventional existence (*saṃvṛtisat*). The former category of real entities includes the ultimate constituent factors such as visible form or feelings, which produce cognition

> without depending on anything else. The latter category of provisional entities includes entities such as a pot or an army, which can produce cognition only in dependence upon a real entity that serves as its basis. This dependence upon real entities may be either direct, as in the case of a pot, which depends directly upon the fundamental material elements (*mahābhūta*) of which it is made, or indirect, as in the case of an army, which depends first upon other provisional entities—that is, its human members—and secondarily upon real entities—that is, the ultimate factors of which these humans are composed.
>
> Here, by "dependence," Saṅghabhadra does not understand causal dependence; all conditioned factors, real entities and provisional entities alike, are causally dependent or are related through conditioning interaction. Rather, "dependence" in the case of a provisional entity refers to the possibility of further analysis; any entity that can be analyzed further into constituent elements is considered "dependent" upon those elements. The possibility of further analysis then becomes the criterion by which conventional (*saṃvṛtisatya*) and absolute truth (*paramārthasatya*) are distinguished. If the notion of a particular entity disappears when that entity is broken (e.g., a pot) or can be resolved by cognition into its components (e.g., water), that entity exists only conventionally. Entities that are not subject either to this further material or mental analysis exist absolutely. Thus, actual existence as a real entity (*dravyasat*) is attributed only to the ultimate constituent factors, which are not subject to further analysis.

Buescher (2005, 75) sums up the difference between the views of the Vaibhāṣhikas and Sautrāntikas regarding what is ultimate as follows:

> The Vaibhāṣikas, as the *Abhidharmakośa* made clear, regarded the aggregates, the sources, and the constituents (or "types") as ultimates, and held that even one atom of "form," for example, qualified as a "form aggregate" (*rūpaskandha*). On the other hand, the Sautrāntikas as described in the *Abhidharmakośa* (and by Śrīlāta) held that, of these three categories, only the constituents (*dhātu*) were ultimates.

For more on the Vaibhāṣhikas' explanations of what is ultimate, see Pruden 1988, 77–80 and 1989, 910–1; Buescher 2005, 66–83; Cox 1995, 133–58; Matilal 1986, 240–50; Newland 1999, 18–22; and Williams 1981.

307 Capable of performing a function (*arthakriyāsamartham, don byed nus pa*): An entity (*dngos po*) performs the function of producing its own specific result, such as later moments of its own continuum or a consciousness perceiving that specific phenomenon. (See Dreyfus 1997, 66.)

Since here Jamgön Kongtrul presents ultimate reality from a perspective that is both Vaibhāṣhika and Sautrāntika, this paragraph combines positions that in Book Seven, Part Two (*TOK*, III:35), he attributes separately. There he says that Vaibhāṣhikas consider the partless moments of cognition and partless minute particles to be ultimate reality, and that the Sautrāntikas' presentation of the two truths is that whatever is ultimately able to perform a function is ultimately existent, and whatever is not ultimately able to perform a function is conventionally existent.

308 Element-derivatives (*'byung 'gyur*) are the five sense objects: visible forms (*rūpa, gzugs*), sounds (*shabda, sgra*), smells (*gandha, dri*), tastes (*rasa, ro*), and tangible objects (*spraṣhṭavya, reg bya*).

309 See n. 302.

310 The formative forces not associated [with forms or mind] (*viprayuktasaṃskāra, ldan min 'du byed*)—often shortened in translation to "non-associated formative forces" (and also translated as "non-associated compositional factors" or "non-associated formations")—are a category of conditioned phenomena and the third of the five bases (the other four being forms, mind, mental events, and unconditioned phenomena).

The *Treasury of Abhidharma* (Chapter 2, verses 35bcd–36ab) lists fourteen types of formative forces not associated [with forms or mind] (*viprayuktasaṃskāra, ldan min 'du byed*): (1) obtainment (or possession) (*prāpti, thob pa*); (2) non-obtainment (or non-possession) (*aprāpti, ma thob pa*); (3) homogeneous character (or equal status) (*sabhāgatā, skal mnyam*); (4) a state of non-discrimination (*asaṃjñika, 'du shes med pa*); (5) absorption (or equipoise) without discrimination (*asaṃjñisamāpatti, 'du shes med pa'i snyoms 'jug*); (6) absorption (or equipoise) of cessation (*nirodhasamāpatti, 'gog pa'i snyoms 'jug*); (7) life-force (or vitality) (*jīvita, srog*); (8–11) the four characteristics (*lakṣhaṇa, mtshan nyid*) of arising (or of birth) (*jāti, skye ba*), aging (*jarā, rga ba*), duration (*sthiti, gnas pa*), and impermanence (*anityatā, mi rtag pa*); (12) the group of names (*nāmakāya, ming gi tshogs*); (13) the group of phrases (*padakāya, tshig gi tshogs*); and (14) the group of letters (or of syllables) (*vyañjanakāya, yi ge'i tshogs*).

See also Pruden 1988, 206–54; and Cox 1995, particularly 67–74. The *Compendium of Abhidharma* lists twenty-three (see Boin-Webb 2001, 18–21), which are also found in Hopkins 1983, 268–71.

311 See n. 326.

312 The sixteen defining characteristics of the four truths (each truth has four characteristics) are discussed in Chapter 2; see pp. 115–119.

313 The four pairs of beings, also called eight kinds of individuals (*skyes bu zung bzhi dang gang zag ya brgyad*), are approachers and abiders who are stream enterers (*rgyun zhugs zhugs pa dang 'bras gnas gnyis*); approachers and abiders who are once returners (*lan cig phyir 'ong zhugs pa dang 'bras gnas gnyis*); approachers and abiders who are nonreturners (*phyir mi 'ong zhugs pa dang 'bras gnas gnyis*); and approachers and abiders who are arhats (*dgra bcom pa zhugs pa dang 'bras gnas gnyis*). They are discussed in A Detailed Explanation of the Gradual Type, pp. 142–149.

314 Incalculable aeon (*asaṃkhyeya-kalpa, bskal pa grangs med pa*): "Incalculable" is the name for the highest enumerated number in ancient India. It is the sixtieth in the series and is equivalent to 10^{59}.

315 Knowledge of the exhaustion [of defilements] and the knowledge of their [subsequent] nonarising (*kṣhayānutpattijñāna, zad mi skye shes pa*) are discussed in the *Treasury of Abhidharma*, in Chapter 6, verses 50 and 67ab, and extensively in Chapter 7. (See Pruden 1989, 991, 1023, and 1087–1134.) *GTCD* says:

- The knowledge of the exhaustion [of defilements], one of the ten types of knowledge, is the confidence that one has relinquished all the factors to be abandoned (*zad pa shes pa/ shes pa bcu'i ya gyal zhig ste rang nyid spang bya thams cad spangs zin pa'i gdeng 'thob par byed pa'i shes pa'o*).
- The knowledge of nonarising, one of the ten types of knowledge, is the knowledge that nonarising suffering is nonarising (*mi skye ba shes pa/ shes pa bcu'i nang gses/ sdug bsngal mi skye ba la mi skye bar shes pa'o*).

316 These are Buddha Shākyamuni's first teachers. See Butön's *History of Buddhism* (Obermiller 1932, 26). Note that *MVP* lists Arāḍha-kālāma for the Tibetan *rGyu rtsal*

byed kyi bu ring 'phur, and Udrako-rāmaputra for the Tibetan *Rangs byed kyi bu lhag spyod,* whereas Obermiller (1932, 26) has Ārāḍa-Kālāma and Udraka Rāmaputra respectively for the same Tibetan.

317 The twenty types of saṅgha are grouped as follows: (1–5) the five types of stream enterers; (6–8) the ten types of once returners; (9–18) the ten types of nonreturners; (19) those who have entered the level of an arhat; (20) the rhinoceros-like pratyekabuddhas (*GTCD*). See also Hopkins 2003, 228–30.

318 For some of the ways Sautrāntikas disagree with Vaibhāṣhikas on this see p. 135. This topic is discussed in the *Treasury of Abhidharma,* Chapter 6, verses 58–60b; see Pruden 1989, 1003–13.

319 Examples of their point are that the Buddha Shākyamuni experienced pain when a thorn pierced his foot and felt ill when he ate some pork. They explain those by saying that the Buddha, like an arhat with remainder, had a remainder of karma.

320 See pp. 132–133 for a list of these seven treatises.

321 *Udānavarga, Ched du brjod pa'i tshoms,* compiled by Dharmatrāta, who lived sometime between 75 BCE and 200 CE (according to Sparham 1986, 19). According to the notes in the Dergé Kangyur, Vaibhāṣhikas considered this to be a sūtra (i.e., the words of the Buddha Shākyamuni), whereas Sautrāntikas considered it a shāstra (i.e., composed by followers of the Buddha). See *Catalogue of the Nyingma Edition of the sDe-dge bKa'-'gyur/bsTan-'gyur,* 1:498. As said there, this is "the Northern Buddhist version of the Pāli and Prakṛit *Dhammapāda.*" See also the translation by Sparham 1986.

322 Among the non-associated formative forces, three are related to this point: the group of names (*nāmakāya, ming gi tshogs*), the group of phrases (*padakāya, tshig gi tshogs*), and the group of letters (*vyañjanakāya, yi ge'i tshogs*). See Pruden 1988, 250–4; Hopkins 1983, 269; and Cox 1995, 160–3.

323 This is the position of the Kashmiri Vaibhāṣhikas and is discussed in the *Explanation of the "Treasury of Abhidharma,"* Chapter 1, commentary for verse 43. See Pruden 1989, 120–2.

324 This is in contrast to the Sautrāntika position that a sense consciousness apprehends an object through the intermediary of its image (or representation; aspect) (*ākāra, rnam pa*), and does not apprehend the object itself. See Dreyfus 1997, 335–9; and Klein 1998, 100–113.

325 The five bases (*mūla, gzhi*) are forms (*rūpa, gzugs*); mind (*chitta, sems*); mental events (*chaitta, sems byung*); formative forces not associated [with forms or mind] (*viprayuktasaṃskāra, ldan min 'du byed*); and unconditioned phenomena (*asaṃskṛita, 'dus ma byas*). Vaibhāṣhikas state that these five are entities (*dngos po*), phenomena (*chos*), existents (*yod pa*), and knowable objects (*shes bya*). They then divide entities into conditioned phenomena (*'dus byas*) and unconditioned phenomena (*'dus ma byas*). Sautrāntikas differ in that they state that phenomena, existents, and knowable objects are equivalent, and then divide phenomena into entities and nonentities (*dngos med*).

326 It seems that Jamgön Kongtrul is drawing on a definition of non-associated formative forces, which can be found in Vasubandhu's *Delineation of the Five Aggregates* (*Pañchaskandha-prakaraṇa, Phung po lnga'i rab tu byed pa;* Toh. 4059; Dg.T. 77:42). There Vasubandhu defines non-associated formative forces as "designations for

states that arise from form or mind" (*gang dag gzugs dang sems las byung ba'i gnas skabs la gdags pa*). In Jamgön Kongtrul's remark "that which bear a state" (*gnas skabs can*) are forms, mind, and mental events to which states (*gnas skabs*)—that is, the non-associated formative forces—are designated.

The point here is that Vaibhāṣhikas state that non-associated formative forces are substantially existent and that they have the same status as forms, minds, and mental events (both of which are positions that the Sautrāntikas do not agree with). I am grateful to Artemus Engle for help with this passage and directing me to this source.

327 Vaibhāṣhikas consider whatever is substantially existent (*dravyasat, rdzas yod*) to be ultimate reality (*paramārthasatya, don dam bden pa*). See also n. 306.

328 Space, analytical cessations, and nonanalytical cessations. See n. 279.

329 A determination (*pariccheda, yongs gcod*) is the result of a negation, which may be either an implicative negation or a nonimplicative negation, and thus a determination (or conclusion) may be either an affirmation or a complete negation. Generally, this term is used to indicate the result of an implicative negation, and as such it refers to the ascertainment of something that remains after the exclusion of other features. For example, if you mistakenly take a striped rope to be a snake, but upon closer inspection see that it is not a snake, you have eliminated, or negated, the rope being a snake, and you have determined the object to be a rope. Note that this term is also translated as "positive determination" or "positive inclusion."

330 Jamgön Kongtrul's wording is precise: unconditioned phenomena are not *conditioned* entities which perform functions. Other Tibetan commentators explain that Vaibhāṣhikas assert that unconditioned phenomena do perform functions although their function is not as defined for conditioned entities (see n. 307). For example, the Geluk commentator Ngawang Palden explains (Hopkins 2003, 242):

> Among the four Buddhist tenet systems, only this system asserts that a permanent phenomenon such as uncompounded space is able to perform a function and thus is an effective thing. For instance, the lack of obstructive contact that space affords performs the function of allowing movement to take place. Since both permanent and impermanent phenomena are asserted to be effective things in this system, functionality is not limited to producing causal sequences as it is in the higher Buddhist schools; instead, as with uncompounded space, functionality can refer to allowing or opening the way for something to occur.

Jamyang Shepa (*'Jam dbyangs bzhad pa*) says (Buescher 2005, 105):

> Vaibhāṣikas assert that the entity of an analytical cessation is a substantially existent, permanent, and virtuous, unconditioned thing. For they assert it as unconditioned in the sense of lacking causes and conditions, a thing (*bhāva*) in that it performs the function of causing an affliction to cease . . .

331 Chapter 2, verse 55d. Toh. 4089; Dg.T. Beijing 79:13. See Pruden 1988, 278.

332 Five faculties (*dbang po lnga*): faculty of faith (*dad pa'i dbang po*); faculty of exertion (*brtson 'grus kyi dbang po*); faculty of mindfulness (*dran pa'i dbang po*); faculty of samādhi (*ting nge 'dzin gyi dbang po*); and faculty of wisdom (*shes rab kyi dbang po*). See Pruden 1988, 157.

333 Simply put, this means that although Vaibhāṣhikas negate the existence of a self of persons, they are incapable of understanding that this nonimplicative negation is

the ultimate reality (or thusness, *tathātā, de bzhin nyid*) of all phenomena, because for them all phenomena are substantially existent.

334 The four great venerable ones (*mahābhadanta, btsun pa chen po*) are Dharmatrāta (*Chos skyob*), Vasumitra (*dByig bshes*), Ghoṣhaka (*dByangs sgrog*), and Buddhadeva (*Sangs rgyas lha*), all of whom lived around the first century CE. The views of these four masters are often cited by Vasubandhu in his *Explanation of the "Treasury of Abhidharma,"* and they are said to be particularly important within the Vaibhāṣhika abhidharma tradition in that they represent four different interpretations of how phenomena exist in the three time periods. Of the four, only Vasumitra's works are found in the Tengyur. See Pruden 1989, 808–10; Willemen et al. 1998, 21–3; and Cox 1995, 139–41.

335 Saṅghabhadra (*'Dus bzang*) (late fourth to early fifth century CE) was a Kashmiri Vaibhāṣhika (or Sarvāstivādin) and contemporary of Vasubandhu, whose abhidharma works, **Nyāyānusāra* and **Abhidharmasamayapradīpikā*, are only extant in Chinese translations by Hsüan-tsang. A shorter work by Saṅghabhadra that is a brief summary of Vasubandhu's *Treasury of Abhidharma* was translated into Tibetan: *An Explanation of the Treatise of the "Treasury of Abhidharma"* (*Abhidharmakoṣhashāstra-kārikā-bhāṣhya, Chos mngon pa mdzod kyi bstan bcos kyi tshig le'ur byas pa'i rnam par bshad pa*) (Toh. 4091). See Cox 1995, 53–60; and Cox 1998, 240–9.

336 *Go cha mtha' yas.* On the basis of the Tibetan, I tentatively identify this person as Anantavarman, who was the author of a commentary on the *Great Exposition* (*Mahāvibhāṣha*). See Cox 1998, 234.

337 For a good discussion of the name Sautrāntika, see Honjō 2003, 321–328. He concludes (324) that "Sautrāntikas are those scholars who belong to the Sarvāstivādin sect, and who claim that Abhidharma was not expounded by the Buddha."

338 *Ye shes la 'jug pa.*

339 *Rab tu byed pa.*

340 *Chos kyi phung po.*

341 Or *Prajñāptibhāṣhya.*

342 *gDags pa'i bstan bcos.* This is said to be the only one of these seven that was translated into Tibetan (Cox 1998, 139n2); it is found in the Peking canon (nos. 5587–9) (Hirakawa 1998, 132) but is not included in Toh. This is the only one of the seven that was partially translated into Chinese (the other six were fully translated into Chinese).

343 *rNam shes kyi tshogs.*

344 Or possibly Devakṣhema (*Lha skyid*).

345 *'Gro ba'i rnam grangs.* Note that *TOK*, II:473.4, ***bGro** ba'i rnam grangs,* should be ***'Gro** ba'i rnam grangs.* (TN)

346 *Khams kyi tshogs.*

347 For overviews of these texts, see Buswell and Jaini 1996, 100–110; and Cox 1998, 171–229. Apart from Sanskrit fragments for some of these works and the *Prajñāptishāstra,* these texts only exist in Chinese translation.

348 This seems to be derived from Vasubandhu's *Explanation of the "Treasury of Abhidharma,"* Chapter 1, commentary for verse 43d. See Dg.T. Beijing 79:123; and Pruden 1988, 122.

349 For a discussion of the meaning and explanations of "hidden" (*lkog na mo*), see Dreyfus 1997, 416–27.

350 Image (*ākāra, rnam pa*) is also translated as "aspect" or "representation." See Dreyfus 1997, 335–9; and Klein 1998, 100–113.

351 Jamgön Kongtrul's wording implies that there are different views on which of the mental events are substantially existent, but I have not found the source for this comment.

352 Such imputedly existent entities (*btags yod kyi dngos po*) are formative forces not associated [with forms or mind]. See n. 310.

353 This is a case where a determination (or what is determined) (*pariccheda, yongs gcod*) is the outcome of a nonimplicative negation. (ALTG)

354 The meditative concentration of resting at ease in the present life (*mthong chos bder gnas kyi bsam gtan*) is one of three types of meditative concentration listed in Kongtrul 1998, 202 (*TOK*, II:124–5). The other two are the meditation aimed at acquiring good qualities (*yon tan sgrub pa'i bsam gtan*), and the meditation of working for the welfare of others (*sems can gyi don la dmigs pa'i bsam gtan*).

355 The *Treasury of Abhidharma* (Chapter 6, verse 56a) states that there are six types of arhats, one of which is called "those who regress" (*parihāṇadharman, yongs su nyams pa'i chos can*). The *Explanation of the "Treasury of Abhidharma"* contains a lengthy discussion of these types and whether they can regress or not. Sautrāntikas argue their point by saying, "If it is possible for one to regress from the state of an arhat, why did the Bhagavat say an arhat could only regress from the higher mental state [i.e., meditative concentration] that abides in the ease, or bliss, of this life? Therefore, the liberation of all arhats is to be considered unwavering" (*gal te yang dgra bcom pa nyid las yongs su nyams pa srid pa zhig tu gyur na/ ci'i phyir bcom ldan 'das kyis thong ba'i chos la bde bar gnas par lhag pa'i sems las byung ba dag kho na las yongs su nyams par 'gyur bar gsungs par gyur te/ de'i phyir dgra bcom pa thams cad kyi rnam par grol ba ni mi g.yo ba yin par khong du chud do*) (Dg.T. Beijing 79:759). See Pruden 1989, 1000–10, particularly 1006–7.

356 Valid cognition (*pramāṇa, tshad ma*): For a definition of valid cognition, see n. 717. For the four forms of valid cognition, see Chapter 10, p. 225; for the forms accepted by Svātantrikas, see n. 676. See also Khenpo Tsültrim Gyamtso 1996b/2000; Dreyfus 1997, 285–327; and Dunne 2004, 15–35.

357 I am reading *de bzhin*, "like that," as *de bzhin nyid*, "thusness" (*TOK*, II:474.18), since that fits the pattern of Jamgön Kongtrul's commentary. This statement is in contrast to his point about Vaibhāṣhikas in the previous section: ". . . they are not able to posit that the nonimplicative negation that is the simple negation of the self of persons is thusness (*tathātā, de bzhin nyid*)" (*TOK*, II:472.15). (This reading was confirmed by ALTG.)

358 Saṅgharakṣhita (*dGe 'dun srung ba*) (early sixth century): According to Tāranātha's *History of Buddhism in India*, Saṅgharakṣhita was a student of Nāgamitra and a teacher of Buddhapālita and Vimuktasena. (See Chimpa and Chattopadhyaya 1970, 151, 186, and 188.) None of his works are included in the Tengyur.

359 Shrīlāta (*dPal len*) (330–410 CE) is thought to have been an older contemporary of Vasubandhu and Saṅghabhadra. Traditionally he is said to have been a student of Kumāralāta and a teacher of Vasubandhu. (See Cox 1995, 41.) His works are not included in the Tengyur.

360 Traditionally it is said that in his *Explanation of the "Treasury of Abhidharma,"* Vasubandhu presents the Sautrāntika point of view, often in the form of a discussion or debate with Vaibhāṣhikas. Vasubandhu's *Explanation of the "Treasury of Abhidharma"* and its commentaries were, and still are, Tibetan scholars' main source for the Sautrāntika view.

361 Shākyaprabha says in his *Luminous* (*Prabhāvatī, 'Od ldan*) (Toh. 4125; Dg.T. Beijing 93:415) that the Sarvāstivādins were the single original order from which the other orders split. Bhāvaviveka says in Chapter 4 of his *Blaze of Reasoning* (*Tarkajvālā, rTog ge 'bar ba*) (Toh. 3856; Dg.T. Beijing 58:361) that the two root orders were the Sthaviras and Mahāsāṅghikas. In the same text, Bhāvaviveka says (Dg.T. Beijing 58:364) that another presentation is that there were three root orders: Sthaviras, Mahāsāṅghikas, and Vibhajyavādins. See also Bareau 1989; Dutt 1978; Hopkins 2003, 210–18; and Obermiller 1932, 94–7.

362 This is the presentation of Vinītadeva in his *Compendium on the Different Orders* (*Samayabhedoparachanachakre Nikāyabhedopadeshanasaṃgraha, gZhung tha dad pa rim par bklag pa'i 'khor lo las sde pa tha dad pa bstan pa bsdus pa*) (Toh. 4140; Dg.T. Beijing 93:1166–71). In his *History of Buddhism* (*Chos 'byung*), Butön says (Obermiller 1932, 95) that "Vinītadeva and the master of *Varṣhāgra-pṛichchhā* assert that there were four root orders." In Hopkins 2003, 210, the latter master is identified as Padma (not to be confused with Padmasambhava from Oḍiyāna), and Hopkins (2003, 1028) identifies the text as *dGe tshul gyi dang po'i lo dri ba* (P5634, vol. 127) and *dGe slong gi dang po'i lo dri ba* (P5649, vol. 127). For the subdivisions of the four orders according to Padma, see Hopkins 1983, 718.

363 In this section I believe that Jamgön Kongtrul has abbreviated Mūlasarvāstivādins twice to Sarvāstivādins (as is often done in Tibetan histories and is done by Butön, upon whom Jamgön Kongtrul draws heavily); however, this should not give the impression that these terms are necessarily to be used interchangeably. Dessein says (Willemen et al. 1998, 88) that "the Sarvāstivāda and Mūlasarvāstivāda communities seem to have been two independent monastic communities." Cox notes (1995, 45n38) that Schmithausen "argues that even though no consensus has yet been reached about the relationship between the Sarvāstivādins and Mūlasarvāstivādins, the simplest explanation for systematic differences and similarities in their literature is to assume that they were separate but interacting groups with their own progressively revised and mutually influenced collections." Yamabe (2003, 225–6) says, "Concerning the exact relationship between the appellations 'Sarvāstivāda' and 'Mūlasarvāstivāda,' Enomoto Fumio has recently suggested that the word 'Mūlasarvāstivāda' represents the Sarvāstivādin claim that the Sarvāstivāda was the root (*mūla*) of the other sects; thus, according to him, 'Mūlasarvāstivāda' does not refer to a subsect of the Sarvāstivāda tradition." See above n. 284. For more on these schools, see Willemen et al. 1998, xi–xiii; and Cox 1995, 23–9.

364 The following presentation draws on Butön's *History of Buddhism* (Obermiller 1932, 96–7) and Pawo Tsuk-lak Trengwa's *Feast for Scholars: A History of the Dharma* (*Chos 'byung mkhas pa'i dga' ston;* 1:62–7) but not exclusively (e.g., some of the information on patch numbers, symbols, and name endings is different, for which Jamgön Kongtrul says he followed "Atīsha's exegesis (*gsung sgros*)," a source I have not been able to identify).

365 The Sanskrit for the name endings is based on *MVP*.

366 The presentation of tenets for this order and the other three is derived from Vinītadeva's *Compendium on the Different Orders* (Dg.T. Beijing 93:1167–71).

367 Prakṛit (or Prakṛita) (*Rang bzhin gyi skad*) is the name for Middle Indo-Aryan languages that began as vernacular dialects and eventually developed into literary languages. It includes regional dialects such as Magadhi.

368 The ascetic practices (*dvādasha dhūta guṇāḥ, sbyangs pa'i yon tan*) are twelve: [wearing] robes made of rags (*phyag dar khrod pa*); [wearing] the three dharma robes (*chos gos gsum pa*); [wearing] felt robes (*phying pa ba dang*); [eating one's meal on] one seat (*stan gcig pa*); begging for alms (*bsod snyoms pa*); not taking food after [having risen from one's seat] (*zas phyis mi len pa*); [dwelling in] a hermitage (*dgon pa ba*); [dwelling in] a forest (*shing drung ba*); [dwelling in] the open (*bla gab med pa*); [dwelling in] charnel grounds (*dur khrod pa*); [remaining in] the sitting posture (*tsog pu ba*); and [sleeping] wherever one happens to be (*gzhi ji bzhin pa*) (*GTCD* and Rigdzin 1986/1993). For a similar list, see also Ñāṇamoli 1979, 59.

369 Mahāsāṅghikas differ from Sarvāstivādins on this point. The latter state that the sixteen moments of seeing the four truths occur gradually. See the *Explanation of the "Treasury of Abhidharma,"* Chapter 6, commentary on verse 27ab for a reference to this difference in views (Pruden 1989, 947 and 1057n169). See also Dutt 1978, 88.

370 Supreme qualities (*chos mchog*) is the fourth and highest stage of the path of junction (*sbyor lam*).

371 Pishācha (or Pisaca) (*Sha za'i skad*), also called Dard languages, is a group of closely related Indo-Iranian languages spoken in Pakistan, Kashmir, and Afghanistan.

372 According to the Vaibhāṣhikas' abhidharma teachings, mind (*chitta, sems*) and mental events (*chaitta, sems byung*) are interrupted during the absorption of cessation (*nirodhasamāpatti, 'gog snyoms*). This was not, however, a universally accepted explanation. See Cox 1995, 113–7; and Schmithausen 1987, 19–20.

373 Apabhraṃsha (or Apabhramsa) (*Zur chag gi skad*) is the name for languages of Northern India spoken in approximately the third to fifth centuries, which differ from literary Prakṛit and evolved into modern languages like Gujarati and Bengali.

374 Inexplicable self [or person] (**avaktavya pudgala, brjod du med pa'i bdag*): Note that the Tibetan term *brjod du med pa'i bdag* is "inexplicable self," whereas the likely Sanskrit equivalent, **avaktavya pudgala,* is "inexplicable person." In translating this as "inexplicable self [or person]," I am following Duerlinger 2003, 61n29:

> The term, *avaktavya,* has been variously translated into English. Most of its translations are meant to convey the idea of being incapable of being spoken about or described. Nowhere, I believe, do the Pudgalavādins [Proponents of Persons] define the term in this way. The meaning of the term is "inexplicable," i.e., incapable of being explained as either other than or the same in existence as the phenomena in dependence upon which it is conceived.

Williams and Tribe sum up (2000, 126) the position advocated by this school regarding an inexplicable self of persons:

> Adherents of the *pudgala* [person] claim that it is neither the same as nor different from the aggregates. If it were the same as the aggregates then the *pudgala* would be conditioned, and when the aggregates were destroyed the person would be destroyed. This would be annihilationist, . . . On the other hand if the *pudgala* were different from the aggregates it would be unconditioned, in fact a Self like the *ātman,* and subject to all the Buddhist criticisms of the concept of a

Self. This would be to fall into the great mistake of eternalism. Thus the *pudgala* is neither identical to nor different from the aggregates, and neither conditioned nor unconditioned. In fact, it is said to be 'indefinable' (*avaktavya*).

Most of our understanding of the Saṃmitīyas' views of an inexplicable self [or person] come from the ninth chapter of Vasubandhu's *Treasury of Abhidharma,* where he devotes one section of his refutation of a self to refuting the Vātsīputrīyas' assertions of an inexplicable person. Vātsīputrīyas, who are one of the five Saṃmitīya orders, are referred to by Vasubandhu as Pudgalavādins, Proponents of Persons. See Pruden 1990, 1314–42. For an in-depth study of this chapter and the views of the Vātsīputrīyas, see Duerlinger 2003.

375 Dutt says (1978, 207n1) ". . . The Sammitīyas [*sic*] count in all the fourteen moments instead of Sarvāstivādins' sixteen; so the thirteenth moment of the Sammitīyas corresponds to the fifteenth of the Sarvāstivādins."

376 *Prātimokṣha-sūtra, So sor thar pa'i mdo.* Toh. 2.

377 For a discussion of the present-day ceremony (*da lta'i cho ga*) and the original ceremony (*sngon chog*) for conferring monastic ordination, see Kongtrul 1998, 89–90.

378 Part 2, Chapter 4, verses 59–60:

> Because it emanates and is a firm abode,
> the emanation (*nirmāṇa*) chakra is the Sthaviras.
> Because it is the source for propounding the dharma,
> the dharmachakra is the Sarvāstivādins.
>
> Since the throat is honored by all,
> the [sam]bhogachakra is the Saṃmitīyas.
> Since great bliss resides at the head,
> the chakra of bliss is the Mahāsāṅghikas.
> What are called "the orders " refer to the body.
>
> *gang phyir sprul pa gnas brtan phyir/ sprul pa'i 'khor lor gnas brtan nyid/ chos ni smra bas byung ba'i phyir/ chos kyi 'khor lor thams cad yod/ gang phyir mgrin par kun bkur phyir/ longs spyod 'khor lo kun bkur nyid/ gang phyir bde chen mgor gnas pas/ bde ba'i 'khor lo dge 'dun che/ sde pa zhes bya skur ru brjod.* Dg.K. 418, 21b.4.

379 The verse 52ab in the fifth chapter of the *Kālachakra Tantra* states:

> The lord of victors proclaims the Sarvāstivādins' [doctrine] from his front [face], and the Saṃmitīyas' from his right one. From his rear face, he speaks the Sthaviras' [teachings], and from his left one, the Mahāsāṅghikas'.
>
> *rgyal ba'i bdag pos mdun nas thams cad yod par smra ba gsungs te g.yas nas mang pos bkur ba'o/ rgyab kyi zhal nas gnas brtan pa ste slar yang dge 'dun phal chen pa ni g.yon gyi zhal nas so.* Dg.T. Beijing 6:200.

380 *Nikāyabhedopadeshanasaṃgraha, sDe pa tha dad bklags pa'i 'khor lo.* Toh. 4140; Dg.T. Beijing 93:1166–7.

381 *Pūrvashailas, Shar gyi ri bo pa,* Eastern Mountain Ones.

382 *Aparashailas, Nub kyi ri bo pa,* Western Mountain Ones.

383 *Haimavatas, Gang rir gnas pa,* Himalaya-Dwellers.

384 *Lokottaravādins, 'Jig rten 'das par smra ba,* Proponents of Worldly Transcendence.

385 *Prajñaptivādins, bTags par smra ba,* Proponents of Designation.

386 *Sarvāstivādins, gZhi kun pa,* Proponents of the Existence of All Bases.

387 *Kāshyapīyas, 'Od srungs pa,* Kāshyapa Followers.

388 *Mahīshāsakas, Sa ston pa* (or *Mang ston pa*), Great Teaching.

389 *Dharmaguptakas, Chos srung pa,* Dharmagupta Followers.

390 *Bahushrutīyas, Mang thos pa,* Much Hearing.

391 *Tāmrashāṭīyas, Gos mar slob ma.*

392 *Vibhajvavādins, rNam par phye ste smra ba,* Propounders of Discernment.

393 *Jetavanīyas, rGyal byed tshal gnas.*

394 *Abhayagirikas, 'Jigs med gnas.*

395 *Mahāvihārins, gTsug lag kang chen gnas,* Dwellers in the Great Vihāra.

396 *Kurukullas, Sa sgrogs ri,* Mount Kurukulla Dwellers.

397 *Avantakas, Srung ba pa,* Avantaka City Dwellers.

398 *Vatsīputrīyas, gNas ma bu pa,* Vatsīputra Followers.

399 *Āryasvapnanirdesha-nāma-mahāyāna-sūtra, 'Phags pa rmi lam bstan pa zhes bya theg pa chen po'i mdo.* Toh. 48. (Short title: *rMi lam lung bstan gyi mdo.*)

400 The five Saṃmitīya orders are generally said to be Saṃmitīyas (also called Kurukullas); Vātsīputrīyas; Bhadrayānīyas (*bZang lam pa,* Bhadrayāna Followers); Uttarīyas (*bLa ma pa,* Uttara Followers); and Dharmaguptakas (*Chos sbas pa*). For more information and different views, see Hopkins 2003, 220–2.

401 *Madhyamakahṛidayavṛittitarkajvālā, dBu ma'i snying po'i 'grel pa rtog ge 'bar ba,* by Bhāvaviveka. Toh. 3856; Dg.T. Beijing 58:364. Note the following differences: Dg.T. Beijing 58:364: *brjod du med par rnam par shes* ***pa drug gis shes*** *par bya ba . . . yongs su gsal bar* ***gyur pa****; TOK,* II:478.13–14: *brjod du med par rnam par shes* ***par bya ba*** *. . . yongs su gsal bar* ***bya ba.***

402 Bhāvaviveka lists (Dg.T. Beijing 58:361–2) the eight Mahāsāṅghika orders as Mahāsāṅghikas; Ekavyaharikas (*Tha snyad gcig pa,* One Convention); Lokottaravādins; Bahushrutīyas; Prajñaptivādins; Chaitikas (*mChod rten pa,* Monument Ones); Pūrvashailas; and Aparashailas.

403 *Dharmottaras, Chos mchog pa,* Dharmottara Followers.

404 The remaining five orders in Bhāvaviveka's list (Dg.T. Beijing 58:362) are Vātsīputrīyas, Bhadrayānīyas, Saṃmitīyas, Dharmaguptakas, and Uttarīyas.

405 *Mahāyānasūtrālaṃkāra, Theg pa chen po mdo sde rgyan,* by Maitreya. Toh. 4020. For example, Chapter 2 (according to the Tibetan chapter numbering) is called Establishing the Mahāyāna (*Theg pa chen po sgrub pa'i skabs*). See Jamspal et al. 2004.

406 Jamgön Kongtrul states (above, p. 134) that Sautrāntikas consider non-associated formative forces and unconditioned phenomena to be imputedly existent (*btags yod*). Although he does not explicitly state it, presumably such Sautrāntikas consider these to be conventionally existent (*kun rdzob du yod pa*). We may assume that

it is this point that Chittamātras would not accept, because in Chapter 6, p. 180, Jamgön Kongtrul states that in the Chittamātra system what is imputedly existent is the imagined characteristic (*kun brtags*), and in Chapter 11, p. 256, Jamgön Kongtrul says that the imagined does not exist conventionally (*kun rdzob du med pa*). Note that *TOK*, II:478.22 ***brtags*** should be ***btags*** (see PKTC).

407 Tib. *Dus 'khor rtsa 'grel*. This is the *Stainless Light* (*Vimalaprabhā, 'Dri med 'od*) by Puṇḍarīka. Toh. 1347. See Wallace 2004, 241–2.

408 *Madhyamakāvatāra, dBu ma la 'jug pa*, by Chandrakīrti. Toh. 3861. Chandrakīrti refutes the inexplicable self asserted by Vātsīputrīyas in Chapter 6, verses 147–9. See Padmakara Translation Group 2002, 297–8; and Goldfield et al. 2005, 391–3.

409 The *Treasury of Abhidharma* states (Chapter 4, verse 14a) that there are eight kinds of vows of individual liberation, which are listed in its commentary as the vows of a monk (*bhikṣhu, dge slong*); nun (*bhikṣhuṇī, dge slong ma*); postulant nun (*shikṣhamanā, dge slob ma*); male novice (*shrāmaṇera, dge tshul*); female novice (*shrāmaṇerikā, dge tshul ma*); male lay practitioner (*upāsaka, dge bsnyen*); female lay practitioner (*upāsikā, dge bsnyen*); and one observing the purificatory fast (*upavāsastha, bsnyen gnas*). See Pruden 1988, 581. These are also listed in Kongtrul 1998, 88–9; and *TOK*, II:38.

410 The nine scriptural categories (*navāṅga pravachana, gsung rab yan lag dgu*) are (1) sūtras (or discourse) section (*sūtra, mdo'i sde*); (2) section of discourses in mixed verse and prose (*geya, dbyangs kyis bsnyad pa'i sde*); (3) section of prophecies (*vyākaraṇa, lung du bstan pa'i sde*); (4) section of verses (*gāthā, tshigs su bcad pa'i sde*); (5) section of meaningful expressions (*udāna, ched du brjod pa'i sde*); (6) section of introductory remarks (*nidāna, gleng gzhi'i sde*); (7) section of extensive teachings (*vaipulya, shin tu rgyas pa'i sde*); (8) section on marvels (*abdhutadharma, rmad du byung ba'i sde*); (9) and section presenting ascertainments (*gtan la phab pa'i sde*) (*GTCD*). See *TOK*, I:348–50.

411 The sixteen aspects of the four truths (each truth has four aspects) are discussed in Chapter 2: The Presentation Summarizing the General Characteristics [of the Four Truths], pp. 115–119.

412 The progression from stream enterer to arhat has two aspects: relinquishment and realization. The process of relinquishment is described in terms of abandoning the mental afflictions associated with the nine levels of the three realms (desire, form, and formless), where the first level is the desire realm, levels two through five are the four concentrations of the form realm, and levels six through nine are the four spheres of the formless realm. Since each level has nine afflictions associated with it—three degrees of large afflictions (i.e., strong large, middling large, and weak large), three degrees of medium afflictions, and three degrees of small afflictions—there are eighty-one afflictions that are the factors to be abandoned. This is discussed in the *Explanation of the "Treasury of Abhidharma,"* Chapter 6, commentary for verses 33–49. See Pruden 1989, 956–86. See also Cox 1992; and Hopkins 1983, 96–109.

413 See the *Treasury of Abhidharma* (Chapter 6, verse 30a); and Pruden 1989, 953. Wangchuk Dorjé (*Youthful Play*, p. 427) clarifies that they have abandoned up to and including five factors: "the term 'up through,' [which could also mean 'up to' in other contexts, here] means '[from] one up through two, three, four, or five'" (*bar du'i sgras ni gcig gam gnyis gsum bzhi dang lnga'i bar bzung ngo*).

414 Once they abandon the sixth factor, they are a once returner.

415 In this context, "moments" (*skad cig*) do not mean the smallest unit of time but rather the time it takes to complete the investigation of each of the sixteen aspects of the four truths. According to the *Treasury of Abhidharma,* the first fifteen moments belong to the path of seeing and the sixteenth moment is the path of meditation. According to the *Compendium of Abhidharma,* all sixteen moments are the path of seeing. See n. 422.

416 The translation "acceptance of phenomena" for *chos bzod* (*dharmakṣhānti*) is based on *GTCD,* which says: "Acceptance of phenomena [means] acceptance of the realization of phenomena. This refers to the uninterrupted path that is the antidote for the factors to be abandoned by the path of seeing. This occurs following the end of supreme qualities, when the phenomena (*dharma, chos*) comprising the desire realm are seen just as they are in terms of the four truths" (*chos bzod/ chos la rtogs pa'i bzod pa ste/ chos mchog gi mjug tu 'dod khams kyis bsdus pa'i chos la bden bzhi ji lta mthong bas mthong spang spangs te bral 'bras nyams su myong ba rnam grol lam mo*).

This term (*dharmakṣhānti, chos bzod*) is also translated as "doctrinal forbearance," "dharma endurance," and "patient acceptance of the dharma," and is explained as such. Levinson states (1994, 190–191), "The 'doctrine' endured by uninterrupted paths and known by paths of release is selflessness." See also the reference from Cox 1992 in the next note.

417 Again, the translation of "knowledge of phenomena" for *chos shes* (*dharmajñāna*) is based on *GTCD,* which says: "Knowledge of phenomena [refers to] the path of release that is actualization of the result of separation, and the relinquishment of the factors to be abandoned by the path of seeing. This occurs when the phenomena (*dharma, chos*) comprising the desire realm are seen just as they are in terms of the four truths" (*chos shes/ 'dod khams kyis bsdus pa'i chos la bden bzhi ji lta mthong bas mthong spang spangs te bral 'bras nyams su myong ba rnam grol lam mo*).

Note that this term is also translated as "doctrinal knowledge" and so on. Cox explains (1992, 99n56): "The term *dharmajñāna* is ambiguous: 'dharma' can refer to the doctrine, as possibly in the *Mahāvibhāṣha* . . . or, 'dharma' can refer to those factors belonging to the realm of desire specifically, as in the *Saṅgītiparyāya,* in which case *anvayajñāna* [subsequent knowledge] would refer to the subsequent knowledge of those factors belonging to the realm of form and the formless realm . . ."

418 Acceptance of phenomena (*dharmakṣhānti, chos bzod*), knowledge of phenomena (*dharmajñāna, chos shes*), subsequent acceptance (*anvayakṣhānti, rjes bzod*), and subsequent knowledge (*anvayajñāna, rjes shes*) form two pairs: acceptance of phenomena and subsequent acceptance, which are called uninterrupted paths (*ānantaryamārga, bar chad med pa'i lam*); and knowledge of phenomena and subsequent knowledge, which are paths of release (*vimuktimārga, rnam par grol ba'i lam*). Uninterrupted paths are when the mental afflictions are abandoned, and paths of release are the state when the abandonment of a particular affliction is experienced. These are likened to throwing out a thief and locking the door.

See the *Explanation of the "Treasury of Abhidharma,"* Chapter 6, commentary for verse 28ab, and Chapter 7, verse 1; Book Nine, Part One (*TOK,* III:482); Cox 1992, particularly 82–91; and Hopkins 1983, 96–9.

419 In this sequence of four moments, the first two moments relate to the desire realm and the last two to the form and formless realms. Thus, in the case of the truth of suffering, the first moment is the acceptance of the phenomena of the truth of suffering as it relates to the desire realm, followed by the moment of the knowledge of the

phenomena of the truth of suffering as it relates to the desire realm. The third and fourth moments are the subsequent acceptance and subsequent knowledge of the truth of suffering as it relates to the form and formless realms. See the *Explanation of the "Treasury of Knowledge,"* Chapter 6, commentary for verses 25cd–27ab. Dg.T. Beijing 79:717–8; and Pruden 1989, 943–7.

420 Followers of faith (*shraddhānusārin, dad pa'i rjes 'brang*) are defined in the *Explanation of the "Treasury of Abhidharma"* (Chapter 6, verse 29ab) as "someone who pursues the meaning [of the dharma] first by being led by another" (*dad pas rjes su 'brang ba ste/ sngon gzhan gyi dring gis don gyi rjes su 'brang ba'i phyir ro*). See Dg.T. Beijing 79:723; and Pruden 1989, 952. See also Chapter 6, verse 63ac; and Pruden 1989, 1016.

This category and most of the following ones are also presented in Asaṅga's *Compendium of Abhidharma,* Chapter 4, sometimes with slightly different explanations than those found in the *Explanation of "Treasury of Abhidharma."* See Dg.T. Beijing 76:268–75; and Boin-Webb 2001, 202–18.

421 Followers of dharma (*dharmānusārin, chos kyi rjes 'brang*) are defined in the *Explanation of the "Treasury of Abhidharma"* (Chapter 6, verse 29ab) as "someone who pursues the meaning of the dharma of the sūtras and so forth first on their own" (*chos kyis rjes su 'brang ba yang de dang 'dra ste/ sngon bdag nyid kho nas mdo la sogs pa'i chos kyi don gyi rjes su 'brang ba'i phyir ro*). See Dg.T. Beijing 79:723; and Pruden 1989, 952.

422 The *Treasury of Abhidharma* (Chapter 6, verse 28cd) states that the first fifteen moments are the path of seeing, and the commentary for this verse explains that the sixteenth moment is the path of meditation. See Dg.T. Beijing 79:222; and Pruden 1989, 950–2. The *Compendium of Abhidharma* (Chapter 2) states that the sixteen moments are the path of seeing. See Dg.T. Beijing 76:235; and Boin-Webb 2001, 145–6.

423 *TOK,* II:480.11: ***dbyen*** should be ***dbye na***. (TN)

424 See the *Treasury of Abhidharma,* Chapter 6, verse 31cd; and Pruden 1989, 954–5.

425 Note that the *Explanation of the "Treasury of Abhidharma"* (Chapter 6, commentary for verse 34ab) makes it clear that seven rebirths is the most they will take at this level but they may take fewer: "Since they may take up to seven rebirths [the root verse says], 'they are reborn seven times at most'" (*tshe bdun gyi bar du skye bas na re ltar thogs na lan bdun pa'o*). See the *Treasury of Abhidharma,* Chapter 6, verse 34ab; and Pruden 1989, 958–60.

426 This might seem to contradict the earlier comment that "the relinquishments of those who abide in the result of a stream enterer are the same as those on the previous level," since those approaching the result of a stream enterer "may have abandoned the fourth or fifth" affliction of the desire realm. However, it seems to be a particular feature of "those born into the same class" that they have not abandoned the fifth factor. See the *Explanation of the "Treasury of Abhidharma,"* Chapter 6, commentary for verse 34cd; and Pruden 1989, 963.

427 Note that verse 34cd of the *Treasury of Abhidharma* (Chapter 6) says that those born into the same class will take two or three more rebirths (*tshe gnyis gsum du rigs nas rigs*). Also the *Explanation of the "Treasury of Abhidharma,"* Chapter 6, commentary for verse 34cd, states that there are two types of "those born into the same class": those who will be reborn two or three times as a god and those who will be reborn

two or three times as a human, depending on whether they attained abiding in the result of a stream enterer as a god or as a human. See Pruden 1989, 963.

428 It is said that there are two types of abiders in the result of a once returner: the seeming abider in the result of a once returner (*phyir 'ong 'bras gnas tsam po ba*) and the special abider in the result of a once returner, who has one interruption for one life (*phyir 'ong 'bras gnas khyad par can tshe gcig bar chad gcig pa bcas*) (*GTCD*). I have not located any reference to a seeming abider in the *Treasury of Abhidharma;* it is, however, a term used in Maitreya's *Ornament of Clear Realization* (*Abhisamayālaṃkāra, mNgon rtogs rgyan*); see Brunnhölzl 2001.

429 The *Explanation of the "Treasury of Abhidharma"* (Chapter 6, commentary for verse 36ac) explains the meaning of the name "those interrupted for one life" (*ekavīchika, tshe gcig bar chad pa*): "'interruption,' meaning what creates an interruption or interval, is used because the nirvāṇa of this person is interrupted by one lifetime, or because the result of a nonreturner is interrupted by one factor of the mental afflictions" (*bar chad ces bya ba ni bar chad byed pa'o/ de'i mya ngan las 'da' ba la tshe gcig gis chod pa'i phyir ram/ phyir mi 'ong ba'i 'bras bu la nyon mongs pa'i rnam pa gcig gis chod pa'i phyir*). See Dg.T. Beijing 79:731; and Pruden 1989: 965.

430 Since the ninth affliction is the last affliction of the desire realm, an abider in the result of a nonreturner does not take rebirth in the desire realm, which is the meaning of "nonreturner": one who does not return to the desire realm. See Pruden 1989, 965.

431 The form realm has seventeen levels, which are grouped according to the four concentrations (*dhyāna, bsam gtan*). Great Brahmā (*Mahābrahmāṇa, Tshangs chen*) is the third level of the first concentration. The *Explanation of the "Treasury of Abhidharma"* states (Chapter 6, commentary for verse 38ab): "A noble being will not take birth in Great Brahmā. Why? Because it is a place of beliefs and where there is only one leader" (*'phags pa ni tshangs chen pa dag gi nang du mi skye ste/ ci'i phyir zhe na/ lta ba'i gnas yin pa'i phyir dang/ gtso bo gcig tu zad pa'i phyir dang*). Dg.T. Beijing 79:733.

Pruden's translation (1989, 968) elaborates: "An Āryan is never reborn among the Mahābrahmas, because this heaven is a place of heresy: one considers Mahābrahma as the creator there; and because only one leader can be found there: an Āryan would be superior to Mahābrahma there."

432 The *Explanation of the "Treasury of Abhidharma"* (Chapter 6, commentary for verse 37ac) specifies that the term *'du byed* here means "application" or "to fully engage": "Those who fully pass beyond misery through application are those who, after they are born [in one of the formless states,] do not put aside their application and continue to fully engage [the path,] and thus fully pass beyond misery" (*mngon par 'du byed pa dang bcas pas yongs su mya ngan las 'da' ba ni skyes nas sbyor ba ma btang zhing mngon par 'du byed pa dang bcas pas yongs su mya ngan las 'da' ba gang yin pa*). See Dg.T. Beijing 79:732; and Pruden 1989, 966–7.

433 Akaniṣhṭha (*'Og min,* Highest or Below None) here means the highest level of the form realm (the eighth level of the fourth concentration), not the buddha realm Akaniṣhṭha.

434 Pinnacle of Existence (*Bhavāgra, Srid pa'i rtse mo*): The fourth and final sphere of the formless realm. Also called the sphere of Neither Discrimination nor Nondiscrimination (*'du shes med min gyi skye mched*).

435 Brahmā Type (*Brahmakāyika, Tshangs ris*) is the first level of the first concentration of the form realm.

436 The four pure states (*gtsang gnas bzhi*) are the first four of the last five levels of the fourth concentration of the form realm (the last being Akaniṣhṭha). Only noble beings are born in these last five levels, hence the name "pure states."

437 I have not been able to locate the source of this quotation and thus am not certain of its meaning. It may be a corruption of verse 38c, Chapter 6, of the *Treasury of Abhidharma*: "Others who go through the formless are of four types" (*gzhan ni gzugs med 'gro rnam bzhi*). See Pruden 1989, 969.

438 There is no bardo, or intermediate state, for those who take birth in the formless realm; they are born there directly. See Wangchuk Dorjé's *Youthful Play*, p. 436.

439 The *Treasury of Abhidharma* says (Chapter 6, verse 38c) that there are four types who go to the formless realm and pass beyond misery. Although the *Explanation of the "Treasury of Abhidharma"* only says that these four are "those who pass beyond misery after birth and the others" (*skyes nas yongs su mya ngan las 'da' ba la sogs pa'i bye brag gis rnam pa bzhi*), Pruden (1989, 966 and 969–70) provides a list of these four: those who pass beyond misery after birth (*upapadyaparinirvāyin*), those who pass beyond misery through application (*sābhisaṃskāraparinirvāyin*), those who pass beyond misery without application (*anabhisaṃskāraparinirvāyin*), and those who rise to a higher state (*ūrdhvasrotas*). This accords with Jamgön Kongtrul's remark, the only difference being that he refers to "those who rise to a higher state" as "three types of leapers" (*'phar gsum*).

440 See the *Treasury of Abhidharma,* Chapter 6, verse 43cd. Dg.T. Beijing 79:739–40; and Pruden 1989, 977–8.

441 See the *Treasury of Abhidharma,* Chapter 6, verse 44. Dg.T. Beijing 79:741; and Pruden 1989, 980–981.

442 All three classifications are presented in the *Compendium of Abhidharma*, Chapter 2 (see Dg.T. Beijing 76:229–30; and Boin-Webb 2001, 135–6). The first classification is presented in the *Treasury of Abhidharma,* Chapter 6, verses 63–64b (see Dg.T. Beijing 79:767; and Pruden 1989, 1016–18).

443 There are six supercognitive abilities (*mngon shes drug*). See n. 252.

444 The *Treasury of Abhidharma* states (Chapter 7, verse 44a) that the supercognitive abilities can only operate on the level (or realm) in which the being who possesses them dwells or on a lower level, but not on a higher level. For example, if an arhat dwells in the form realm, his or her supercognitive abilities will operate in the form and desire realms but not in the formless realm. See Pruden 1990, 1161.

445 The *Compendium of Abhidharma* explains (Chapter 2) that ornamented cessation is attained by those with twofold liberation, and unornamented cessation is attained by those liberated by means of wisdom. See Dg.T. Beijing 76:229; and Boin-Webb 2001, 135–6. See also Chapter 2, p. 114.

446 The translation follows PKTC reading *de nyid* ***zad***; *TOK*, II:483.22 has *de nyid* ***phrad.***

447 The *Treasury of Abhidharma* (Chapter 8, verses 18c–19b) discusses a "skipping" approach to the meditative absorptions as opposed to a sequential approach. See Pruden 1990, 1248–50.

448 The *Compendium of Abhidharma* states (Chapter 4) that there are two kinds of stream enterers: the gradual type (*rim gyis pa*) and the instantaneous type (*cig char ba*). The instantaneous type abandons the afflictions that are experienced in the three realms all at once. Two results are attributed to this type: the result of a stream enterer and the result of an arhat. See Dg.T. Beijing 76:274–5; and Boin Webb 2001, 218.

449 The first line is Chapter 6, verse 24d. Toh. 4089, f. 19b4. The second line is Chapter 3, verse 94d. Toh. 4089, f. 10b2. See Pruden 1989, 942, and 1988, 482.

450 Jamgön Kongtrul uses *pratyekabuddha* (*rang sangs rgyas*) and *pratyekajina* (*rang rgyal*, self[-realized] victor) interchangeably; however, I have used *pratyekabuddha* in all cases since it is well known. For a discussion of these names, see n. 456.

451 The sixteen aspects of the four truths (each truth has four aspects) are discussed in Chapter 2: The Presentation Summarizing the General Characteristics [of the Four Truths], pp. 115–119.

452 The twelve links of dependent origination (*dvādashāṅga pratītyasamutpāda, rten 'brel bcu gnyis*) are (1) ignorance (*avidyā, ma rig pa*); (2) karmic formative forces (*saṃskarakarma, 'du byed kyi las*); (3) consciousnesses (*vijñāna, rnam shes*); (4) names and forms (*nāmarūpa, ming gzugs*); (5) six sense spheres (*āyatana, skye mched*); (6) contact (*sparsha, reg pa*); (7) feelings (*vedanā, tshor ba*); (8) craving (*tṛiṣhṇā, sred pa*); (9) grasping (*upādāna, len pa*); (10) existence (*bhava, srid pa*); (11) birth (*jāti, skye ba*); and (12) aging and death (*jarāmaraṇa, rga shi*).

453 Pratyekabuddhas realize the absence of a self of persons (*pudgalanairātmya, gang zag gi bdag med*) and half the absence of self-entity of phenomena (*dharmanairātmya, chos kyi bdag med*). The realization of the absence of a self-entity of phenomena has two aspects: that the perceived object (*gzung ba*) has no self-entity and that the perceiver (*'dzin pa*) has no self-entity. Pratyekabuddhas are said to only realize the former, thus they only realize half the absence of self-entity of phenomena.

454 *Akṣhayamati-nirdesha-ṭīkā, bLo gros mi zad pas bstan pa'i mdo 'grel.* Toh. 3994.

455 The translation follows PKTC reading ***rkyen** rtogs; TOK,* II:485.9 has ***rgyan** rtogs.*

456 Salomon notes (2000, 9n9), "Instant enlightenment stimulated by an external cause (Skt. *nimitta* or *pratyaya*) is typical of the pratyeka-buddha legends associated by the commentaries with the verses of the Rhinoceros Sūtra. This fact has been offered (Norman 1983) in support of the theory that the original term for such buddhas was *pratyaya-buddha*, "enlightened by an external cause," and that the term *pratyeka-buddha*, "solitarily enlightened," results from a later and historically inaccurate Sanskritization." See Norman 1983.

Jamyang Shepa (in Hopkins 2003, 355–6) provides a detailed (Tibetan) presentation of the etymology of *pratyekabuddha*: "In the Sanskrit original of Solitary Realizer (*rang sangs rgyas*) *pratyekabuddha*, *eka* is used for 'one' [or 'alone']; *buddha* is used for 'realize' (*rtogs pa*) or 'understand' (*khong du chud pa*). Hence, they are Solitary Realizers because of becoming buddhafied alone—that is to say, they 'realize suchness'—without scripture. [In another etymology] they are Realizers (*buddha*) of Conditionality (*prati*, that is, *prayaya*) through understanding the reverse process and so forth [of the twelve links] of dependent-arising within observing a skeleton in a cemetery . . ." Hopkins notes (2003, 356nb), "Thus the term 'buddha' that is part of their name does not mean that they are Buddhas; rather, it means 'realizer.'"

For a detailed overview of the descriptions of pratyekabuddhas and their path, see Ray 1994, 213–50.

457 This and the following quotations are found in Haribhadra's *[Revised Edition of the] "Prajñāpāramitā Sūtra in Twenty-five Thousand Lines"* (*Pañchaviṃshatisāhasrikā-prajñāpāramitā, Shes rab kyi pha rol ru phyin pa stong phrag nyi shu lnga pa*). Toh. 3790; Dg.T. Beijing 50:827–8.

458 Treatises on the Bhūmis (*sa sde*) are a collection of five texts by Asaṅga: (1) *Bhūmis of Yogic Practice* (*Yogāchārabhūmi, rNal 'byor spyod pa'i sa*); (2) *Compendium of Ascertainments* (*Nirṇayasaṃgraha, gTan la dbab pa'i bsdu ba*); (3) *Compendium of Bases* (*Vastusaṃgraha, gZhi bsdu ba*); (4) *Compendium of Enumerations* (*Paryāyasaṃgraha, rNam grangs bsdu ba*); and (5) *Compendium of Explanations* (*Vivaraṇasaṃgraha, rNam par bshad pa'i bsdu ba*). Toh. 4035–42.

459 *Abhisamayālaṃkāra, mNgon rtogs rgyan,* by Maitreya. Chapter 2, verse 82. Toh. 3786. Note in the second line that *TOK*, II:487.3 ***rtogs** pa* should be ***rtog pa***.

460 See Chapter 3, p. 149.

461 *TOK*, II:487.15: *bse **la** rva gcig* should be *bse **ru la** rva gcig* according to PKTC.

462 It may be the case that both the single horn of the Indian rhinoceros and the rhinoceros' solitary habits are the similes for the pratyekabuddhas' habit of dwelling alone. For a discussion of the term *khaḍgaviṣhāṇa*, see Salomon 2000, 10–14.

463 The six topics of training (*bslab par bya ba'i gnas drug*) are the first topics presented in Mipham's *Gateway to Knowledge* (*mKhas 'jug*). See Schmidt 1997.

464 Those in their final phase of cyclic existence (*srid pa tha ma pa*) are not compelled to take rebirth in cyclic existence owing to their karma. They are either individuals who are about to attain arhatship or they are tenth bhūmi bodhisattvas (*srid pa tha ma pa/ srid pa'i gnas 'dir las kyi dbang gis slar skye ba len mi dgos pa'i phyir na srid pa tha ma pa ste/ nyan rang dgra bcom 'thob ka ma'i gang zag dang/ sa bcu'i byang chub sems dpa' rnams*) (*GTCD*).

465 The three castes are brahmins, warriors (*kṣhatriyas*), and merchants (*vaishyas*).

466 The "final perfection" (*prāntakoṭika, rab mtha'*), which is the fourth meditative concentration (*bsam gtan bzhi pa*), is discussed in the *Treasury of Abhidharma*, Chapter 7, verse 41ac. See Dg.T. Beijing 79:824–5; and Pruden 1990, 1155–6.

467 This is stated in the *Treasury of Abhidharma,* Chapter 6, verse 24ab. See Dg.T. Beijing 79:716; and Pruden 1989, 941. For more on the knowledge of the exhaustion [of defilements] and the knowledge of their [subsequent] nonarising (*kṣhayānutpattijñāna, zad mi skye shes pa*), see n. 315.

468 Three doors to liberation (*vimokṣhamukhatraya, rnam thar sgo gsum*) are emptiness (*shūnyatā, stong pa nyid*), absence of characteristics (*animitta, mtshan ma med pa*), and absence of expectancy (*apraṇihita, smon pa med pa*). See also n. 756.

469 *Ajātashatru-kaukṛittyavinodana, Ma skyes dgra'i 'gyod pa bsal ba'i mdo.* Toh. 216.

470 Three yānas (those of the shrāvakas, pratyekabuddhas, and bodhisattvas) are discussed in such sūtras as the *Eight Thousand Stanza Perfection of Wisdom Sūtra* (*Aṣhṭa-sāhasrikāprajñāpāramitāsūtra, Shes rab kyi pha rol tu phyin pa brgyad stong pa'i mdo*) and *Lotus Sūtra* (*Saddharmapuṇḍarīka-nāma-mahāyāna-sūtra, Dam pa'i chos pad ma dkar po zhes bya ba theg pa chen po'i mdo*).

471 Mikyö Dorjé (*Mi bskyod rdo rje*) (1507–1554), the eighth Karmapa, was renowned as a scholar. He wrote four of the five great treatises on the Sūtrayāna studied in the Karma Kagyu tradition: (1) *Chariot of the Dakpo Kagyu Siddhas: A Commentary on*

the "Entrance to the Middle Way" (*dBu ma la 'jug pa'i rnam bshad dpal ldan dus gsum mkhyen pa'i zhal lung dvags brgyud sgrub pa'i shing rta*); (2) *Repose of the Noble Ones: A Commentary on the "Ornament of Clear Realization"* (*Shes rab kyi pha rol tu phyin pa'i man ngag gi bstan bcos mngon par rtogs pa'i rgyan gyi 'grel pa rje btsun ngal gso*); (3) *Bestowing the Fulfillment of Accomplishment and Happiness: A Commentary on the "Treasury of Abhidharma"* (*Chos mngon pa mdzod kyi 'grel pa grub bde'i dpyid 'jo*); and (4) *Disk of the Sun: A Detailed Commentary on the "Root Vinaya Sūtra"* (*'Dul ba mdo rtsa ba'i rgya cher 'grel pa nyi ma'i dkyil 'khor*).

472 Jamgön Kongtrul cites *Praises of Madhyamaka* (*dBu ma la bstod pa*), which seems to be an alternative title for Nāgārjuna's *Praises of the Inconceivable One* (*Achintyastava, bSam gyis mi khyab par bstod pa*) (Toh. 1128; Dg.T. Beijing 1:228). The quotation is not found in that text; however, it similar enough to verse 27 of Nāgārjuna's *Praises of the Transcendent One* (*Lokātītastava, 'Jig rten las 'das par bstod pa*) (Toh. 1120; Dg.T. Beijing 1:197) to consider it to be a quotation from that text. The differences in the wording between Nāgārjuna's *Praises of the Transcendent One* and *TOK* do not change the meaning.

Dg.T. Beijing 1:197: *mtshan ma med* ***la ma zhugs*** *par/ thar pa med ces gsungs pa'i phyir/ de phyir khyod kyis theg chen* ***rnams/ ma lus par ni de nyid bstan.*** *TOK*, II:489.22: *mtshan ma med* ***pa ma rtogs*** *par/* ***khyod kyis*** *thar pa med* ***par*** *gsungs/ de phyir khyod kyis theg chen* ***las/ de ni tshang bar bstan pa lags.***

473 Āchārya Shūra (or Āchārya Vira, *sLob dpon dpa' bo*) (ca. second to third century), also known as Ashvaghoṣha (*rTa dbyangs*), was a Mahāyāna master and contemporary of Nāgārjuna.

474 Chapter 1, verse 11ab. Toh. 3786, f. 2a7; Dg.T. Beijing 49:4.

475 Chapter 20, verses 59–60. Toh. 4020, f. 35a3–4; Dg.T. Beijing 70:881. See Jamspal et al. 2004, 310.

476 The twofold of absence of self-entity is the absence of a self of persons (*pudgalanairātmya, gang zag gi bdag med*) and the absence of a self-entity of phenomena (*dharmanairātmya, chos kyi bdag med*).

477 See n. 314.

478 These are discussed in Chapter 2, pp. 100–103.

479 According to *GTCD*, the ten strengths (*stobs*) of a buddha are the strength of (1) knowing what is the case and what is not the case; (2) knowing the maturation of karma; (3) knowing the various inclinations [of beings]; (4) knowing the various dispositions [of beings]; (5) knowing the various faculties [of beings]; (6) knowing the path that leads everywhere; (7) knowing the meditative concentrations, samādhis, absorptions, and so forth; (8) knowing previous lives; (9) knowing death and rebirth; and (10) knowing the exhaustion of defilements.

The four fearlessnesses (*mi 'jigs pa*) of a buddha are fearlessness regarding (1) realization, (2) relinquishment, (3) teaching the dharma to overcome obstacles, and (4) teaching the path of renunciation.

The eighteen unique qualities of a buddha (*sangs rgyas kyi chos ma 'dres pa*) are buddhas (1) do not have confusion; (2) are not noisy; (3) are not forgetful; (4) always abide in equipoise; (5) do not have the perception [of things] as discrete; (6) do not have equanimity lacking in analysis; (7) do not have intentions that decline; (8) do not have diligence that diminishes; (9) do not have mindfulness that decreases; (10) do not have wisdom that degenerates; (11) do not have samādhi that declines; (12) do not have a liberation that regresses; (13) have physical activity that is preceded by and followed through with primordial wisdom; (14) have verbal activity that is preceded by and followed through with primordial wisdom; (15) have mental activity that is preceded by and followed through with primordial wisdom; (16) see the past through dispassionate, unobstructed primordial wisdom; (17) see the future through dispassionate, unobstructed primordial wisdom; and (18) see the present through dispassionate, unobstructed primordial wisdom.

These excellent qualities manifest with the attainment of the dharmakāya and are known as the thirty-two excellent qualities that are the result of separation (or freedom) (*bral ba'i 'bras bu'i yon tan*), which indicate the separation from, or relinquishment of, the mental afflictions. They are presented in the *Highest Continuum;* see Fuchs 2000, 218–26; and Holmes 1999, 242–58.

480 *Prajñāpāramitā-saṃchayagāthā, Shes rab kyi pha rol tu phyin pa sdud pa* (also known as *'Phags pa mdo sdud pa*). Toh. 13.

481 *Mahāyāna-saṃgraha, Theg pa chen po bsdus pa,* by Asaṅga. Toh. 4048, f. 2b6–7; Dg.T. Beijing 76:5. This is the summarizing verse for the *Compendium of the Mahāyāna's* ten chapters. See Keenan 1992, 12–3. These topics also form the basis for the presentation of one of three main sections in the Chittamātra chapter: The Summary of Its Seven Bases. See Chapter 6, pp. 177–185.

482 Vajrayāna is the subject of Part Four of Book Six (*Systems of Buddhist Tantra,* Kongtrul 2005). Jamgön Kongtrul lists it here to show that the Mahāyāna has two modes (even though he only discusses one of them in this part). This heading is the first root verse in Book Six, Part Four (Kongtrul 2005, 72): "[Here is presented] the resultant indestructible way of secret mantra."

483 The outline heading here is slightly different from when the section is presented (see p. 166).

484 Elevated states (*abhyudaya, mngon mtho*): the god and human realms in which happiness is experienced.

485 Definitive excellence (*niḥshreyasa, nges legs*): states of lasting happiness, in other words, the states of liberation (*thar pa*) and omniscience (*thams cad mkhyen pa*).

486 See also the Introduction, p. 17, for a brief discussion of the meaning of "philosophical" (*lakṣhaṇa, mtshan nyid*) in this context.

487 The Pāramitāyāna is called the cause-based portion of the Mahāyāna path (in contrast to the Vajrayāna, called the result-based part of the path), because the Pāramitāyāna takes the causes of awakening (the six pāramitās and so forth) as the path, whereas the Vajrayāna takes the results of awakening (the kāyas and primordial wisdoms) as the path. Jamgön Kongtrul's comment that the cause-based part of the Mahāyāna alone serves as the path to nonabiding nirvāṇa is in keeping with the position of the eighth Karmapa, Mikyö Dorjé (see *Chariot of the Dakpo Kagyu Siddhas,* pp. 17–50), but is not held universally. For Tsongkhapa's view that buddhahood cannot be attained through the practice of the Pāramitāyāna alone, that only through practicing the Vajrayāna can it be attained, see Dalai Lama et al. 1977, 60–70; Cozort 1986, 26; and Hopkins 2003, 687–92 (which includes Tak-tsang Lotsāwa's objection to this view) and 1009–10.

Jamgön Kongtrul adds the comment here that "the instrumental case [in the root verse, translated as "through" (*yis*),] connects these lines with the next ones." Although it is part of the main text, I place this comment in the endnotes because it is relevant only to those reading the Tibetan text. Also note that the addition of "practitioners" in the root verse is in keeping with Jamgön Kongtrul's point.

488 The outline heading here is slightly different from when the section is first mentioned (see p. 165). For the sake of consistency, I am using the first form, "A Detailed Account of the Systematic Presentation [of the Pāramitāyāna]," *rnam gzhag **rgyas par smos pa*** (*TOK,* II:491.11), as opposed to what is here, "The Actual Systematic Presentation," *rnam gzhag **dngos*** (*TOK,* II:492.2).

489 "The two types of bodhichitta" means either conventional (or relative) bodhichitta (*kun rdzob byang chub kyi sems*) and ultimate bodhichitta (*don dam byang chub kyi sems*), or the two types of conventional bodhichitta, aspirational bodhichitta and engaged bodhichitta (*smon 'jug byang chub sems*).

490 Reading ***drang** nges* as ***grangs** nges* (*TOK,* II:492.18), which is the spelling used for this topic (*TOK,* II:496.8).

491 See Kongtrul 1998, 200–204.

492 Chapter 5, verses 436–437b. Toh. 4158, f. 123a7–b1.

493 Generosity's opposite is miserliness (*ser sna*); ethical conduct's opposite is immorality (*tshul 'chal*); patience's opposite is anger (*zhe sdang*); exertion's opposite is laziness (*le lo*); meditative concentration's opposite is distraction (*rnam g.yeng*); and wisdom's opposite is impaired awareness (*shes 'chal*) (*GTCD*).

494 The three spheres (*trimaṇḍala, 'khor gsum*) are agent, object, and action.

495 Chapter 17, verse 8. Toh. 4020, f. 21b3; Dg.T. Beijing 70:851.

496 *Ornament of the Mahāyāna Sūtras*, Chapter 17, verse 15. Toh. 4020, f. 21b7–22a1; Dg.T. Beijing 70:851. Note that in the second line Dg.T. Beijing 70:851 reads: *dbul ba 'dor bar **byed pa;*** and *TOK,* II:493.10 has: *dbul ba 'dor bar **bya ba.***

497 I believe that *dāridrya* is what Jamgön Kongtrul means and may well have written, rather than *dāridrā* (*TOK,* II:493.14), which may be a printing error introduced at some point.

498 See, for example, the *Compendium of the Mahāyāna,* Chapter 4; and Keenan 1992, 76.

499 Each of the six pāramitās has three types. The three of generosity are to give material aid (*zang zin*), to give the dharma (*chos*), and to protect others from their fears (*mi 'jigs pa*). The three of ethical conduct are to restrain one's unwholesome behavior (*nyes spyod sdom pa*), to acquire good qualities (*dge ba chos sdud pa*), and to work for the benefit of others (*sems can don byed pa*). The three of patience are to withstand harm (*gnod pa*), to accept hardships (*dka' ba*), and to fathom emptiness (*stong nyid*). The three of diligence are armor-like (*go cha*) diligence, the application (*sbyor ba*) of diligence, and insatiable (*chog mi shes pa*) diligence. The three of meditative concentration are to rest at ease in the present life (*mthong chos bder gnas*), to achieve good qualities (*yon tan sgrub pa*), and to focus on the welfare of others (*sems can gyi don la dmigs pa*). The three of wisdom are mundane (*'jig rten*) wisdom, lower transmundane (*'jig rten 'das dman*) wisdom, and higher transmundane (*'jig rten 'das mchog*) wisdom; or they are the wisdoms that arise through study (*thos pa*), critical reflection (*bsam pa*), and meditation (*sgom pa*). See Kongtrul 1998, 201–3; and *TOK,* II:124–5.

500 Verse 44. Toh. 3786, f. 3b4–5; Dg.T. Beijing 49:7. Note the following differences in the first two lines: Dg.T. Beijing: ***de dag so sor sbyin la sogs/ rnam pa drug tu*** *bsdus pa yis/; TOK,* II:493.23: ***sbyin pa la sogs rnam drug la/ de dag so sor*** *bsdus pa yis/.*

501 Chapter 19, verse 40. Toh. 4020, f. 30a1–4; Dg.T. Beijing 70:869.

502 Chapter 20, verses 28–29. Toh. 4020, f. 33b5–6; Dg.T. Beijing 70:878.

503 *Ornament of the Mahāyāna Sūtras*, Chapter 20, verse 42. Toh. 4020, f. 34a7; Dg.T. Beijing 70:879.

504 "Abiding in the final [equipoise] with compassion" (*mtha' la snying rje ldan gnas*) means to abide in the fourth meditative concentration with limitless compassion, according to Vasubandhu's *Commentary on the "Ornament of the Mahāyāna Sūtras"* (*Sūtrālaṃkāra-vyākhyā, mDo sde rgyan gyi bshad pa*). Dg.T. Beijing 70:1414.

The fourth meditative concentration (*bsam gtan bzhi pa*) is the final level of meditative concentration in the form realm, and the fourth of the nine successive levels of abiding in meditative equipoise (*mthar gyis gnas pa'i snyoms par 'jug pa dgu*). It is also called the "final perfection" (*prāntakoṭika, rab mtha'*); see n. 466.

505 A similar list is given in Book Five, Part Three (*TOK*, II:126). See Kongtrul 1998, 203, where these are called "the six noble components."

506 Chapter 20, verses 30–31. Dg.T. Beijing 70:878.

507 Chapter 20, verses 32–33. Dg.T. Beijing 70:878. Note the following spelling variations:

Verse 32, line two: Dg.T. Beijing: **bzhin mdzes pa ni** (with Peking and Nar editions noted as *bzhin* ***gyis mdzes***); *TOK*, II:495.12–15: ***bzhin gyi mdzes ni.*** Verse 32, line three: Dg.T. Beijing: ***'phral***; (with Peking and Nar editions noted as ***'bral***); *TOK*: ***phra*** *la.*

Verse 33, line three: Dg.T. Beijing: *sems dpa'* ***rnams*** *dag; TOK*: *sems dpa'* ***rnam*** *dag.* Verse 33, line five: Dg.T. Beijing: *sbyor rnams* ***kyi****; TOK*: *sbyor rnams* ***kyis.***

508 Chapter 5, verse 438. Toh. 4158, f. 123b1–2; Dg.T. Beijing 96:328. In line two, the translation follows Dg.T. Beijing: *bzod pas* ***mdangs ldan****; TOK,* II:496.3: *bzod pas* ***gzugs bzang.***

509 The form kāyas (*rūpakāya, gzugs sku*) are the sambhogakāya (*longs spyod rdzogs pa'i sku*) and the nirmāṇakāya (*sprul pa'i sku*).

510 The three trainings (*shikṣhā, bslab pa*) are the training in ethical conduct (*shilashikṣhā, tshul khrims kyi bslab pa*), the training in samādhi (*samādhishikṣhā, ting nge 'dzin gyi bslab pa*), and the training in wisdom (*prajñāshikṣhā, shes rab kyi bslab pa*). See Chapter 6, p. 184.

511 Chapter 17, verse 7. Toh. 4020, f. 21b2–3; Dg.T. Beijing 70:851.

512 *Ornament of the Mahāyāna Sūtras*, Chapter 17, verse 14. Toh. 4020, f. 21b7; Dg.T. Beijing 70:851.

513 Chapter 19, verse 67. Toh. 4020, f. 31a2; Dg.T. Beijing 70:872. In line two the translation follows Dg.T. Beijing: *yang dag* ***gnas pa****; TOK,* II:497.1: *yang dag* ***dmigs pa.***

514 *Saṃdhinirmochanasūtra; dGongs pa nges par 'grel pa zhes bya ba theg pa chen po'i mdo.* This is the final statement of the Bhagavat in Chapter 3, The Questions of Suvishuddhamati. Toh. 106, f. 9b2. See Powers 1995, 49.

515 See Book Eight, Part One (*TOK*, III:110–136).

516 For discussion of the term Chittamātra (*Sems tsam pa*; Mere Mind, Mind-Only, or Mere Mentalism), see n. 519. For discussion of the name "Proponents of Cognition" (*Vijñaptivādin* or *Vijñaptika, rNam rig smra ba*), see n. 520.

517 For discussion of the term Mādhyamikas (*dBu ma pa*; Those of the Middle, or Centrists), see n. 604. For the use of the name "Proponents of the Absence of a Nature" (or "Proponents of Entitylessness," or "Proponents of Non-Nature") (*Niḥsvabhāvavādin, Ngo bo nyid med par smra ba*), see Chapter 7, p. 201.

518 The outline heading here is slightly different from when the section is presented (see p. 195).

519 The term *chittamātra* (*sems tsam*; mind only) appears in texts such as the *Descent into Laṅkā Sūtra* and *Sūtra Unraveling the Intention*, but it does not seem to have been used in Indian Buddhist texts to denote a system of thought. In Tibet, however, it became a common term for the philosophical tenet system of those known in India as Yogāchāras (*rNal 'byor spyod pa*, Yoga Practitioners) and Proponents of Consciousness (*Vijñānavādin, rNam shes smra ba*). For an overview of the use of the term in Indian Buddhism, see Lindtner 1997.

520 Proponents of Cognition (*Vijñaptivādin* or *Vijñaptika, rNam rig smra ba*). The use of this term to denote a school of thought probably evolved from the expression "cognition only" (*vijñaptimātra, rnam rig tsam*), which is found, for example, in the *Sūtra Unraveling the Intention* (Chapter 8); see Powers 1995, 155. Although it seems that "Proponents of Cognition" is used interchangeably with Proponents of Consciousness (*Vijñānavādin, rNam shes smra ba*), the latter is more common in Indian Buddhist texts. For example, the *Tibetan-Sanskrit Dictionary* (Negi 2001; vol. 7, pp. 3165 and 3175) lists four instances of *Vijñānavādin* (*rNam par shes par smra ba*) but only one for the form *Vijñaptimātravādin* (*rNam par rig pa tsam du smra ba*, Proponents of Mere Cognition), and none for *Vijñaptivādin*; and *Vijñānavādin* is found in the *MVP*, whereas *Vijñaptivādin* or *Vijñaptimātravādin* are not. I am grateful to Karl Brunnhölzl for help with this information.

For more references relating to this term, see below n. 533. For Shākya Chokden's statement that it is wrong to regard Proponents of Cognition and Chittamātras as the same, see Chapter 11, p. 266.

521 *Aṣhṭasāhasrikāprajñāpāramitāsūtra, Shes rab kyi pha rol tu phyin pa brgyad stong pa'i mdo.* (Toh. 12; ACIP KD0012.) This quotation is not found in this text, but it does appear in the *Descent into Laṅkā Sūtra* and the *Sūtra on the Ten Bhūmis* (*Dashabhūmikasūtra, Sa bcu pa'i mdo*).

522 Yogāchāras (*rNal 'byor spyod pa*, Yoga Practitioners). Early uses of this term designated Buddhist practitioners in general, but it later came to be associated with the works attributed to Maitreya, Asaṅga, and Vasubandhu, possibly having been derived from the title of Asaṅga's *Yogāchārabhūmi* (*rNal 'byor spyod pa'i sa, Bhūmis of Yogic Practice*). The first, or at least an early, use of "Yogāchāra" as referring to a school of thought is found in Bhāvaviveka's *Lamp of Wisdom* (*Prajñāpradīpa, Shes rab sgron ma*), and his *Heart of the Middle Way* (*Madhyamakahṛidayakārikā, dBu ma'i snying po'i tshig le'ur byas pa*) and its auto-commentary, *Blaze of Reasoning* (*Tarkajvālā, rTog ge 'bar ba*). This became the most common term in India for followers of the thought of Maitreya, Asaṅga, and Vasubandhu, followed by "Proponents of Consciousness" (*Vijñānavādin, rNam shes smra ba*). See Hanson 1998, 3–11; and Davidson 1985, 51.

523 Although here Jamgön Kongtrul attributes this verse to the *Abhidharma Sūtra* (*Chos mngon pa'i mdo*), it is in fact one of the summarizing verses of the *Compendium of the Mahāyāna.* It is also cited in Chapter 5, p. 165, where it is correctly attributed to the *Compendium of the Mahāyāna.* I have, therefore, attributed it here to the *Compendium of the Mahāyāna.* See Dg.T. Beijing 76:5; and Keenan 1992, 12–3.

This verse summarizes the subject matter (and titles) of the ten chapters of the *Compendium of the Mahāyāna*. Jamgön Kongtrul condenses these into the seven bases (*gzhi bdun*) of the Mahāyāna path by combining the three trainings into one topic and the relinquishments and primordial wisdoms into one topic, the result.

524 This section is drawn primarily from the *Compendium of the Mahāyāna*, Chapter 1. See Dg.T. Beijing 76:6–30; and Keenan 1992, 15–37.

525 This is the final statement of the Bhagavat in Chapter 5, The Questions of Vishālamati. Toh. 106, f. 13b7. See Powers 1995, 77. It is also quoted in the *Compendium of the Mahāyāna*, Chapter 1.

526 Appropriating consciousness (*ādānavijñāna, len pa'i rnam shes*).

527 The *Abhidharma Sūtra* (*Chos mngon pa'i mdo*) is no longer available except for quotations found in other texts. One such text is the *Compendium of the Mahāyāna*, which states that it is based on the *Abhidharma Sūtra*. This quotation is found in the *Compendium of the Mahāyāna*. See Dg.T. Beijing 76:7; and Keenan 1992, 15.

528 Afflictive phenomena (*saṃklesha, kun nyon*) can mean saṃsāra in a general sense; more specifically it is the fifty-three phenomena listed in the Prajñāpāramitā sūtras, along with the fifty-five purified phenomena. For a list of these phenomena, see Hopkins 1983, 201–12.

529 Dependent origination that is the differentiation of the nature [into phenomena] (**svabhāvavibhāgaḥpratīyasamutpādaḥ, ngo bo nyid rnam par 'byed pa'i rten cing 'brel 'byung*): Jamgön Kongtrul describes this type of dependent origination in Book Six, Part Two (*TOK*, II:426) as referring to the fact that "all outer and inner phenomena emanate from the ālaya consciousness" (*phyi nang gi chos thams cad kun gzhi'i rnam par shes pa las sprul*).

In his *Compendium of the Mahāyāna*, Asaṅga says, "All phenomena arise in dependence upon the ālaya. This is [what is meant by] the differentiation of the nature [into phenomena]" (*gang kun gzhi rnam par shes pa la brten nas chos rnams 'byung ba de ni ngo bo nyid rnam par 'byed pa can*). See Dg.T. Beijing 76:15; and Keenan 1992, 22.

530 This section draws heavily from the *Compendium of the Mahāyāna*, Chapter 2. See Dg.T. Beijing 76:30–56; and Keenan 1992, 39–61. Points are also drawn from the *Sūtra Unraveling the Intention*, Chapters 6 and 7, and Maitreya's *Differentiation of the Middle and the Extremes* (*Madhyāntavibhaṅga, dBus mtha' rnam 'byed*), Chapters 1 and 3.

Other sources for the three characteristics, or natures, are the *Descent into Laṅkā Sūtra*; Maitreya's *Ornament of the Mahāyāna Sūtras*; and Vasubandhu's *Thirty Verses* (*Triṃshikākārikā, Sum bcu pa*) and *Exposition of the Three Natures* (*Trisvabhāvanirdesha, Rang bzhin gsum nges par bstan pa*). See also Chapter 11, pp. 255–257; Boquist 1993; Brunnhölzl 2004, 463–91; and Hopkins 1999, 2002, and 2003.

531 Three characteristics (*trilakṣhaṇa, mtshan nyid gsum*). Also known as "three natures" (*trisvabhāva, rang bzhin gsum*).

532 "Imagination of what is unreal" (*abhūtaparikalpa, yang dag min rtog* or *yang dag pa ma yin pa'i kun tu rtog pa*) is a term used for the dependent characteristic in the *Differentiation of the Middle and the Extremes*, Chapter 1, specifically, verses 1, 5, 8, and 11. For verse 8, see below n. 534; verses 1 and 2 are quoted in Chapter 11, p. 253.

Verse 5 says: "The imagined, the dependent, and the consummate are explained to be, respectively, referents (*artha, don*), the imagination of what is unreal, and the absence of duality" (*brtags pa dang ni gzhan dbang dang/ yongs su grub pa nyid kyang ngo/ don phyir yang dag min rtog phyir/ gnyis po med pa'i phyir bshad do*). See Dg.T. Beijing 70:902–3.

Simply put, the imagination of what is unreal is the aspect of the dependent nature that creates the sense of duality (*gnyis snang*). It could also be said that it is a term used for the dependent nature in its impure state. (See p. 181 for the two divisions of the dependent nature.) "Imagination" (*parikalpa, kun rtog*) includes both conceptual and nonconceptual cognition (*rnam rig*) or perception (*blo*) and the perceived referents, thus "imagination" is not identical with "thought" or "concept" (*vikalpa, rnam rtog*). As Urban and Griffiths say (1994, 14): "*Parikalpa* [imagination] . . . has the potential to be pure and error-free; *vikalpa* [thought] does not: it is what produces defilement and error in the flow of concepts and percepts."

Urban and Griffiths (1994, 12) also quote Sthiramati's explanation in his *Sub-Commentary on the "Differentiation of the Middle and the Extremes"* (*Madhyāntavibhaṅga-ṭīkā, dBus dang mtha' rnam par 'byed pa'i 'grel bshad*) of Chapter 1, verse, 1:

> The compound 'unreal comprehensive construction' [or the imagination of what is unreal] may be understood to indicate that the duality comprehensively constructed either by it or in it is unreal. The term 'unreal' indicates that the extent to which something is comprehensively constructed in terms of a dichotomy between subject and object is the extent to which it does not exist. The term 'comprehensive construction' indicates that the extent to which an object is comprehensively constructed is the extent to which it is not found.

They observe (12–3): "There is . . . an especially close relationship between *abhūtaparikalpa* [imagination of the unreal] and the relative (*paratantra*) aspect of experience . . . and this in turn suggests that when . . . *parikalpa or parikalpana* . . . [are used] it may sometimes denote, descriptively, the simple fact of the flow of experience, with all its finally illusory phenomenal properties of division between subject and object, 'appearances,' as MV-ṭ [Sthiramati's *Sub-Commentary*] puts it, 'that consist in objects, living beings, and selves and representations' . . . Such locutions leave open the possibility that the phenomenally rich series of mental images that usually constitutes the flow of experience may occur without being accompanied by a sharp phenomenological distinction between subject and object . . . We might say that *parikalpa*[*na*] [imagination] and *abhūtaparikalpa* [imagination of the unreal] have a dual use: they can be used to denote both an undefiled nonerroneous flow of experience, and a defiled and mistaken set of percepts and concepts that results from constructive action upon that flow."

Nagao says (1991, 53): "The actualities of daily life are here [in the *Madhyāntavibhaṅga* I.1] summed up as 'unreal notions,' which are a discrimination between, and attachment to, two things—the subject grasping and the object grasped (*grāhaka, grāhya*). This two-ness, though indispensable for discrimination or conceptualization, does not have any reality at all; here, emptiness is found to belong to the 'unreal notion' or 'imagination.' (The adjective 'unreal' is used to qualify the notions or imagination that singles out as existent things that are 'non-reals,' that is, 'empty.')"

Boquist states (1993, 69): "To account for the fact of illusion, Maitreya introduces the concept of 'the imagination of the unreal' (*abhūtaparikalpa*). Ignorance and illusion require a mind and this mind constitutes the imagination of the unreal subject (*grāhaka*) and object (*grāhya*) expressed as a duality (*dvaya*). This very act of cognition is the dependent being (*paratantrasvabhāva*), which is real while the cognitive images reflecting the bifurcation into duality make up the imagined nature (*parikalpitasvabhāva*), which is unreal. The imagination's sole reality is the pure and unified awareness expressed as emptiness, suchness, or pure mind, which is within it and in which it resides. This absence of discriminative thinking is the consummated nature (*parinișhpannasvabhāva*)."

For more discussion of this term, see Kochumuttom 1982, 29–72 and 222–4; Nagao 1991; Boquist 1993; Urban and Griffiths 1994; Hopkins 1999, 305–10; Mathes 2000; and Brunnhölzl 2004, 464–5. Note that this term is translated in various ways, including "unreal ideation," and "unreal comprehensive construction."

533 For a useful article on the term *vijñapti* (*rnam rig*; "cognition") see Hall 1986. For a list of nine ways that this term has been translated by Western and Asian scholars, see Hopkins 2003, 309–10nb.

534 This is related to the statement in the *Differentiation of the Middle and the Extremes,* Chapter 1, verse 8ab: "The imagination of what is unreal is mind as well as mental events belonging to the three realms" (*yang dag ma yin kun rtog ni/ sems dang sems byung khams gsum pa*). See Dg.T. Beijing 70:903; Anacker 1984/1998, 214; and Kochumuttom 1982, 238–9.

535 "Substantially established" (*dravyasiddha, rdzas su grub pa*) and "substantially existent" (*dravyasat, rdzas su yod pa*) are synonyms in the Chittamātra system presented here by Jamgön Kongtrul. "Substantially established" is used to describe both the dependent characteristic and the consummate characteristic, and, therefore, neither term is *necessarily* synonymous with "truly existent" (*bden par grup pa*). (ALTG)

536 Imagined [characteristics] (*parikalpita, kun brtag*) are everything that is imputed on the basis of the dependent nature: all conceptual labels, universals (or generally characterized phenomena) (*spyi mtshan*), the idea of a self or of true existence. This term is also translated as "imputational character" and "imaginary nature."

537 Floaters (*kesha/ keshoṇḍuka, skra shad* [*'dzag pa*]; "falling hairs"): In the West, floaters, or *muscae volitantes*, are not considered the result of an eye disease (*timira, rab rib*) as they are said to be in Indian and Tibetan Buddhist texts. Nevertheless, the definitions of floaters and *muscae volitantes* seem to fit the traditional descriptions. Floaters: "a bit of optical debris (as a dead cell or a cell fragment) in the vitreous humor or lens that may be perceived as a spot before the eye"; *muscae volitantes* ("flying flies"): "spots before the eyes, usually in the form of dots, threads, beads, or circles, due to cells and cell fragments in the vitreous humor and lens" (*Webster's Third New International Dictionary Unabridged*). For a more complete account, see Brunnhölzl 2004, 871n273.

538 The horns of a rabbit are a traditional example of something that simply does not exist.

539 "The consummate" (*parinișhpanna, yongs grub*) is also translated as "perfected," "perfectly existent," "thoroughly established," and so on.

540 An example of such teachings is found in the *Heart Sūtra*: "There are no forms, no feelings, no discriminations, no formative forces, no consciousness, no eye, no ear, . . ."

541 The same divisions and, for the most part, similar explanations are found in Longchen Rabjam's (*kLong chen rab 'byams*) *The Precious Treasury of Philosophical Systems* (*Grub mtha' mdzod*) (forthcoming translation by Richard Barron), and Kedrup Jé's (*mKhas grub rje*) *Great Digest* (*sTong thun chen mo*) (see Cabezón 1992a, 67–8). Jamyang Shepa's *Great Exposition of Tenets* (*Grub mtha' chen mo*) (see Hopkins

2003, 374–8) and Chang-kya Rolpé Dorjé's *Beautiful Ornament of Philosophical Tenet Systems* (*Grub mtha' mdzes rgyan*, 122–4) present the same divisions and similar explanation for the imagined and the dependent. In Book Six, Part Two, Jamgön Kongtrul provides these and other categorizations; see *TOK*, II:413–5.

542 "The appearance of the dualism of perceived objects and perceiving subject for the nonconceptual sense consciousnesses" (*rtog med dbang shes la gzung 'dzin gnyis snang*) means that the perceiving subject and its object appear to the sense consciousnesses as two discrete, separate things (*tha dad du snang ba*). The sense object is not the imagined, nor is the perceiving subject (the sense consciousness), but their appearance as a dualistic subject and object, separate and cut off from each other, is a nominal imagined characteristic (ALTG). See n. 544.

543 The description of the dependent nature as pure and impure is found in a number of Yogāchāra texts, for example, the *Differentiation of the Middle and the Extremes*, Chapter 1, verse 21: "If that [i.e., the dependent nature] were not defiled, all beings would be liberated. If it were not pure, efforts would yield no results" (*gal te nyon mongs de ma gyur/ lus can thams cad grol bar gyur/ gal te rnam dag de ma gyur/ 'bad pa 'bras bu med par 'gyur*). See Dg.T. Beijing 70:904; Anacker 1984/1998, 221; and Kochumuttom 1982, 245–6. See also the *Compendium of the Mahāyāna*, Chapter 2 (Dg.T. Beijing 76:40; and Keenan 1992, 47).

544 The implication of Jamgön Kongtrul's statements (see also n. 542) is that there is a difference between "the appearance of the dualism of perceived object and perceiving subject" (*gzung 'dzin gnyis snang*) and "dualistic appearance" (*gnyis snang*). Not all dualistic appearance is the dualistic appearance of an object and a subject. The dependent nature (cognition, or mind and mental events) appears as a duality (*gnyis su snang ba*) in that it has an externally oriented aspect and an internally oriented aspect (*kha phyi bltas dang nang bltas*). Putting this another way, in the Chittamātra system, all cognitions are both other-awareness (*gzhan rig*) and reflexive awareness (*rang rig*), but such cognition does not involve an ascertainment of a duality or split. The ascertainment (*nges pa*) of a duality of perceiver and percept, that is as split into two discrete, separate things, is considered the imagined characteristic. (ALTG)

545 Cognition during the subsequent state (*rjes shes*) is the mental state following a period of meditative equipoise, which technically is called a "subsequent state of attainment" (*pṛiṣhṭhalabdha, rjes thob*). See n. 747.

546 The division of the consummate into unchanging and unerring is specified in the *Differentiation of the Middle and the Extremes*, Chapter 3, verse 11bc: "The consummate has two aspects: its unchanging [aspect] and its unerring [aspect]" (*'gyur med phyin ci ma log pa/ yongs su grub pa rnam pa gnyis*). See Dg.T. Beijing 70:907; and Anacker 1984/1998, 237.

547 For a discussion of the path (*mārga, lam*) and its observed objects (*ālambana, dmigs pa*) as part of the consummate nature, see Brunnhölzl 2004, 465–9.

548 The analogy of an illusion (*māyā, sgyu ma*) is widely used in Buddhist texts; one frequently quoted source is Vasubandhu's *Exposition of the Three Natures*, verses 27–30. Jamgön Kongtrul is clearly drawing from these verses:

> Through the power of [the magician's] mantra, a magical creation
> appears like an elephant,
> [but] only an image appears—
> there is no elephant that exists. (27)

The imagined nature is like the elephant.
The dependent is like that image.
The nonexistence of the elephant there
is the consummate [nature]. (28)

From the fundamental mind,
imagination of what is unreal appears as a duality.
Since duality does not exist at all,
there simply exists an image. (29)

The fundamental consciousness is like the mantra.
Thusness is like the wood.
Conception is like the image of the elephant.
Duality is like the elephant. (30)

sngags mthus sgyu ma byas pa yis/ ji nas glang po snang gyur pa/ rnam pa tsam zhig snang bar 'dod/ glang po kun du yod ma yin/
brtags pa'i rang bzhin glang po 'dra/ gzhan dbang de'i rnam lta bu'o/ de la glang po dngos med gang/ de 'dra yongs su grub par 'dod/
rtsa ba'i sems las gnyis bdag tu/ yang dag ma yin kun rtog snang/ gnyis po shin tu med pas na/ de ni rnam pa tsam du yod/
rtsa ba'i rnam shes sngags dang 'dra/ de bzhin nyid ni shing 'dra 'dod/ rnam rtog glang po'i rnam pa 'dra/ gnyis ni ngag po lta bu'o. Dg.T. Beijing 77:31–2.

(Vasubandhu did not write an auto-commentary and no one else wrote a commentary.) Note that "fundamental mind" (*rtsa ba'i sems*) is the ālaya consciousness.

Nagao (1991, 71-72) observes, "It should be clear from the magic show simile that the difference between the other-dependent nature and the imagined nature is very subtle and delicate; the former is compared to an elephant form and the latter to an attachment to that form. The difference is established on the basis of whether 'attachment' is operative or not. The difference between the other-dependent and consummated natures is likewise subtle. When the other-dependent nature ceases to be the cause for the delusory imagination to appear, it is identified with the consummated nature, the difference being whether such a cause is operative or not. The three natures, then, are neither different from each other nor identical to each other; or, rather, they are both different and identical at one and the same time."

See Nagao 1991, 69–72; Boquist 1993, 126–8; Garfield 2002, 128–51; and Tola and Dragonetti 2004, 226–7. This example is also used in the *Ornament of the Mahāyāna Sūtras,* Chapter 12, verse 15; see Jamspal et al. 2004, 122.

549 This section is drawn from the *Compendium of the Mahāyāna,* Chapter 3, and Vasubandhu's *Commentary on the "Compendium of the Mahāyāna"* (*Mahāyāna-saṃgraha-bhāṣhya, Theg bsdus 'grel pa bshad pa*). See Keenan 1992, 63–72.

550 See Chapter 5, p. 172.

551 The *Compendium of the Mahāyāna* (Chapter 6) states that the three types of ethical discipline (*shīla, tshul khrims*) are the ethical discipline of restraint (*sdom pa'i tshul khrims*), the ethical discipline of gathering the virtuous qualities (*dge ba'i chos sdud pa'i tshul khrims*), and the ethical discipline that benefits others (*sems can gyi don bya ba'i tshul khrims*). See Dg.T. Beijing 76:77; and Keenan 1992, 87.

552 The training in higher concentration (*adhichittaṃshikṣhā, lhag pa'i sems kyi bslab pa*) is often called the training in higher samādhi (*lhag pa ting nge 'dzin gyi bslab pa*).

553 The *Compendium of the Mahāyāna* (Chapter 7) says that there are four types of concentration: illuminating the Mahāyāna (*theg pa chen po snang ba*); accumulating all merit (*bsod nams thams cad yang dag par bsags pa*); the king of samādhis, "sustaining excellence" (*ting nge 'dzin gyi rgyal po bzang skyong*); and the heroic stride (*dpa' bar 'gro ba*). See Dg.T. Beijing 76:79; and Keenan 1992, 89.

554 This is the topic of Chapter 8 in the *Compendium of the Mahāyāna*.

555 The results of relinquishments and primordial wisdom are the topics of Chapters 9 and 10 in the *Compendium of the Mahāyāna*.

556 These five attributes of the dharmakāya are presented in Chapter 10 of the *Compendium of the Mahāyāna*. See Dg.T. Beijing 76:92–3; and Keenan 1992, 105–7.

557 The bhūmis (levels or grounds) and paths are presented in Book Nine, Part One (*TOK*, III:464–508).

558 For the five Dharma Treatises of Maitreya (*Byams pa'i chos sde*), see n. 807; for additional information, see nn. 809 and 811. For Dolpopa Sherab Gyalsten's views on the categorization of the five Treatises, see Chapter 6, p. 192 and Chapter 11, p. 251. For Shākya Chokden's views, see Chapter 11, pp. 250, 252–253, and 263. For Jamgön Kongtrul's statement, see Chapter 11, p. 262.

559 Asaṅga (*Thogs med*) (late fourth century to early fifth century) was an Indian master born in Gandhāra who is considered to be the founder of the Yogāchāra system. Traditional accounts state that he was Vasubandhu's older half-brother, and that after many years of retreat he received teachings directly from the future buddha Maitreya, which include the Five Treatises of Maitreya. Additionally he is credited with having composed a number of other major treatises, such as the *Compendium of Abhidharma, Compendium of the Mahāyāna,* and the Treatises on the Bhūmis (see n. 458). For bibliographic details, see Willis 2002, 4–12.

560 Vasubandhu (*dByig gnyen*) (late fourth century to early fifth century) was an Indian master born in Gandhāra. Traditional accounts state that he was Asaṅga's half-brother, and that he first studied the abhidharma in Gandhāra and later in Kashmir, after which he wrote the *Treasury of Abhidharma* and its auto-commentary, *Explanation of the "Treasury of Abhidharma."* Following this he is said to have been "converted" to the Mahāyāna teachings by Asaṅga and to have written a number of famous treatises considered part of the Yogāchāra tradition, some of which are included in the collection known as the Eight *Prakaraṇa* Treatises: (1) *Explanation of the "Ornament of the Mahāyāna Sūtras"* (*Sūtrālaṁkārāvyākhyā, mDo sde rgyan gyi bshad pa*); (2) *Commentary on the "Differentiation of the Middle and the Extremes"* (*Madhyāntavibhaṅgaṭīkā, dBus dang mtha' rnam par 'byed pa'i 'grel pa*; (3) *Commentary on the "Differentiation of Phenomena and Their Nature"* (*Dharmadharmatāvibhaṅgavṛitti, Chos dang chos nyid rnam par 'byed pa'i 'grel pa*); (4) *Principles of Explanation* (*Vyākhyayukti, rNam par bshad pa'i rig pa*); (5) *Delineation of Achieving Actions* (*Karmasiddhiprakaraṇa, Las grub pa'i rab tu 'byed pa*); (6) *Delineation of the Five Aggregates* (*Pañchaskandhaprakaraṇa, Phung po lnga'i rab tu 'byed pa*); (7) *Twenty Verses* (*Viṃshakākārikā, Nyi shu pa'i tshig le'ur byas pa*); and (8) *Thirty Verses* (*Triṃshikākārikā, Sum cu pa'i tshig le'ur byas pa*). See Anacker 1984/1998 for a detailed biography of Vasubandhu and translations of five of these eight texts.

Recent studies by Japanese and Western scholars have shown that in his *Explanation of the "Treasury of Abhidharma"* Vasubandhu at times takes positions that are similar to the *Bhūmis of Yogic Practice* (*Yogāchārabhūmi*), a seminal Yogāchāra work, when criticizing particular points of the Vaibhāṣhikas' doctrine. See Kritzer 2003b and 2005.

561 For other perspectives on whose views are represented by the Chittamātra system, see The Masters Who Assert Those [Chittamātra Positions], p. 191.

562 Dreyfus (1997, 433) makes the following remarks about Proponents of Real Images (or True Aspectarians) (*Satyākāravādin, rNam bden pa*), and Proponents of False Images (or False Aspectarians) (*Alīkākāravādin, rNam rdzun pa*):

> Concerning the notion of aspect, Dharmakīrti's Indian and Tibetan followers can be divided into two categories: those who hold that aspects are real entities, the True Aspectarians (*satyākāravādin, rnam bden pa*), and those who deny it, the False Aspectarians (*alīkārāvādin, rnam par rdzun par smra ba*). The former view is compatible with a so-called Sautrāntika view that perception provides undistorted access to the external world. Since external objects exist, the cognition that validates them, perception, must be undistorted. And so must the aspects that provide the basis for the conceptual interpretation of reality brought about by perception. Consequently, the adoption of a Sautrāntika view commits one to a True Aspectarian view of perception.
>
> The converse, however, is not true. The adoption of a True Aspectarian view does not commit one to the Sautrāntika acceptance of the reality of external objects. Thinkers who deny the reality of the external world hold that perception is mistaken, since objects appear to us as existing independent of their perception. These thinkers differ, however, on the degree of distortion. Among these thinkers the True Aspectarians, who take a Mind-Only view, hold that perception is mistaken with respect to the externality of its objects. According to their view, this distortion does not affect the nature of perception itself. The objective aspect held by a mental state is substantially identical with consciousness and hence real. The False Aspectarians reject this distinction and hold that the representation of objects in consciousness is itself a deluded construct. For them, aspects do not really exist, but are superimposed on the luminous nature of consciousness. Such a nature is ineffable, utterly beyond the duality of subject and object. Thus this view is described by Śākya Chok-den as Yogācāra but not as Mind-Only.

See Dreyfus 1997, 433–6. Tillemans comments (1990, 41–2 and 42n92):

> Satyākāravādins [Proponents of Real Images] (viz. Dignāga and Dharmakīrti) who, as their name implies, maintained the reality of these images, held that the raw sense-data which present themselves to perception, such as impressions of blue, etc., are real and possess dependent natures (*paratantrasvabhāva*) in that they are inseparable from consciousness, which is itself real. These *ākāra* [images] are then misinterpreted as external entities by conceptualization and thus subsequently, through the influence of a cognition different from simple perception, they acquire false or "thoroughly imagined natures" (*parikalpitasvabhāva*).
>
> The opposite Vijñānavāda position is that of the Alīkākāravādins [Proponents of False Images] who profess that the given data, or *ākāra,* while conventionally existent, are themselves deceptive in that they are falsely of two sorts, subjective (i.e. *grāhakākāra*) and objective (*grāhyākāra*). Only the pure non-dual consciousness is real . . . To take Bodhibhadra's explanation, the Alīkākāravādin maintains that the *ākāra* [images] themselves are not *paratantra* [dependent] but *parikalpitasvabhāva* [the imagined nature]: the raw given which one sees is itself unreal; it is only the self-awareness, or *svadaṃvedana,* which is fully real.

See also below, n. 565.

563 The *Sūtra Unraveling the Intention* (Chapter 6) uses a crystal as a simile for the dependent nature:

> Guṇākara, it is like this: When a clear crystal is in contact with the color blue, it appears to be a [blue] precious stone, such as a sapphire or *indranīla.* Since sentient beings incorrectly take [the clear crystal] to be a [blue] precious stone, such as a sapphire or *indranīla,* they are confused. When it is in contact with the color red, it appears to be a [red] precious stone, such as a ruby. Since sentient beings incorrectly take [the clear crystal] to be a [red] precious stone, such as a ruby, they are confused . . .
>
> Guṇākara, it is like this: Like the clear crystal in contact with a color, the dependent characteristic should be viewed as [being in contact with, or influenced by,] the habitual tendencies for conventions, which are imagined characteristics. It is like this: See that taking the dependent characteristic to be the imagined characteristics is like the simile of incorrectly taking a clear crystal to be a sapphire, *indranīla,* or ruby. Guṇākara, it is like this: the clear crystal should be viewed as the dependent characteristic . . .
>
> *yon tan 'byung gnas 'di lta ste dper na/ shel shin tu gsal ba ni gang gi tshe tshon sngon po dang phrad par gyur pa de'i tshe ni nor bu rin po che an da rnyil dang/ mthon ka chen/ po lta bur snang bar 'gyur zhing/ nor bu rin po che an da rnyil dang/ mthon ka chen por log par 'dzin pas kyang sems can rnams rnam par rmongs par byed do/ gang gi tshe tshon dmar po dang phrad par gyur pa de'i tshe ni nor bu rin po che pad-ma rā ga lta bur snang bar 'gyur zhing/ nor bu rin po che pad-ma rā ga ru log par 'dzin pas sems can rnams rnam par rmongs par byed do/ . . . yon tan 'byung gnas 'di lta ste dper na/ shel shin tu gsal ba tshon dang phrad pa de lta bur ni gzhan gyi dbang gi mtshan nyid la kun brtags pa'i mtshan nyid kyi tha snyad kyi bag chags su blta bar bya'o/ 'di lta ste/ dper na/ shel shin tu gsal ba la nor bu rin po che an da rnyil dang/ mthon ka chen po . . . gser du log par 'dzin pa lta bur ni gzhan gyi dbang gi mtshan nyid la kun brtags pa'i mtshan nyid du 'dzin pa blta bar bya'o/ yon tan 'byung gnas/ 'di lta ste/ dper na/ shel shin tu gsal ba de nyid lta bur ni gzhan gyi dbang gi mtshan nyid blta bar bya'o.*

See Powers 1995, 84–5.

564 Appearances are real in being the mind (*snang ba sems su bden pa*): The Proponents of Real Images' statement that appearances (i.e., forms, sounds, smells, tastes, and tangible objects) are real in being mind means that they consider perceived images (*gzung ba'i rnam pa*) to be real in that they are an intrinsic quality of mind, or inseparable from mind, which is itself real. Both Proponents of Real Images and Proponents of False Images assert that what appears is not other than mind, but they differ as to whether those appearances *are* mind (i.e., are an intrinsic part of mind) or not (ALTG). See Āchārya Sherab Gyaltsen 2003, Chapter 7. See also n. 562 above.

565 The doxographical categories of Proponents of Real Images (*Satyākāravādin, rNam bden pa*) and Proponents of False Images (*Alīkākāravādin, rNam rdzun pa*) are found in later Indian Buddhist works, where, in the context of Yogāchāra, the term "Proponents of Images" (*Sākāravādin, rNam pa dang bcas pa*) is sometimes used for Proponents of Real Images, and "Proponents of Nonexistent Images" (*Nirākāravādin, rNam pa med pa*) for Proponents of False Images (Jamgön Kongtrul states the latter on p. 189). Note that in a pan-Buddhist context "Proponents of Images" is used for both Sautrāntika and Yogāchāra Proponents of Real Images, and "Proponents of Nonexistent Images" are either Vaibhāṣhikas, because they do not posit "images" (in which case the term is better translated as

Proponents of No Images), or Yogāchāra Proponents of False Images, because they do not accept that images are real. (Also note that the categories of Proponents of Images and Proponents of No Images are used in non-Buddhist Indian philosophical circles.)

Bodhibhadra in his *Commentary on the "Compendium on the Heart of Primordial Wisdom"* (*Jñānasārasamuchchaya-nāma-nibandhana, Ye shes snying po kun las btus pa zhes bya ba'i bshad sbyar*) (Dg.T. Beijing 57:895) states:

> There are two types of Yogāchāras: Proponents of Images and Proponents of Nonexistent Images. The master Dignāga and others assert the positions of Proponents of Images. They teach that the image is the dependent (*paratantra, gzhan dbang*), as is said [in Dignāga's *Examination of Objects of Observation* (*Ālambanaparīkṣhā, dMigs pa brtags pa*), verse 6ac]: "The entity of the inner knowable object, which appears as if it were external, is the referent." They discuss [only] six modes of consciousness.
>
> Proponents of Nonexistent Images include the master Asaṅga and others. They state that images are the imagined (*parikalpita, kun brtags*) [and] are like the floaters seen by the visually impaired, since it is said [in the *Compendium of the Mahāyāna,* Chapter 8]: "If referents were to exist as referents, there could be no nonconceptual wisdom. If that [wisdom] does not exist, the attainment of buddhahood is not feasible." And [in the same text]: "Where nonconceptual wisdom occurs, no object appears. One must comprehend that there are no referents. Since they do not exist, there is no cognition." They state that there are eight modes of consciousness, [although] some say that there is [just] one [mode of consciousness], which is [a position also held by] some Proponents of Images.
>
> *'dir rnal 'byor spyod pa ni rnam pa gnyis te/ rnam pa dang bcas pa dang/ rnam pa med pa'o/ de la rnam pa dang bcas pa ni slob dpon phyogs kyi glang po la sogs pa dag gi 'dod pa ste/ rnam pa gzhan gyi dbang du ston pas ji skad du/ nang gi shes bya'i ngo bo ni/ phyi rol ltar snang gang yin de/ don yin zhes bya ba la sogs pa ste rnam par shes pa'i tshogs drug tu smra ba'o.*
>
> *rnam pa de med pa ni slob dpon 'phags pa thogs med la sogs pa ste/ de dag rnam pa kun tu brtags pa rab rib can gyis skra shad la sogs pa ltar smra bas/ don ni don du grub 'gyur na/ mi rtog ye shes med par 'gyur/ de med pas na sangs rgyas nyid/ thob par 'thad pa ma yin no/ de de bzhin du/ mi rtog ye shes rgyu ba la/ don kun snang ba med phyir yang/ don med khong du chud par bya/ de med pas na rnam rig med/ ces brjod cing rnam par shes pa'i tshogs brgyad dang/ kha cig gcig pur smra ba ste/ gcig pu nyid ni rnam pa dang bcas pa dag la yang kha cig go.*

(See Kajiyama 1998, 154; Tola and Dragonetti 2004, 36; and Keenan 1992, 98.) Readers should be aware that the views on classifying the thought of Dignāga and Dharmakīrti are very varied and complicated, ranging from the above to that they were Mādhyamikas. For a discussion of different doxographical categorizations of Dharmakīrti's thought, see Dreyfus 1997, 20–21 and 428–42.

Mokṣhākaragupta in his *Discourse on Logic* (*Tarkabhāṣhā, rTog ge'i skad*) also divides Yogāchāras into Proponents of Images and Proponents of Nonexistent Images. See Kajiyama 1965 and 1998, 148 and 154–8. Maitrīpa in his *Precious Garland of Suchness* (*Tattvaratnāvalī, De kho na nyid kyi rin chen phreng ba*) (Dg.T. Beijing 26:340–2) divides Yogāchāras into Proponents of Images and Proponents of Nonexistent Images.

Tillemans says (1990, 41n91), "Note that amongst later Vijñānavādins, Ratnākaraśānti becomes the principal representative of Alīkākāravāda [Proponents of

False Images], whereas Jñānaśrīmitra is probably the principal Satyākāravādin [Proponent of Real Images]." (Ratnākarashānti refers in the colophon to his *Instructions that Ornament the Middle Way (Madhyamakālaṃkāropadesha, dBu ma rgyan gyi man ngag)* to his teachings as being that of the "Mahāyāna Mādhyamika [Proponents of] Cognition" (*Mahāyāna vijñapti madhyamaka, Theg chen rnam rig dbu ma*). Although it seems clear from a number of his works that Ratnākarashānti was a Proponent of False Images, he may not have considered himself a Chittamātra as distinct from a Mādhyamika. Nevertheless most of his writings are included in the Chittamātra (*sems tsam*) section of the Tengyur. See Ruegg 1981, 122–4.)

According to Ruegg (1981, 110), Dharmapāla and his students Ratnakīrti and Jñānashrīmitra were Proponents of Real Images. Dreyfus says (1997, 364) that Dharmottara was a Proponent of False Images.

See also n. 562 above for remarks concerning the views of Proponents of Real Images and Proponents of False Images.

566 In his *Ornament of the Middle Way* (*Mādhyamakālaṃkāra, dBu ma rgyan*), Shāntarakṣhita presents Yogāchāra views (verses 44 and 52) and then refutes them (verses 45–51 and 53–60). Although he does not identify proponents of these views either in his root text or in his auto-commentary (nor does Kamalashīla in his *Commentary on the Difficult Points of the "Ornament of the Middle Way"*), later commentators identify the three Real Image subschools (Split-Eggists, Proponents of Perceptual Parity, and Non-Pluralists) and the Proponents of False Images as the ones refuted by these verses. Thus Shāntarakṣhita's text and its commentaries are sources for understanding these positions. See Blumenthal 2004, 120–34 and 268–74; and Padmakara Translation Group 2005, 236–61.

567 Split-Eggists (*sGo nga phyed tshal pa*) (more literally, "Egg-Split-in-Half-ists") is also translated as "Half-Eggists." The Geluk commentator Ngawang Palden says (Hopkins 2003, 420) that Brahmin Shaṃkarānanda (*bram ze bDe byed dga' ba*) is a proponent of this system. See Shāntarakṣhita's *Ornament of the Middle Way*, verses 46–47; Blumenthal 2004, 120–4; and Padmakara Translation Group 2005, 240–2.

568 *The Explanation of "Differentiating the Sugata's Texts"* (*Sugatamatavibhaṅgabhāṣhya, bDe bar gshegs pa'i gzhung rnam par 'byed pa'i bshad pa*) (Toh. 3900; Dg.T. Beijing 63:995–6) is by Jetāri (or Jitāri) (*dGra las rgyal ba*) (ca. eleventh century). His root text, *Differentiating the Sugata's Texts* (*Sugatamatavibhaṅgakārikā, bDe bar gshegs pa'i gzhung rnam par 'byed pa'i tshig le'ur byas pa*) (Toh. 3899), contains only eight verses, all of which are almost identical to verses 21–28 of Āryadeva's *Compendium on the Heart of Primordial Wisdom* (*Jñānasārasamuchchaya, Ye shes snying po kun las btus pa*). See Mimaki 2000, 234–5.

Ruegg states (1981, 100) that Jetāri "was counted by doxographers as a Yogācāra-Svātantrika-Madhyamaka (Samala-Alīkākāra branch [Proponents of Staining False Images]). His *Sugatamatavibhaṅga-kārikās* and *Bhāṣya* deal with the four main schools of Buddhist thought . . . In the *Bhāṣya* Jitāri endeavours in particular to demonstrate that Dharmakīrti was in agreement with Nāgārjuna and that he taught the Madhyamaka."

The translation follows Dg.T. Beijing: *nang du snang ba'i shes pa 'di gzhan yin la phyi rol du snang ba yang gzhan kho na'o/ gnyis po de la yang gnyis med pa yin te/ rang rig pa tsam yin pa'i phyir ro/ de'i stobs kyis byung ba'i rnam par rtog pas ni de dag la gzung ba dang 'dzin pa'i ngo bor sgro btags pa.*

Compare with *TOK*, II:505.12–15: *yang kha cig ni nang du snang ba'i rnam par shes pa de nyid kyang gzhan yin la phyi rol tu snang ba de nyid kyang gzhan yin te de gnyis kyang so so rang rig pa tsam yin pa'i phyir ro/ kun tu rtog pa de gnyis kyi stobs kyis byung bas gzung ba dang 'dzin pa'i ngo bo gnyis su sgro btags so,* "For some, the consciousness that appears internally and what appears externally are different from each other, but they are both simply intuitive reflexive awareness. Conceptuality, which arises through the force of those two, exaggeratedly considers them to be the two entities of percept and perceiver."

569 Proponents of Perceptual Parity (or Proponents of Equal Numbers of Percepts and Perceivers) (*gZung 'dzin grangs mnyam pa*). Ngawang Palden says (Hopkins 2003, 420) that Shākyabuddhi [in his commentary on Dharmakīrti's *Commentary on (Dignāga's) "Compilation of Prime Cognition"*] is a proponent of this system. See Shāntarakṣhita's *Ornament of the Middle Way,* verse 49; Blumenthal 2004, 124–5; and Padmakara Translation Group 2005, 243–5. Mipham states that perceptual parity is the view favored by Shāntarakṣhita on a conventional level, though not as these Chittamātras express it. See n. 572.

570 *TOK,* II:505.19: ***snang*** *tshogs* should be ***sna*** *tshogs.* (TN)

571 *dBu ma rang 'grel,* that is, *Madhyamakālaṃkāra-vṛitti, dBu ma'i rgyan gyi 'grel pa,* by Shāntarakṣhita. Toh. 3885; Dg.T. Beijing 62: 929. The translation follows Jamgön Kongtrul's citation of this passage, which adds a clarifying phrase. *TOK,* II:506.1: *rigs mi mthun pa'i shes pa* ***du ma cig car 'byung ba*** *bzhin du 'byung ngo zhes smra.* Compare with Dg.T. Beijing: *rigs mi mthun pa'i shes pa bzhin du 'byung ngo zhes smra,* "They arise in the same way that dissimilar-type cognitions do."

572 As said above (n. 569), Mipham states that Shāntarakṣhita holds the view of perceptual parity on a conventional level or as an imputation, but not in the way these Chittamātras do. (Although Shāntarakṣhita does not identify them and Kamalashīla calls them "some Yogāchāras," later commentators call them Proponents of Perceptual Parity). Thus in this statement Shāntarakṣhita presents their position and its weakness, which he says is that they assert that multiple consciousnesses of the same type (for example, cognitions of the color blue) can occur simultaneously. Shāntarakṣhita points out that this contradicts the Buddha's statements that it is impossible for two minds to occur simultaneously and that every being has only one mindstream. Mipham comments, "In our system, cognitions arise in numbers corresponding to the [cognized] images, but these are not [cognitions of] similar types. Thus it is not a case of many [cognitions of] similar types arising simultaneously" (*rang lugs la rnam pa'i grangs bzhin shes pa du ma skye yang rigs mthun du mi 'gyur bas rigs mthun du ma lhan cig mi skye ba'i tshul*) (Tibetan in Doctor 2004, 368; my translation). For Mipham's full analysis of this topic based on Shāntarakṣhita's *Auto-Commentary for the "Ornament of the Middle Way,"* see Mipham in Doctor 2004, 258–67 and 368–71; and Padmakara Translation Group 2005, 197–201 and 243–5.

573 Non-Pluralists (or Proponents of Varieties without [Cognitive] Plurality) (*sNa tshogs gnyis med*). "Varieties" are the diverse appearances that manifest, and "without plurality" means that the perceiving consciousness is singular (ALTG).

Ngawang Palden states (Hopkins 2003, 420) that Dharmakīrti is a proponent of this system; however, Dreyfus points out (1997, 434) that even in the Geluk tradition there are different views on this matter: "Kay-drup asserts that Dharmakīrti is a True Aspectarian . . . Gyel-tsap . . . claims that Dharmakīrti is a False Aspectarian." See Shāntarakṣhita's *Ornament of the Middle Way,* verses 50–51; Mipham in Doctor 2004, 372–4; Blumenthal 2004, 125–7; and Padmakara Translation Group 2005, 245–6.

574 See Dg.T. Beijing 62:931.

575 Mipham restates Shāntarakṣhita's remark as: "They state that the entities of the varieties [of appearances] are apprehended by just a single consciousness, in the same way that [a single consciousness apprehends the various colors of] an onyx" (*gang dag nor bu gzi bzhin tu rnam par shes pa gcig kho nas sna tshogs gyi ngo bo* ***bzung*** *ngo zhes*). Compare with *TOK,* II:506.5 and Dg.T. Beijing 62:931: *gang dag nor bu gzi bzhin tu rnam par shes pa gcig kho nas rnam par shes pa gcig kho nas sna tshogs kyi ngo bo* ***blangs*** *so zhes.* See Mipham in Doctor 2004, 374; and Padmakara Translation Group 2005, 246.

576 This general statement of the assertion of the Proponents of False Images specifically expresses the view of the Proponents of Non-Staining False Images, not the Proponents of Staining False Images, possibly because most scholars say that the view of the Proponents of Staining False Images is not really in keeping with the positions of Proponents of False Images (ALTG). In support of this, see Chang-kya Rolpé Dorjé in Hopkins 2003, 425.

577 "Proponents of False Images" (*Alīkākāravādin, rNam rdzun pa*) is also translated as "False Aspectarians." As stated above (n. 565), Ratnākarashānti and Dharmottara are considered to be Proponents of False Images. See also n. 562; and Ratnākarashānti in Kajiyama 1998, 148 and 154–8.

In his *Ornament of the Middle Way,* Shāntarakṣhita presents the positions of Proponents of False Images in verse 52 and refutes them in verses 53–60; see Blumenthal 2004, 127–34; and Padmakara Translation Group 2005, 247–61.

In his commentary on the *Ornament of the Middle Way,* Mipham says, "The authentic Chittamātras are the Proponents of Real Images, and thus they [may be considered to] have a sound approach. [Nevertheless,] since Proponents of False Images assert that outer referents are not real as mind, they are slightly closer [to understanding that things are] empty of reality, and thus they provide, as it were, a link to Madhyamaka. For that reason they are ranked higher [than Proponents of Real Images]. However, since their [position] is quite illogical on a conventional level, the conventional level of things should be asserted only according to [the positions of] Proponents of Real Images" (*de ltar na sems tsam mtshan nyid pa ni rnam bden pa yin pas rnam bden pa 'di gzhung brling zhing/ rnam brdzun pa phyi don sems su'ang mi bden par 'dod pas bden stong la cung nye bas dbu ma dang/ mtshams sbyor lta bu yin pas go rim gyis 'di gong mar bzhag kyang/ tha snyad la mi 'thad pa chen po 'ong bas tha snyad rnam bden pa kho na ltar khas blang bar bya ba yin ni*). See Mipham in Doctor 2004, 380–2; and Padmakara Translation Group 2005, 249–50.

Dreyfus notes that Shākya Chokden considers Proponents of False Images to be Yogāchāras, not Chittamātras, and that Gorampa considers Proponents of False Images to hold the best view of Chittamātras. See Dreyfus 1997, 433 and 557n14.

578 This statement is almost identical to one Jamyang Shepa makes in his *Great Exposition of Tenets* (*Grub mtha' chen mo*) (579.2–3), which suggests that there is a common source for this statement (which I have not been able to locate): *dri bcas ni rnam shes di rnams* ***sim gdung*** *sogs kyi 'dzin rnam du* ***don dam par*** *gnas kyang/ ma rig pa'i mthus phyi rol gyi gzung ba'i rnam par snang bas rnam shes rang gi* ***ngo bo rdzun pa'am 'khrul pa*** *des gos par smra bas dri bcas su 'dod de,* "Some say that although consciousnesses are, ultimately, the perceiving aspect of pleasure, pain, and so forth, the force of ignorance causes them to appear as outer perceived images, and thus the entity of consciousness is tainted by falsity or confusion. Therefore, they are called Proponents of Staining False Images." See also Hopkins 2003, 425.

579 Jamyang Shepa states: "Proponents of Non-Staining [False Images] assert—in accordance with [Maitreya's] *Ornament of the Mahāyāna Sūtras* and [Dharmakīrti's] *Commentary on Valid Cognition*—that since stains are adventitious, they do not exist in the slightest way in the entity of mind, which is like a pure crystal globe" (*mdo sde rgyan dang rnam 'grel ltar dri ma glo bur ba yin pas sems kyi ngo bo la cung zad kyang med pa shel sgong dag pa lta bur 'dod pa dri med lugs yin pa'i phyir*). See *Great Exposition of Tenets,* 579.1; and Hopkins 2003, 424–5.

580 According to Jamyang Shepa (*Great Exposition of Tenets,* 577–9), it is "reputed" in Tibet that the divisions into Proponents of Staining False Images and Proponents of Non-Staining False Images rest on their assertions regarding whether buddhas experience the stains of dualistic appearances or not; however the scholar-siddhas of India explain that these divisions are based upon whether they assert that the entity of mind is tainted by dualistic appearances or not. Jamyang Shepa says he regards the Tibetan explanation as incorrect since the second presentation accords with texts such as Dignāga's *Compendium on Valid Cognition* (*Pramāṇasamuchchaya, Tshad ma kun btus*) and Dharmakīrti's *Commentary on Valid Cognition.* See Hopkins 2003, 424.

Compare this with Kajiyama 1998, 154–5:

> According to Ratnākaraśānti . . . all the Yogācārins must be *sākārvādins* [Proponents of Images] so far as the cognition of common people is concerned. A problem, however, appears in regard to an emancipated person, who is supposed to have acquired *nirvikalpakajñāna* or non-conceptual, supermundane knowledge. Some Yogācārins thought that knowledge of an emancipated person is free from the fetter of cognitum and cognizer and accordingly is clear like a pure crystal without specks. And they thought this clear, imageless knowledge is the essence of cognition, regarding images as false, unreal specks born from our *vāsanā* [habitual tendencies]. This is the essential of the *nirākārajñānavāda* [that is, of stating that there is cognition without images] held by some of the Yogācārins. But others from the same school criticized this theory saying that what is not real can be never manifested, since otherwise a sort of the unfavourable doctrine of *asatkhyāti* [what is nonexistent appearing] would follow. Every cognition, so long as it is knowledge, must have an image, and there is no harm in that an emancipated person's knowledge is with an image, if he is freed from conceptual thinking. This is the essential point of the *sākārajñānavāda* [Proponents of Images].

581 I am unable to verify whether Lakṣhmī is the Kashmiri scholar Lakṣhmī[kara] referred to on p. 200.

582 Karma Tinlé Choklé Namgyal (*Karma phrin las phyogs las rnam rgyal*) (1456–1539) was a student of the seventh Karmapa, Chödrak Gyamtso (*Chos grags rgya mtsho*) (1454–1506), and teacher of the eighth Karmapa, Mikyö Dorjé (*Mi bskyod rdo rje*) (1507–1554). Source not found.

583 See n. 807.

584 Butön, for example, placed *The Ornament of Clear Realization* in the Prajñāpāramitā (*shes phyin*) section of the Tengyur (the collection of Indian commentaries translated into Tibetan) and the other four Treatises of Maitreya in the Chittamātra (*sems tsam*) section.

585 Dignāga (*Phyogs glang*) (late fifth to mid sixth century) was the Indian master who systematized Buddhist logic and epistemology (*pramāṇa, tshad ma*) in such works as

his *Compendium on Valid Cognition* (*Pramāṇasamuchchaya, Tshad ma kun btus*). See also n. 565.

586 Dharmakīrti (*Chos kyi grags pa*) (ca. seventh century). Although not a direct student of Dignāga (traditionally Dharmakīrti is said to have been a student of Ishvarasena, Dignāga's student), Dharmakīrti is considered Dignāga's son in that he was the one to clarify and elaborate Dignāga's teachings and is considered to have been the master of them. His works include the Seven Treatises on Valid Cognition (*tshad ma sde bdun*): (1) *Analysis of Relations* (*Sambhandhaparīkṣhā, 'Brel pa brtag pa*); (2) *Ascertainment of Valid Cognition* (*Pramāṇavinishchaya, Tshad ma rnam par nges pa*); (3) *Commentary on Valid Cognition* (*Pramāṇavārttikakārikā, Tshad ma rnam 'grel gyi tshig le'ur byas pa*); (4) *Drop of Reasoning* (*Nyāyabinduprakaraṇa, Rigs pa'i thigs pa zhes bya ba'i rab tu byed pa*); (5) *Drop of Reasons* (*Hetubindunāmaprakaraṇa, gTan tshigs kyi thigs pa zhes bya ba rab tu byed pa*); (6) *Principles of Debate* (*Vādanyāya, rTsod pa'i rigs pa*); and (7) *Proof of Other Continua* (*Saṃtānāntarasiddhināmaprakaraṇa, rGyud gzhan grub pa zhes bya ba'i rab tu byed pa*). See also n. 565.

587 For a discussion of different views on the doxographical categorization of Dharmakīrti, see n. 573; and Dreyfus 1997, 433–8.

588 Nāgārjuna (*kLu sgrub*) (ca. second century CE) was the Indian master regarded as the founder of the Madhyamaka system. The works traditionally attributed to him are classified in three groups: Collection of Reasonings (*Rigs tshogs*), Collection of Praises (*bsTod tshogs*), and Collection of Advice (*gTam tshogs*). It would be the texts found in the Collection of Praises that some would consider as reflecting the views of both the Proponents of Real Images and the Proponents of False Images. For a list of some of the texts included in the Collection of Praises see n. 856. For a list of the texts in the Collection of Reasonings see n. 592. For more information on Nāgārjuna's life and works, see Walser 2005, particularly 60–79; Mabbett 1998; and Ruegg 1981, 4–9.

589 Vasubandhu wrote the *Treasury of Abhidharma* as an explication of the Kashmiri-Vaibhāṣhika abhidharma system (as stated in Chapter 8, verse 40), but he did not always agree with their positions, which he demonstrated in his auto-commentary, *The Explanation of the "Treasury of Abhidharma."* Thus he serves as an illustration of the fact that teachers sometimes compose texts on philosophical systems that do not reflect their own positions.

590 The great omniscient dharma lord of Jonang (*Jo nang chos rje kun mkhyen chen po*) is one of many ways that Jamgön Kongtrul refers to Dolpopa Sherab Gyaltsen (*Dol po pa shes rab rgyal mtshan*) (1292–1361). See n. 815; and Stearns 1999.

591 Maitreya's five Dharma Treatises are grouped as three: the two *Ornaments*, the two *Differentiations*, and the *Highest Continuum*. Thus, the middle texts are *Differentiation of the Middle and the Extremes* and *Differentiation of Phenomena and Their Nature*. See nn. 807, 809, and 811.

592 The Collection of Reasonings (*rigs tshogs*) are (1) *Fundamental Treatise on the Middle Way* (*Prajñā-nāma-mūlamadhyamakakārikā, dBu ma rtsa ba'i tshig le'ur byas pa shes rab*); (2) *Rebuttal of Objections* (*Vigrahavyāvartanīkārikā, rTsod pa bzlog pa'i tshig le'ur byas pa*); (3) *Seventy Verses on Emptiness* (*Shūnyatāsaptati, sTong nyid bdun cu pa*); (4) *Sixty Verses on Reasoning* (*Yuktiṣhaṣhṭikā, Rigs pa drug cu ba*); and (5) *Thorough Grinding* (*Vaidalya-sūtra, Zhib mo rnam 'thag*). Note that ***rig** tshogs* should be ***rigs** tshogs* (*TOK*, II:508.20).

593 Tāranātha states in his *Presentation of the Scriptures for the "Ornament of the Shentong-Madhyamaka"* (*gZhan stong dbu ma'i rgyan gyi lung sbyor ba;* 168.7–169.1), "It was well known that there were five hundred Yogāchāra masters, such as the great venerable Avitarka, Jñānatala, and others. Their treatises were not translated into Tibetan, in the same way that the treatises of the eighteen orders [were not translated into Tibetan]" (*btsun pa chen po a bi tarka dang/ dzanyanya na ta la sogs pa rnal 'byor spyod pa'i slob dpon lnga brgya byung bar grags pa ltar yin par mngon no/ de dag gi bstan bcos ni bod du ma 'gyur ba yin te/ sde pa bco brgyad kyi bstan bcos rnams bzhin no*).

In his *History of Buddhism in India,* Tāranātha makes a similar statement (Chimpa and Chattopadhyaya 1970, 98–100): "There were about five hundred preachers of the Doctrine like *mahābhaṭṭāraka* Avitarka, Vigatarāgadvaja, Divyākaragupta, Rāhulamitra, Jñānatala, *mahā-upāsaka* Saṇgatala and others . . . All [those] Mahāyānī-s [*sic*] were followers of the path of *yogacaryā* [that is, they were Yogāchāra-Chittamātras (*rnal 'byor spyod pa sems tsam pa*)]." Tāranātha also states (ibid., 102) that Rāhulabhadra (who, as Nāgārjuna's teacher, is considered first to second century CE) studied with Avitarka, so we may conclude that these Yogāchāra teachers lived during the first century CE.

See also Book Four, Part One (*TOK*, I:401–3). For some other thoughts on this matter, see Kapstein 2000a, 118.

594 For a comprehensive overview of which masters have been considered Chittamātra or Yogāchāra and who was criticized by the Mādhyamikas, see Brunnhölzl 2004, 491–5.

595 For Vaibhāṣhikas and Sautrāntikas, the truly existing substratum (*gzhi rten bden grub*) is the irreducible partless particles and instants of consciousness; for Chittamātras, it is reflexively aware, self-illuminating cognition, empty of the duality of percept and perceiver.

596 Realists (or Proponents of [Truly] Existing Entities; "Substantialists") (*Vastusatpadārthavādin, dNgos por smra ba* or *dNgos po yod par smra ba*): In Buddhist philosophy, the term "Realists" is used for those who assert the true existence of entities (what the entities are differs according to the school). It should be understood that these schools, of course, do not use the term for themselves: Chittamātras do not consider themselves Realists. Thus, this statement should be understood to be from the perspective of the Madhyamaka systems.

597 *TOK,* II:509.11: ***rig** tshogs* should be ***rigs** tshogs.*

598 *Pradarshanānumatoddeshaparīkṣhā, Rang gi lta ba'i 'dod pa mdor bstan pa yongs su brtag pa* by Narendrakīrti (*Mi'i dbang po grags pa*). This is also known as *Āryamañjushrīpradarshana, 'Phags pa 'jam dpal gyi rang gi lta ba.* P4610; and Dharma 4530. (Not listed in Toh.)

599 *Jñānasārasamuchchaya, Ye shes snying po kun las btus pa,* by Āryadeva, verse 26ab. Toh. 3851, f. 27b2; Dg.T. Beijing 57:853. Dg.T. Beijing reads *gzung dang 'dzin pa* ***las*** *grol ba'i/ rnam shes dam pa'i don du yod. TOK*, II:509.20–21 has *gzung dang 'dzin pa* ***rnam*** *grol ba'i/ rnam* ***par*** *shes* ***pa don*** *dam yod.* See Mimaki 2000, 240.

600 These two lines appear in Jetāri's *Differentiating the Sugata's Texts* as verse 6ab (Dg. T. Beijing 63:885), with the simple difference that the second line reads ***shes pa*** *dam pa'i don du yod* (instead of *rnam shes*).

601 Jetāri's *Differentiating the Sugata's Texts* (verse 8ab) reads *rnam shes* ***don dam yin pa ru/ de yang mkhas rnams*** *mi bzhed de* (Dg.T. Beijing 63:885). Note the slight difference with *TOK,* II:509.22: *rnam shes* ***de yang don dam du/ yod par mkhas rnams*** *mi bzhed de.* Āryadeva makes a similar statement in his *Compendium on the Heart of Primordial Wisdom*, verse 29ab: *rnam shes dam pa'i don ldan pa/ de yang brten rnams mi 'dod de.* See Mimaki 2000, 240.

602 The outline heading here is slightly different from when the section is first mentioned (see Chapter 6, p. 176). For the sake of consistency, I am using the first form, "An Explanation of the Madhyamaka System," *dbu ma'i* ***lugs bshad pa*** (*TOK*, II:497.17), as opposed to what is here, "A Systematic Presentation of Madhyamaka," *dbu ma'i* ***rnam par gzhag pa*** (*TOK*, II:510.2).

603 The translation combines the outline headings that appear here and when the topic is presented (see Chapter 12, p. 272). Here it is, "A Synopsis of Its Ground, Path, and Fruition," ***gzhi lam 'bras gsum*** *mdor bsdu ba* (*TOK,* II:510.4); and when the topic is presented it is, "A Synopsis of What Is Taught in All Madhyamaka Systems," ***dbu ma rnams kyi bstan bya*** *mdor bsdu ba* (*TOK,* II:559.10).

604 Mādhyamikas (Those of the Middle, or Centrists) (*dBu ma pa*). The Dzogchen Ponlop Rinpoche comments (2003, 230–1):

> Madhyamaka has become well-known in Western literature as the Middle Way school. However, the term *madhyamaka* can also mean "not even a middle." There is a difference between a "middle path" and a path that is "not even a middle" . . .
>
> Within this tradition, we typically refer to the four extremes, [which can be summarized] into the two extremes of eternalism and nihilism. If we totally refute both of these extremes through the intellectual path of reasoning and reflecting, then how can we say, "This is the middle"? For example, if we were to knock down all four walls of a room and entirely take away the ground, then we would not be able to point to a spot as the middle of the room since there would no longer be a room. The concept of "the middle" is dependent on the existence of sides. Thus, we cannot continue to cling to a "middle path" because Nāgārjuna's philosophy precludes clinging to any side or extreme. There is no middle whatsoever at this point. Accordingly, there is no reference point at all.

Brunnhölzl remarks (2004, 32):

> In the West, *Madhyamaka* is usually translated as "middle way," but the word "way" does not have any correlate in either the Sanskrit term nor its Tibetan equivalent *uma. Madhya* means "middle or center," *-ma* is an emphasizing affix, and *-ka* refers to anything that deals with or expresses this middle, be it texts, philosophical systems, or persons. (The latter are mostly called "Mādhyamika," though.) Thus, Madhyamaka means "that which deals with (or proclaims) the very middle/center." The corresponding Tibetan term *Uma* usually also refers to "the very middle." Some masters, such as the Eighth Karmapa Mikyö Dorje, interpret the syllable *ma* as a negative and thus take the whole term to mean that there is not (*ma*) even a middle (*u*) between the extremes.

As for the use of the term to denote a philosophical school, according to Huntington (2003, 74), "So far as we know at present Bhāvaviveka is responsible for first appropriating the word *madhyamaka* as the name of a philosophical system or school that advocated specific tenets."

605 *Ratnakūṭa, dKon mchog brtsegs pa.* This is the name of a section of the Kangyur (Toh. 45-93). This quotation is from the *Kāshyapa Chapter Sūtra* (*Kāshyapa-parivarta-sūtra, 'Od srung gi le'u zhes bya ba'i mdo*). Toh. 87.

606 The shorter *Ornament of the Middle Way* (*dBu ma rgyan chung*) is possibly either Ratnākarashānti's *Instructions that Ornament the Middle Way* (*Madhyamakālaṃkāropadesha, dBu ma rgyan gyi man ngag*) (Toh. 4085; Dg.T. Beijing 78) or his *Commentary that Ornaments the Middle: Establishing the Middle Path* (*Madhyamakālaṃkāra-vṛitti-madhyamaka-pratipadāsiddhi-nāma, dBu ma rgyan gyi 'grel pa dbu ma'i lam grub pa zhes bya ba*) (Toh. 4072; Dg.T. Beijing 78); however, this quotation does not appear in either of those works.

Āryadeva's *Compendium on the Heart of Primordial Wisdom*, verse 28, is very similar: *yod min med min yod med min/ gnyis ka'i bdag nyid kyang min pas/ mtha' bzhi las grol dbu ma pa/ mkhas pa rnams kyi de kho na'o.* Compare with *TOK*, II:510.13: *yod pa ma yin med pa'ang min/ gnyis kyang ma yin gnyis med min/ mtha' bzhi dag dang bral ba la/ dbu ma pa zhes rab tu brjod.* Given that Jamgön Kongtrul has just quoted Āryadeva's text (see Chapter 6, p. 193), it possible that this citation could be from Āryadeva as well. (I am grateful to Karl Brunnhölzl for help with the information provided here.)

607 Two truths (*satya, bden pa*): As explained above (n. 189), since the Sanskrit term *satya* means what is experienced as true or real, here "truth" is used in the sense of an empirical truth or actual truth, not in the sense of a formal truth or logical truth. "Truth" is used throughout this translation for the familiar categories of "the four truths" or "two truths," and "reality" in most other cases.

608 *Prajñā-nāma-mūlamadhyamakakārikā, dBu ma rtsa ba'i tshig le'ur byas pa shes rab ces bya ba*, by Nāgārjuna. Chapter 25, verse 3. Toh. 3824, f. 16a6–7. See Garfield 1995, 73 and 323–4; and Khenpo Tsültrim Gyamtso 2003, 164–5.

609 *Nirupama-stava* (or *Niraupamyastava*), *dPe med par bstod pa,* by Nāgārjuna, verse 6. Toh. 1119; Dg.T. Beijing 1:191. This is one of the Four Praises (*Chatuḥstava, bsTod pa bzhi*); see n. 856. Note the following minor differences: Dg.T. Beijing: *rnam byang ro gcig* ***gyur rig pas/ chos dbyings mngon par dbyer med pa/ kun du rnam par dag par gyur.*** *TOK*, II:512.3–4: *rnam byang ro gcig* ***nyid du mkhyen/ chos kyi dbyings dang dbyer med pas/ khyod ni kun nas rnam dag gyur.***

610 *Suvarṇaprabhāsottamasūtra, gSer 'od dam pa'i mdo.* Toh. 556, f. 167a5–6.

611 For thorough and excellent overviews of the classifications of Madhyamaka in Indian and Tibetan works, see Ruegg 1981, 58–9; Ruegg 2000, 23–41 and 55–72; and Brunnhölzl 2004, 331–41. See also Phuntsho 2005, 42–54 and 238n38; and Vose 2005.

612 Butön, in his *History of Buddhism* (II.135), uses this threefold classification: Buddhapālita and Chandrakīrti are Prāsaṅgika-Mādhyamikas, Mādhyamikas Who Employ Worldly Consensus. The master Bhāvaviveka and others are Sautrāntika-Mādhyamikas. Jñānagarbha, Shrīgupta, Shāntarakṣhita, Kamalashīla, Haribhadra, and others are Yogāchāra-Mādhyamikas (*sangs rgyas bskyang dang zla grags dbu ma thal 'gyur 'jig rten grags sde spyod pa'i dbu ma/ slob dpon bha bya la sogs mdo sde spyod pa'i dbu ma/ yes shes snying po/ dpal sbas/ zhi ba 'tsho/ padma'i ngang tshul/ seng ge bzang po la sogs pa rnal 'byor spyod pa'i dbu ma*). See Obermiller 1932, 133–4.

According to Mimaki (1983, 161–2), the fourteenth-century Kadampa master Upa Lo-sel (*dBus pa blo gsal*) also employed this threefold classification with the following two differences from Butön: Upa Lo-sel does not refer to Mādhyamikas

Who Employ Worldly Consensus as Prāsaṅgikas, and he lists Jñānagarbha as a Mādhyamika Who Employs Worldly Consensus. (Upa Lo-sel also gives the twofold classification of Svātantrika and Prāsaṅgika.)

Yeshé Dé (*Ye shes sde*), who lived in the early ninth century, is credited with writing the first Tibetan doxography, *Distinctions of the View* (*lTa ba'i khyad pa*), in which he refers to Sautrāntika-Madhyamaka and Yogāchāra-Madhyamaka, with Bhāvaviveka and Shāntarakṣhita being the representatives of those respectively.

613 *Sautrāntika-Mādhyamikas (*mDo sde spyod pa'i dbu ma*), *Yogāchāra-Mādhyamikas (*rNal 'byor spyod pa'i dbu ma*), and Mādhyamikas Who Employ Worldly Consensus (*Lokaprasiddhi, 'Jig rten grags sde spyod pa'i dbu ma pa*) are distinguished on the basis of how they present conventional reality. It became normative in Tibet after the time of Tsongkhapa to treat Sautrāntika-Madhyamaka and Yogāchāra-Madhyamaka as divisions of Svātantrika-Madhyamaka (see Chapter 9 in general, and specifically n. 705), and to consider Mādhyamikas Who Employ Worldly Consensus as Prāsaṅgika-Madhyamaka, which is discussed most specifically in Chapter 10 under the heading A Brief Account of Chandrakīrti's Exegetical System, pp. 224–230.

614 I use the form "Bhāvaviveka" for both the Tibetan *Legs ldan 'byed* and Bhavya (*Bha bya*) because it is the most commonly used one in North American scholarship. However, as Eckel says (2003, 196n10), "There has been a great deal of discussion about the proper form of this important philosopher's name. 'Bhāvaviveka' has come down to us from La Vallée Poussin's edition of Candrakīrti's PPMV [*Mūlamadhyamakavṛittiprasannapadā*]. There also is good evidence, however, for the forms Bhavya and Bhāviveka. A useful summary of the complex and contradictory evidence for the name of Bhāvaviveka or Bhavya can be found in Lindtner (1995): 37–65. Recent manuscript discoveries suggest that the proper form of the name is almost certainly Bhāviveka. See Yonezawa (2001a): 26 [in *Facsimile Edition of a Collection of Sanskrit Palm-Leaf Manuscripts in Tibetan dBu med Script*. Tokyo: The Institute for Comprehensive Studies of Buddhism, Taishō University]."

See also Ruegg 1990, 69n1; and below, nn. 628 and 694.

615 Shāntarakṣhita (*Zhi ba 'tsho*) (eighth century) was the Bengali master invited to Tibet by King Trisong De-tsen (*Khri srong sde btsan*) in 763. He was the first major teacher of philosophy in Tibet and wrote the *Ornament of the Middle Way*, *Commentary on the "Ornament of the Middle Way," Compendium on Suchness* (*Tattvasaṃgraha, De kho na nyid bsdus pa*), and other works. See Padmakara Translation Group 2005, especially 2–5; and Blumenthal 2004, 25–30.

616 Chandrakīrti (*Zla ba grags pa*) (sixth to seventh century) is credited in Tibet with delineating the Prāsaṅgika Madhyamaka system (*dbu ma thal 'gyur*), which he did by clarifying the thought of Nāgārjuna's *Fundamental Treatise on the Middle Way* (*Mūlamadhyamakakārikā, dBu ma rtsa ba shes rab*) in two well-known commentaries, *Lucid Words* (*Mūlamadhyamakavṛittiprasannapadā, dBu ma'i rtsa ba'i 'grel pa tshig gsal ba*) and *Entrance to the Middle Way* (*Madhyamakāvatāra, dBu ma la 'jug pa*). Put very simply, in these texts he upheld the use of consequences (*prasaṅga, thal 'gyur*) by Buddhapālita and refuted the use of independently [verifiable] reasonings (*svatantra, rang rgyud pa'i gtan tshig*) as put forth by Bhāvaviveka. See Padmakara Translation Group 2002, particularly 4–5 and 20–32. On the importance of Chandrakīrti in Tibet from the fourteenth century onwards, see Vose 2005. For a summary of his influence in India, see Brunnhölzl 2004, 340–1.

617 The division of Mādhyamikas into Those Who Logically Establish Illusion (*sGyu ma rigs grub pa*) and Proponents of Complete Nonabiding (*Rab tu mi gnas par smra ba*) on

the basis of their assertions concerning the ultimate is a subject of much discussion in Tibet. Some, such as Tak-tsang Lotsāwa (*sTag tshang lo tsā ba*), equate the first with Svātantrikas and the latter with Prāsaṅgikas (see Phuntsho 2005, 239n38). Others, such as Ngok Loden Sherab (*rNgog blo ldan shes rab*) and Do-drup Dam-chö (*rDo grub dam chos*), reject the classification altogether (see Iaroslav 2000, 50; Phuntsho 2005, 238n38; and Ruegg 2000, 33n60). Tsongkhapa concurs with Ngok Loden Sherab on the unsuitability of these divisions in relation to ultimate reality, calling them "not a good approach." For Tsongkhapa's explanation, see *The Great Treatise on the Stages of the Path to Enlightenment,* Cutler and Newman 2002, 115–6. (There is, however, controversy concerning the exact meaning of Tsongkhapa's statement; see Hopkins 2003, 800na.) For Ke-drup Jé's views, see Cabezón 1992, 89—90.

Longchen Rabjam in his *Precious Treasury of the Supreme Yāna* (*Theg pa'i mchog rin po che'i mdzod*) applies both subcategories to Svātantrikas. He states that "Those Who Logically Establish Illusion" (*sgyu ma rigs grub tu 'dod pa*) is one of many names used for the lower Svātantrika (*rang rgyud 'og ma*), and "[Proponents of] Complete Nonabiding" is one of many names used for the higher Svātantrika (*rang rgyud gong ma*). For Shākya Chokden's comments on these divisions, see Iaroslav 2000, 84n197.

It seems that in Tibet the terms used here, "Those Who Logically Establish Illusion" and "Proponents of Complete Nonabiding," are used interchangeably with "Proponents of Illusionlike Nonduality" (*Māyopamādvayavādin, sGyu ma ltar gnyis med du smra ba*) and "Proponents of the Complete Nonabiding of All Phenomena" (*Sarvadharmāpratiṣhṭhānavādin, Chos thams cad rab tu mi gnas par smra ba*), which Jamgön Kongtrul lists separately. See Cabezón 2003, 307n2.

618 Kamalashīla (*Padma'i nang tshul*) (740–795) was a student of Shāntarakṣhita. He was invited to Tibet during the reign of King Trisong De-tsen, where he is famous for successfully debating with Heshang Moheyan (*Hā shang Mahāyāna*) at Samyé monastery, which established the gradual approach of Indian Buddhism as predominant in Tibet. Among his many works are the three-part text on meditation called the *Stages of Meditation of the Middle Way* (*Bhāvanākrama, dBu ma'i sgom rim gsum*) and commentaries on Shāntarakṣhita's works, such as *Commentary on the Difficult Points of the "Ornament of the Middle Way"* (*Madhyamakālaṃkārapañjikā, dBu ma rgyan gyi dka' 'grel*).

619 Khenpo Tsültrim Gyamtso Rinpoche explains that illusion (*sgyu ma*) refers to the union of appearances and emptiness. These masters use reasonings to establish that the ultimate truth is the unity, or combination (*tshogs pa*), of phenomena and their absence of existence, their emptiness.

620 Buddhapālita (*Sangs rgyas bkyangs*) (early sixth century) was a student of Saṅgharakṣhita, with whom he studied Nāgārjuna's works. He is most well-known for his commentary on Nāgārjuna's *Fundamental Treatise on the Middle Way,* called *Buddhapālita's Commentary on the "Fundamental Treatise on the Middle Way"* (*Buddhapālita-mūlamadhyamakavṛitti, dBu ma rtsa ba'i 'grel pa Buddhapālita*), which is preserved only in Tibetan translation. Chandrakīrti's defense of Buddhapālita's work against Bhāvaviveka's criticism led to the later distinctions and classifications of Svātantrika-Madhyamaka and Prāsaṅgika-Madhyamaka. See Chapter 9, p. 218; Ruegg 1981, 60–1; and Chimpa and Chattopadhyaya 1970,186–8.

621 Ratnākarashānti (*Rin chen 'byung gnas zhi ba*) (early eleventh century) was a great Mahāyāna master who resided as the eastern gate-keeper at Vikramashīla. Over

thirty of his works on tantras, prajñāpāramitā, philosophy, and epistemology (*pramāṇa, tshad ma*) are included in the Tengyur. He was also one of the eighty-four mahāsiddhas, in which context he is referred to simply as Shāntipa (see J. Robinson 1979, 60–4). Ratnākarashānti was a contemporary of Jñānashrīmitra and Ratnakīrti, and one of Atīsha's teachers, and, according to Tāranātha's *History of Buddhism in India*, a student of Nāropa. See Chimpa and Chattopadhyaya 1970, 295 and 299–300.

622 According to Ruegg (1981, 123), Ratnākarashānti divides Mādhyamikas into those who state that conventional [reality] is an image of cognition (*kun rdzob shes pa'i rnam par smra ba*) and those who state that conventional [reality] is habitual tendencies (*kun rdzob bag chags su smra ba*) in his *Presentation of the Three Vehicles* (*Triyānavyavasthāna, Theg pa gsum gyi rnam bzhag*) (Toh. 3712; P4535, f. 114a).

623 Maitrīpa (also known as Avadhūta Advayavajra, *gNyis med rdo rje*) discusses these classifications in his *Precious Garland of Suchness* (Toh. 2240; Dg.T. Beijing 26:336).

Maitrīpa (1007-1085) studied with Nāropa, Ratnākarashānti, and Jñānashrīmitra before seeking out the siddha Shavari (or Shabara), from whom he heard mahāmudrā teachings. Maitrīpa was one of Marpa Lotsāwa's two principal teachers, and one of Kyungpo Naljor's (*Khyung po rnal 'byor*) teachers (see Nālandā Translation Committee 1982, 26–32 and 58; and Zangpo 2003, 50–6 and 241–4). His teachings and set of twenty-five texts known as Teachings on the Absence of Mental Fabrications (*Amanasikāroddesha, Yid la mi byed pa ston pa*) (Toh. 2229–52) are the source of the sūtra mahāmudrā teachings taught by Gampopa and passed down through the Kagyu lineage. See Tatz 1987. Maitrīpa also recovered two of Maitreya's texts, *Highest Continuum* and *Differentiation of Phenomena and Their Nature*; see Roerich 1949, 347; and n. 811 below.

624 According to Ruegg (2000, 34–5) and Brunnhölzl (2004, 335), this twofold division of Proponents of Illusionlike Nonduality (*Māyopamādvayavādin, sGyu ma ltar gnyis med du smra ba*) and Proponents of the Complete Nonabiding of All Phenomena (*Sarvadharmāpratiṣhṭhānavādin, Chos thams cad rab tu mi gnas par smra ba*) is also found in Chandrahari's *Jewel Garland* (*Ratnamālā, Rin po che'i phreng ba*), "alluded to" in Ashvagoṣha's *Stages of Meditation on the Ultimate Mind of Enlightenment* (*Paramārtha-bodhichittabhāvanākrama, Don dam byang sems sgom pa'i rim pa*), and listed in the Kagyu master Gampopa's *Beauty of Community Dharma* (*Tshogs chos legs mdzes ma*).

For Padma Karpo's explanation of these categories, see Brunnhölzl 2004, 337. For an overview of these categories as used by Tibetan masters in the eleventh through thirteenth centuries, see Tauscher 2003, 209–11. See also n. 617.

625 Lakṣhmīkara uses these terms in *Illuminating the Meaning of "The Five Stages"* (*Pañchakrama-vṛittārthavirochana, Rim pa lnga'i don gsal bar byed pa*). Toh. 1842; Dg.T. Beijing 19.

626 Mother of the Victors (*rgyal ba'i yum*) is a name for the Prajñāpāramitā scriptures based on the reference to Prajñāpāramitā (the perfection of wisdom) as the mother of all buddhas.

627 Mādhyamika Proponents of the Absence of a Nature (*Niḥsvabhāvavādin, Ngo bo nyid med par smra ba'i dbu ma [pa]*). Also translated as "Proponents of Entitylessness" or "Proponents of Non-Nature."

628 Bhāvaviveka makes this distinction in his *Precious Lamp of Madhyamaka* (*Madhyamaka-ratna-pradīpa, dBu ma rin po che'i sgron ma*) (Dg.T. Beijing 57:1539). The

Tibetan tradition attributes the authorship of this text to the famous sixth-century Bhāvaviveka, rather than an eighth-century master of the same name. On the reasons for attributing this text to the later Bhāvaviveka, see Ruegg 1981, 66n214 and 106n339. For a justification of this being composed by the sixth-century Bhāvaviveka, see Lindtner 1982. See also Chapter 7, n. 614.

629 The terms "broad" (*rags pa*) and "subtle" (*phra ba*) may be interpreted not as comments on the merits of the individual systems but as descriptions of how easy or difficult it is to understand these systems (ALTG).

Here Jamgön Kongtrul uses these descriptive categories to refer to Rangtong and Shentong. In Chapter 9, p. 219, he uses them to refer to the two subdivisions of Svātantrika-Madhyamaka, the so-called Sautrāntika-Svātantrika-Mādhyamikas and Yogāchāra-Svātantrika-Mādhyamikas, calling the first "the broad, outer Mādhyamikas," and the latter "the subtle, inner Mādhyamikas."

630 Dolpopa Sherab Gyaltsen (*Dol po pa shes rab rgyal mtshan*) (1292–1361), is considered to be the first to widely employ the terms Rangtong (Intrinsic Emptiness, Empty-of-Self, or Self-Empty) (*Rang stong*) and Shentong (Extrinsic Emptiness, Empty-of-Other, Other-Emptiness) (*gZhan stong*). See also n. 815.

Jamgön Kongtrul's statements are similar to those made by Tāranātha in his *Essence of Shentong* (*gZhan stong snying po*): "There are two [kinds] of Mādhyamikas: ordinary Mādhyamikas and great Mādhyamikas. The ordinary [Madhyamaka] is known in this land of Tibet as Rangtong and [its followers] are known in both India and Tibet as Proponents of the Absence of a Nature . . . Great Madhyamaka is known in Tibet as Shentong, and is the Vijñapti-Madhyamaka (Madhyamaka of [the Proponents of] Cognition)" ([178.3:] *dbu ma pa la dbu ma phal pa dang/ dbu ma chen po gnyis kyi phal po ni bod yul 'dir rang stong du grags shing rgya bod gnyis kar du ngo bo nyid med par smra ba zhes grags pa ste/* . . . [179.5:] *gnyis pa dbu ma chen po ni/ bod du gzhan stong du grags pa rnam rig gi dbu ma ste*). See Hopkins 2007, 55 and 62.

631 *Svātantrikas (Those [Who Use] Independently [Verifiable Reasons], or Autonomists) (*Rang rgyud pa*) and *Prāsaṅgikas (Consequentialists or Apagogists) (*Thal 'gyur pa*): The use of the terms Svātantrika and Prāsaṅgika to categorize Mādhyamikas is not found in works by Indian Buddhists (with two exceptions for Svātantrika as noted below). Pa-tsap Lotsāwa Nyima Drak (*Pa tshab lo tsā ba Nyi ma grags*) (eleventh century) is said to be the first to use these two terms, but since his works are no longer available, the earliest source for distinctions between Svātantrika and Prāsaṅgika is the Sakya master Sonam Tsemo's (*bSod nams rtse mo*) (1142–1182) *Commentary on the "Entrance to the Bodhisattva's Way of Life"* (*Byang chub sems dpa'i spyod pa la 'jug pa'i 'grel pa*). By the fourteenth and fifteenth centuries these had become accepted and were the commonly used divisions for Madhyamaka in Tibet.

Nevertheless, there has been much disagreement regarding their validity as classifications and their meaning. Butön, for example, considered them "an artificial Tibetan conceptual creation (*bod kyi rang bzo*) without much merit" (Dreyfus and McClintock 2003, 1–5), whereas Tsongkhapa argues that they are founded upon distinctions made in Chandrakīrti's *Lucid Words* and are not Tibetans' own fabrications (Cutler and Newland 2002, 116). On the origin of the controversy between Svātantrikas and Prāsaṅgikas, see Brunnhölzl 2004, 392–421 and 438–44; Della Santina 1986, 59–93; Ruegg 2000, 23–72; and Vose 2005, 24–99. For Mikyö Dorjé's views on the Svātantrika-Prāsaṅgika distinction, see Brunnhölzl 2004, 341–92, particularly 360–73. For Tsongkhapa's views, see Eckel 2003, 173–203; and Thurman 1984. For Ke-drup Jé's perspective, see Cabezón 1992. For Jamyang Shepa's account, see Hopkins 2003, 457–505; and Lopez 1987, 55–81. For Mipham's perspective, see Padmakara Translation Group 2005, 6–20.

The two known uses of Svātantrika in Indian works are as follows: The terms Svātantrika (*rang rgyud pa*) and Svātantrika-Madhyamaka (*dbu ma rang rgyud pa*) are found in the eleventh-century Kashmiri Jayānanda's *Commentary on the "Entrance to the Middle Way"* (*Madhyamakāvatāraṭīkā, dBu ma la 'jug pa'i 'grel bshad*) as the identification of Chandrakīrti's opponents, but he does not use the term Prāsaṅgika (*thal 'gyur pa*). (Jayānanda simply refers to Chandrakīrti's own doctrine as Madhyamaka.) See Ruegg 2000, 20n38. Yoshimizu says (2003, 276n3) that the other reported use is "that the **Lakṣaṇaṭīkā* gives Bhāviveka the appellation *svatantrasādhanavādin*. This text is supposed to have been composed earlier than the last quarter of the eleventh century . . ." (See Yoshimizu reference for more information.)

For Jamgön Kongtrul's presentation of the differences between Svātantrikas and Prāsaṅgikas, see pp. 212-216; and for his brief account of the source of the divisions, see Chapter 9, p. 218.

632 For some discussion of the term "independently [verifiable]" (*svatantra, rang rgyud/ rang dbang*), see n. 691.

633 Three modes (*trairūpya/ trirūpa, tshul gsum*): see n. 757.

634 Established through the power of [their relationship to real] things (*dngos stobs kyis grub pa*): see n. 707.

635 Realists (or Proponents of [Truly] Existing Entities; Substantialists) (*Vastusatpadārthavādin, dNgos por smra ba* or *dNgos po yod par smra ba*): see n. 663.

636 In this simple presentation of the reasons for dividing Rangtong-Madhyamaka into Svātantrika and Prāsaṅgika, Jamgön Kongtrul returns to the core issues and implicitly rejects positions taken by Tsongkhapa and his followers (but for a fuller picture, see also the section on the differences between Svātantrika and Prāsaṅgika, pp. 212–216). In this regard, overall it seems that his views are in keeping with those expressed by Mikyö Dorjé and the Sakya scholars Rongtön Sheja Kunrik (*Rong ston shes bya kun rig*) (1367–1449) and Gorampa Sonam Seng-gé (*Go rams pa bsod nams seng ge*) (1429–1489). For an overview of the positions of Tsongkhapa, Rongtönpa, and Gorampa, see Cabezón 2003, 296–307. For Tsongkhapa's "reevaluation," see Yoshimizu 2003, 257–88. For Mikyö Dorjé's perspective, see Brunnhölzl 2004, 333–444.

A brief account of the historical aspects of the Svātantrika-Prāsaṅgika split is given in Chapter 9, p. 218.

637 Views (*dṛiṣhṭi, lta ba*) and mental afflictions (*klesha, nyon mongs pa*) are of five kinds each. The five views are (1) the view, or belief, in the perishing collection [i.e., the aggregates, as being a self] (*satkāyadṛiṣhṭi, 'jig tshogs la lta ba*); (2) a view holding to an extreme (*antagrahādṛiṣhṭi, mthar 'dzin gyi lta ba*); (3) wrong views (*mithyādṛiṣhṭi, log lta*); (4) holding a view to be supreme (*dṛiṣhṭiparāmarsha, lta ba mchog 'dzin*); and (5) holding an ethical conduct or a discipline to be supreme (*shīlavrataparāmarsha, tshul khrims brtul zhugs mchog 'dzin bcas*).

The five mental afflictions are (1) desire (*rāga, 'dod chags*); (2) anger (*pratigha, khong khro*); (3) pride (*māna, nga rgyal*); (4) ignorance (*avidyā, ma rig pa*); and (5) doubt (*vichikitsā, the tshom*). (ALTG notes)

638 Objectively real (*rang mtshan du bden pa*) could also be translated as "real in terms of their own specific characteristics." For the Prāsaṅgika position on what constitutes the two obscurations, see Chapter 10, pp. 245–246.

639 The two obscurations (*sgrib gnyis*) are the afflictive obscurations (*kleṣhāvaraṇa, nyon sgrib*) and the cognitive obscurations (*jñeyāvaraṇa, shes bya'i sgrib pa*).

640 Reflection is the subject of Book Seven, and meditation is the subject of Book Eight.

The refutation of a self-entity of phenomena employs the four, or five, great Madhyamaka reasons (*dbu ma'i rigs chen bzhi'am lnga*), and the refutation of a self of persons uses the sevenfold reasoning [using the analogy of] a chariot (*shing rta rnam bdun gyi rigs pa*) (ALTG notes). Thus, although Jamgön Kongtrul says that the way the two types of self-entity are refuted is explained extensively in the section on reflection, in fact he explains the refutation of a self-entity of phenomena in more detail here: in this chapter's presentation of the reasons (see pp. 209–211), and in Chapter 10's even more detailed presentation of the five great reasons (see pp. 235–240).

Refutation of a self of persons is discussed in some detail in Chapter 10 (see p. 240), but in more detail in Book Seven, Part Three (*TOK*, III:69–77). See also Book Seven's entire section on The Analysis of the Absence of Self-Entity (*bdag med dngos dpyad pa*) (*TOK*, III:65–80).

The vipashyanā section of Book Eight, Part One, discusses meditation on the twofold absence of self-entity (*TOK*, III:126–9).

641 Useful and readable presentations of Madhyamaka debate and reasoning (as practiced in Tibet) are found in Brunnhölzl 2004, 172–272 (which includes many sections from this book), and Dreyfus 2003, 195–228. For a discussion of the issues related to "the subject" (*dharmin, chos can*) in Madhyamaka reasonings, see McClintock 2003, particularly 145–150; Tillemans 2003; and Yotsuya 1999, 73–4. For some discussion of the issues related to subjects in independently [verifiable] reasonings, see n. 691.

642 Valid cognition (*pramāṇa, tshad ma*): For a definition of valid cognition, see n. 717. For the four forms of valid cognition, see Chapter 10, p. 225; for the forms accepted by Svātantrikas, see n. 676. See also Khenpo Tsültrim Gyamtso 1996b/2000; Dreyfus 1997, 285–327; and Dunne 2004, 15–35.

The translation follows *TOK*, II:515.3: *rgol phyir rgol gnyis ka'i tshad* ***mas ma grub****;* PKTC has *rgol phyir rgol gnyis ka'i tshad* ***mas grub****.*

643 Heterologous set (or non-concordant class; dissimilar class) (*vipakṣha, mi mthun phyogs*) is that which does not correspond to the predicate. Generally speaking, this is everything that is the opposite of the predicate in a proof statement. In the argument, "A sprout, the subject, does not exist inherently, because . . . ," the heterologous set is everything that does exist inherently.

644 See n. 537.

645 Unafflicted ignorance (*nyon mongs pa can ma yin pa'i ma rig pa*) is "an equivalent for the cognitive obscurations, that is, the latent tendencies of clinging to reality plus the clinging to the fact that phenomena lack reality and are illusionlike" (Brunnhölzl 2004, 95).

646 The translation follows PKTC reading *nyes pa*; *TOK*, II:515.13 has *zhes pa*.

647 Chapter 2, verse 222ab. Toh. 4210, f. 116a3; Dg.T. Beijing 97:520. See R. Jackson 1993, 431. Note that *TOK*, II:515.22 should be *sun* ***phyung****,* not *sun* ***dbyung****.*

648 Afflictive phenomena (*saṃklesha, kun nyon*): see n. 528.

649 The nonexistence of a self of persons is discussed in Chapter 2, p. 120.

650 This refers to the discussion of why appearances are not objects of negation on p. 206.

651 A proof of a fact (*don sgrub pa*) means that the predicate of the probandum is a defining characteristic, as in the statement, "sound is momentary, because it is produced." A proof of a convention (*tha snyad sgrub pa*) means that the predicate of the probandum is a definiendum, as in the statement, "sound is impermanent, because it is produced" (Khenpo Tsültrim Gyamtso 1996a/1999, 103–4).

Jamgön Kongtrul only discusses proofs of facts here because Mādhyamikas, for the most part, do not use proofs of conventions. (ALTG)

652 A nonimplicative negation (*prasajyapratiṣhedha, med dgag*) is one that does not indicate or imply anything in place of its object of negation. The other main type of negation used in Indo-Tibetan debate is an implicative negation (*paryudāsapratiṣhedha, ma yin dgag*), which implies or affirms something in place of the object of negation.

653 The first type of nonimplicative negation negates the existence of a nature of things, such as the aggregates, constituents, and sense spheres. The second type of nonimplicative negation negates, for example, the mere existence of imagined things, such as a permanent self, or it negates just "nature" (which is separate from an object). (ALTG)

654 For more on determinations (or [positive] determinations) (*pariccheda, yongs gcod*), see n. 329.

655 *Vigrahavyāvartanī, rTsod pa zlog pa,* by Nāgārjuna; verses 29–30. Toh. 3828; Dg.T. Beijing 57:77. The translation of these verses is based on Nāgārjuna's auto-commentary (Dg.T. Beijing 57:350). See Bhattacharya 1978, 113–5.

656 This seems to be a combination of verse 64cd in *Rebuttal of Objections* (Dg.T. Beijing 57:80) and a paraphrase of its explanation in the *Commentary on the "Rebuttal of Objections"* (*Vigrahavyāvartanī-vṛitti, rTsod pa zlog pa'i 'grel pa*) (Toh. 3832; Dg.T. Beijing 57:365). Verse 64cd is *de la tshig ni med ces par/ go bar byed kyi skye sel min. TOK,* II:517.12: *rang bzhin med pa go bar byed pa yin gyi skye ba sel ba ma yin no.*

657 The vajra sliver reasoning (*vajrakaṇahetu, rdo rje gzegs ma'i gtan tshigs*) is also called "the reasoning that negates arising from the four extremes" (*mtha' bzhi skye 'gog gi gtan tshig*).

658 Reasonings that negate the arising of [a result] existent [at the time of its cause] and the arising of [a result that is] nonexistent [at the time of its cause] (**satasatutpāda-pratiṣhedhahetu, yod med skye 'gog gi gtan tshigs*).

659 Reasonings that refute arising from the four possibilities (*chatuṣhkoṭyutpāda-pratiṣhedhahetu, mu bzhi skye 'gog gi gtan tshigs*).

660 Reasonings that [demonstrate that a phenomenon] is neither a single unit nor a plurality (*ekānekaviyogahetu, gcig du bral gyi gtan tshigs*).

661 *Shālistambha-sūtra, Sa lu ljangs pa'i mdo.* Toh. 210.

662 These four reasonings are presented in many treatises:

The vajra sliver reasoning (the analysis of causes) is found in Nāgārjuna's *Fundamental Treatise on the Middle Way;* the sixth chapter of Chandrakīrti's *Entrance to the Middle Way;* the ninth chapter of Shāntideva's *Entrance to the Bodhisattva's Way of Life*; and Kamalashīla's *Stages of Meditation.*

The analysis of results (whether results exist at the time of their cause or not) is presented in Nāgārjuna's *Fundamental Treatise on the Middle Way* and his *Seventy Verses on Emptiness (Shūnyatāsaptati, sTong nyid bdun cu pa)*; Chandrakīrti's *Entrance to the Middle Way;* and Shāntideva's *Entrance to the Bodhisattva's Way of Life.*

The analysis of both (the four possibilities) occurs in Jñānagarbha's *Differentiation of the Two Truths (Satyadvaya-vibhaṇga, bDen gnyis rnam 'byed);* Shāntarakṣhita's *Commentary on the "Differentiation of the Two Truths" (Satyadvayavibhaṅgavṛitti, bDen gnyis rnam par 'byed pa'i 'grel pa)* and his *Commentary on the Difficult Points of the "Differentiation of the Two Truths" (Satyadvayavibhaṅgapañjika, bDen gnyis rnam par 'byed pa'i dka' 'grel);* Kamalashīla's *Illumination of the Middle Way (Madhyamakāloka, dBu ma snang ba)* and his *Establishing that All Phenomena Are Without Nature (Sarvadharmāsvabhāvasiddhi, Chos thams cad rang bzhin med par grub pa)*; Haribhadra's *Illumination of the "Ornament of Clear Realization" (Abhisamayālaṃkārālokā, mNgon par rtogs pa'i rgyan gyi snang ba).*

The analysis of a nature (unity and plurality) is found in Nāgārjuna's *Seventy Verses on Emptiness*; Āryadeva's *Four Hundred Verses (Chatuḥṣhataka, bZhi brgya pa)*; Dharmakīrti's *Commentary on Valid Cognition*; Shrīgupta's *Commentary on Entering Suchness (Tattvāvatāravṛitti, De kho na la 'jug pa'i 'grel pa)*; Shāntarakṣhita's *Ornament of the Middle Way*; the first volume of Kamalashīla's *Stages of Meditation*; and Jetāri's *Differentiating the Sugata's Texts* and his *Explanation of "Differentiating the Sugata's Texts."*

Bhāvaviveka's *Summary of the Meaning of the Middle Way (Madhyamakārthasaṃgraha, dBu ma'i don bsdus pa)* is the first known synopsis of three of these reasonings and the reasoning of dependent origination (he omits the analysis of the four possibilities). Atīsha presents a more detailed overview of the same four reasonings in his auto-commentary on the *Lamp for the Path to Enlightenment (Bodhipathapradīpa, Byang chub lam gyi sgron ma)*. Kamalashīla discusses the five reasonings in his *Illumination of the Middle Way*. For the scriptural sources for the reason of dependent origination, see n. 670.

663 Realists (or Proponents of [Truly] Existing Entities; or "Substantialists") (*Vastusatpadārthavādin, dNgos por smra ba* or *dNgos po yod par smra ba*): Here this means any Buddhist or non-Buddhist proponents of a philosophical tenet system that asserts the true existence of something, be it a self, partless particles, or the primal substance (*prakṛiti*). From a Madhyamaka perspective, all non-Madhyamaka Buddhist schools are Realists.

664 These four negations are presented in more detail in Chapter 10, pp. 235-239.

665 A more detailed treatment of the vajra sliver reasoning is found in two sections of Chapter 10: pp. 226–228 and pp. 235–239.

666 The horns of a rabbit are a traditional example of something that cannot be produced by any cause or conditions because they simply do not exist.

667 The three conditions (*rkyen gsum*) are visual forms (the object condition), the eye sense faculty (the dominant condition), and the just-ceased preceding moment of eye consciousness (the proximate condition). Often a fourth condition is listed, which is, simply put, prior moments of eye consciousness (the causal condition).

668 The analysis of a nature is presented somewhat more fully in Chapter 10, p. 235.

669 The reasoning of dependent origination (*pratītyasamutpādanyāya, rten 'brel gyi rigs pa*) is also discussed in Chapter 10, p. 239, as the fifth of the five great reasons.

670 *Anavataptanāgarāja-paripṛicchā-sūtra, kLu'i rgyal po ma dros pas zhus pa'i mdo.* Toh. 156.

In addition to this sūtra, the reasoning of dependent origination is presented in the *Sūtra on Dependent Origination* (*Pratītyasamutpādasūtra, rTen cing 'brel bar 'byung ba'i mdo*); Nāgārjuna's *Seventy Verses on Emptiness, Rebuttal of Objections, Sixty Verses on Reasoning,* and *Fundamental Treatise on the Middle Way;* and Chandrakīrti's *Entrance to the Middle Way.*

671 Negative entailment (*vyatirekavyāpti, ldog khyab*) is the third mode of a correct reason. (It is also translated as "negative concomitance," "reverse entailment," or "reverse pervasion.")

Khenpo Tsültrim Gyamtso's *Classifications of Reasons* (*rTags rigs*) (86) defines it as "A reason that has been determined not to be present in a single instance of the heterologous set" (*mi mthun pa'i phyogs kho na la yod par nges pa'i gtan tshigs*). Heterologous set (or non-concordant class) (*vipakṣha, mi mthun phyogs*) is that which does not correspond to the predicate.

In the case of the five Madhyamaka reasonings, from the perspective of their meaning, the predicate is the absence of any nature (*rang bzhin med pa*); thus the heterologous set would be an existent nature. Since there is no such thing as an existent nature, it is not possible to say that the reason employed (such as that of dependent origination) is not present in a single instance of the heterologous set. See also Brunnhölzl 2004, 885n582.

672 What is to be pervaded (*khyab par bya ba*) means a specific item, and its pervader (*khyab par byed pa*) is a larger, general set that includes it. In this case, "no link" (*'brel pa med pa*) between those two means that since there is no inherent nature of things in general, there is no specific instance of an inherent nature that can be discussed either. (ALTG)

673 Chapter 6, verse 79. Toh. 3861, f. 208a2. Note that in the second line (*TOK,* II:520.11) ***bde*** should be ***med.*** (TN)

674 *Entrance to the Middle Way,* Chapter 6, verse 81. Toh. 3861, f. 208a3.

675 [Sheer] sophistry (*sun 'byin phyin ci log tu rgol ba*): more literally, "an attack, or form of disputation, that [uses] a fallacious [means of] invalidation."

676 Valid forms of cognition (*pramāṇa, tshad ma*): For a definition of valid cognition, see n. 717. Of the four valid means of cognition (see Chapter 10, p. 225), Svātantrikas follow Dignāga's and Dharmakīrti's systematization in accepting only two forms of valid cognition: direct perceptual valid cognition (*pratyakṣhapramāṇa, mngon sum tshad ma*) and inferential valid cognition (*anumāṇapramāṇa, rjes dpag tshad ma*). There are also two modes of valid cognition for the Svātantrikas according to the object: conventional and ultimate. Their assertions about conventional valid cognition conform with their views of conventional reality, which are aligned with either the Sautrāntikas or Yogāchāras. Ultimate valid cognition is the ultimate inferential valid cognition that arises from the investigation of the ultimate (which occurs on the path of junction) and ultimate direct valid cognition, which is yogic direct valid cognition (ALTG). See Khenpo Tsültrim Gyamtso 1996b/2000; Dreyfus 1997, 285–327; Dunne 2004, 15–35; and Pettit 1999, 108.

677 *Madhyamakaprajñāvatāra, dBu ma shes rab la 'jug pa,* by Chandrakīrti, verse 1. Toh. 3863; Dg.T. Beijing 60:929. The colophon of this text states that it was written by the great master Chandrakīrti and translated by the author himself and the lotsāwa Gö-khukpa Lha-tsé (*'Gos khug pa lha btsas*), who lived in the eleventh century. The

author of this text was the eleventh-century Chandrakīrti, known in the Tibetan tradition as "the lesser Chandrakīrti," who was a disciple of Jetāri (ca. eleventh century), one of the teachers of Atīsha. (He is sometimes referred to by Western scholars as Chandrakīrti III; see Vose 2005, 39–40.)

678 Chapter 6, verse 118. Toh. 3861, f. 210a2–3.

679 Superimposition (*samāropa, sgro 'dogs*) means to impute true existence to that which is nonexistent (*med par yod 'dzin gyi kun btags*). Denial (*apavāda, skur 'debs*) is to regard conventionally existent phenomena as nonexistent [meaning one denies their conventional existence] (*tha snyad du yod pa'i chos rnams yod pa min pa'am med par 'dzin pa*). (*GTCD*)

680 *Entrance to the Middle Way,* Chapter 6, verse 117. Toh. 3861, f. 210a1–2.

681 See Chapter 10, p. 225 for more explanation on the irrelevance of proofs that are equivalent to the probandum (*sgrub byed bsgrub bya dang mtshung pa'i ma grub pa*).

682 The four types of reasons and the four valid means of cognition are discussed in Chapter 10, pp. 225–228. It is worth noting that Brunnhölzl points out (2004, 897n817):

> According to Rongtön's commentary on *The Entrance into Centrism* (*Nges don rnam nges*), Consequentialists employ, for example, "inferences acknowledged by others" (Tib. *gzhan grags kyi rjes dpag*), which can be seen as the Consequentialist equivalent of autonomous reasoning (*Rong ston shes bya kun rig*, n.d., pp. 77-78). He further explains: "What is the difference between 'inferences acknowledged by others' and autonomous inferences? In a probative argument that establishes an autonomous thesis, the three modes are ascertained. [In inferences] acknowledged by others, it is for the sake of eliminating the wrong ideas of opponents that one states as the reason what these others accept, without however establishing any thesis in an independent way (*rang dbang du*)." (pp. 83-84).
>
> "Autonomous reasons are rejected, but we do not deny 'what is to be proven' and 'the means to prove' as mere imputations. . . . Thus, a reason (which is like [the reflection of] the moon in water) makes an opponent (who is like an illusion) realize what is to be proven (which is like a dream)." (pp. 74-75).
>
> As for the difference between autonomous reasonings and mere absurd consequences . . . the latter do not have to involve the correct three modes. This means that they are just unwanted consequences that follow from another position that was wrong in the first place. Thus, they are logically correct, but their explicit meaning must be false, since it is just an absurd outgrowth of a previous false statement. If these consequences (such as "if things arose from themselves, then it would follow that they arise endlessly and pointlessly") are supplemented with a reason that is the opponent's explicit or implicit position (such as "because these things exist already"), the second and third modes usually do apply (at least for the opponent).

683 Valid forms of cognition that function by virtue of [their relationship to real] things (*vastubalapravṛittānumāna, dngos po stobs zhugs kyi tshad ma*): see n. 707. For discussion of the term "independently [verifiable]" (*svatantra, rang rgyud/ rang dbang*), see n. 691.

684 Note that in The System Common to Prāsaṅgikas and Svātantrikas, p. 208, Jamgön Kongtrul says "[For Svātantrikas and Prāsaṅgikas, the probandum] is only an exclu-

sion (*viccheda, rnam gcod*), merely the elimination of the object to be negated, and simply free from conceptual elaborations; they have no probandum that is something [positively] determined (*yongs gcod kyi bsgrub bya*)." For more on determinations (*pariccheda, yongs gcod*), see n. 329.

685 See Chapter 9, p. 221.

686 There are six extant commentaries, four of which are found in the Tengyur: the *Fearless Commentary* (*Mūlamadhyamaka-vṛitti-akutobhayā, dBu ma rtsa ba'i 'grel pa ga las 'jigs med*); Buddhapālita's *Buddhapālita's Commentary on the "Fundamental [Treatise on] the Middle Way"* (*Buddhapālita-mūlamadhyamakavṛitti, dBu ma rtsa ba'i 'grel pa Buddhapālita*); Bhāvaviveka's *Lamp of Wisdom* (*Prajñapradīpa, Shes rab sgron ma*); and Chandrakīrti's *Lucid Words* (*Prasannapadā, Tshig gsal*). Two are preserved in Chinese: *Chung-lun* by the Indian master known as Ch'ing-mu and *Ta-sheng chung-kuan shih-lun* by Sthiramati.

The earliest commentary on Nāgārjuna's work by a commonly accepted known author is Buddhapālita's *Buddhapālita's Commentary on the "Fundamental Treatise on the Middle Way."* The *Fearless Commentary* (*Akutobhayā*) is the earliest known commentary, but the traditional attribution of authorship to Nāgārjuna is not accepted by followers of Tsongkhapa, by many in the Sakya tradition, and by some modern scholars.

There is mention of other (no longer extant) commentaries by Yogāchāra masters (indicating the importance of Nāgārjuna's work for them): Guṇamati, Dharmapāla, and his student Devasharman. See Huntington 1986; Ruegg 1981, 47–9, 48n120; Tillemans 1990, 57–8n123; and Brunnhölzl 2004, 905n948.

687 For some discussion of the history of these two terms and sources for various opinions regarding them, see n. 631. For an overview of earlier categorizations of Madhyamaka, see Chapter 7, pp. 199–200.

688 Chapter 1, verse 1.

689 In *Buddhapālita's Commentary on the "Fundamental Treatise on the Middle Way"* (*Buddhapālita-mūlamadhyamakavṛitti, dBu ma rtsa ba'i 'grel pa Buddhapālita*). For a summary of this text, see Potter 2003, 286–305.

690 Bhāvaviveka criticized Buddhapālita in his *Lamp of Wisdom*. The root statements (*rtsa ba'i sbyor ba*) are Nāgārjuna's statements that things do not arise (1) from themselves, (2) from a thing other than themselves, (3) from both themselves and something other than themselves, and (4) without any cause. For an analysis of Bhāvaviveka's critique of Buddhapālita, see Ames 2003, 46–8.

691 Independently [verifiable] (*svatantra, rang rgyud/ rang dbang*): There are two aspects to examine to understand the issues and ensuing controversies surrounding this term: the meaning of "independently [verifiable]" (or, as it is often translated "autonomous"), and how—that is, on what level—proof statements, inference, and valid cognition are independently [verifiable]. For a useful analysis of the positions of Bhāvaviveka, Chandrakīrti, and Tsongkhapa, see Yotsuya 1999, 47–72, where he states (72 and 65):

> In the *PMV* [*Lamp of Wisdom*] Bhāvaviveka uses the term *svatantra* (*rang dbang*) [independent] variously to describe the reasoning (or inference) of Nāgārjuna, of Bhāvaviveka himself or of his opponent, viz. the Vātsīputrīya. The term *svatantra* seems to connote 1) that Nāgārjuna demonstrates his own doctrinal position by means of a reasoning, 2) that the argument his opponent presents

is based upon Bhāvaviveka's own position, and 3) that the reasoning is valid or correct.

Although Candrakīrti does not give a definition of the term *svatantra* (*rang rgyud*), his usage can be more clearly elucidated. In Candrakīrti's critique of svatantra-reasoning (in its wider sense) the term *svatantra* connotes that a reasoning which demonstrates one's own position is employed on the basis of a subject, etc., established in common for both parties in a debate. And the term *svatantra* is considered to be used especially to emphasize that the subject, etc., are accepted by the proponent, viz. the Mādhyamika himself.

According to Tsongkhapa, in contrast, the term *svatantra* (*rang rgyud*) connotes that the subject, etc., are established by virtue of self-character, that is, ultimately.

> In [one] . . . passage [of Chandrakīrti's *Lucid Words*] an important aspect of a svatantra-reasoning is clearly explained: namely, a svatantra-reasoning is a reasoning which is fully equipped with a proposition, a logical reasoning and a logical example. More precisely, it is a reasoning whose elements are established for both parties. By means of it, one proves the content of the thesis, such as non-origination from self, or refutes the thesis of one's opponent. This contrasts with refutation by means of a reasoning whose elements are established for the opponent alone, i.e. the pure prasaṅga-method [that is, consequences].

Generally speaking, anything that is "independently verifiable," "autonomous," or simply "independent" exists by virtue of its own nature (*bhāva, svabhāva*); that is, it is "real" in some sense. In the case of so-called independently verifiable proof statements, the question is whether the term means that the elements involved—the subject, evidence, and examples—are real, i.e., have independent existence. (As just shown, Yotsuya's analysis is that Bhāvaviveka did not intend such acceptance.) Another issue of contention for Mādhyamikas is whether the use of such reasonings implies their acceptance of this "independent reality" as their opponents accept it, in accordance with the Indian debate rule for inferences or probative arguments (*prayoga[vākya], sbyor ba['i ngag]*) whereby the subject must be acknowledged in common by both opponents (*mthun snang du grub pa*). As Yotsuya says (1999, 73), "Within the milieu of Indian Buddhist logic, it was generally considered impossible for a person to demonstrate his doctrinal position or refute that of his opponent by means of an inferential statement whose subject, etc., were not accepted in common by both parties."

Bhāvaviveka's use of independently [verifiable] proof statements has given rise to much commentary, extrapolation of other positions, and disagreement, since, of course, anyone who is a Mādhyamika does not agree with a Realist on the matter of whether subjects and so forth exist in reality. Thus, independently [verifiable] reasonings (and independently [verifiable] theses, *rang rgyud kyi dam bca'*) and what is or is not implied by their use is a pivotal difference between the approach of Bhāvaviveka and that of Chandrakīrti; and these are explained and understood differently by the various Tibetan scholars and traditions.

Readers should refer to Brunnhölzl 2004, 373–92, Eckel 2003, McClintock 2003, Yoshimizu 2003, and Yotsuya 1999, for explanations and citations that support that, for Bhāvaviveka, Shāntarakṣhita, and Kamalashīla, the use of independently [verifiable] reasoning or valid cognition when debating with Realists does not entail the acceptance of the Realists' views regarding the reality of the subjects for the debate. For example, McClintock says (2003, 145, 150):

> My contention is that Śāntarakṣita and Kamalaśīla have a different understanding of autonomous inference, one that dispenses with the metalogical requirement that all elements in the inference be established as appearing similarly (*mthun snang du grub pa*) as mKhas grub [or Ke-drup] understands this requirement . . . Śāntarakṣita and Kamalaśīla understand agreement concerning the subject of a debate to come about through a shared participation in some form of error . . . Thus, even when his realist opponents have a different *intellectual* understanding of the elements involved in an inference—including, most significantly, the manner in which these elements are established to appear—a Mādhyamika can still, due to a primordial ignorance shared with others, find some common ground from which to begin the dialectical process of demonstrating that unassailably real natures do not exist . . . Yet as a Mādhyamika, one will always be keenly aware that *no* autonomous inference *at any level* is ever anything more than provisional.

Drawing from the Kagyu system, Brunnhölzl (2004, 347) presents Mikyö Dorjé's view as follows:

> For a reasoning to be an autonomous reasoning, the Eighth Karmapa says, it does not matter whether others accept the three modes or not. When a debater generates an inferential cognition in another debater in such a way that the first debater himself or herself pronounces the three modes, then these three modes are autonomously or independently pronounced as such by the first debater and not in dependence on others.

Brunnhölzl notes here (2004, 897n815):

> This is obviously an interpretation of the term "autonomous" (*svatantra/rang rgyud*) that is different from the Gelukpa understanding (the latter requiring the three modes in relation to phenomena that are established through their own specific characteristics and a corresponding valid cognition). Mikyö Dorje's explanation of the term "autonomous" seems furthermore to hinge on the double meaning of *svatantra/rang rgyud*, since this can also mean "one's own continuum." Inasmuch as all reasonings employed by Consequentialists arise and are pronounced within their own personal continua, such reasonings are "autonomous" in this sense, since they clearly do not arise or are pronounced within the continua of others. Thus, the above passage could also be read, ". . . these three modes are stated as such by the first debater's own continuum (*rang rgyud*) and not by the continuum of others (*gzhan rgyud*)."

For analyses of the perspectives of Tsongkhapa and his followers, see Cabezón 2003; Eckel 2003; Ruegg 2000, 233–304; Yoshimizu 2003; and Yotsuya 1999. See also Hopkins 1983; and Lopez 1987.

For a definition of the subject property (*pakṣhadharmatā/-tva, phyogs chos*), see n. 757.

692 In his *Lucid Words*, Chandrakīrti critiques Bhāvaviveka's criticisms of Buddhapālita. For studies of this, see Brunnhölzl 2004, 392–421; Yotsuya 1999, 73–107; and Hopkins 1983, 469–530.

693 For the reasons why Chandrakīrti, not Buddhapālita, is considered the founder of the Prāsaṅgika school, see Lopez's reference (1987, 231) to Chang-kya Rolpé Dorjé's explanation.

694 Bhāvaviveka (*Legs ldan 'byed pa*) (sixth century) was the Mādhyamika master retrospectively considered to be the originator of the Svātantrika-Madhyamaka school, said to have been the abbot of fifty monasteries in the region of Dhānyakaṭa, in South India. He excelled in debate and was the first to use the dialectical methods developed by Dignāga in a Madhyamaka context, which are found in his *Lamp of Wisdom*. He is also considered the first to make the distinction between a "nominal ultimate" (*paryāyaparamārtha, rnam grangs pa'i don dam*) and "non-nominal ultimate" (*aparyāyaparamārtha, rnam grangs ma yin pa'i don dam*), as found in his *Summary of the Meaning of the Middle Way* (*Madhyamakārthasaṃgraha, dBu ma'i don bsdus pa*).

Bhāvaviveka criticizes the view of the three natures in Chapter 25 of his *Lamp of Wisdom* (*Prajñāpradīpa, Shes rab sgron ma*). His *Heart of the Middle Way* (with its auto-commentary, *Blaze of Reasoning*) is noted for its refutation of Yogāchāra (fifth chapter) and for being the first Buddhist compendium of both Buddhist and non-Buddhist Indian philosophical systems (it may be the first of this type of text in all of Indian philosophical writing). His works are only preserved in Tibetan translation. See Eckel 1992, 2–15; and Ruegg 1981, 61–7. For information on the form of his name and authorship of texts, see also nn. 614 and 628.

695 Shrīgupta (*dPal sbas*) (seventh century) was a contemporary of Dharmakīrti and teacher of Jñānagarbha. He wrote the *Commentary on Entering Suchness* (*Tattvāvatāravṛitti, De kho na la 'jug pa'i 'grel pa*), which uses the reasoning of being neither a unity nor a plurality to demonstrate that the suchness of all things is their absence of any nature (see Ruegg 1981, 67–8). Butön considers Shrīgupta to be a Yogāchāra-Madhyamaka (see Obermiller 1932, 134).

696 Jñānagarbha (*Ye shes snying po*) (eighth century) was a master at Nālandā, student of Shrīgupta, and the ordaining abbot and teacher of Shāntarakṣhita. He wrote the *Differentiation of the Two Truths* (*Satyadvaya-vibhaṇga, bDen gnyis rnam 'byed*). See Eckel 1987. Butön considers Jñānagarbha to be a Yogāchāra-Madhyamaka (see Obermiller 1932, 134).

697 See n. 615.

698 See n. 618.

699 Vimuktisena (*rNam grol sde;* or Āryavimuktisena, *'Phags pa rnam grol sde*) (early sixth century) was a master of the Prajñāpāramitā literature, who wrote the earliest extant commentary on the *Ornament of Clear Realization*. He is considered a contemporary of Dignāga and Bhāvaviveka, a student of Vasubandhu, and (by some) the originator of the Yogāchāra-Svātantrika-Madhyamaka synthesis. See Ruegg 1981, 101.

700 Haribhadra (*Seng ge bzang po*) (late eighth century) was a student of Vairochanabhadra and Shāntarakṣhita, and the author of the renowned *Illumination of the "Ornament of Clear Realization"* (*Abhisamayālaṃkārālokā, mNgon rtogs pa'i rgyan gyi snang ba*). Ruegg says (1981, 102), "By some doxographers Haribhadra is considered to belong to the Nirmala-Alīkākāra branch [Proponents of Non-Staining False Images] of Yogāchāra-Svātantrika-Madhyamaka."

701 Buddhajñānapāda ([*Sang rgyas*] *Ye shes zhabs*) (ca. thirteenth century) was invited to Tibet in 1200. He wrote a Madhyamaka text, *Entering the Victor's Path* (*Jinamārgāvatāra, rGyal ba'i lam la 'jug pa*), and a commentary on the *Abhisamayālaṃkāra, The Garlands of Wisdom Lamps* (*Prajñāpradīpāvalī, Shes rab sgron ma'i 'phreng ba*). See Ruegg 1981, 117.

702 Dīpaṇkarabhadra, more commonly known in Tibet as Atīsha (982–1054), was a Bengali master who studied with Bodhibhadra, Jetāri, Kṛiṣhṇāpāda, Ratnākarashānti, and Dharmakīrti of Suvarṇadvīpa. He went to Tibet in 1042, where he taught widely and worked closely with a number of translators, including Rinchen Zangpo (*Rin chen bzang po*), on the translation of treatises by Bhāvaviveka, Chandrakīrti, Dharmapāla, Vasubandhu, and others. One of his most well-known works is *Lamp for the Path to Enlightenment* (*Bodhipathapradīpa, Byang chub lam gyi sgron ma*). See Sherburne 2000; and Ruegg 1981, 110–1. On the difficulties of classifying Atīsha's thought, see Brunnhölzl 2004, 334–5.

703 Vitapāda (*sMan zhabs*) wrote nine texts translated into Tibetan, which are included in the tantra section of the Tengyur and mainly seem to be associated with the Guhyasamāja tantras.

704 Thagana (*Tha ga na*) was, according to Tāranātha (Chimpa and Chattopadhyaya 1970, 290), a contemporary of Prajñākaragupta (ca. ninth century). Chimpa and Chattopadhyaya note that Thagana was one of the eighty-four siddhas; he "belonged to eastern India and was a preceptor of Śanti-pā."

Note that *TOK*, II:524.18 *thag na* should be *tha* ***ga*** *na*. (PKTC)

705 Sautrāntika-[Svātantrika-]Mādhyamikas (Middle Way Proponents [of Independently Verifiable Reasons] Who [Accord with] Followers of the Sūtras) (*mDo sde spyod pa'i dbu ma [rang rgyud] pa*); and Yogāchāra-[Svātantrika-]Mādhyamikas (Middle Way Proponents [of Independently Verifiable Reasons] Who [Accord with] Yoga Practitioners) (*rNal 'byor spyod pa'i dbu ma [rang rgyud] pa*). This distinction is based upon their presentations of conventional reality.

The division of Svātantrikas into Sautrāntika-Svātantrika-Mādhyamikas and Yogāchāra-Svātantrika-Mādhyamikas became well established in the fourteenth and fifteenth centuries in Tibet with Tsongkhapa's *Essence of Eloquence* (*Legs bshad snying po*) and his student Ke-drup Jé's *Introduction to the Buddhist Tantric Systems* (*rGyud sde spyi'i rnam par gzhag pa rgyas par brjod*). See respectively Thurman 1984, 266–77; and Lessing and Wayman, 1968, 90.

It is not known whether these were models accepted at the time, though a precedence is evident in a late thirteenth- to mid-fourteenth-century Bön work, *Clarifying the Doors of Bön* (*Bon sgo gsal byed*), by Tretön Gyaltsen Pal (*Tre ston rgyal mtshan dpal*). This being a Bön work, of course, implies that the subdivisions were made in Buddhist works of that time; see Mimaki 1983, 164–7.

Longchenpa in his *Precious Treasury of the Supreme Yāna* divides Svātantrika into lower Svātantrika (*rang rgyud 'og ma*) and higher Svātantrika (*rang rgyud gong ma*), which Mipham follows in his *Compendium of Philosophical Tenet Systems* (*Yid bzhin mdzod kyi grub mtha' bsdus pa*) (see Phuntsho 2005, 238n38).

706 Bhāvaviveka makes this distinction in his *Precious Lamp of Madhyamaka* (Dg.T. Beijing 57:1539). See also nn. 628 and 629. Note that in Chapter 7, p. 201, Jamgön Kongtrul uses these descriptive categories to refer to Rangtong and Shentong.

707 Established through the power of [their relationship to real] things (also translated as "operating by the power of facts") (*dngos stobs kyis grub pa;* and **vastubalapravṛitta, dngos po stobs zhugs*): On this technical phrase, Tillemans comments (1999a, 28–9):

> The usual types of inferences which we associate with Dignāga and Dharmakīrti, such as those of sound's impermanence and the like, are said to be *vastubalapravṛittānumāna* [inferences functioning through the force of real

entities] in that they derive their truth from the fact that the reason—being a product (*kṛtakatva*)—is in reality, or objectively, related with the property—impermanence—and qualifies the subject, sound . . . (Often, for convenience, we will adopt a less literal translation for this technical term, i.e., "objective inference." The point here, very briefly, is that the usual or paradigmatic type of inference in Dharmakīrti is one which functions objectively, or "by the force of real entities," in that it can and should be evaluated purely on the basis of facts and states of affairs, and not in any way because of belief, acceptance or faith in someone or his words.)

Since the use of reasons established through the power of [their relationship to real] things is one of the key issues said to separate Svātantrikas and Prāsaṅgikas, the Svātantrika view on the ontological status of "things" (*vastu, dngos po*) is important. To understand their position, we must look at their presentation of conventional reality, which distinguishes between correct and mistaken conventional reality, and their presentation of ultimate reality (see pp. 220–222), and identify the context in which "reasons are established through the power of [their relationship to real] things." It is the view of Mikyö Dorjé, as stated in Brunnhölzl 2004 (361–2), that Svātantrikas only accept "established through the power of [their relationship to real] things" on a conventional level, and that these "real" things are illusionlike, dependently originated entities.

Note that *TOK,* II:525.5 *dngos po* ***stong*** should be *dngos po* ***stobs***. (TN)

708 Longchenpa discusses these four positions regarding the two truths in the Svātantrika section of his *Precious Treasury of Philosophical Systems* (*Grub mtha' mdzod*); see forthcoming translation by Richard Barron. Longchenpa's analysis is such that the third alternative in Jamgön Kongtrul's list (the fourth in Longchenpa's)—that the two truths are discrete simply as a negation of their sameness—is considered to be the inevitable conclusion reached by Svātantrikas.

For further discussion of whether the two truths are one or different, see Brunnhölzl 2004, 88-94. For a succinct comparison of the views of Chapa Chökyi Seng-gé (*Phya pa chos kyi seng ge*), Tsongkhapa, and others on the differences between the two truths, see Tauscher 2003, 235 and 253n100.

709 An isolate (or reverse; distinguisher) (*vyatireka, ldog pa*) is a conceptual object and refers to the conceptual process of isolation or elimination, which operates whenever we think of something. For example, when we think "impermanent phenomena," we conceptually exclude or eliminate everything that is not an impermanent phenomenon, and we isolate the notion of "impermanent phenomena." The point here is that the truths are simply synonyms in the same way that "Fourteenth Dalai Lama" and "Tenzin Gyatso" are simply different names for the same person.

710 Capable of performing a function (*arthakriyāsamartham, don byed nus pa*): see n. 307.

711 "To appear [to its cognizing subject] in a way that is consistent with its respective class [of phenomena]" (*rang rang gi rigs pa mthun par snang ba*) means that objects—i.e., particulars, or specifically characterized phenomena (*svalakṣhaṇa, rang mtshan*)—that are misperceived, such as snow mountains appearing to be yellow for someone with jaundice, do not qualify as correct conventional reality. (ALTG)

712 See n. 537.

713 A nonimplicative negation that excludes [the possibility that the subject] does not possess [the quality of emptiness] (*mi ldan rnam gcod kyi med dgag*): This type of negation excludes the possibility that phenomena have any kind of real existence

without implying anything in its place. It is formulated by excluding the possibility that phenomena do not possess the "quality" of emptiness. Although this does mean that phenomena possess the quality of emptiness (and this form of negation does explicitly emphasize that all phenomena are empty), from the point of view of the way the negation is stated, it means that they do not really possess any quality. (I am grateful to both Āchārya Lama Tenpa Gyaltsen and Karl Brunnhölzl for help on this point.)

714 *Satyadvaya-vibhaṅga, bDen gnyis rnam 'byed,* by Jñānagarbha. Toh. 3881; Dg.T. Beijing 62. Jñānagarbha uses the terms "approximate ultimate" (*don dam dang mthun pa'i don dam*) and "non-nominal ultimate" (*rnam grangs ma yin pa'i don dam*). See Eckel 1992, 71–2 and 112n9.

The primary source for the twofold presentation of the ultimate seems to be Bhāvaviveka's *Summary of the Meaning of Madhyamaka* (*Madhyamakārthasaṃgraha, dBu ma'i don bsdus pa*) and the third chapter of his *Blaze of Reasoning,* in which texts he uses the terms "nominal ultimate" (*paryāyaparamārtha, rnam grangs pa'i don dam*) and "non-nominal ultimate" (*aparyāyaparamārtha, rnam grangs ma yin pa'i don dam*). See Lindtner 1981, 200n14; and Eckel 2003, 202n48.

These divisions are presented in Shāntarakṣhita's *Ornament of the Middle Way* (see Padmakara Translation Group 2005, 108–9 and 294–311) and Longchenpa's *The Precious Treasury of Philosophical Systems* (see Barron forthcoming).

715 For another statement of the position of some Svātantrikas regarding fruition, see Chapter 8, p. 216.

716 The outline heading here is slightly different from when the section is presented (see Chapter 10, p. 233). For the sake of consistency, I am using the second form, "The Specific Explanation of Ground, Path, and Result [in Madhyamaka]," *gzhi lam 'bras gsum bye brag tu* ***bshad*** (*TOK,* II:533.15), as opposed to what appears here, "The Specific Classifications of Ground, Path, and Result [in Madhyamaka]," *gzhi lam 'bras gsum bye brag tu* ***dbye*** (*TOK,* II:527.8).

717 The four valid means of cognition (*pramāṇa, tshad ma*) were propounded by the Nyāyas (Logicians) and became widely accepted in Indian philosophical circles (see Dreyfus 1997, 293–4). Of these four, Buddhists, as followers of the epistemological treatises of Dignāga and Dharmakīrti, only accept direct perception and inference as valid forms of cognition. Broadly speaking, Chandrakīrti and his followers were the exception and accepted the use of all four in debate with others.

Khenpo Tsültrim Gyamtso (1996b/2000) says, "the general definition of valid cognition is 'a new and undeceiving awareness'" (*gsar du mi bslu ba'i rig pa tha snyad tshad ma spyi'i mtshan nyid*); and "the definition from the point of view of dispelling wrong ideas is 'an awareness which clarifies what was not known [previously]'" (*ma shes don gsal gyi rig pa log rtog bsal ba'i dbang du byas pa'i mtshan nyid*). (In the following paragraphs, the definitions for direct perceptual valid cognition and inferential valid cognition are from Khenpo Tsültrim Gyamtso 1996b/2000.)

(1) Direct perceptual valid cognition (*pratyakṣhapramāṇa, mngon sum tshad ma*) is defined as "a nonconceptual and nonmistaken awareness" (*rtog pa dang bral zhing ma 'khrul pa'i rig pa*). It is of four types: sense direct perception (*indriya pratyakṣha, dbang po'i mngon sum*), mental direct perception (*mānasapratyakṣha, yid kyi mngon sum*), reflexively aware direct perception (*rang rig mngon sum*), and yogic direct perception (*yogi pratyakṣha, rnal 'byor mngon sum*). For definitions of these subcategories, see the *Classifications of Mind* and Book Six, Part One (*TOK,* II:233–4).

Generally, Tibetan commentators agree that on a conventional level Prāsaṅgikas accept sense, mental, and yogic direct perceptions, but they disagree about whether Prāsaṅgikas accept reflexively aware direct perception. Tsongkhapa, for example, states that Prāsaṅgikas do not accept reflexive awareness, not even conventionally (this is one of the "eight difficult points"; see p. 247 and n. 803 for related sources); whereas Mipham states that Prāsaṅgikas do accept reflexively aware direct perception conventionally (see Pettit 1999, 129 and 497n451). According to Āchārya Lama Tenpa Gyaltsen (ALTG), Mikyö Dorjé often criticizes reflexive awareness, but he does not make a clear statement on whether the Prāsaṅgikas accept it conventionally or reject it completely. It is generally understood that Mikyö Dorjé's refutations of reflexive awareness are only refutations on the level of slight analysis.

(2) Inferential valid cognition (*anumāṇapramāṇa, rjes dpag tshad ma*) is of two types: inference for oneself (*rang don rjes dpag*) and inference for others (*gzhan don rjes dpag*). Inference for oneself is defined as "an awareness newly realizing that which is to be proven by a reason having the three modes" (*tshul gsum pa can gyi rtags las bsgrub bya gsar du rtogs pa'i rig pa*). It arises in dependence upon the three basic types of reasons: reasons of nature (*'bras bu'i gtan tshigs*), reasons of results (*rang bzhin gyi gtan tshigs*), and reasons of imperception (*ma dmigs pa'i gtan tshig*). Inference for others is defined as "A sentence construction fully clarifying for others the fact seen by the disputant himself, [i.e.,] a reason having the three modes" (*rgol ba rang nyid kyi mthong pa'i don tshul gsum pa can gyi gtan tshigs gzhan la rab tu gsal bar byed pa'i tshig sbyor*). See Khenpo Tsültrim Gyamtso 1996a/1999; Brunnhölzl 2004, 178–81; Dreyfus 1997, 316–27; Dunne 2004, 25–35; and Matilal 1998, 108–16.

(3) Scriptural authority (or verbal testimony) (*āgama, lung*) as a valid means of cognition is also called "inferential valid cognition of conviction" (*yid ches rjes dpag tshad ma*). Dreyfus says (1997, 294), "*Nyāya-sūtra* I.1.7 explains the epistemological status of testimony: 'Verbal testimony (*śabda*) is the communication (*upadeśa*) from a trustworthy person (*āpta*).'" For Buddhists, the status of scriptural authority as a form of valid cognition is a topic of much discussion. Some consider it a form of inference, others do not. It is generally said to be the means for cognizing that which is extremely hidden (*atyantaparokṣha, shin tu lkog gyur*). See Tillemans 1999a, 28-32 and 37–51; Tillemans 1999b, 395–404; and Dunne 2004, 230–45.

(4) Analogy (or analogical induction) (*upamāṇa, nye bar 'jal ba*) is the use of examples to bring about cognition of something formerly unknown. Dreyfus says (1997, 529n41) that Buddhist epistemologists consider this to be a form of inference. See also Dunne 2004, 145–7.

718 For comments on the relationship between inferences based on what is commonly acknowledged by others and independently [verifiable] reasonings, see n. 682.

719 [Demonstrations to the opponent of] the irrelevance of proofs that are equivalent to the probandum are also called "the circularity of the argument" or "showing a reason to be invalid because it merely reiterates the thesis."

For a similar presentation of these four reasons with some additional comments, see Brunnhölzl 2004, 351–4.

720 Gorampa (*Go ram pa bsod nams seng ge*) (1429–1489) was one of the most famous Sakya scholars and a critical opponent of Tsongkhapa (1357–1419).

721 Serdokpa Dön-yö Pal (*gSer mdog pa don yod dpal*) is also known as Silung Paṇchen (*Zi lung paṇ chen*) and Serdok Paṇchen Shākya Chokden (*gSer mdog paṇ chen shākya mchog ldan*) (1428–1509). He was a Sakya master and student of the seventh Karmapa, Chödrak Gyamtso. As we can see from Jamgön Kongtrul's liberal quoting of Shākya Chokden's works in Chapter 11, he is one of the major sources for Jamgön Kongtrul's presentation of Shentong. It also seems that much of Chapters 9 and 10 are drawn from Shākya Chokden's *The Dharma Treasury of an Ocean of Scriptures and Reasonings Ascertaining the Middle Way* (*dBu ma rnam par nges pa'i chos kyi bang mdzod lung dang rigs pa'i rgya mtsho*). See also Dreyfus 1997, 27–9; Iaroslav 2000; and Mathes 2004.

722 In his *Entrance to the Middle Way,* Chandrakīrti devotes a large section of Chapter 6 to refuting the four possible causes for arising as a demonstration that phenomena have no self-entity (*dharmanairātmya, chos kyi bdag med*). The Sāṃkhyas' position that things arise from themselves is refuted in verses 8c–13. The refutation of the idea held by some Buddhists that things arise from something other than themselves is presented in verses 14–21 (further discussions and ramifications of this refutation are found in verses 22–97). The Jains' view that things arise from both themselves and from things other than themselves is refuted in verse 98. The Chārvākas' assertion that things arise without cause is refuted in verses 99–103. See Huntington 1989, 158–69; Padmakara Translation Group 2002, 183–266; and Goldfield et al. 2005, 35–305.

The vajra sliver reasoning is also discussed later in this chapter. See The Explanation of the Way [the Two Truths] Are Established, pp. 236–238.

723 Sāṃkhyas (Calculators or Enumerators) (*Grangs can pa*) are followers of the oldest of the "orthodox" philosophical schools, that is, schools that take the Vedas as authoritative. The Vedic sage Kapila is traditionally said to be the founder of the Sāṃkhya school (though this is not verified), which also serves as the philosophical system for Patañjali's system of Yoga.

Sāṃkhyas posit a metaphysical dualism between the ultimates of *prakṛiti* (primal matter) (*rang bzhin*) and *puruṣha* (person or ātman) (*skyes bu*). They believe that, with the exception of *puruṣha,* everything is a manifestation of, or transformation within, *prakṛiti,* the primal matter. In that way, all results can be said to be fundamentally identical with their causes, and Sāṃkhyas are said to hold the position that things arise from themselves. See Hiriyanna 1932, 267–97; Hiriyanna 1948, 106–28; Hopkins 1983, 321–6; and Brunnhölzl 2004, 795–6.

724 "The entailment is not definite" (or "[the reason's] entailment [of the consequence] is not ascertained") (*de la khyab pa ma nges pa*) means that Sāṃkhyas do not accept that their statement (used here as the reason) entails the consequence Prāsaṅgikas have stated. In other words, they do not accept that a result being present at the time of its cause necessarily means that its arising is pointless.

725 When Sāṃkhyas say, "Those two [cases] are not comparable (*de gnyis mi mtshungs*)," they are objecting to the way Prāsaṅgikas apply their thesis (things arise from themselves) to both unmanifest results (e.g., sesame oil present within a sesame seed prior to its extraction) and manifest results (e.g., the extracted sesame oil).

726 The Prāsaṅgikas' point is that the consequences they already stated, which show the absurdity of saying that something already existent arises again, would apply to

a vase as a lump of clay. The Sāṃkhyas' attempt to clarify their position and avoid accepting the Prāsaṅgikas' consequences amounts to nothing more than a restatement of their original position albeit with qualifications. In short, the Sāṃkhyas have not brought anything new to their argument.

727 Inferences based on what is commonly acknowledged by others refer to the everyday experience and understanding of people in the world, such as that planting seeds and tending crops will produce a harvest. Sāṃkhyas do not want, for example, to accept the consequence that if things arise from themselves, they will arise in a meaningless fashion, because then any work, like farming, would be useless and unjustified. Sāṃkhyas are now left with no argument to support their view that things arise from themselves.

728 Mādhyamikas consider the Buddhist Realists to be Vaibhāṣhikas and Sautrāntikas, who believe, as is described in their abhidharma texts, that discrete results arise from existent, discrete causes. Mādhyamikas also regard Chittamātras who consider the ālaya consciousness to be truly existent to be Realists. See also n. 596.

729 The refutation of arising from other comes down to the fact that for two things to be inherently different from each other (*rang bzhin gyis gzhan*) they have to exist at the same time. ("Other" here does not mean simply a notion of otherness that we impute to objects.) If they exist at the same time, they cannot be in a cause and result relationship with each other. For a more detailed refutation of production from other, see pp. 236–237.

730 By saying that the entailment is not definite, Realists mean that even though they say one thing arises from something entirely different from itself, they do not accept the consequence the Prāsaṅgikas have stated. In other words, for these Realists, a sprout arising from a seed and a sprout and a seed being inherently other are not mutually exclusive (*'gal ba*).

731 Here Realists are simply adding a qualification to their position that things arise from something other than themselves and as such, it is merely a restatement of their original position. The Prāsaṅgikas' reply means that the previous consequences would apply to something that has the potential to produce a result.

732 Nirgranthas ("Those Freed from Bondage") (Tib. *gCer bu pa,* Naked Ones) is a common name in Buddhist works for Jains (Followers of the Victor) (*rGyal ba pa*), specifically for the *Digambaras* (Sky-Clad Ones), who were the naked ascetics (all other Jains are known as *Shvetāmbaras*, White Clad Ones). The founder of Jainism was Vardhamāna Mahāvīra, also known as Jina (the Victor), a contemporary of the Buddha. Jains observe a strict ethical code of five vows—nonviolence (*ahiṃsā*), truth (*satya*), not stealing (*asteya*), chastity (*brahmacharya*), and renunciation (or non-possessiveness) (*aparigraha*). See Hiriyanna 1932, 155–73; Hiriyanna 1948, 57–70; and Brunnhölzl 2004, 798.

733 Chapter 6, 98ab. Toh. 3861, f. 209a1–4.

734 Hedonists (or Materialists) (*Lokāyata, ['Jig rten] rgyang 'phen pa*)—more well-known as Chārvākas (probably "Sweet[-Talkers]") (*Tshu rol mdzes pa*)—belong to an ancient philosophical tradition, possibly dating from 600 BCE, whose works have not survived. Chārvākas only accept direct perception as a valid means of cognition or knowledge. Thus they do not accept any causality that is not directly perceptible, or the existence of past and future lives. They were denounced by all other philosophical traditions of their time for what were considered immoral views. See Hiriyanna,

1932, 187–95; Hiriyanna 1948, 57–60; Hopkins 1983, 237–330; and Brunnhölzl 2004, 798–9.

735 Hedonists do not accept the Prāsaṅgikas' consequence that something that arises without a cause is something that cannot be perceived directly by the senses.

736 A blue water lily (*Nymphaea stellata*) [growing] in the sky (*nam mkha'i utpa la*) is one of the traditional examples of something that does not exist at all.

737 The most effective way to refute the notion that things arise without any causes is to point out that things *sometimes* arise. If things had no causes, they would either always arise or never at all, that is, there would be no reason for them to appear or not appear. We can see, however, that this is not the case: things appear when their specific causes and conditions are present. (ALTG)

738 *Bodhichittavivaraṇa-nāma, Byang chub sems 'grel pa zhes bya ba,* by Nāgārjuna, verse 21cd. Toh. 1800, f. 39a5; Dg.T. Beijing 18:110. The verse in full reads: [Things] perform functions due to being similar to objects. Is this not like an offense [committed] while dreaming? When we awaken from the dream [we see that dream objects and waking objects] do not differ in their performance of functions (*don mtshungs pa yis don byed pa/ rmi lam gnod pa bzhin min nam/ rmi lam sad pa'i gnas skabs la/ don byed pa la khyad par med*). See Lindtner 1986, 41.

739 Worldly conventionality (*'jig rten kun rdzob*) includes both the average person's notions and experiences of conventional reality and non-Buddhist philosophical and scientific ideas about it. Yogic conventionality (*rnal 'byor kun rdzob*) is what is experienced by Buddhist yogic practitioners, beginning with their initial stage of slight analysis and conceptual understanding of emptiness, through the appearances and realizations they experience as noble beings. These divisions of conventional reality are discussed in Book Seven, Part Two (*TOK*, III:31–2).

For the Svātantrikas' division of conventional reality into correct and mistaken, see Chapter 9, p. 221. For further discussion of worldly and yogic conventional realities, and conventional reality and mere conventionality, see Brunnhölzl 2004, 94-9.

740 Chandrakīrti differentiates between conventional reality (*saṃvṛitisatya, kun rdzob bden pa*) and mere conventionality (*saṃvṛitimātra, kun rdzob tsam*) in his auto-commentary to *Entrance to the Middle Way,* Chapter 6, verse 28. See Huntington 1989, 232–3n47. See also Goldfield et al. 2005, 79.

741 Chapter 6, verse 23. Toh. 3861, f. 205a3.

742 Chapter 6, verse 29. Toh. 3861, f. 205a5–6; Dg.T. Beijing 60:565. Note the following spelling mistakes: *TOK,* II:531.9: *rnam* ***btags*** *pa* should be *rnam* ***brtags*** *pa;* and *de* ***ni*** *bdag nyid* should be *de* ***nyid*** *bdag nyid.*

743 Collection of Madhyamaka Reasonings (*dBu ma rigs tshogs lnga*) is a collective name for five texts by Nāgārjuna. See n. 592.

744 Tak-tsang Lotsāwa (*sTag tshang lo tsā ba Shes rab rin chen*) (b. 1405) was a famous scholar of the Sakya tradition who is well known for his vigorous refutation of Tsongkhapa, founder of the Geluk tradition.

745 Reading ***rig*** *shes* as ***rigs*** *shes* (*TOK,* II:532.1) following this spelling in the next sections and Khenpo Tsültrim Gyamtso Rinpoche's explanation.

746 For a brief description of conventions that are suitable for common consensus (*grags rung gi tha snyad*), see Chapter 8, p. 207.

747 Subsequent state of attainment (*prishthalabdha, rjes thob*) is the period following meditative equipoise. Although often translated as "post-meditation," it refers to the level of realization of emptiness that is attained when emerging from meditative equipoise. Bodhisattvas then apply this realization to seeing the illusionlike nature of all appearances and experiences while they engage in the six pāramitās. A synonym for the subsequent state of attainment is "the samādhi in which [appearances are seen to be] illusionlike" (*sgyu ma lta bu'i ting nge 'dzin*).

748 Mother [Sūtras] (*mātṛi/ mātā, yum*): "mother" is an epithet for Prajñāpāramitā, the perfection of wisdom, and also is a way of referring to the Prajñāpāramitā Sūtras.

749 Chapter 22, verse 11. Toh. 3824, f. 13b1–2.

750 Verses 9cd–12. Dg.T. Beijing 60:930. On the authorship of the text, see n. 677. Note that for verse 11c, the translation follows Dg.T. Beijing: *bsgom* ***pa*** *med; TOK,* II:533.5: *bsgom* **bya** *med.* For verse 12a, the translation follows Dg.T. Beijing: *de yi* ***don*** *ni; TOK,* II:533.5: *de yi* ***blo*** *ni.*

751 Chandrakīrti, in his *Entrance to the Middle Way* (Chapter 6, verse 80ab), says, "Conventional reality serves as the method; ultimate reality is what develops from the method" (*tha snyad bden pa thabs su gyur pa dang/ don dam bden pa thabs byung gyur pa ste*). See Huntington 1989, 162; Padmakara Translation Group 2002, 79 and 80–1; and Goldfield et al. 2005, 237.

This explanation of the two truths as method and the outcome of method should be understood in terms of the perceiving subject, our minds, not in terms of objects, such as appearances and their emptiness. The designation of the conventional reality as method and ultimate reality as the outcome indicates the way an understanding of the two truths develops in our minds—it is not that conventional reality is the cause of the ultimate nor is it that the ultimate is the result of the conventional reality. (ALTG)

752 *TOK,* II:534.11: ***gtam*** *tshigs* should be ***gtan*** *tshigs.*

753 Reasons of the imperception of something connected [to the predicate of the negandum] (*saṃbhandhānupalabdhihetu, 'brel zla ma dmigs pa'i gtan tshigs*): Something connected to the predicate of the negandum (*dgag bya'i chos*) may be (1) its nature (*rang bzhin*), (2) any of its results (*'bras bu*), (3) any of its causes (*rgyu*), or (4) a larger category to which it belongs (*khyab byed*).

An example of a reason of the imperception of a result connected to the predicate is: "In this smoke-free room, there is no fire, because no smoke is perceived through any form of valid cognition." The predicate of the negandum is "there is a fire." The fact that a result (smoke) connected to the phenomenon in question (fire) is not perceived in this room serves as the reason that negates the existence of this phenomenon (fire).

See Khenpo Tsültrim Gyamtso 1996a/1999; and Brunnhölzl 2004, 180–1.

754 Reasons of the perception of something contradictory [to the predicate of the negandum] (*viruddhopalabdhihetu, 'gal zla dmigs pa'i gtan tshigs*): Something that is contradictory to the predicate of the negandum may be (1) its nature (*rang bzhin*), (2) its result (*'bras bu*), or (3) a subset of it (*khyab bya*).

An example of using a reason of the perception of something whose nature is contradictory to the predicate is: "Right next to a hot fire, there is no lasting sensation of coldness, because a hot fire is perceived there." The predicate of the negandum is "a lasting feeling of coldness." The fact that something whose nature is contradictory (a hot fire) to the phenomenon in question (an ongoing sensation of cold) is perceived serves as the reason that negates the existence of this phenomenon (an ongoing sensation of cold).

Or to use the reasoning of dependent origination: "Outer and inner phenomena do not come into being, because they are dependently originated." The predicate is "come into being." The perception of something contradictory (phenomena being dependently originated) to the predicate serves as the reason to negate it.

755 The five reasons are also presented in Chapter 8; see pp. 209–211.

756 The three doors to liberation (*vimokṣhamukhatraya, rnam thar sgo gsum*) are avenues, or ways, to liberation presented in the Prajñāpāramitā literature. Here these three doors are demonstrated through the first three forms of analysis: By analyzing the nature of phenomena, we understand it to be emptiness (*shūnyatā, stong pa nyid*); that is emptiness as a door to liberation. By analyzing phenomena in terms of their causes, we see that they actually have no defining characteristics, and this absence of characteristics (*animitta, mtshan ma med pa*) serves as a door to liberation. By analyzing phenomena in terms of their results, we recognize that they do not really come into being, and this leads us to the absence of expectancy (*apraṇihita, smon pa med pa*) as a door to liberation.

757 In Buddhist logic, three modes (or criteria) (*trairūpya/ trirūpa, tshul gsum*) are examined to determine whether a reason is valid or not: the subject property, the positive entailment, and the negative entailment. These are concerned with the reason's relationship to the subject and to the predicate. If they are determined to be correct, the reason is a valid means to establish what is to be proven. The following definitions are from Khenpo Tsültrim Gyamtso's *Classifications of Reasons* (86).

1. The subject property (*pakṣhadharmatā/-tva, phyogs chos*) is defined as "a reason that valid cognition has determined to be present in all instances of the flawless subject in question in a corresponding formulation" (*shes 'dod chos can skyon med kyi steng du 'god tshul dang mthun par yod pa nyid du tshad mas nges pa'i gtan tshigs*). Simply put, it means that the reason is a property, or quality, of the subject (that is, the subject is either equivalent to the reason or a subset of it).
2. Positive entailment (*anvayavyāpti, rjes khyab*) is defined as "a reason that has been determined to be present only in the homologous set [of the predicate]" (*mthun pa'i phyogs kho na la yod par nges pa'i gtan tshigs*). Simply put, the reason is equivalent to the predicate or a subset of it.
3. Negative entailment (*vyatirekavyāpti, ldog khyab*) is defined as "a reason that has been determined not to be present in a single instance of the heterologous set" (*mi mthun pa'i phyogs kho na la yod par nges pa'i gtan tshigs*). (See also n. 671.)

For more discussion of the three modes, see Khenpo Tsültrim Gyamtso 1996a/1999; Brunnhölzl 2004, 177–9; Dreyfus 1997; Dunne 2004; Matilal 1998, 6–7 and 90–94; and Perdue 1993.

758 The vajra sliver reasoning is presented at some length earlier in this chapter. See A Brief Account of Chandrakīrti's Exegetical System, pp. 226–228.

759 This means that if something actually arises it will do so through one of these four ways (from itself, from something other than itself, from both, or causelessly)—there is no fifth possibility. (ALTG)

760 Nāgārjuna's opening statement of his *Fundamental Treatise on the Middle Way* (see Chapter 9, p. 218) states that things do not arise from any of the four possibilities, but he does not discuss this matter any further. Chandrakīrti, however, refutes arising from the four extremes in great detail in Chapter 6 of his *Entrance to the Middle Way*. See Huntington 1989, 158–69; Padmakara Translation Group 2002, 183–266; and Goldfield et al. 2005, 35–305.

761 See also n. 723.

762 Object-consistent consciousnesses (or factually concordant types of consciousness) (*shes rig don mthun*) are the six consciousnesses, which always arise in keeping with their respective objects (that is, an eye consciousness will arise only with a physical form as its object, never a sound). Vaibhāṣhikas explain that the six consciousnesses arise from their four conditions (*pratyaya, rkyen*): object condition (*dmigs rkyen*); dominant condition (*bdag rkyen*); proximate condition (*de ma thag rkyen*); and causal condition (*rgyu'i rkyen*). For example, an eye consciousness arises from visual forms (its object condition), the eye sense faculty (its dominant condition), the just-ceased preceding moment of eye consciousness (its proximate condition), and, simply put, prior moments of eye consciousness (its causal condition).

The scriptural source for this is the *Treasury of Abhidharma*, Chapter 2, verse 64a: "Mind and mental events arise from the four [conditions]." See Pruden 1988, 305.

Note that at *TOK*, II:536.1 *shes* ***rigs*** *don mthun* should be *shes* ***rig*** *don mthun*.

763 "Most [other] entities" mean non-associated formative forces (*ldan min 'du byed*) and forms (*gzugs*), which are the phenomena other than the consciousnesses, mental events, and unconditioned phenomena.

The *Treasury of Abhidharma*, Chapter 2, verse 64c says, "Other [phenomena] arise from the two." Vasubandhu explains that "other" phenomena are non-associated [formative forces] and forms, and that "the two" are causal conditions and dominant conditions. See Pruden 1988, 306. For information on non-associated formative forces, see n. 310.

Jamgön Kongtrul says, "Most [other] entities arise from their causal and dominant conditions," to exclude the Vaibhāṣhikas' category of permanent entities (*rtag pa'i dngos po*), which are unconditioned phenomena (ALTG). See Chapter 3, p. 131.

764 For a synopsis of the key point in the refutation of arising from other, see n. 729.

765 This is a terse statement of an absurd consequence that Prāsaṅgikas deduce from the assertion that phenomena actually arise from something other than themselves. To state this in a fuller way:

If it were the case that phenomena arise from things that are other than themselves, anything could arise from anything, because both the causes of a specific thing and what are not its causes are equal in being "other" than the particular result. For example, a rice sprout could arise as easily from a barley seed as from a rice seed, because a barley seed and a rice seed are equally other than the rice sprout. Another frequently stated absurd consequence is that flames would arise from darkness.

For a thorough presentation of this line of refutation, see Chapter 6 of Chandrakīrti's *Entrance to the Middle Way*, specifically verses 14–21, in Huntington 1989; Padmakara Translation Group 2002; and Goldfield et al. 2005.

766 Here, a substantial [cause] (*upādāna[hetu]*, *nyer len [gyi rgyu]*) is a direct cause (*dngos rgyu*), which produces its own particular result. For example, a sunflower

seed is the substantial cause for a sunflower sprout. Substantial causes by definition must precede their results. This is an important clarification because, of the six causes and four conditions (all of which contribute to the arising of a result and some of which may exist at the same time as the result), it is the substantial cause that is the focus of this debate (ALTG). (Note that substantial cause is also translated as "primary cause" or "perpetuating cause.")

767 In his *Entrance to the Middle Way,* Chandrakīrti refutes the idea that a cause and its result are simultaneous; see verses 18–20 of Chapter 6.

768 This is a reference to the third of the five great reasons. See p. 238.

769 The four possibilities (*chatuṣhkoṭi, mu bzhi*) are (1) that only one result manifests from just a single cause; (2) that numerous results are produced by only one cause; (3) that a single result comes from many causes; and (4) that many results could arise from many causes.

770 See Chapter 8, p. 210.

771 Chapter 7, verse 16ab. Toh. 3824, f. 4a5.

772 Chapter 6, verse 32. Toh. 3861, f. 205b5.

773 The absence of a self of persons is discussed in more detail in Book Seven, Part Three (*TOK,* III:69–77).

774 Chapter 6, verse 151. Toh. 3861, f. 211b4–5; Dg.T. Beijing 60:579. The translation follows Dg.T. Beijing: *yan lag la* ***min*** *yang lag dag der* ***min****; TOK,* II:538.6: *yan lag la* ***med*** *yang lag dag der* ***med****.*

775 The Buddha used the analogy of a cart to illustrate that a "self" is just a conventional designation; see, for example, *The Connected Discourses of the Buddha* (Bodhi 2000, 230). It is also used by Nāgasena in *The Questions of King Milinda* (see Rhys Davids 1890, 43–5).

Nāgārjuna in his *Fundamental Treatise on the Middle Way* (Chapter 22, verses 1–8) presents a fivefold analysis. Chandrakīrti also presents this fivefold analysis in his *Entrance to the Middle Way,* Chapter 6, verses 121–136, and then he adds two more points in verses 150d–162.

776 Other-exclusion (or elimination; elimination of other) (*anyāpoha, gzhan sel*): Generally speaking and put very simply, the term "other-exclusion" indicates that the conceptual mind apprehends its object by way of exclusion. For example, when we think "rose," our minds eliminate all that is not rose to arrive at the general object "rose." This theory of exclusion, *apoha,* was first introduced in Buddhist works by Dignāga in his *Compendium on Valid Cognition,* and discussed by Dharmakīrti and later Shāntarakṣhita and Kamalashīla. For more on *apoha* theory in the works of Dharmakīrti, Shāntarakṣhita, and the Tibetan traditions, see Dreyfus 1997, particularly Chapters 11–13. For a comparison of Dignāga and Dharmakīrti, see Katsura 1995. See also Bronkhorst 1999; Tillemans 1999, 209–46; and Dunne 2004.

777 PKTC has ***tshig*** *spros pa; TOK,* II:538.19 has ***cho ga*** *spros pa.* The translation follows the latter, although either reading seems feasible.

778 See n. 679.

779 *Bodhicharyāvatāra, Byang chub sems dpa'i spyod pa la 'jug pa;* Chapter 9, verse 34. Toh. 3871; Dg.T. Beijing 61:1020. See Brunnhölzl 2004, 653–4; and Padmakara Translation Group 1997, 142.

780 *Dashabhūmikasūtra, Sa bcu pa'i mdo.* Toh. 44:31. (This is Chapter 31 of the *Avataṃsaka Sūtra, Phal po che.*)

781 In his *Entrance to the Middle Way,* Chandrakīrti presents the path to awakening in ten chapters, which correlate the ten bhūmis with the ten pāramitās (generosity, ethical conduct, patience, diligence, meditative concentration, wisdom, methods, strength, aspirations, and primordial wisdom). See Huntington 1989; and Padmakara Translation Group 2002.

782 *Satyadvayāvatāra, bDen pa gnyis la 'jug pa;* verse 7ab. Toh. 3902; Dg.T. Beijing 63: 1051. See Lindtner 1981, 194; and Sherburne 2000, 353.

783 From the perspective of the subsequent state of attainment (i.e., not the state of meditative equipoise), we speak of the primordial wisdom of the first bhūmi, the primordial wisdom of the second bhūmi, and so on. Because primordial wisdom is the basis, or ground, for the pāramitās of the bhūmis, the primordial wisdom of the first bhūmi is equivalent to the pāramitā of generosity, the primordial wisdom of the second bhūmi to the pāramitā of ethical conduct, and so on. (ALTG)

784 For example, in Book Ten, Part One, Jamgön Kongtrul distinguishes the sambhogakāya in terms of the actual (*dngos*) sambhogakāya and the nominal (*btags*) sambhogakāya. (See *TOK,* III:598.)

785 Chapter 11, verse 17. Toh. 3861, f. 216b3–4. Note that Dg.T. Beijing 60:590 reads *sems 'gags* ***pas*** *de*; *TOK,* II:540.13 has *sems 'gags* ***pa*** *de.*

786 In his commentary on the *Entrance to the Middle Way,* Mikyö Dorjé explains that "cessation of mind" (*sems 'gag pa*) means that the clinging of mind and mental events (*sems dang sems 'byung ba'i 'dzin pa*) and the delusive appearances of ignorance have dissolved. The conventional expression "cessation" simply refers to such dissolution. He makes the point that any other position would involve the extremes of permanence or nihilism, e.g., it would be the extreme of nihilism to state that the mind and mental events exist up through the tenth bhūmi and then cease with the attainment of buddhahood.

It should be noted that the term cessation (*'gags pa*) has two senses: (1) cessation as elimination (*spangs pa'i 'gags pa*), which is also called cessation that is the interruption of continuity (*rgyun chad pa'i 'gag pa*), and (2) cessation as a transformation (*gnas gyur ba'i 'gags pa*). Mikyö Dorjé makes it clear that cessation means transformation (in the sense of transforming the distorting influence of ignorance), not elimination (ALTG). See *The Chariot of the Dakpo Kagyu Siddhas,* pp. 672–3.

787 Jetsün Drakpa Gyaltsen (*rJe btsun grags pa rgyal mtshan*) (1147–1216), the third patriarch in the Sakya tradition.

788 Sakya Paṇḍita (*Sa skya paṇḍita*) (1182–1251) was the fourth and most famous of the Sakya tradition's patriarchs. Sakya Paṇḍita was not only a great master of the Sakya School, he was a pioneer in the introduction of Sanskrit poetics in the Tibetan language, the inventor of the Mongolian alphabet, and the one responsible for developing much of the scholastic disciplines of the Tibetan monastic tradition. Sakya Paṇḍita wrote many influential works and was instrumental in making the ten sciences complete in Tibet. Some of his works include the *Discrimination of the Three Vows* (*sDom gsum rab dbye*), *Treasury of Valid Means of Cognition* (*Tshad ma rigs pa'i gter*) and *Treasury of Well-Spoken Advice* (*Legs par bshad pa rin po che'i gter*). The source of this citation was not found.

789 Silung Paṇchen (*Zi lung paṇ chen*) is more commonly known as Serdok Paṇchen Shākya Chokden (*gSer mdog paṇ chen shākya mchog ldan*). Jamgön Kongtrul also calls him Serdokpa Dön-yö Pal (*gSer mdog pa don yod dpal*). See n. 721.

790 Chapter 11, verse 11d. Dg.T. Beijing 60:590 reads *shes bya* ***thugs su chud***; *TOK*, II:541.2 has *shes bya* ***thams cad mkhyen***.

791 Legends of wish-fulfilling gems (*chintāmaṇi, yid bzhin gyi nor bu*) and wish-granting trees (*kalpataru/ kalpa-vṛikṣha, dpag bsam gyi shing*) were well known in ancient India.

792 Chapter 11, verse 18. Toh. 3861, f. 216b5–6.

793 This point is discussed on p. 229.

794 *Yuktiṣhaṣhṭikā, Rigs pa drug bcu pa*, by Nāgārjuna, verse 35ab. Toh. 3825; Dg.T. Beijing 57:54. The translation follows Dg.T. Beijing: ***rgyal ba rnams kyis gang*** *gsungs pa; TOK*, II:542.5: ***gang tshe sangs rgyas rnams*** *gsungs pa.*

795 Verse 390ab. See Fuchs 2000, 289.

796 The three spheres (*trimaṇḍala, 'khor gsum*) are agent, object, and action.

797 The one hundred [and eight] concepts related to percepts and perceivers (*gzung 'dzin gyi rnam rtog brgya rtsa brgyad*) are grouped into four sets of nine: (1) nine concepts related to percepts concerned with afflictive phenomena (*kun nas nyon mongs gzung rtog*); (2) nine concepts related to percepts concerned with purified phenomena (*rnam byang gzung rtog*); (3) nine concepts related to apprehending perceivers as substantially existent persons (*rdzas yod kyi gang zag du 'dzin pa'i 'dzin rtog*); and (4) nine concepts related to apprehending perceivers as imputedly existent beings (*btags yod kyi skyes bur 'dzin pa'i 'dzin rtog*). These thirty-six concepts pertain to each of the three realms, making 108 concepts. For a complete list and discussion, see the *Ornament of Clear Realization* and its commentaries.

798 Verse 35ab. Dg.T. Beijing 96:291 reads *ji srid phung por 'dzin yod* ***par***/ *de srid de la ngar 'dzin yod; TOK*, II:542.11: *ji srid phung por 'dzin yod* ***pa.***

799 See also Brunnhölzl 2004, 421–38; Padmakara Translation Group 2002, 310–14; and Lopez 1988a.

800 Chapter 11, verse 45c.

801 A garuda stūpa (*mkha' lding gi mchod sdong*) is another example of an inanimate object that is of benefit to beings. Once in ancient India during an outbreak of leprosy, a master built stūpas with images of garudas on them. He recited the appropriate mantras and made aspirations that these stūpas would cure all lepers who circumambulated them, and, as a result, all those afflicted with leprosy who circumambulated those stūpas were cured. (ALTG)

802 I was unable to locate this exact passage in Āryadeva's texts, but a similar one occurs in his *Madhyamaka: Conquering Delusions* (*Madhyamaka-bhramaghāta, dBu ma 'khrul pa 'joms pa*) (Toh. 3850; Dg.T. Beijing 57:849):

> In that way, when one is awake, conventional consciousness
> is not seen since the eye of intelligence has opened
> and the sleep of ignorance has gone.
>
> *de bzhin kun rdzob shes pa dag/ blo gros mig ni bye gyur ching/ mi shes nyid dang bral gyur nas/ sad pa'i tshe na mi gzigs so.*

Compare with *TOK,* II:542.22: *ma rig rmong pa'i gnyid sad na/ 'khor ba 'di dag mi dmigs so.* I am grateful to Karl Brunnhölzl for locating this. Note that this passage is also found in Bhāvaviveka's *Blaze of Reasoning* (see Lindtner 1982).

803 Here, "a later generation of Tibetans" (*bod phyi rabs pa*) specifically means Tsongkhapa Lo-zang Drakpa (*Tsong kha pa blo bzang grags pa*) (1357–1419) and the Geluk school, who are known as the "later Mādhyamikas" (in contrast to the "early Mādhyamikas," which refers to the followers of the Madhyamaka traditions in Tibet prior to the time of Tsongkhapa and to those who continue these traditions). (ALTG)

These eight great, uncommon theses (*thun mong ma yin pa'i dam bca' chen po brgyad*) are Tsongkhapa's "eight difficult points of the Prāsaṅgika-Madhyamaka" (*dbu ma thal 'gyur gyi dka' gnas brgyad*), which he considers to be a summary of the ways in which the Prāsaṅgika system is distinct from other Buddhist philosophical tenets.

The primary sources for these are Tsongkhapa's *Illumination of the Thought* (*dGongs pa rab gsal*); and Gyaltsap Jé's *Notes on the Eight Difficult Points* (*dKa' gnas brgyad kyi zin bris*) (see Ruegg 2002, 139–255); and Gyaltsap Jé's *Aide-Mémoire for the Eight Great Difficult Points of the "Fundamental [Treatise on] the Middle Way"* (*dBu ma'i rtsa ba'i dka' gnas chen po brgyad kyi brjed byang*). In an earlier work, *Essence of Eloquence* (*Legs bshad snying po*), Tsongkhapa presents seven points that distinguish the Prāsaṅgika system (see Thurman 1984, 288–344; and Ruegg 2002, 146–7). For overviews of these eight points, the various lists, and the Geluk works in which they are found, see Cozort 1998, 58–63; and Ruegg 2002, 142–52.

Although each of these primary sources lists eight points, there are some discrepancies between them, and Jamgön Kongtrul's list of eight does not correspond to any of them exactly in terms of content or order. Nevertheless, the elements in his list match those in Tsongkhapa's *Illumination of the Thought* with just one exception: whereas Tsongkhapa's list includes "an uncommon way of positing the three times due to [disintegration being a functioning thing]" (*de'i rgyu mtshan gyis dus gsum gyi 'jog tshul thun mong ma yin pa*), Jamgön Kongtrul's does not. Instead, Jamgön Kongtrul has "the existence of things by way of their own characteristics is not accepted even as a convention" (*tha snyad du'ang rang gi mtshan nyid kyis grub par khas mi len pa*) (A1), which is found in both texts by Gyaltsap Jé (see ACIP S5426).

Jamgön Kongtrul's presentation of these as "four theses associated with refutation and four theses associated with affirmation" (*dgag phyogs kyi dam bca' bzhi/ sgrub phyogs kyi dam bca' bzhi*) is similar to Gyaltsap Jé's comment that these constitute "four theses involving acceptance and four positions involving non-acceptance" (*khas len pa'i dam bca' bzhi dang mi len pa'i dam bca' bzhi*) (see ACIP S5426; and Ruegg 2002, 158).

These points have been the subject of much discussion and, of course, refutation. Numerous Geluk teachers have written on these, ranging from Chang-kya Rolpé Dorjé in his *Beautiful Ornament of Philosophical Tenet Systems* (see Cozort 1998, 429–78) to Jamyang Shepa, who presents a list of sixteen points in eight pairs in his *Great Exposition of Tenets* (see Hopkins 2003, 927–47; and Cozort and Preston 2003, 258–71). Brunnhölzl presents (2004, 557–62) Mikyö Dorjé's assessment of these. Mipham's views are discussed in Pettit 1998, 128–33; and Dreyfus and McClintock 2003, 324–8.

804 For the sake of comparison, the following is a list of Tsongkhapa's enumeration of the eight uncommon theses in his *Illumination of the Thought* (ACIP S5408@124B):

(1-2) [The Prāsaṅgika system] has an uncommon way of refuting an ālaya consciousness that is separate in essence from the six modes of consciousness and reflexive awareness (*tshogs drug las ngo bo tha dad pa'i kun gzhi rnam shes dang rang rig 'gog lugs thun mong ma yin pa*).

(3) It does not accept the use of independently [verifiable] probative arguments to generate [an understanding of] the view of suchness in the mindstream of opponents (*rang rgyud kyi sbyor bas phyir rgol gyi rgyud la de kho na nyid kyi lta ba skyed pa khas mi len pa*).

(4) It is necessary to accept external objects in the same way that cognition is accepted (*shes pa khas len pa bzhin du phyi rol gyi don yang khas blang dgos pa*).

(5) Shrāvakas and pratyekabuddhas realize that entities have no nature (*nyan rang la dngos po rang bzhin med par rtogs pa yod pa*).

(6) Clinging to a self-entity of phenomena is posited as an affliction (*chos kyi bdag 'dzin nyon mongs su 'jog pa*).

(7) Disintegration is a [functioning] thing (*zhig pa dngos po yin pa*).

(8) Therefore, [this system] has an uncommon way of positing the three times (*de'i rgyu mtshan gyis dus gsum gyi 'jog tshul thun mong ma yin pa*).

805 Although it seems that Jamgön Kongtrul regards Mikyö Dorjé's position on these eight points to be mostly the same as Shākya Chokden's (that is, that he rejects seven of the eight points), many present-day Kagyu scholars say that as pedagogical conventions, Mikyö Dorjé agrees with four or five of Tsongkhapa's eight points. Brunnhölzl states (2004, 559):

> There is no question that Karmapa Mikyö Dorjé denies that Consequentialists [Prāsaṅgikas] have a philosophical system of their own, let alone unique distinctive features of such a system. However, his explanations so far also clearly show that, when the points in Tsongkhapa's above lists are understood as mere pedagogic and expedient conventionalities to counteract wrong views from the perspective of others, contrary to what one might expect, the Karmapa in fact agrees with more of these points . . . than he denies.

The four or five points that Mikyö Dorjé agrees with (as conventions) are A1, possibly A3, A4, B2, and B4. Regarding A2, Mikyö Dorjé agrees that independently verifiable reasons are not accepted even as conventions from one's own perspective (i.e., as a Prāsaṅgika), but he does accept their use for others. In his *Chariot of the Dakpo Kagyu Siddhas,* Mikyö Dorjé refutes that B1 (the acceptance of external objects) is an assertion of the Prāsaṅgika system, and refutes the idea of B3 (disintegration is a functioning thing) completely. (ALTG)

Some Kagyu scholars feel that Mikyö Dorjé does not make a clear statement about A3 (to them, it seems that he accepts reflexive awareness on the level of no analysis), while others say that since he is a Prāsaṅgika he does not accept reflexive awareness even as a convention (because Prāsaṅgikas only cite what is commonly acknowledged in the world as their presentation of conventional reality, and reflexive awareness is only posited by philosophical systems).

806 This section is drawn in part from Tāranātha's *Essence of Shentong* (*gZhan stong snying po*), 182.1–.6. See Hopkins 2007, 77–8.

807 The Dharma Treatises of the exalted Maitreya (*Byams pa'i chos sde*) are the following five texts: (1) *Ornament of Clear Realization* (*Abhisamayālaṃkāra; mNgon rtogs rgyan*); (2) *Ornament of the Mahāyāna Sūtras* (*Mahāyānasūtrālaṃkāra, Theg pa chen po mdo sde rgyan*); (3) *Differentiation of the Middle and the Extremes* (*Madhyāntavibhaṅga, dBus mtha' rnam 'byed*); (4) *Differentiation of Phenomena and Their Nature* (*Dharmadharmatāvibhaṅga, Chos dang chos nyid rnam 'byed*); and (5) *Highest Continuum* (*Mahāyānottaratantrashāstra, Theg pa chen po rgyud bla ma'i bstan bcos*).

This is the order in which Maitreya taught these texts to Asaṅga according to Jamgön Kongtrul's *Irrepressible Lion's Roar: A Commentary on the Highest Continuum* (*rGyud bla ma'i 'grel pa phyir mi ldog pa seng ge'i nga ro,* hereafter cited as *Irrepressible Lion's Roar*) (2005, 6–7). For a history of the transmission of these texts and their translation into Tibetan, see Jamgön Kongtrul's Introduction in his *Irrepressible Lion's Roar* (2005, 4–10); Hookham 1991, 266–72; Roerich 1949, 347–50; and Book Four, Part One (*TOK*, I:407–10).

808 In addition to recording Maitreya's Dharma Treatises, Asaṅga wrote *An Explanation of the "Highest Continuum"* (*Mahāyānottaratantra-shāstra-vyākhyā, Theg pa chen po rgyud bla ma'i bstan bcos rnam par bshad pa*). Vasubandhu wrote *An Explanation of the "Ornament of the Mahāyāna Sūtras"* (*Sūtrālaṃkāra-vyākhyā, mDo sde'i rgyan gyi bshad pa*); *A Commentary on the "Differentiation of the Middle and the Extremes"* (*Madhyāntavibhaṅga-ṭīkā, dBus dang mtha' rnam par 'byed pa'i 'grel pa*); and *A Commentary on the "Differentiation of Phenomena and Their Nature"* (*Dharmadharmatāvibhaṅga-vṛitti, Chos dang chos nyid rnam par 'byed pa'i 'grel pa*).

809 Jamgön Kongtrul makes a similar statement in his *Irrepressible Lion's Roar* (8): "The general philosophical tenet system of the definitive-meaning Madhyamaka and three Dharma Treatises of Maitreya were spread widely by many excellent disciple lineages, such as [those originating with] Dignāga and Sthiramati. Because it was difficult for others to fathom, the uncommon [philosophical tenet system of] these [texts of Maitreya] was transmitted orally to supreme disciples, and the texts of the *Highest Continuum* and *Differentiation of Phenomena and Their Nature* were hidden as treasures. Thus, the two Ornaments and the *Differentiation of the Middle and the Extremes* were translated and explained by Lotsāwa Pal-tsek (*Lo tsā ba dPal brtsegs*) and Shang Yeshé Dé (*Zhang ye shes sde*) during the period of the early spreading [of the dharma]." See also Hookham 1991, 269–70.

Sthiramati (*Blo gros brtan pa*) (ca. 470–550) was one of Vasubandhu's main students, who wrote ten texts that are included in the Tengyur, including commentaries on the *Ornament of the Mahāyāna Sūtras, Differentiation of Phenomena and Their Nature,* and works by Vasubandhu.

810 Zu Gawé Dorjé (*gZus dga' ba'i rdo rje*) was an eleventh-century translator who studied with the great Kashmiri paṇḍita Sajjana (or Sañjana). He wrote a commentary on the *Highest Continuum* according to the teachings of Sajjana and an explanation of the *Differentiation of Phenomena and Their Nature.* See *Irrepressible Lion's Roar,* pp. 8–9; and see also n. 811.

811 Tsen Kawoché (*bTsan kha bo che*) (b. 1021) was a translator who studied the five Dharma Treatises of Maitreya with the Kashmiri paṇḍita Sajjana (or Sañjana). According to Jamgön Kongtrul's *Irrepressible Lion's Roar* (8–10), Maitrīpa recovered the *Highest Continuum* and *Differentiation of Phenomena and Their Nature* and transmitted all five treatises to the paṇḍita Ānandakīrti, who taught them to the Kashmiri paṇḍita Sajjana. When Tsen Kawoché received these teachings from Sajjana, Zu Gawé Dorjé served as the translator. The line of transmission that ensued from Tsen Kawoché and Zu Gawé Dorjé is known as "the meditative tradition of Maitreya's Dharma Treatises," and is differentiated from the line of transmission that passed from the paṇḍita Sajjana to Ngok Lotsāwa Loden Sherab (*rNgog lo tsā ba blo ldan shes rab*), known as "the tradition of hearing and reflection." The Kagyu and Nyingma traditions have relied more on the meditative tradition of Tsen Kawoché and Zu Gawé Dorjé, whereas the exegetical tradition of Ngok Lotsāwa has been maintained in the Geluk system.

Some of Tsen Kawoché's teachings were preserved by the Jonang master Kunga Drolchok (*Kun dga' grol mchog*) (1507–1566) in his *Instructions on the Shentong View* (*gZhan stong gi lta khrid*). Stearns (1999, 88) says, "Tsen Kawoché . . . is often thought to be the first Tibetan to have taught what later came to be known as the Zhentong view." See Stearns 1999, 42–3 and 88–9; and Roerich 1949, 347–8.

812 Yumo Mikyö Dorjé (*Yu mo mi bskyod rdo rje*) (b. 1027) was a Kālachakra master and student of the Kashmiri paṇḍita Somanātha (*Zla ba mgon po*). He is considered a forefather of the Jonang tradition. He wrote a recently recovered set of four texts called The Four Bright Lamps (*gSal sgron skor bzhi*), which discuss the completion stage practices of the Kālachakra system (the six branches of union). According to Stearns (1999, 44) these texts discuss "some of the same themes that Dolpopa later elaborated," without using the key terms, such as "empty of other" (*gzhan stong*). Nevertheless, Tāranātha states that Yumo Mikyö Dorjé "was the founder of the Mantra-Shentong philosophical tenet system" (*sngags kyi gzhan stong grub mtha'i srol ka phye*) (*Requisite Sources for the Dharma Cycle of the Glorious Kālachakra, dPal dus kyi 'khor lo'i chos bskor gyi byung khungs nyer mkho*, II:8.2).

Stearns also points out (1999, 44) that "the Geluk master Thukan Lozang Chögyi Nyima (1737–1802) much later states in *A Crystal Mirror of Philosophical Systems* (*Grub mtha' shel gyi me long*) that Yumowa was the originator of the Shentong teachings, which he so named, and that they were passed down orally until the time of Dolpopa as a hidden doctrine (*lkog pa'i chos*) without any written texts."

813 Rangjung Dorjé (*Rang byung rdo rje*) (1284–1339) was the third Karmapa and author of many famous works on tathāgatagarbha, Kālachakra Tantra, Dzogchen, and Vajrayāna, including *The Profound Inner Reality* (*Zab mo nang don*). For some discussion of the differences between Rangjung Dorjé's Shentong view and Dolpopa's, see Mathes 2004, 288–94. It is clear from Rangjung Dorjé's writings that he regarded the systems that developed from Nāgārjuna and Maitreya (which are now being called Rangtong-Madhyamaka and Shentong-Madhyamaka, respectively) to be equal. See a quotation from Rangjung Dorjé in Book Seven, Part Two (*TOK*, III:24) and Brunnhölzl's (2007) work on Rangjung Dorjé.

814 Omniscient Drimé Özer (*Kun mkhyen dri med 'od zer*), also known as Longchen Rabjam (*kLong chen rab 'byams*) (1308–1364), was one of the greatest Nyingma masters and author of many works, including the Seven Treasuries (*mDzod bdun*). For a bibliography, see Thondup 1996, 109–17. For some points on the relationship of Longchenpa's teachings to Shentong, see Stearns 1999, 51–2.

815 Dolpopa Sherab Gyaltsen (*Dol po pa shes rab rgyal mtshan*) (1292–1361) is generally considered to be the first to use the terms "Shentong" (*gzhan stong*) and "Rangtong" (*rang stong*) extensively. For an excellent overview of Dolpopa's proclamation of Shentong as the highest expression of the Madhyamaka view, see Stearns 1999, 45–55.

For a survey of the Shentong tradition in Tibet, see Stearns 1999, 41–77; for use of the term "Shentong" prior to Dolpopa, see Stearns 1999, 42–5 and 50–1. See also Kapstein 1992a, 23–4; Kapstein 2000a, 106–19; Mathes 2004, 285–328; and Hopkins 2006.

816 For differences between Shākya Chokden's Shentong views and Dolpopa's, see Tāranātha's *Twenty-one [Differences Regarding] the Profound Meaning* (*Zab don nyer gcig pa/ Zab don khyad par nyer gcig pa*, hereafter cited as *Twenty-one Differences*), trans. Mathes 2004, 294–310; and Hopkins 2007, 117–36. See also n. 721.

817 Tāranātha (*sGrol ba'i mgon po*) (1575–1634) is the most famous Jonang teacher after Dolpopa and one of the major sources for Jamgön Kongtrul's presentation of Shentong-Madhyamaka. Additionally, Taranatha was a Kālachakra master, one of the last major Tibetan translators of Vajrayāna texts from Sanskrit, and he wrote a well-known history of Buddhism (*History of Buddhism in India,* Chimpa and Chattopadhyaya 1970). For further material relating to Tāranātha's Shentong views, see Mathes 2000 and 2004; and Hopkins 2007.

818 Shākya Chokden states this perspective in his *Great Path of the Nectar of Emptiness* (*sTong nyid bdud rtsi'i lam po che*, hereafter cited as *Nectar of Emptiness*) (179.2) as follows:

> To summarize, the view expressed by Asaṅga does not differ in terms of its essence; there are, however, two contexts in which the philosophical tenets [found in the Treatises of Maitreya] are incompatible. The expositions of the thought of the first Dharma Treatises of Maitreya state that ultimately there are three yānas, and they do not make any mention of a bhūmi on which the habitual tendency of ignorance is present or that birth can take place through undefiled karma. The expositions of the thought of the *Highest Continuum* are the opposite.
>
> *mdor na thogs med zhabs kyis bzhad ba'i lta ba rang gi ngo bo la khyad par med kyang/ grub mtha'i mi mthun pa'i skags gnyis byung ste/ byams pa'i chos dang po rnams kyi dgongs pa 'grel ba na mthar thug gi theg pa gsum yin pa dang/ ma rig bag chags kyi sa dang zag med kyi las kyis skye ba len pa zhes bya ba'i bshad pa mi mdzad la/ rgyud bla ma'i dgongs pa 'grel ba na ni/ snga ma las zlog ste bshad pas so.*

Note that Shākya Chokden says "the first Dharma Treatises of Maitreya," not "the first three" (*byams chos dang po gsum*) as Jamgön Kongtrul does. This may indicate that Jamgön Kongtrul bases his statement of Shākya Chokden's position on Tāranātha's *Twenty-one Differences*. There Tāranātha says (211.5–212.3) that the second difference between Shākya Chokden and Dolpopa is that Shākya Chokden considers the *Ornament of Clear Realization* to teach both Rangtong and Shentong tenet systems, and that the remaining four Dharma Treatises of Maitreya teach only Shentong. These four have two [exegetical] modes: (1) The *Highest Continuum* teaches that ultimately there is one yāna and that a cut-off potential (*rigs chad*) is refuted. (2) The other three treatises [*Ornament of the Mahāyāna Sūtras, Differentiation of the Middle and the Extremes,* and *Differentiation of Phenomena and Their Nature*] teach that ultimately there are three yānas and that there is a cut-off potential. See Mathes 2004, 297; and Hopkins 2007, 121.

This is in contrast to Dolpopa's view that all five Dharma Treatises teach only Shentong (see p. 251 and n. 823).

819 The translation follows PKTC reading ***'chad** tshul; TOK,* II:544.14 has ***'char** tshul.*

820 The *Highest Continuum* teaches that arhats who have attained nirvāṇa without remainder still have the potential (*nus pa*) for ignorance, even though they have abandoned ignorance. They are said to dwell on the bhūmi with the habitual tendencies of ignorance (*ma rig bag chags kyi sa*), since they have only abandoned afflicted ignorance but not unafflicted ignorance (see n. 645). The *Highest Continuum* explains that arhats will enter the Mahāyāna path, and that they do so by taking birth in a mental body through the force of undefiled karma (*zag med las kyi skye ba*

len pa). This is stated in the Fifth Vajra Point, verse 225. See Fuchs 2000, 209 and Khenpo Tsültrim's explanation in annotation 26, 344.

The *Highest Continuum* also teaches that bodhisattvas on the impure bhūmis (the first bhūmi through the seventh) dwell on the bhūmi with the habitual tendencies of ignorance and take birth through undefiled karma. The main support (*gzhi*) for their taking rebirth is their habitual tendencies of ignorance, but that is not the impetus (*nus pa*) for taking rebirth; they take rebirth through the strength of their previous aspiration prayers (*smon lam*) and their samādhi. When bodhisattvas reach the three pure bhūmis (the eighth bhūmi through the tenth), they continue to take rebirth through undefiled karma.

821 Reading *thos bsam* ***gyis*** *spros pa gcod pa,* instead of *TOK,* II:544.18: *thos bsam* ***gyi*** *spros pa gcod pa.*

822 Sugatagarbha ("heart of those gone to bliss") (*bde bar gshegs pa'i snying po*) is also translated as "buddha nature." On the meaning of *garbha* (heart; essence; or seed), Tāranātha says (*Essence of Shentong,* 187.3) that *garbha* (*snying po*) means "what resides within and is hidden" (*khong na gnas pa dang sbas pa*) and is "unchanging" (*mi 'gyur ba*). Brunnhölzl says (2004, 865n189), "In its original meaning, the Sanskrit term *garbha* signifies the space within some enclosure or sheath (it also came to mean "embryo," "seed," and, later, "essence"). Ruegg states (1995, 167 and 170) that *garbha* is interpreted in the Indian and Tibetan traditions as seed or embryo, whereas the Sino-Japanese tradition understands it as womb (*tsang*).

823 This is a paraphrase of Tāranātha's statement concerning Dolpopa's view. It is the second point of difference in the *Twenty-one Differences* (212.2): "The five Dharma Treatises of Maitreya do not contain different tenets at all. The tenets of what is known as Rangtong are not explained even in The *Ornament of Clear Realization.* The *Ornament of the Sūtras* and the others do not explain that there is an eternal cut-off potential or that ultimately there are three yānas" (*byams chos sde lnga la grub mtha' so so ba ye med/ rang stong par grags pa'i grub mtha' mngon rgyan nas kyang ma bshad/ mdo rgyan sogs nas kyang/ gtan nas rigs chad pa dang mthar thug theg gsum ma bshad*). (See Mathes 2004, 297–8; and Hopkins 2007, 121.)

Compare with *TOK,* II:545.5–7: *byams chos sde lnga kar lta ba mi 'dra ba med/ rang stong gi lta ba mgnon rgyan nas ma bshad/ mthar thug theg gsum dang rigs chad gang du'ang 'chad pa med.*

For some discussion of Tāranātha's interpretation of the cut-off potential presented in the *Ornament of the Mahāyāna Sūtras* (Chapter 4, verse 11), see Mathes 2000, 218.

824 This paragraph is a paraphrase of a section in Shākya Chokden's *Establishing the Unity of the Definitive Meaning* (*Nges don gcig tu bsgrub pa,* hereafter cited as *Unity of the Definitive Meaning*), 538.2–.4.

Elsewhere in his *Unity of the Definitive Meaning,* Shākya Chokden states (588.2): "Later Tibetans say the view of the three middle Treatises of Maitreya is that of the Chittamātra" (*bod phyi ma na re/ byams chos bar pa gsum gyi lta ba sems tsam du gnas pa yin te*).

825 See Chapter 6, pp. 186–190; and Chapter 6, nn. 562, 565, and 577.

826 *Unity of the Definitive Meaning,* 538.5–9.4. The opening sentence of the citation is slightly different, but the translation follows *TOK* because it seems that Jamgön Kongtrul intentionally simplified it. *TOK,* II:545.14: *rgyud bla ma'i lta ba sems tsam gyi lta ba yin par 'dod na.*

Compare with *Unity of the Definitive Meaning,* 538.5: *byams chos phyi ma nas bstan pa'i lta ba 'di grub mtha' smra ba bzhir phye ba'i sems tsam gyi lta ba yin par 'dod na,* "Those who assert that the view taught in the last Dharma Treatise of Maitreya is the Chittamātra view that is one of the four basic philosophical tenet systems . . ."

827 The translation follows *Unity of the Definitive Meaning,* 539.1 reading *mang po* ***dag***; *TOK,* II:546.2 has *mang po* ***dang***.

828 The four Synopses (*bsDu ba bzhi*) by Asaṅga are *Synopsis of Ascertainment* (*Nirṇayasaṃgraha, gTan la dbab pa bsdu ba*); *Synopsis of Bases* (*Vastusaṃgraha, gZhi bsdu ba*); *Synopsis of Enumerations* (*Paryāyasaṃgraha, rNam grangs bsdu ba*); and *Synopsis of Explanations* (*Vivaraṇasaṃgraha, rNam par bshad pa bsdu ba*).

829 The two Compendia (*sDom rnam gnyis*) by Asaṅga are *Compendium of Abhidharma* (*Abhidharmasamuchchaya, mNgon pa kun btus*); and *Compendium of the Mahāyāna* (*Mahāyāna-saṃgraha, Theg pa chen po bsdus pa*).

830 This section is from Tāranātha's *Essence of Shentong* (182.6–187.3), with a few modifications, which are noted. (The root verses are Jamgön Kongtrul's composition.) See Hopkins 2007, 78–92. For an analysis of Tāranātha's interpretation of the three natures in his *Essence of Shentong,* see Mathes 2000.

831 *Madhyāntavibhaṅga, dBus mtha' rnam 'byed,* by Maitreya. Chapter 1, verses 1–2. Toh. 4021, f. 40a2–3; Dg.T. Beijing 70:902. See Anacker 1984/1998, 212–3; Hopkins 1999, 182–93 and 305–12; Hopkins 2002, 342–7, and 2007, 78–80 (which compare Tāranātha's reading of this verse with Tsongkhapa's interpretation); Kochumuttom 1982, 235–6; and Mathes 2000, 197–207.

832 The bracketed words are based on Vasubandhu's explanation in his *Commentary on the "Differentiation of the Middle and the Extremes"* (*Madhyāntavibhaṅga-ṭīkā, dBus dang mtha' rnam par 'byed pa'i 'grel pa*). Toh. 4027; Dg.T. Beijing 71:4. Vasubandhu comments on the first three lines of verse 2 (the order of the first two lines are reversed in the translation) as follows:

> "Not empty" refers to emptiness and the imagination of what is unreal. "Not non-empty" refers to duality, that is, percept and perceiver. "All" refers to what is called "the imagination of what is unreal" (which is the conditioned) and to "emptiness" (the unconditioned). "Exists" refers to the imagination of what is unreal; "not exist," duality; and "exists," the imagination of what is unreal existing within emptiness and that [emptiness] also existing within the imagination of what is unreal.
>
> *stong pa ma yin zhes bya ba ni stong pa nyid dang yang dag pa ma yin pa kun tu rtog pas so/ mi stong min zhes bya ba ni/ gnyis pa ste/ gzung ba dang 'dzin pas so/ thams cad ces bya ba ni yang dag pa ma yin pa kun tu rtog pa zhes bya ba 'dus byas dang stong pa zhes bya ba 'dus ma byas so/ yod pas zhes bya ba ni yang dag pa ma yin pa kun tu rtog pa'o/ med pas zhes bya ba ni gnyis pa'o/ yod pas na zhes bya ba ni yang dag pa ma yin kun tu rtog pa la stong pa nyid yod pa dang/ de la yang yang dag pa ma yin pa kun tu rtog pa yod pa'o.*

For discussion of the term "imagination of what is unreal" (*abhūtaparikalpa, yang dag ma yin pa'i kun rtog*), see n. 532.

833 The *Essence of Shentong* (183.1) has *kun rdzob* ***bden pa gtan la 'bebs*** *pa'i dbang du byas nas,* "From the perspective of ascertaining conventional reality . . ." The translation follows *TOK,* II:546.21: ***dang po*** *kun rdzob* ***kyi spros pa gcod*** *pa'i dbang du byas nas.*

834 In other words, conventional reality is free from the extreme of permanence because superimposed, mutually dependent phenomena do not exist conventionally.

835 "That which bears reality" (or "something possessing a quality") (*dharmin, chos can*) is a term used to indicate that phenomena possess the quality (*chos*) of dharmatā (*chos nyid*), i.e., their reality or true nature, emptiness. Sometimes this term is simply translated as "phenomenon."

836 The *Differentiation of the Middle and Extremes* discusses the status of the three natures in Chapter 3. For example, verse 3 states:

> The three natures are [respectively] always nonexistent,
> existent but not suchness,
> and the existent and nonexistent suchness.
> [That is how] the three natures are asserted [to be].
>
> *ngo bo nyid gsum rtag med dang/ yod kyang kho na ma yin dang/ yod dang med de kho na ste/ ngo bo nyid ni gsum du 'dod.* Dg.T. Beijing 70:906.

Also Chapter 3, verse 7ab says:

> [The three natures are respectively] the emptiness of the nonexistent,
> the emptiness of what does not exist [as it appears to be], and the natural emptiness.
>
> *dngos med de dngos ma yin dang/ rang bzhin gyis ni stong par 'dod.* Dg.T. Beijing 70:907.

See Anacker 1984/1998, 232–4.

837 Chapter 15, verse 34.

838 Inherent absence (*niḥsvabhāva, ngo bo nyid med pa*) is presented in the *Sūtra Unraveling the Intention* (*Saṃdhinirmochanasūtra, dGongs pa nges par 'grel pa*), Chapter 7; see Powers 1995, 98–105. It is also found in Asaṅga's *Compendium of Abhidharma*, Chapter 4; see Boin-Webb 2001, 193. This term is also translated as "non-nature," "absence of own-being," or "lack of nature." See also Khenpo Tsültrim Gyamtso 1986; Mathes 2000, 215–7; Hopkins 2002, 103; and Brunnhölzl 2004, 470.

Imagined characteristics do not exist by way of their own characteristics. The nature that they do not have is to be existent by way of their own characteristics.

839 Dependent characteristics do not arise on their own. Thus, the nature they do not have is to come into being in and of themselves, because they arise in dependence on numerous causes and conditions.

840 The consummate nature is the ultimate because it is transmundane primordial wisdom (*'jig rten las 'das pa'i ye shes*). It is inherent absence, or non-nature, in that it is the nature that is devoid of percepts and perceivers (*yongs su grub pa'i ngo bo nyid de/ de bas na gzung ba dang 'dzin pa med pa'i ngo bo nyid yin pa'i phyir ngo bo nyid med pa'o*). Sthiramati's *Sub-Commentary on the "Thirty Verses"* (*Triṃshikaṭīkā, Sum cu pa'i 'grel bshad*); Dg.T. Beijing 78:133–4.

841 This citation is almost identical to the widely quoted twenty-third verse in Vasubandhu's *Thirty Verses* (*Triṃshikākārikā, Sum bcu pa*). Toh. 4055; Dg.T. Beijing 77:55.

The translation follows Dg.T. Beijing 77:55: *ngo bo nyid ni rnam gsum* ***gyis****/ ngo bo nyid med rnam gsum la/* ***dgongs*** *nas chos rnams thams cad* ***kyi/ ngo bo nyid med*** *bstan pa yin. TOK,* II:549.1–3: *ngo bo nyid ni rnam gsum* ***gyi****/ ngo bo nyid med rnam gsum la/* ***brten*** *nas chos rnams thams cad* ***la/ rang bzhin med par*** *bstan pa yin,* "On the basis of the three types of inherent absence of the three kinds of natures, it is taught that all phenomena have no nature."

842 This ends Jamgön Kongtrul's quotation from *Essence of Shentong.* In this last section there are a number of small but sometimes significant differences. I have followed Jamgön Kongtrul because all his changes seem quite deliberate. Note the following differences:

TOK, II:549.8: After *ngo bo nyid med pas khyab par bzhed cing*, three lines of *Essence of Shentong* (185.4–.7) are omitted. See Hopkins 2007, 89–92.

TOK, II:549.11: After *'di ni* the following is added: *kun rdzob kyi chos de rnams gang dang yang ma 'brel ba ste*, ". . . has no connection to any such conventional phenomena."

TOK, II:549.14: *phyogs dus* ***sogs spros pa*** *thams cad dang bral ba'****i phyir rang bzhin gyis rtag pa*** ("since . . . [the consummate nature] is inherently permanent"). *Essence of Shentong*, 186.2: *phyogs dus thams cad dang bral ba/* ***rang gi ngo bos kun rdzob kyi chos nyid dang ma 'brel ba yin no***, "In terms of its very nature, [the consummate nature] does not involve the dharmatā of conventionality."

TOK, II:549.16: ***chos thams cad*** *kyi chos nyid yin pa'i phyir* ("Since it is the dharmatā of all phenomena . . ."). *Essence of Shentong*, 186.2: ***chos nyid*** *kyi chos nyid yin pa'i phyir*, "Since it is the dharmatā of dharmatā . . ." Hopkins (2007, 92nc) notes that the Smanrtsis Shes rig Dpemzod edition reads the same as *TOK*: ***chos thams cad*** *kyi chos nyid.*

843 The topics connected to the ground are the two truths; those relating to the path are the six pāramitās, five paths, and ten bhūmis; and those related to the result are buddhahood with its three kāyas. The two truths are presented in Book Seven, Part Two; the pāramitās are presented in Chapter 5 of this book; the paths and bhūmis are the topics of Book Nine, Part One; and fruition of Book Ten, Part One.

844 Subsequent state of attainment (*pṛiṣhṭhalabdha, rjes thob*): see n. 747.

845 Inanimate emptiness (*kanthāshūnya, bem stong*) means the emptiness or nonexistence of matter, a nothingness (*ci yang med pa*) with no sentience.

846 190.6–192.4. See Hopkins 2007, 102–10.

847 This seems to be a paraphrase of the passage in the *Descent into Laṅkā Sūtra.* See ACIP KL0107@136A; and Suzuki 1932, 69.

848 Tīrthikas ("forders") (*mu stegs pa*) is a term used for non-Buddhist spiritual practitioners in India. Jamgön Kongtrul explains that it means that they remain at the edge (*mu*) of, or on a rung (*stegs*) to, liberation; that is, they approach liberation, but they are not on the path to the true nirvāṇa (Book Six, Part One; *TOK*, II:335).

849 The Fourth Vajra Point, verse 28. The full verse reads:

> Because the primordial wisdom of buddha[hood] is present in all sentient beings,
> [because] the stainless nature is nondual,
> and because the buddha-potential is named after its result,
> all beings are said to possess the buddha-*garbha* (heart).

> *sangs rgyas ye shes sems can tshogs zhugs phyir/ rang bzhin dri med de ni gnyis med de/*
> *sangs rgyas rigs la de 'bras nyer brtags phyir/ 'gro kun sangs rgyas snying po can du gsungs.*

850 "The strength of knowing what is the case and what is not the case" (*gnas dang gnas ma yin pa mkhyen pa'i stobs*) is one of the ten strengths (*stobs bcu*), which are part of the dharmakāya's thirty-two excellent qualities of separation (*bral ba'i yon tan*). See n. 479.

851 The scriptural traditions of the two great chariot[-systems] (*shing rta'i chen po gnyis kyi gzhung lugs*) are those of Nāgārjuna and Asaṅga.

852 Nāgārjuna's system emphasizes from the "outer," or objective, side, that the ultimate nature is emptiness, whereas Maitreya and Asaṅga's system emphasizes from the "inner," or subjective, side, that the ultimate nature is nondual primordial wisdom. (ALTG)

853 *Nectar of Emptiness*, 206.3–.5.

854 *Nectar of Emptiness*, 172.6–175.

855 See n. 592.

856 Nāgārjuna's Collection of Praises (*bsTod pa'i tshogs*) includes a number of texts, such as *Praises of the Dharmadhātu* (*Dharmadhātustava, Chos dbyings bstod pa*) and *Praises of the Vajra of Mind* (*Chittavajra-stava, Sems kyi rdo rje bstod pa*), and the sub-collection called Four Praises (*Chatuḥstava, bsTod pa bzhi pa*), which are *Praises of the Transcendent One* (*Lokātīta-stava, 'Jig rten las 'das pa'i bstod pa*); *Praises of the Incomparable One* (*Nirupama-stava* or *Niraupamyastava, dPe med par bstod pa*); *Praises of the Inconceivable One* (*Achintyastava, bSam gyis mi khyab par bstod pa*); and *Praises of the Ultimate* (*Paramārtha-stava, Don dam par bstod pa*). See Lindtner 1986, 236.

857 Āryavimuktisena wrote *A Commentary on the "Ornament of Clear Realization"* (*Abhisamayālaṃkāra-vṛitti, mNgon par rtogs pa'i rgyan gyi 'grel pa*). See also n. 699.

858 Haribhadra wrote the *Illumination of the "Ornament of Clear Realization"* (*Abhisamayālaṃkārālokā, mNgon rtogs pa'i rgyan gyi snang ba*). See also n. 700.

859 Abhayākaragupta (*'Jigs med 'byung gnas sbas pa*) (late eleventh to early twelfth century) resided at Vikramashīla. His *Ornament of Clear Realization* commentary is called *Moonlight of Key Points* (*Marmakaumudī, gNad kyi zla 'od*). He also wrote over thirty works that are included in the Tengyur and collaborated on the translation of over one hundred texts. Some of his more well-known writings are *Kernels of Key Instructions* (*Upadesha-mañjarī, Man ngag snye ma*), a commentary on the *Sampuṭa-mahātantra* (a shared explanatory tantra), and *Ornament of the Sage's Thought* (*Munimatālaṃkāra, Thub pa'i dgongs pa'i rgyan*), an encyclopedic work on Mahāyāna Buddhism. See Ruegg 1981, 114-5.

860 Dharmapāla (*Chos skyong*) (530–561) was a Yogāchāra master who resided at Nālandā. Tāranātha states (Chimpa and Chattopadhyaya 1970, 213) that he was a student of Dignāga, whereas modern scholars believe "he may have been a grand-pupil of Dignāga" (see Tillemans 1990, 8). In addition to his commentaries on the works of Vasubandhu and Dignāga, his major contributions are his defense of the Yogāchāra positions in his commentary on Āryadeva's *Four Hundred Verses* (Chapter 10), written in response to Bhāvaviveka's *Lamp of Wisdom*, and his influence on the Chinese scholar Hsüan-Tsang's work on Yogāchāra, *Chéng wéi shí lùn*. None of Dharmapāla's works were translated from Sanskrit into Tibetan but they are preserved in Chinese translations (however his commentary on *Ornament of Clear Realization* does not seem to have been translated into Chinese). See Tillemans 1990, 8–13; and Brunnhölzl 2004, 492–4.

861 *Fundamental Treatise on the Middle Way,* Chapter 24, verse 18. Note the following differences: Dg.T. Beijing is: *de ni brten nas* ***gdags*** *pa ste/ de* ***nyid*** *dbu ma'i lam yin no; TOK,* II:554.16: *de ni brten nas* ***brtags*** *pa ste/ de* ***ni*** *dbu ma'i lam yin no.*

862 Chapter 1, verse 2cd. See above n. 832.

863 Chapter 11, verse 55ab.

864 The translation follows *TOK,* II:555.6 reading *dbang* ***tha ma'i*** *lta bar bshad pa'i phyir* ("a view for those of lesser acumen"); *Nectar of Emptiness* (174.4) has *dbang* ***za ba'i*** *lta bar bshad pa'i phyir* ("a pretentious view"). This is probably a deliberate change by Jamgön Kongtrul, not a spelling mistake. (ALTG)

865 *TOK,* II:555.7: ***des*** *don* should be ***nges*** *don.* (See *Nectar of Emptiness,* 174.5.)

866 Jamgön Kongtrul refers to the source of this quotation as *Establishing the Unity of the Two Modes* (*Tshul gnyis gcig sgrub*). Since this citation is found verbatim in Shākya Chokden's *Establishing the Unity of the Definitive Meaning* (585.4–589.1), obviously "*Establishing the Unity*" (*gcig sgrub*) refers to that text.

Tāranātha wrote a text called *Entry to the Definitive Meaning: Distinguishing the Two Modes* (*Tshul gnyis rnam par 'byed pa nges pa'i don gyi 'jug ngogs*), which sets out the differences between the Rangtong and Shentong systems. The text begins by distinguishing how Rangtong and Shentong proponents regard the Yogāchāra scriptural system. There Tāranātha refers to the Yogāchāra scriptural system as that of the Proponents of Cognition (Vijñaptivādins), which for Shentong proponents is not synonymous with Chittamātras (as Tāranātha explains). Thus, I take "*Two Modes*" (*tshul gnyis*) as referring to this work by Tāranātha. (For another citation where Tāranātha uses the term Vijñapti[vādins] in connection with Shentong and Madhyamaka, see n. 630.)

On the other hand, it could be that *Establishing the Unity of the Two Modes* should be *Establishing the Unity of the Two Traditions* (*Srol gnyis gcig bsgrub*), which may be an alternative short title for Shākya Chokden's work derived from its full title: *An Extensive Commentary on the Treatise Establishing the Unity of the Definitive Meaning Through the Explanation of the Distinction Between the Two Traditions of the Great Charioteers* (*Shing rta chen po'i srol gnyis kyi rnam par dbye ba bshad nas nges don gcig tu bsgrub pa'i bstan bcos kyi rgyas 'grel*). In that case, the translation should read, ". . . as is discussed in detail in the *Establishing the Unity of the Two Modes.*"

867 Chapter 5, verse 19ab. Note that the first line should read *chos kyi dbyings* ***ni*** *ma gtogs pa'i; TOK,* II:556.10: *chos kyi dbyings* ***las*** *ma gtogs pa'i.*

868 This quotation is found in the *Compendium of the Mahāyāna.* See Dg.T. Beijing 76:7; and Keenan 1992, 15. See n. 527.

869 Part One, Chapter 8, verse 41cd.

870 This quotation is almost identical to lines in the *Vajrapañjarā* (*rDo rje gur*), Chapter 6: "Outside of the precious mind, there are no buddhas and no persons" (*rin chen sems las phyir gyur pa'i/ sang rgyas med cing* ***gang zag*** *med*) (Dg.K. 419, f. 44.4). *TOK,* II:556.13: *rin chen sems las phyir gyur pa'i/ sang rgyas med cing* ***sems can*** *med.*

871 The *Sūtra on Ultimate Emptiness* (*Paramārthashūnyatā-sūtra, Don dam pa stong nyid kyi mdo*) is not found in the Kangyur, but there are two sūtras with similar names: *Great Sūtra on Emptiness* (*Shūnyatā-nāma-mahāsūtra, mDo chen po stong pa nyid*) (Toh. 290) and *Great Sūtra on Great Emptiness* (*Mahāshūnyatā-nāma-mahāsūtra, mDo chen po stong pa nyid chen po*) (Toh. 291). A similar and often-quoted passage is found in the *Great Sūtra on Emptiness* (Dg.K., vol. Sha, 153a.1):

Ānanda, it is like this: It is correctly seen that the absence of one thing in something else is [that latter thing's] emptiness of that [first thing]. What remains there exists there. Know this to be correct and exactly how it is.

kun dga' bo de lta bas na gang la gang med pa de ni stong ngo zhes bya bar yang dag par rjes su mthong yang/ de la lhag ma gang yod pa de de la yod do/ zhes bya bar yang dag pa ji lta ba bzhin du rab tu shes te.

(Note that the phrase "middle way" does not appear in this sūtra in either the Tibetan or the Pāli recensions.)

Compare with *TOK,* II:556.20–23: *gang na gang med pa de ni des stong pa nyid yin la/ 'di la lhag ma gang yin pa de ni 'dir yod pa ste/ 'di ni dbu ma'i lam stong pa nyid la lta ba yang dag pa phyin ci ma log pa'o.*

Both the *Great Sūtra on Emptiness* and *Great Sūtra on Great Emptiness* are found in the Pāli Canon: *The Shorter Discourse on Voidness* (*Cūḷasuññata Sutta*) and *The Greater Discourse on Voidness* (*Mahāsuññata Sutta*) (*Majjhima Nikāya* 121 and 122). See Ñāṇamoli and Bodhi 2005, 965–78.

For a discussion of this passage, its context, and applications, see Nagao 1991, 52–60.

872 *Mādhyamakālaṃkāra, dBu ma rgyan,* by Shāntarakṣhita. The first two lines are not in this text (and have not been located in another text); the last four lines are verse 92. See Padmakara Translation Group 2005, 363.

873 *Kāyatrayāvatāramukha, sKu gsum la 'jug pa'i sgo.* Toh. 3890; Dg.T. Beijing 63:12. According to Tāranātha's *History of Buddhism in India* (Chimpa and Chattopadhyaya 1970, 148 and 151), Nāgamitra (*kLu'i bshes gnyen*) was a student of Rāhulamitra and teacher of Saṅgharakṣhita.

874 *Madhyamakālaṃkāropadesha, dBu ma rgyan gyi man ngag.* Toh. 4085; Dg.T. Beijing 78:604. The translation follows Dg.T. Beijing: *byams pa thogs med kyis* ***gsungs shing/*** *klu sgrub* ***kyis kyang*** *bzhed pa yi/ tshad ma lung dang ldan pa* ***yis/*** *bden pa gnyis 'dir bshad pa bya. TOK,* II:557.7–.8: *byams pa thogs med kyis* ***bshad cing/*** *klu sgrub* ***kyang ni*** *bzhed pa yi/ tshad ma lung dang ldan pa* ***yi/*** *bden pa gnyis 'dir bshad pa bya.*

875 For a discussion of the meaning of E and VAṂ, see Kongtrul 2005,188–97.

876 *Pañchakrama, Rim pa lnga pa,* by Nāgārjuna, is a commentary on the *Guhyasamāja Tantra.* Toh. 1802.

877 The Three Commentaries by Bodhisattvas (*Sems 'grel skor gsum* or *Byang chub sems dpa'i 'grel ba*) are three commentaries on the tantras: (1) *The Stainless Light* (*Vimalaprabhā, 'Dri med 'od*) by Puṇḍarīka (a *Kālachakra Tantra* commentary) (Toh. 1347); (2) *The Commentary that Summarizes the Hevajra Tantra* (*Hevajrapiṇḍārthaṭīkā; Kye'i rdo rje bsdus pa'i don gyi rgya cher 'grel pa*) by Vajragarbha (a *Hevajra Tantra* commentary) (Toh. 1180); and (3) *The Commentary that Summarizes the Condensed Chakrasaṃvara Tantra* (*Lakṣhābhidhānāduddhṛitalaghutantrapiṇḍārthavivaraṇa*), also known as Vajrapāṇi's *Commentary on the Upper* [*Section*] (*Phyag rdor stod 'grel*), by Vajrapāṇi (a *Chakrasaṃvara Tantra* commentary) (Toh. 1402).

878 Generation stage (*utpattikrama, bskyed rim*) and completion stage (*utpannakrama* [or *saṃpannakrama*], *rdzogs rim*) are the two phases of Vajrayāna practice. These practices are discussed in other sections of the *Treasury of Knowledge,* for example, Kongtrul 2005, 98, 240–2, and passim; and Book Eight, Part Three (*TOK,* III:275–464). See also Harding 1996; and Ray 2001, 209–57.

879 The maṇḍalas are the supports (*rten*) and the deities are what are supported (*rten pa*) by those maṇḍalas.

880 The state of unification (*zung 'jug*) is the unification of luminosity (*'od gsal*) and the illusory body (*sgyu lus*), which occurs in two stages: the state of unification of training (*slob pa'i zung 'jug*) and the state of unification that is beyond training (*mi slob pa'i zung 'jug*). The first corresponds to the first bhūmi and the latter to complete buddhahood (KTGR). See also Kongtrul 2005, 477n78.

881 Subsequent state of attainment (*pṛiṣhṭhalabdha, rjes thob*): see n. 747.

882 "Grasping the whole" (*piṇḍagraha, ril 'dzin, ril por/bur 'dzin pa*) and "successive destruction" (*anuvināsha, rjes gzhig*) are two forms of meditative concentration discussed in Nāgārjuna's *Five Stages* (*Pañchakrama, Rim lnga*) (which presents the completion stage practices of the Guhyasamāja cycle); they are also part of the luminosity practice of the Six Dharmas (*chos drug*). See Book Eight, Part Three (*TOK*, III:270–1); and Book Eight, Part Four (*TOK*, III:362). These names are also translated as the "quick dissolution and gradual dissolution" and "total dissolution and sequential dissolution."

883 Reading (*TOK*, II:558.20) *rang stong gi tshul* ***dang*** as *rang stong gi tshul* ***ni*** on the advice of ALTG.

884 Reading *TOK*, II:558.24 *lhan cig* ***byed*** *pa bde ba chen po'i ye shes* as *lhan cig* ***skyes*** *pa bde ba chen po'i ye shes* following KTGR's oral commentary. "Connate" (*sahaja, lhan cig skyes pa*) is also translated as "innate," and "co-emergent."

885 Self-blessing (*rang byin rlabs*): see Kongtrul 2005, 476n73.

886 For discussions related to illustrative primordial wisdom (also translated as "example-wisdom" or "example pristine awareness") (*dpe'i ye shes*), the primordial wisdom of unified bliss and emptiness (*bde stong zung 'jug gi ye shes*), and the connate primordial wisdom of melting bliss (*zhu bde lhan skyes kyi ye shes*), see Kongtrul 2005, 27–9, 231–3, and passim.

887 In Book Seven, Part Three (*TOK*, III:84–6), Jamgön Kongtrul also discusses the differences between the Mantra-Madhyamaka and Sūtra-Madhyamaka approaches.

888 The translation combines the outline headings that appear here and when the topic is first mentioned (see Chapter 7, p. 138). Here it is, "A Synopsis of What Is Taught in All Madhyamaka Systems," ***dbu ma rnams kyi bstan bya*** *mdor bsdu ba* (*TOK*, II:559.10); and when the topic is first mentioned it is, "A Synopsis of Its Ground, Path, and Fruition," ***gzhi lam 'bras gsum*** *mdor bsdu ba* (*TOK*, II:510).

BIBLIOGRAPHY OF WORKS CITED BY THE AUTHOR

ACIP	Electronic files of the Asian Classics Input Project (www.acip.org)
AP	*Asian Philosophy*
AS	*Asiatische Studien*
Dg.T. Beijing	The collated sDe dge edition of the bsTan 'gyur. Beijing: Krung go'i bod kyi shes rig dpe skrun khang, 1995–2005.
IIJ	*Indo-Iranian Journal*
JAOS	*Journal of American Oriental Society*
JIABS	*Journal of the International Association of Buddhist Studies*
JIBS	*Journal of Indian and Buddhist Studies (Indogaku bukkyōgaku kenkyū)*
JIP	*Journal of Indian Philosophy*
P	*A Comparative Analytical Catalogue of the Kanjur Division of the Tibetan Tripitaka: Edited in Peking during the K'ang-hsi Era, and At Present Kept in the Library of the Otani Daigaku Kyoto*, 3 vols., The Otani Daigaku Library, Kyoto, 1930-1932. Otani University Shin-Buddhist Comprehensive Research Institute: Tibetan Works Research Project, 2005. http://web.otani.ac.jp/cri/twrp/tibdate/Peking_online_search.html
PEW	*Philosophy East and West*

Toh. A Complete Catalogue of the Tibetan Buddhist Canons. Edited by Ui, Suzuki, Kanakura, and Tada. Sendai, Japan: Tohoku University, 1934.

TJ *The Tibet Journal*

WZKS *Wiener Zeitschrift für die Kunde Südasiens*

† indicates a work cited by the author that was consulted by the translator

Scriptures

Abhidharma Sūtra
Abhidharmasūtra
Chos mngon pa'i mdo
not extant

Condensed Perfection of Wisdom Sūtra
Prajñāpāramitā-saṃchayagāthā
Shes rab kyi pha rol tu phyin pa sdud pa/ 'Phags pa mdo sdud pa
Toh. 13
English translation: Edward Conze. 1973. *The Perfection of Wisdom in Eight Thousand Lines & Its Verse Summary*. Bolinas, CA: Four Seasons Foundation.

Descent into Laṅkā Sūtra †
Laṅkāvatārasūtra
Lang kar gshegs pa'i mdo
Toh. 107; ACIP KL0107
English translation: D. T. Suzuki. 1932. *The Lankavatara Sutra*. Repr., London: Routledge and Kegan Paul, 1973.

Eight Thousand Stanza Perfection of Wisdom Sūtra †
Aṣhṭasāhasrikāprajñāpāramitāsūtra
Shes rab kyi pha rol tu phyin pa brgyad stong pa'i mdo
Toh. 12; ACIP KD0012
English translation: Edward Conze. 1973. *The Perfection of Wisdom in Eight Thousand Lines & Its Verse Summary*. Bolinas, CA: Four Seasons Foundation.

Genuine Golden Light Sūtras
Suvarṇaprabhāsottamasūtra/ Ārya-suvarṇaprabhāsottama-sūtrendrarāja-nāma-mahāyāna-sūtra
gSer 'od dam pa'i mdo/ 'Phags pa gser 'od dam pa mdo sde'i dbang po'i rgyal po zhes bya ba theg pa chen po'i mdo
Toh. 556

Glorious Two-Part Hevajra Tantra/The King of Tantras, Called the Glorious Hevajra †
Hevajra-tantra-rāja-nāma
dPal brtag pa gnyis pa/ Kye'i rdo rje zhes bya ba rgyud kyi rgyal po (part I); Kye'i rdo rje mkha' 'gro ma dra ba'i sdom pa'i rgyud kyi rgyal po (part II)
Toh. 417 and Toh. 418
English translation: D. L. Snellgrove. 1959. *The Hevajra Tantra: A Critical Study*. London: Oxford University Press.
Also: G. W. Farrow and I. Menon. 1992. *The Concealed Essence of the Hevajra Tantra*. Delhi: Motilal Banarsidass.

Kālachakra Tantra/ Glorious Kālachakra, the King of Tantras: Issued from the Supreme, Original Buddha (by Mañjushrī Yashas) †
Laghutantra/ Paramādibuddhoddhṛita-shrīkālachakra-nāma-tantrarāja
bsDus pa'i rgyud/ mChog gi dang po'i sangs rgyas las phyung ba rgyud kyi rgyal po dpal dus kyi 'khor lo
Toh. 362 and 1346; Dg.T. Beijing 6
English translation (chapter 1): John Newman. 1987. "The Outer Wheel of Time: Vajrayāna Buddhist Cosmology in the Kālacakra." PhD diss., University of Wisconsin.
Also (chapter 2): Vesna A. Wallace. 2004. *The Kālacakratantra: The Chapter on the Individual together with the* Vimalaprabhā. Editor-in-chief, Robert A. F. Thurman. Treasury of the Buddhist Sciences. New York: American Institute of Buddhist Studies, Columbia University.
Also (chapter 3): Jensine Andresen. 1997. "Kālacakra: Textual and Ritual Perspectives." PhD diss., Harvard University.
Also (chapter 5): James F. Hartzell. 1997. "Tantric Yoga: A Study of the Vedic Precursors, Historical Evolution, Literatures, Cultures, Doctrines, and Practices of the Eleventh-Century Kaśmīri Śaivite and Buddhist Unexcelled Tantric Yogas." PhD diss., Columbia University.

Questions of the Nāga King Anavatapta Sūtra
Anavataptanāgarāja-paripṛicchā-sūtra
kLu'i rgyal po ma dros pas zhus pa'i mdo
Toh. 156

Rice Seedling Sūtra
Shālistambha-sūtra
Sa lu ljangs pa'i mdo
Toh. 210

Stacks of Jewels/ Kāshyapa Chapter Sūtra
Ratnakūṭa/ Kāshyapa-parivarta-sūtra
dKon mchog brtsegs pa/ 'Od srung gi le'u zhes bya ba'i mdo
Toh. 87

Sūtra Dispelling the Remorse of [King] Ajātashatru
Ajātashatru-kaukṛittyavinodana
Ma skyes dgra'i 'gyod pa bsal ba'i mdo
Toh. 216

Sūtra of a Teaching Given in a Dream
Āryasvapnanirdesha-nāma-mahāyāna-sūtra
rMi lam lung bstan gyi mdo/ 'Phags pa rmi lam bstan pa zhes bya theg pa chen po'i mdo
Toh. 48

Sūtra on the Heavily Adorned Arrangement
Ārya-ghanavyūha-nāma-mahāyāna-sūtra
rGyan stug/ 'Phags pa rgyan stug po bkod pa zhes bya ba theg pa chen po'i mdo
Toh. 110

Sūtra on the Ten Bhūmis
Dashabhūmikasūtra
Sa bcu pa'i mdo
Toh. 44:31
English translation: M. Honda. 1968. "An Annotated Translation of the 'Daśabhūmika.'" In *Studies in South, East and Central Asia,* Śatapitaka Series 74, ed. D. Sinor, 115–276. New Delhi: International Academy of Indian Culture.

Sūtra Unraveling the Intention †
Saṃdhinirmochanasūtra
dGongs pa nges par 'grel pa zhes bya ba theg pa chen po'i mdo
Toh. 106; ACIP KD0106
English translation: John C. Powers. 1995. *Wisdom of Buddha: The Saṃdhinirmocana Mahāyāna Sūtra.* Berkeley: Dharma Publishing.

TREATISES

Āryadeva
Compendium on the Heart of Primordial Wisdom †
Jñānasārasamuchchaya
Ye shes snying po kun las btus pa
Toh. 3851; Dg.T. Beijing 57
English translation (verses 20–28): Katsumi Mimaki. 2000. "*Jñānasārasamuccaya* kk⁰ 20–28: *Mise au point* with a Sanskrit Manuscript." In *Wisdom, Compassion, and the Search for Understanding: The Buddhist Studies Legacy of Gadjin M. Nagao,* ed. Jonathan A. Silk, 233–244. Honolulu: University of Hawaii Press.

Asaṅga
Compendium of Abhidharma †
Abhidharmasamuchchaya
Chos mngon pa kun las btus pa
Toh. 4049; Dg.T. Beijing 76
French translation: Walpola Rāhula. 1971. *La Compendium de la superdoctrine (philosophie) (Abhidharmasamuccaya) d'Asaṅga.* Paris: École Française d'Extrême-Orient.
English translation of the French: Sara Boin-Webb. 2001. *Abhidharmasamuccaya: The Compendium of the Higher Teaching (Philosophy).* Fremont, CA: Asian Humanities Press.

Compendium of the Mahāyāna †
Mahāyāna-saṃgraha
Theg pa chen po bsdus pa
Toh. 4048; Dg.T. Beijing 76
English translation from the Chinese: John P. Keenan. 1992. *The Sum-*

mary of the Great Vehicle. BDK English Tripiṭaka 46-III. Berkeley: Numata Center for Buddhist Translation and Research.

Atīsha

Entrance to the Two Truths †

Satyadvayāvatāra

bDen pa gnyis la 'jug pa

Toh. 3902; Dg.T. Beijing 63

English translation: Chr. Lindtner. 1981. "Atiśa's Introduction to the Two Truths, and Its Sources." *JIP* 9:161–214.

Also: Richard Sherburne. 2000. In *The Complete Works of Atīśa Śrī Dīpaṁkara Jñāna, Jo-bo-rje: The* Lamp for the Path *and* Commentary, *together with the Newly Translated* Twenty-five Key Texts, 353–359. Repr., Delhi: Aditya Prakashan, 2003.

Bhāvaviveka

Blaze of Reasoning/ Blaze of Reasoning: Commentary on the "Heart of the Middle Way" †

Tarkajvālā/ Madhyamakahṛidayavṛittitarkajvālā

rTog ge 'bar ba/ dBu ma'i snying po'i 'grel pa rtog ge 'bar ba

Toh. 3856; Dg.T. Beijing 58

English translation (chapter 3): Shōtarō Iida. 1980. *Reason and Emptiness.* Tokyo: Hokuseido.

Bodhibhadra

Commentary on the "Compendium on the Heart of Primordial Wisdom" †

Jñānasārasamuchchaya-nāma-nibandhana

Ye shes snying po kun las btus pa zhes bya ba'i bshad sbyar

Toh. 3852; Dg.T. Beijing 57

Chandrakīrti

Entrance to the Middle Way †

Madhyamakāvatāra

dBu ma la 'jug pa

Toh. 3861; Dg.T. Beijing 60

English translation (chapters 1–5): Jeffrey Hopkins. 1980. *Compassion in Tibetan Buddhism.* Ithaca, NY: Snow Lion Publications.

Also (chapter 6): Stephen Batchelor. 1983. *Echoes of Voidness.* London: Wisdom Publications.

Also: C. W. Huntington, Jr. 1989. *The Emptiness of Emptiness.* Honolulu: University of Hawaii Press.

Also: Padmakara Translation Group. 2002. *Introduction to the Middle Way: Chandrakīrti's 'Madhyamakāvatāra' with Commentary by Jamgön Mipham*. Boston: Shambhala Publications.

Also: Jürgen Stöter-Tillmann and Acharya Tashi Tsering. 1997. *Rendawa Shönnu Lodrö's Commentary on the "Entry into the Middle": Lamp which Elucidates Reality*. Dalai Lama Tibeto-Indological Series 23. Sarnath, India: Central Institute of Higher Tibetan Studies.

Also (chapter 6): Ari Goldfield, Jules Levinson, Jim Scott, and Birgit Scott. 2005. *The Moon of Wisdom: Chapter Six of Chandrakīrti's "Entering the Middle Way."* Ithaca, NY: Snow Lion Publications.

Commentary on the "Sixty Verses on Reasoning" †
Yuktiṣhaṣhṭikā-vṛitti
Rigs pa drug cu pa'i 'grel pa
Toh. 3864; Dg.T. Beijing 60

Chandrakīrti, the lesser
Entrance to the Wisdom of the Middle Way †
Madhyamakaprajñāvatāra
dBu ma shes rab la 'jug pa
Toh. 3863; Dg.T. Beijing 60

Dharmakīrti
Commentary on Valid Cognition †
Pramāṇavārttikakārikā
Tshad ma rnam 'grel gyi tshig le'ur byas pa
Toh. 4210; Dg.T. Beijing 97
English translation (chapter 2): Masatoshi Nagatomi. 1957. "A Study of Dharmakīrti's Pramāṇavārttika: An English Translation and Annotation of the Pramāṇavārttika, Book I." PhD diss., Harvard University.

Dharmatrāta
Collection of Meaningful Expressions
Udānavarga
Ched du brjod pa'i tshoms
Toh. 326 and 4099; Dg.T. Beijing 83
English translation: Gareth Sparham. 1986. *The Tibetan Dhammapada*. London: Wisdom Publications.

Haribhadra

[Revised Edition of the] "Prajñāpāramitā Sūtra in Twenty-five Thousand Lines" †

Pañchaviṃshatisāhasrikāprajñāpāramitā

Shes rab kyi pha rol ru phyin pa stong phrag nyi shu lnga pa

Toh. 3790; Dg.T. Beijing 50–1

Jetāri

Differentiating the Sugata's Texts †

Sugatamatavibhaṅgabhāṣhya

bDe bar gshegs pa'i gzhung rnam par 'byed pa'i bshad pa

Toh. 3900; Dg.T. Beijing 63

Jñānagarbha

Differentiation of the Two Truths †

Satyadvaya-vibhaṅga

bDen gnyis rnam 'byed

Toh. 3881; Dg.T. Beijing 62

English translation: Malcolm David Eckel. 1987. *Jñānagarbha on the Two Truths: An Eighth Century Handbook of Madhyamaka Philosophy.* Repr., Delhi: Motilal Banarsidass, 1992.

Maitreya

Differentiation of the Middle and the Extremes †

Madhyāntavibhaṅga

dBus mtha' rnam 'byed

Toh. 4021; Dg.T. Beijing 70

English translation: F. Th. Stcherbatsky. 1971. *Madhyāntavibhāga, Discourse on Discrimination between Middle and Extremes ascribed to Bodhisattva Maitreya and Commented by Vasubandhu and Sthiramati.* Calcutta: Indian Studies Past and Present.

Also (chapter 1): Thomas Kochumuttom. 1982. *A Buddhist Doctrine of Experience.* 27–89. Repr., Delhi: Motilal Banarsidass, 1999.

Also: Stefan Anacker. 1984/1998. *Seven Works of Vasubandhu.* 211–273. Rev. ed. Delhi: Motilal Banarsidass.

Highest Continuum/ The Mahāyāna Treatise of the Highest Continuum †

Mahāyānottaratantrashāstra

Theg pa chen po rgyud bla ma'i bstan bcos

Toh. 4024; Dg.T. Beijing 70

English translation: E. Obermiller. 1931. "Sublime Science of the Great Vehicle to Salvation." *Acta Orientalia* 9: 81–306.

Also: J. Takasaki. 1966. *A Study on the Ratnagotravibhāga.* Rome: Istituto Italiano per il Medio ed Estremo Oriente.

Also: Ken Holmes and Katia Holmes. 1985. *The Changeless Nature.* Eskdalemuir, Scotland: Karma Drubgyud Darjay Ling.

Also: Rosemarie Fuchs. 2000. *Buddha Nature: The Mahayana Uttaratantra Shastra.* Ithaca, NY: Snow Lion Publications.

Ornament of the Mahāyāna Sūtras †
Mahāyānasūtrālaṃkāra
Theg pa chen po mdo sde rgyan
Toh. 4020; Dg.T. Beijing 70
English translation: L. Jamspal et al. 2004. *The Universal Vehicle Discourse Literature (Mahāyānasūtrālaṁkāra).* Editor-in-chief, Robert A. F. Thurman. Treasury of the Buddhist Sciences. New York: American Institute of Buddhist Studies, Columbia University.

Ornament of Clear Realization †
Abhisamayālaṃkāra
mNgon rtogs rgyan
Toh. 3786; Dg.T. Beijing 49
English translation: Edward Conze. 1954. *Abhisamayālaṃkāra.* Serie Orientale Rome. Rome: Istituto Italiano per il Medio ed Estremo Oriente.

Nāgāmitra
Entrance to the Three Kāyas †
Kāyatrayāvatāramukha
sKu gsum la 'jug pa'i sgo
Toh. 3890; Dg.T. Beijing 63

Nāgārjuna
Commentary on Bodhichitta †
Bodhichittavivaraṇa-nāma
Byang chub sems 'grel
Toh. 1800; Dg.T. Beijing 18
English translation: Chr. Lindtner. 1997. *Master of Wisdom: Writings of the Buddhist Master Nāgārjuna.* 32–71. Berkeley: Dharma Publishing.

Fundamental Treatise on the Middle Way †
Prajñā-nāma-mūlamadhyamakakārikā
dBu ma rtsa ba'i tshig le'ur byas pa shes rab ces bya ba
Toh. 3824; Dg.T. Beijing 57
English translation: Frederick Streng. 1967. *Emptiness: A Study in Religious Meaning.* Nashville, TN: Abingdon Press.
Also: Kenneth Inada. 1970. *Nāgārjuna: A Translation of His Mūlamadhyamakakārikā.* Tokyo: Hokuseido Press.
Also: David J. Kalupahana. 1986. *Nāgārjuna: The Philosophy of the Middle Way.* Albany, NY: State University of New York Press.
Also: Jay L. Garfield. 1995. *The Fundamental Wisdom of the Middle Way: Nāgārjuna's Mūlamadhyamakakārikā.* New York: Oxford University Press.
Also: Stephen Bachelor. 2000. *Verses from the Center: A Buddhist Vision of the Sublime.* New York: Riverhead Books.

Praises of the Incomparable One †
Nirupama-stava/ Niraupamyastava
dPe med par bstod pa
Toh. 1119; Dg.T. Beijing 1

Praises of the Transcendent One †
Lokātītastava
'Jig rten las 'das par bstod pa
Toh. 1120; Dg.T. Beijing 1
English translation: Chr. Lindtner. 1997. *Master of Wisdom: Writings of the Buddhist Master Nāgārjuna.* 2–11. Berkeley: Dharma Publishing.

Precious Garland/ Precious Garland of Advice for the King †
Ratnāvalī/ Rājaparikathāratnāvalī
Rin chen 'phreng ba/rGyal po la gtam bya ba rin po che'i phreng ba
Toh. 4158; Dg.T. Beijing 96
English translation: John Dunne and Sara McClintock. 1997. *The Precious Garland: An Epistle to a King.* Boston: Wisdom Publications.
Also: Jeffrey Hopkins. 1998. *Buddhist Advice for Living and Liberation: Nāgārjuna's Precious Garland.* 94–164. Ithaca, NY: Snow Lion Publications.

Rebuttal of Objections †
Vigrahavyāvartanī
rTsod pa zlog pa
Toh. 3828; Dg.T. Beijing 57
English translation: K. Bhattacharya. 1978. *The Dialectical Method of Nāgārjuna: Vigrahavyāvartanī.* 4th ed. Repr., Delhi: Motilal Banarsidass, 2002.

Sixty Verses on Reasoning †
Yuktiṣhaṣhṭikākārikā
Rigs pa drug cu pa'i tshig le'ur byas pa
Toh. 3825; Dg.T. Beijing 57
English translation: Chr. Lindtner. 1997. *Master of Wisdom: Writings of the Buddhist Master Nāgārjuna.* 72–93. Berkeley: Dharma Publishing.

Narendrakīrti
Synopsis of the View Asserted by Mañjushrī
Pradarshanānumatoddeshaparīkṣhā/ Āryamañjushrīpradarshana
Rang gi lta ba'i 'dod pa mdor bstan pa yongs su brtag pa/ 'Phags pa 'jam dpal gyi rang gi lta ba
P4610; Dharma 4530

Puṇḍarīka
Root Commentary on the Kālachakra Tantra/ Stainless Light
Vimalaprabhā-nāma-mūlatantrānu-sāriṇī-dvādashasāhasrikā-laghu-kālacakra-tantrarāja-tīkā
Dus 'khor rtsa 'grel/ bsDus pa'i rgyud kyi rgyal po dus kyi 'khor lo'i 'grel bshad rtsa ba'i rgyud kyi rjes su 'jug pa stong phrag bcu gnyis pa dri ma med pa'i 'od ces bya ba
Toh. 1347; Dg.T. Beijing 6

Ratnākarashānti
Commentary that Ornaments the Middle: Establishing the Middle Path †
Madhyamakālaṃkāra-vṛitti-madhyamaka-pratipadāsiddhi-nāma
dBu ma rgyan gyi 'grel pa dbu ma'i lam grub pa zhes bya ba
Toh. 4072; Dg.T. Beijing 78

Instructions that Ornament the Middle Way †
Madhyamakālaṃkāropadesha

dBu ma rgyan gyi man ngag
Toh. 4085; Dg.T. Beijing 78

Shāntarakṣhita

Commentary on the "Ornament of the Middle Way"/ Auto-Commentary for the "[Ornament of] the Middle Way" †
Madhyamakālaṃkāra-vṛitti
dBu ma'i rgyan gyi 'grel pa/ dBu ma rang 'grel
Toh. 3885; Dg.T. Beijing 62
English translation: Masamichi Ichigō. 1989. "Śāntarakṣita's Madhyamakālaṃkāra." In *Studies in the Literature of the Great Vehicle,* eds. Luis O. Gómez and Jonathan A. Silk, 141–240. Ann Arbor: University of Michigan.

Ornament of the Middle Way †
Mādhyamakālaṃkāra
dBu ma rgyan
Toh. 3884; Dg.T. Beijing
English translation: James Blumenthal. 2004. *The Ornament of the Middle Way: A Study of the Madhyamaka Thought of Śāntarakṣita.* Ithaca, NY: Snow Lion Publications.
Also: Thomas H. Doctor. 2004. *Speech of Delight: Mipham's Commentary on Śāntarakṣita's "Ornament of the Middle Way."* Ithaca, NY: Snow Lion Publications.
Also: Padmakara Translation Group. 2005. *The Adornment of the Middle Way: Shāntarakṣhita's Madhyamakalankara with Commentary by Jamgön Mipham.* Boston: Shambhala Publications.

Shāntideva

Entrance to the Bodhisattva's Way of Life †
Bodhicharyāvatāra
Byang chub sems dpa'i spyod pa la 'jug pa
Toh. 3871; Dg.T. Beijing 61
English translation: Marion Matics. 1970. *Entering the Path of Enlightenment.* New York: Macmillan.
Also: Stephen Batchelor. 1979. *A Guide to the Bodhisattva's Way of Life.* Repr., Dharamsala, India: Library of Tibetan Works and Archives, 1993.
Also: Kate Crosby and Andrew Skilton. 1996. *The Bodhicharyāvatāra.* Oxford: Oxford University Press.

Also: Padmakara Translation Group. 1997. *The Way of the Bodhisattva.* Boston: Shambhala Publications.

Also: Vesna A. Wallace and B. Alan Wallace. 1997. *A Guide to the Bodhisattva Way of Life.* Ithaca, NY: Snow Lion Publications.

Also (chapter 9): Karl Brunnhölzl. 2004. *The Center of the Sunlit Sky: Madhyamaka in the Kagyü Tradition.* Nitartha Institute Series. Ithaca, NY: Snow Lion Publications.

Vasubandhu

Commentary on the "Teachings Requested by Akṣhayamati"
Akṣhayamati-nirdesha-ṭīkā
bLo gros mi zad pas bstan pa'i mdo 'grel
Toh. 3994; Dg.T. Beijing 66

Explanation of the "Treasury of Abhidharma" †
Abhidharmakosha-bhāṣhya
Chos mngon pa'i mdzod kyi bshad pa
Toh. 4090; Dg.T. Beijing 79
French translation: Louis de la Vallée Poussin. 1971. *L'Abhidharmakośa de Vasubandhu.* 6 vols. Brussels: Institut Belge des Hautes Études Chinoises.
English translation of the French: Leo M. Pruden. 1988–1990. *Abhidharmakośabhāṣyam.* 4 vols. Berkeley: Asian Humanities Press.

Thirty Verses/ Treatise on Cognition-Only in Thirty Verses †
Triṃshikākārikā/ Sarvā-vijñāna-mātradeshaka-triṃshika-kārikā
Sum bcu pa/ Thams cad rnam rig tsam du ston pa sum cu pa'i tshig le'ur byas pa
Toh. 4055; Dg.T. Beijing 77
English translation: Thomas Kochumuttom. 1982. *A Buddhist Doctrine of Experience.* 127–163. Repr., Delhi: Motilal Banarsidass, 1999.
Also: Stefan Anacker. 1984/1998. *Seven Works of Vasubandhu.* 181–189. Rev. ed. Delhi: Motilal Banarsidass.

Treasury of Abhidharma †
Abhidharmakoshakārikā
Chos mngon pa'i mdzod kyi tshig le'ur byas pa
Toh. 4089; Dg.T. Beijing, 79
French translation: Louis de la Vallée Poussin. 1971. *L'Abhidharmakośa de Vasubandhu.* 6 vols. Brussels: Institut Belge des Hautes Études Chinoises.

English translation of the French: Leo M. Pruden. 1988–1990. *Abhidharmakośabhāṣyam.* 4 vols. Berkeley: Asian Humanities Press.

Vinītadeva

Compendium on the Different Orders †

Samayabhedoparachanachakre nikāyabhedopadeshanasaṃgraha

sDe pa tha dad bklag pa'i 'khor lo/ gZhung tha dad pa rim par bklag pa'i 'khor lo las sde pa tha dad pa bstan pa bsdus pa

Toh. 4140; Dg.T. Beijing 93

Tibetan Works

Jetsün Drakpa Gyaltsen (*rJe btsun grags pa rgyal mtshan*)

[Jeweled] Tree/ Jeweled Tree: The Clear Realizations of the Tantras

lJon shing/ rGyud kyi mngon par rtogs pa rin po che'i ljon shing

Serdok Paṇchen Shākya Chokden (*gSer mdog paṇ chen shākya mchog ldan*)/ Silung Paṇchen (*Zi lung paṇ chen*)

Establishing the Unity of the Definitive Meaning/ An Extensive Commentary on the Treatise Establishing the Unity of the Definitive Meaning Through the Explanation of the Distinction Between the Two Traditions of the Great Charioteers †

Nges don gcig tu bsgrub pa/ Shing rta chen po'i srol gnyis kyi rnam par dbye ba bshad nas nges don gcig tu bsgrub pa'i bstan bcos kyi rgyas 'grel

In the Complete Works (gsung 'bum) of gSer-mdok Pan-chan Śākya-mchog-ldan, vol. 2: 471–619

Thimphu, Bhutan: Kunzang Tobgey, 1975

Great Path of the Nectar of Emptiness: An Explanation of Profound Peace, Free from Elaborations †

Zab zhi spros bral gyi bshad pa stong nyid bdud rtsi'i lam po che

In the Complete Works (gsung 'bum) of gSer-mdok Pan-chan Śākya-mchog-ldan, vol. 4: 107–207

Thimphu, Bhutan: Kunzang Tobgey, 1975

Tāranātha

Essence of Shentong †

gZhan stong snying po
Collected Works of Jo-nang rje-btsun Tāranātha
In the Collected Works of Jetsün Tāranātha, vol. 18: 171–193
Sichuan, China: 'Dzam than dgon, 2000?
English translation: Jeffrey Hopkins. 2007. *The Essence of Other-Emptiness.* 23–115. In collaboration with Lama Lodrö Namgyel. Ithaca, NY: Snow Lion Publications.

Twenty-one [Differences Regarding] the Profound Meaning †
Zab don nyer gcig pa/ Zab don khyad par nyer gcig pa
In the Collected Works of Jetsün Tāranātha, vol. 18: 209–222
Sichuan, China: 'Dzam than dgon, 2000?
English translation: Klaus-Dieter Mathes. 2004. "Tāranātha's 'Twenty-One Differences with regard to the Profound Meaning'—Comparing the Views of the Two *gŹan sToṅ* Masters Dol po pa and Śākya mChog ldan." *JIABS* 27, no. 2: 285–328.
Also: Jeffrey Hopkins. 2007. *The Essence of Other-Emptiness.* 117–36. In collaboration with Lama Lodrö Namgyel. Ithaca, NY: Snow Lion Publications.

REFERENCE BIBLIOGRAPHY

INDIC TEXTS

Vajrapañjarā
Vajrapañjarā/ Ārya-ḍākinī-vajrapañjarā-mahātantrarāja-kalpa-nāma
rDo rje gur/ 'Phags pa mkha' 'gro ma rdo rje gur zhes bya ba'i rgyud kyi rgyal po chen po'i rtag pa
Toh. 419

Ajitamitra
Extensive Commentary on the "Precious Garland"
Ratnāvalī-ṭīkā
Rin po che'i phreng ba'i rgya cher bshad pa
Toh. 4159; Dg.T. Beijing 96

Āryadeva
Madhyamaka: Conquering Delusions
Madhyamaka-bhramaghāta
dBu ma 'khrul pa 'joms pa
Toh. 3850; Dg.T. Beijing 57

Asvabhāva
Explanation of the "Compendium of the Mahāyāna"
Mahāyāna-saṃgrahopanibandhana
Theg chen bsdus pa'i bshad sbyar
Toh. 4051; Dg.T. Beijing 76

Ashvaghoṣha
Stages of Meditation on the Ultimate Mind of Enlightenment
Paramārtha-bodhichitta-bhāvanā-kramavarṇa-saṃgraha
Don dam pa byang kyi sems sgom pa'i rim pa yi ger bris pa
Toh. 3912; Dg.T. Beijing 64

Bhāvaviveka

Heart of the Middle Way
Madhyamakahṛidayakārikā
dBu ma'i snying po'i tshig le'ur byas pa
Toh. 3855; Dg.T. Beijing 58

Lamp of Wisdom: A Commentary on the "Fundamental [Treatise on] the Middle Way"
Prajñāpradīpa-mūlamadhyamaka-vṛitti
dBu ma'i rtsa ba'i 'grel pa shes rab sgron ma
Toh. 3853; Dg.T. Beijing 57

Precious Lamp of Madhyamaka
Madhyamaka-ratna-pradīpa
dBu ma rin po che'i sgron ma
Toh. 3854; Dg.T. Beijing 57

Chandrahari

Jewel Garland
Ratnamālā
Rin po che'i phreng ba
Toh. 3901; Dg.T. Beijing 63

Chandrakīrti

Lucid Words
Mūlamadhyamakavṛittiprasannapadā
dBu ma'i rtsa ba'i 'grel pa tshig gsal ba
Toh. 3860; Dg.T. Beijing 60

Dignāga

Examination of Objects of Observation
Ālambanaparīkṣhā
dMigs pa brtags pa
Toh. 4205; Dg.T. Beijing 97

Jetāri

The Explanation of "Differentiating the Sugata's Texts"
Sugatamatavibhaṅgabhāṣhya
bDe bar gshegs pa'i gzhung rnam par 'byed pa'i bshad pa
Toh. 3900; Dg.T. Beijing 63

Kamalashīla
Commentary on the Difficult Points of the "Ornament of the Middle Way"
Madhyamakālaṃkārapañjikā
dBu ma rgyan gyi dka' 'grel
Toh. 3886; Dg.T. Beijing 62

Lakṣhmī
Illuminating the Meaning of "The Five Stages"
Pañchakrama-vṛittārthavirochana
Rim pa lnga'i don gsal bar byed pa/ Rim pa lnga'i grel pa'i don gsal bar byed pa
Toh. 1842; Dg.T. Beijing 19

Maitrīpa/ Advayavajra
Precious Garland of Suchness
Tattvaratnāvalī
De kho na nyid kyi rin chen phreng ba
Toh. 2240; Dg.T. Beijing 26

Nāgārjuna
Commentary on the "Rebuttal of Objections"
Vigrahavyāvartanī-vṛitti
rTsod pa zlog pa'i 'grel pa
Toh. 3832; Dg.T. Beijing 57

Sahajavajra
Compendium of Positions
Sthiti-samuchchaya
gNas pa bsdus pa
Toh. 2227; Dg.T. Beijing 26

Shākyaprabha
Luminous
Prabhāvatī/ Ārya-mūlasarvāstivādi-shrāmaṇera-kārikā-vṛitti-prabhāvatī
'Od ldan/ 'Phags pa gzhi thams cad yod par smra ba'i dge tshul gyi tshig le'ur byas pa'i 'grel pa 'od ldan
Toh. 4125; Dg.T. Beijing 93

Sthiramati
Sub-Commentary on the "Differentiation of the Middle and the Extremes"
Madhyāntavibhaṅga-ṭīkā

dBus dang mtha' rnam par 'byed pa'i 'grel bshad
Toh. 4032; Dg.T. Beijing 71

Sub-Commentary on the "Ornament of the Mahāyāna Sūtras"
Sūtrālaṃkāra-vṛitti-bhāṣhya
mDo sde rgyan gyi 'grel bshad
Toh. 4034; Dg.T. Beijing 72

Sub-Commentary on the "Thirty Verses"
Triṃshikaṭīkā
Sum cu pa'i 'grel bshad
Toh. 4070; Dg.T. Beijing 78

Vasubandhu

Commentary on the "Differentiation of the Middle and the Extremes"
Madhyāntavibhaṅga-ṭīkā
dBus dang mtha' rnam par 'byed pa'i 'grel pa
Toh. 4027; Dg.T. Beijing 71

Commentary on the "Ornament of the Mahāyāna Sūtras"
Sūtrālaṃkāra-vyākhyā
mDo sde rgyan gyi bshad pa
Toh. 4026; Dg.T. Beijing 70

Commentary on the "Compendium of the Mahāyāna"
Mahāyāna-saṃgraha-bhāṣhya
Theg bsdus 'grel pa bshad pa
Toh. 4050; Dg.T. Beijing 76

Delineation of the Five Aggregates
Pañchaskandha-prakaraṇa
Phung po lnga'i rab tu byed pa
Toh. 4059; Dg.T. Beijing 77

Exposition of the Three Natures
Trisvabhāvanirdesha
Rang bzhin gsum nges par bstan pa
Toh. 4058; Dg.T. Beijing 77

Principles of Exegesis
Vyākhyāyukti
rNam bshad rigs pa
Toh. 4061; Dg.T. Beijing 77

Yashomitra
Sub-Commentary on the "Treasury of Abhidharma"
Abhidharmakoṣhaṭīka
Chos mngon pa'i mdzod kyi 'grel bshad
Toh. 4092; Dg.T. Beijing 80

Tibetan Works

Anonymous
Nighaṇṭu
sGra sbyor bam po gnyis pa
Toh. 4347; Dg.T. Beijing 115

Butön (*Bu ston*)
History of Buddhism
Bu ston chos 'byung/ bDe bar gshegs pa'i bstan pa'i gsal byed chos kyi 'byung gnas gsung rab rin po che'i mdzod
Bauddhanath, Nepal: Padma Karpo Translation Committee edition, 2005

Chang-kya Rolpé Dorjé (*lCang skya rol pa'i rdo rje*)
Beautiful Ornament of Philosophical Tenet Systems/ A Systematic Presentation of Philosophical Tenet Systems: The Beautiful Ornament for the Meru of the Muni's Teachings
Grub mtha' mdzes rgyan/ Grub pa'i mtha' rnam par bzhag pa thub bstan lhun po'i mdzes rgyan
Xining, China: Krung go bod kyi shes rig dpe skrun khang, 1998

Dolpopa Sherab Gyaltsen (*Dol po pa shes rab rgyal mtshan*)
Mountain Dharma: Ocean of the Definitive Meaning
Ri chos nges don rgya mtsho
Beijing: Mi rigs dpe skrun khang, 1998

Gampopa (*sGam po pa*)
The Jewel Ornament of Liberation
Thar pa rin po che'i rgyan
Chengdu, China: Si khron mi rigs dpe skrun khang, 1989

Gyaltsap Jé, Dharma Rinchen (*rGyal tshab rje dar ma rin chen*)
Aide-Mémoire for the Eight Great Difficult Points of the "Fundamental [Treatise on] the Middle Way"
dBu ma'i rtsa ba'i dka' gnas chen po brgyad kyi brjed byang
ACIP S5426

Gyamtso, Khenpo Tsültrim, Rinpoche (*mKhen po tshul khrims rgya mtsho rin po che*)
Classifications of Mental States; Classifications of Reasons/ The Presentation of the Classifications of Mental States; The Presentation of the Classifications of Reasons/ Presentation of Mind and Reasons: The Essence of the Ocean of Texts on Reasoning
bLo rig; rTags rigs/ bLo rig gi rnam gzhag; rTags rigs kyi rnam gzhag/ bLo rtags kyi rnam gzhag rigs gzhung rgya mtsho'i snying po
New York: Nitartha *international* Publications, 1997

Kongtrul Lodrö Tayé, Jamgön (*'Jam mgon Kong sprul blo gros mtha' yas*)
Irrepressible Lion's Roar: A Commentary on the "Highest Continuum"
rGyud bla ma'i 'grel pa/ Theg pa chen po rgyud bla ma'i bstan bcos snying po'i don mngon sum lam gyi bshad srol dang sbyar ba'i rnam par 'grel ba phyir mi ldog pa seng ge nga ro
Seattle: Nitartha *international* Publications, 2005

Light of the Stainless Vajra Moon: Instructions on the View of Shentong, the Great Madhyamaka
gZhan stong dbu ma chen po'i lta khrid rdo rje zla ba dri ma med pa'i 'od zer
In rGya chen bka' mdzod, vol. 8: 735–765
Paro, Bhutan

A Non-Sectarian History of the Dharma
Ris med chos kyi 'byung/ Ris med chos kyi 'byung gnas mdo tsam smos pa blo gsal mgrin pa'i mdzes rgyan
In rGya chen bka' mdzod, vol. 9: 69-99
Paro, Bhutan

Revealing the Indestructible Vajra Secrets: An Elucidation of the Word-Meaning of the "Two-Part King of Tantras, the Glorious Hevajra"
dPal kye'i rdo rje'i rgyud kyi rgyal po brtag pa gnyis pa'i tshig don rnam par 'grol ba gzhom med rdo rje'i gsang ba 'byed pa
Seattle: Nitartha *international* Publications, 2005

The Treasury of Knowledge (TOK)/ Infinite Ocean of Knowledge
Shes bya mdzod/ Shes bya mtha' yas pa'i rgya mtsho/ Theg pa'i sgo kun las btus pa gsung rab rin po che'i mdzod bslab pa gsum legs par ston pa'i bstan bcos shes bya kun khyab
Beijing: Mi rigs dpe skrun khang, 1982
Bauddhanath, Nepal: Padma Karpo Translation Committee edition, 2000 (input of Zhechen Publications edition, a photographic reproduction of the original 4 vol. Palpung woodblock-print, 1844)

Jamyang Shepa (*'Jam dbyangs bzhad pa*)
Great Exposition of Tenets/ Explanation of Tenets: Sun of the Land of Samantabhadra Brilliantly Illuminating All of Our Own and Others' Tenets and the Meaning of the Profound [Emptiness], Ocean of Scripture and Reasoning Fulfilling All Hopes of All Beings
Grub mtha' chen mo/ Grub mtha'i rnam bshad rang gzhan grub mtha' kun dang zab don mchog tu gsal ba kun bzang zhing gi nyi ma lung rigs rgya mtsho skye dgu'i re ba kun skong
In the Collected works of 'Jam-dbyangs-bzhad-pa'i-rdo-rje (Reproduced from prints from the bKra shis 'khyil blocks), vol. 14
South India, 1995

Longchen Rabjam (*kLong chen rab 'byams*)
Precious Treasury of the Supreme Yāna
Theg pa'i mchog rin po che'i mdzod
Electronic file, input by James Valby

Mikyö Dorjé (*Mi bskyod rdo rje*)
The Chariot of the Dakpo Kagyu Siddhas: A Commentary on the "Entrance to the Middle Way," Oral Teachings of the Glorious Dusum Khyenpa
dBu ma la 'jug pa'i rnam bshad dpal ldan dus gsum mkhyen pa'i zhal lung dvags brgyud grub pa'i shing rta
Seattle: Nitartha *international* Publications, 1996

Mipham Gyamtso, Ju (*'Ju mi pham rgya mtsho*)
Clarifying the Abiding Nature: An Ornament for Nāgārjuna's Thought
dBu ma rtsa ba'i shes rab ba'i mchan 'grel gnas lugs rab gsal klu dbang dgongs rgyan
unknown

Feast of the Nectar of the Supreme Yāna: An Explanation of the Thought of the "Ornament of the Mahāyāna Sūtras"

Theg pa chen po mdo sde'i rgyan gyi dgongs don rnam par bshad pa theg mchog bdud rtsi'i dga' ston
unknown

Garland of Light Rays: A Commentary on the "Shāstra of Differentiation of the Middle and the Extremes"
dBus dang mtha' rnam par 'byed pa'i bstan bcos kyi 'grel ba 'od zer phreng ba
unknown

Gateway to Knowledge
mKhas 'jug
Xining, China: mTsho sngon mi rigs dpe skrun khang, 1988

A Teaching to Delight My Guru Mañjughoṣha: A Commentary on the "Ornament of the Middle Way"
dBu ma rgyan gyi rnam bshad 'jam dbyangs bla ma dgyes pa'i zhal lung
In Thomas H. Doctor. 2004. *Speech of Delight: Mipham's Commentary on Śāntarakṣita's "Ornament of the Middle Way."* Ithaca, NY: Snow Lion Publications.

Ngul-chu Tokmé (*dNgul chu thogs med*)
An Ocean of Eloquent Explanations: A Commentary on "Entrance to the Bodhisattva's Way of Life"
Byang chub sems dpa'i spyod pa la 'jug pa'i 'grel pa legs bshad rgya mtsho
Sarnath, India: Sakya Students Union, Central Institute of Higher Tibetan Studies, 1988

Pawo Tsuk-lak Trengwa (*dPa' bo gtsug lag phreng ba*)
Feast for Scholars: A History of the Dharma
Chos 'byung mkhas pa'i dga' ston/ Dam pa'i chos kyi 'khor lo bsgyur ba rnams kyi byung ba gsal bar byed pa mkhas pa'i dga' ston
Sarnath, India: Vajra Vidya Library, 2003

Serdok Paṇchen Shākya Chokden (*gSer mdog paṇ chen shākya mchog ldan*)/ Silung Paṇchen (*Zi lung paṇ chen*)
The Dharma Treasury of an Ocean of Scriptures and Reasonings Ascertaining the Middle Way
dBu ma rnam par nges pa'i chos kyi bang mdzod lung dang rigs pa'i rgya mtsho

In the Complete Works (gsung 'bum) of gSer-mdok Pan-chan Śākya-mchog-ldan, vols. 14–15
Thimphu, Bhutan: Kunzang Tobgey, 1975

An Elucidation of the Definitive Meaning of the Five Dharma Treatises of Maitreya
Byams chos lnga'i nges don rab tu gsal ba
In the Complete Works (gsung 'bum) of gSer-mdok Pan-chan Śākya-mchog-ldan, vol. 11: 1–37
Thimphu, Bhutan: Kunzang Tobgey, 1975

Opening a Chest of Treasures: A Treatise That Clarifies the Progressive Path of the Five Dharma Texts of Maitreya
Byams chos lnga'i lam gyi rim pa gsal bar byed pa'i bstan bcos rin chen sgrom 'byed
In the Complete Works (gsung 'bum) of gSer-mdok Pan-chan Śākya-mchog-ldan, vol. 11: 39–155
Thimphu, Bhutan: Kunzang Tobgey, 1975

Tāranātha (*sGrol ba'i mgon po*)
Entry to the Definitive Meaning: Distinguishing the Two Modes
Tshul gnyis rnam par 'byed pa nges pa'i don gyi 'jug ngogs zhes bya ba nyung ngu rnam gsal dag cing tshang pa
In the Collected Works of Jetsün Tāranātha, vol. 18: 195–208
Sichuan, China: 'Dzam than dgon, 2000?

Ornament of Shentong-Madhyamaka
gZhan stong dbu ma'i rgyan
In the Collected Works of Jetsün Tāranātha, vol. 18: 109–129
Sichuan, China: 'Dzam than dgon, 2000?

Presentation of the Scriptures for the "Ornament of the Shentong-Madhyamaka"
gZhan stong dbu ma'i rgyan gyi lung sbyor ba
In the Collected Works of Jetsün Tāranātha, vol. 18: 131–170
Sichuan, China: 'Dzam than dgon, 2000?

Requisite Sources for the Dharma Cycle of the Glorious Kālachakra
dPal dus kyi 'khor lo'i chos bskor gyi byung khungs nyer mkho
In the Collected Works of Jetsün Tāranātha, vol. 2
Sichuan, China: 'Dzam than dgon, 2000?

Thubten Nyima

Outline of "The Encompassment of All Knowledge"

Shes bya kun khyab kyi sa bcad

Sichuan, China: Si khron mi rigs dpe skrun khang, 1990

Tsongkhapa (*Tsong kha pa blo bzang grags pa*)

Illumination of the Thought/ Illumination of the Thought of the "Entrance to the Middle Way"

dGongs pa rab gsal/ dBu ma la 'jug pa'i rgya cher bshad pa dgongs pa rab gsal

ACIP S5408

Wangchuk Dorjé (*dBang phyug rdo rje*)

Feast for the Fortunate: An Easy Way into the "Chariot of the Dakpo Siddhas," A Commentary on the "Entrance [to the Middle Way]"

'Jug ṭikā dvags brgyud grub pa'i shing rta bde bar 'dren byed skal bzang dga' ston

Sarnath, India: Vajra Vidya Library, 2003

Youthful Play: An Explanation of the "Treasury of Abhidharma"

mNgon par mdzod kyi rnam bshad gzhon nu rnam rol/ Chos mngon pa mdzod kyi rnam par bshad pa chos mngon rgya mtsho'i snying po mkhyen rtse'i zhal lung gzhon nu rnam rol legs bshad chos mig rnam 'byed grub bde'i shing rta zhes bya ba bzhugs so

Sarnath, India: Vajra Vidya Library, 2003

Zhang, Yisun et al., ed.

Great Tibetan-Chinese Dictionary

Bod rgya tshig mdzod chen mo

3 vols. Beijing: Mi rigs dpe skrun khang, 1985

Other Works and Translations

A Comparative Analytical Catalogue of the Kanjur Division of the Tibetan Tripitaka: Edited in Peking during the K'ang-hsi Era, and At Present Kept in the Library of the Otani Daigaku Kyoto. 3 vols. The Otani Daigaku Library, Kyoto, 1930-1932. 2005. Otani University Shin-Buddhist Comprehensive Research Institute: Tibetan Works Research Project. http://web.otani.ac.jp/cri/twrp/tibdate/Peking_online_search.html

Ames, William L. 1982. "The Notion of Svabhāva in the Thought of Candrakīrti." *JIP* 10: 161–177.

———. 1986a. "Bhāvaviveka's Prajñāpradīpa: Six Chapters." PhD diss., University of Washington.

———. 1986b. "Buddhapālita's Exposition of the Madhyamaka." *JIP* 14: 313-348.

———. 2003. "Bhāvaviveka's Own View of His Differences with Buddhapālita." In *The Svātantrika-Prāsaṅgika Distinction: What Difference Does a Difference Make?*, eds. Georges B. J. Dreyfus and Sara L. McClintock, 41–66. Boston: Wisdom Publications.

Anacker, Stefan. 1984/1998. *Seven Works of Vasubandhu*. Rev. ed. Delhi: Motilal Banarsidass.

Aramaki, Noritoshi. 2000. "Toward an Understanding of the *Vijñaptimātratā*." In *Wisdom, Compassion, and the Search for Understanding: The Buddhist Studies Legacy of Gadjin M. Nagao*, ed. Jonathan A. Silk, 39–60. Honolulu: University of Hawaii Press.

Arnold, Dan. 2005. *Buddhists, Brahmins, and Belief: Epistemology in South Asian Philosophy of Religion.* New York: Columbia University Press.

Bareau, André. 1989. "Hīnayāna Buddhism." Trans. David M. Weeks. In *Buddhism and Asian History*, 195–214. New York: Macmillan.

Barron, Richard, trans. 2003. *The Autobiography of Jamgön Kongtrul: A Gem of Many Colors.* Ithaca, NY: Snow Lion Publications.

———, trans. forthcoming. *The Precious Treasury of Philosophical Systems.* Junction City, CA: Padma Publishing.

Bastow, David. 1994. "The Mahā-Vibhāṣa Arguments for Sarvāstivāda." *PEW* 44, no. 3: 489–499.

Batchelor, Stephen, trans. 1979. *A Guide to the Bodhisattva's Way of Life.* Repr., Dharamsala, India: Library of Tibetan Works and Archives, 1993.

Beal, Samuel, trans. 1884. *Si-Yu-Ki: Buddhist Records of the Western World.* 2 vols. in one. Repr., Motilal Banarsidass, 2004.

Bechert, Heinz. 1973. "Notes on the Formation of Buddhist Sects and the Origins of Mahāyāna." In *German Scholars on India: Contributions to Indian Studies*, vol. 1: 6–18. Varanasi: Chowkhamba Sanskrit Series Office.

Bhattacharya, K. 1978. *The Dialectical Method of Nāgārjuna: Vigrahavyāvartanī.* 4th ed. Repr., Delhi: Motilal Banarsidass, 2002.

Blumenthal, James. 2004. *The Ornament of the Middle Way: A Study of the Madhyamaka Thought of Śāntarakṣita.* Ithaca, NY: Snow Lion Publications.

Bodhi, Bhikkhu, trans. 2000. *The Connected Discourses of the Buddha: A Translation of the Saṃyutta Nikāya.* Boston: Wisdom Publications.

Boin-Webb, Sara, trans. 2001. *Abhidharmasamuccaya: The Compendium of the Higher Teaching (Philosophy).* Fremont, CA: Asian Humanities Press.

Boquist, Åke. 1993. *Trisvabhāva: A Study of the Development of the Three-nature-theory in Yogācāra Buddhism.* Lund Studies in African and Asian Religions 8. Lund: University of Lund.

Broido, Michael. 1985. "Padma Karpo on the Two Satyas." *JIABS* 8, no. 2: 7-59.

———. 1988. "Veridical and Delusive Cognition: Tsongkhapa on the Two Satyas." *JIP* 16: 29-63.

———. 1989. "The Jo-nang-pas on Madhyamaka: A Sketch." *TJ* 14, no. 1: 86-91.

Bronkhorst, Johannes. 1993. *The Two Traditions of Meditation in Ancient India.* Repr., Delhi: Motilal Banarsidass, 2000.

———. 1999. "Nāgārjuna and *Apoha.*" In *Dharmakīrti's Thought and Its Impact on Indian and Tibetan Philosophy. Proceedings of the Third International Dharmakīrti Conference, Hiroshima, November 4-6, 1997,* ed. S. Katsura, 17–23. Vienna: Verlag der Österreichischen Akademie der Wissenschaften.

Brunnhölzl, Karl, trans., ed., and ann. 2001. *A Commentary on the Perfection of Knowledge, The Noble One's Resting at Ease.* Halifax, Nova Scotia: Nitartha Institute.

———, trans., ed., and ann. 2002a. *The Presentation of Grounds, Paths, and Results in the Causal Vehicle of Characteristics in "The Treasury of Knowledge" (Shes bya kun khyab mdzod,* ch. 9.1 and 10.1*).* Halifax, Nova Scotia: Nitartha Institute.

———, trans., ed., and ann. 2002b. *The Presentation of Madhyamaka in "The Treasury of Knowledge" (Shes bya kun khyab mdzod,* Selected passages from ch. 6.3, 7.2, and 7.3*).* Halifax, Nova Scotia: Nitartha Institute.

———. 2004. *The Center of the Sunlit Sky: Madhyamaka in the Kagyü Tradition.* Nitartha Institute Series. Ithaca, NY: Snow Lion Publications.

———. 2007. *In Praise of Dharmadhātu.* Ithaca, NY: Snow Lion Publications.

Buescher, John B. 2005. *Echoes from an Empty Sky: The Origins of the Buddhist Doctrine of the Two Truths*. Ithaca, NY: Snow Lion Publications.

Bugault, G. 1983. "Logic and Dialectics in the *Mādhyamikakārikās*." *JIP* 11, no. 1: 7-76.

Buswell, Robert E., Jr., and Robert M. Gimello, eds. 1992. *Paths to Liberation: The Mārga and Its Transformations in Buddhist Thought*. Studies in East Asian Buddhism 7. Honolulu: Kuroda Institute, University of Hawaii Press.

Buswell, Robert E., Jr., and Padmanabh S. Jaini. 1996. "The Development of Abhidharma Philosophy." In *Encyclopedia of Indian Philosophies*, vol. 7, ed. Karl H. Potter, 73–119. Repr., Delhi: Motilal Banarsidass, 1998.

Cabezón, José I. 1990. "The Canonization of Philosophy and the Rhetoric of Siddhānta in Tibetan Buddhism." In *Buddha Nature: A Festschrift in Honor of Minoru Kiyota*, eds. Paul J. Griffiths and John P. Keenan, 7–26. Reno, NV: Buddhist Books International.

———. 1992a. *Dose of Emptiness: An Annotated Translation of the* sTong thun chen mo *of mKhas grub dGe legs dpal bzang*. Repr., Delhi: Sri Satguru Publications, 1993.

———. 1992b. "Vasubandhu's *Vyākhyāyukti* on the Authenticity of the Mahāyāna Sūtras." In *Texts in Context: Traditional Hermeneutics in South Asia*, ed. Jeffrey R. Timm, 221–243. Albany: State University of New York Press.

———. 2001. "Authorship and Literary Production in Classical Buddhist Tibet." In *Changing Minds: Contributions to the Study of Buddhism and Tibet in Honor of Jeffrey Hopkins*, ed. Guy Newland, 233–263. Ithaca, NY: Snow Lion Publications.

———. 2003. "Two Views on the Svātantrika-Prāsaṅgika Distinction in Fourteenth-Century Tibet." In *The Svātantrika-Prāsaṅgika Distinction: What Difference Does a Difference Make?*, eds. Georges B. J. Dreyfus and Sara L. McClintock, 289–316. Boston: Wisdom Publications.

Cabezón, José I., and Roger Jackson, eds. 1996. *Tibetan Literature: Studies in Genre, Essays in Honor of Geshe Lhundrup Sopa*. Ithaca, NY: Snow Lion Publications.

Callahan, Elizabeth M., trans. 2001. *Mahāmudrā: The Ocean of the Definitive Meaning*. Seattle: Nitartha *international* Publications.

Chimpa, Lama, and Alaka Chattopadhyaya, trans. 1970. *Tāranātha's History of Buddhism in India*. Repr., Motilal Banarsidass, 1990.

Coghlan, Ian. 2002. "The Translation and Introduction to the First Two Chapters of the mDzod 'Grel mNgon pa'i rGyan by mChim 'Jam pa'i dbYangs." PhD diss., Latrobe University.

Conze, E. 1973. *The Perfection of Wisdom in Eight Thousand Lines & Its Verse Summary*. Bolinas, CA: Four Seasons Foundation.

———. 1975. *The Large Sūtra on the Perfection of Wisdom*. Berkeley: University of California Press.

Cox, Collett. 1988. "On the Possibility of a Non-existent Object of Perceptual Consciousness." *JIABS* 11, no. 1: 31–88.

———. 1992. "Attainment through Abandonment: The Sarvāstivādin Path of Removing Defilements." In *Paths to Liberation: The Mārga and Its Transformations in Buddhist Thought,* eds. Robert E. Buswell, Jr., and Robert M. Gimello, 63–105. Studies in East Asian Buddhism 7. Honolulu: Kuroda Institute, University of Hawaii Press.

———. 1995. *Disputed Dharmas: Early Buddhist Theories on Existence.* Studia Philologica Buddhica Monograph Series XI. Tokyo: International Institute for Buddhist Studies.

———. 1998. "Kaśmīra: Vaibhāṣika Orthodoxy." In *Sarvāstivāda Buddhist Scholasticism,* Handbook of Oriental Studies, Charles Willemen, Bart Dessein, and Collett Cox. Leiden: E. J. Brill.

Cozort, Daniel. 1986. *Highest Yoga Tantra.* Ithaca, NY: Snow Lion Publications.

———. 1998. *Unique Tenets of the Middle Way Consequence School*. Ithaca, NY: Snow Lion Publications.

Cozort, Daniel, and Craig Preston. 2003. *Buddhist Philosophy: Losang Gönchok's Short Commentary to Jamyang Shayba's "Root Text on Tenets."* Ithaca, NY: Snow Lion Publications.

Cruise, Henry. 1983. "Early Buddhism: Some Recent Misconceptions." *PEW* 33, no. 2: 149–165.

Cutler, Joshua W. C., and Guy Newland, eds. 2000. *The Great Treatise on the Stages of the Path to Enlightenment.* Vol. 1. Ithaca, NY: Snow Lion Publications.

———. 2002. *The Great Treatise on the Stages of the Path to Enlightenment.* Vol. 3. Ithaca, NY: Snow Lion Publications.

Dalai Lama, Tenzin Gyatso. 1975. *The Buddhism of Tibet.* Trans. and ed. Jeffrey Hopkins. Repr., Ithaca, NY: Snow Lion Publications, 1987.

———. 1992/2000. *The Meaning of Life: Buddhist Perspectives on Cause and Effect.* Trans. Jeffrey Hopkins. Rev. ed. Somerville, MA: Wisdom Publications.

———. 2005. *The Universe in a Single Atom.* New York: Morgan Road Books.

Dalai Lama, Tsong-ka-pa, and Jeffrey Hopkins. 1977. *Tantra in Tibet.* Trans. and ed. Jeffrey Hopkins. Ithaca, NY: Snow Lion Publications.

D'Amato, Mario A. 2000. "The Mahāyāna-Hīnayāna Distinction in the *Mahāyānasūtrālaṃkāra*: A Terminological Analysis." PhD diss., University of Chicago.

———. 2003. "Can all Beings Potentially Attain Awakening? *Gotra*-Theory in the *Mahāyānasūtrālaṃkāra.*" *JIABS* 26, no. 1: 115–138.

Davidson, Ronald M. 1985. "Buddhist Systems of Transformation: *Āśraya-parivṛtti/-parāvṛtti* among the Yogācāra." PhD diss., University of California.

———. 1990. "An Introduction to the Standards of Scriptural Authenticity in Indian Buddhism." In *Chinese Buddhist Apocrypha,* ed. Robert E. Buswell, Jr., 291–325. Repr., Delhi: Sri Satguru Publications, 1992.

Della Santina, Peter. 1986. *Madhyamaka Schools in India: A Study of the Madhyamaka Philosophy and of the Division of the System into the Prāsaṅgika and Svātantrika Schools.* Repr., New Delhi: Motilal Banarsidass, 1995.

Dessein, Bart. 1999. *Saṃyuktābhidharmahṛdaya: Heart of Scholasticism with Miscellaneous Additions.* Buddhist Tradition Series, 3 vols. Delhi: Motilal Banarsidass.

———. 2003. "Sautrāntika and the Hṛdata Treatises." *JIABS* 26, no. 2: 287–320.

Doctor, Thomas H. 2004. *Speech of Delight: Mipham's Commentary on Śāntarakṣita's "Ornament of the Middle Way."* Ithaca, NY: Snow Lion Publications.

Douglas, Nik, and Meryl White. 1976. *Karmapa: The Black Hat Lama of Tibet.* London: Luzac.

Dreyfus, Georges B. J. 1997. *Recognizing Reality: Dharmakīrti's Philosophy and Its Tibetan Interpretations.* Albany: State University of New York Press.

———. 2003. *The Sound of Two Hands Clapping: The Education of a Tibetan Buddhist Monk.* Berkeley: University of California Press.

Dreyfus, Georges B. J., and Sara L. McClintock, eds. 2003. *The Svātantrika-Prāsaṅgika Distinction: What Difference Does a Difference Make?* Boston: Wisdom Publications.

Dudjom Rinpoche, Jikdrel Yeshe Dorje. 1991. *The Nyingma School of Tibetan Buddhism: Its Fundamentals and History*. Trans. and ed. Gyurme Dorje and Matthew Kapstein. Boston: Wisdom Publications.

Duerlinger, James. 2003. *Indian Buddhist Theories of Persons: Vasubandhu's "Refutation of the Theory of a Self."* RoutledgeCurzon Critical Studies in Buddhism. London: RoutledgeCurzon.

Dunne, John D. 2004. *Foundations of Dharmakīrti's Philosophy*. Boston: Wisdom Publications.

Dutt, Nalinaksha. 1978. *Buddhist Sects in India*. Repr., Delhi: Motilal Banarsidass, 1987.

Dzogchen Ponlop, Rinpoche. 1998. *Tenets Sourcebook: Hīnayāna Tenets*. Trans. Elizabeth Callahan. Halifax, Nova Scotia: Nitartha Institute.

———. 2001. *An Exposition of the Presentation of the Philosophical Systems of the Great Vehicle: An Exposition that Reveals the Presentation of the Philosophical Systems of the Chittamatrikas of the Great Vehicle*. Trans. Karl Brunnhölzl, Tyler Dewar, and Scott Wellenbach. Halifax, Nova Scotia: Nitartha Institute.

———. 2003. *Wild Awakening*. Boston: Shambhala Publications.

Dzogchen Ponlop, Rinpoche, and Āchārya Lama Tenpa Gyaltsen. 2001. *The Gateway that Reveals the Philosophical Systems to Fresh Minds: An Exposition that Reveals the Presentation of the Philosophical Systems of Our Own Buddhist Faction in a Slightly Elaborate Way*. Trans. Karl Brunnhölzl. Halifax, Nova Scotia: Nitartha Institute.

Eckel, Malcolm D. 1978. "Bhāvaviveka and the Early Mādhyamika Theories of Language." *PEW* 28, no. 3: 323–337.

———. 1985. "Bhāvaviveka's Critique of Yogācāra Philosophy in Chapter XXV of the *Prajñāpradīpa*." In *Indiske Studier V*, ed. Chr. Lindtner, 24–75. Copenhagen: Akademisk Forlag.

———. 1987. *Jñānagarbha on the Two Truths: An Eighth Century Handbook of Madhyamaka Philosophy*. Repr., Delhi: Motilal Banarsidass, 1992.

———. 1992. *To See the Buddha: A Philosopher's Quest for the Meaning of Emptiness*. Princeton, NJ: Princeton University Press.

———. 2003. "The Satisfaction of No Analysis: On Tsong kha pa's Approach to Svātantrika-Madhyamaka." In *The Svātantrika-Prāsaṅgika Distinction:*

What Difference Does a Difference Make? eds. Georges Dreyfus and Sara L. McClintock, 173–203. Boston: Wisdom Publications.

Farrow, G. W., and I. Menon, trans. 1992. *The Concealed Essence of the Hevajra Tantra.* Delhi: Motilal Banarsidass.

Frauwallner, Erich. 1995. *Studies in Abhidharma Literature and the Origins of Buddhist Philosophical Systems.* Trans. Sophie Francis Kidd. Albany, NY: State University of New York Press.

Fuchs, Rosemarie, trans. 2000. *Buddha Nature: The Mahayana Uttaratantra Shastra.* Ithaca, NY: Snow Lion Publications.

Fukuda, Takumi. 2003. "Bhadanta Rāma: A Sautrāntika before Vasubandhu." *JIABS* 26, no. 2: 255–286.

Garfield, Jay L., trans. and comm. 1995. *The Fundamental Wisdom of the Middle Way: Nāgārjuna's Mūlamadhyamakakārikā.* New York: Oxford University Press.

———. 1997. "Vasubandhu's 'Treatise on the Three Natures': Translated from the Tibetan Edition with a Commentary." *AP* 6, no. 2: 133–154.

———. 2002. *Empty Words: Buddhist Philosophy and Cross-Cultural Interpretation.* New York: Oxford University Press.

Goldfield, Ari, Jules Levinson, Jim Scott, and Birgit Scott, trans. 2005. *The Moon of Wisdom: Chapter Six of Chandrakirti's Entering the Middle Way.* Ithaca, NY: Snow Lion Publications.

Gombrich, Richard. 1988. *Theravāda Buddhism: A Social History from Ancient Benares to Modern Colombo.* London and New York: Routledge.

———. 1990. "Recovering the Buddha's Message." In *Earliest Buddhism and Madhyamaka*, eds. David Seyfort Ruegg and Lambert Schmithausen, Panels of the VIIth World Sanskrit Conference, 5–23. Leiden: E. J. Brill.

Gómez, Luis O. 1976. "Proto-Mādhyamika in the Pāli Canon." *PEW* 26, no. 2: 137–165.

———. 2000. "Two Jars on Two Tables: Reflections on the 'Two Truths.'" In *Wisdom, Compassion, and the Search for Understanding: The Buddhist Studies Legacy of Gadjin M. Nagao*, ed. Jonathan A. Silk, 95–136. Honolulu: University of Hawaii Press.

Griffiths, Paul J. 1986. *On Being Mindless.* La Salle, Illinois: Open Court.

———. 1990. "Omniscience in the Mahāyānasūtrālaṅkāra and Its Commentaries." *IIJ* 33: 85–120.

———. 1999. "Asaṅga: *Abhidharmasamuccaya.*" In *Encyclopedia of Indian Philosophies, Volume VIII: Buddhist Philosophy from 100 to 350 A. D.*, ed. Karl Potter, 435–525. Repr., Delhi: Motilal Banarsidass, 2002.

Guenther, Herbert V., trans. and ann. 1959. *The Jewel Ornament of Liberation.* Repr., Boulder, CO: Shambhala Publications, 1971.

Gyaltsen, Sherab, Āchārya. 1998. *Commentary on "The Presentation of the Classifications of Reasons."* Trans. Elizabeth Callahan. Halifax, Nova Scotia: Nitartha Institute.

———. 2002. *Commentary on "The Gateway that Reveals the Philosophical Systems to Fresh Minds."* Trans. Tyler Dewar. Halifax, Nova Scotia: Nitartha Institute.

———. 2003. *Commentary on "The Chittamatra Philosophical System: An Exposition of the Presentation of the Philosophical Systems of the Chittamatrikas of the Great Vehicle."* Trans. Tyler Dewar. Halifax, Nova Scotia: Nitartha Institute.

Gyaltsen, Tenpa, Āchārya Lama. 1999. *Tagrig Overview.* Trans. Elizabeth Callahan. Halifax, Nova Scotia: Nitartha Institute.

———, compiled. 1999. *Collected Topics: A Presentation of Objects, Subjects, and Methods that Lead to Cognition of Objects and Subjects.* Trans. Karl Brunnhölzl and the Nitartha Translation Group. 5th ed. Halifax, Nova Scotia: Nitartha Institute.

———. 2002. *Commentary on "The Presentation of Madhyamaka in 'The Treasury of Knowledge.'"* Trans. Karl Brunnhölzl. 2nd ed. Halifax, Nova Scotia: Nitartha Institute.

Gyamtso, Khenpo Tsültrim, Rinpoche. 1986. *Progressive Stages of Meditation on Emptiness.* Trans. Shenpen Hookham. Oxford: Longchen Foundation.

———. 1992. *A Presentation of the Two Truths in the Three Yānas and the Mahāyāna Philosophical Traditions.* Trans. Jules B. Levinson. Halifax, Nova Scotia: Nālandā Translation Committee.

———. 1995. *Talks and Songs on the Progressive Stages of Meditation on Emptiness.* Trans. Susanne Schefczyk. Kathmandu: Marpa Translation Committee.

———. 1996a/1999. *The Presentation of the Classifications of Reasons Called: The Essence of the Ocean of Texts on Logic.* Trans. Āchārya Sherab Gyaltsen and Ari Goldfield. Rev. ed. Halifax, Nova Scotia: Nitartha Institute.

———. 1996b/2000. *The Presentation of the Classifications of Mental States Called: The Essence of the Ocean of Texts on Reasoning.* Trans. Karl Brunnhölzl and Chryssoula Zerbini. Rev. ed. Halifax, Nova Scotia: Nitartha Institute.

———. 2003. *The Sun of Wisdom: Teachings on the Noble Nāgārjuna's "Fundamental Wisdom of the Middle Way."* Trans. and ed. Ari Goldfield. Boston: Shambhala Publications.

Hall, Bruce Cameron. 1986. "The Meaning of Vijñapti in Vasubandhu's Concept of Mind." *JIABS* 9, no. 1: 7–23.

Hanson, Elena F. 1998. "Early Yogācāra and Its Relation to Nāgārjuna's Madhyamaka: Change and Continuity in the History of Mahāyāna Buddhist Thought." PhD diss., Harvard University.

Harding, Sarah, trans. 1996. *Creation and Completion: Essential Points of Tantric Meditation.* Boston: Wisdom Publications.

Harris, Ian Charles. 1991. *The Continuity of Madhyamaka and Yogācāra in Indian Mahāyāna Buddhism.* Leiden: E. J. Brill.

Hirabayashi, Jay and Shotaro Iida. 1977. "Another Look at the Mādhyamika versus Yogācāra Controversy Concerning Existence and Non-existence." In *Prajñāpāramitā and Related Systems,* ed. Lewis Lancaster, 341–60. Berkeley: Berkeley Buddhist Studies.

Hirakawa, Akira. 1978. *Index to the Abhidharmakośabhāṣya.* Part Three: Tibetan-Sanskrit. Tokyo: Daizo Shuppan Kabushikikaisha.

———. 1990. *A History of Indian Buddhism: From Śākyamuni to Early Mahāyāna.* Trans. and ed. Paul Groner. Honolulu: University of Hawaii Press.

Hiriyanna, M. 1932. *Outlines of Indian Philosophy.* Repr., Delhi: Motilal Banarsidass, 2000.

———. 1948. *The Essentials of Indian Philosophy.* Repr., Delhi: Motilal Banarsidass, 2000.

Holmes, Ken, and Katia Holmes, trans. 1985. *The Changeless Nature.* Eskdalemuir, Scotland: Karma Drubgyud Darjay Ling.

———, trans. 1995. *Gems of Dharma, Jewels of Freedom.* Forres, Scotland: Altea Publishing.

———. 1999. *Maitreya on Buddha Nature.* Forres, Scotland: Altea Publishing.

Honjō, Yoshifumi. 2003. "The Word Sautrāntika." *JIABS* 26, no. 2: 321–330.

Hookham, S. K. 1991. *The Buddha Within: The Tathāgatagarbha Doctrine According to the Shentong Interpretation of the Ratnagotravibhaga*. Albany: State University of New York Press.

Hopkins, Jeffrey. 1980. *Compassion in Tibetan Buddhism.* Ithaca, NY: Snow Lion Publications.

———. 1983. *Meditation on Emptiness*. London: Wisdom Publications.

———. 1987. *Emptiness Yoga.* Repr., Delhi: Motilal Banarsidass, 1997.

———. 1996. "The Tibetan Genre of Doxography: Structuring a Worldview." In *Tibetan Literature: Studies in Genre, Essays in Honor of Geshe Lhundrup Sopa,* eds. José I. Cabezón and Roger Jackson, 170–186. Ithaca, NY: Snow Lion Publications.

———. 1999. *Emptiness in the Mind-Only School of Buddhism.* Berkeley: University of California Press.

———. 2002. *Reflections on Reality: The Three Natures and Non-Natures in the Mind-Only School.* Berkeley: University of California Press.

———. 2003. *Maps of the Profound: Jam-yang-shay-ba's "Great Exposition of Buddhist and Non-Buddhist Views on the Nature of Reality."* Ithaca, NY: Snow Lion Publications.

———. 2005. *Absorption in No External World: 170 Issues in Mind-Only Buddhism.* Ithaca, NY: Snow Lion Publications.

———. 2006. *Mountain Doctrine: Tibet's Fundamental Treatise on Other-Emptiness and the Buddha Matrix.* Ithaca, NY: Snow Lion Publications.

———, trans. and ann. 2007. *The Essence of Other-Emptiness.* In collaboration with Lama Lodrö Namgyel. Ithaca, NY: Snow Lion Publications.

Hopkins, Jeffrey, and Geshe Lhundrup Sopa. 1976. *Practice and Theory of Tibetan Buddhism.* New York: Grove Press. Rev. ed., *Cutting through Appearances: Practice and Theory of Tibetan Buddhism,* Ithaca, NY: Snow Lion Publications, 1989.

Huntington, C. W., Jr. 1983. "The System of the Two Truths in the Prasannapadā and the Madhyamakāvatāra: A Study in Madhyamaka Soteriology." *JIP* 11, no. 1: 77–107.

———. 1986. "The Akutobhayā and Early Indian Buddhism." PhD diss., University of Michigan.

———. 1989. *The Emptiness of Emptiness.* Honolulu: University of Hawaii Press.

———. 2003. "Was Candrakīrti a Prāsaṅgika?" In *The Svātantrika-Prāsaṅgika Distinction: What Difference Does a Difference Make?* eds.

Georges Dreyfus and Sara L. McClintock, 67–91. Boston: Wisdom Publications.

Hurvitz, Leon. 1976. *Scripture of the Lotus Blossom of the Fine Dharma.* New York: Columbia University Press.

Iaroslav, Komarovski, trans. 2000. *Three Texts on Madhyamaka by Shakya Chokden.* Dharamsala, India: Library of Tibetan Works and Archives.

Ichigō, Masamichi. 1985. *Madhyamakālaṁkāra of Śāntarakṣita with his own commentary or Vṛtti and with the subcommentary or Pañjika of Kamalaśīla.* Kyoto: Bun'eidō.

———. 1989. "Śāntarakṣita's *Madhyamakālaṁkāra.*" In *Studies in the Literature of the Great Vehicle,* eds. Luis O. Gómez and Jonathan A. Silk. Ann Arbor: University of Michigan Press.

———. 2000. "Śāntarakṣita and Bhāvaviveka as Opponents of the Mādhyamika in the *Madhyamāloka.*" In *Wisdom, Compassion, and the Search for Understanding: The Buddhist Studies Legacy of Gadjin M. Nagao,* ed. Jonathan A. Silk, 147–170. Honolulu: University of Hawaii Press.

Ichimura, Shohei, et al. 1996. "Mahāvibhāṣā: Summary." In *Encyclopedia of Indian Philosophies, Volume VII: Abhidharma Buddhism to 150 A.D.*, ed. Karl Potter et al., 512–568. Repr., Delhi: Motilal Banarsidass, 1998.

Jamspal, L., et al., trans. 2004. *The Universal Vehicle Discourse Literature (Mahāyānasūtrālaṁkāra).* Editor-in-chief, Robert A. F. Thurman. Treasury of the Buddhist Sciences. New York: American Institute of Buddhist Studies, Columbia University.

Jackson, David P. 1985. "Madhyamaka Studies among the Early Sa-skya-pas." *TJ* 10, no. 2: 20-34.

———. 1994. *Enlightenment by a Single Means: Tibetan Controversies on the "Self-Sufficient White Remedy."* Vienna: Verlag der Österreichischen Akademie der Wissenschaften.

Jackson, Roger R. 1993. *Is Enlightenment Possible? Dharmakīrti and rGyal tshab rje on Knowledge, Rebirth, No-Self and Liberation.* Ithaca, NY: Snow Lion Publications.

Jones, Elvin W. 1978. "Buddhist Theories of Existents: The System of Two Truths." In *Mahāyāna Buddhist Meditation,* ed. Minoru Kiyota, 3–45. Repr., Delhi: Motilal Banarsidass, 1991.

Kajiyama, Yuichi. 1965. "Controversy between the *sākāra-* and the *nirākāra-vādins* of the Yogācāra school—some materials." *JIBS* 14, no. 1: 26–37.

———. 1978. "Later Mādhyamikas on Epistemology and Meditation." In *Mahāyāna Buddhist Meditation,* ed. Minoru Kiyota, 114–143. Repr., Delhi: Motilal Banarsidass, 1991.

———. 1998. *An Introduction to Buddhist Philosophy: An Annotated Translation of the Tarkabhāṣā of Mokṣākaragupta.* Wiener Studien zur Tibetologie und Buddhismuskunde, Heft 42. Vienna: Arbeitskreis für Tibetische und Buddhistische Studien Universität Wien.

Kalupahana, David J. 1974. "The Buddhist Conception of Time and Temporality." *PEW* 2, 181–191.

Kaplan, Stephen. 1990. "A Holographic Alternative to a Traditional Yogācāra Simile: An Analysis of Vasubandhu's Trisvabhāva Doctrine." *The Eastern Buddhist* 23: 56-78.

Kapstein, Matthew T. 1988. "Mipham's Theory of Interpretation." In *Buddhist Hermeneutics,* ed. D. S. Lopez, 149–174. Honolulu: University of Hawaii Press.

———. 1992a. *The 'Dzam-thang Edition of the Collected Works of Kun-mkhyen Dol-po-pa Shes-rab rgyal-mtshan: Introduction and Catalogue.* Delhi: Shedrup Books.

———. 1992b. "The Illusion of Spiritual Progress." In *Paths to Liberation: The Mārga and Its Transformations in Buddhist Thought,* eds. Robert E. Buswell, Jr. and Robert M. Gimello, 193–224. Studies in East Asian Buddhism 7. Honolulu: Kuroda Institute, University of Hawaii Press.

———. 2000a. *The Tibetan Assimilation of Buddhism: Conversion, Contestation, and Memory.* New York: Oxford University Press.

———. 2000b. "We are all Gzhan stong pas." *Journal of Buddhist Ethics* 7: 105–125.

———. 2001. *Reason's Traces: Identity and Interpretation in Indian and Tibetan Buddhist Thought.* Boston: Wisdom Publications.

Katsura, Shōryū. 1995. "Dignāga and Dharmakīrti on *Apoha*." In *Studies in the Buddhist Epistemological Tradition. Proceedings of the Second International Dharmakīrti Conference, Vienna, June 11-16, 1989,* ed. E. Steinkellner, 129–146. Vienna: Verlag der Österreichischen Akademie der Wissenschaften.

Katz, N. 1983. "Tibetan Hermeneutics and the *yāna* Controversy." In *Contributions on Tibetan and Buddhist Religion and Philosophy: Proceedings of the Csoma de Körös Symposium Held at Velm-Vienna, Austria, 13–19 September 1981,* eds. E. Steinkellner and H. Tauscher, 107-130. Repr., Delhi: Motilal Banarsidass, 1995.

Keenan, John P. 1989. "Asaṅga's Understanding of Mādhyamika: Notes on the *Shung-chung-lun*." *JIABS* 12, no. 1: 93–107.

———. 1992. *The Summary of the Great Vehicle*. BDK English Tripiṭaka 46-III. Berkeley: Numata Center for Buddhist Translation and Research.

Kimura, Toshihiko. 1999. "A New Chronology of Dharmakīrti." In *Dharmakīrti's Thought and Its Impact on Indian and Tibetan Philosophy. Proceedings of the Third International Dharmakīrti Conference, Hiroshima, November 4-6, 1997*, ed. S. Katsura, 209–214. Vienna: Verlag der Österreichischen Akademie der Wissenschaften.

King, Richard. 1994. "Early Yogācāra and Its Relationship with the Madhyamaka School." *PEW* 44, no. 4: 659–683.

———. 1998. "Vijnaptimatrata and the Abhidharma context of early Yogācāra." *AP* 8, no. 1: 5-18. http://ccbs.ntu.edu.tw/FULLTEXT/JR-ADM/richard.htm

Klein, Anne C. 1991. *Knowing, Naming, and Negation*. Ithaca, NY: Snow Lion Publications.

———. 1998. *Knowledge and Liberation*. Ithaca, NY: Snow Lion Publications.

Kochumuttom, Thomas A. 1982. *A Buddhist Doctrine of Experience*. Repr., Delhi: Motilal Banarsidass, 1999.

Kongtrul Lodrö Tayé, Jamgön. 1995. *The Treasury of Knowledge: Myriad Worlds*. Trans. International Translation Committee of Kalu Rinpoché. Ithaca, NY: Snow Lion Publications.

———. 1998. *The Treasury of Knowledge: Buddhist Ethics*. Trans. International Translation Committee of Kalu Rinpoché. Ithaca, NY: Snow Lion Publications.

———. 2005. *The Treasury of Knowledge: Systems of Buddhist Tantra*. Trans. Kalu Rinpoché Translation Group (Elio Guarisco and Ingrid McLeod). Ithaca, NY: Snow Lion Publications.

———. forthcoming. *The Treasury of Knowledge: Journey and Goal*. Trans. Kalu Rinpoché Translation Group (Richard Barron). Ithaca, NY: Snow Lion Publications.

Krasser, Helmut. 2001. "On Dharmakīrti's Understanding of *Pramāṇabhūta* and His Definition of *Pramāṇa*." *WZKS* 45: 173–199.

Kritzer, Robert. 1999. *Rebirth and Causation in the Yogācāra Abhidharma*. Wiener Studien zur Tibetologie und Buddhismuskunde, Heft 44. Vienna: Arbeitskreis für Tibetische und Buddhistische Studien Universität Wien.

———. 2003a. "General Introduction [to the issue of the *Journal of the International Association of Buddhist Studies* entitled *The Sautrāntikas*]." *JIABS* 26, no. 2: 201–224.

———. 2003b. "Sautrāntika in the *Abhidharmakośabhāṣya*." *JIABS* 26, no. 2: 331–384.

———. 2005. *Vasubandhu and the Yogācārabhūmi: Yogācāra Elements in the Abhidharmakośabhāṣya.* Studia Philologica Buddhica Monograph Series XVIII. Tokyo: International Institute for Buddhist Studies.

Lamotte, Étienne. 1988. *History of Indian Buddhism: from the Origins to the Śaka Era.* Trans. Sara Webb-Boin. Publications de L'Institut Orientaliste de Louvain 36. Louvain-la-Neuve: Institut Orientaliste.

Lang, Karen C. 2003. *Four Illusions: Candrakīrti's Advice for Travelers on the Bodhisattva Path.* New York: Oxford University Press.

Lati Rinbochay. 1980/1986. *Mind in Tibetan Buddhism.* Trans. and ed. Elizabeth Napper. 3rd ed. Ithaca, NY: Snow Lion Publications.

Lessing, F. D., and Wayman, Alex. 1968. *Introduction to the Buddhist Tantric Systems.* 2nd ed. Repr., Delhi: Motilal Banarsidass.

Levinson, Jules Brooks. 1994. "The Metaphors of Liberation: A Study of Grounds and Paths according to the Middle Way Schools." PhD diss., University of Virginia.

Lindtner, Christian. 1981. "Atiśa's Introduction to the Two Truths, and Its Sources." *JIP* 9: 161–214.

———. 1982. "*On the Authenticity of Madhyamakaratnapradīpa.*" *WZKS* 26: 172-184.

———. 1986. *Master of Wisdom: Writings of the Buddhist Master Nāgārjuna.* Berkeley: Dharma Publishing.

———. 1995. "Bhavya's *Madhyamakahṛdaya (Pariccheda Five) Yogācāra-tattvaviniścaya-āvatāra.*" *Adyar Library Bulletin* 59: 37–65.

———. 1997. "*Cittamātra* in the Indian Mahāyāna until Kamalaśīla." Repr., in *A Garland of Light: Kambala's Ālokamāla.* Fremont, CA: Asian Humanities Press, 2003.

———. 2003. *A Garland of Light: Kambala's Ālokamāla.* Fremont, CA: Asian Humanities Press.

Lopez, Donald S., Jr. 1987. *A Study of Svātantrika.* Ithaca, NY: Snow Lion Publications.

———. 1988a. "Do *Śrāvakas* Understand Emptiness?" *JIP* 16: 65-105.

———. 1988b. "On the Interpretation of the Mahāyāna Sūtras." In *Buddhist Hermeneutics,* ed. Donald S. Lopez, Jr., 47–70. Honolulu: University of Hawaii Press.

———. 1992. "Paths Terminable and Interminable." In *Paths to Liberation: The Mārga and Its Transformations in Buddhist Thought,* eds. Robert E. Buswell, Jr. and Robert M. Gimello, 147–192. Studies in East Asian Buddhism 7. Honolulu: Kuroda Institute, University of Hawaii Press.

———. 1996a. *Elaborations on Emptiness.* Princeton: Princeton University Press,

———. 1996b. "Polemical Literature (dGag lan)." In *Tibetan Literature,* eds. José Cabezón and Roger Jackson, 17-28. Ithaca, NY: Snow Lion Publications.

———. 2001. "Painting the Target. On the Identification of the Object of Negation (dgag bya)." In *Changing Minds: Contributions to the Study of Buddhism and Tibet in Honor of Jeffrey Hopkins,* ed. Guy Newland, 63-81. Ithaca, NY: Snow Lion Publications.

Mabbett, Ian. 1998. "The Problem of the Historical Nagarjuna Revisited." *JAOS* 118, no. 3: 332–346.

Mahāvyutpatti. Ed. Sakaki. 2 vols. Kyoto, 1916–25 and 1928.

Mathes, Klaus-Dieter. 2000. "Tāranātha's Presentation of *trisvabhāva* in the *gŹan stoṅ sñiṅ po.*" *JIABS* 23, no. 2: 195–223.

———. 2004. "Tāranātha's 'Twenty-One Differences with regard to the Profound Meaning'—Comparing the Views of the Two *gŹan sToṅ* Masters Dol po pa and Śākya mChog ldan." *JIABS* 27, no. 2: 285–328.

Matilal, Bimal K. 1971/2005. *Epistemology, Logic, and Grammar in Indian Philosophical Analysis.* New ed., Delhi: Oxford University Press.

———. 1986. *Perception: An Essay on Classical Indian Theories of Knowledge.* Repr., Delhi: Oxford University Press, 2002.

———. 1998. *The Character of Logic in India.* Albany: State University of New York Press.

McClintock, Sara L. 2003. "The Role of the 'Given' in the Classification of Śāntarakṣita and Kamalaśīla as Svātantrika-Mādhyamikas." In *The Svātantrika-Prāsaṅgika Distinction: What Difference Does a Difference Make?,* eds. Georges B. J. Dreyfus and Sara L. McClintock, 125–171. Boston: Wisdom Publications.

McEvilley, Thomas. 1981. "Early Greek Philosophy and Mādhyamika." *PEW* 31, no. 2: 141–164.

———. 2002. *The Shape of Ancient Thought.* New York: Allworth Press.

Mimaki, Katsumi. 1983. "The *Blo gsal grub mtha'* and the Madhyamaka Classification in Tibetan *Grub mtha'* Literature." In *Contributions on Tibetan and Buddhist Religion and Philosophy: Proceedings of the Csoma de Körös Symposium Held at Velm-Vienna, Austria, 13–19 September 1981,* eds. E. Steinkellner and H. Tauscher, 161-167. Repr., Delhi: Motilal Banarsidass, 1995.

———. 1987. "Āryadeva." In *The Encyclopedia of Religion,* ed. Mircea Eliade et al., 1:431a–432a. New York: MacMillan.

———. 2000. "*Jñānasārasamuccaya* kk^0 20–28: *Mise au point* with a Sanskrit Manuscript." In *Wisdom, Compassion, and the Search for Understanding: The Buddhist Studies Legacy of Gadjin M. Nagao,* ed. Jonathan A. Silk, 233–244. Honolulu: University of Hawaii Press.

Monier-Williams, Sir Monier. 1899. *A Sanskrit-English Dictionary.* Repr., Delhi: Asian Educational Services, 1999.

Moriyama, Seitetsu. 1991. "The later Mādhyamika and Dharmakīrti." In *Studies in the Buddhist Epistemological Tradition. Proceedings of the Second International Dharmakīrti Conference, Vienna, June 11-16, 1989,* ed. E. Steinkellner, 199–210. Vienna: Verlag der Österreichischen Akademie der Wissenschaften.

Müller, Charles. 2004. "The Yogācāra Two Hindrances and their Reinterpretations in East Asia." *JIABS* 27, no. 1: 207–235.

Murti, T. R. V. 1955. *The Central Philosophy of Buddhism: A Study of the Madhyamaka System.* Repr., Delhi: Munshiram Manoharlal Publishers, 2003.

Nagao, Gadjin. 1991. *Mādhyamika and Yogācāra. A Study of Mahāyāna Philosophies.* Ed., collated, and trans. Leslie Kawamura. Repr., Delhi: Sri Satguru Publications, 1992.

Nālandā Translation Committee. 1982. *The Life of Marpa the Translator.* Boulder: Prajñā Press.

Ñāṇamoli, Bhikkhu, trans. 1979. *The Path of Purification (Visuddhimagga) by Bhadantācariya Buddhaghosa.* Fourth ed. Kandy, Sri Laṅkā: Buddhist Publication Society.

Ñāṇamoli, Bhikkhu, trans., and Bhikkhu Bodhi, ed. and rev. 2005. *The Middle Length Discourses of the Buddha: A Translation of the Majjhima Nikāya.* 3rd ed. Boston: Wisdom Publications.

Negi, J. S. 2001. *Tibetan-Sanskrit Dictionary.* Vol. 7. Sarnath, India: Central Institute of Higher Tibetan Studies.

Newland, Guy. 1999. *Appearance and Reality: The Two Truths in the Four Buddhist Tenet Systems*. Ithaca, NY: Snow Lion Publications.

———. 2001. "Ask a Farmer: Ultimate Analysis and Conventional Existence in Tsong kha pa's *Lam rim chen mo*." In *Changing Minds: Contributions to the Study of Buddhism and Tibet in Honor of Jeffrey Hopkins*, ed. Guy Newland, 49-62. Ithaca, NY: Snow Lion Publications.

Norman, K. R. 1983. "The Pratyeka-buddha in Buddhism and Jainism." In *Buddhist Studies: Ancient and Modern*, eds. Philip Denwood and Alexander Piatigorsky, 92–106. Collected Papers on South Asia 4. London: Curzon Press.

———. 1990. "Aspects of Early Buddhism." In *Earliest Buddhism and Madhyamaka*, eds. David Seyfort Ruegg and Lambert Schmithausen, Panels of the VIIth World Sanskrit Conference, 24–35. Leiden: E. J. Brill.

———. 1996. "Solitary as Rhinoceros Horn." *Buddhist Studies Review* 13: 133-142.

Nyingma Edition of the sDe-dge bKa'-'gyur and bsTan-'gyur: Research Catalogue and Bibliography. 8 vols. Oakland, CA: Dharma Press, 1980.

Obermiller, E., trans. 1931. *The Jewelry of Scripture by Bu ston*. Repr., Delhi: Classics India Publications, 2000.

———, trans. 1932. *History of Buddhism in India and Tibet*. Repr., Delhi: Paljor Publications. 1999.

Olson, Robert F. 1974. "Candrakīrti's critique of Vijñānavāda." *PEW* 24, no. 1: 405-411.

Oxford English Dictionary (Second Edition). 1994. Oxford: Oxford University Press.

Padmakara Translation Group, trans. 1997. *The Way of the Bodhisattva*. Boston: Shambhala Publications.

———, trans. 2001. *Treasury of Precious Qualities: A Commentary on the Root Text of Jigme Lingpa by Longchen Yeshe Dorje, Kangyur Rinpoche*. Boston: Shambhala Publications.

———, trans. 2002. *Introduction to the Middle Way: Chandrakīrti's 'Madhyamakāvatāra' with Commentary by Jamgön Mipham*. Boston: Shambhala Publications.

———, trans. 2005. *The Adornment of the Middle Way: Shantarakshita's Madhyamakalankara with Commentary by Jamgön Mipham*. Boston: Shambhala Publications.

Patt, David. 1993. "Elucidating the Path to Liberation: A Study of the Commentary on the 'Abhidharmakośa' by the first Dalai Lama." PhD diss., University of Wisconsin.

Perdue, Daniel. 1993. *Debate in Tibetan Buddhism.* Ithaca, NY: Snow Lion Publications.

Pettit, John W. 1999. *Mipham's Beacon of Certainty: Illuminating the View of Dzogchen, the Great Perfection.* Boston: Wisdom Publications.

Phuntsho, Karma. 2005. *Mipham's Dialectics and the Debates on Emptiness: To Be, Not to Be or Neither.* London: RoutledgeCurzon.

Pind, Ole Holten. 2001. "Why the Vaidalyaprakaraṇa Cannot be an Authentic Work of Nāgārjuna." *WZKS* 45: 149–172.

Potter, Karl. 1991. *Presuppositions of India's Philosophies.* Delhi: Motilal Banarsidass.

———, ed. 1999. *Encyclopedia of Indian Philosophies, Volume VIII: Buddhist Philosophy from 100 to 350 A. D.* Repr., Delhi: Motilal Banarsidass, 2002.

———, ed. 2003. *Encyclopedia of Indian Philosophies, Volume IX: Buddhist Philosophy from 350 to 600 A. D.* Delhi: Motilal Banarsidass.

Potter, Karl, with Robert E. Buswell, Jr., Padmanabh S. Jaini, and Noble Ross Reat, eds. 1996. *Encyclopedia of Indian Philosophies, Volume VII: Abhidharma Buddhism to 150 A. D.* Repr., Delhi: Motilal Banarsidass, 1998.

Powell, James K., II. 1998. "The Great Debate in Mahāyāna Buddhism: The Nature of Consciousness." PhD diss., University of Wisconsin.

Powers, John, trans. 1995. *Wisdom of Buddha: The Saṇdhinirmocana Mahāyāna Sūtra.* Berkeley: Dharma Publishing.

Pruden, Leo M., trans. 1988–1990. *Abhidharmakośabhāṣyam.* 4 vols. Berkeley: Asian Humanities Press.

Przyluski, Jean. 1940. "Dārṣṭāntika, Sautrāntika and Sarvāstivādin." *Indian Historical Quarterly* 16: 246–254.

Ray, Reginald A. 1994. *Buddhist Saints in India: A Study in Buddhist Values & Orientations.* New York: Oxford University Press.

———. 2001. *Secret of the Vajra World: The Tantric Buddhism of Tibet.* Boston: Shambhala Publications.

Rhys Davids, T. W., trans. 1890. *The Questions of King Milinda: Part I.* Repr., Delhi: Motilal Banarsidass, 2003.

———. 1894. *The Questions of King Milinda: Part II.* Repr., Delhi: Motilal Banarsidass, 1999.

Rigzin, Tsepak. 1986/1993. *Tibetan-English Dictionary of Buddhist Terminology*. 2nd ed. Dharamsala, India: Library of Tibetan Works and Archives.

Roberts, Peter, trans. 2001. *Transcending Ego: Distinguishing Consciousness from Wisdom* of Rangjung Dorje, the third Karmapa, with a Commentary by Thrangu Rinpoche. Delhi: Sri Satguru Publications.

Robinson, James B., trans. 1979. *Buddha's Lions: The Lives of the Eighty-Four Siddhas*. Berkeley: Dharma Publishing.

Robinson, Richard H. 1976. *Early Mādhyamika in India and China*. Repr., Delhi: Motilal Banarsidass, 1978.

Roerich, George N., trans. 1949. *The Blue Annals*. Repr., Delhi: Motilal Banarsidass, 1979.

Ruegg, David Seyfort. 1963. "The Jo nang pas: A School of Buddhist Ontologists according to the Grub mtha' shel gyi me long." *JAOS* 83: 73-91.

———. 1977. "The Uses of the Four Positions in the *Catuṣkoṭi* and the Problem of the Description of Reality in Mahāyāna Buddhism." *JIP* 5, no. 1: 1–71.

———. 1981. *The Literature of the Madhyamaka School of Philosophy in India*. Wiesbaden: Otto Harrassowitz.

———. 1983. "On the Thesis and Assertion in the Mādhyamika/dBu Ma." In *Contributions on Tibetan and Buddhist Religion and Philosophy: Proceedings of the Csoma de Körös Symposium Held at Velm-Vienna, Austria, 13–19 September 1981,* eds. E. Steinkellner and H. Tauscher, 205-241. Repr., Delhi: Motilal Banarsidass, 1995.

———. 1988. "A Kar ma bka' brgyud Work on the Lineages and Traditions of the Indo-Tibetan dbu ma (Madhyamika)." In *Orientalia Josephi Tucci Memoriae Dicata,* eds. Gnoli and L. Lanciotti, 1249-1280. Rome: Istituto Italiano per il Medio ed Estremo Oriente.

———. 1990. "On the Authorship of Some Works Ascribed to Bhāvaviveka/ Bhavya." In *Earliest Buddhism and Madhyamaka,* eds. David Seyfort Ruegg and Lambert Schmithausen, Panels of the VIIth World Sanskrit Conference, 59–71. Leiden: E. J. Brill.

———. 1991. "On *Pramāṇa* Theory in Tsoṅ kha pa's Madhyamaka Philosophy." In *Studies in the Buddhist Epistemological Tradition. Proceedings of the Second International Dharmakīrti Conference, Vienna, June 11-16, 1989,* ed. E. Steinkellner, 281–330. Vienna: Verlag der Österreichischen Akademie der Wissenschaften.

———. 1995. "Some Reflections on the Place of Philosophy in the Study of Buddhism." *JIABS* 18, no. 2: 145-181.

———. 2000. *Three Studies on the History of Indian and Tibetan Madhyamaka Philosophy: Studies in Indian and Tibetan Madhyamaka Thought, Part 1.* Wiener Studien zur Tibetologie und Buddhismuskunde, Heft 50. Vienna: Arbeitskreis für Tibetische und Buddhistische Studien Universität Wien.

———. 2002. *Two Prolegomena to Madhyamaka Philosophy. Candrakīrti's Prasannapadā Madhyamaka-vṛttiḥ on Madhyamakakārikā I.1 and Tsoṅ kha pa blo bzang grags pa/rgyal tshab dar ma rin chen's dka' gnad/gnas brgyad kyi zin bris. Studies in Indian and Tibetan Madhyamaka Thought Part 2.* Wiener Studien zur Tibetologie und Buddhismuskunde, Heft 54. Vienna: Arbeitskreis für Tibetische und Buddhistische Studien Universität Wien.

———. 2004. "Aspects of the Investigation of the (Earlier) Indian Mahāyāna." *JIABS* 27, no. 1: 3–62.

Salomon, Richard. 2000. *A Gāndhārī Version of the Rhinoceros Sūtra: British Library Kharoṣṭhī Fragment 5B.* Gandharan Buddhist Texts 1. Seattle: University of Washington Press.

Schaeffer, Kurtis. 1995. "The Enlightened Heart of Buddhahood: A Study and Translation of The Third Karma pa Rang byung rdo rje's Work on *Tathāgatagarbha*, The De bzhin gshegs pa'i snying po gtan la dbab pa." Master's thesis, University of Washington.

Scherrer-Schaub, Christina. 2002. "Enacting Words: A Diplomatic Analysis of the Imperial Decrees (*bkas bcad*) and their Application in the *sGra sbyor bam po gñis pa* Tradition." *JIABS* 25, nos. 1–2: 263–340.

Schmidt, Erik Hein, trans. 1997–2002. *Gateway to Knowledge.* 3 vols. Hong Kong: Rangjung Yeshe Publications.

Schmithausen, Lambert. 1976. "On the Problem of the Relation of Spiritual Practice and Philosophical Theory in Buddhism." In *German Scholars on India: Contributions to Indian Studies,* vol. 2: 235–250. Delhi: Nachiketa Publications.

———. 1987. *Ālayavijñāna: On the Origin and the Early Development of a Central Concept of Yogācāra Philosophy*. 2 vols. Tokyo: International Buddhist Institute for Buddhist Studies.

———. 2000. "On Three *Yogācārabhūmi* Passages Mentioning the Three *Svabhāvas* or *Lakṣaṇas*." In *Wisdom, Compassion, and the Search for*

Understanding: The Buddhist Studies Legacy of Gadjin M. Nagao, ed. Jonathan A. Silk, 245-263. Honolulu: University of Hawaii Press.

Sherburne, Richard. 2000. *The Complete Works of Atīśa Śrī Dīpaṁkara Jñāna, Jo-bo-rje: The* Lamp for the Path *and* Commentary, *together with the Newly Translated* Twenty-five Key Texts. Repr., Delhi: Aditya Prakashan, 2003.

Siderits, Mark. 1980. "The Madhyamaka Critique of Epistemology I." *JIP* 8: 307-336.

———. 1981. "The Madhyamaka Critique of Epistemology II." *JIP* 9: 121-160.

Silk, Jonathan A. 2000. "*The Yogācāra Bhikṣu.*" In *Wisdom, Compassion, and the Search for Understanding: The Buddhist Studies Legacy of Gadjin M. Nagao,* ed. Jonathan A. Silk, 265–314. Honolulu: University of Hawaii Press.

Skilling, Peter. 2000. "Vasubandhu and the *Vyākhyāyukti* Literature." *JIABS* 23, no. 2: 296–350.

Smith, E. Gene. 2001. *Among Tibetan Texts. History and Literature of the Himalayan Plateau.* Boston: Wisdom Publications.

Snellgrove, David, trans. 1959. *The Hevajra Tantra: A Critical Study.* London: Oxford University Press.

———. 1987. *Indo-Tibetan Buddhism.* Boston: Shambhala Publications.

Sparham, Gareth. 1986. *The Tibetan Dhammapada.* London: Wisdom Publications.

———. 2001. "Demons on the Mother." In *Changing Minds: Contributions to the Study of Buddhism and Tibet in Honor of Jeffrey Hopkins,* ed. Guy Newland, 193–214. Ithaca, NY: Snow Lion Publications.

———. 2003. *Ocean of Eloquence: Tsong kha pa's Commentary on the Yogācāra Doctrine of Mind.* Albany: State University of New York Press.

Stearns, Cyrus. 1995. "Dol-po-pa Shes-rab rgyal-msthan and the Genesis of the *gzhan stong* Position in Tibet." *AS* 49, no. 4: 829–852.

———. 1999. *The Buddha from Dolpo.* Albany: State University of New York Press.

Stöter-Tillmann, Jürgen, and Acharya Tashi Tsering. 1997. *Rendawa Shönnu Lodrö's Commentary on the "Entry into the Middle": Lamp which Elucidates Reality.* Dalai Lama Tibeto-Indological Series 23. Sarnath, India: Central Institute of Higher Tibetan Studies.

Sutton, Florin Giripescu. 1991. *Existence and Enlightenment in the Laṇkāvatāra-sūtra: A Study in the Ontology and Epistemology of the Yogācāra-School of Mahāyāna-Buddhism.* Repr., Delhi: Sri Satguru Publications, 1992.

Suzuki, D. T., trans. 1932. *The Lankavatara Sutra.* Repr., London: Routledge and Kegan Paul, 1973.

Tatz, Mark. 1987. "The Life of the Siddha-Philosopher Maitrīgupta." *JAOS* 107, no. 4: 695–711.

Tauscher, Helmut. 1999. "Phya pa chos kyi seng ge's Opinion on Prasaṅga in his *Dbu ma'i shar gsum gyi stong thun.*" In *Dharmakīrti's Thought and Its Impact on Indian and Tibetan Philosophy. Proceedings of the Third International Dharmakīrti Conference, Hiroshima, November 4-6, 1997,* ed. S. Katsura, 387–393. Vienna: Verlag der Österreichischen Akademie der Wissenschaften.

———. 2003. "Phya pa chos kyi seng ge as a Svātantrika." In *The Svātantrika-Prāsaṅgika Distinction: What Difference Does a Difference Make?*, eds. Georges B. J. Dreyfus and Sara L. McClintock, 207–256. Boston: Wisdom Publications.

Thondup, Tulku. 1996. *Masters of Meditation and Miracles.* Boston: Shambhala Publications.

Thurman, Robert. 1984. *Tsong Khapa's Speech of Gold in the Essence of True Eloquence.* Repr., Delhi: Motilal Banarsidass, 1989.

Tillemans, Tom. 1990. *Materials for the Study of Āryadeva, Dharmapāla, and Candrakīrti: The Catuḥśataka of Āryadeva, Chapters XII and XIII, with the Commentaries of Dharmapāla and Candrakīrti: Introduction, Translation, Sanskrit, Tibetan and Chinese Texts, Notes.* 2 vols. Wiener Studien zur Tibetologie und Buddhismuskunde, Heft 24. Vienna: Arbeitskreis für Tibetische und Buddhistische Studien Universität Wien.

———. 1999a. "How Much of a Proof is Scripturally Based Inference (*Āgamāśritānumāna*)?" In *Dharmakīrti's Thought and its Impact on Indian and Tibetan Philosophy. Proceedings of the Third International Dharmakīrti Conference, Hiroshima, November 4-6, 1997,* ed. S. Katsura, 395–404. Vienna: Verlag der Österreichischen Akademie der Wissenschaften.

———. 1999b. *Scripture, Logic, Language: Essays on Dharmakīrti and His Tibetan Successors.* Boston: Wisdom Publications.

———. 2003. "Metaphysics for Mādhyamikas." In *The Svātantrika-Prāsaṅgika Distinction: What Difference Does a Difference Make?*, eds.

Georges B. J. Dreyfus and Sara L. McClintock, 93–123. Boston: Wisdom Publications.

Tola, Fernando, and Carmen Dragonetti. 1983. "The Trisvabhāvakārikā of Vasubandhu." *JIP* 11: 225-266.

———. 2004. *Being as Consciousness: Yogācāra Philosophy of Buddhism.* Delhi: Motilal Banarsidass.

Tulku, Ringu. 2006. *The Ri-me Philosophy of Jamgön Kongtrül the Great: A Study of the Buddhist Lineages of Tibet.* Boston: Shambhala Publications.

Ueda, Yoshifumi. 1967. "Two Main Streams of Thought in Yogācāra Philosophy." *PEW* 17: 155-165.

Ui, Hakuju, Munetada Suzuki, Yensho Kanakura, and Tokan Tada, eds. 1934. *A Complete Catalogue of the Tibetan Buddhist Canons (Bkah-hgyur and Bstan-hgyur).* Sendai, Japan: Tohoku Imperial University.

Urban, Hugh B., and Paul Griffiths. 1994. "What else Remains in Śūnyatā: An Investigation of Terms for Mental Imagery in the Madhyāntavibhāga-corpus." *JIABS* 17, no. 1: 1–25.

Vetter, Tilmann. 2001. "Once Again on the Origin of Mahāyāna Buddhism." Trans. and ed. Anne MacDonald. *WZKS* 45: 59–90.

Vose, Kevin Alan. 2005. "The Birth of Prāsaṅgika: A Buddhist Movement in India and Tibet." PhD diss., University of Virginia.

Waldron, William S. 2003. *The Buddhist Unconscious: The Ālaya-vijñāna in the Context of Indian Buddhist Thought.* RoutledgeCurzon Critical Studies in Buddhism. London: RoutledgeCurzon.

Wallace, Vesna A., trans. 2004. *The Kālacakratantra: The Chapter on the Individual together with the "Vimalaprabhā."* Editor-in-chief, Robert A. F. Thurman. Treasury of the Buddhist Sciences. New York: American Institute of Buddhist Studies, Columbia University.

Walser, Joseph. 2002. "Nāgārjuna and the *Ratnāvalī.* New Ways to Date an Old Philosopher." *JIABS* 25, nos. 1-2: 209–262.

———. 2005. *Nāgārjuna in Context: Mahāyāna Buddhism and Early Indian Culture.* New York: Columbia University Press.

Wangdu, Pasang, and Hildegard Diemberger. 2000. *dBa' bzhad: The Royal Narrative Concerning the Bringing of the Buddha's Doctrine to Tibet.* Vienna: Verlag der Österreichischen Akademie der Wissenschaften.

Webster's Third New International Dictionary Unabridged. 2000. Springfield, MA: Merriam-Webster.

Willemen, Charles, Bart Dessein, and Collett Cox. 1998. *Sarvāstivāda Buddhist Scholasticism.* Handbook of Oriental Studies. Leiden: E. J. Brill.

Williams, Paul. 1980. "Some Aspects of Language and Construction in the Madhyamaka." *JIP* 8: 1-45.

———. 1981. "On the Abhidharma Ontology." *JIP* 9: 227–257.

———. 1983a. "A Note on Some Aspects of Mi bskyod rdo rje's Critique of Dge lugs pa Madhyamaka." *JIP* 11: 125–145.

———. 1983b. "On Rang Rig." In *Contributions on Tibetan and Buddhist Religion and Philosophy: Proceedings of the Csoma de Körös Symposium Held at Velm-Vienna, Austria, 13–19 September 1981,* eds. E. Steinkellner and H. Tauscher, 321–332. Repr., Delhi: Motilal Banarsidass, 1995.

———. 1989. *Mahāyāna Buddhism: The Doctrinal Foundations.* London: Routledge.

———. 1998. *The Reflexive Nature of Awareness: A Tibetan Madhyamaka Defence.* Repr., Delhi: Motilal Banarsidass, 2000.

———, with Anthony Tribe. 2000. *Buddhist Thought: A Complete Introduction to the Indian Tradition.* London: Routledge.

Willis, Janice Dean. 1979. *On Knowing Reality: The Tattvārtha Chapter of Asaṅga's Bodhisattvabhūmi.* Repr., Delhi: Motilal Banarsidass, 2002.

Wilson, Joe B. 1984. "The Meaning of Mind in the Mahāyāna Buddhist Philosophy of Mind-Only (Chittamātra): A Study of a Presentation by the Tibetan Scholar Gung-tan Jam-bay-yang (gung-thang-'jam-pa'i-dbyangs) of Asaṅga's Theory of Mind-Basis-of-All (ālayavijñāna) and Related Topics in Buddhist Theories of Personal Continuity, Epistemology, and Hermeneutics." PhD diss., University of Virginia.

Wynne, Alexander. 2004. "The Oral Transmission of the Early Buddhist Literature." *JIABS* 27, no. 1: 97–128.

Yamabe, Nobuyoshi. 2003. "On the School Affiliation of Aśvaghoṣa: 'Sautrāntika or Yogācāra'?" *JIABS* 26, no. 2: 225–254.

Yoshimizu, Chizuko. 2003. "Tsong kha pa's Reevaluation of Candrakīrti's Criticism of Autonomous Inference." In *The Svātantrika-Prāsaṅgika Distinction: What Difference Does a Difference Make?*, eds. Georges B. J. Dreyfus and Sara L. McClintock, 257–288. Boston: Wisdom Publications.

Yotsuya, Kodo. 1999. *The Critique of Svatantra Reasoning by Candrakīrti and Tsong-kha-pa: A Study of Philosophical Proof According to Two Prāsaṅgika*

Madhyamaka Traditions of India and Tibet. Tibetan and Indo-Tibetan Studies 8. Stuttgart: Franz Steiner Verlag.

Zangpo, Ngawang. 2003. *Timeless Rapture: Inspired Verse of the Shangpa Masters*. Ithaca, NY: Snow Lion Publications.

INDEX

Hīnayāna/Mahāyāna distinctions, 163
in Madhyamaka system, 198–99
nonabiding, 166, 174
path and, 119
in Prāsaṅgika system, 245
in Pratyekabuddhayāna, 154–55, 156
with remainder, 122, 156, 198
in Sautrāntika system, 135
in Secret Mantra, 270, 271
Shrāvakayāna, distinctions in, 33, 121–22, 129
in Vaibhāṣhika system, 131
without remainder, 122, 156, 198
non-associated formative forces. *See* formative forces, non-associated
Non-Pluralists, 25, 39, 50, 187, 188, 360n573
Non-Staining False Images, Proponents of, 25, 39, 50, 189, 190
nonexistents, 181, 189
nonimplicative negation, 263, 311n155, 320n248
in Chandrakīrti's system, 224
in Chittamātra system, 181
probandum, role in, 207–8, 373nn652–53
in Sautrāntika system, 121–22, 134, 135
in Shentong system, 48, 252, 259
in Shrāvakayāna, 111–12
in Svātantrika system, 52, 222, 382–83n713
in Vaibhāṣhika system, 132
nonreturners, 113, 141, 145–48
nonsectarian movement. *See* Rimé (nonsectarian) movement
Nyingma school, 12, 28, 29

object-universals, 181
obscurations, two, 126, 325n293
antidote for, 171
Hīnayāna/Mahāyāna distinctions, 162, 163
Rangtong view of, 205
once returners, 113, 141, 144–45
origins of suffering, 32, 91, 92–93, 96
general characteristics of, 116–17
karma and, 98–99
mental afflictions and, 97–98
See also karma
Ornament of Clear Realization (Maitreya)
doxographical classification, 19, 46, 251
on pāramitās, 169
on pratyekabuddhas, 36, 155
Rangtong commentaries on, 263
Ornament of the Mahāyāna Sūtras (Maitreya), 140
on emptiness, 256
in Kongtrul's work, 36, 37, 46, 47
on pāramitās, 169, 170, 171, 173
on shamatha and vipashyanā, 174
Ornament of the Middle Way (Shāntarakṣhita), 20, 39
on the four extremes, 196
on mind, 267
other-exclusion, 240, 391n776

Pa-tsap Lotsāwa Nyima Drak, 21, 22, 28
Padma, 35
Pañchakrama. *See Five Stages* (Nāgārjuna)
pāramitās
in Chittamātra path, 183–84
distinctions, 171–72
divisions of, 168–69, 347n499
four characteristics of, 168, 347n493
Hīnayāna/Mahāyāna distinctions, 163
six genuine aspects, 170–71
training in, 167–74
Pāramitāyāna, 36–37, 346n487
characteristics, 17–18, 165–166
Kongtrul's classification of, 50–51
tenet systems of, 174 (*See also* Chittamātra; Madhyamaka)
training in, 166–67 (*See also* pāramitās, training in)
paratantra. *See* dependent characteristic
parikalpita. *See* imagined characteristic
pariniṣhpanna. *See* consummate characteristic
path
characteristics of, 118–19
in Chittamātra system, 183
phenomena of, 127
Prāsaṅgika/Svātantrika differences in, 215–16
shrāvaka view of, 128
term, meaning of, 118–19, 322n267
truth of, 32, 91, 92–93
paths, five, 114, 128, 141, 183